A New Scramble for Africa?

A New Scramble for Africa?

Imperialism, Investment and Development

Edited by
Roger Southall and Henning Melber

UNIVERSITY OF KwaZulu-Natal Press

Published in 2009 by University of KwaZulu-Natal Press
Private Bag X01
Scottsville 3209
South Africa
E-mail: books@ukzn.ac.za
Website: www.ukznpress.co.za

© 2009 University of KwaZulu-Natal

Reprinted 2010

ISBN 978-1-86914-171-4

Managing editor: Sally Hines
Editor: Christopher Merrett
Typesetting: Patricia Comrie
Indexer: Abdul S. Bemath
Maps and diagrams: M Design
Cover design: M Design
Cover photograph: Elaine Gilligan, FoE EWNI (Friends of the Earth – England, Wales and
    Northern Ireland): Shell's corporate activities in the Niger Delta have caused pollution
    from oil spills and gas flares, devastating local communities who up to now have not
    received compensation

Nordiska Afrikainstitutet
The Nordic Africa Institute

DAG HAMMARSKJÖLD FOUNDATION

Printed and bound by Interpak Books, Pietermaritzburg

Contents

Preface

This volume follows the footsteps and imprints of two earlier joint projects, which were fruitful in visible ways. Based on collaboration between the Democracy and Governance Research Programme of the South African Human Sciences Research Council (HSRC) represented by Roger Southall, and the project on Liberation and Democracy in Southern Africa (LiDeSA) at the Nordic Africa Institute represented by Henning Melber, we earlier co-produced the volumes *Limits to Liberation in Southern Africa: The Unfinished Business of Democratic Consolidation* (*Journal of Contemporary African Studies* 21(2), 2003; Cape Town: HSRC Press, 2003) and *Legacies of Power: Leadership Change and Former Presidents in African Politics* (Cape Town: HSRC Press and Uppsala: The Nordic Africa Institute, 2006). Given the warm welcome extended to both publications, we felt encouraged to continue our teamwork.

The project of exploring 'the new scramble for Africa', the results of which are presented here, was originally conceptualised during late 2005 as a result of our participation in the emerging debate about the impact of increased external demand for the continent's resources as well as the effects of this on intra-continental constellations. On occasion of the XVI World Congress of Sociology towards the end of July 2006 in Durban, the continued discussion about the project's framework was joined by John Daniel, who had also been actively involved in the two earlier publication projects. As before, he remained a loyal and valuable debating partner, who shared his ideas with us throughout the implementation of the project.

The Africa Department of the Swedish International Development Agency (Sida) had already decided at the end of 2005, through its established collaboration with the Nordic Africa Institute, to offer us generous financial support for turning our ideas into reality, although both of us moved on during the course of the project to new institutions: Roger Southall left the HSRC for the Sociology of

Work Unit/Department of Sociology at the University of the Witwatersrand in 2007, while Henning Melber had by late 2006 moved on to the Dag Hammarskjöld Foundation in Uppsala. The continuation of the project was turned into an integral part of the Foundation's long-standing commitments to the global South and Africa in particular.

During 2007, the project was financially administered by the Institute for Security Studies (ISS) in Pretoria/Tshwane, to which the editors remain immensely grateful. Further generous support was granted by the South African office of the Friedrich Ebert Foundation under Werner Rechmann for a workshop, at which we discussed first draft chapters in June 2007. Given the continuous shift in global trends and African developments, the thematic focus of the volume was constantly readjusted against the background of emerging social and political realities.

This volume was finally ready for submission to publishers in June 2008. By this time, the Nordic Africa Institute had adopted a new strategy whereby it would cease to publish its own hard copy books. The Institute, however, continued through the publication department's head Birgitta Hellmark-Lindgren to support the project and our initiatives to link up with alternative publishers. We are correspondingly grateful to Glenn Cowley and his team at the University of KwaZulu-Natal Press who agreed to enter a publishing arrangement ensuring widest possible distribution of this volume. We greatly appreciate the support provided by Sally Hines, who took care of the final production stages. We also thank our three external reviewers for their comments on the manuscript, which contributed to the quality of the end result, although ultimately of course, what appears in print remains our responsibility.

We gratefully acknowledge the support of all the individuals and institutions who have contributed to making this volume a reality. In particular, we would like to thank all our authors, who have not only generously contributed their own ideas but who have patiently responded to the often pedantic demands of the editorial process. We trust that the final results presented in the following pages justify their combined efforts. As close collaborators in this third joint project, both of us feel encouraged to consider a further collaborative enterprise. It is our hope that readers do not consider this as a threat.

Finally, we are proud to declare that the Dag Hammarskjöld Foundation was enabled to make a substantial donation from our contributors' honoraria to the Methodist Church in downtown Johannesburg. Under Bishop Paul Verryn, this church has played a magnificent role in offering shelter and support to the victims of the disturbing wave of xenophobic violence against perceived foreigners that erupted in South Africa towards the project's conclusion.

Roger Southall and Henning Melber
Johannesburg and Uppsala
March 2009

Abbreviations

AAC	Anglo-American Corporation
AAG	Anglo-American Group
AAMS	Associated African and Malagasy States
ACBF	African Capacity Building Foundation
ACOTA	African Contingency Operations Training and Assistance
ACP	African, Caribbean and Pacific
ACR	African Consolidated Resources
ACRF	African Crisis Response Force
ACRI	African Crisis Response Initiative
AEC	African Economic Community
AES	Applied Energy Services Corporation (US and UK)
Afreximbank	African Export-Import Bank
AFRICA	Action for Resisting Invasion, Colonialism and Apartheid
AFRICOM	Africa Command (US)
AGC	African Global Capital (South Africa)
AGOA	African Growth and Opportunity Act (US)
AGRA	Alliance for a Green Revolution for Africa
ANC	African National Congress (South Africa)
ANOC	Asian national oil company
ANT	Armée Nationale Tchadienne (Chad)
AOPIG	African Oil Policy Initiative Group
APRM	African Peer Review Mechanism
AU	African Union
BCEAO	Banque des États de l'Afrique de l'Ouest
BDC	Banco Desenvolvimento e Comercio (Mozambique)
BEAC	Banque des États de l'Afrique Centrale
BEE	Black Economic Empowerment
BLNS	Botswana, Lesotho, Namibia and Swaziland

BSAC	British South Africa Company
CAMEC	Central African Mining and Exploration Company
CAP	Common Agricultural Policy
CAR	Central African Republic
CBD	Convention on Biological Diversity
CCSRP	Collège de Contrôle et de Surveillance de Ressources Pétrolières (Chad)
CdK	Compagnie du Katanga
CDR	Conseil Démocratique Révolutionnaire (Chad)
CEMAC	Central African Economic and Monetary Community
CENTCOM	Central Command (US)
CET	common external tariff
CFA	Communauté Financière Africaine
CFAO	Compagnie Française de l'Afrique Occidentale
CII	Confederation of Indian Industries
CJTF-HOA	Combined Joint Task Force-Horn of Africa (US)
CNOOC	China National Offshore Oil Corporation
CNPC	China National Petroleum Corporation
COMESA	Common Market of Eastern and Southern Africa
CPA	Comprehensive Peace Agreement (Sudan)
CREC	China Railway Engineering Company
CSIRO	Commonwealth Scientific and Industrial Research Organisation (Australia)
CSK	Comité Special du Katanga
DFA	Department of Foreign Affairs
DRC	Democratic Republic of Congo
DTI	Department of Trade and Industry (South Africa)
EAC	East African Community
EADB	East African Development Bank
EBA	Everything But Arms
EC	European Commission
ECA	Economic Commission for Africa
ECA	European Court of Auditors
ECDPM	European Centre for Development Policy Management
ECMG	External Compliance Monitoring Group (Chad)
ECOWAS	Economic Community of West African States
EDF	European Development Fund

EEC	European Economic Community
EER	Energy and Equity Resources (Nigeria)
EEZ	exclusive economic zone
EIB	European Investment Bank
EIBI	Export-Import Bank of India
ELISA	Ethiopian Leather Industries Association
EPA	Economic Partnership Agreement
ESA	Eastern and Southern Africa
EU	European Union
EUCOM	European Command (US)
EUFOR	European Union Force
FA	fisheries agreement
FAD	fish aggregation device
FAO	Food and Agriculture Organisation
FARDC	Forces Armées de la Republic Democratic du Congo
FDI	foreign direct investment
FIDH	Fédération Internationale des Ligues des Droits de l'Homme
FOCAC	Forum on China-Africa Cooperation
FPA	fisheries partnership agreement
FQML	First Quantum Minerals (Canada)
FRELIMO	Frente de Libertação de Moçambique or Mozambique Liberation Front
FTA	free trade agreement
FUC	Front Uni pour la Changement (Chad)
GATT	General Agreement on Trade and Tariffs
GDP	Gross Domestic Product
GMO	genetically modified organism
GNP	Gross National Product
GNPOC	Greater Nile Petroleum Operating Company (Sudan)
GPOI	Global Peace Operations Initiative
GSM	Global Systems for Mobile Communication
GSP	generalized system of preferences
GSSP	Guardes Specials de Sécurité Présidentiele (DRC)
HIPC	highly indebted poor country
HPCL	Hindustan Petroleum Corporation Ltd
HSRC	Human Sciences Research Council (South Africa)
IAG	International Advisory Group (Chad)

IAGS	Institute for the Analysis of Global Security
IBSA	India-Brazil-South Africa
ICBC	Industrial and Commercial Bank of China
ICR	implementation completion report
ICT	information and communications technology
IDC	Industrial Development Corporation (South Africa)
IFI	international financial institution
IGG	Inspector General of Government (Uganda)
IMF	International Monetary Fund
Implats	Impala Platinum
IOC	Indian Oil Corporation
IOR	Indian Ocean Rim
IOTC	Indian Ocean Tuna Commission
IPR	intellectual property right
ITEC	Indian Technical and Economic Co-operation
ITU	International Telecommunications Union
IUU	illegal, unregulated and unreported
JEM	Justice and Equality Movement (Sudan)
Johncom	Johnnic Communications (South Africa)
JRC	junior resource company
JSE	Johannesburg Stock Exchange
kg	kilogramme
KPRC	Kaduna Refinery and Petrochemical Company
LDC	least developed country
LDWF	long distant waters fleet
LNG	liquefied natural gas
LOC	line of credit
MAP	Millennium African Renaissance Programme
mbd	million barrels per day
MCA	Millennium Challenge Account
MDG	Millennium Development Goal
MDRI	Multilateral Debt Relief Initiative
MEG	Metals Economics Group
MEND	Movement for the Emancipation of the Niger Delta (Nigeria)
MFA	multi-fibre-agreement
MFN	most-favoured nation
MNC	multinational company

MOSOP	Movement for the Survival of Ogoni People (Nigeria)
MOU	memorandum of understanding
MPLA	Movimento Popular de Libertação de Angola or Popular Liberation Movement of Angola
MPS	Mouvement Patriotique du Salut (Chad)
MRAG	Marine Resources Assessment Group
MTN	Mobile Telephone Networks (South Africa)
mua	million units of account
NAI	New African Initiative
NAIL	New African Investments Limited (South Africa)
NAM	Non-Aligned Movement
NAMA	non-agricultural market access
NATA	North American Tuli Association
NATO	North Atlantic Treaty Organisation
NDU	National Defence University (China)
NEPAD	New Partnership for African Development
NFC	Non-Ferrous Metals Industry Corporation China)
NGO	non-governmental organisation
NIEO	New International Economic Order
NIPL	Nile Independent Power Limited (Uganda)
NIZA	Netherlands Instititute for Southern Africa
NNPC	Nigerian National Petroleum Corporation
NOC	national oil corporation
NRM	National Resistance Movement (Uganda)
NSSF	National Social Security Fund (Uganda)
OAU	Organisation of African Unity
ODA	official development assistance
OECD	Organisation for Economic Co-operation and Development
OEEC	Organisation for European Economic Co-operation
OMEL	ONGC Mittal Energy Limited (India)
OML	oil mining licence
OMNC	oil multinational company
ONGC	Oil and Natural Gas Company (India)
OPEC	Organisation of Petroleum Exporting Countries
OVL	ONGC Videsh (India)
PACOM	Pacific Command (US)
PDD25	Presidential Decision Directive 25 (US)

PDP	People's Democratic Party (Nigeria)
PEPFAR	President's Emergency Plan for Aids Relief (US)
PGM	platinum group metal
PIC	prior informed consent
PLA	People's Liberation Army (China)
PSA	production sharing agreement
PSC	production sharing contract
PSI	Pan-Sahel Initiative
PTC	Post and Telecommunications Corporation (Zimbabwe)
RDP	Reconstruction and Development Programme (South Africa)
REC	regional economic community
RENAMO	Resistência Nacional Moçambicana or National Mozambican Resistance Movement
RFC	Rassemblement des Forces pour le Changement (Chad)
RST	Roan Selection Trust
SAB	South African Breweries
SACP	South African Communist Party
SACU	Southern African Customs Union
SADC	Southern African Development Community
SARS	South African Revenue Service
SEATINI	Southern and Eastern African Trade, Information and Negotiations Institute
SHT	Société des Hydrocarbures du Tchad
SIMAB	Smithsonian Institution Monitoring and Assessment of Biodiversity (US)
Sinopec	China Petroleum and Chemical Corporation
SLA	Sudanese Liberation Army
SME	small-scale and micro enterprise
Socomin	Société Congolaise Minière
SPLM	Sudan Peoples Liberation Movement
SSA	sub-Saharan Africa
Stanbic	Standard Bank of South Africa
SWAPO	South West African People's Organisation (Namibia)
TAC	total allowable catch
TCIL	Telecommunications Consultants India Limited
TDCA	Trade, Development and Co-operation Agreement
TEAM-9	Techno-Economic Approach for Africa-India Movement

TI	Transparency International
TSCTI	Trans-Sahara Counter-Terrorism Initiative
UFDD	Union des Forces pour la Démocratie et le Développement (Chad)
UFDDF	Union des Forces pour la Démocratie et le Développement Fondamentale (Chad)
UFPD	Union des Forces pour le Progrès et la Démocratie (Chad)
UMHK	Union Minière du Haute Katanga
UN	United Nations
UNCLOS	United Nations Convention on the Laws of the Seas
UNCTAD	United Nations Conference on Trade and Development
UNEP	United Nations Environment Programme
UNITA	União Nacional para a Independência Total de Angola or Nation Union for the Total Independence of Angola
UPOV	Union for the Protection of New Varieties of Plants
US	United States (of America)
USAID	United States Agency for International Development
WAGPP	West African Gas Pipeline Project
WIPO	World Intellectual Property Organisation
WSF	World Social Forum
WTO	World Trade Organisation
WWF	World Wide Fund for Nature
ZCCM	Zambian Consolidated Copper Mines
ZTE	Zhong Xing Telecommunication Equipment Company (China)

A New Scramble for Africa?

Henning Melber and Roger Southall

Something big was happening in Africa during the early years of the twenty-first century. More global investment was flowing into the continent than at any time since at least the 1960s and local stock exchanges were booming. There was a significant inflow of foreign capital investment, an improved outflow of exports, more focus upon Africa as a market and higher rates of economic growth. Most importantly, there was a modest increase in the average per capita income in many African countries affected by the new engagement. All told, this was an encouragingly different picture from that painted by *The Economist* at the turn of the millennium when Africa was depicted as 'the hopeless continent'.[1] To be sure, there continue to be major instances of civil war, political strife bordering on genocide, autocratic repression, democratic reversals and economic collapse – Chad, Sudan, Kenya, Somalia and Zimbabwe, Guinea, Guinea-Bissau and Madagascar – among others. Although many naïve expectations accompanying the wave of democratisation that washed through much of Africa during the 1990s have been confounded, the first decade of our new century was clearly one of much greater economic dynamism than *The Economist* anticipated.

Observers agree that the higher levels of economic growth recorded in most African countries were due, directly or indirectly, to increasing global demand for the continent's resources; notably for oil, but also for gas and other energy sources, minerals, metals and natural products such as fish and timber. There is further agreement that this increased demand has been driven, above all, by the sudden appearance of China as an economic actor, whose dramatic burst of industrialisation has fuelled the global upswing of the last few years. Africa was regarded during the immediate post-Cold War era as an undisputed sphere of Western influence. Yet this geopolitical map is now being challenged by China and other emerging industrial actors from the South such as India and Brazil. Worse still, as far as the hitherto dominant powers are concerned, the increased Chinese presence also constitutes a challenge to codes of conduct prescribed in numerous treaties, international documents and aid conditionalities, and formally promoted by the Western powers. Ironically, in contrast to various African regimes that manifestly rejoice in the greater freedom for manoeuvre the more fluid situation brings, some post-imperial commentators now warn of the dangers of Africa becoming subject to a new phase of imperialism. While the imperial imagery evoked is often sensationalist, a more substantial approach to increased external involvement in the continent is that of a new scramble reminiscent of the high-handed antics of the European imperial powers that divided up Africa between them in the penultimate decade of the nineteenth century. It is to an examination of this perspective that this book is devoted.

The idea of a new scramble remains highly contested. For a start, there is substantial debate about the extent to which the recent era of greater growth and investment in Africa represents the inauguration of a new and significant phase in the continent's historical trajectory. After all, there have been so many false starts in post-colonial Africa that any analyst is well advised to regard the significance and potential longevity of new beginnings with suspicion. Yet more substantially, while there is near consensus that dramatically rising global demand for natural resources triggered the surge of growth in Africa, there is far less agreement about the long-term effects of the current impact by external actors. This is understandable, for apart from variant ideological and theoretical assumptions that underlie analyses of patterns of growth and development (or lack of them) in contemporary Africa, the changes identified with the new scramble (if that is what is taking place) are remarkably recent, and hence challenge easy categorisation. It is for this reason that the present collection seeks to promote discussion about whether the new era is best characterised as primarily one of renewed and changing imperialism(s); new investment and opportunity; or development.

The initial debate is about whether the new scramble has been unleashing a new round of competition and conflict between imperial powers in Africa. There is, on the one hand, a prominent perspective which argues that the upsurge of investment and external activity in Africa is analogous to historical processes that culminated in the Berlin Conference of 1884–5; and that just as the challenge to Britain and France by the rising industrialised powers of Germany and Italy set off the scramble for African possessions and empire, so today the new scramble is promoting competition for raw materials and influence in Africa between the established industrial powers of the West and the rising industrial powers of the East and South. Central to this analysis is the fear and prognosis that the new scramble will extend, deepen or transform Africa's subordination to external capitalist powers; and hence inhibit, if not negate, the continent's prospects for growth and development, even though it is recognised that there is no desire or quest on the part of imperial powers for direct political control as there was during the late nineteenth and early twentieth centuries. If this is a renewed age of imperialism, then it is manifestly one of informal, not formal, empire.

Even within this broad approach, largely endorsed by the editors of this book, there is substantial debate not merely about the different elements and weights of historical continuity and discontinuity, similarity and dissimilarity; but also around the question of whether the behaviour of the new actors in Africa can usefully or correctly be interpreted as imperialist. Thus, whereas there is a long tradition of analysis of US and European policies in Africa as imperialist (or neo-imperialist) that lends itself easily to examination of Western engagement in the new scramble, there is no established body of literature that provides an equivalent basis for analysing the activities of China or India in a similar way. That is not to say there is any shortage of analysts who choose to depict the growing presence of China in Africa as embodying a new imperialism.[2]

Yet apart from the strident repudiation of imperialist motives by the Chinese government, and the importance of recognising the diversity of Chinese actors (huge state firms, private capitalist ventures and small traders, for example) and hence admitting a variety of Chinese motives in Africa, depiction of Chinese involvement as imperialist suggests we must similarly apply such analysis to the engagements of, for instance, the Indian state and Indian companies. If, as is suggested in some quarters, rapid South African investment expansion into the rest of the continent similarly suggests a new form of imperialism (or sub-imperialism), then we need to pose major questions about the relationship between the South African state and South African and international capital, and between economic, political and military power. In short, the questions come thick and fast. This is not to say there are no credible answers, only that they both overlap and compete. In other words, while we may easily view the new African scramble as a product of increased global competition for natural resources, political hegemony and military power between established (and declining) and new (and rising) Great Powers (and associated lesser powers), many argue that the jury is still out as to whether China (or India, or whoever) constitutes a new force of imperialism (Marks 2006).

The alternative approach to the new scramble recognises that it is largely a product of rapidly increasing global demand for natural resources contingent upon the rise, in particular, of China and India as industrial powers. From this perspective, traditional Western dominance in Africa in spheres such as oil, minerals, finance and manufacturing is being challenged by the recent arrival of new actors, with all the opportunities and costs that might be expected from a period of new and rapid capitalist growth. Globally this may imply, as argued for instance by British historian Niall Ferguson (2004), that the age of American informal empire is coming to an end, despite the desperate need for some Great Power to establish order over unruly smaller states in a highly troubled and dangerously unstable world. Yet this approach tends to deny, even if the post-9/11 war on terror is urging the US to militarise and extend its alliances in Africa, that the Americans and other Western actors display any seriously imperial ambitions in Africa. They may want to carve out areas of influence, it is argued, but wish to minimise long-term direct involvement in African states, save for extending and securing their direct investments and sources of supply. The new scramble, in other words, is primarily about investment and business. Meanwhile, some commentators from this perspective join many left-wing critics in arguing that, paradoxically, Western imperialism is being succeeded by Chinese imperial-like behaviour.[3] Others, even bodies like the World Bank, present Chinese, Indian and other new actors as providing the competition for African resources that can spark an era of African growth and renewal (Broadman 2007). Overall, this approach maintains that there is a great variety of external actors in Africa today; both old and new, with variant motivations, interested in short- and long-term benefits. There is thus no great sense or advantage in characterising or understanding their actions as imperial. The contemporary world is far more complex than it was during the late nineteenth century and there is no serious comparison between the initial and new scrambles, however inviting the latter label might be.

What is largely lost in the clash of ideas about the new scramble is the paradoxical possibility that both major approaches, while variant and opposed to each other in many ways, can also be mutually supportive. Or in short, if renewed imperialism involves investment, then it may also promote capitalist development. Of course, this may not be to the liking of many critics of imperialism, who while concerned to condemn the negative aspects of external involvements in Africa are less comfortable when considering whether these might have historically progressive consequences. Yet, as we explore in some greater depth in the conclusion, analysis of the present scramble would appear to need less Lenin and more Marx: that is, we need to move beyond the focus of Africa's under-development towards one that centres on development and growth. Such a perspective would not, it must be stressed, imply an acceptance of anything that goes and an endorsement of any and every prescription put forward by the World Bank or similar agencies. Quite the reverse, for it would rather combine critique of purely exploitative, external, probably extractive ventures, that have outrageously negative consequences for host communities with careful assessment of external involvements with progressive and developmental possibilities.

Indeed, it is precisely in this direction that some of the more sensitive assessments of the impact of the present wave of Chinese and Indian investment in Africa are going. It also involves a rigorous analysis of the class consequences entailed. On the one hand, the dramatic extension of Chinese aid to Africa, much of which is focused upon the provision and extension of infrastructure (including road and railway building, in the tradition of Cecil Rhodes), although designed to facilitate the more efficient and profitable extraction of oil and minerals, may well do much to boost local business. On the other hand, as emphasised by the American-Chinese scholar Lee (2008), it may simultaneously stimulate an active response by African workers, demanding of Chinese employers that they live up to the progressive rhetoric of their socialist past. In short, the argument here is that any analysis of imperialism, as much as that of investment, must also seek to engage with the problematic of development.

This collection raises many more questions than it provides answers and we are only too well aware of various inadequacies. Thus, although some attention is granted in passing to North Africa, the volume as a whole is largely focused upon parts of sub-Saharan Africa, even though it is recognised that, for instance, the linkage between oil extraction and the US-led war on terror demands that the continent be treated as a whole. Likewise, the focus upon external engagements with Africa has, we are uncomfortably aware, somewhat underemphasised African agency and response.[4] While sharing a common problem, the collection is also unashamedly diverse.

Our own approach, as reflected in our contributions, although leaning strongly towards an interpretation that endorses the idea of Africa being subject to an historically distinct and new round of imperialist engagement, nonetheless attempts to grapple with numerous complexities and contradictions of the present moment, however unsatisfactorily. Our contributors, meanwhile, adopt variant perspectives that range from enthusiastic endorsements of the idea of the new scramble as renewed imperialism, to those who either explicitly or implicitly challenge it and who present the new era as one of investment and (uneven) opportunity.

Nevertheless, the volume centres on the idea that whatever the nature and outcome of the new interest and investment in contemporary Africa, something big is happening and there is an urgent need for us as analysts to seek to understand it. As readers will notice, this collection was brought together before the onset of the recession in the global economy which is widely described as rivaling that of the 1930s in its severity. However, we do not believe that this in any way negates the idea of a 'scramble for Africa', even if, for the moment, it might reduce its intensity (although even that is questionable). There are a number of factors at play.

Despite the marked decline of projected economic growth rates as a direct result of the global economic crisis, African economies have been so marginal to the international economic system that they have been less affected than other regions. Perhaps because of the strictures of the era of structural adjustment from the mid-1970s through to the 1990s, Africa's banking system has been so conservatively managed that it has had almost no exposure to the sub-prime market that has wreaked so much damage elsewhere in the world. To be sure, unlike other African countries, South Africa is being adversely affected, not because of it having a banking sector which has been any less conservative, but because it has been running a sizeable balance of payments deficit which has been financed by foreign investment, and this is now flowing back out of the country. Furthermore, unlike other African countries, South Africa has relied on raising huge loans on international markets to fund ambitious infrastructural projects. For instance, the state electricity supplier, Eskom, needs to raise more than US$30 million over the next five years, but has now had to delay issuing bonds because of current market conditions. Nonetheless, the South African government remains committed to a significant shift in its spending pattern towards long-term infrastructural investment. Meanwhile, the fall in commodity prices, notably oil, but also diamonds and copper, will hit a range of countries, but many observers feel that these are going to be only relatively short-term effects, not least because 'China has an almost insatiable appetite for markets' (Plaut 2008). To be sure, whereas the International Monetary Fund (IMF) was predicting a growth rate of 6–7% average growth rate for African countries before the late 2008 financial meltdown, it has now revised that forecast down to between 3–5%. But that compares remarkably well with advanced industrialised countries, which are in the eye of the storm, for their growth rates are facing collapse in the midst of a recession and economies might even shrink.

One reason why the African performance can expect to compare relatively well internationally is that the African market is continuing to grow apace, and continues to attract international attention. According to one recently published review (Mahajan 2008, summarised by Mann 2009):

- Home to 900 million consumers, Africa remains one of the fastest-growing markets in the world.
- 220 million Africans live in areas where GDP growth in 2006 was more than 6%.
- Africa has some of the poorest nations in the world, but is wealthier across the continent than India. Average gross national income per capita across all 53 nations in 2006 was about $1066, $200 more than India.
- While it is true that the top four on the 2007 list of Africa's largest companies were based in metals, mining, oil or gas, consumer goods companies such as SAB Miller, telecom companies (MTN, Orascom Telcom, Itissalat Al Magrib, Telkom) and banks (Standard, Absa, First Rand) and real estate (Liberty International) are amongst the top twenty.

Meanwhile, apart from the increasing attraction of its status as a market for foreign-made consumer goods, Africa is slowly but surely benefiting from something of a peace dividend with the wind down of various long-running conflicts (even though some situations, as in Darfur, Somalia, and in the north-east of the Democratic Republic of Congo, remain desperate). This is bringing with it higher rates of infrastructural investment, which are likely to continue. Having said this, the new credit crunch might, however, exacerbate old problems and bring another debt spiral into force. The decline of financial sources to be invested from the outside might also reinforce the 'old' patterns of competition and dependency, even among new players. Further, we may well observe a renaissance of the IMF, which under a slightly modified management structure will be back in the arena as an influential agency. Both the conference of African ministers and central bank governors convened in Dar es Salaam on 10/11 March 2009, as well as the summit of the G20 in London on 2 April 2009, reinforced in different but complementary ways the role of the international financial institutions. While recent trends had suggested that development in large parts of the African continent would in the future be less dependent on the IMF, the opposite seems now to become a likely development. While neo-liberalism is ailing, it is far from being dead (cf. Bond 2009). It is also no longer the time for generous gifts of friendship to be exchanged in return for favours as a new form of investment.

This will clearly limit the windows of opportunity, which China and other emerging new global players had provided in recent years to African elites. We seem to be back to an era, where it is 'business as usual', no matter with whom (Melber 2008; Polgreen 2009). However, despite all the (not so) new hampering factors, most of all, Africa remains home to major reserves of scarce minerals. Global demand for these may fall off significantly in the near future. When – as it will – demand again picks up, the new scramble for Africa's wealth and resources will commence with vigour anew.

Notes

1. *Economist* 13 May 2000.
2. On the whole, such analysts come from the political left, with most such commentaries published in the electronic media. For a taste, see Cheng (2007) and Van der Walt and Schmidt (2007).
3. Valuable collections debating the notion of Chinese involvement in Africa as imperialist include Alden, Large and Soares de Oliveira (2008), Ampiah and Naidu (2008) and Games (2005). The influential South African commentator, Moeletsi Mbeki, is also manifestly ambiguous about the Chinese role, claiming that while offering opportunity it is replicating the classical exchange of raw materials for manufactured imports (as cited in Marks 2006).
4. See as a subsequent effort based in part on the chapters in this volume Southall (2008).

References

Alden, C., D. Large and R. Soares de Oliveira (eds). 2008. *China Returns to Africa: A Rising Power and Continent Embrace.* London: Hurst.

Ampiah, K. and S. Naidu (eds). 2008. *Crouching Tiger, Hidden Dragon? Africa and China.* Pietermaritzburg: University of KwaZulu-Natal Press.

Bond, P. 2009. 'Realistic postneoliberalism: a view from South Africa.' In: *Postneoliberalism: A beginning debate.* Development Dialogue, no. 51, January, edited by U. Brand and N. Sekler. Uppsala: The Dag Hammarskjöld Foundation: 193–210.

Broadman, H. 2007. *Africa's Silk Road: China and India's New Economic Frontier.* Washington: World Bank.

Cheng, E. 2007. 'Is China Africa's new imperialist power?' *Green Left Weekly* 4 Mar. http://www.greenleft.org.au/2007/701/36384.

Ferguson, N. 2004. *Empire: How Britain Made the Modern World.* London: Penguin.

Games, D. 2005. 'Chinese: the new imperialists in Africa'. *Business Day* 11 July.

Lee, C.K. 2008. 'Casualisation and precariousness of labour in Africa'. Paper presented to Sociology of Work Unit, University of the Witwatersrand, 2 Sep.

Mahajan, V. 2008. *Africa Rising: How 900 million African Consumers Offer more than you Think*. Pennsylvania: Wharton School Publishing.

Mann, I. 2009. 'Rise and rise of Africa', *Sunday Times* (Johannesburg) 1 Mar.

Marks, S. 2006. 'China in Africa: the new imperialism?' *Pambuzuka News* 2 Mar. http://www.pambuzuka.org/en/category/features/32132.

Melber, H. 2008. 'China in Africa: a new partner or another imperialist power?' *Afrika Spectrum* 43(3): 393–402.

Plaut, M. 2008. 'Can Africa gain in credit crisis?' 21 Oct. http://news.bbc.co.uk/2/hi/africa/7682724.stm.

Polgreen, L. 2009. 'As Chinese investment in Africa drops, hope sinks'. *The New York Times* 26 Mar.

Southall, R. 2008. 'The 'new scramble' and labour in Africa'. *Labour, Capital and Society* 41(2): 128–55.

Van der Walt, L. and M. Schmidt. 2007. 'Is China Africa's new imperialist power?' *Power to the People!* 11 Nov. http://power-2-people.blogspot.com/2007/11-is-china-africa's-new-imperialist-power.

CHAPTER ONE

Scrambling for Africa?

Continuities and Discontinuities with Formal Imperialism

Roger Southall

The idea that recent years have seen a new scramble for Africa has become increasingly commonplace, yet curiously there has been little systematic investigation of an approach that demands not just an analysis of the present, but also of the past. But the question whether external involvements replicate aspects of imperialism, or whether they are qualitatively different, refuses to go away. This opening chapter therefore seeks to provide a framework for pursuit of this debate by simultaneously examining the grounds for comparison between the first and new scrambles, while outlining the principal features of the rush for Africa's resources and the global dynamics that lie behind it.

The Scramble for Africa in Retrospect

'The Scramble for Africa,' writes Thomas Pakenham in his magisterial volume, 'bewildered everyone, from the humblest African peasant to the master statesmen of the age' (Pakenham 1991: xxiii). Africa had been known to Europe since Roman times, but by the mid-1870s it was still mysterious. As far as Europe was concerned, the continent was largely unexplored, its geography unknown, its land vacant. If there were states and rulers, they were African. If there were treasures, they were buried in African soil. So, beyond the European trading sites along the coastal fringes of the continent, and the strategically important colonies in Algeria and Southern Africa, 'Europe saw no reason to intervene' (Pakenham 1991: xxiii). Yet suddenly, within half a generation, the scramble gave Europe virtually the whole continent: 30 new colonies and protectorates, ten million square miles of territory, and 110 million new subjects.

Africa was sliced up like a cake, the pieces swallowed by five rival nations –
Germany, Italy, Portugal, France and Britain, with Spain taking some scraps –
and Britain and France were at one another's throats. At the centre, exploiting
the rivalry, stood one enigmatic individual and self-styled philanthropist, controlling the heart of the continent: Leopold II, King of the Belgians. By the end of
the century, Pakenham continues, the passions generated by the scramble had
poisoned the political atmosphere in Europe, brought Britain and France to the
brink of hostilities, and precipitated a bloody and extended war between Britain
and the Boers – 'one of the most humiliating in British history' (1991: xxiii).

Pakenham asks, 'Why this undignified rush by the leaders of Europe to build
empires of Africa?' His immediate answer is that historians provide three types of
explanation. First, Eurocentric approaches like John Hobson's (and later Lenin's)
theory that the need of the European capitalist powers to export surplus capital
was the driving force behind expansion into Africa. Second, Afrocentric
explanations place emphasis on sub-imperialisms, by which we take it Pakenham
means the expansion of empire as a result of actions by imperialists on the ground
in Africa acting beyond the immediate control of their chancelleries in Europe.
Third, there is an argument for combinations of the two. Broadly speaking, we
might say, these explanations range from those that view the scramble (and empire)
as a product of the economic logic and rivalry of the international capitalist
system; to those that, in the tradition of Seeley (1883), portray it as, if not actually
an accidental outcome of diverse historical events, then following inexorably from
the political logic of the expansion of the most successful nation states of their
time.[1] Yet, as Pakenham argues, not only is there no *general* explanation (his italics)
acceptable to historians; there is not even agreement whether there should be
one. Having said that, he then goes on to suggest that the scramble can be
understood in terms of Livingstone's three Cs: commerce, Christianity and
civilisation; 'a triple alliance of Mammon, God and social progress'. However,
while Livingstone's hope in the mid-nineteenth century was that it would be
trade, rather than the gun, that would liberate Africa, the paper, or informal,
imperialism it promoted was soon to prove inadequate and within a short space
of time, it was a fourth C, conquest, that came to predominate.

It would be presumptuous to offer a condensation, synthesis or review of
different approaches of historians to the scramble. All that is necessary here is to
isolate certain aspects of this dramatic onset of formal imperialism in Africa.

First, whatever historical perspective we adopt, it is necessary to distinguish
underlying, long-term causations of European imperial expansion, of which the

scramble was a particular historical expression. Suffice it to say that, as indicated by Pakenham, approaches to this issue fall into two major camps. The one is fundamentally the Marxian approach that, building from Hobsonian/Leninist foundations, gives primacy to economic factors, stressing competition between the leading capitalist powers of Europe for raw materials, markets and investment opportunities as the dominant dynamic. In short, the outward movement of European investment is underlain by the drive for capital accumulation. In contrast, the other pole of argument is more inclined to stress multi-causality, along the lines of Livingstone's three Cs. Economic drivers are by no means excluded, but there is a greater tendency to emphasise political factors (such as the pursuit of national glory) or social factors (the missionary desire to save souls) as independent, and often conflicting, variables. However, what is important is to point out that there is considerable overlap of explanations.

The second aspect of the scramble, which follows from the above, is that its origins and early dynamics lay in Europe rather than Africa (Oliver and Atmore 1996: 100). To be more precise, it was the articulation of capitalist industrialisation and state formation in western Europe that was to promote the race for African empire. The only Great Powers in western Europe during the first 65 years of the nineteenth century were Britain and France. However, while possessing considerable military strength, France was well behind Britain, the most advanced capitalist nation, in terms of commerce and manufacturing. This led France to pursue a protectionist policy in favour of her own merchants in her existing colonies, which were little more than trading posts: in Senegal from 1815; and from the 1840s in Guinea, Ivory Coast, Dahomey (now Benin), Gabon and Madagascar. Meanwhile, Germany and Italy did not yet exist as separate and unified states, while of the lesser powers, Denmark (in 1850) and Holland (from 1867) actually abandoned their trading posts in the Gold Coast during the course of the nineteenth century, 'leaving only Portugal as a minor competitor with France and Britain' (Oliver and Atmore 1996: 100).

Momentum towards the partition of Africa increased from the 1870s. There were, of course, important facilitating factors. Thus while the capitalist quest for raw materials, of which a far greater range was required in more quantity than ever before, enhanced interest in the tropics:

> New technology immeasurably cheapened the cost of expansion and conquest in Africa. Medical discoveries enabled Europeans to live there far more safely, avoiding the sacrifice in lives so typical of early

attempts at colonization. Precision arms, which in turn depended on advances in the European machine tool industry, presented European armies with an enormous new advantage over Africans . . . It was significant too that the commercial expansion of the era of legitimate trade had as one by-product the rise of European-controlled armies of African troops prepared to fight for small wages and the prospect of loot (Freund 1984: 89).

Against this background, it was a sharpening of Anglo-French rivalry in West Africa, where both nations had long-established trading interests, that propelled the extension of empire. Hitherto, neither country had an economic motive to annex large territories: British dominance benefited from free trade, whilst even protectionist France found that her trading settlements in West Africa were a financial burden. From the 1870s, however, France's desire to penetrate the interior by steamship (where rivers were navigable), railway and telegraph in order to corner the greater part of West African trade stimulated a similar British response; not least through the entrepreneur, George Goldie, who amalgamated the British firms trading in the Niger Delta and subjected the French to ruinous commercial competition. In turn, this prompted France to feel that its commercial companies needed political support. Meanwhile, with the French busily engaged in pacifying Tunisia, the British effectively occupied Egypt in 1882 in order to safeguard British-French dual control of that nation's finances and free passage through the newly-constructed Suez Canal.

The increased rivalry encouraged France and Britain to consider consolidating their possessions, notably through the offer of Gambia by Britain in exchange for control over the coastline from Sierra Leone to Cameroon. However, this fell foul of the sudden appearance upon the African scene of two new European actors, Germany and King Leopold II of Belgium. In essence, both wanted to play catch-up. Germany, which had more or less caught up with Britain industrially by the 1860s, determined not to be left out of the thrust for Africa while there were still remaining areas to be colonised (Wehler 1970).[2] Consequently, after discreetly encouraging a number of sorties by German explorers into Africa to establish a presence, Chancellor Otto von Bismarck proclaimed German protectorates over Togo, Cameroon and South West Africa in 1884. Similarly, while the bourgeoisie of Belgium showed only limited interest in overseas expansion, Leopold, from a mixture of motives, looked to establish a commercial monopoly in the Congo, a vast area into which the established powers had hitherto declined to venture. In turn, the British responded by supporting the claims of Portugal, a backward state in which it had strong commercial interests, to Angola and the mouth of the Congo river. The result of these developments was

> to force all the European powers, including Britain and France, to look far beyond their immediate economic needs. What each power feared was that its rivals would keep the trade of their new colonies to themselves by enclosing them within high tariff (or customs) barriers. Therefore each power felt compelled to enter the scramble for territory in order to reserve the largest possible sphere for its own activities (Oliver and Atmore 1996: 103).

However, as Freund (1984: 90) observes, there was a strong co-operative streak to this competition between European powers. As far as all major capitalist interests were concerned, it was far better, if their own nation could not or would not occupy a territory, that some rival power should establish efficient colonial power.

It was in this context that Bismarck called a conference in Berlin in 1884–5 of the main European powers. Formally, its mission was to secure free navigation along the Niger and Congo rivers, but its grander motivation was to reach some kind of European agreement about the carving up of Africa already under way. Although it did not lead to the definition of colonial boundaries as such, it had two important outcomes. First, it recognised Leopold's authority over the Congo basin in exchange for his guarantee of free access to European traders and missionaries. This led to Leopold's proclamation of the Congo Free State in 1885 as his personal kingdom. Second, following Germany's proclamation of protectorates, the Berlin Conference agreed that a European claim to any part of Africa would only be recognised by other European governments if it was effectively occupied by that particular power. This was a deliberate tactic to undermine British claims to informal spheres of influence. Within days of the end of the conference, Bismarck put this principle into practice by proclaiming a German protectorate, German East Africa (later renamed Tanganyika) in the heart of the British sphere of influence in that region. The scramble had begun.

The two decades that followed were to see the delineation of the internal boundaries of colonial Africa; a process that, with only minor exceptions, was completed with the final absorption of the Boer republics of Transvaal and Orange Free State into the Union of South Africa in 1910 (until that is, the victorious

Allies divided the German African territories amongst themselves after the First World War). Yet as Shillington (1989: 306) notes, the acquisition of territory was not the same as effective occupation, and this period was notable not only for the extension of colonial rule (through co-operative as well as by competitive means)[3] but also for the widespread, if uneven, resistance by Africans to European conquest. To be sure, we must beware a trite conquest and resistance paradigm. Military conquest, on occasion of the most brutal kind (notably the genocidal policies perpetrated by German colonialism in South West Africa and Tanganyika in the early twentieth century) there most certainly was. Yet 'Conquest was, in fact, but one aspect of a slow process of infiltration, much of which was completely bloodless' (Oliver 2000: 214). On the ground, colonialism depended heavily upon a mix of the co-operation and compliance of local populations.

Nonetheless, this process of conquest carried within itself the seeds of its own destruction. Indeed, retrospectively we can say that the European occupation of Africa was over within a relatively short period of time. European domination provoked African nationalist response and the majority of Africans regained their political freedom, albeit through the dubious vehicles of new states defined by colonial boundaries, within a period of 70 years. To be sure, the pace of the European withdrawal initially came as a surprise even to the European powers themselves. Not unexpectedly, there was concerted military resistance to African nationalism, especially in those territories physically dominated by white settler minorities (Algeria, Kenya and Rhodesia) and in Portuguese Africa, retained by a backward colonial regime until the costs of its overseas wars resulted in its overthrow by progressive forces within the military in 1974. There was also a long-running attempt by Africa's largest white minority, located in South West Africa and South Africa, to resist the tide of history, its resolve stiffened by its political autonomy and by concerted support from Western powers.[4] Yet even this defiance met its match, not least because ultimately it lost the support of the former colonial powers and the US, and accommodated to African majority rule: South West Africa as Namibia in 1990; and South Africa in 1994.

The colonial withdrawal was propelled not only by the costs of containing African demands for independence, which billowed after the Second World War, but also by the declining economic utility of empire. As we have seen, the scramble is associated above all with the partitioning of Africa into discrete colonial economic estates. Lenin, famously, viewed the territorial expansion of empire as a result of the maturation of capitalism, notably its shift from competitive to monopoly capitalism. Monopolies were driven by the need to limit or abolish competition. Hence it was natural to want to reserve the right to trade or invest in particular areas exclusively, seizing territory in undeveloped parts of the world from which competition from the nationals of other capitalist powers could be excluded. Furthermore, late-developing capitalisms (notably of Germany) having maximised the returns from the meagre territories left to them by the major powers would compel their states to demand a repartition of the world, a demand that led inexorably to war. The uneven rates of development of the capitalist powers required a periodic reallotment of the undeveloped world between them. Ultimately, this would stimulate revolt by colonised peoples, as well as by the proletariats of the advanced nations of the colonial empires themselves. However, as Strachey (1959: 109) was to put it, there was 'a miscalculation at the very centre of Lenin's theoretical structure,' for history was to demonstrate that while the mighty capitalist nations of the world might clash, they proved able to divest themselves of their empires without the catastrophic effects predicted for them.

They were able to do so because Lenin's predictions of the immiseration of the working classes within advanced capitalism turned out to be wrong. This was not unrealistic if applied to the Britain of 1900–14, on which Lenin founded his model. However, he was in error to ascribe it to capitalism in general. As Strachey describes it, he failed to comprehend the economic consequences of democracy: advanced capitalism proved much more capable of adapting to the economic and political demands of wage earners than Lenin gave credit for. Yet there were also other aspects of this adaptability which gave the capitalist powers confidence that the economic structures of imperialism they had put in place could survive a colonial withdrawal.

Empires in Africa were constructed around extensive systems of imperial preference and protection. However, despite considerable differences in the nature of rule between the British, French, Belgians and Portuguese, their empires were founded upon the commonalities of colonial economic exploitation. As Freund (1984: 112) puts it:

> Colonial rule began with an act of political expropriation, with the use or threat of force, to extract surplus from Africa in the form of either direct labour or the product of labour which could then be commoditised. The state acted as tribute-taker rather than an organizing agency for capitalist producers as in a developed capitalist society. This was indeed plunder pure and simple, but it could not yield any great wealth. Capitalism demanded the further development

of commodity production and the circulation of goods from which firms in the metropolitan countries could benefit. Where possible colonialism was about pressing forward the social and economic conditions, the development of class forces that could lead to capitalist production itself.

He continues:

At the heart of the economic task of the colonial state lay the problem of labour. To open Africa to effective capital penetration, the most central issue which underlay all others, and which to some extent explains the need for conquest itself, was to prize open the labour resources of the continent, to redirect them functionally, socially and geographically in order to create a surplus from which capital could benefit (Freund 1984: 114).

Amin (1972) identified colonial capitalism operating across three broad zones: Africa of the colonial trade economy, dominant in West Africa, founded upon the unequal exchange of agricultural commodities produced by peasants for the products of metropolitan capitalist industry; Africa of the concession-owning companies, mainly in central Africa, where metropolitan capital used either force or economic persuasion to induce African labour to produce agricultural products on plantations; and Africa of the labour reserves in southern and eastern Africa, where, because there was great mineral wealth, metropolitan capital required the creation of a migrant proletariat to provide labour. Here, the costs of social reproduction were subsidised by the subsistence economy of migrants' families within demarcated native areas to the benefit of the mines, settler agriculture and manufacturing industries in South Africa, the Rhodesias and Kenya. The implementation of these models of exploitation was uneven (for instance, South Africa was the only country in which capitalist production became generalised) and they overlapped untidily across Amin's three zones. Nonetheless, there proved over the long term to be a contradiction: the cost of maintaining the colonial state.

Much has been made of the apparent paradox between the eagerness of venture capital to establish outposts in Africa and the reluctance of the governments of the most advanced capitalist countries, notably Britain and France, to impose their direct rule upon African peoples during the first seven decades of the nineteenth century. The basic reason was that they had little reason to: the era of legitimate commerce between metropolitan merchant interests and African trading communities that succeeded the brutalities of slavery provided for profitable exchange without the military, political, ideological and financial costs of a colonial state. However, this comfortable situation was transformed by the scramble and the introduction of its doctrine of possession by effective occupation. The late nineteenth century challenge to their commercial domination of spheres of influence compelled the dominant powers to match their rivals by establishing the formal panoply of empire. Yet, from the very beginning such expansion was more often than not based upon a notion of parsimony, with metropolitan governments devolving the tasks of conquering African societies, acquiring territory and ruling colonies to chartered companies.

It was only when this system proved unprofitable or otherwise untenable (in most territories during the late 1890s or early 1900s) that home governments stepped into the breach. Thereafter, in their different ways, the colonial powers gradually extended their functions from the collection of taxes and mobilisation of labour to the provision of infrastructure and rudimentary educational and social services. In few places, with the exception of settler colonies where governments diverted resources for the benefit of white minorities, did the colonial state depart significantly from nineteenth century notions of the minimalist state. It was only after the Second World War, when African participation did much to stimulate ideas of political equality, that Britain and France began to think diffidently about colonial welfare and development; and it was not long afterwards that the mounting political, military and psychological costs of containing African nationalism encouraged them to evacuate their empires earlier than they had anticipated.

One additional reason for the rapid pace of decolonisation was pressure from the US, the Western world's creditor nation, whose ideological (albeit myopic) aversion to colonialism served as a convenient front for its own capitalist enterprises, notably in mining, eager to gain access to investment opportunities in Africa and Asia. Another was the confidence which the major capitalist powers, except Portugal, had in the continuity of economic structures established during colonialism. This was to be summarised by influential post-colonial thinkers (notably Rodney 1972) in terms of dependence and underdevelopment: the idea that patterns of domination and exploitation had become so deeply established under colonialism that they could survive formal decolonisation: the functions of the colonial state were now undertaken by compliant political classes, a phenomenon termed neo-colonialism. For such thinkers, the remedy to dependence lay in the delinking of the former colonies from metropolitan capital by revolutionary nationalist regimes. In practice, however, such few attempts as were made invariably ran aground on the shoals of Western hostility, impractical economics, lack of developmental alternatives, self-interested leadership, and the demobilisation and subversion of revolutionary regimes. The result was that former colonial nations in Africa remained heavily dependent upon their links with former colonial powers, although increasingly this dependence was to become multilateralised under US hegemony. It is the challenge to this by a new generation of late-industrialising countries of the South that is giving rise to analyses proposing a new scramble for Africa.

A New Scramble for Africa?

There has been no shortage of recent proclamations about a new scramble for Africa. Indeed, it has become a stock phrase, bandied about as much by global statesmen and sober Western economists as by investigative journalists and left-inclined analysts. A sampling of media headlines and content is instructive. We have, for instance, Kofi Annan, when United Nations (UN) Secretary-General, noting in 2006 that foreign investment in Africa had increased by 200% over the last five years, but lamenting that it was still focused on extracting natural resources rather than developing local economies.[5] Statements that Africa is seeing an 'unprecedented boom in oil and gas investment,'[6] that rising prices for minerals are leading international companies to 'hot' new destinations,[7] and that there are major profits to be made in capturing the continent's financial markets[8] abound. However, what has really attracted the media's attention are the changing international dynamics that appear to lie behind this: notably the arrival of China, and to a lesser extent India and other players from the South, as rivals to the US and Western countries for Africa's raw materials, markets and allegiances.[9] While this is viewed as embodying both economic cost and opportunity for Africa, it is also seen as presenting major challenges to good governance and environmental and military security.[10] Interestingly, too, the scramble for African resources, notably its oil, is very much located in a global context of resource scarcity and international competition reaching into hitherto marginalised or bypassed areas, notably the Arctic and other oceans.[11] While much of the media treatment is informative, albeit often highly ideologically charged, it needs to be thoroughly digested for us to approach a more systematic understanding of the proclaimed new scramble for Africa. Fortunately, the foundations for a more informed analysis are at hand, located within an increasing flow of academic analyses produced by concerned authors and institutes.

Rather than attempt to summarise the literature, this chapter seeks to locate our understanding of the new scramble politically and historically. Consequently, it will proceed, first, by outlining the major features of the perceived scramble as presented by leading authors who treat it, implicitly or explicitly, as an outcome of a latest phase of imperialism; second, by providing an overview of the counterpoint provided by international agencies and the participants in the scramble themselves; third, by seeking to advance understanding through a systematic comparison of the present scramble with the original scramble for Africa; and fourth, by considering policy options open to African actors to minimise the cost and maximise the opportunities provided by the scramble.

Bracking and Harrison (2003) argue that imperialism provides a far more useful starting point than globalisation for understanding Africa's relation with the world political economy. Whereas the latter implies an expansion of global capitalist relations that is uplifting for even the world's poorer states, the notion of imperialism is embedded in critique. It 'refuses to accept that bourgeois civilization has lived up to its own historic claims of progress' and 'reveals that capitalist development in Africa fails to be developmental,' for the continent is subject to 'external dominance and socially-damaging and extraverted forms of accumulation' (Bracking and Harrison 2003: 9). They therefore present imperialism as

- the inexorable expansion of capitalism as a socio-economic system on a world scale;
- the necessarily competitive, expansionist and warlike character of developed capitalist states;
- the unequal nature of capitalist expansion and the reproduction on a world scale of socio-economic inequalities;
- the creation on a world scale of structures of inequality of power and wealth not only in the economic, but also social, political, legal and cultural spheres; and
- the generation, through the very process of capitalist expansion, of movements of resistance and anti-imperialism.

There is a massive amount of writing on Africa based upon such assumptions.

The depiction of a present scramble for Africa as new is not universally accepted. Margaret Lee (2006), a contributor to the present volume and one of the few writers to attempt a comprehensive analysis of the topic, is insistent upon referring to the twenty-first century scramble for Africa rather than the new scramble. Her argument is that, as Melber (2007) has put it, the present situation is one of "Old wine in new bottles;" in other words that the continuities of imperialism underlying the present situation outweigh the latter's newness. Against that, she divides her analysis almost equally between the scramble for Africa's resources and markets by the western powers and by China. She thus characterises the present era as one of 'head on collision' (Lee 2006: 317), and concludes that 'China is the new imperialist power in Africa, committed not only to pillaging and investing in ways that would benefit China, but also perpetuating Africa's continued instability by exporting Chinese armaments to Africa and by building armament factories on the continent' (Lee 2006: 325). Melber (2007) similarly emphasises the critical difference introduced by Chinese involvement and foresees that in the near future 'India, Brazil and Russia (as well as a number of actors such as Malaysia and Mexico) are likely to increase competition for limited markets and resources'. He queries whether the focus upon 'the at times appallingly imperialist nature of the Chinese expansion into Africa' is not a one-sided narrative that seeks to direct attention away from the past history and present practice of Western imperialism. However, he also argues that the present scramble in Africa follows on from the collapse of what he terms the Soviet empire, the end of the Cold War and the inauguration of 'a new global order for hegemonic rule' by the US. The offensive by China for African markets and resources thus constitutes a 'new stage of competing forces on the continent' that by implication suggests it is part of a larger Chinese challenge to US hegemony.

Whether we emphasise continuity (Lee) or discontinuity (Melber), it is the idea of the new scramble for Africa that has taken deepest root. Yet the importance lies far less in the terminology than the content, about which most analysts in this tradition are largely agreed. The end of the Cold War and the rapidly rising status of China have led to the hugely intensified global struggle for control of resources, matched by an aggressive assertion of what Foster refers to as the new US imperial grand strategy: 'Recent US attempts to establish a stronger alliance with India, with Washington bolstering India's status as a nuclear power are clearly part of this New Great Game for control of South Central Asia – reminiscent of the nineteenth century Great Game between Britain and Russia for control of this part of Asia' (2006: 5). In turn, the new Great Game between the world's Great Powers is matched by the new scramble for Africa. We shall return to this theme below.

The Scramble for Resources

The recent rush by external powers to profit from Africa's wealth of natural resources is the most remarked upon aspect of the new scramble by far. 'With oil, gas, timber, diamonds, gold, coltan and bauxite,' remarks Turner (2007), 'Africa is home to some of the largest deposits of natural resources in the world'. However, while her stress upon the inherent wealth of the continent (as opposed to its customary characterisation as inherently impoverished) is welcome, her list is unnecessarily limited and should be extended by reference to Africa's marine, water and ecological resources as well. In broad terms, the thrust of the literature can be summarised as follows.

Oil and Gas

There is near unanimity that the new scramble in Africa has been galvanised by the Great Powers' urgent search for energy security in response to increased global demand for fossil fuels in view of projected shortages and anticipated threats to supply from existing sources. As of 2004, the US Department of Energy cited Africa as having 7% of the world's proven oil resources and being responsible for 11% of total production. Africa holds 7% of the world's proven natural gas reserves with supply set to rise by 5% each year from 2003 to 2030 (Lee 2006: 314). Compared with other world regions, therefore, Africa is presently a relatively modest player, but the bare statistics understate its importance.

First, there is expected to be a massive increase in global demand. According to the Institute for the Analysis of Global Security (IAGS), world consumption, driven by greater oil use in China and India, will rise by 60% from 2002 levels by 2020.[12] It will therefore be strategically imperative for all competing Great Powers to secure their access to oil.

Second, the overwhelming bulk of known oil reserves (66% according to the IAGS) are held in Middle Eastern countries (including Libya), many of whose regimes are hostile or potentially hostile to the US. The US and other western powers are therefore seeking to decrease their dependence upon the Middle East as a region of supply. Given that oil production in Russia (6% of proven oil reserves) is already declining, the US is looking to Africa, notably its producers in North Africa (Algeria, Mauritania, Chad and Sudan) and along the Gulf of Guinea (Nigeria, Angola, Equatorial Guinea, Gabon and São Tomé and Príncipe) for an increase in supply from around 15% in 2006 to between 25% and 35% within 10–15 years.[13] Other powers are acting similarly and Africa has attracted investments from virtually all the major oil companies in Europe and the US, not least because the continent is poorly surveyed and may yet reveal staggering potential: in Angola recent discoveries suggest that its production could soon match that of Kuwait. In addition, because crude oil from West Africa is of a light quality it is particularly attractive to importers. Meanwhile, China is presently drawing around 30% of its oil imports from Africa and accounts for 50–60% of oil exports from Sudan and 25% of oil exports from Angola; It is also sourcing further oil supplies from Nigeria, Algeria and Equatorial Guinea, and looking to sign deals with other countries such as Chad, the Central African Republic and Congo (Lee 2006: 318–20).

Africa's known gas reserves have grown strongly over the past 20 years and in 1995 totalled about 6.3 trillion cubic metres with potential reserves estimated at 17.65 trillion cubic metres by 2010. Of proven gas reserves, 78% are in Nigeria with the balance concentrated in Algeria, Egypt, Libya, Angola, Mozambique, Namibia and Tanzania. However, total gas production in Africa of about 80 billion cubic metres per annum is small in relation to reserves, with Algeria accounting for two thirds. Most of this is exported to Europe, with inland use of gas being concentrated in Nigeria, South Africa, Angola and Gabon. Most of the gas produced in sub-Saharan Africa is flared, although the oil companies, notably in Nigeria, are looking to recover this and use it in power generation (Turner 2007).

Imperialism in the twentieth century was closely associated with the Great Powers' struggle for the control of oil in the Middle East – 'for sheer wealth,' observed Strachey (1959: 155), there had never been anything in history like it. With the US and other Western countries attempting to reduce their dependence on the Middle East, and with China's demand for oil rising dramatically, oil and gas are at the fore of the new scramble for Africa (Klare and Volman 2006). The outcome has been what Shaxson (2007) has termed the 'dirty politics of oil': the paradox of poverty from plenty and the effective dispossession of local communities in oil-producing areas, deals with despots at the cost of democracy (White and Taylor 2001) and environmental despoliation. Further, the determination of the US to secure its access to African oil, gas, other energy sources and minerals is leading to its extension of a formidable apparatus of political and military alliances with strategically placed countries in Africa, often justified by reference to the war on terror (Abramovici 2004). In this book, the scramble for Africa's oil, the militarisation it is pulling in its wake, the repressive politics it fosters and its impact upon the continent's peoples is dealt with variously by Martin Rupiya and Roger Southall, Cyril Obi, and Simon Massey and Roy Máy (chapters seven to nine). Their contributions highlight not merely the absolute centrality of oil to the new scramble, but its pursuit by an unholy combination of international financial institutions, states, companies and African elites with little regard for either the welfare of local inhabitants or the ecology within which they live.

Uranium

According to the International Atomic Energy Agency, in 2005 Africa had 18% of the world's recoverable uranium resources. After a massive fallback following the Chernobyl nuclear disaster in 1986, demand for uranium has increased dramatically in recent years as a major dimension of the global war for energy security. Production in Africa is largely accounted for by just four countries – Niger (the world's largest producer after Canada and Australia), Gabon, Namibia and South Africa (where uranium is extracted from certain gold mines as a by-product) – with production undertaken principally by French, Australian, Canadian and South Africa companies. But there is revival of lapsed projects in the Democratic Republic of Congo (DRC), Algeria and Morocco and frenzied exploration for new deposits is taking place across the continent, in countries as diverse as Central African Republic, Guinea, Malawi, Uganda and Zambia. While Western companies are taking the lead, China is becoming an increasingly significant actor and is competing especially with Russia for deals in Namibia and Niger. These include the actual or potential takeover of Western operations.[14]

Other Minerals

Africa hosts about 30% of the planet's known mineral reserves, including gold (40%), cobalt (60%) and platinum (90%), as well as significant supplies of diamonds, manganese, chromium, copper, nickel, bauxite and other minerals. Production is concentrated in South Africa, Ghana, Zimbabwe, Tanzania, Zambia and the DRC, although other countries, including Angola, Botswana, Namibia, Sierra Leone and Zambia, are also heavily dependent upon the export of minerals.

The scramble for minerals was at the heart of late nineteenth-century imperialism and provided a major foundation for Western support for white minority rule and apartheid during the latter part of the twentieth century. Historically, production has been dominated by British, Australian, Canadian, South African and European firms, although since 1945 the US, which has become increasingly dependent on foreign sources for almost all non-fuel minerals, has loomed increasingly large as a consumer. The US war machine is heavily dependent upon imports from Africa of cobalt, manganese, chromium and platinum essential to the manufacture of defence equipment. US dependence upon Africa was accentuated during the Cold War by the fact that, between them, the former Soviet Union and Africa accounted for over 90% of world platinum, manganese and chromium. Consequently, the political volatility of the latter region constituted a major factor behind US support for some very dubious regimes.

This factor cannot be discounted today, for China is becoming not only a rapidly increasing consumer of Africa's minerals, but also a significant investor in mines and mining-related infrastructure, notably in Zambia, Zimbabwe and the DRC (Lee 2006). Indeed, in early 2007 the heads of a over dozen Western mining companies, meeting in Switzerland, complained that they were increasingly being cut out of deals by Chinese state-owned companies because the Chinese were linking investment in mining to the provision of huge incentives, such as the building of dams, stadiums, roads, railways and power stations at discounted rates. Complaining that Africa was being raped and pillaged by China, they therefore appealed to the UN and World Bank to mandate that African countries insist that mining investment deals incorporate high environmental and safety standards, areas in which political, legislative and legal pressure has compelled Western mining companies to raise their game.

In chapter ten of this volume, Wilson Prichard stresses the continuity of the present boom in minerals with similar moments in the past, arguing the cyclical nature of mining's historical development. Thus while he notes the more favourable competitive dynamics that underlie the present boom, notably the arrival of mining investment from China, India and South Africa, he argues that this does not fundamentally change the regulatory challenges facing African countries if they are to maximise their benefit. Indeed, as Jana Hönke demonstrates in chapter eleven, while the industry has become multinationalised, the increasing competition between firms brought about by the entry of new players such as China is forcing mining companies in remote areas to assume state-like functions regarding the maintenance of order, a role played in colonial times by charter companies ironically evoked by Chinese state-backed companies in Africa today.

Forestry

African forests, long a victim of foreign harvesting, are today under pressure as never before. According to a Food and Agriculture Organisation (FAO) review of some 46 countries in Africa, the area of forest cover decreased by around 0.7% per annum during the period 1990–2005. The extent of decrease is in all probability worse than this as information was missing from the FAO study from most of the countries of the Congo basin, representing the second largest area of tropical primary forest in the world. Export of forest products from sub-Saharan Africa declined from almost nine million cubic metres in 1996 to about 4.3 million in 1998 (later data is difficult to obtain), probably reflecting the gradual depletion of prime logging areas. Against that, there was an increase in wood removals from 500 million cubic metres in 1990 to 661 million in 2005, stemming from increased production of fuel wood.[15]

Most of the logging is done by a bewildering array of large and small, mostly European companies, many of which hold generous concessions granted by African governments; or even by warlords such as Charles Taylor, a factor deemed to have prolonged the civil war in Liberia (Johnston 2004). Much logging is done illegally, with the American Forest and Paper Association estimating recently that in Cameroon, Equatorial Guinea, Gabon, Ghana and Liberia, 30% of production is suspicious. Other estimates put it as high as 50% in Ghana and Cameroon and up to 100% in Liberia. Exports to southern Europe dominate, but China is rapidly becoming a major destination for timber from Cameroon, DRC, Equatorial Guinea, Gabon, Liberia and Mozambique. A high proportion of such exports (70% from Gabon and 90% from Equatorial Guinea) is illegal (Turner 2007).

Fisheries

In Africa nearly ten million people depend on fishing, fish farming, fish processing and trading fish. Fishing produces 7.3 million tonnes of fish per year, more than 90% caught by small-scale fishermen. Fish provides about 19% of animal proteins consumed in Africa, although fish consumption per capita in sub-Saharan Africa is the lowest of all regions of the world and declining. Fish also provide exports worth some $2.7 billion annually. Historically, Africa's rivers, lakes and coastline have provided a rich harvest for local fishing communities, while trade to the interior has offered the benefits of fish consumption to many living far from fishing sites.

However, in recent decades various factors, notably population expansion and urbanisation, have disrupted the balance of supply and demand. While some fisheries have declined because of pollution and environmental degradation, the greatest impact upon fish catch and fish availability in local markets has been due to over-exploitation. In particular, the growth of industrial fishing by foreign fleets, catching huge quantities off Africa's once fish-rich coasts, has raised most concern. Some fleet owners have negotiated agreements with coastal states that provide for the payment of a licence fee or a share of income to the host nation, but many have not. Such illegal, unregulated and unreported (IUU) fleets, mainly from Europe and the Far East, fish within African territorial limits, which extend to 200 kilometres offshore, with impunity since few coastal states (Nigeria and South Africa being two exceptions) have the aircraft and naval vessels to spot, arrest and fine or impound intruders.[16] These themes are pursued in chapter thirteen by Andre Standing on the impact of European Union (EU) access agreements on fishing, The bottom line is that they allow for the plunder of Africa's fishing stocks with too little regard for either the future or the present interests of Africa's fishing communities and nations.

Agro and Indigenous Resources

Africa remains one of the richest sources of biodiversity on the planet, but is increasingly under assault from international interests seeking to privatise key resources and monopolise production. Corporations and energy-hungry countries, in collaboration with African governments and business elites, are pouring money into Africa for agro-fuel crop production and stimulating a land rush reminiscent of Europe's initial colonial expansion. Europe, Japan and the US are very active, working their agro-fuel interests into multilateral and bilateral aid, trade and investment agreements, but they are being joined by the state-owned companies of emerging powers such as Brazil and China. The largest proportion of such investments is focused around large-scale plantation agriculture and tightly integrated into transnational corporate networks. Such investments tend to consume the most fertile land and lead to the exclusion of small-scale African farmers. Meanwhile, Africa is also increasingly the victim of bio-piracy from multinational firms which, after illegally acquiring biological resources (plants, marine life and microbes), are developing and patenting products that generate massive profits without due benefit to the countries of origin (Mushita and Thompson 2007). After providing a survey of this territory, Carol Thompson in chapter twelve argues that the enclosure and dispossession fostered by multi-nationals in Africa needs to be unscrambled by a mix of alternative legal regimes, alternative science and organised resistance.

Markets and Trade

The EU and US are currently locked in a trade war for more favourable access to African markets for their subsidised products. Although a mere 1% increase in Africa's share of world exports would be worth more than five times the continent's share of aid and debt relief, Western politicians are reluctant to practise the trade liberalisation that they preach as this requires confronting protectionist interests at home. The EU has led the way with an attempt to renegotiate its relations with the African, Caribbean and Pacific (ACP) countries through Economic Partnership Agreements (EPAs), four of which have been devised for sub-Saharan Africa. However, while the EU maintains that EPAs are designed to increase trade and render EU-African trade relations compatible with the liberalising demands of the World Trade Organisation (WTO), critics and many African governments respond that EPAs favour Europe, facilitate further dumping of EU subsidised products and undermine Africa's existing regional arrangements (Stevens 2006; Goodison 2007). The US has countered by the formulation and repeated updating of the African Growth and Opportunity Act (AGOA) of 2000 that provides for preferential access to its market. This has allowed for an increase in African exports, notably by African-based, but not African-owned, textile companies. However, US trade with Africa continues to revolve overwhelmingly around the import of oil, minerals and natural resources in exchange for the export of high technology goods and machinery. Meanwhile, trade with China has increased dramatically, so that it is now the continent's third most important trading partner behind the US and France, but ahead of Britain. However, the trade balance overwhelmingly favours China, whose provision of cheap products – often sold in local markets and often by Chinese traders – is having a devastating impact upon segments of African business, notably in clothing and textiles (Lee 2006; Melber 2007). These themes are dealt with by Margaret Lee (chapter four) on European and Henning Melber (chapter three) on US and Chinese interests, while Sanusha Naidu (chapter five) on India and John Daniel and Mpume Bhengu (chapter six) on South Africa add detail on country-based strategies to penetrate African markets.

Arms

The African defence market has traditionally been dominated by European countries, Russia and the US. During the immediate post-Cold War period, arms sales to Africa decreased. However, defence spending by African states is again set to rise from $13.9 billion in 2007 to more than $15.9 billion in 2011. These figures disguise the fact that some African countries are increasing their defence spending at a rate significantly above the average. According to one report, the confluence of burgeoning security requirements and vast oil and gas reserves in the context of high energy prices has led to the emergence of African nations that are today demonstrating procurement characteristics reminiscent of the Middle

East three decades ago. Consequently, competition in these expanding African defence markets can be expected to be fierce with China emerging as a growing player for its willingness to make sales without attaching strings. Indeed, as noted by Martin Rupiya and Roger Southall in chapter seven, increasing US demand for oil in Africa and the perceived need to counter China's influence is leading to a steadily growing American military presence. China's arms deals have come under particular criticism for reasons that include indiscriminate provision of weapons to dictatorial regimes (Zimbabwe), the building of arms factories in return for access to oil (Sudan) and sales to both sides in a war (between Ethiopia and Eritrea) as well as to rebel factions in war-torn countries (Burundi). However, while China no less than the US appears guilty of fuelling wars and abetting dictatorial governments, arms exports to Africa from China remain considerably less than those from the US, Russia, Britain and France. Indeed, during the Blair years, British arms sales to Africa quadrupled (Campbell 2008; Lee 2006; Taylor 2007).

Other Resources

There are numerous other aspects of the new scramble that could be valuably explored, such as multinational companies securing major construction deals (often funded by long-term loans to African governments by the World Bank), the privatisation of utilities and the systematic recruitment of Africa's skilled human resources. All can be said to have ambiguous, if not deleterious, consequences for Africa, not least in the corruption they so often foster as instanced by the case of Uganda, explored in chapter fifteen by Roger Tangri.

The Impact upon Africa of the New Scramble

The thrust of the new scramble is to systematise the exploitation of Africa's natural resources and markets. This has characterised the continent's relations with the outside world since the beginnings of imperialism and has in recent times been promoted by the neo-liberalisation of the continent, a broad overview of which is provided by Vishwas Satgar in chapter two. Initially, the post-Cold War era appeared to inaugurate a wave of democratisation in Africa underpinned by economic reforms that promised growth and development. Such hopes were encouraged by the transformation of the Organisation of African Unity (OAU) into the African Union (AU), promising better continental governance, and the launch of the New Partnership for African Development (NEPAD), promising better economics. Critics argue that the promise has not been realised. Many democratic gains have been reversed by elites. African growth rates have improved, but highly unevenly and at the cost of increasing internal inequality. Foreign investment has become more varied and has increased, but is underpinned by deals between governments, multinational companies and African elites that are often corrupt, enrich a small minority and subvert the general welfare, while also concentrating upon the extraction of resources rather than developing local economies. Foreign extractive activity is overwhelmingly damaging to the environment and local communities; and emerging trade relations with the US, EU and China appear more likely to extend, rather than diminish, Africa's global disadvantage. Finally, the growing securitisation of the new scramble, notably by the US as part of the war on terror, appears destined to fuel local wars, lessen rather than extend human security, and undermine human rights. However, this is not always how the major participants in the new scramble view it.

The very fact that the idea of the new scramble for Africa has been so widely appropriated, even into the discourse of dominant organs of the Western media, indicates that something new is happening and that Africa's relations with external powers are undergoing significant changes, both quantitative and qualitative. However, given that today no external actor will own up to, and indeed will decry, imperialism, there is a need to legitimate imperialist or imperial-like relations in alternative clothing of benevolence. If Africa, as *The Economist* implied, lacks hope, then it needs to be given hope; if Africa is impoverished, it must be given aid; if Africa is undeveloped, then it must be developed; and if Africa is badly governed, then it needs good governance. Or as Lee (2006: 305–10) has it, Africa needs to be saved. Whatever the precise terminology, Africa is projected as an other, a cross between a wayward child and a tragic victim of historical circumstance that can only be helped from outside to pull up its own bootstraps by well-intentioned nations. From this perspective, it is only rivals of dubious intention (for Western nations, the Chinese or other new intruders; and for the Chinese, Western nations) that engage in imperialism and are responsible for detrimental aspects of the new scramble. The ideological justification is that they do imperialism; we do development. However, as Lee (2006) points out, the two faces of the new scramble are inextricably intertwined.

Lee (2006) provides a wide-ranging account of the saving Africa profile. Africa is to be rescued by the Western powers from its potential slide into the abyss, primarily through increased development assistance:

> The rescuing is to be done through a myriad programmes, including the United Nations Millennium Development Goals (MDGs); the US African Growth and Opportunity Act; President George W.

Bush's Millennium Challenge Account; and Prime Minister Tony
Blair's Commission for Africa. As *The Economist* (December 18, 2004)
notes, "Everyone from Kofi Annan and George Bush to Jacques
Chirac and Mr Blair would like to be known as the politician who
broke the back of global poverty" (Lee 2006: 305).

Of course, the actors change, but the play continues to run, one of its latest
episodes being the G8 Africa Action Plan that promised an increase of official
development assistance to $12 billion a year.

Margaret Lee has provided in chapter four an overview of these different
programmes, along with notes about their internal inconsistencies, their
unevenness, the tendency to favour some countries over others and, not least, the
failure of most Western countries to honour their aid promises. While the goals
of such programmes are ambitious (for instance, the MDGs were adopted by the
heads of state of 147 countries in 2000, their major objective being to halve
extreme poverty by 2015) and include some valuable initiatives (commitments to
the doubling of aid to sub-Saharan Africa under the MDGs, writing off debt for
highly-indebted countries and massively increasing African access to health and
education), they tend to be rather larger on rhetoric than action. This may be in
part because they are complemented first by Western promotion of good
governance via aid conditionalities; and second, by emphasis upon economic
self-help. In contrast to the statist development strategies so common after
independence, this requires an unambiguous commitment of African states to
strategies of capitalist development. From this perspective, the Western
engagement with Africa comes as a package. As Hurt (2007: 365) opines of Blair's
Report of the Commission on Africa, 'Ultimately the report urges Africa to
embrace the good governance agenda so that it can benefit economically from a
liberalized world trade system and the continued transnationalisation of
production'.

Lee (2006: 310) refers to the saving Africa profile as 'a convenient disguise to
mask the real intentions of the Western powers to have continued access to the
markets and natural resources of Africa'. However, the argument here is rather
that the two faces of the new scramble co-exist, with the motivations of almost all
external actors simultaneously embodying good intention, self-interest, naked
imperialism and outright hypocrisy. We can even make useful comparison with
Pakenham's four Cs. In place of civilisation, there is emphasis upon development,
the collapse of the Soviet model now permitting promotion of capitalism as the

only road to modernity. Commerce translates into the advantages of globalisation and the opportunities offered to Africa by increased exchange with the West. Although Christianity is no longer explicit in official discourse, where it has been replaced by the secular gospel of democratisation, it is surely no coincidence that emphasis on Africa as a theatre in a global struggle against Islamic jihad is accompanied by a massive thrust into the continent by American evangelical churches. Finally, while overt conquest is no longer regarded as respectable, it appears inevitable that the militarisation of the new scramble by the US under the guise of securitisation of allied regimes will outlast the demise of the adminis-tration of President George W. Bush.

That the Chinese do not subscribe to the good governance agenda in no way alters the fundamental thrust of the equivalent of the 4 Cs. Nor should the Chinese approach be viewed as less paradoxical than that of the West. Their gospel of non-intervention in the internal affairs of African countries, yoked as it is to crude elevation of socio-economic over political and human rights, is so imbalanced in its de facto support for despotic regimes from Sudan to Zimbabwe that at some point it is likely to translate into substantial disaffection on the ground with perceived Chinese imperialism. However, while an effort to trace the lineages of the 4 Cs can be instructive, it is more helpful to compare the original and new scrambles in terms of the characteristics of the former as already identified.

The First and New Scrambles Compared

Imperialism and empire are unfashionable words, yet they are both evoked by the popularity of references to the new scramble. It follows that they need to be taken seriously for the patterns of continuing global inequality suggest that the underlying relations of imperialism did not disappear with the passing of formal colonial rule. We need to draw these out if we are to understand the underlying, long-term causes of the new scramble.

Arrighi (1978) has pointed out that the theories of imperialism that served as a guide for Marxists in interpreting the trends and events of the first half of the twentieth century had by the 1970s been overtaken by history. Whereas Lenin and others had predicted that monopoly capitalism would lead inexorably to war between the leading capitalist nations (a prediction that served well enough to explain the conflicts of both 1914–18 and 1939–45), this perspective sat uneasily with the Cold War (where conflict seemed more likely between the capitalist and communist Great Powers) but more particularly with the kind of world economic order that developed under US global hegemony. This was in considerable part shaped by workers' struggles along both the social democratic and Marxist trajectories that forced a fundamental, reformist reorganisation of world capitalism at the end of the Second World War. However, while this stabilised capitalism in the West through the incorporation of the working class both politically and economically, it also resulted in a strengthening of the unity of the world market and a tendency to decentralise industrial production in less-developed regions of the global economy. Capitalism, in short, was becoming more internationalised, a process much hastened by the collapse of the Soviet Union. The existing Marxist theories of imperialism had therefore become obsolete

> for the simple reason that world capitalism as instituted under US hegemony was no longer generating the tendency towards war among capitalist powers that constituted their specific *explanandum*. And to the extent that the system of nation-states was actually ceasing to be the primary form of political organization of world capitalism, the obsolescence of these theories would become permanent (Arrighi 2002: 9).

A major attempt to update the theory of imperialism has been offered by Hardt and Negri. Their basic thrust is that imperialism has been replaced by empire, 'a *decentred* and *deterritorialising* apparatus of rule that progressively incorporates the entire global realm within its open, expanding frontiers' (Hardt and Negri 2000: xii; original emphasis). Unlike previous empires, the empire of postmodern times has no boundaries nor centre of power. Rather, sovereignty is now 'composed of a series of national and supranational organisms united under a single logic of rule' that operate within an interlocking regulatory framework. Empire has thus done away with the nation state as an effective power structure, so that today even the US cannot act as a centre of gravity for imperialism. Meanwhile, 'the tendential realization of the world market' destroys any notion that today a region or market can 'isolate or de-link itself from the global networks of power in order to create the conditions of the past and develop as the dominant capitalist countries once did' (Hardt and Negri 2000: 284). The counterpoint is the multitude, the new global working class that, simultaneously empowered and liberated by global-isation, must abandon local struggles and 'touch immediately on the global level' (Hardt and Negri: 55).

Hardt and Negri's book *Empire* has been much praised for providing a radicalised understanding of globalisation and for highlighting its progressive political potentialities. However, two fundamental criticisms stand out. The first is the over-inclusiveness of the multitude. As Arrighi (2002) observes, popular protests against the emergent world state, as at the Seattle meeting of the WTO in 1999, were as much a struggle between North and South as they were between capital and labour. Second, Hardt and Negri too easily dismiss the US as a locus of imperialist power and as a 'pre-eminent guardian of the capitalist order world-wide' (Munck 2001). While it is certainly true that US hegemony is being eroded economically by amongst others the EU and China, the US still constitutes a military power of unprecedented proportions.[17] Given that the leading capitalist powers are increasingly interdependent, with Chinese growth, for instance, fuelled by the sale of manufactured goods to the US, this may mean that inter-imperialist war becomes logically less likely. Against this, a neo-conservative attempt by the US to protect its hegemony militarily, as demonstrated by the wars in Afghanistan and Iraq and continued sabre rattling towards Iran, could lead to massive destruction and instability (Arrighi 2002).

According to Harvey (2003) the latest world historical phase is characterised by the new imperialism of the US. His framework is based upon an understanding of capitalist imperialism as a contradictory fusion of 'the politics of state and empire' (imperialism as a political project on the part of actors whose power is based in command of a territory) and 'the molecular processes of capital accumulation in space and time' (imperialism as a diffuse political-economic process in which command over and use of capital takes primacy) (Harvey 2003:26). In practice, while the two logics are often complementary, they also frequently tug against each other. Over the long term, however, the process of capital accumulation needs a political power to protect property. Consequently, 'if the accumulation of power must necessarily accompany the accumulation of capital then bourgeois history must be a history of hegemonies expressive of ever larger and continuously more expansive power' (Harvey 2003: 34).

After 1945, the geographical expansion of capital accumulation was dis-tinguished by the rise of US hegemony. From 1970, the latter was characterised by neo-liberalism and the flight of Western capital to countries where labour was cheaper than at home (see chapter two by Vishwas Satgar). By the late 1990s, however, US capitalism was in the throes of crisis, marked by a dramatic decline in asset values. Either there had to be a dramatic devaluation of capital to promote exports; or new areas of capital accumulation needed to be opened up in areas such as China. It was in this context that the US administration under President George W. Bush shifted to neo-conservatism, towards coercion rather than consent and a more overtly imperial vision of the US role in the world. This was based upon a reliance on the US's unchallengeable power, notably through military command over global oil resources. The logic of this was that 'whoever controls the Middle East controls the global oil spigot and whoever controls the global oil spigot can control the global economy, at least for the near future' (Harvey 2003: 19). Following 9/11, the Iraq war was an inexorable outcome.

Harvey proposes the notion of the spatio-temporal fix, whereby crises of capitalist accumulation – the lack of means to bring together profitably simultaneous surpluses of capital and labour, as during the Great Depression – are resolved. Such surpluses can be absorbed either by temporal displacement – investment in long-term projects at home; by spatial displacements – the opening up of new markets, new production capacities and new resource, social and labour possibilities elsewhere; or combinations of both (Harvey 2003: 109). However, capitalist accumulation always retains a dual character. On the one hand, it operates in the commodity market and in the places – factories, mines and farms – where capital value is produced. On the other, it involves accumulation by dispossession.

For Harvey, following Rosa Luxemburg, accumulation by dispossession is a product of the unequal relations between capitalism and non-capitalist modes of production as exhibited under colonialism. With neo-liberalism, accumulation by dispossession became systematised at the global level by various means: the corporatisation and privatisation of public utilities and the reversal of social rights won by class struggle; commodification and privatisation of land in the South; biopiracy (the pillaging of the world stockpile of genetic resources); and the escalating depletion of the global commons, for example oceans and forests. This released assets, including labour power, at low or zero cost and turned them over to capital for profitable use. Accumulation by dispossession thus re-emerged from the shadowy position it had held prior to 1970 to become a major feature within capitalist logic. The collapse of the Soviet Union and the opening up of China entailed a massive release of hitherto unavailable assets into the mainstream of capital accumulation. However, while the 'gargantuan programme of what is in essence a truly primitive form of accumulation in China' (Harvey 2003: 209) may drive capitalist growth capable of absorbing much of the world's surplus, it is simultaneously viewed as a massive looming threat to US hegemony. The resulting neo-conservative agenda has been to contain this threat by the extension of military power and control of oil spigots. However, even though the influence of the neo-conservatives is today increasingly under challenge, it will be difficult for successor administrations to reverse this process along more rational lines – for instance, towards a sort of global New Deal – because of the overwhelming political strength of the US ruling class and its military-industrial complex.

It would be unwise to discount various analyses that ascribe improving economic performance in Africa to factors such as better governance and economic management, reduced conflict, debt relief, targeted anti-poverty policies and so on, even though it is necessary to debate them. Chege, for one, stresses that higher growth rates are not merely restricted to Africa's oil-driven economies.[18] Even so, there is overwhelming evidence that the fundamentals of Africa as a producer and exporter of raw materials and an importer of capital goods and consumables are largely unchanged. These fundamentals reflect the dual character of capital accumulation as proposed by Harvey. What has altered, however, is the external global environment, which has so dramatically changed the competition for Africa's resources.

Key Features of the New Scramble

As during the late nineteenth century, the dynamics of the new scramble clearly lie outside Africa in the changing global power shifts and strategies outlined by Harvey: the spatial opening up of new of sites of capital accumulation in the South, the increasingly fluid and global nature of financial flows, the erosion of US hegemony, the struggle for access to oil and the increasingly imperial thrust of US military policy. In Africa, the recent emergence of China as an investor and trading partner, alongside its own (sometimes) imperial-like strategies towards individual African regimes, is only the most obvious example. Other new actors, notably India whose engagements are portrayed in chapter five by Sanusha Naidu, are also appearing. Another important feature is the emergence of South African capital as a significant player in the scramble for, most notably, energy, mineral resources, and financial, construction and retail markets. Indeed, as John Daniel and Mpume Bhengu argue in chapter six, in many ways South Africa – in economic, if not strategic, terms – remains an equal player to China and certainly much more important than any other rival from the South. However, whether or not South Africa constitutes a sub-imperial power remains a matter for debate, not least with regard to which imperial power it is in thrall. Nonetheless, what is undisputable is that South African capital is itself increasingly internationalised, notwithstanding its not insignificant black empowerment element; and that South Africa is becoming an increasingly important site for take off into the rest of Africa for foreign capital.

A further point, not usually stressed but highlighted in chapter fourteen by Roger Southall and Alex Comninos, is that because of the amount of capital and advanced technology required to engage in the most advanced thrusts of the new scramble, it is only African state companies that have the resources and autonomy to engage on anything like equal terms with the multinationals and Chinese state-linked companies. Even the larger South African black empowerment companies are closely tied to white financial or mineral capital. Otherwise, African capitalist success has remained restricted largely to areas of investment from which multinationals have exited, such as local manufacturing; or which they have ignored until recently, such as cellular telephony.

The major difference between the first and new scrambles clearly lies in the territorial aspect. Partition of Africa and formalisation of empire occurred in the late nineteenth century as the outcome of political rivalry between the west European Great Powers, the flag preceding trade as much as the reverse. This was for a mix of motives that ranged from the desire for national glory, the fear of being excluded and the need to exclude rival nations; to the opportunity to appropriate African riches, markets and labour. The borders resulting from that partition are today fiercely protected by African successors to the colonial powers. The legitimacy of the state, and politicians' control of and access to resources, relies upon its supposed embodiment of nation, however hollow that claim is in reality. The political, economic and human costs of the lack of fit between nation and state are one of the most widely commented upon aspects of contemporary Africa. Indeed, much of the policy of the former colonial powers has been directed at maintaining the integrity of territorial boundaries, propping up state machineries and containing the dynamics of disintegration. Such strategies range from direct military support and intervention to recent support for democratisation. However, while post-colonial spheres of influence, notably the informal division into Francophone and Anglophone Africa, are today becoming more porous as patterns of foreign investment are increasingly internationalised, there are few regrets at the retreat from formal to informal empire.

There are, however, two caveats. First, while their formal retreat from Africa allowed the former colonial powers to reduce or eliminate the political costs of continuing occupation, the financial burden of maintaining the colonial state was not shed so easily. The continuing dependence of the large majority of African states upon donors for foreign aid to supplement their budgets left them acutely vulnerable to external influence in determining the allocation of their expenditure. Aid therefore became a vital tool in the arsenal of the foreign policy of the Western powers, to be granted or withdrawn as they deemed fit. Conditionality has become the major instrument utilised by bodies like the International Monetary Fund (IMF) and the World Bank for requiring loan recipients to conform to their economic strictures; and by donor governments for demanding good governance. Indeed, multinational companies sometimes indulge in strategic philanthropy in order to protect their investments (Barnes 2005).

Given the waywardness of often corrupt African leaders, conditionality is not without its virtues and to some extent it is a response by Western politicians to demands for accountability from their own electorates. Nonetheless, especially with the increasing multilateralisation of aid, dispensed as it is by a host of state and non-state actors (non-governmental organisations (NGOs), foundations, churches and so on) it has become highly politicised, with the US under President George W. Bush, for instance, counterbalancing its military expansion into Africa by emerging as the continent's single largest source of aid for fighting HIV/AIDS (Smith 2004). Donors thus often scramble to dispense aid as leverage for political influence or for clearing the path for investments. However, it is precisely this aspect that is threatened by the Chinese, for they formally eschew conditionality and grant their aid without strings. Their position is that their commitment in Africa is long-term, notably the provision of infrastructure such as roads, railways, buildings and stadiums, and that human rights are better served by resultant economic development than political conditionalities. Yet this is merely a variation of the aid game, for Chinese aid projects on the whole appear to be an accompaniment to investment by Chinese companies; or an inducement to Chinese access to oil, minerals or other raw materials (Tull 2006). How Western governments are going to react, and how China is going to respond to African governments that fail to keep their part of any perceived bargain, is a matter for speculation.

The second caveat is that political partitioning has been succeeded by the economic division of Africa into zones. This operates at several levels. First, Africa as a whole is increasingly subject to the strictures of the WTO, which has emerged as the broker drawing up comprehensive, binding global rules for the exchange of goods. Suffice it to say, their emphasis upon free trade and intellectual property rights favours rich countries over poor and the North over the South. Second, the adoption by the AU of NEPAD, whose rationale is to open up African markets by adopting rules of good governance, was designed to secure increased flows of Western aid, trade and investment. Then third, in contrast to the WTO and NEPAD, which provide the overarching framework for Africa's international trade, there is the systematisation of competitive trade preference zones by the US under AGOA and by the EU in the form of EPAs. Overall, the comprehensive restructuring of the African political economy that has occurred since the 1970s is due to structural adjustment programmes, the erosion of the spheres of influence of former colonial powers and the post-Cold War rewriting of global trade and investment rules. These are the major factors facilitating and structuring the new scramble in Africa, although they have been supplemented by the massive changes in technology, transport and communications that have drawn Africa so much closer to other global markets.

Lee (2006: 325) is not alone in depicting African leaders as serving as 'conduits for naked imperialism' and actively participating in pillaging. To be sure, a key difference of the new scramble compared with its predecessor is that today, external actors negotiate with formally sovereign states for access to resources, rather than crudely appropriating them. If this is imperialism, argues John Daniel, then it is 'imperialism by consent' rather than grand larceny.[19] So the crucial mechanism of new forms of imperialism in Africa appears to be compradorism, the willing accession of leaders to deals with external forces that are of advantage to them but operate at great cost to the general welfare of their fellow African citizens. Thus heinously corrupt leaderships in oil- and mineral-rich African countries are notorious for structuring deals with multinational companies that enable them to appropriate revenues and redirect into them into foreign bank accounts, lavish consumption, private businesses or political patronage. Governments lacking accountability to their peoples prove happy to enter defence agreements with the US in exchange for the strengthening of their militaries and their hold on power. At continental and national levels, African leaders have acceded to rules and regulations that entrench, restructure and extend global relations of inequality, risking the opening up of their economies in exchange for uncertain advantages. Political and economic elites are complicit in asset stripping, ranging from acceptance of commissions for facilitating external access to local resources to active participation in schemes for exporting Africa's riches without due regard to the general interest (see again chapter fifteen by Roger Tangri).

Yet the reality faced by African leaders is a daunting one. Leaving aside the patrimonial basis of power in many African countries, which requires that leaderships provide rewards for their clienteles, African governments are confronted by the dilemmas of promoting the development of their economies amidst global conditions of acute disadvantage. Broadly speaking, their options have narrowed considerably since independence, when socialism and de-linking from the West, perhaps supported by the Soviet Union, appeared credible alternatives. In the wake of rapid globalisation and IMF and World Bank entrenchment of neo-liberal economics, African leaders now have little option but attempt to make capitalism work for their countries under highly unfavourable conditions. One of the latter is the absence of a significant African capitalist class capable of offering competition to foreign companies in spheres other than local manufacturing, commerce and tourism. This in turn renders them subject to the urgencies of competing for foreign investment, an imperative that can so easily turn into a race to the bottom in terms of relaxed tax conditions as well as labour and environmental standards. Meanwhile, they have to weigh the necessity of balancing the budget against the political protests that often accompany popular resistance to foreign competition and exploitation.

It is often remarked that the new scramble is widening choices for African governments and promoting prospects for development. Two factors, in particular, are said to present themselves. First, the increase in trade with and investment from China, India and other countries from the South is reducing US and Western political leverage and economic dominance over the continent. Second, projected global scarcities raise the prospect of Africa exploiting resource (inter)nationalism and joining bodies such as the Organisation of Petroleum Exporting Countries (OPEC). Indeed, Russia is already said to be working with Nigeria and Algeria to establish an international gas cartel, while major oil producers from the Middle East are known to be looking to Africa to develop relationships that could increase their weight as resource suppliers globally (Holslag 2008). There is no doubt that these are, potentially, exciting opportunities and perhaps a step on the road to the realisation of Harvey's global New Deal. However, the consideration of such possibilities is postponed to the conclusion.

Notes

1. Whereas Seeley initially laments that 'There is something very characteristic in the indifference which we show towards this mighty phenomenon of the diffusion of our race and the expansion of our state. We seem, as it were, to have conquered and peopled half the world in a fit of absence of mind' (1883: 10); he later cites the expansion of the US and Russia 'as examples of the modern tendency towards enormous political aggregations, such as would have been impossible but for the modern inventions which diminish the difficulties caused by time and space' (1883: 334). Whereas the US and Russia were continuous land powers, the expansion of what he termed Greater Britain was dependent upon domination of the seas.

2. Wehler stresses that Bismarck's push into Africa was motivated in considerable part to protect German merchants, who faced rising protective tariffs abroad, and was subsequently justified by a strategy of social imperialism that sought to displace middle-class lack of security to the colonies.

3. Recall, for instance, the Heligoland-Zanzibar Treaty of 1890 between Germany and the United Kingdom. The former gained Heligoland in the North Sea, the Caprivi Strip and freedom to acquire the coast around Dar es Salaam in exchange for handing over the small sultanate of Wituland on the Kenyan coast and northern parts of East Africa; and pledged not to interfere in Zanzibar, over which Britain finally gained control following the Anglo-Zanzibar War in 1896.

4. Lest we forget: the major Western powers stood solidly behind white power in southern Africa, despite their increasing discomfort as the years went by with apartheid as both ideology and a strategy for political stability. Their support was military, economic and political, conforming to or evading internationally imposed sanctions upon Rhodesia and South Africa as it suited them. After the Portuguese withdrew from Africa in the mid-1970s, the US in particular lent systematic undercover support to rebel movements in both Angola and Mozambique, while more generally the Western powers worked extensively to deny legitimacy to liberation movements. It was only after defeat loomed large for the Smith regime in Rhodesia, white rule was threatened in South Africa by growing internal black resistance, and the Soviets signalled their withdrawal from Africa towards the end of the Cold War that the US sought settlements in Angola, Mozambique, South West Africa and South Africa itself. I am grateful to Carol Thompson for urging me to stress this point.

5. 'UN's Annan warns of new scramble for Africa'. *New Zealand Herald* 2 July 2006.

6. Dino Mahtani, 'The new scramble for Africa's resources'. *Financial Times* 28 Jan. 2008.

7. 'Oz geologists I presume: gold's price boom is leading mining companies to 'hot' new destinations'. *Financial Mail* (Johannesburg) 23 Dec. 2005; 'Great expectations for continent's hidden asset'. *Financial Mail* (Johannesburg) 9 Dec. 2005; 'Manganese rush in the Kalahari'. *Business Day* (Johannesburg) 11 Sep. 2006.

8. 'Investors eye Africa's privatizing banks'. *Business Day* 24 Mar. 2005.

9. 'Threat, ally or model? China looms large in Africa's future'. *Business Day* 31 Mar. 2005; 'China's new scramble for Africa'. *The American* 22 Nov. 2006; 'Beware the "Chindia" effect'. *Mail & Guardian* (Johannesburg) 14–20 Oct. 2005; 'US and China in Africa: arrival of partners or predators?' *Business Day* 11 Aug. 2006; 'Why China is winning in Africa'. *Business Day* 2 Jan. 2007; 'Africa could lose out to Bric firms'. *Star* (Johannesburg) 24 Jan. 2006; 'China and the US in Africa: scramble for an African response'. *Business Day* 26 June 2007.

10. 'The scramble for Africa's oil'. *New Statesman* (London) 17 June 2007; 'Scramble for Africa'. *The Guardian* 2 May 2007.

11. 'Expectations high for deep underwater reserves'. *Financial Mail* 7 Oct. 2005; 'Deep land claims'. *Financial Mail*, 9 Nov. 2007; 'Melting ice wastes spark new scramble for the Arctic's riches'. *Business Day* 20 Aug. 2007.

12. Institute for the Analysis of Global Security, 'The future of oil', 2004. http://www.iags.org/futureofoil.html.

13. General James Jones, head of the US European Command, speaking before the Senate Armed Services Committee in Mar. 2006, cited by Thompson (2007).
14. Associated Press Business News. 2007. 'Uranium exploration in Africa by country' http:news.moneycentral.msn.com/ticker/article.aspx?Feed=AP&Date+20071226&1; StockInterview.com. 'Russia and China battle over African uranium'. http://www.stock interview.com/News/05222007/African-Uranium-Russia-China-Batt.
15. J. Holmberg, Natural resources in sub-Saharan Africa: assets and vulnerabilities: a contribution to the Swedish Government White Paper on Africa commissioned by the Nordic Africa Institute, 2007.
16. 'Focus on . . . fisheries in Africa'. New Agriculturalist Online 1 Nov. 2005. http://www. new-agri.co.uk/05-6/focuson/focuson1.html.
17. President George W. Bush's military budget for 2009 ran to $515 billion. Adjusted for inflation this was higher than at any time since the Second World War. If supplementary outlays and spending on the military elsewhere in his overall budget are included, US spending would exceed $1 trillion, roughly half the British economy (Cornwall 2008).
18. M. Chege, Concept note for the first sub-Saharan Africa HDR: building state capability in Africa: institutional reforms for stability, economic growth and societal transformation. Mimeo, 2007.
19. Private communication to the author, 28 May 2008.

References

Abramovici, P. 2004. 'United States: the new scramble for Africa'. *Review of African Political Economy* 31(102): 685–90.

Amin, S. 1972. 'Underdevelopment and dependence in black Africa: origins and contemporary forms'. *Journal of Modern African Studies*, 10(4): 503–24.

Arrighi, G. 1978. 'Towards a theory of capitalist crisis'. *New Left Review* 111: 3–24.

——. 2002. 'Lineages of empire'. *Historical Materialism* 10(3): 3–16.

Barnes, S. 2005. 'Global flows: terror, oil and strategic philanthropy'. *Review of African Political Economy* 32(104–5): 235–52.

Bracking, S. and G. Harrison. 2003. 'Africa, imperialism and new forms of accumulation'. *Review of African Political Economy* 30(95): 5–10.

Campbell, K. 2008. 'Growth forecast for key African defence markets'. *Engineering News* (Johannesburg) 18 Jan.

Cornwall, R. 2008. 'White House marches to iron triangle's beat. *Sunday Independent* 17 Feb.

Foster, J. 2006. 'A warning to Africa: the new U.S. imperial grand strategy'. *Monthly Review* 58(2): 1–12.

Freund, B. 1984. *The Making of Contemporary Africa: The Development of African Society Since 1800*. Basingstoke: Macmillan.

Goodison, P. 2007. 'EU trade policy and the future of Africa's trade relationship with the EU'. *Review of African Political Economy* 34(112): 247–66.

Hardt, M. and A. Negri. 2000. *Empire*. Cambridge, Mass: Harvard University Press.

Harvey, D. 2003. *The New Imperialism*. Oxford. Oxford University Press.

Holslag, J. 2008. 'The new scramble for Africa'. *Europe's World* 21 Feb. http://www.europesworld.org/EWSettings/Article/tabid/78/Default.aspx?Id=16d5d99d-ad2e-43f6-a51c-1dad3aOcfe82.

Hurt, S. 2007. 'Mission impossible: a critique of the Commission for Africa'. *Journal of Contemporary African Studies* 25(3): 355–68.

Johnston, P. 2004. 'Timber booms, state busts: the political economy of Liberian timber'. *Review of African Political Economy* 31(101): 441–56.

Klare, M and D. Volman. 2006. 'America, China and the scramble for Africa's oil'. *Review of African Political Economy* 33(108): 297–309.

Lee, M. 2006. 'The 21st century scramble for Africa'. *Journal of Contemporary African Studies* 24(3): 303–30.

Melber, H. 2007. 'The new scramble for Africa's resources'. *Pambazuka News* 8 Feb. http://www.pambazuka.org/en/category/comment/39693.

Munck, R. 2001. 'Review of Hardt and Negri's "Empire"'. *Cultural Logic* 3(2).

Mushita, A. and C. Thompson. 2007. *Biopiracy of Biodiversity: Global Exchange as Enclosure*. Lawrenceville, N.J.: Africa World Press.

Oliver, R. 2000. *The African Experience: From Olduvai Gorge to the 21st Century*. London: Phoenix.

Oliver, R. and A. Atmore. 1996. *Africa since 1800*. Cambridge. Cambridge University Press, 4th ed.

Pakenham, T. 1992. *The Scramble for Africa*. Johannesburg. Jonathan Ball.

Rodney, W. 1972. *How Europe Underdeveloped Africa*. Dar es Salaam: Tanzanian Publishing House.

Seeley, J. 1883. *The Expansion of England*. London: Macmillan (1931 printing).

Shaxson, N. 2007. *Poisoned Wells: The Dirty Politics of African Oil*. London: Palgrave Macmillan.

Shillington, K. 1989. *History of Africa*. Basingstoke: Macmillan.

Smith, G. 2004. 'US aid to Africa'. *Review of African Political Economy* 31(102): 698–703.

Stevens, C. 2006. 'The EU, Africa and economic partnership agreements: unintended consequences of policy leverage'. *Review of African Political Economy* 44(3): 441–58.

Strachey, J. 1959. *The End of Empire*. London: Gollancz.

Taylor, I. 2007. 'Arms sales to Africa: Beijing's reputation at risk'. *China Brief* 5 April. http://www.jamestown.org.china/china_brief/article.php?articleid=2373306.

Thompson, C. 2007. Scramble for Africa's oil'. *New Statesman* 17 June.

Tull, D. 2006. 'China's engagement in Africa: scope, significance and consequences'. *Journal of Modern African Studies* 44(3): 459–80.

Turner, M. 2007. 'Scramble for Africa'. *The Guardian* (London) 2 May.

Wehler, H-R. 1970. 'Bismarck's imperialism, 1862–1890'. *Past and Present* 48: 119–55.

White, G. and S. Taylor. 2001. 'Well-oiled regimes: oil and uncertain transitions in Algeria and Nigeria'. *Review of African Political Economy* 28(89): 323–44.

CHAPTER TWO

Global Capitalism and the Neo-Liberalisation of Africa

Vishwas Satgar

Africa has experienced almost 500 years of capital penetration, from the era of merchant capital through the slave trade and colonialism to neo-colonialism. Over the past three decades, however, the continent has witnessed a departure from this trajectory with new historical conditions and dynamics of accumulation taking root. Changes in global capitalism, due to the crisis of the 1970s, brought to the fore a new set of requirements for capital accumulation. During this period the increasing international mobility of capital, the further integration of the global market and the restructuring of global production have re-organised world capitalism. This chapter begins by contrasting the dynamics of colonial accumulation that informed the late nineteenth century scramble for Africa with the new dynamics of neo-liberal global restructuring. It argues that the new scramble for Africa obtains its meaning only in relation to an understanding of today's neo-liberal global economy.

While Africa's political economy is not unique, there are particularities and complexities that need to be highlighted to allow a more nuanced understanding of the forces shaping the continent. Through this analysis I attempt to situate the origins, development and logic of a neo-liberal Africa and challenge many of the common sense understandings about the failures of post-colonial development. More importantly, this chapter specifies the effect of Afro-neo-liberalism on continental accumulation processes, ideological concepts of control and state forms, while recognising that the embrace of neo-liberalism was not inevitable, but engendered under particular historical conditions.[1] These conditions produced more than a neo-liberal moment by conditioning a structural shift in which Africa has been disciplined to accept neo-liberal capitalism as its development path, albeit indigenised.

At the same time, the neo-liberalisation of Africa is not without its contradictions. Contemporary neo-liberal Africa coexists with an illiberal Africa. This is a part of Africa that is driving the commodity boom for natural resources, such as oil, stimulating continental growth and generating large amounts of financial resources, but is exempt from neo-liberal standards of Anglo-American style market democracy. It is that part of Africa that is most conflict ridden, tied into extractive global circuits, politically authoritarian and resistant to democratisation. In addition, the neo-liberalisation of Africa has also been affected by the securitisation of global accumulation due to the US-led war on terror. This further reinforces the illiberal side of Africa and involves an unprecedented US military presence through the new Africa command. It also imposes US pre-emptive conditionalities on aid and trade on the poorest countries on the African continent. This is neo-liberalisation through US supremacy and not through hegemonic intrusions. In short, Afro-neo-liberal capitalism – the new concept of control shaping continental restructuring by the transnationalised fraction of the African ruling classes – together with US-imposed neo-liberal accumulation is setting the rules and determining the conditions for the new scramble for Africa.

The First Scramble for Africa, Current Dynamics of Global Restructuring and Neo-Liberalism

The late nineteenth century colonial carve up of Africa by European countries at the Berlin Conference of 1884–5 continued a process of transplanting modernity and its various capitalist forms onto the African continent. This process was effected by the different kinds of colonialism that took root and was an outcome of the global expansion of capital due to industrialisation. Africa was linked into a global division of labour as a supplier of primary commodities, a role it continues to fulfil up to the present. In this sense, the first scramble for Africa has had consequences that still endure. Nonetheless, despite this continuity, it is important to understand the basis for capital expansion in the late nineteenth century world order and how this differs from that of the early twenty-first century.

The first important feature distinguishing the basis of capitalist expansion in the late nineteenth century from the present was the emergence of monopoly capital. This was observed by the liberal Hobson and various Marxists such as Hilferding, Bukharin, Lenin and Luxemburg. The emergence of monopolies, married to nation states, provided the basis for intense competition for markets and raw materials generating rivalries between economically advanced capitalist centres. This also served to explain the basis for war and conflict. However, unlike the national monopolies of finance capital in the late nineteenth century, the forms of capital driving the world economy today are transnational. Transnational capital is grounded in post-Fordist production structures that operate on a cross-border basis and constitute the emergence of a global economy (Cox 1997). Such forms of transnational capital originated in the crisis of accumulation of the 1970s and have been central to restructuring production, financial flows and the global division of labour. More specifically, global restructuring has developed production systems and value chains that cut across national spaces, but have been unevenly organised through the concentrated triadic investment flows between North America, Europe and Japan, as well with parts of Latin America and Asia, particularly China. Hence, the nature of rivalry today is not inter-imperialist but global. This is observable on the African continent in various sectors as transnational capital scrambles to capture resources to meet the needs of a global capitalism.

The second important distinguishing feature of capitalist expansion in the nineteenth century lies in the historical structures that served as the basis for world order and the foundation for British hegemony (Arrighi 1993).[2] Britain's victory over Napoleon in 1815 gave it control of the Westphalian inter-state system, which it transformed to its advantage. The rise of an industrial bourgeoisie, control of the world market, and the expansion into and extraction of tribute from non-Western colonies was such that the city of London grew into the centre of global finance. This served to enhance the hegemonic capacities of Britain in the nineteenth century. However, by the time of the Berlin Conference, British hegemony was in decline and being challenged by both Germany and the US. Germany at this point was attempting to emulate the territorial empire building of Britain, a factor that gave particular impetus to the carving up of Africa and ensured a fragile balance of power in Europe. Subsequently, after the Second World War, the US emerged as the dominant capitalist power and proceeded to build a new world order, the Pax Americana. It was maintained through the Bretton Woods system, managed by the World Bank and International Monetary Fund (IMF) anchored in mass Fordist production relations and the Keynesian welfare state (Cox 1987). However, unlike the British, US hegemony was extended through the promotion of decolonisation; a process of incorporation conditioned by the Communist threat during the Cold War; and by capital investment, military alliances, institutional linkages and dense networks across the developed capitalist states (Panitch and Gindin 2006). This integration, restructuring and co-ordination of the capitalist core continues to this day.

A final distinguishing feature of capital expansion relates to the ideological dimension. In the nineteenth century, British hegemony expressed itself through the credible assertion that the growth of its power reflected a universal rather than a mere national interest. Arrighi (1993: 174) suggests that 'central to this hegemonic claim was a distinction between the power of rulers and the "wealth of nations" subtly drawn in the liberal ideology propagated by the British intelligentsia. In this ideology, the expansion of the power of British rulers relative to other rulers was presented as the motor force of a universal expansion of the wealth of nations'. In other words, the ideology of free trade was effectively tied to wealth creation and fostered a dependency on the British market that reproduced its power. By the end of the Second World War the British-led world order came to an end and was replaced by the Pax Americana. Its ideological articulations and coercive practices broke with British free trade and laid the basis for the internationalisation of US monopolies.

By the 1970s, however, the Pax Americana began to unravel. Its crisis was organic and hence went to the heart of capitalist accumulation. In the words of Overbeek and Van der Pijl (1993: 14), the crisis of the 1970s 'was a fundamental crisis of "normality" affecting all aspects of the post-war order: social relations of production, the composition of the historical bloc and its concept of control, the role of the state, and the international order'. They argue that capital's response had to be comprehensive and hence the restructuring was accompanied by a newly-constituted project of hegemony. Neo-liberalism had to locate itself as the national or general interest, while in fact it was the narrow fractional interest of transnational capital.

Since the 1970s the neo-liberalisation of the world order has had to confront contending ideological forms and models of national political economy. Neo-liberalism in the 1980s had to overcome the developmentalism of the Third World, bureaucratic and centrally planned Soviet socialism and the regulatory regime of European social democracy. By the beginning of the twenty-first century the war on terror also became an important element in the ideological construction of neo-liberalism: in other words, global accumulation had to be securitised. This has also meant that a US-led world order is increasingly based on coercion. The notion of US supremacy most appropriately describes the shift from hegemonic consent to the coercive politics of the past decade and a half (Gill 2003). For Gill this means neo-liberalism is an instrument of power, more appropriately understood as disciplinary neo-liberalism. This 'involves the increasing use of market based structures to secure social discipline and organise distribution and welfare, for example in capital and labour markets, with the costs of adjustment forced upon the weakest by the strong, backed by the coercive apparatus of the state' (Gill 2003: 25).

However, in the transition from the US-led Pax Americana to a US-led neo-liberalisation of the world it is important to put in perspective the main goals of this project. While neo-liberalism was presented as a solution for the accumulation crisis of the 1970s, affirming the centrality of market-led development, free enterprise and a possessive individualism, it was also intended to ensure the following: first, the restoration of US leadership and hegemony in the world; second, the construction of a seamless global market for trade and financial flows, deepening commodification through intellectual property rights and capital; third, a model of primitive accumulation in which the market is unleashed on society and nature such that the structural power of capital, particularly finance capital, prevails; fourth, restructuring of state forms and regional economies to meet the requirements of global capitalism in a disciplined way; and fifth, subordination of all subaltern and working-class forces to the rule of capital.

However, today the US brand of hegemonic neo-liberalism is in crisis. The Washington consensus has unravelled through its development failures, the social crisis inflicted on the world through mass poverty and inequality, the internal contradictions of the US economy, and the impasse in World Trade Organisation (WTO) negotiations. Nonetheless, this does not mean the end of neo-liberalism, but rather its articulation into new forms, such as the poverty reduction paradigms of the World Bank and IMF. Moreover, the ideological renewal of neo-liberalism is also being conditioned by post-9/11 security imperatives. The war on terror has compelled the US to recognise the importance of excluded states and hence it is attempting to ensure its informal empire is firmly entrenched in the South and that its values restructure these states (Panitch and Gindin 2006: 37). It means that the new scramble for Africa is also about the US scramble to ensure that the states on the continent are disciplined to ensure loyalty in the war on terror, management of global crises and the reproduction of global capitalism.

The nineteenth century scramble for Africa's resources was directly related to the expansion of capital through colonialism. This was conditioned by the existence of various historical structures and forces – relations of production, hegemonic state forms and ideologies – that enabled penetration of the African continent. Today, Africa is confronting a new expansion or globalising form of capitalist penetration, but in a post-colonial context. Consequences of the old scramble are still prevalent, but reality requires coming to terms with a new wave of capitalist penetration shaped by transnational capital, US supremacy and the ideological prescriptions of a new concept of control: in short, transnational neo-liberalism. Africa today is confronted by the formation of a global capitalism in the image of the US.

Great Transformation: Afro-Neo-Liberal Capitalism and the Disciplining of Africa

Given the uneven development of the global economy, Africa's structural location is in the underdeveloped South. The way African ruling classes have ideologically internalised neo-liberalism and engaged transnational capital has to take account of particular modes of social relations of production. In other words, neo-liberalism has had to take on African characteristics and express itself through ideological forms and constructs championed by Africa's ruling blocs in national and regional politics. For instance, an IMF-led structural adjustment programme in Uganda under Yoweri Museveni is hailed in popular political rhetoric as the *Bonna Baggagawale*, the Prosperity For All Programme. In post-apartheid South Africa, structural adjustment has been home grown, legitimised through the rhetoric of the Reconstruction and Development Programme (RDP). While this process of neo-liberalisation has been uneven, it has produced an Afro-neo-liberal capitalism over three decades on the African continent.

For Gill (2003), the moment of neo-liberalisation represents a civilisation shift. It is about the deepening of commodification into the nooks and crannies of everyday life, in an extremely intensive way. The myth of capitalist progress thus marches under the banner of market civilisation. Afro-neo-liberal capitalism is an ideological expression of the shift in the *longue durée* to a global market civilisation. In the current situation on the African continent, it is a response of the ruling classes to the organic crisis of the continent; a crisis that has its roots in the failed post-colonial transition from structurally-determined underdevelopment to economic development. This has been a long crisis, multifaceted and contradictory, as it spanned early post-colonial independence and reached into the neo-liberalised present.

The making of Afro-neo-liberal capitalism has been a violent and brutal process, consisting of three overlapping post-colonial conjunctures. These are: first, the defeat of actual and potentially radical post-colonial state-led development projects – revolutionary nationalist, African socialist and Marxist-Leninist; second, the debt crisis and national adjustment; and third, limited democratisation and continental restructuring to meet the requirements of transnational capital.

Some commentators blame Fanon's ghost, or middle-class betrayals, for the neo-liberalisation of Africa, reducing failed post-colonial development to various state based pathologies such as South African sub-imperialism, the predatory state, criminalised state and neo-patrimonialism. Reality has been flattened out and complexity homogenised.[3] Hence it was argued by the World Bank that neo-liberalisation was the only solution to some of these state centric pathologies. But are such single factor causal arguments sufficient to explain Africa's great transformation and structural shift to market-led development? The disciplining of Africa has involved a dialectical interplay between US-led Cold War forces with continental and national forces. Africa's embrace of neo-liberalisation reflects the defeat of progressive political agency on the continent. This defeat and its implications for structural change is brought into perspective below utilising Gramsci's interpretative approach of the different levels of force that constitute the disciplining of Africa – the economic, political and coercive (Gramsci 1971: 175–85).

First, at the time of their independence Africa's post-colonial economic structures were poorly diversified and extroverted; that is, skewed to meet the needs of colonial economies (Mengisteab 1996). Originally, cash crops were the main economic products, but later minerals and oil become important national exports. Moreover, Africa's pre-colonial state boundaries were never firmly fixed and did not fit into some kind of idealised cultural map. Various disruptions – drought, war and trade – affected them. However, this history does not take away from the argument that economically viable African states required territorial unity. Although some anti-colonial leaders attempted to avoid Balkanisation to the point of proposing greater unity across colonial territorial boundaries, the majority of nationalist leaders preferred to accept the colonial map of Africa and small states obtained sovereign, internationally recognised status. Furthermore, although inward industrialisation was attempted as a crucial accumulation strategy in many countries, this did not confront the structural weaknesses of the inherited economy and also failed to break out of the colonial mould of the state. Thus, according to Mkandawire (2005: 168), 'the phase of import substitution industrialisation was too short – in most countries it was less than a decade'. Ultimately, post-colonial Africa was locked into structurally-dependent economic relations. The seeds for this were sown in the decolonisation process and ensured economic control remained in the hands of neo-colonial forces, while most of

Africa's politically liberated majorities had to be content with citizenship and inherited weak states.

By the 1980s, the cumulative impact of oil price shocks in the 1970s, falling primary commodity prices, drought and reduced global demand due to substitution contributed to Africa's debt crisis. However, the global event that ensnared Africa in the debt trap was rising interest rates in the US in the early 1980s. This move by the US Federal Reserve drove up the costs of loan finance to Africa and firmly tied the continent into the debt crisis. As a consequence, Africa became a net exporter of capital and growth rates were in negative digits.[4] Hence, the first wave of structural adjustment failed according to trade and investment indicators. Africa's great transformation, being the deepest and most aggressive, began displaying morbid symptoms of de-industrialisation and stagnation. The structural weaknesses and the debt crisis of the 1980s did not just hit non-capitalist states, but even those like Kenya that were seen as models of capitalist development. African debt undermined many economic and social development gains made through post-colonial development.

The disciplining of Africa continued at a political level. The narrowing of space for autonomous development by post-colonial African states links directly to the way demands by countries of the South for global economic restructuring were received by the US-led bloc in the United Nations in the early 1970s. These demands required greater redistribution through improved terms of trade, access to markets and the regulation of multinationals to ensure beneficial development. For the US-led bloc, these demands represented a grave threat to the sovereignty of capital and by the late 1970s, the demands for a New International Economic Order (NIEO) were defeated (Van der Pijl 1993). As a result, the NIEO-inspired Lagos Plan of Action, put forward by African countries in the early 1980s, which emphasised an alternative development path based on self-reliance, regional integration and endogenous industrial development, was stillborn. The debt crisis of the 1980s effectively undermined the last vestiges of economic sovereignty available to African states. Despite this, the World Bank claimed that the cause of failed adjustment was the African state and the fact that insufficient time was given to adjustment (Mkwandire 2005: 162). This gave rise to full-blown adjustment of the African state.

The great transformation to bring about Afro-neo-liberal capitalism had devastating consequences. First, the de-territorialising and disembedding of the African market meant rolling back state intervention. Structural adjustment was aggressively championed through strategies like privatisation, liberalisation and monetarism. It was as though the already ravaged African state had to walk through a bonfire: it had to be subsumed by the market. Second, African states remade racial and ethnic cleavages in the context of economic crisis. Ethnic and reactionary nationalisms came to the fore: Africa turned on itself even more and civil wars broke out in the 1990s in Liberia, Sierra Leone, Angola and Rwanda. Many of these conflicts were the result of failed attempts to achieve market democracies or took on the characteristics of resource wars.[5]

Third, secular economic decline continued and by the mid- to late-1990s most commentators and development actors including the World Bank were willing to accept the failures of adjusting the African state and economy (Cheru 2002; Mengisteab and Logan 1995; Mkandawire 2005 and 2006; Nyang'Oro 1999). The poverty, social polarisation, suffering and inequality this engendered further undermined the legitimacy of several already disintegrating states. This gave rise to a wave of resistance and democratisation. These processes were uneven, but swept away one-party states and numerous military dictatorships after the collapse of the Soviet Union (Southall 2003). Before 1990 Africa had only seven countries – Morocco, Senegal, Botswana, Zimbabwe, Tunisia, Egypt and Mauritius – with multi-party systems, albeit limited in some way. Between 1990 and 1997 peaceful changes of government took place in more than 40 countries through competitive multi-party elections (Cheru 2002: 33).

Strengthened by events in South Africa in 1994, this wave of democratisation held out numerous radical possibilities and gave rise to ideological battles about the kind of democracy appropriate to Africa. While many attempted to defend popular democracy over narrow liberal electoral democracy, the constitutionalism that emerged from this process in most instances premised democratisation on a separation of the economic and the political. The ideological argument that enabled this was anchored in an interpretation of post-colonial Africa that conflated state intervention with authoritarianism: democracies had, therefore, to ensure the freedom of the market even if state intervention in some instances had a great deal of economic merit (Mkandawire 2006: 16). This meant that a Rousseauian politics of mobilised general will easily descended into a Hobbesian nightmare in many countries. The second independence, or democratisation movement, of Africa engendered a new constitutionalism, but in the main locked in private property rights, insulated policymaking processes from mass-based politics and further transformed the African state into a student of good governance under the external surveillance of donors (Abrahamsen 2000; Sachikonye 1995; Shivji 1991). In a sense, the democratisation wave from below exposed the African state's major weakness: it was not counter-hegemonic and instead it gave rise to a neo-liberalised state rendered an effective prisoner to transnational capital and trade flows.

The coercive factor in post-colonial Africa also played a crucial disciplining role. This happened through counter-revolution and was part of Cold War anti-communism. Coups, covert operations, assassinations, support for dictators, low-intensity destabilisation and the fomenting of civil wars were used to prevent the emergence of successful state-led development projects or autonomous development paths (Heller 2006; Hobsbawm 1995). Post-colonial ruling classes made this even easier when many squandered the legitimacy gained from national independence by narrowing the space for mass involvement in development. Many of the first- and second-generation post-colonial ruling blocs replaced the masses with the state as the motive force for change.[6] State-centric development widened the gap between leaders and the masses and this easily opened the door for counter-revolution.

Cold War forces on the African continent insidiously targeted political movements with the potential to emerge as counter-hegemonic. One of the first Cold War operations on the African continent to stem the tide of supposed communism was the 1961 assassination of Patrice Lumumba, the first prime minister of Congo. This pioneer of African unity was not a communist, but a radical nationalist who threatened colonial interests. He was assassinated by Belgian forces and replaced, with US backing, by Mobutu Sese Seko. Kwame Nkrumah, leader of a liberated Ghana, an advocate of African socialism and fervent proponent of continental unity and anti-imperialism was toppled in a Western-backed coup in 1966. Amilcar Cabral, one of the great revolutionary leaders in the liberation struggle of Guinea-Bissau and Cape Verde, was assassinated in 1973 on the eve of a liberation breakthrough.[7]

Southern Africa also became an important theatre for Cold War conflict. Reagan's roll back strategy in the Third World gave support to Jonas Savimbi's National Union for the Total Independence of Angola (UNITA) forces and the National Mozambican Resistance Movement (RENAMO) in the 1980s. The South African apartheid regime assisted these forces through military incursions, intelligence and logistical support. Savimbi's UNITA was able to destabilise Angola, led by the Popular Liberation Movement of Angola (MPLA) for almost three decades. Fighting only stopped when Savimbi was killed in 2002, by which time it was clear that the MPLA had abandoned its commitment to a Marxist-Leninist project. In the struggle for Mozambique's liberation from Portuguese colonialism,

Eduardo Mondlane, one of the top leaders of the Mozambique Liberation Front (FRELIMO), was assassinated in 1969. However, the destabilisation of Mozambique and FRELIMO only ended with the death of Samora Machel in 1986 in a dubious plane crash over South Africa; and after FRELIMO entered into a peace agreement with South Africa, abandoned its Marxist-Leninist orientation and embraced multi-party democracy (Christie 1989; Hall and Young 1997).

According to Hobsbawm (1995: 251) the Cold War ended at a Washington summit in 1987, but was only recognised as such after the dissolution of the Soviet Union in 1991. In Africa it did not end with the collapse of eastern Europe or the negotiated transition in South Africa; but with the assassination of Chris Hani, General Secretary of the South African Communist Party (SACP) on 10 April 1993 and the subsequent degeneration and capture of his party by an authoritarian populist faction.[8] The counter-revolution in Africa destroyed countries, dislocated populations and shattered the lives of millions of ordinary people. The violent disciplining of Africa through destabilisation during the Cold War and its consequences cannot be excluded from an understanding of how state-led development projects failed or were blocked.

All of these historical factors – economic, political and coercive – shifted the relations of forces against an autonomous development path for Africa. The disciplining of Africa produced an Afro-neo-liberal capitalism that has attempted to legitimise neo-liberal accumulation strategies within ruling class projects of economic and political reform. It has inserted itself into the common sense of most African citizens through various cultural, political and social idioms and practices. In this way, Afro-neo-liberal capitalism indigenises neo-liberalism and restructures African economies, state forms, state-society relations, historical blocs and international relations to harmonise with its goals. At the same time, Afro-neo-liberal capitalism as a concept of control, excludes alternative development options for Africa such as delinking, autocentric development, self-reliant development and even African capitalism. It is presented by ruling historical blocs as a solution to Africa's organic crisis and embodies the national or general interests of society – an African solution to an African problem.

In various national and regional economic spaces, the core of neo-liberalism has had to co-exist with various ideological constructs, some hegemonic and some not, and establish forms of rule buttressing the power of ruling classes. This mixing of ideological elements has brought various national and regional paradigms of development under its sway and has hybridised with the ideological projects of political agents to structure and extend the reach of transnational capital and a global pattern of accumulation. In western Europe, for example, a heartland of capitalism, the restructuring of capital had a double effect. For Van Appeldoorn (2002) it spawned and made a transnational fraction of capital, which then utilised its structural power to defeat projects that would have introduced greater national regulation and protection from global competition.

In other parts of the world, neo-liberalisation had to be internalised in a way that solicits consent and is rooted in the common sense mentalities of various civil society structures.[9] However, this has not always been done through a democratic politics in countries of the South. From Chile to China, neo-liberalisation has been imposed through authoritarian means.[10] In other contexts, non-hegemonic strategies of passive revolution that limit mass social and political forces from influencing restructuring have been utilised.[11] The irony of neo-liberal accumulation strategies is that they are not development orientated. Privatisation, liberalisation, public-private partnerships, surveillance-based good governance, a truncated individual rights based discourse and regular elections are all strategies to entrench the power of capital over society and the state. This is the essence and logic of the new scramble for Africa.

The Illiberal Side of Neo-Liberalism: Africa's Petro-States

Africa has seven oil producing economies in which net oil exports make up 30% or more of total exports (International Monetary Fund 2007). Besides these oil-dependent economies there is a host of other countries that have discovered oil and are poised to emerge as petro-states. This boom in oil exploration and extraction has been a recent phenomenon and precipitated a geopolitical shift from North Africa – Algeria and Libya were early oil producers – to the Gulf of Guinea (Watts 2006; chapter eight by Cyril Obi in this book). The commodity boom over the past few years on the African continent is driven by oil producers. According to the IMF, Africa's growth crisis has been broken and the improvement in the continent's growth rate from just over 3% in 2001 to 6% in 2007 is bound to increase further (International Monetary Fund 2007).

However, while the growth data is wielded as affirmation of the restructuring of Africa's political economy, it conceals the illiberal side of neo-liberalism and Afro-neo-liberal capitalism. Most of the petro-states in sub-Saharan Africa – Sudan, Chad and most of West Africa – are some of the most authoritarian countries on the continent. A non-hegemonic politics of domination, combining dictatorship and fraud, prevails. States have international recognition, but internally sovereignty stands on imaginary stilts due to their deep legitimacy crises. Alongside formal state institutions, a parallel form of oil governance operates, based on the relationship between ruling classes, transnational oil companies and transnational banks (Shaxson 2007). Various extractive mechanisms come together in this axis of oil governance, but most striking is the use of selective elements of disciplinary neo-liberalism. For instance, all these oil economies have liberalised their oil industries and, while state oil corporations exist, in most instances they are locked into public-private partnerships that fit directly into the axis: that is, they extract oil for the benefit of the ruling classes and transnational capital (Watts 2006). Africa's oil wealth and its petro dollars are being drained away (see chapters eight and nine by Massey and May and Obi in this book).

The selective use of disciplinary neo-liberalism also extends to the sphere of consumption. In this regard, liberalisation has been crucial in ensuring that imports are plentiful to meet the conspicuous consumption of the ruling classes. This includes luxury cars, the latest *haute couture* and the necessities for palatial homes and expensive restaurants (Shaxson 2007). This elite consumption takes place in a context of large slums together with deepening poverty, inequality, abysmal human development trends and sharp social cleavages (Shaxson 2007; Watts 2006). Africa's petro-states are poised to become increasingly wealthy with growing global demand for oil and increasing prices. It is estimated that Africa's oil revenues per annum under current market conditions range between $90 and $100 billion (Shaxson 2007: 238) making them larger than total global aid flows. Yet there is increasing human misery and environmental destruction, concentrated in these petro-states but also afflicting Africa more broadly.

It is in the petro-states that wars are waged and thoroughgoing democratisation is a pipe dream. Attempted democratisation, as in Nigeria, has been managed from above and is not conducive to bringing people into the political process to influence economic policy and development choices. The axis of oil governance still rules. More generally, the disciplinary dictatorships of Africa's petro-states have ensured that the outer trenches and earthworks of civil society are rudimentary and pacified. With primitive accumulation concentrated on oil extraction, the development of agricultural production and manufacturing has been constrained in most of these economies. In the end, the axis of oil governance buys out some social forces and unleashes coercion and fear on the rest in order to maintain a conducive business climate and stability.

In short, the illiberal realities of Africa's petro-states contradict the utopian expansion of market democracy and Afro-neo-liberal capitalism. These states seem to be an acceptable exception for the US-led transnational historical bloc promoting the neo-liberalisation of the global economy as long as the investment and oil output from them aggregates into growth for Africa and ultimately the global economy, on the one hand; and massive oil profits are made for transnational capital, on the other. The transnational scramble for Africa's oil resources harmonises with the selective deployment of neo-liberal accumulation strategies by Africa's petro-states. This enables the use of global market economic force, combined with fraud, patronage and coercion, to give the relations that make up the axis of oil governance a disciplinary, dictatorial character. Ultimately, these free market based disciplinary dictatorships have produced a horror-ridden dystopia for the majority of their citizens.

US Supremacy and the Securitisation of Neo-Liberalism in Africa

Prior to 9/11, the administration of President George W. Bush publicly acknowledged a growing energy crisis in the US. However, instead of choosing a renewable energy path to solve it, Bush favoured continued oil import dependency (Klare 2003). His national energy policy projected that by 2020 the US will have to increase imports from 11 million barrels per day (mbd) to 18.5 mbd, an increase of 7.5 mbd or the equivalent of the total current oil consumption of India and China (Klare 2003: 169). Both in terms of present and future oil consumption, the US remains the largest oil consumer on the planet. Consequently, its energy policy choice under the Bush regime has also meant that US security is directly tied into ensuring steady, uninterrupted oil imports. It means foreign deliveries of oil to the US cannot be impeded by war, revolution or civil disorder and that these energy supply imperatives will extend to all major supply regions, including Africa.

After 9/11, security imperatives gained primacy in US foreign policy. This is reflected in the evolution of the post Washington consensus into a 'with us' or 'against us' emphasis, through numerous presidential pronouncements and a decisive policy shift in the *National Security Strategy* of 2006. This strategy affirms that Africa holds growing geostrategic importance. The broad objectives underpinning Africa's importance are clearly articulated: 'The United States recognises that our security depends upon partnering with Africans to strengthen fragile and failing states and bring ungoverned areas under the control of effective democracies . . . Through improved governance, reduced corruption, and market reforms, African nations can lift themselves toward a better future' (USA 2006: 42). These intentions have to be read together with the rest of the strategy, which explicitly links development support measures, trade and aid, to US security concerns.

The securitisation of the post-Washington consensus has two crucial aspects. First, it tightens the intersection between energy, security and foreign policy in the US. Second, following Soederberg (2006) and based on the objectives of the NSS document, it is clear that the post-Washington consensus intends to confront threats facing neo-liberal globalisation through greater control and surveillance. It is about pre-empting, through unilateralism rather than multilateralism, the development challenges facing failed and weak states. In this way, the security of the US is managed by bringing excluded states, particularly African, into global capitalism in a disciplined way and on the neo-liberal terms of the US.

Moreover, an unprecedented and very purposeful executive decision was taken in 2007 by the US government regarding the establishment of an integrated Africa military command structure (chapter seven by Rupiya and Southall in this book). Concrete steps were taken to establish such an Africa command structure during 2008. Inserted into the African context these securitised post-Washington consensus policy positions represent a new dimension in which the relations of force are seriously changed. What are the possible implications of a securitised neo-liberal post-Washington consensus for Africa?

First, it means Africa's petro-states have a geopolitical significance that far outweighs the rest of Africa. Currently, it is estimated that Africa produces 12% of the world's liquid hydrocarbon, about one in four barrels of oil outside North America (Vines 2006: 64). Most forecasts suggest that Africa's contribution to global oil production is likely to increase tremendously by the end of the decade due to growing global demand, its low sulphur content during refining and the ease of export from the Gulf of Guinea to the eastern seaboard of the US. At a geopolitical and policy level, increasing oil imports from Africa breaks US dependence on Persian Gulf oil supplies, an important consideration for the influential US Council on Foreign Relations (Victor 2006). Currently, Africa supplies the US with nearly 20% of its petroleum needs and given the energy choices made by the Bush government, supplies from Africa are going to balloon. As the US reduces its import dependence on Persian Gulf states, securing the supply of Africa's oil is an absolute necessity. In sub-Saharan Africa the US is targeting the largest oil producers, Nigeria and Angola, that together account for close to 50% of output. Forty billion dollars has been invested by oil transnationals in West Africa over the last decade with a further $50 billion injection expected before the end of the decade (Lyman and Morrison 2006; Watts 2006).

Second, a securitised neo-liberal post-Washington consensus implies that any prospect of utilising Africa's oil wealth for continental development is contained.

Oil nationalism linked to pan-Africanism is an unlikely prospect. Many of the petro-states have been disciplined by the first Gulf War and the subsequent invasion of Iraq, which has confirmed the willingness of the US to utilise its awesome military strength to secure what it wants. Moreover, the globalisation of domestic human rights abuses from the US, including the curtailment of civil liberties and political rights, has been encouraged by the infamous Patriot Act of 2001. The US's emphasis on combating domestic and global terrorism in this way is bound to strengthen the authoritarian impulses of Africa's petro-states and repressive regimes more generally.[12] The alliances formed between the US and many of these regimes, both for oil and the war on terror, will likely translate into a conducive business climate at all costs.

Third, both the US approach to protection of its oil interests in the Persian Gulf and its counter-attacks waged under the pretext of the war on terror, suggest an invasive disposition that could develop into a visible presence and meddling in internal politics. The US has already started militarising its relations with numerous African petro-states. According to Klare (2003: 177), Washington has made numerous African petro-states eligible for military aid and is planning a potential base located at the heart of the West African oil spigot, probably on the island of São Tomé e Príncipe. This approach will likely breed hostility and invite Islamic extremists to escalate armed conflict. Given the fragile nature of the states the US is targeting on the continent, there is potential for many Iraqs. Reminiscent of the Cold War era, Africa is likely to be further destabilised by superpower-incited armed conflict.

Finally, the securitised post-Washington consensus will utilise aid and trade on the African continent to ensure pre-emptive action against threats to neo-liberalism. For example, the Millennium Challenge Account (MCA) and Corporation were established by President George W. Bush as a US response to the financing challenges of the UN Millennium Development Goals for the poorest countries in the World. Through the MCA, countries have to conform to sixteen criteria to obtain assistance. According to Soederberg (2006), the criteria not only affirm the golden straightjacket of neo-liberalism, but the funding mechanism fits in with a unilateral practice linked directly to the US President. Soederberg further highlights the distinction between loan finance and MCA provisioning of performance-based grants. The latter is an alternative to loan-based practices that give recipients greater latitude over spending. Conversely, performance-based grant financing provides for greater control, surveillance and influence. In the context of securitisation, this coercive logic will also extend to trade and other bilateral relations through the American Growth and Opportunities Act (AGOA). This means the failed African state will have to accept all the pathologies imputed to it at a common sense and policy discourse level, implying surrender to the paternalism of a securitised post-Washington consensus. This is nothing short of a supremacist project, similar to but different from the first scramble for Africa.

Conclusion

The international economy over the past three decades has experienced a shift that has laid the basis for global capitalist structures of accumulation to emerge. Global neo-liberal restructuring is establishing a global market civilisation and attempting to end the era of national capitalism and autonomous development. The new scramble for Africa cannot be understood outside this process. Transnational fractions of Africa's ruling classes have embraced and internalised neo-liberalism as a new concept of control and ensured that an African version of neo-liberal capitalism is organised. A neo-liberalism with African characteristics has emerged: Afro-neo-liberal capitalism.

This has intensified and deepened Africa's integration into global extractive circuits. This process has developed through various post-colonial conjunctures in which Africa has been disciplined to accept Afro-neo-liberal capitalism as its development path. At the same time, the vulnerabilities of the political and economic dimensions of Afro-neo-liberal capitalism have to co-exist with an illiberal Africa, in particular its petro-states. These petro-states are driving growth on the continent, but are essentially disciplinary dictatorships with extremely tenuous political and social orders. In addition, global mutations in US-led neo-liberalisation, informed by the war on terror, have produced a securitised post-Washington consensus. In the African context this means Afro-neo-liberal capitalism is likely to give way to a neo-liberalisation imposed through US supremacy. This will further reveal the crisis of hegemony facing a US-led world order and the limits of the neo-liberal project. The dialectic that flows from this recognises an intensification of resistance as the likely outcome. This might determine the future of the US in the twenty-first century as the new scramble for Africa's resources, markets and state forms intensifies.

Notes

1. The macro-restructuring project on the African continent through the AU and NEPAD is further deepening Africa's integration into the global political economy. This is being mediated by class agency, in particular the role of a transnational fraction of the African ruling class. This class fraction has been formed in the process of national economic restructuring, through globalising sectors linked into transnational production and financial circuits and through processes of ideological articulation in global institutions both multilateral and private. The ideological outlook and strategic orientation of this class fraction is expressed through an indigenised variety of neo-liberalism – Afro-neo-liberalism. This is shaping continental restructuring and integration with the global economy and is reflected in various policies, institutions and practices. This hypothesis is central to my PhD project undertaken through the Department of International Relations, University of the Witwatersrand, entitled 'Africa's Adjustment to Transnational Capital: The Political Economy of the AU-NEPAD'. I draw on it for this paper to show how the rise of Afro-neo-liberalism is part of the disciplining of Africa.

2. The term hegemony is not used by Arrighi in a neo-Gramscian way, which refers to consent amongst social forces (states, transnational class fractions, media, professional classes and so on) that make up a transnational historical bloc. Arrighi uses hegemony in a state-centric way very similar to theorists in the neo-Realist tradition of international relations.

3. The sub-imperialism argument has been made by Patrick Bond (2004a and b) and is his consistent explanation for Africa's woes. Fanon's ghost is invoked in Bond (2005). Regarding pathologies of the state in Africa, while corruption and state failure clearly exist, I share the view of Mamdani (2005) that the state that has really failed in the post-colonial context is an inherited colonial state that generated racial and ethnic identities. The African failed state thesis attempts to explain a social reality by being ahistoric and blind to wider external and systemic realities.

4. According to Tlemcani (2005: 31), Africa's debt stood at $500 billion in the first few years of the new millennium. At the same time, 50% of Africa's savings was moved offshore. This capital flight deprives Africa of important financial resources for development that could break its dependence on international financial institutions if redirected.

5. Using the term resource wars, Klare (2001) helps to explain the new geopolitical dynamics underpinning conflict in the post-Cold War context, particularly with regard to the economisation of US security policy and the nature of resources themselves – limited supply, increasing demand and conflicts about ownership. In the African context, rival elites – ethnic and religious – struggle to control national endowments like water, oil, timber, diamonds and land. This has been at the root of various conflicts.

6. This would include Kenneth Kaunda's Zambia and Julius Nyerere's Tanzania and their attempts at African socialism from above. In the second generation, Gerry Rawlings of Ghana and Yoweri Museveni of Uganda are interesting in the way they moved from radical promises and commitments to fervent neo-liberalism.

7. There is an important literature that tells this tragic story: see Birmingham (1990), Chabal (2002), Davidson (1981), De Witte (2001) and Ray et al (1980).

8. See Forrest (2008). Moreover, Williams (2008) highlights the extent to which the renewal of socialist thinking in the SACP during the 1990s was merely a theoretical exercise for most and did not lead to the serious development of counter-hegemonic generative politics.

9. See Prasad (2006) for a comparative historical analysis of the development of neo-liberal policies.

10. Fernandez (1993) provides a tragic account of how Chile was violently and brutally made the guinea pig of the first country based neo-liberal experiment led by an authoritarian military regime which he characterises as a neo-liberal dictatorship. Also see Harvey (2005) regarding the neo-liberalisation of China.

11. Restructuring in Mexico, Spain, Australia and parts of eastern Europe are examples of passive revolutions. See Overbeek (1993) and Soederberg, Menz and Cerny (2005).

12. The Patriot Act of 2001 was enacted to 'deter and punish terrorist acts in the United States and around the world, to enhance law enforcement investigatory tools, and for other purposes'. It has ten titles that deal with the following issues: (I) enhancing domestic security against terrorism; (II) enhanced surveillance procedures; (III) international money laundering abatement and anti-terrorist financing; (IV) protecting the border; (V) removing obstacles to investigating terrorism; (VI) providing for victims of terrorism, public safety officers and their families; (VII) increased information sharing for critical infrastructure protection; (VIII) strengthening the criminal laws against terrorism; (IX) improved intelligence; and (X) miscellaneous.

References

Abrahamsen, R. 2000. *Disciplining Democracy: Development Discourse and Good Governance in Africa*. London: Zed Books.

Arrighi, G. 1993. 'The three hegemonies of historical capitalism'. In: *Gramsci, Historical Materialism and International Relations*, edited by Stephen Gill. Cambridge: Cambridge University Press.

Birmingham, D. 1990. *Kwame Nkrumah: The Father of African Nationalism*. Athens: Ohio University Press.

Bond, P. 2004a. 'The ANC's "left turn" and South African sub-imperialism'. *Review of African Political Economy* 31(102): 599–616.

———. 2004b. *Talk Left, Walk Right: South Africa's Frustrated Global Reforms*. Pietermaritzburg: University of KwaZulu-Natal Press.

———. (ed.). 2005. *Fanon's Warning: A Civil Society Reader on the New Partnership for Africa's Development*. Trenton, NJ: Africa World Press.

Chabal, P. 2002. *Amilcar Cabral: Revolutionary Leadership and People's War*. London: Hurst.

Cheru, F. 2002. *African Renaissance: Roadmaps to the Challenge of Globalisation*. London: Zed Books.

Christie, I. 1989. *Samora Machel: A Biography.* London: Panaf.

Cox, R. 1997. 'A perspective on globalisation' In: *Globalisation: Critical Reflections,* edited by J. H. Mittelman. Boulder: Lynne Rienner.

Davidson, B. 1981. *No Fist Is Big Enough To Hide The Sky.* London: Zed Books.

De Witte, L. 2001. *The Assasination of Lumumba..* London: Verso.

Forrest, D. 2008. 'A bigot with his eye on the Cabinet?' *Mail and Guardian* 19 Aug.

Fernandez, J. 1993. 'Chile: the laboratory experiment of international neo-liberalism'. In: *Restructuring Hegemony in the Global Political Economy: The Rise of Transnational Neo-liberalism in the 1980s,* edited by H. Overbeek. London: Routledge.

Gill, S. 2003. *Power and Resistance in the New World Order.* New York: Palgrave Macmillan.

Gramsci, A. 1971. *Selections from the Prison Notebooks,* edited by Q. Hoare and G. Nowell Smith. London: Lawrence and Wishart.

Hall, M. and T. Young. 1997. *Confronting Leviathan: Mozambique Since Independence.* Athens: Ohio University Press.

Harvey, D. 2005. *A Brief History of Neo-Liberalism.* Oxford: Oxford University Press.

Heller, H. 2006. *The Cold War and the New Imperialism: A Global History, 1945–2005.* New York: Monthly Review Press.

Hobsbawm, E. 1995. *Age of Extremes: The Short Twentieth Century 1914–1991.* London: Abacus.

International Monetary Fund. 2007. *Regional Economic Outlook: Sub-Saharan Africa.* Washington: IMF.

Klare, M. T. 2001. *Resource Wars.* New York: Henry Holt.

——. 2003. 'Blood for oil: the Bush-Cheney energy strategy'. In: *Socialist Register: The New Imperial Challenge,* edited by L. Panitch and C. Leys. London: Merlin.

Leys, C. 2003. *Market Driven Politics: Neo-Liberal Democracy and the Public Interest.* London: Verso.

Lyman, P. and J. Morrison. 2006. *More Than Humanitarianism: A Strategic US Approach to Africa.* Washington: Council on Foreign Relations.

Mamdani, M. 2005. 'Identity and national governance. In: *Towards a New Map For Africa,* edited by B. Wisner, C. Toulmin and R. Chitiga London: Earthscan.

Mengisteab, K. 1996. *Globalization and Autocentricity in Africa's Development in the 21st Century.* Trenton, NJ: Africa World Press.

Mengisteab, K. and I. K. Logan. 1995. *Beyond Economic Liberalization in Africa: Structural Adjustment and the Alternatives.* London: Zed Books.

Mkandawire, T. 2005. 'The global economic context'. In: *Towards a New Map For Africa,* edited by B. Wisner, C. Toulmin and R. Chitiga. London: Earthscan.

——. 2006. *Disempowering New Democracies and the Persistence of Poverty.* Geneva: United Nations Research Institute for Social Development.

Nyang'Oro, J. 1999. 'Hemmed in?: the state in Africa and global liberalisation'. In: *States and Sovereignty in the Global Economy,* edited by D. Smith, D. Solinger and S. Topik London: Routledge.

Overbeek, H. (ed.). 1993. *Restructuring Hegemony in the Global Political Economy: The Rise of Transnational Neo-Liberalism in the 1980s.* London: Routledge.

Overbeek, H. and K. Van der Pijl. 1993. 'Restructuring capital and restructuring hegemony: neo-liberalism and the unmaking of the post-war order'. In: *Restructuring Hegemony in the Global Political Economy: The Rise of Transnational Neo-liberalism in the 1980s*, edited by H. Overbeek. London: Routledge.

Panitch, L. and S. Gindin. 2006. 'The unique American empire'. In: *The War on Terrorism and the American 'Empire' after the Cold War*, edited by A. Colas and R. Saull. London: Routledge.

Prasad, M. 2006. *The Politics of Free Markets: The Rise of Neo-Liberal Economic Policies in Britain, France, Germany and the United States*. Chicago: University of Chicago Press.

Ray, E. et al. 1980. *Dirty Work: The CIA in Africa*. London: Zed Books.

Sachikonye, L. 1995. *Democracy, Civil Society and the State: Social Movements in Southern Africa*. Harare: SAPES Trust.

Shaxson, N. 2007. *Poisoned Wells: The Dirty Politics of African Oil*. Basingstoke: Palgrave Macmillan.

Shivji, I. 1991. *State and Constitutionalism: An African Debate*. Harare: SAPES Trust.

Soederberg, S. 2006. 'The war on terrorism and American empire: emerging development agendas'. In: *The War on Terrorism and the American 'Empire' after the Cold War*, edited by A. Colas and R. Saull. London: Routledge.

Soederberg, S., G. Menz and P. Cerny (eds.). 2005. *Internalizing Globalisation: The Rise of Neo-Liberalism and the Decline of National Varieties of Capitalism*. New York: Palgrave Macmillan.

Southall, R. 2003. *Democracy in Africa: Moving Beyond a Difficult Legacy*. Pretoria: HSRC Press.

Tlemcani, R. 2005. 'Reflections on the question of political transition in Africa: the police state'. In: *Liberal Democracy and its Critics in Africa*, edited by T. Lumumba-Kasonga. London: Zed Books.

United States of America (USA). 2006. *National Security Strategy*. Washington: White House.

Van Apeldoorn, B. 2002. *Transnational Capitalism and the Struggle over European Integration*. London: Routledge.

Van Der Pijl, K. 1993. 'The sovereignty of capital impaired: social forces and codes of conduct for multinational corporations'. In: *Restructuring Hegemony in the Global Political Economy: The Rise of Transnational Neo-Liberalism in the 1980s*, edited by H. Overbeek. London: Routledge.

Victor, D. 2006. *National Security Consequences of US Oil Dependency*. Washington: Council on Foreign Relations.

Vines, A. 2006. 'The scramble for resources: African case studies. *South African Journal of International Affairs* 13(1): 63–75.

Watts, M. 2006. 'Empire of oil: capitalist dispossession and the scramble for Africa'. *Monthly Review* 58(4): 1–17.

Williams, M. 2008. *The Roots of Participatory Democracy: Democratic Communists in South Africa and Kerala, India*. Basingstoke: Palgrave Macmillan.

CHAPTER THREE

Global Trade Regimes and Multi-Polarity

The US and Chinese Scramble for African Resources and Markets

Henning Melber

The first decade of the twenty-first century has seen Africa moving from acute marginality to greater centrality within the global political economy. This was a product of progressive political changes within the continent and a dramatic increase in external demand for its natural wealth. This chapter will examine these changes with particular regard to the contrasting nature and impact of US and Chinese trading and other economic activities in Africa since the year 2000 as well as the African response. With the collapse of the financial markets and the effects of the subsequent recession, the temporary honeymoon has come to an end. Since late 2008 global demand and world market prices for most of Africa's natural resources have been in dramatic decline again. As an ongoing process, its end is not in sight and beyond the scope of this chapter's analysis. The question to be answered, however, is to what extent the temporary bonanza had so far benefited the ordinary African people. As it is suggested, the winners were largely again not the needy ones.

Africa Since the End of the Bipolar World

The collapse of the Soviet empire and the end of more than 40 years of confrontation was by no means the end of history. The subsequent consolidation of US hegemony during the 1990s and its impact on the global order resulted in substantial changes for the African continent. The economic paradigms implemented by the World Bank and International Monetary Fund (IMF) consolidated their globally-dominant power. The quasi-mystical notion of good governance was consecrated as gospel (Abrahamsen 2000), providing a powerful ideological instrument to legitimate development policies and place them firmly under the control of donor (often in reality, creditor) countries and international institutions. Meanwhile, the World Trade Organisation (WTO) emerged as the broker responsible for devising and implanting comprehensive and binding rules for the global exchange of goods.

From the beginning of this century, significant intra-African dynamics complemented the changes in global arrangements. The arrival of democracy in South Africa and Nigeria enabled the two economic powerhouses south of the Sahara to cast off their pariah status. Based on internal and international acceptance, they were now able to assume leadership roles in international policy arenas. Thus from 2000, Presidents Thabo Mbeki and Olusegun Obasanjo emerged (with active, if at times intermittent, support from other major continental players such as Senegal, Algeria and Egypt) as new figureheads representing the collective interests of the South and, in particular Africa, vis-à-vis the industrialised West. Originally tasked to negotiate debt cancellation arrangements, they moved on to seek new forms of interaction based on the acknowledged socio-economic premises defined by the WTO. As junior, yet newly influential, partners in the global market they became the architects of what was finally termed the New Partnership for Africa's Development (NEPAD),[1] whose basic thrust was to render the continent more competitive and attractive to international investment using a heady mix of liberalisation, export orientation, infrastructural development, regional collaboration and good governance. The new quality of NEPAD as a blueprint for Africa's future was in the hitherto unprecedented claim by political leaders for collective responsibility over policy issues. The notion of good governance was explicitly recognised as a substantial ingredient for socio-economic development. The NEPAD document welcomed that 'across the continent, democracy is spreading, backed by the African Union, which has shown a new resolve to deal with conflicts and censure deviation from the norm'. As it states further, NEPAD 'has, as one of its foundations, the expansion of democratic frontiers and the deepening of the culture of human rights' (for the full document, see Bond 2005). NEPAD's strong emphasis on democracy and governance made it genuinely different from earlier initiatives to promote, propagate and seek external support for African development.[2]

After a considerable incubation period and intensive political negotiations behind closed doors this blueprint was upgraded to the status of an official economic programme and institution of the African Union (AU). The AU itself was the product of a parallel transformation of the Organisation of African Unity (OAU) that had brought about significant corrections to hitherto established principles of continental policy. Most importantly, it moved away from the hitherto entrenched principle of non-intervention by the continental organ in the internal affairs of member states. In the years that have followed, the AU has provided some reasonable evidence that it can be 'an important forum for collective action' as well as 'a veritable platform for multilateral diplomacy' (Sesay 2008: 32).

Invested with confidence, trust and substantive political support by the G8 states at their 2001 summit in Genoa, the NEPAD's architects were able to bring back home the reassuring message that the industrial West was on board and willing to support the initiative. This contributed to NEPAD's acceptance within Africa as well as by the United Nations, which in a General Assembly resolution officially recognised it as the economic programme for Africa. However, while this appears an unblemished success, in reality key policy issues were either buried completely or otherwise watered down. While NEPAD's endorsement of good governance discourse played to the Western gallery, it nonetheless represented a significant breach with the OAU's de facto unquestioning acceptance of autocratic rule by African despots and oligarchs.

The AU constitution was adopted at the same summit in Durban at which NEPAD was incorporated into its lexicon. It introduced a hitherto absent collective responsibility, justifying joint intervention for specified reasons. This has provided several broadly positive outcomes, as cases of mediation of violent conflict in Darfur, the Democratic Republic of Congo (DRC), the Ivory Coast, Liberia, Togo and the Comoro Islands have shown in different ways, such as conflict reduction or enhanced political legitimacy. Similarly, collective African policy responses to the crises in Kenya and Zimbabwe have moved beyond the earlier tendency to abstain from involvement in internal policy matters of AU member states. In contrast to this new responsibility, the African Peer Review Mechanism (APRM), conceptualised by NEPAD as a cornerstone for the enhancement of good governance, has met with distinctly mixed results and failed to meet expectations (Fombad and Kebonang 2006).

Whereas the APRM process is regarded as having enjoyed some reasonable success in both evaluating and deepening democracy in countries such as Ghana, Cameroon, Rwanda and South Africa, all of whom willingly agreed to undergo peer review of their state of governance, its limits have been demonstrated by an inability to influence governments unwilling to participate. This has highlighted the failure of both the AU and NEPAD to deal with major crises. The single most prominent disappointment has been the inability of new continental initiatives to take any determined action against clear breaches of human rights and good governance in Zimbabwe for far too long, before finally refusing to offer legitimacy to Mugabe's coercively induced re-election as president in June 2008. In contrast, the demand for democracy and respect for constitutional principles articulated by the NEPAD blueprint as a prerequisite for sustainable socio-economic development may have been an important contributing factor to the introduction of term limits for rulers. An increasing number of African heads of state have vacated their offices peacefully and more or less voluntarily (Southall and Melber 2006), although there remain many who continue to cling to power as both Kenya and Zimbabwe showed in 2008.

NEPAD – Trade as Aid?

There existed much goodwill and optimism in the early stages of NEPAD. Many observers and stakeholders such as Western governments, aid agencies and international non-governmental organisations (NGOs) were prepared to support an initiative perceived as signalling new determination to achieve greater self-reliance. However, this initial optimism gradually became disillusion, as principle gave way to pragmatism. NEPAD seems to have become little more than a veneer obscuring a pact among elites in the African South and the G7/8 North.[3]

Whilst boasting bold ambitions for the promotion of self-sustaining growth, development and democracy, NEPAD seems increasingly to have become little more than an agency to channel aid funds into development projects. These claim to be driven by a desire for enhanced regional collaboration, but in reality pay little more than lip service. For a start, the programmes and policies funded under NEPAD are implemented mainly by countries and not by regional bodies. Hence NEPAD in effect more often undermines than strengthens Africa's regional institutions. This is so notwithstanding the fact that NEPAD attributes substantial relevance to regional bodies when identifying ways and means to achieve socio-economic goals.

NEPAD claims that its agenda is 'based on national and regional priorities and development plans,' which ought to be prepared 'through participatory processes involving the people' (Bond 2005: 126). So far, however, no visible signs in the Southern African Development Community (SADC), the Economic Community of West African States (ECOWAS) or any other regional organisation indicate collective, multilateral efforts aimed at a united approach to relations with the outside world. Nor has NEPAD so far translated its noble aims into practical steps. The blueprint emphasises sub-regional and regional approaches and stresses 'the need for African countries to pool their resources and enhance regional development and economic integration . . . to improve international competitiveness' (Bond 2005: 153). But the crux of the matter lies there: an emphasis on promoting international competitiveness as the key to attracting investment and hence development comes at the expense of the self-sustainability of local economies and people. As Bond (2005: 134) in his annotated critique of NEPAD points out, integration in Africa should as a priority 'meet the socio-economic and environmental needs of its citizenries' instead of seeking to create a more efficient export platform'.

NEPAD claims further to enhance the provision of essential regional goods as well as the promotion of intra-African trade and investment, with another focus on 'rationalising the institutional framework for economic integration' (Bond 2005: 153). But again, such an approach neglects the local and internal in favour of the global and external orientation. The implementation of NEPAD appears, therefore, to have had the adverse effect of increasing the outward orientation of regional blocs at the expense of internal consolidation.

NEPAD defines a strengthening of African regional markets as a stepping stone to greater integration into the global economy and not as a goal in itself. It thus fails to acknowledge that 'what Africa needs is a regional integration strategy which is neither defined by liberalisation nor market mechanisms, but which nurtures first and foremost a policy, institutional and instrumental framework which will allow the regional market to function' (Hayman 2003: 8–9). Instead, the NEPAD document itself through its market access initiative advocates an external orientation, identifying a need for negotiations for 'more equitable terms of trade for African countries within the WTO multilateral framework' (para 188). This is proclaimed by NEPAD as offering 'an historic opportunity for the developed countries of the world to enter into a genuine partnership with Africa, based on mutual interest, shared commitments and binding agreements' as stated in the concluding paragraphs (para 205) of the document.

It was the United Nations (UN) Secretary-General Kofi Annan who used the opportunity of an invitation to the informal part of the G8 summit in 2003 to summarise in a letter to heads of state and government his concerns over the unsolved problems concerning such partnership.[4] He reminded the club of eight that eighteen months earlier, at the WTO negotiations in Doha, a new round of trade negotiations was agreed upon that would, for the first time, treat the needs and interests of developing countries as a priority. The distortions of trade in agricultural products created by massive subsidies and a variety of (tariff and non-tariff) barriers, as well as the measures protecting pharmaceutical manufacturing capacity – both serving the interests of stakeholders in the industrialised world – were identified as areas requiring urgent attention. Annan illustrated the current discrepancies with reference to World Bank figures, which disclosed that Organisation for Economic Co-operation and Development (OECD) members spent $311 billion in 2001 alone on agricultural subsidies. These, in combination with other forms of protectionism in industrialised countries, cost farmers and the agro-industry in the developing world upwards of $30 billion a year.[5]

Despite such sobering figures, some observers share the view that 'there is tremendous potential for economic gains from specialisation and trade within Africa which might, in turn, open up new export possibilities to the world'; provided the required harmonisation of trade rules and a much improved transportation infrastructure are achieved (Loxley 2003: 122). But critics of NEPAD are concerned that, despite Western commitment to liberalisation of trade under the WTO, the reality is that in practice many African commodities and goods are effectively rendered uncompetitive in Western markets by a variety of unfair practices and regulations, ranging from high tariffs and quotas to a variety of non-tariff barriers. The question is therefore how this challenge should be met and what strategies should be pursued to overcome, or at least reduce, the obstacles.[6] The complexity of trade constellations clearly demands far more preparation and research than NEPAD's advocates and other protagonists of trade liberalisation seem to have done.

Multi-Polar Tendencies and the Competition for African Resources

Systematic new efforts to access African markets and resources became visible with the adoption of the African Growth and Opportunity Act (AGOA) by the outgoing Clinton administration. Through this initiative, the US openly underlined the relevance of the African dimension for its external trade relations: Africa ranks higher than eastern Europe in the US trade balance. The breakdown of the AGOA trade volume, however, shows that with the exception of a few smaller niches (such as temporary opportunities created for export by the African-based, although rarely African-owned, textile industry with preferential access to the US market) the trade volume mainly comprises exports to Africa of US-manufactured high technology goods and machinery in return for the import of oil, strategic minerals and other natural resources that meet the demands of US industries.

Soon after AGOA was enacted, the trade department at the European Union (EU) headquarters in Brussels initiated negotiations for a re-arrangement of its relations with the African, Caribbean and Pacific (ACP) countries through Economic Partnership Agreements (EPAs, for a critical assessment of which, see chapter four by Margaret Lee in this book). The declared aim was to meet demands for WTO compatibility. The EPA negotiations have since then entered critical stages, encountering resistance from many among the ACP countries. They are afraid of losing existing trade preferences and feel that Brussels is seeking to impose a one-sided trade regime in its own interests by redrawing the map of regional configurations in Africa in line with EU interests, while denying the declared partners the right to autonomous negotiations.

Both initiatives, AGOA and the EPA negotiations, seem to reflect less a concern with fairer trade than securing preferential access to relevant markets (Melber 2005 and 2006), although competition between the EU and US to secure preferential trade agreements with South Africa (successfully negotiated by the former during the late 1990s and currently facing an impasse with regard to the latter) illustrates that the industrialised West can have distinctly divergent interests when it comes to securing trading links with particular countries. Meanwhile, however, the new offensive pursued by Chinese agencies, expanding aggressively into African markets and seeking access to fossil energy resources and other minerals and metals, adds to the rivalry. In a matter of time, too, Indian, Brazilian and Russian firms, as well as actors from other countries such as Malaysia and Mexico, are likely to add further pressure on limited markets and resources. This new stage of competing forces on the continent has resulted in a plethora of analyses dealing with the impact of Chinese practices.[7]

With the exception of controversies around EPAs and emerging concerns over the extension of a US military canopy over Africa, European and US policies and interests seem to feature in Western reportage much less prominently than the impact of recent Chinese activity. Such selective narrative tends to downplay, if not ignore, the damaging effects to Africa of the imbalance of existing global power structures. Indeed, it is increasingly commonplace that much of the criticism directed towards China in Africa is more an indicator of Western fear of being challenged in territory historically considered as its own backyard than motivated by genuine concern for African development prospects.

A recent example of the interests guiding decision making was the discussion around the European-African summit in Lisbon in December 2007. The overwhelming majority of EU member states were prepared to accept the presence of Zimbabwe's President Robert Mugabe in violation of their own sanctions imposed upon him and leading members of his regime. This was partly motivated by the concern that his exclusion could result in a boycott by most African countries, weaken Europe's status among African governments and thereby strengthen Chinese influence. China's presence in Africa alongside the arrival of other new interests competing for business and investment opportunities is having far-reaching effects upon US and EU perspectives of their relations with the continent.

The US Trade Policy Offensive

In official US understanding, 'AGOA is the cornerstone of the Administration's trade and investment policy toward sub-Saharan Africa, aimed at promoting free markets, expanding U.S.-African trade and investment, stimulating economic growth and facilitating sub-Saharan Africa's integration into the global economy' (Office of the United States Trade Representative 2007: 7).

Interestingly, there has been very limited analytical focus upon US trade policy through AGOA since the early stages of its implementation. After an initial period of critical reflection, little has been researched, published or even discussed with regard to this trade regime and its effects on African economies.[8] Instead, US interests have been almost exclusively acknowledged in terms of the emerging security architecture (as described by Rupiya and Southall in chapter seven of this book), which, it is proposed, is geared to access to and control over oil and other energy resources (Barnes 2005; Foster 2006; Klare and Volman 2006). AGOA as a complementary strategy is largely omitted from these scenarios, while a recent monograph on the policy of the Bush administration in Africa offers little more than a brief, albeit critical, mention (just two pages) on AGOA (Copson 2007: 34–6). However, as AGOA is central to US concerns, this clearly needs redress.

AGOA was originally adopted as title I of the Trade and Development Act of 2000 under the outgoing Clinton administration as part of the 'trade not aid' paradigm and it has been extended several times by President George W. Bush.[9] The benefits of AGOA differ among African countries depending on their resources. Ironically, in those countries allocated least developed status under AGOA that receive additional preferential treatment, external incoming capital, mainly from east Asian countries, has managed to exploit the opportunities created for supplying the US market with cheap textiles. This has doubtful benefits for the host countries in terms of employment, revenue and development potential.

Provisional insights into the consequences of AGOA are illuminating. As the executive summary of the administration's annual report on AGOA for 2002 suggests,[10] the US is sub-Saharan Africa's largest single market, purchasing 27% of the region's exports in 2000 with imports having increased by 61.5% over the previous two years. Meanwhile, US exports to sub-Saharan African countries grew 17.5% in 2001 to nearly $7 billion and were in that year higher than to all the former Soviet Union and eastern European countries combined. But a breakdown of the commodities shows the development flaws behind the statistics, for the bulk of trade value of US exports comprised aircraft, oil and gas field equipment, alongside motor vehicles and parts. Sub-Saharan Africa in return supplies a growing share of US oil and other energy imports. Under AGOA, the US imported $3.7 billion of liquid natural gas, $2.8 billion of crude oil and $271.5 million in refined petroleum products in 2001. The remaining products accounted for less than 10% of the total (Van Grasstek 2003: 9). AGOA, not surprisingly, reproduces and reinforces already skewed trade relations. Hence its advantages seem limited. Successes claimed by AGOA include growing exports to the US of frozen fruit sorbets from South Africa, birdseed from Ethiopia, wood carvings and handicrafts from West Africa, and various items of apparel from around the continent (Copson 2007: 35).

The implication of the skewed nature of US-African trade is that it is far more suited to US interests than to African development potential. This is illustrated by the fact that the main beneficiaries of AGOA trade, accounting for 92% of duty-free benefits, were, according to the 2002 report, Nigeria (with $5.7 billion of benefits), Gabon ($938.7 million) and South Africa ($923.2 million). As Thompson (2004: 468) has pointed out, by 2004 only six out of a total of then 37 eligible participating countries had recorded modest positive gains from AGOA, mainly from increased exports in the textile and apparel sectors. Only in Kenya and South Africa had exports from other sectors, primarily agricultural products, been able to rise substantially under AGOA. Thus whereas in 2005, AGOA reported an overall increase of imports from African partner countries into the US of 44%, this came about mainly as a result of soaring oil imports that increased in value by 53%. Meanwhile, non-oil exports from African countries to the US market fell by 16%, mainly as a direct and immediate result of the expiration of the Multi Fibre Agreement (MFA) and the subsequent decline of imports of apparel (Copson 2007: 35).

The latest figures available for 2006 (Office of the United States Trade Representative 2007) showed that US-sub-Saharan Africa two-way total trade (exports plus imports) increased by 17% to almost $71.3 billion. US exports rose by 17% to $12.1 billion. Again, the increase was due to exports in machinery, aircraft, vehicles and parts and electrical machinery. US imports rose also by 17% to $59.2 billion, due to increases in imports of platinum, diamonds, iron and steel, but mainly because of a 20% increase in the value of crude oil. These trends confirm the earlier patterns of a classical trade imbalance, exchanging value-added goods for raw materials. The US

> remained sub-Saharan Africa's largest single-country export market, accounting for nearly 30 percent of the region's total exports in 2005 ... U.S. imports from sub-Saharan Africa under AGOA, including its GSP provisions, totalled $44.2 billion in 2006, up 16 percent from 2005, mostly as a result of increased oil imports. AGOA non-oil imports increased by seven percent to $3.2 billion in 2006 – rebounding from a decline of 16% in 2005 – as several sectors (footwear, fruits, nuts, prepared vegetables, cut flowers) experienced increases (Office of the United States Trade Representative 2007).

Of the top five African destinations for US products in 2006, exports rose to South Africa (by 14%), Nigeria (38%), Angola (67%, partly due to aircraft sales) and Equatorial Guinea (96%, mainly for oil field and related equipment); while those to Kenya dipped (by 17%, due to a decline in aircraft sales). US imports from oil producing countries continued to increase: Nigeria (by 15%), Angola (38%), Republic of Congo (91%), Chad (28%) and Equatorial Guinea (11%), but imports from South Africa also increased (28%). Notably, petroleum products accounted for the largest portion of AGOA imports with 93%. With regard to imports of non-petroleum related commodities, minerals and metals increased by 21% to $596.3 million and agricultural products by 33% to $360.8 million; while textile and apparel imports declined by 11% to $1.3 billion. In total, US trade with sub-Saharan Africa between 2003 and 2006 almost doubled in terms of exports (from $6.8 to 12.1 billion) while imports more than doubled from $25.6 billion to $59.1 billion.

Textiles remained, despite a decline, the second single largest African export product to the US market under AGOA. But textiles represent less than 5% of total exports from sub-Saharan Africa to the global economy and, as noted above, have developed largely as a result of short-term investment by largely east Asian capital interests expanding into temporary market niches. In Madagascar, companies from Singapore, Hong Kong and China established factories to gain access to the US market under AGOA. Similarly, the textile industry in Lesotho, Malawi, Mauritius, Namibia and Swaziland is largely, if not exclusively, dependent upon foreign investors. Often, such investment has been induced by host governments who offer an array of attractions such as industrial parks, ready-made factory shells, tax holidays and friendly industrial relations environments. Under such preferential treatment schemes the public fiscus rarely benefits. The usual pattern is for initial investments and running costs to be substantially subsidised by public revenue rather than profits providing tax income. Hence the textile sector in Lesotho, largely owned by foreign companies operating under a six-year tax exemption, emerged within less than four years under AGOA with 40 000 workers as the largest source of employment and overtook the export of migrant labour to South Africa. But this came at a price (Bahadur 2004), with appalling employment conditions in what critics deemed to be sweat shops:

> The Lesotho Clothing and Allied Workers Union claims that the success of the industry is also attributable to the gross exploitation of labour, as companies ignore local laws protecting workers, which they can do with impunity since top government officials are share holders with the foreign companies. Poor working conditions, unduly long working hours, low wages and anti-union activities are said to characterise the industry (Loxley 2003: 126).

Nor is such employment secure, for textile factories in present global conditions are notoriously footloose and fancy free. In Lesotho, for instance, textile employment dropped from 55 000 in 2005 to 35 000 in 2007 as a result of increased Asian competition and a short-term appreciation in the value of country's currency, which is tied to the value of the South African Rand.

A further example of the dubious advantages provided by the expansion of African textiles under AGOA is provided by the opening of a large factory, Ramatex, by a Malaysian-owned company in Windhoek, Namibia, during 2001–2. It was founded upon dismally low labour standards, which resulted in a strike in 2003, and other business practices of a questionable ethical nature. But this was tolerated by the authorities at the expense of the taxpayer since revenue had to cover the state subsidies dished out to make Windhoek an attractive location in competition with neighbouring countries. It has since then become a sad, but classic, example of worst practice (Jauch, 2006; LaRRI 2003; Mwilima 2007; Winterfeldt 2007).

In mid-2004 Windhoek municipality had to intervene because of constant environmental violations and pollution of reservoirs. Furthermore, the illegal employment of several hundred unqualified workers imported from Bangladesh by unscrupulous dealers in migrant labour challenged the presumption that textile investment was providing employment for labour already available within Namibia's desperately poor economy. The Ramatex saga, claimed the director of the trade union-affiliated Labour Resource and Research Institute, showed the ugly face of global capitalism:

> Protected by the blind faith of host countries that foreign investment will solve their development problems, these corporations drive down labour and environmental standards in what has been described as a "race to the bottom" . . . It is a tragic irony that Namibia plays host to such abuses . . . Just over a decade after Independence, we now see a return to the migrant labour system in a new globalised, and perhaps even more vicious form. Like under colonial rule, workers who revolt against their inhuman conditions are simply deported to their "homelands". Previously back to Ovamboland, now back to Bangladesh, China or the Philippines (Jauch 2004).

The 6 000 jobs originally created in 2002–3 had declined after retrenchments in 2005 and 2006 to 3 600 workers in the textile industry as a whole. Ramatex itself closed down one of its subsidiaries with 1 600 employees as a direct result of the termination of the MFA. As a footloose enterprise, it could relocate operations easily and did so without hesitation once the opportunities faded. The bitter end for the remaining workforce came after less than six years of operation in March 2008 when the company locked out its workers and left Namibia without prior warning, literally overnight. Earlier on, it had started to ship its movable equipment to a new factory in Cambodia while denying any plans to close down.

The Namibian state and the Windhoek municipality had provided Ramatex with subsidies estimated at $40 million. The AGOA website showed that Ramatex's revenue was $78.8 million in 2004 and $33.8 million in 2006, of which it spent 11% and 16% respectively on wages. In denial of these figures, the managing director declared that labour and imported raw material costs were too high to justify continued production. The Namibian government, which had consistently defended Ramatex against all criticism, had to admit that it had no binding agreement with the Malaysians and no other option but to stand by and watch helplessly as the factory was closed down.[11]

Under such circumstances, AGOA does less to fuel a local African economy than to provide a platform for the unreasonable profit of external investors taking advantage of a highly uneven form of liberalisation. Ironically, too, it is precisely the Everything But Arms (EBA) preferential trade arrangements by the EU and preferential access to the US market under AGOA, in particular for textiles and apparel, which have served as an incentive for Asian capital to invest in short-term businesses in Africa:

> While Chinese firms may be very focused on efficiency considerations at an operational level, it seems rather unlikely they would locate in Africa without AGOA and EBA . . . Indeed, the density of trading and distribution companies in the population of firms from the major investing countries, whether from the North or the South, seems to confirm the longevity of a very old pattern of trade driven business relations with SSA (Henley et al. 2008: 13).

With the end of the MFA at the beginning of 2005 according to WTO rules, the textile and apparel industries in China, India and other Asian countries were increasingly able to compete freely with AGOA-favoured African products. The textile boom, especially in Lesotho, Namibia and Swaziland, was thus of a short-term nature and offered little evidence that it could adapt to changing market conditions. The losers were once again those at the receiving end. Having been promised that trade is better than aid, these countries were in short order to experience that, under conditions provided by AGOA, trade principally aids foreign investors willing to maximise profit from short-term investments under temporary windows of opportunity. As a WTO analysis had predicted:

> The countries that are most likely to lose market shares are those located far from the major markets and which have had either tariff and quota-free access to the United States and EU markets, or which have had non-binding quotas. These countries will undoubtedly face adjustment challenges (Nordås 2004: 345).

The harsh realities of so-called adjustment challenges have since then included the loss of tens of thousands of employment opportunities, often created with local taxpayers' money through public subsidies only a few years earlier, in several African countries.[12] The expected result of the MFA termination was, despite transitional measures to soften the impact through limited interim benefits for African-based producers, a marked decline in an industry which always had short-term horizons:

> The simple facts are that the full incorporation of China and Eastern Europe into the world trading system over the next decade will more than double the number of workers in the global economy in just ten years time. The AGOA legislation passed in 2004 provides some preferential access for certain categories of African textiles until 2008, but there is no evidence that any African state will be able to build up viable domestic textile industries capable of competing with Chinese producers before that deadline (Martin 2004: 589).

The sobering experiences of examples such as Ramatex indicate severe limits to the highly unequal partnerships established within the framework of AGOA-stimulated short-term foreign investments:

> The new (or not so new) economic rationale of liberalism is characterised by neglect of genuine social responsibility. Contrary to its claim, liberalism does not halt marginalisation. Nor can it prevent further exacerbation of internal social structural inequalities and contradictions of a dependent economy and society in the globalisation process in the long run. On the contrary, economic and social marginalisation comes along with globalisation, as long as the conditional framework of globalisation follows the well-established pattern dictated by the capitalist accumulation process over the past five centuries (Winterfeldt 2007: 68).

Effects of the Trade as Aid Paradigm

Recent trends indicate less rather than more regional co-operation and integration, at least in macro-economic terms, among the official membership of bodies such as SADC. Political and security interests might promote, with increased support by the G8, the strengthening of initiatives towards closer regional collaboration to reduce armed conflicts and secure more stability. But such stability continues to be perceived as regime security and regional configurations have not yet provided any convincing evidence that the political leadership, or local capital for that matter, is geared towards a progressive new regionalism. At best, they document 'predominantly state-driven visions of responsive, responsible but neo-liberal development' in which 'agendas are . . . set and implemented, via the primary route of individual national plans and financial transfers . . . This is hardly a radical prescription for reconfiguring inappropriate colonial and post-colonial legacies to promote development at the regional or continental scales!' (Simon 2003: 71).

Notwithstanding such bleak prognosis, external support for further positive regional interdependence remains possible by means of both bi- and multilateral forms of co-operation. But, as Kivimäki and Laakso (2002: 176) summarise, this requires more than merely opening up to the global economy. Rather, it would have to re-visit matters of regional economic collaboration and seek involvement of the majority of the African population in the countries concerned. However, current initiatives by the EU and US under the WTO offer little or no promise of contributing to such a desirable tendency.

The challenge is to contribute towards sustainable development by offering African partners a globally-conducive environment that will secure them a fairer share in the world economy and international policy making processes. Only on such a basis might viable scenarios for fair partnership be discussed, negotiated and formulated.

It has been suggested by Hurt (2004: 171) that neo-liberalism in trade is pre-eminently compatible with the interests of political elites as well as outward-oriented fractions of capital within both the EU and, to a lesser extent, African states. Consequently, international conditions make it difficult to redefine African-European relations positively. On the basis of the evidence it is not easy to counteract such a conclusion convincingly.

Conventional development paradigms and discourses still advocated within the OECD cultivate the assumption that regional collaboration is an inherently positive factor favouring economic growth. Yet at the same time, OECD member countries are actively involved in undercutting any supportive environment that would enhance regional co-operation. Thus sub-Saharan Africa continues to face the risk that, despite impressive economic growth rates under the current boom in natural resources, companies investing in the continent may 'remain marginal trading outposts of the world's manufacturers' (Henley et al. 2008: 13), an outcome consistent with early predictions by some observers that AGOA would provide only limited and passing benefits (Shapouri and Trueblood 2003; Van Grassteek 2003). After all, 'if multilateralism and leading regional trade initiatives remain stalled, then Competitive Liberalization may amount to little more than bilateral opportunism masquerading as high principle'.[13]

China: The Dragon Goes Abroad

As mentioned earlier, rapid Chinese expansion into the economies of sub-Saharan Africa has triggered an avalanche of recent studies. However, these have too often been based on sweeping generalisations rather than carefully researched reality.[14] Nor have distinctions been made between the policies and practices of the Chinese government, state agencies, companies and capital across different sectors. The limited scope of this chapter prevents the presentation of a picture that sufficiently recognises the different strategies, aims and impacts of different Chinese actors, even while it seeks to locate their activities in Africa within the context of global competition for the continent's resources.

During the US-Africa Business Summit in Cape Town in November 2007, Professor Yang Guang from the Institute of West Asian and African Studies of the Chinese Academy of Social Sciences informed the audience that the total number of Chinese companies operating on the continent today exceeds 800. Some 100 of these are state-owned and most others receive state support while operating privately. He valued Chinese investment by the end of 2006 at $11.7 billion.[15]

Trade between China and Africa has accelerated dramatically since the turn of the century. According to Wang (2007: 5), Africa's exports to China increased between 2001 and 2006 at over 40% per annum to reach $28.8 billion. During the same period imports from China quadrupled to $26.7 billion, leaving a small trade surplus for Africa. The bulk of Sino-African trade, some 85%, takes place with sub-Saharan Africa. It reproduces a classical skewed pattern: raw materials on the one side (from Africa), and value-added manufactured products on the other (from China). In 2006, oil and gas accounted for 62% of Africa's exports to China. Oil supply from Africa is currently estimated to cover a third of China's annual consumption. Non-petroleum minerals and metals rank second (13%) on the export list. This means that 75% of all exports to China are oil, gas, minerals and metals. In contrast, Africa imports mainly manufactured products from China (45%) and machinery and transport equipment (31%). Meanwhile, Chinese exports to Africa include a considerable amount of weaponry: China ranks among the top suppliers of arms to African customers.

The increased demand for primary goods by emerging economies, notably China, has contributed to a dramatic increase in world market prices that has positively affected the terms of trade for African countries. The beneficiaries are not only African economies, but also new enterprises established from abroad. Amongst the most prominent of the latter are Chinese multinationals (Corkin

2007). They have left their major mark in the energy sector, notably through operations undertaken by Sinopec in Angola, the China National Offshore Oil Corporation (CNOOC) in Nigeria and Kenya and the China National Petroleum Corporation (CNPC) in Sudan. In the telecommunications sector, meanwhile, the state-owned Zhong Xing Telecommunication Equipment Company (ZTE) and the private multinational Huawei are challenging the dominance of British, French and South African companies. In addition, Chinese companies have secured major government tenders in the construction sector in several African countries. In earlier days the Chinese earned a reputation for building sports stadiums as a sign of friendship and transport infrastructure in support of enhanced trade links between independent African countries and the outside world: the most prominent was TAZARA, the railway line connecting Zambia with Tanzania. They have moved on to build more sports complexes and railway lines as well as state houses and government offices, major roads, dams, harbours, airports and other infrastructural projects: 'Following the "going global" strategy and dovetailing with the Chinese government's foreign aid programs to African countries, these projects are often financed by Chinese government loans' (Corkin 2007: 21).[16]

By 2007 China had already emerged as the African continent's third largest trading partner, behind the US and France but ahead of the United Kingdom. From $5 billion worth of trade with Africa in 1997, Sino-African trade was hitting $55.5 billion in 2006 and has been estimated to top the $110 billion mark by 2011 according to a senior economist at the Chinese Ministry of Commerce (Taylor 2007: 379). Thus the Zambian Copperbelt mining industry, a product of British colonialism, has now become Chinese dominated, while so-called Chinatowns have become visible in many African cities.[17]

The Ambiguities of Chinese Policy

While multilateralism is claimed to be the guiding principle for regulation of the global market by the G7 and OECD countries, the Chinese expansion into Africa is underpinned by the construction of strong bilateral relations between Beijing and African regimes. Given the hugely improved market conditions for African natural resources offered by Chinese and other recent industrialisation, this development is strongly welcomed by African governments as it enhances their scope for manoeuvre. In theory, too, favourable market conditions and the Chinese arrival should work to the benefit of ordinary African people. However, that presumes that the African elites benefiting from unequal structures of trade and investment are willing to put the public interest before their own. Yet it is here that the moral and political thrust of Chinese policy falls down, for the foundation of Chinese foreign policy in Africa is one that emphasises the sovereignty of governments and commits Beijing to non-interference. It was precisely the abandonment of such principles that characterised the evolution of the OAU into the AU, pointing the way towards an era of greater democracy, transparency and accountability by rulers. In contrast, however, the reality is that the Chinese gospel of non-interventionism is warmly welcomed by the autocratic leaders and oligarchies that continue to rule the roost in the majority of African countries, especially those in possession of vast natural resources.

It must be noted in passing that the non-interference paradigm is by no means the firm foreign policy principle the Chinese government claims. After all, Beijing boosts its image in Africa by referring to itself as a staunch past supporter of anti-colonial liberation movements, yet its strategy at the time was manifestly built upon political solidarity rather than non-interference. Indeed, from the time of the Bandung Conference of 1954 onwards, Chinese ambitions to assume a hegemonic role in the South, later stoked by Sino-Soviet rivalry, were founded upon a necessarily proactive, interventionist role in African countries and were at times guided by disastrous misjudgements that resulted in costly adventures, not least in terms of human lives sacrificed.[18] More recently, the strong Chinese response to the radically anti-Chinese populism of Zambian presidential candidate Michael Sata (who, according to observers, only emerged during the 2006 elections as a significant contender because he voiced such popular sentiments) testified to China's inconsistency. Angered by the attacks, the Chinese ambassador threatened that if Sata were elected, all assistance to Zambia would be withdrawn (Erdmann 2007: 493, 497).[19]

Given such a mixed track record, a Chinese public relations exercise initiated at the World Social Forum (WSF) in Nairobi in January 2007 (in the Chinese-built sports arena on the outskirts of the capital) backfired when quasi-NGO members known to be semi-official policy representatives of the government were confronted by an outburst of anger by social movement activists from various countries. They accused the Chinese of bailing out despotic and authoritarian regimes like Zimbabwe through economic deals, depicting China as worse than the old colonial and imperialist powers; and criticised them for generating profits at the expense of small traders and unskilled workers victimised by new and unfair competition (Bello 2007).[20]

Such social movement activists critical of Beijing's policy and the Chinese expansion into African societies are by no means less critical of Western imperialism. However, for many of them and many more other people on the ground, the Chinese arrival is greeted with marked ambivalence 'While African populations are aware of the dangers and the risks of China's rising expansion . . . they also seem fascinated and attracted by the incomparable facility of Chinese to adapt to any situation. And the hope of new jobs and social development helps also to welcome new friends' (Legault 2008: 42).

However, China's image as an alternative to imperialist and neo-colonial Western interests might increasingly be tested against harsh business realities. The activists articulating their frustration at the WSF in Nairobi were not the only ones disillusioned. China's insensitivity to popular movements and their protest against illegitimate forms of rule was illustrated in spectacular fashion in May 2008 with the delivery of Chinese military equipment to Zimbabwe via what was dubbed the ship of shame. The Zanu-PF government's defeat by the opposition in the March 2008 parliamentary elections offered an unambiguous indication that the majority of ordinary people had turned against the regime in spite of brutal repression. Preparing for a further clamp down, the military command was anxiously awaiting the hastily-shipped freight of six containers only to learn that workers in Mozambique, South Africa, Namibia and Angola through their trade unions refused to unload and transport it to Zimbabwe. Nonetheless, despite organised resistance by trade unions and civil society, an appeal by the SADC chairperson, incredulous worldwide attention and an original indication by the Chinese government that it had ordered the ship to return home without offloading, unconfirmed reports later suggested that weapons had been clandestinely delivered after a long odyssey of several weeks along the southern African coast. The three million rounds of assault rifle ammunition, 3 000 mortar rounds and 1 500 rocket-propelled grenades were allegedly unloaded in the Congolese port of Ponta Negra (Pointe-Noire) and airlifted by a freight charter company (Maletsky 2008). The general secretary of the South African Transport and Allied Workers Union described this as 'a serious lack of respect for international solidarity' and 'an injustice to the people of Zimbabwe'. He stated further that 'Both the Chinese government and . . . the state-owned shipping company . . . have regrettably demonstrated that profiteering remains the overriding consideration over human solidarity and saving lives' (Maletsky 2008).[21]

It is apparent that transparency and accountability cannot be found among the core values cultivated in African-Chinese links. Instead, these emerging relations seem to offer an exit option from demands for good governance. Chinese policy might be better served by fostering a political and economic environment that includes emphasis upon corporate governance that would be favourable to investment over the long term. Put differently, 'China cannot afford to put all its eggs in government baskets' (Amosu 2007); at least, not as long as these governments are not held accountable by the rule of law in a society regulated by checks and balances.

China's role in future deals and collaboration with African partners should be measured against the words of one of her former leaders. In his speech at a special session of the United Nations General Assembly, Deng Xiaoping stated in 1974:

> If capitalism is restored in a big socialist country, it will inevitably become a superpower . . . If one day China should change her colour and turn into a superpower, if she too should play the tyrant in the world, and everywhere subject others to her bullying, aggression and exploitation, the people of the world should identify her as social-imperialism, expose it, oppose it and work together with the Chinese people to overthrow it (Manji and Marks 2007: ix).

In contrast to these clear words, the present Chinese policy of non-interference accords poorly with demands for the protection of human rights and the promotion of democracy. However, notwithstanding embarrassments such as the recent Zimbabwe debacle, which may have come about as a result of a disjunction between the Chinese state and Chinese private capital, there are emerging signs of a shift with China moving away from its 'defensive insistence on solidarity with the developing world to an attempt to balance its material needs with its acknowledged responsibilities as a major power' (Kleine-Ahlbrandt and Small 2008: 56).

What's in it for Africa?

Given the history of African relations with the outside world and recent European and US initiatives to maintain their interests, much of the concern expressed in the West about the expansion of Chinese interests into Africa and their collaboration with local elites is evidence either of hypocrisy or amnesia, or both. After all, the Chinese penetration is only giving another face to capitalism, no more and no less self-interested than similar Western involvements. Consequently, it is necessary to guard against any tendency to characterise the entire China-Africa relationship simply by its worst aspects and by crude extrapolation to demonise China; and present Western engagements in the continent as un-ambiguously morally and ethically superior (Mohan 2008: 155–6).

Against the historical background of centuries of exploitation of Africa it should come as no surprise that many among the wretched of the earth are pinning their hopes for a better life upon a new actor, who, representing the global South, might offer an alternative. This is at present more wishful thinking than socio-economic and political reality, but understandable from the perspective of those who, for far too long, have been marginalised by global development. Yet it is less acceptable when articulated by analysts who take a strongly anti-imperialist stance against the West, but at the same time welcome the Chinese offensive uncritically as a window of opportunity. Such a selective view ignores the class nature and interests involved: they remain an integral part of emerging exchange relations and show little difference so far to the established practices of exploitation. Despite the bonanza of the new scramble, poverty remains a structurally embedded phenomenon in African societies and hence a continuous challenge. Meanwhile, although the new rivalry is providing African leaderships with improved bargaining options and new choices, this can have the unfortunate by-product of strengthening undemocratic governments. After all, for both the US and China, as for most other external interests, it remains largely business as usual. Over and above this re-drawing of the political map, reminiscent of the Cold War era, the economic realities have not really changed significantly.

The resource curse still looms for those economies currently benefiting from the upswing in demand. Windfall profits, positive terms of trade and trade balances, as well as unusually high economic growth rates do not yet in themselves indicate sustainable positive change towards poverty reduction and secure livelihoods for the majority of the people. Inequalities and social disparities might well increase further in midst of a growing segment of beneficiaries able to siphon off revenue incomes for their private enrichment.

Institutional quality and sound economic policies remain substantial in-gredients for a development paradigm benefiting the majority of people. Governing access to resources through appropriate rent and revenue management policies as well as by improving policy design and implementation (in a sense, truly good governance practices) is as important as a diversification of the economy and the creation of human and social capital (Wohlmuth 2007: 11). Relatively weak African states and their governments on the one hand and major international corporations on the other are highly unequal partners. Furthermore, even if the former are drawn into comprador relationships, in many cases neither the governments nor the people in the resource rich areas are aware of the cash flow generated by the exploitation of raw materials: 'In settings where initial political and economic institutions are relatively weak, dependence on primary commodities, especially natural resources such as oil, appears to have encouraged predatory government behaviour and rent-seeking, deterring the development of stable, democratic institutions that are conducive to growth' (Jerome and Wohlmuth 2007: 201).

The question is not so much a choice between Europe, the US, China or any other actors interested in African resources. The challenge lies in setting a new course to make optimal use of the new scenario for the majority of the people on the continent. As Amosu (2007) concludes, 'Don't focus so much on the elephants. The future of Africa lies with the grass'.

Notes

1. From the African Renaissance coined in the late 1990s by South Africa's President Thabo Mbeki emerged the Millennium African Renaissance Programme (MAP). The Compact for African Recovery by the Economic Commission for Africa (ECA) and the Omega Plan by Senegal's President added to the substance of the document, adopted as the New African Initiative (NAI) at the OAU Summit in July 2001 in Lusaka. An Implementation Committee of Heads of State renamed a revised version in Abuja during October 2001 in the New Partnership for Africa's Development (NEPAD).

2. See among many critical analyses Bond (2005), Melber (2002 and 2004), Nyong'o, Aseghedech and Lamba (2002) and Taylor (2005).

3. The initiative known today as G7/8 started originally in 1975 at a meeting set up by French President Giscard d'Estaing. Leaders of France, Germany, Japan, the United Kingdom, the US and Italy met near Paris to discuss issues of common concern, at that time mainly the oil crisis. Since then, the informal gathering has become an annual mid-year event, including Canada as a seventh member state. The 1997 summit invited Russia (attending as an observer from the 1990s) to join the group. Hence from 1998 it had become a G8 summit, in which the EU holds observer status and is represented by the President of the Commission and the leader of the country holding the EU presidency at the time.

4. United Nations document of 29 May 2003 (http://allafrica.com).

5. In contrast to the G7/8, the Organisation for Economic Co-operation and Development (OECD) comprises some 30 industrialised countries accepting representative democracy and free market economics. It was originally formed in 1948 as the Organisation for European Economic Co-operation (OEEC) to assist implementation of the post-Second World War Marshall Plan and later extended membership to non-European states. It was reformed 1961 into the OECD.

6. See among others the summaries by Wade (2003) and Ochieng and Sharman (2004).
7. See the review articles by Taylor (2007) and Mohan (2008) as well as the bibliographic overview by Melber (2008). Recent studies presenting rather measured views on the ambiguities of the subject include Davies (2007), Holslag (2007) and Tjønneland et.al. (2006) as well as some chapters in Ampiah and Naidu (2008).
8. The US-American African Studies Association had for a few years a limited number of presentations relating (at times rather uncritically) to AGOA. At its 50th annual conference in New York in Oct. 2007, however, not a single paper dealt with AGOA. Similarly, the World Social Forum (Nairobi, Jan. 2007) discussed both the European EPAs and Chinese economic interests in Africa in several panels and related activities, while not a single event focussed on AGOA.
9. AGOA is US law and was enacted without negotiation with African states. Sole ownership and power of definition therefore rests with the US administration, which is free to interpret and apply AGOA according to its exclusive understanding. AGOA, which was launched with a limited time span, has been regularly renewed, the last time on 20 Dec. 2006 when President George W. Bush signed the Africa Investment Incentive Act (AGOA IV). As of Jan. 2007, a total of 38 African countries had been declared AGOA beneficiaries with 26 countries eligible to receive AGOA apparel benefits.
10. Documented in *epd-Entwicklungspolitik* 10 May 2003: 48–53 (see also www.agoa.gov/) and commented upon by Veney (2003).
11. 'Multinational cuts and runs in Namibia' *Mail & Guardian* 8 Mar. 2008, as posted on http://www.agoa.info/news.php?story=910 (accessed on 23 May 2008).
12. For Lesotho, Madagascar and Swaziland see Fontaine (2007). For the negative effects on the southern African garment industry and possible measures to limit the damage see De Haan and Vander Stichele (2007).
13. S. Evenett and M. Meier. An interim assessment of the U.S. trade policy of competitive liberalization. Unpublished. 24 July 2006: 23.
14. Although this situation is definitely changing for the better as shown by Ampiah and Naidu (2008).
15. H. Kilbey. 'Why China beats its competitors'. Allafrica.com News, 16 Nov. 2007. http://allafrica.com/stories/200711160638.html.
16. Much empirical evidence on Chinese political and economic activities illustrating the massive expansion into sub-Saharan African countries is presented in a number of country cases in the annual *Africa Yearbook* published for the fourth consecutive year (Mehler, Melber and Van Walraven 2008).
17. Windhoek as the rather provincial capital of Namibia, with an estimated population of some 200,000 people, many of them with little to no purchasing power, already has two separate Chinatowns. The massive impact of Chinese business operations in Namibia during recent years is analysed in detail by Dobler (2007).
18. The anecdotal evidence presented at different places in the sobering demystification of Chairman Mao by Chang and Halliday (2006) testifies to this.
19. Note however that following the untimely death of Zambia's President Levy Mwanawasa, Sata declared in Sep. 2008 during the presidential election campaign his intention to

seek close and friendly relations with Chinese business partners operating as investors in his country (http://africa.reuters.com/wire/news/usnL823623.html).

20. Attending the session, I can confirm the report. The Chinese charm offensive was a disastrous failure and an obvious indicator of frustration in some countries with the growing Chinese presence. A volume by African scholars and activists on the subject launched at the same occasion in Nairobi testifies further to the at best mixed reactions to the newly emerging constellation (Manji and Marks 2007).

21. The Chinese government dismissed the news as unsubstantiated reports and further investigations could indeed not confirm the delivery. But the fact remains that the cargo might have only been prevented from reaching its destination because of popular protest and organised workers' solidarity in several SADC countries. As a result of its documented willingness to continue support to the Zanu-PF government, the Chinese image was seriously damaged further in the eyes of concerned southern African civil society and human rights actors campaigning in solidarity with the Zimbabwean people against a regime clinging to power by all violent means.

References

Abrahamsen, R. 2000. *Disciplining Democracy: Development Discourse and Good Governance in Africa*. London: Zed Books.

Amosu, A. 2007. 'China in Africa: it's (still) the governance, stupid'. *Foreign Policy in Focus* 9 Mar. http://www.fpif.org/fpiftxt/40658.

Ampiah, K. and S. Naidu (eds). 2008. *Crouching Tiger, Hidden Dragon?: Africa and China*. Pietermaritzburg: University of KwaZulu-Natal Press.

Bahadur, A. 2004. 'Taking the devils rope . . . AGOA'. *South African Labour Bulletin* 28(1): 39–42.

Barnes, S. 2005. 'Global flows: terror, oil and strategic philanthropy'. *African Studies Review* 40(2): 1–22.

Bello, W. 2007. 'China provokes debate in Africa'. *Foreign Policy in Focus* 9 Mar. http://www.fpif.org/fpiftxt/4065.

Bond, P. (ed). 2005. *Fanon's Warning: A Civil Society Reader on The New Partnership for Africa's Development*. Trenton, N.J.: Africa World Press.

Chang, J. and J. Halliday. 2006. *Mao: The Unknown Story*. London: Vintage.

Copson, R. 2007. *The United States in Africa: Bush Policy and Beyond*. London: Zed Books.

Corkin, L. 2007. 'China's emerging multinationals in Africa'. *The Africa Journal* Spring: 20–2.

Davies, P. 2007. *China and the End of Poverty in Africa: Towards Mutual Benefit?* Uppsala: Diakonia.

De Haan, E. and M. Vander Stichele. 2007. *Footloose Investors: Investing in the Garment Industry in Africa*. Amsterdam: Centre for Research on Multinational Corporation.

Dobler, G. 2007. 'Old ties or new shackles?: China in Namibia'. In: *Transitions in Namibia: Which Changes for Whom?* edited by H. Melber. Uppsala: Nordic Africa Institute: 94–109.

Erdmann, G. 2007. 'Zambia'. In: *Africa Yearbook. Volume 3: Politics, Economy and Society South of the Sahara in 2006*, edited by A. Mehler, H. Melber and K. van Walraven. Leiden: Brill: 491–500.

Fombad, C and Z. Kebonang. 2006. *AU, NEPAD and the APRM: Democratisation Efforts Explored*. Uppsala: Nordic Africa Institute.

Fontaine, T. 2007. 'End of quotas hits African textiles'. *IMF Survey Magazine* 5 July. http://www.imf.org/external/pubs/ft/survey/so/2007/NEW075A.htm.

Foster, J. 2006. 'A warning to Africa: the new U.S. imperial grand strategy'. *Monthly Review* 58(2): 1–12.

Hayman, R. 2003. 'Wooing the West or championing Africa?: NEPAD's vision for African integration. In: *The New Partnership for Africa's Development (NEPAD): Internal and External Visions*, edited by R. Hayman, K. King and S. McGrath. Edinburgh. Centre of African Studies, University of Edinburgh: 1–22.

Henley, J. et al. 2008. *Foreign Direct Investment from China, India and South Africa in Sub-Saharan Africa: A New or Old Phenomenon?* Helsinki: UN-WIDER.

Holslag, J. 2007. *Friendly Giant?: China's Evolving Africa Policy*. Brussels: Brussels Institute of Contemporary China Studies.

Hurt, S. 2004. 'The European Union's external relations with Africa after the Cold War: aspects of continuity and change'. In: *Africa in International Politics: External Involvement on the Continent*, edited by I. Taylor and P. Williams. London: Routledge: 155–73.

Jauch, H. 2004. 'No justice for the poor: a reflection on the deportation of Bangladeshi workers at Ramatex'. *The Namibian* 17 Sep.

——. 2006. 'Africa's clothing and textile industry: the case of Ramatex in Namibia'. In: *The Future of the Textile and Clothing Industry in Sub-Saharan Africa*, edited by H. Jauch and R. Traub-Merz. Bonn: Friedrich-Ebert-Stiftung: 212–26.

Jerome, A. and K. Wohlmuth. 2007. 'Nigeria's commodity dependence and options for diversification: an introduction'. In: *Africa: Commodity Dependence, Resource Curse and Export Diversification*, edited K. Wohlmuth et al. Berlin: LIT: 199–224.

Kivimäki, T. and L. Laakso. 2002. 'Conclusions and recommendations'. In: *Regional Integration for Conflict Prevention and Peace Building in Africa: Europe, SADC and ECOWAS*, edited by L. Laakso. Helsinki. Department of Political Sciences, University of Helsinki: 170–7.

Klare, M. and D. Volman. 2006. 'America, China and the scramble for Africa's oil'. *Review of African Political Economy* 108: 297–309.

Kleine-Ahlbrandt, S. and A. Small. 2008. 'China's new dictatorship diplomacy: is Beijing parting with pariahs? *Foreign Affairs* 87(1): 38–56.

LaRRI. 2003. *Ramatex: On the Other Side of the Fence*. Windhoek: Labour Resource and Research Institute.

Legault, G. 2008. 'Africa's newest friends'. *China Rights Forum* 1: 40–2.

Loxley, J. 2003. 'Imperialism and economic reform in Africa: what's new about the new partnership for Africa's development (NEPAD)?' *Review of African Political Economy* 30(95): 119–28.

Maletsky, C. 2008. ' "Ship of Shame" cargo delivered to Zimbabwe'. *The Namibian* 20 May.

Manji, F. and S. Marks (eds). 2007. *African Perspectives on China in Africa*. Nairobi: Fahamu.

Martin, W. 2004. 'Beyond Bush: the Future of Popular Movements and US Africa Policy'. *Review of African Political Economy* 31(102): 585–97.

Mehler, A., H. Melber and K. van Walraven (eds). 2008. *Africa Yearbook. volume 4: Politics, Economy and Society South of the Sahara in 2007.* Leiden: Brill.

Melber, H. 2002. 'The New Partnership for Africa's Development (NEPAD): old wine in new bottles?' *Forum for Development Studies* 29(1): 186–209.

——. 2004. 'The G8 and NePAD: more than an elite pact?' University of Leipzig Papers on African Politics and Economics (ULPA), no. 14.

——. (ed). 2005. *Trade, Development, Cooperation: What Future for Africa?* Uppsala: Nordic Africa Institute.

——. 2006. 'The EU and regional integration in Africa: a critical appraisal of the economic partnership agreements'. In: *Africa, Regional Cooperation and the World Market*, by M. Brüntrup, H. Melber and I. Taylor. Uppsala: Nordic Africa Institute: 40–51.

——. 2008. 'Selected bibliography'. In: *Perspectives on Africa Today: A Swedish -Chinese-African Dialogue*, by K. Marklund and K. Odqvist. Stockholm: Institute for Security and Development Policy: 23–9.

Mohan, G. 2008. 'China in Africa: a review essay'. *Review of African Political Economy* 35(115): 155–66.

Mwilima, N. 2007. 'Has Namibia benefited from AGOA?' *The Namibian* 7 Dec.

Nordås, H. 2004. *The Global Textile and Clothing Industry Post the Agreement on Textiles and Clothing.* Geneva: World Trade Organisation.

Nyong'o, P., G. Aseghedech and D. Lamba (eds). 2002. *New Partnership for Africa's Development (NEPAD): A New Path?* Nairobi. Heinrich Böll Foundation.

Ochieng, C. and T. Sharman. 2004. *Trade Traps: Why EU-ACP Economic Partnership Agreements Pose a Threat to Africa's Development.* London: Actionaid International.

Office of the United States Trade Representative. 2007. *2007 Comprehensive Report on U.S. Trade and Investment Policy Toward Sub-Saharan Africa and Implementation of the African Growth and Opportunity Act.* Washington: Office of the United States Trade Representative.

Sesay, A. 2008. *The African Union: Forward March or About Face-Turn?* Uppsala: Department of Peace and Conflict Research, Uppsala University.

Shapouri, S. and M. Trueblood. 2003. The African Growth and Opportunity Act (AGOA): Does It Really Present Opportunities? Paper to the International Conference on Agricultural Policy Reform and the WTO: Where Are We Heading? Capri (Italy), 23–26 June.

Simon, D. 2003. 'Regional development-environment discourses, policies and practices in post-apartheid southern Africa'. In: *The New Regionalism in Africa*, edited by A. Grant and F. Söderbaum. Aldershot: Ashgate: 67–89.

Southall, R. and H. Melber. (eds). 2006. *Legacies of Power: Leadership Transition and the Role of Former Presidents in African Politics.* Cape Town: HSRC Press.

Taylor, I. 2005. *NEPAD: Towards Africa's Development or Another False Start?* Boulder: Lynne Rienner.

———. 2007. 'China and Africa: towards the development of a literature: review article'. *Afrika Spectrum* 42(2): 379–88.

Thompson, C. 2004. 'US trade with Africa: African growth and opportunity?' *Review of African Political Economy* 31(101): 457–74.

Tjønneland, E. et al. 2006. *China in Africa: Implications for Norwegian Foreign and Development Policies*. Bergen: Chr. Michelsen Institute.

Van Grasstek, C. 2003. *The African Growth and Opportunity Act: A Preliminary Assessment: A Report Prepared for the United Nations Conference on Trade and Development*. New York: United Nations (UNCTAD/ITCD/TSB/2003/1).

Veney, C. 2003. 'Renaissance für wen? Das US-Gesetz für Wachstum und Chancen in Afrika (AGOA). *epd-Entwicklungspolitik* 10: 39–42.

Wade, R. 2003. *What Strategies are Viable for Developing Countries Today? The World Trade Organization and the Shrinking of "Development Space"*. London: Crisis State Programme, Development Research Centre, London School of Economics.

Wang, Jian-Ye. 2007. *What Drives China's Growing Role in Africa?* Washington: International Monetary Fund.

Winterfeldt, V. 2007. 'Liberated economy? the case of Ramatex Textiles, Namibia'. In: *Transitions in Namibia: Which Changes for Whom?*, edited by H. Melber. Uppsala: Nordic Africa Institute: 65–93.

Wohlmuth, K. 2007. 'Abundance of natural resources and vulnerability to crises, conflicts and disasters: an introduction'. In: *Africa: Commodity Dependence, Resource Curse and Export Diversification*, edited by K. Wohlmuth et al. Berlin: LIT: 3–48.

CHAPTER FOUR

Trade Relations between the European Union and Sub-Saharan Africa under the Cotonou Agreement

Repartitioning and Economically Recolonising the Continent?

Margaret C. Lee

Those who say that the EPAs are pushed because we want access to ACP markets are wrong! It is ridiculous! We want to implement change in Africa, increase their share in world trade, make sure Africa does not disappear from the radar screen. We want Africa to develop.

We are not dumping poultry parts in Africa. The parts exported to Africa are parts not meant for consumption here. They would not be fed to animals . . . parts that would be dumped in the sea.

These two statements are from interviews with high-ranking officials in the Directorate-General of Trade of the European Commission[1] eager to argue that prospective trade agreements between the European Union (EU) and the African, Caribbean, and Pacific (ACP) countries are intended to be developmental and are not about the EU member states gaining greater access to their markets.

This chapter will argue the opposite: that in fact the proposed new trade agreements are primarily about increased market access for EU member states as has been the case since the founding of the European Economic Community (ECC) in 1957. More specifically, it will propose that the EU, in order to have continued access to Africa's markets, has sought to repartition the continent initially into three, and later four, regional economic zones. While the literature on theses zones – known as Economic Partnership Agreements (EPAs) – is voluminous, few authors have examined the implications of this repartitioning, which I argue is akin to an attempt to recolonise Africa economically. While some scholars might think this notion unrealistic given the current scramble for Africa by numerous powers, several activists and scholars have made reference to this idea. They include Goodison (2007 a-c) and Kamidza (2005). Stoneman and Thompson (2007: 112) use milder but equivalent terminology, suggesting that both the US and the EU have as their goal 'maximising trade dominance' in southern Africa. The notion of colonising is still relevant as is evident from the front cover of a recent issue of *The Economist*.[2] It is therefore relevant that an analysis of this new relationship with the EU is placed within the context of both repartition and economic recolonisation of Africa. It is a perspective that means I am embarking on new and untested terrain within the debate about the new scramble for Africa.

The foundation of this new relationship rests with the post-Lomé convention signed in Cotonou between the EU and the ACP countries in June 2000. The Cotonou agreement guides economic and political relations between the EU and ACP countries between 2000 and 2020; and replaces the Lomé Conventions that informed EU-ACP economic and political relations between 1975 and 2000. Among the major objectives of the Cotonou Agreement, according to EC spokesmen, is the greater integration of Africa into the global economy. This is to be accomplished by spearheading development and enhancing regional economic integration through the creation of either four free trade areas (FTAs);[3] or, ideally, four customs unions.[4] However, the argument here is that, in essence, the EU proposes a new partition of the continent reminiscent of the nineteenth century scramble for Africa.

EU-Africa Trade Relations in Historical Perspective, 1957–2000

EU-Africa trade relations between 1957 and 2000 were based on neo-colonial patterns that were a reflection of the economic structural linkages developed as a result of European invasions, slavery and later colonial rule. These patterns dictated that African countries would continue to export raw materials to Europe and import expensive European products, often made from the very resources exported from Africa (Montana 2003).

In return for maintaining these asymmetric and unequal trade relationships, African countries were rewarded with financial assistance, allegedly designed to help them develop (for example, by diversifying their exports to reduce dependence on primary products); and preferential access to the EU market for their products, provided they did not compete with EU products. Some products – including beef and veal, rum and sugar that competed with European producers – Africans were able to export under special protocols. Countries were assigned a certain export allocation and in return were paid prices above the international market level. For example, countries that exported under the sugar protocol received earnings that were two to three times the actual international market value of their product.

Although this may have appeared a positive relationship, it was not. This was largely because in the end the colonial linkages of structural dependence were maintained and forced African countries to continue to export primary products to Europe, thus hindering industrialisation and economic development. Therefore what was to become a dysfunctional relationship was laid with the creation of the ECC. Under part IV of the Treaty of Rome, France convinced the member states[5] to provide association status to its African colonies (Brown 2002: 40). This association status was achieved, although both Holland and West Germany were bitterly opposed to it. It was the final issue to be dealt with before the treaty was finalised. France was pleased because it allowed a continuation of its relationship with African colonies and its precarious status as a world power. It also meant that France could share the burden of maintaining the relationship with other EEC member states.

With the Treaty of Rome, colonies and overseas dependencies of member states, without being consulted, were given associate status under article 131 of part IV. The French were effectively given the authority to determine the type of relationship that was to be established and to control policy. As a result of this association, France was able not only to maintain its imperial preferences, but also to transfer them to the other EEC states and the newly-created Common Market. Associated countries and territories were provided with equal access to the EEC market at tariff levels that were preferential; and similarly the EEC market had access to the markets of the associates. The EEC was also to provide aid to the associates to the amount of 581.25 million units of account (mua) from the first European Development Fund (Brown 2002: 41).

Following the independence of the French colonies in 1960, the EEC decided that it wished to renew the association arrangement. This continuation of the relationship with France's former colonies was achieved through the Yaoundé Conventions (I and II) of 1963 and 1969. Eighteen African states (later nineteen)[6] accepted the EU's offer of renewed association. They became known as the group of Associated African and Malagasy States (AAMS). Yaoundé I (1963–9) was signed in July 1963 giving most AAMS exports preferential entry into the EU with the exception of products covered by the Common Agricultural Policy (CAP). A second European Development Fund (EDF) allocation of 730 mua of aid was made, a large percentage of the increase representing loans from the European Investment Bank (EIB) (Brown 2002: 42). In return, the AAMS had to give the EU greater access to their markets (Montana 2003: 75).[7]

Yaoundé II (1969–74) was signed in 1969 and included a third allocation by the EDF of 918 mua of aid, 65 mua of which was to compensate partially for a decrease in the prices of commodities on the international market. Like Yaoundé I, the structural trade relations of inequality were maintained, along with preferential access to each other's markets. However, the conventions did not result in the greater integration of the economies of the EU and AAMS (Brown 2002: 42; Montana 2003: 77).

Although trade relations between the EEC/EC[8] were formally based on reciprocity and non-discrimination, Yaoundé was criticised as being a neocolonial arrangement (Montana 2003: 81; Nunn and Price 2004: 203 and 211) that encouraged division among African countries. Indeed, according to Kwame Nkrumah, first president of Ghana, the Treaty of Rome signalled the beginning of neocolonialism: the association was a system of collective colonialism that was stronger and more dangerous than the earlier agreement it was intended to replace.

Britain's accession to the EC[9] in 1973 once again resulted in the renegotiation of relations with Africa. Britain argued that the EC had to include its ACP Commonwealth partners (Lee 2003: 193). The new agreement, the Lomé Convention, was signed in February 1975 and was divided into two major components: financial and technical assistance, which consisted of the National Indicative Programme and the Regional Indicative Programme; and trade, which consisted of a non-reciprocal discriminatory trade agreement that required a waiver to the most-favoured nation (MFN)[10] principle of the General Agreement on Trade and Tariffs (GATT)/World Trade Organisation (WTO) and special protocols for beef and veal, sugar, bananas and rum. There were to be four Lomé Conventions: Lomé I (1975–80); Lomé II (1980–5); Lomé III (1985–90); and Lomé IV (1990–2000). Given limitations of space, it is impossible to explore their complexity and systematised imbalances.[11]

Throughout Lomé, EU-Africa trade relations remained the same with Africa continuing to export primary products to the EU and the EU exporting processed products to Africa. In practice, the EU discouraged African countries from industrialising because of direct competition with its own producers. Meanwhile, EU technical and financial assistance was not designed to correct the supply-side constraints that prevented African products from being competitive. It was during Lomé IV (1993) that the EEC became the EU.[12]

The continued commitment on the part of the EU to importing ACP raw materials, along with the extension of preferences to other developing countries including former members of the Soviet Union, contributed to the failure of Lomé to meet its objectives. Between 1978 and 2002, ACP exports to the EU decreased from over 7% to less than 3%; and of these exports, five products (petroleum, diamonds, cocoa, fish and wood products) represented 60% of total exports from only nine countries. Supply-side constraints under Lomé included rules of origin,[13] sanitary and phyto-sanitary standards,[14] poor transport, lack of access to telecommunication infrastructure, low labour productivity, lack of economies of scale and the absence of functioning capital markets. Despite such disadvantages, the European Commission (EC), representing the EU, continues to argue that the ACP countries themselves are primarily at fault for failing to deliver the expected results (Goodison and Stoneman 2005: 20). Consequently, the proposed resolution to this problem is through the creation of reciprocal preferential trade agreements with the ultimate goal being to lock in policy reforms. This is reminiscent of the World Bank's open regionalism, which argues that North-South FTAs are likely to be more economically advantageous than South-South agreements (Lee 2005: 73–4).

By Lomé III (1985–90), the EU no longer pretended to have an equal partnership relationship with the ACP countries. It had bought into the neo-liberal orthodoxy of free trade, privatisation and less government intervention. Conditionality, as imposed by the international financial institutions, the International Monetary Fund (IMF) and World Bank, had become a pillar of the EU approach towards its ACP partners (Lee 2003: 195; Nunn and Price 2004: 213). By Lomé IV, conditionality was not only increased, but in 1991 fifteen states experienced the withholding of Lomé structural adjustment funds because of their failure to adopt satisfactory economic reform programmes. Such conditionality was further extended in 1995 as human rights, democratic principles and the rule of law became central gateways to access to Lomé funding. This policy brought 'Lomé further in line with the wider global development framework . . . demonstrating both a consensual and coercive aspect to the process' (Nunn and Price 2004: 217).

Meanwhile, the EU was committed to ensuring the advantageous positioning of European multinationals in ACP countries. As Nunn and Price (2004: 212–13) further note, 'While recognizing the dependency of many states on a few primary commodities, these (Lomé) regimes supported European MNCs heavily involved in the production of ACP exports'.[15] In terms of Lomé, an investment framework was put in place that was deemed to encourage 'fair and equitable treatment for investors, clear, stable and predictable investment conditions including insurance and guarantee systems'. The facilitating role that the EC gave itself to complement the above framework was, according to Nunn and Price (2004: 217–18), related to a decrease in European investment in mining companies in the developing world in the 1970s. With a view to providing investment stabilisation and protection frameworks the EC then encouraged institutions such as the International Financial Corporation and the World Bank to increase their endeavours. Multinational exporters were treated with the same privileges accorded local exporters, thus further decreasing the incentive for the EU to tackle the problem of supply-side constraints that hindered increased industrialisation in ACP countries, especially in Africa.

In conjunction with the above was the commitment to ensure that EU countries continued to have access to African markets. It was proclaimed that

> FTAs are economically beneficial, especially where they help the EU to bolster its presence in the faster growing economies of the world, which is our overriding interest . . . FTAs are coming to be seen as an indicator of the strength of our relationship with a country or region [and] the level of tariffs in many of our partner countries, particularly the newly industrialised and developing countries, remains high . . . It, therefore, can seem obviously in our interest to persuade such countries to enter into FTAs with the Union, enabling us to encourage both tariff elimination and deregulation . . . The EU also has an interest in supporting deeper integration in southern Africa, with the full involvement of South Africa (Commission of the European Communities 1995).

The Cotonou Agreement, 2000–20

The Cotonou Agreement marked a major watershed in EU-ACP relations because, among other things, it was to replace non-reciprocal with reciprocal trade agreements. These were to be in the form of EPAs or FTAs, due to come into force no later than 1 January 2008.

The stated objectives of the Cotonou Agreement include: first, poverty reduction through enhanced economic and trade co-operation, development aid and political dialogue; second, institutionalisation of democratic principles; third, respect for the rule of law and human rights; fourth, good governance, including greater non-state actor participation; fifth, more efficient project co-operation; sixth, greater peace building efforts; seventh, conflict prevention and resolution; and eighth, support for regional integration. This last appears to be the cornerstone of the agreement.

The Lomé arrangements[16] were to remain in force until 31 December 2007. Then, according to the agreement, as from 1 January 2008 there would be four regional EPAs in place in Africa.[17] Although, according to one EC official, considerable debate attended the feasibility of this time frame and although 'there would not be full functioning EPAs' according to the timetable there would, however, 'be a clearer strategy for regional integration and an understanding to go in a certain direction.' He further noted that 'The substance of the EPAs will be around market access and which countries will be willing to move toward EPAs . . . all the ACP countries under the EPAs will be offered Everything But Arms (EBA)'.[18]

In addition to replacing non-reciprocal with reciprocal trade agreements, EPAs were to be asymmetrical and have special and differential treatment: for example, taking into account the needs of least developed countries (LDCs). They were also to contribute to Africa's economic development; enhance regional integration and Africa's integration into the global economy; and, perhaps most contentious, include the Singapore issues established in Singapore at a World Trade Organisation (WTO) ministerial meeting in 1996 – competition policy, investment, transparency in government procurement and trade facilitation. Inclusion of the Singapore issues is contentious because, with the exception of trade facilitation, they have been removed from WTO negotiations.

Prior to November 2007, the central thrust of the EPAs was the plan to create either four free trade areas or four customs unions in sub-Saharan Africa. The latter was the preferred option as it would result in four trade regimes with common external tariffs. By contrast, free trade areas were deemed less desirable because even if the regions agreed to EPAs, the EU would have to establish separate trade regimes with each individual member of the EPA region (see notes 1 and 2). In an EC-commissioned report, the authors concluded that it is not likely that customs unions will be established with the EPA regions since it is not realistic to expect that common external tariffs will be created (Fontagne, Mitaritionna and Laborde

2008: 47) Alavi, Gibbon and Mortensen (2007: 14) note that in essence, 'ACP countries are supposed to reduce their tariffs in return for market access to the EU'.

Although the EU argues that it has not wavered from its declared objectives, critics have suggested that the EPAs are a smokescreen for its attempt to secure greater market access in Africa. In this context, several issues are at stake. The first is the notable fact that the entire new EU-ACP relationship is not being guided, as previously, by the office of the EC's Director-General for Development, but instead by the EC's Director-General for Trade (Kamidza 2005). This has caused conflict both within the two entities and between the EU and the ACP countries (Meyn 2007; Alavi, Gibbon and Mortensen 2007).

Second is inclusion of the Singapore issues in the EPA negotiations. As these are not deemed to be in the best interest of developing countries, the EU is being heavily criticised for attempting to get bilaterally what it cannot get at the multilateral level.[19] It is argued by critics that the Cotonou Agreement is not WTO compatible and is thus illegal since it discriminates against WTO member countries that do not have non-reciprocal access to the EU market (Alavi, Gibbon and Mortensen 2007: 14–15; Lee 2004: 6; Matambalya 2001: 39–45; Onguglo and Ito 2003; Ramonet 2008: 1; Stevens 2006: 443–44; Storey 2006: 335). According to the provisions of the WTO, member countries that are in the process of creating an FTA or a customs union are allowed to discriminate against outsiders and in favour of member states only if certain provisions are in place. These include market access covering goods under article XXIV. With respect to EPAs, this means that 'substantially all' trade must be liberalised between ACP countries and the EU and this must happen within 'a reasonable length of time' (Stevens 2006: 444).

For Nunn and Price (2004: 215), the 'Cotonou Agreement embodies perhaps the most radical element of reform in the redesigning of the Lomé development framework, namely WTO compliance through the liberalization of the non-reciprocal preferential trade regime'. This major shift represents the most recent phase in the continuous reconfiguration of EU-ACP relations that places it on a par with the much wider global development framework designed to reinforce the notion of rules-based multilateral liberalisation. In the final analysis, EU-ACP relations have been completely integrated into the neo-liberal model of accumulation (Meyn 2007:19). In short, the Cotonou Agreement appears to have made the world safer for European capital. According to Christian Aid (2005: 2), the results of the EPAs are not hard to imagine. With their diverse range of products and muscle in the marketplace, European producers can outstrip ACP rivals in their domestic markets. European producers have enjoyed decades of subsidies, support and protection from their governments and have built strong, lean, competitive industries . . . ACP countries – especially those in Africa, whose problem is not only that they can't sell enough but that they don't produce enough – have not. They stand to lose existing industries and the potential to develop new ones as products from Europe flood their markets.

The debate around EPAs is intense (Goodison 2007c; Safo 2007). Suffice it to say, EPAs have created division among EU countries and there exists a strong Stop EPA campaign. Those involved in the debate include, among others, non-governmental development agencies, civil society, leaders in the ACP countries, the Blair Commission, the British government, and the EU and EC. Indeed, to the dismay of the EU, even the United Kingdom's Departments of Trade and Industry and International Development have criticised EPAs, arguing that

> The European Commission clearly wants to use EPAs as a tool to open markets and further its own interests. This is not good. EPAs in their current form would be detrimental to development. They are free trade agreements by any other name and are currently designed to get the most for Europe without the necessary considerations of the negative effects on weaker developing country partners (Elliott 2005).

The United Kingdom report, along with other critical commentaries, forced the EU Trade Commissioner, Peter Mandelson, to announce that the EC's approach would be modified to reinforce the development component of EPAs (Alavi, Gibbon and Mortensen 2007).

Repartitioning the Continent

Stevens argues that the literature to date on EPAs can be divided into two areas (2006: 442). One consists of the economic effects of the prospective policy changes envisaged by the EU; while the other relates to the ability of the EU to use leverage to get the ACP countries to the negotiating table. The debate around these issues has been placed within the context of whether the ACPs should liberalise and if so whether they should be forced to do so. However, what is missing is discussion about the repartitioning of the African continent. This has been dealt with by only a handful of commentators such as Kamidza (2005) who comments that 'these new regional configurations are likely to produce . . . results comparable to the 1884–5 Berlin Conference which [carved] Africa into small but controllable states solely for the benefit of Europe;' (but see also Melber 2006: 45).

As the map below indicates, the EPAs were to be divided into four regions as follows

- ECOWAS (Economic Community of West African States – 16 countries) EPA: Ghana, Burkina Faso, Benin, Ivory Coast, Guinea-Bissau, Senegal, Niger, Nigeria, Mauritania, Mali, Togo, Cape Verde, Gambia, Guinea, Liberia, and Sierra Leone;
- CEMAC (Central African Economic and Monetary Community – 8 countries) EPA: Cameroon, Congo-Brazzaville, Democratic Republic of the Congo (DRC),[20] Gabon, Equatorial Guinea, Central African Republic, Chad, and São Tomé and Príncipe;
- ESA (Eastern and Southern Africa – 15 countries) EPA: Burundi, Comoros, Ethiopia, Eritrea, Djibouti, Kenya, Madagascar, Malawi, Mauritius, Rwanda, Seychelles, Zimbabwe, Sudan, Uganda and Zambia;
- SADC-minus (Southern African Development Community – 8 countries): Angola, Mozambique, Tanzania, Botswana, Lesotho, Namibia, Swaziland and South Africa).[21]

According to EC officials, there were internal debates about proposed EPA regions and basically two viewpoints. The first felt that the EU should favour small core regional bodies that were serious about regional integration, namely the East African Community (EAC), SADC and the Southern African Customs Union (SACU). The second felt that sub-Saharan Africa should be divided into three regions. This view won the debate. However, the countries of what was to be the ESA EPA would not agree to become one regional entity.[22]

The ACP countries wanted one binding agreement that would inform all EPA agreements. The rationale was that the ACP group had always functioned as one united group since the first Lomé Convention and they wanted to lay a common foundation for all the EPAs. This was especially the case since the ACP countries felt that the ongoing negotiations with the EC were complex and demanding and solidarity should be maintained and enhanced as long as possible.[23] It was hoped that during the first phase of negotiations an ACP-EU Agreement would focus on

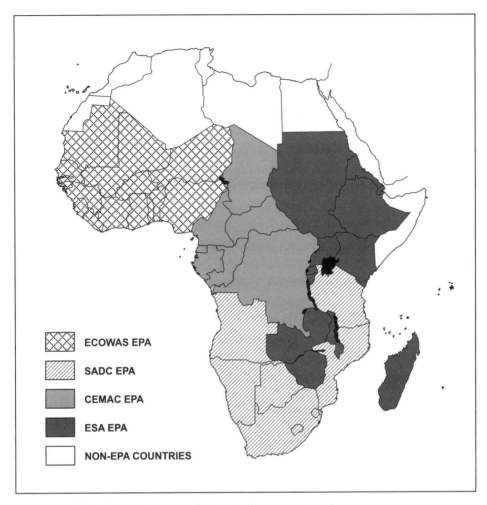

Figure 4.1 Map of proposed ecomomic partnership agreement regions.

issues of concern to all ACP countries, including the objectives and principles of the EPAs. This was to take place between September 2002 and 2003, when phase two would begin (Bilal 2002).

The second phase of the negotiations was to handle specific regional and national issues, including tariff negotiations and sectoral matters. In the end, African diplomats expressed their disappointment at the refusal of the EU to allow for a binding agreement with the entire ACP group (Fraser 2003).

Although the EU argues that EPAs can be created with regional economic organisations that become FTAs, the preferred situation, as previously noted, is for them to become customs unions. In the case of southern and eastern Africa the EU-SADC-minus EPA and the EU-ESA EPA, the following factors are relevant:

- SACU, comprising Botswana, Lesotho, Namibia, Swaziland and South Africa, has a common external tariff;
- South Africa has negotiated an FTA with the EU. Consequently, because Botswana, Lesotho, Namibia and Swaziland are members of SACU they are de facto members of the EU-SA FTA or the EU-SA Trade, Development and Co-operation Agreement (TDCA) of 1999;
- The SADC FTA was launched in August 2008 among eleven of the fourteen member states. Angola, the DRC and Malawi are scheduled to join the FTA later. SADC is scheduled to become a customs union by 2010, a common market by 2015, a monetary union by 2016 and have a single currency by 2018;
- COMESA (Common Market for Eastern and Southern Africa), whose nineteen-strong membership overlaps with SADC, has a FTA and is now scheduled to become customs union by June 2009;
- EAC, which includes Kenya, Tanzania, Uganda, Burundi and Rwanda, became a customs union in 2005.

In other words, in southern and eastern Africa there exist two customs unions (SACU and EAC), two FTAs (COMESA and SADC), and prospectively two new customs unions (COMESA 2009 and SADC 2010). Clearly, rescrambling this particular egg would be immensely complicated. For instance, the longstanding and extremely contentious rivalry between SADC and COMESA should have been enough to warn the EC against any notion of an ESA EPA. The EC admits that it was determined that since COMESA was a stronger and less political organisation than SADC, the former would lead the process.[24] However, this decision was made without any reference to SADC and was accordingly rejected.

Whatever the motivations of the EU, the guidelines of the ACP countries reinforce the importance to build and then consolidate intra-ACP regional co-operation as a precursor to establishing FTAs with the EU. The guidelines further note that the ACP countries do not have the capacity to liberalise trade relations between themselves and with the EU simultaneously. Consequently, they reject the EC's notion of open regionalism, which is at the foundation of the approach to EPA negotiations (*ACP Guidelines* 2002: 25).

In addition to the above, governments in southern Africa, as well as other ACP colleagues, argue that if EPAs are going to be development oriented, they must transcend the perception that they are just FTAs. Instead, measures must be put in place that create structural transformation of economies with a view to increasing the prospects of ACP countries producing more value-added goods, notwithstanding the fact that:

> the free-trade context threatens to make this impossible . . . At times, the EC appears to agree with this view, stressing that the EPA approach will allow trade and development assistance to be linked. However, speaking in the Caribbean in April 2004, the [former] EU Trade Commissioner, Pascal Lamy, stressed that the EC does not have a mandate to 'negotiate development finance as part of EPAs'. What is more, Commission spokespersons have repeatedly said that no additional funding will be made available to any ACP countries until all existing EDF funds have been spent (Goodison and Stoneman 2005: 23).

Undermining Regional Economic Integration

As previously noted, at the core of the Cotonou Agreement is the further incorporation of Africa into the global economy though regional integration. The first phase is to enhance integration among ACP regions, to be followed by increased economic integration between regions and the EU. As the EC notes, at the heart of the EPA concept is the notion of creating integrated regional markets with development at the centre (Storey 2006: 337).

Many critics, however, have argued that the EU strategy will undermine regional economic integration in Africa. For example, Melber (2006: 45–6) notes that the EU's proposed strategy of dividing Africa into groups to negotiate is not only a hindrance to the co-ordination of Africa's trade policies, but reinforces the legacy of colonial economic relationships. Ochieng and Sharman (2004: 3) argue similarly that the EPA initiative 'has created new regional groupings that are inconsistent with, and undermine, existing African economic and political blocs. Reducing regional integration to trade liberalisation undermines the broader socio-economic and political objectives of existing bodies'.

Meanwhile, Kamidza concludes (2005) that EPAs have hampered regional integration efforts: they attempt to bundle African countries into new regional political structures while splitting existing regional economic organisations and rendering them less capable of entering trade negotiations collectively. In short, the EPA process can be seen as an effort at divide and rule. In addition, the EPAs are likely to result in

revenue losses, possibly resulting in the worsening of the regional
debt situation; de-industrialisation; increased unemployment;
increased poverty; fragmentation of export and tariff regimes; loss
of export competitiveness; undermining of local agricultural and
industrial production arising from EU and US dumping; more trade
diversion than trade creation; and undermining existing regional
economic strategies (Lee 2004: 6).

For West Africa, it is estimated that a large percentage of the manufacturing
sector would collapse and the financial sector be weakened (Goodison 2007a:
149). It has been estimated that the ECOWAS EPA would lose $365 million in
revenue from exports to the EU; possibly a greater decline in intra-regional trade
than across any other regional economic organisation in sub-Saharan Africa. In
terms of revenue losses for West Africa, the estimated figure is over $985 million
(Karingi et al. 2005: 49–50 and 56). In the case of Nigeria, which did not sign an
interim EPA (see below), it is estimated that between January and March 2008,
the cocoa industry would have lost $5 million (Boyle 2008: 4).

In addition, a report estimates that as a result of EPAs the SADC region could
experience losses of more than $13 million in exports while revenue losses for
imports would total more than $153 million (Karingi et al. 2005: 14–15).

The EU has consistently argued that EPAs will enhance Africa's development
and that with newly created WTO-compatible trade regimes Africa will experience
first, increased domestic and foreign investment; second, technology transfer and
enhanced economic relations with the EU; third, the development of more
competitive trade regimes that will result in gradual integration into the global
economy; and fourth, economic development (for example, removal of supply-
side constraints to trade) and reduction in poverty levels. With respect to the
latter, however, even EC officials agree that billions of euros are needed for Africa
to overcome supply-side constraints, money the EU is not committed to providing,
even though it did provide such assistance to former countries of the Soviet Union
that joined the EU.

The EC has argued in response that sub-Saharan Africa has too many regional
economic communities (RECs) and that their overlapping membership is one of
the greatest hindrances to regional integration. While the need for rationalisation
is clear, there is a strong argument on the one hand that African countries do not
have the prerequisites for regional integration as proposed by the EU (Lee 2003).
On the other hand the issues of conflicting and overlapping RECs need to be
addressed before they are absorbed into EPAs.

Some have argued that the EU has threatened ACP countries with loss of development aid and other financial support if they refuse to accede to EPAs (Kamidza 2005). This suggestion is adamantly denied by the EC.[25] However, Sanoussi Bilal (2007: 2), the co-ordinator of programmes of the European Centre for Development Policy Management (ECDPM) on ACP-EU economic trade co-operation, argues that the majority of ACP countries were reluctant to engage in EPA negotiations and the major reason they became involved was to retain their EU preferential market access. For these countries, the EPAs are not deemed to be an opportunity but a destiny, a price that has to be paid in order to continue access to Europe's markets.

The SA-EU FTA, which came into force in January 2000, was supposed to be the model for future EU EPAs, although some EC officials deny this (Wellmer 2007). However, as South Africa negotiated with the EU as a developed country, and the other countries of eastern and southern Africa are either developing or least developing countries, any potential association with South Africa and the EPAs was politically problematic. For a start, even though they were not represented at the negotiating table, as members of SACU Botswana, Lesotho, Namibia and Swaziland became de facto parties to the agreement, even though it had serious negative implications for them.

In defence of the ongoing criticism that the EU has created further divisions between SADC and COMESA, one EC official noted that:

> The intention of the EU was to deepen integration in eastern and southern Africa, not split the region. The hope was that eventually eastern and southern Africa would become one customs union. The opinion of the EU is that Africa needs to become more serious about regional integration. The overall objective of the EU was to force Africa to rationalise the integration process. The EU also wanted there to be a clear cut approach towards regional integration. Although the process has not moved in the direction that the EU anticipated, it still feels that it's the right direction and there exists a great deal of movement towards the goals and objectives of the EU and EPAs. According to COMESA, the EPAs have helped tremendously in terms of movement towards at least the discussion towards deeper integration.[26]

The issue of African dependence on EU development assistance and the fear of losing it appear to be at the core of the decision by many African countries to continue to negotiate the EPAs. Yet, as observed by Jane Narunga of the Southern and Eastern African Trade, Information and Negotiations Institute (SEATINI):

> Ugandan negotiators don't know what they are doing. All countries are to work on the development component of the proposed EPAs. They haven't taken a holistic approach. There is a feeling that they are not really negotiating. They are not dealing with the reality of the EPAs and what the EU really plans. The EU has really high stakes and is funding the entire operation. So they see this as just part of development.[27]

The most disconcerting issue for the EU was the fact that Tanzania, a member of the East African Customs Union, had refused to join the ESA EPA. This was especially problematic because in order for the EPAs to go into force, each African country can be a member of only one customs union. Another reality is that most countries in eastern and southern Africa are LDCs, which means they are not required to reduce tariffs and participate in FTAs under WTO rules. More significantly, trade experts have pointed out that while overlapping FTAs are technically possible, overlapping customs union are not.

Goodison and Stoneman (2005) argue that a number of countries in southern Africa are threatened by the introduction of reciprocal trade preferences that will favour EU exports over a large percentage of trade for both national and regional markets. This includes, in particular, food and agricultural products, especially in Zimbabwe, Zambia, Swaziland and Namibia. The CAP reform process is increasing the competitiveness of EU agricultural goods as a result of changes in aid provision:

> Dismantling border protection in this context could expose local agricultural producers and food manufacturers to highly price-competitive (albeit economically inefficient competition), leading to a radical downsizing of the agro-processing industry in Southern Africa where it exists, and effectively preventing its emergence elsewhere. This would then have important knock-on effects on agricultural incomes, as prices for basic agricultural raw materials stagnate (Goodison and Stoneman 2005: 23-4).

Goodison and Stoneman argue that it is obvious that under the EPAs, EU exports will increase since tariffs will be removed and goods from the EU will be more competitive through third country suppliers. However, the opposite is not obvious: namely, how the EPAs will result in increased southern African exports to the EU. This is because it is not clear whether the EU will deal with first, a number of issues including restrictions on residual market access arising out of strict rules of origin; second, the continuous rise in food safety standards; and third, the fact that many supply-side constraints remain. Furthermore, although the EC assumes that there will be an increase in investment flows in southern Africa, resulting in the enhancement of trade and international competitiveness, this cannot be guaranteed. While it appears reasonable that EU-southern African trade will increase under the EPAs, this will probably only benefit consumers, international traders and European producers rather than bringing about what is really needed – ACP economic structural development and transformation. Finally, the non-LDCs will experience considerable barriers to trade. If the worst case scenario were to happen, which Goodison and Stoneman argue (2005: 28) is not unduly pessimistic, 'Southern Africa's exports of food and agriculture products to the EU could be largely suspended'.

Increased EU Market Access

The concerns that the economic 'recolonisation' of Africa which is underway under the two effects of CAP reform and the EU's free-trade area policy can be illustrated by the spate of take-overs which took place in the dairy sector in South Africa in the middle of the 1990s, in the expectation of the impending conclusion of the TDCA. Within an 18-month period, two-thirds of South Africa's dairy-processing sector had been take over or passed into partnership with European dairy companies, with the major European players Danone and Parmalat actively competing with each other to buy up most of the sector (Goodison 2007a: 150).

Possibly concerned about the above, the British government in March 2005 argued against the EU using the EPAs to leverage the immediate opening of access to developing country markets and suggested that ACP countries should be given a minimum of 20 years to allow for full import liberalisation (Storey 2006: 359).

Over the last few years, cheap imported chicken from both the US and EU has flooded the Ghanaian market, with imports from the EU coming from farmers who received generous subsidies. As a result the demand for local poultry has collapsed, affecting the economic stability of over 400 000 farmers. In 2004, an estimated 40 000 tons of such chicken was exported to Ghana. Thus whereas in

1992 Ghanaian farmers supplied 95% of the poultry consumed in the country, by 2001 this figure had dropped to 11%. Other countries seriously affected by the export of EU frozen chicken include Cameroon, Togo, Senegal and South Africa (Atarah 2005; Christian Aid 2005: 17–18). In addition to undermining the chicken industry in Ghana, the seas of Ghana have been emptied by EU fishing vessels (see chapter thirteen by André Standing in this book). Goodison reports (2007b: 291) that increased production of low-priced EU cereals as a result of CAP reforms have increased the export of both cereal-based products and poultry into West Africa since 1995.

An estimated 600 000 small-scale dairy farmers in Kenya have had to compete with imports of EU milk powder and other dairy products. Similarly, in western Kenya those involved in the sugar industry are threatened by the import of refined sugar from the EU. This has posed a major threat to the ability of the country to develop its own industrial sugar refining capacity. In the beef industry, small-scale farmers in both Namibia and Botswana are experiencing serious problems due to the dumping of EU beef on the market.[28] In Senegal, the tomato industry has been devastated by cheap EU imports (Christian Aid 2005: 17).

The literature is full of examples of the devastating consequences of US and EU dumping, structural adjustment programmes and new trade rules under the WTO, as well as the potential further devastating consequence of EU-Africa EPAs.

One EC official acknowledged that there was a contradiction between the EU's denial that its primary interest is in increasing access to the African market and the reality of EU dumping on the continent. However, he argued that once the EPAs are implemented, dumping would stop.[29] Against this, the Cotonou Agreement neither obliges the EU to reduce its dumping nor does it have a safeguard clause for the ACP countries. Furthermore, as noted by Berthelot (2006: 1), 'the EU cheats brazenly with the WTO rules, which allows it to practice a massive agricultural dumping highly detrimental to ACPs'. Although in theory the ACP countries can prosecute the EU for breaking WTO dumping rules, few ACP countries have the financial resources to bring the EU before the WTO. In any case, such prosecution is likely to take place once the damage to a particular sector has already been done.

Kamidza argues that Europe has a problem of overproduction, not only of products but also of services. Creating EPAs through FTAs between countries that are unequal politically and economically in the guise of one size fits all neo-liberal policies offers an answer to the problem. He further notes that this is being done in conjunction with the international financial institutions (IFIs) to shift the Africa-Europe trade relations from non-reciprocity to reciprocity thereby removing the developmental component that characterized the previous Lomé Conventions. Since EPAs seek to replace past special preferences, they are viewed as a vehicle for exerting EU's political influences to her former colonies. Withdrawing these preferences suits Europe's political interests well, especially given that the 25-member body is increasingly becoming sensitive to the demands of the new member-states, which are reluctant to be guided by past colonial relationships (Kamidza 2005: 10).

Benefits do not automatically stem from trade liberalisation in isolation from other policy matters. In the ultimate analysis, the EPAs prioritise freer trade over fair trade and fail to address the role of trade liberalisation in providing opportunities and betterment for the poor.

African Leaders Challenge the EPAs

'The unimaginable has happened, to the displeasure of arrogant Europe. Africa, thought to be so poor that it would agree to anything, has said no in rebellious pride. No to the straitjacket of the Economic Partnership Agreements (EPAs), no to the complete liberalization of trade, no to the latest manifestations of the colonial pact' (Ramonet 2008: 1).

As the 31 December 2007 deadline for the signing of the EPAs was drawing close, EU Trade Commissioner Peter Mandelson continued to insist that there was no alternative to the EPAs that would not leave the ACP countries worse off than under the Lomé regime. In fact, contrary to the provisions of Cotonou, the EU had never presented any alternatives to the ACP countries as stipulated in the agreement. The only way forward, according to the EU, was EPAs. In a September 2007 interview, Mandelson noted (2007: 1–3) that no plan B was available to enhance access by ACP countries to markets in Europe nor the development benefits outlined in the proposed EPAs. He also observed that since the WTO waiver that had allowed the Cotonou preferences to remain was to expire at the end of 2007, the EU would have to fall back on the generalized system of preferences (GSP), which would be a significant step backwards with respect to preferential access and opportunities. This statement is indeed ironic since one of the promises made to the ACP countries with respect to the EPAs was that none of them would be worse off under Cotonou than the Lomé regime.

Clearly under the GSP the non-LDCs would be worse off. With the GSP, all developing countries are offered some tariff reductions on products entering the EU market. The products, however, are very specific and must not compete with EU products. Understandably, therefore, the ACP countries do not see this as a viable alternative to the preferential access to the EU market that they have enjoyed under Lomé and continued to enjoy until the end of 2007.

The EC estimated that reversion to the GSP would cost West Africa in excess of €1 billion of exports and Central Africa more than €360 million. Meanwhile, the Overseas Development Institute has calculated that under the GSP, exports attracting a new tariff of 10% or less would represent a transfer from the ACP countries to the EU of 2.6 times the amount the EDF committed to health projects in 2005.[30]

As far as the EU is concerned, the LDCs that decline to sign an EPA may continue to participate in the EBA initiative. From 2001, the EU has provided all LDCs with duty free access to the EU market with the exception of arms, sugar, rice and bananas. Beginning in 2006, these (minus arms) were to be permitted gradual duty free entry into the EU. Although on paper this appears generous, even the EU admits that because of the more stringent rules of origin under the EBA, most ACP countries continued to export to the EU under the Cotonou Agreement. In addition, the EBA is non-contractual, which means that at any given time the EU can change the agreement or rescind it. It is therefore less predictable than Cotonou.

By November 2007, the EPAs were in such danger of not being signed that the EC began to offer two-step EPAs. As time ran out, the EC began to have second thoughts about threatening to end their trade privileges if ACPs did not sign a comprehensive EPA by the year-end deadline. Instead, it announced it was willing to offer interim deals that included goods only. Other important and controversial issues such as trade in services or steps to enhance competitiveness could, the EU suggested, be negotiated during a second stage in 2008 (Rampa 2007: 1).[31]

The issue of the EPAs came to an unexpected explosive point during the second EU-Africa Summit, which took place in Lisbon in December 2007. Although EPAs were not officially on the agenda (De Bergh 2007-8: 20), massive pressure was placed upon African countries to sign them by 31 December. In response, Abdoubye Wade, president of Senegal, stormed out of the meeting denouncing the EPAs and accusing the EU of using strong-arm tactics. With President Thabo Mbeki of South Africa supporting Wade, African Union (AU) chairperson Alpha Oumar Konaré warned about the divisive consequences the EPAs would have for the regional integration process in Africa and declared that they would have a negative impact on Africa's industries and rural poor.

This necessitated rethinking on the part of the EU. Indeed, at the summit French president Nicolas Sarkozy lent support to African countries that were vehemently opposed to the EPAs by noting that 'he was in favor of globalization but not the despoliation of countries that had nothing left'.[32] Meanwhile, Britain announced that it was trying to secure a temporary arrangement that would ensure no African nation was worse off from 1 January 2008. As a result of such backtracking, the EC president José Manuel Barroso was forced to heed the demand by African countries for further discussions on the EPAs, scheduling these for February 2008.

The only region to sign a full EPA by 31 December 2007 was the Caribbean and it was suggested that this followed 'a mixture of blatant bullying, bribery, cajolery, deception, intellectual dishonesty and plain bluff' (Thomas 2008). However, when it came to the crunch, most African non-LDCs, reluctantly initialed interim EPAs in order to preserve their current market access to the EU. The exceptions were South Africa, which will continue to export to the EU under the TDCA; and Nigeria, Gabon and Congo, which will now have to export to the EU under the GSP. Otherwise, as summarised by the ECDPM, by the end of January 2008 the situation was as follows:

- the EAC (Kenya, Tanzania, Burundi, Uganda and Rwanda) decided to form its own EPA region and signed an interim agreement with the EU. An interim agreement only requires that trade in goods be covered in order to comply with WTO rules;
- other countries that initialed interim agreements in the ESA EPA region were Seychelles, Zimbabwe, Mauritius, Comoros and Madagascar. However, Zambia, Djibouti, Eritrea, Ethiopia and Malawi will be exporting to the EU under the EBA regime;
- an interim agreement was initialed by Namibia, Botswana, Mozambique, Lesotho and Swaziland in the SADC EPA region, with Angola planning to follow their lead;
- in Central Africa, the only country that initialed an interim agreement was Cameroon, the only non-LDC in the region. The LDCs that will export to the EU under the EBA include the Central African Republic, Chad, DRC, Equatorial Guinea and São Tomé and Príncipe;

- in West Africa, Ivory Coast and Ghana initialed an interim agreement in order to prevent the imposition of tariffs on major exports, including bananas and cocoa (Kabuletta and Hanson 2007-8: 1). However, Nigeria opted to export to the EU under the GSP+ regime. Although Cape Verde graduated from LDC status on 1 January 2008, it will be allowed to export to the EU for three years under the EBA regime. The LDCs from this region that will export to the EU under the EBA include Benin, Burkina Faso, Gambia, Guinea, Guinea-Bissau, Liberia, Mali, Mauritania, Niger, Senegal, Sierra Leone and Togo.

The interim agreements contain clauses that stipulate negotiations towards creating full EPAs will continue in 2008. ECDPM acknowledges that a result of the EPAs will be that ACP countries will likely experience losses in tariff revenues and will face adjustment costs as a result of the need to restructure their economies. They will also need support with respect to their productive capacities if they are going to be able to take advantage of new export opportunities. In this regard, the EC has indicated that development assistance under the EDF will continue along with assistance under special programmes that deal with sensitive products such as bananas, sugar and rice. This will be provided from EU budget funding. In addition, the ACP countries have requested other EPA funding complementary to EDF funding, so that funds will not be diverted from development areas to projects related to trade. In addition, the EU has made a serious commitment to increasing trade-related assistance to €2 billion annually by 2010.

Meanwhile, consistent with the joint EU-Africa strategy endorsed at the summit there are three priorities related to the trade and regional integration partnership. It was agreed that such integration could be achieved by:

- ensuring that EPAs support Africa's regional and continental integration agenda as defined in the Abuja Treaty establishing the African Economic Community;
- improving coherence and convergence between African integration processes and EPAs; and
- enhancing the role of the AU in monitoring EPAs and the Euro-Mediterranean Partnership.

However, De Bergh (2007-8) argues that the EC's decision on a fall back position to create bilateral agreements 'as a provisional solution, to be enlarged into a comprehensive regional agreement in 2008' placed African countries between a rock and a hard place. Either, they had to conclude an EPA individually, at the cost of alienating regional partners and disrupting regional integration, a politically (and for some legally) untenable option; or, they could align with their respective region by refusing to sign bilateral EPAs. This would result in a substantive increase of EU tariffs as of 1 January 2008 under the less advantageous GSP, an economically costly option that would damage their development prospects.

An alternative to creating more divisions, De Bergh suggested, would have been for the EU to continue negotiations into 2008. It is indeed ironic that the American African Growth and Opportunity Act (AGOA) has been in existence without a WTO waiver and in many respects AGOA is more discriminatory than the Cotonou Agreement, yet this has been extended to 2015.[33] So, like the US, the EU could possibly continue the Cotonou trade preferences without a waiver since the EPA negotiations have gone beyond the end of 2007. As Christian Aid (2005: 6) notes:

> The resulting one-sided or non-reciprocal trade arrangement could be made WTO-legal if European member states were prepared to instruct the Commission to argue for changes to WTO law. The rules governing regional and preferential trade agreements between developed and developing countries need rewriting. Europe has already promised to support measures to make 'special and differential treatment' for developing countries more effective in the ongoing Doha round of talks.

In the final analysis, when the EU started negotiating the EPAs in 2002, they seemingly began to undermine the effort by the AU to rationalise African RECs that had commenced in 2001 with the Abuja Treaty. It aims to create one African Economic Community (AEC) and the AU had identified eight RECs to begin this process. As previously noted, it is the opinion of this author that the EU model of regional economic integration, whether through the EU EPAs or the AU, will not be successful. However, what has become clear is that the interim EPAs have only served to create more divisions among various regional economic organisations (Hanson and Julian 2008: 14–15). In this regard, the EU will never be successful in repartitioning or economically recolonising the continent.

The one positive outcome of EU efforts in this regard is that it has forced African leaders to become more serious about the need to rationalise regional economic organisations and find an African solution to the failure to integrate the continent economically. This, however, is going to be a daunting task as global economic powers – US, EU, China, India and Brazil – have all joined the fray, scrambling for Africa's resources. The unfortunate reality is that African leaders are not only allowing this to happen, but are active participants in the process. It is frightening to contemplate that at the end of Africa's current commodity boom the continent may well be worse off than before it began. This is highly possible given that amidst the billions of dollars changing hands on the continent, not one leader is spearheading an industrial revolution with these monetary resources. Through attempts to repartition the continent and economically recolonise it, global powers such as the EU are interested only in temporary gains. But who can blame them for trying if African leaders themselves are complicit in the process?

Notes

1. EC, Brussels, 27 Feb. 2006.
2. 'The new colonialists: a 14-page special report on China's thirst for resources', 15–21 Mar. 2008.
3. An FTA consists of an agreement among member states of a regional economic organisation to remove most tariffs when trading among themselves. Each country, however, continues to maintain its own tariffs when trading with countries that are not members of the FTA.
4. In a customs union, the members of the regional economic organisation determine one common external tariff (CET) on each product that enters the FTA. For example, all flour that is imported into the region is imported under the same tariff regime. The EU would like the four proposed regions to be customs unions so they can negotiate one set of tariffs with the entire regional economic organisation. Otherwise, under a FTA, they have to negotiate a separate tariff regime with each country with whom they sign an EPA.
5. Belgium, Federal Republic of Germany, France, Italy, Luxemburg and the Netherlands.
6. Mauritania, Senegal, Mali, Niger, Upper Volta (now Burkino Faso), Ivory Coast, Dahomey (now Benin), Togo, Cameroon, Chad, Gabon, the Central African Republic, Congo-Brazzaville, Congo-Leopoldville (DRC), Rwanda, Burundi, Somalia, Madagascar and Mauritius.
7. He argues that a FTA was created between the EU and each of the associates.
8. The ECC became the European Community in the late 1960s.
9. Ireland and Denmark also joined at the same time.
10. This principle can be found in Article 1 of GATT/WTO and it stipulates that one member must give to all members the same most favourable treatment. This is part of the non-discrimination principle.

11. But see Brown 2002; Crawford 1996; Lee 2003; Montana 2003; Davenport, Hewitt and Koning, 1995; Nunn and Price 2004; Parfitt 1996; Stevens 1996; Wellmer 1998.

12. The EU currently consists of 27 independent states and is the most successful regional economic organisation in the world. It has created an economic union with one single currency, the Euro, although not all member states have adopted it.

13. Rules of origin stipulated the amount of local value that must be added to goods under a FTA in order for ACP countries to export to the EU duty free. This is done to prevent 'non-partner countries from trans-shipping goods to take advantage of the lower tariffs offered within a free trade agreement' (Ravenhill 2005: 423). For more detail see Brown 2002: 61 and Lee 2003: 202.

14. Food safety standards: see Stoneman and Thompson 2007: 236–7 for an in-depth explanation.

15. These included multinational companies such as German Saarbergwerk, Belgian Petrofina and Royal Dutch Shell in the ACP mineral sector; Tate and Lyle, Booker McConnell and Unilever in the agricultural sector, particularly the Caribbean and African plantations; and many conglomerates operating across sectors like Brook Liebig's involvement in tea, coffee and cattle rearing in Africa (Nunn and Price 2004: 213).

16. This means in essence Lomé V since the Lomé Convention provisions remained in force until 31 Dec. 2007.

17. The two other EPAs are the Caribbean and the Pacific.

18. Interview, 28 Feb. 2006.

19. Unequal partners: how EU-ACP economic partnership agreements (EPAs) could harm the development prospects of many of the world's poorest countries. Oxfam briefing note, Sep. 2006.

20. The DRC was originally a member of the ESA EPA.

21. Although South Africa was initially only an observer to the SADC-minus EPA as a result of its existing FTA with the EU, it was allowed to join the SADC-minus EPA on 12 Feb. 2007.

22. Interview, 28 Feb. 2006.

23. It was estimated that there were more than 24 areas of common concern that needed to be addressed in the ACP guidelines at the ACP-EU level.

24. Interview, 28 Feb. 2006.

25. EC official at EPA seminar, Africa Institute of South Africa, 25 Oct. 2007, Pretoria.

26. Interview, 28 Feb. 2006.

27. Interview with Jane Narunga, 22 Mar. 2006.

28. EPAs will destroy small scale farmers' livelihoods in Africa: memorandum to the European Commission by EPA Watch, 13 Apr. 2005.

29. Interview, 27 Feb. 2006.

30. *Trade Negotiations Insights* 6(6) 2007: 2.

31. For a detailed chronology of the events leading up to the final outcome of the EPA negotiations see *Trade Negotiation Insights* Sep. 2007 to Jan. 2008.

32. *New York Times* 9 Dec. 2007.

33. Agritrade Monthly News Update Apr. 2007: 4.

References

ACP Guidelines and the EU Negotiating Mandate: A Comparison. 2002. Brussels: European Research Office.

Alavi, A., P. Gibbon and N. J. Mortensen.2007. EC-ACP Economic Partnership Agreements (EPAs): Institutional and Substantive Issues. Copenhagen: Danish Institute for International Studies.

Atarah, L. 2005. 'Playing chicken: Ghana vs. the IMF'. CropWatch 14 June.

Berthelot, J. 2006. 'David and Goliath: argument against the Economic Partnership Agreements (EPAs) between the European Union and the African, Caribbean and Pacific countries'. Solidarité 19 Dec.

Bilal, S. 2002. The Future of ACP-EU Trade Relations: An Overview of the Forthcoming Negotiations. Brussels: ECDPM.

Boyle, J. 2008. 'Nigerian cocoa processors to lose millions'. Trade Negotiations Insights 7(2): 4.

Brown, W. 2002. The European Union and Africa: The Restructuring of North-South Relations. London: Tauris.

Christian Aid. 2005. For Richer or Poorer: Transforming Economic Partnership Agreements between Europe and Africa. London: Christian Aid.

Commission of the European Communities. 1995. Free Trade Areas: An Appraisal. Brussels: EC.

Crawford, G. 1996. 'Whither Lomé?: the mid-term review and the decline of partnership'. Journal of Modern African Studies 34(3): 503–18.

Davenport, M., A. Hewitt and A. Koning. 1995. Europe's Preferred Partners?: The Lomé Countries in World Trade. London: Overseas Development Institute.

De Bergh, M-L. 2007–8. 'EPAs and the EU-Africa Strategy: (in)coherence?' Trade Negotiations Insights 6(8): 20–21.

Elliott, L. 2005. 'EU move to block trade aid for poor'. The Guardian 19 May.

Fontage, L., C. Mitaritionna and D. Laborde. 2008. An Impact Study of the EU-ACP Economic Partnership Agreements (EPAs) in the Six ACP Regions. Paris: CEPII-CIREM.

Fraser, A. 2003. 'SADC split by EU trade talks'. ACTSA Trade and Development Update 3(2).

Goodison, P. 2007a. 'The future of Africa's trade with Europe: "new" EU trade policy'. Review of African Political Economy 34(111): 139–51.

——. 2007b. 'What is the future for EU-Africa agricultural trade after CAP reform?' Review of African Political Economy 34(112): 279–95.

——. 2007c. 'EU trade policy and the future of Africa's trade relationship with the EU'. Review of African Political Economy 34(112): 247–66.

Goodison, P. and C. Stoneman. 2005. 'Trade, development and cooperation: is the EU helping Africa?' In: Trade, Development Cooperation: What Future for Africa, edited by H. Melber. Uppsala: Nordic Africa Institute.

Hanson, V. and M. Julian 2008. 'EPA negotiations update'. Trade Negotiations Insights 7(2): 14–15.

Kabuletta, P. and V. Hanson. 2007–8. 'Good from far but far from good'. Trade Negotiations Insights 6(8): 1–2.

Kamidza, R. 2005. 'Economic partnership agreements negotiations process: whose interest?' *Seatini Bulletin* 8(8) June. http://www.seatini.org/bulletins/8.8.php.

Karingi, S. et al. 2005. *The EU-SADC Economic Partnership Agreement: A Regional Perspective.* Addis Ababa: Economic Commission for Africa.

Lee, M. C. 2003. *The Political Economy of Regionalism in Southern Africa.* Cape Town: University of Cape Town Press.

——. 2004. 'The US and EU: undermining regional economic integration in Africa'. *News from the Nordic Africa Institute:* 5–8.

——. 2005. 'An assessment of the G8 commitment to trade and regional integration in Africa'. In: *Freedom, Prosperity, and Security: The G8 Partnership with Africa: Sea Island 2004 and Beyond.* New York: Council on Foreign Relations.

Mandelson, P. 2007. 'EPAs: there is no plan B: an interview with Peter Mandelson'. *Trade Negotiations Insights* 6(5): 1–3.

Matambalya, F.A.S.T. 2001. *The New EU-ACP Partnership: Consequences for Eastern and Southern Africa.* Dar es Salaam: Mkuki Na Nyota.

Melber, H. 2006. 'The EU and regional integration in Africa: a critical appraisal with special reference to the economic partnership agreements. In: M. Brüntrup/H. Melber/ I. Taylor, *Africa, Regional Cooperation and the World Market: Socio-Economic Strategies in Times of Global Trade Regimes.* Uppsala: Nordic Africa Institute, 40–51

Meyn. M. 2007. *EPAs: Are the Trade and Development Dimensions Compatible?* London: Overseas Development Institute.

Montana, I. M. 2003. 'The Lomé Convention from inception to the dynamics of the post-Cold War, 1967–1990s'. *African and Asian Studies* 2(1): 63–97.

Nunn, A. and S. Price. 2004. 'Managing development: EU and African relations through the evolution of the Lomé and Cotonou Agreements'. *Historical Materialism* 12(4): 203–30.

Ochieng, C. and T. Sharman. 2004. *Trade Traps: Why EU-ACP Economic Partnership Agreements Pose a Threat to Africa's Development.* London: Action Aid International.

Onguglo, B. and T. Ito. 2003. *How to Make EPAs WTO Compatible?: Reforming the Rules on Regional Trade Agreements.* Maastricht: European Centre for Development Policy Management.

Parfitt, T. 1996. 'The decline of Eurafrica: Lomé's mid-term review'. *Review of African Political Economy* 23(67): 53–66.

Ramonet, I. 2008. 'Africa says no – and means it'. *Le Monde Diplomatique* Jan.

Rampa, F. 2007. 'EU offers ACP "two-step" EPAs: where does development stand?' *Trade Negotiations Insights* 6(7): 1–3.

Ravenhill, J. 2005. *Global Political Economy.* Oxford: Oxford University Press.

Safo, A. 2007. 'Don't sign the EPAs: civil society condemns fruitless deals'. *Trade Negotiations Insights* 6(6): 10.

Stevens, C. 1996. 'The single European market: opportunities and challenges in trade'. In: *Africa and Europe: The Changing Economic Relationship,* edited by O.O. Ojo. London: Zed Books.

——. 2006. 'The EU, Africa and economic partnership agreements: unintended consequences and policy leverage'. *Journal of Modern African Studies* 44(3): 441–58.

Stoneman, C. and C. Thompson. 2007. 'Trade partners or trading deals: the EU & US in Southern Africa'. *Review of African Political Economy* 34(111): 227–45.

Storey, A. 2006. 'Normative power Europe?: economic partnership agreements and Africa'. *Journal of Contemporary African Studies* 24(3): 331–46.

Thomas, C. 2008. 'Guyana and the wider world: suckered: the economic partnership agreement (EPA) as massive manipulation'. *Stabroek News* 20 Jan.

Wellmer, G. 2007. 'South African free trade experiences with the European Union'. *World Economy and Development in Brief, Special Report* 3: 1–9.

CHAPTER FIVE

India's Engagements in Africa

Self-Interest or Mutual Partnership?

Sanusha Naidu

The Commerce between India and Africa will be of ideas and services, not manufactured goods against raw materials after the fashion of western exploiters (Mahatma Gandhi).[1]

If both sides are able to synergise energies and initiatives and adapt to a changing world, the 21st century could surely belong to them (Rao Inderjit Singh, former Indian Minister of State for External Affairs).[2]

Africa is a success story waiting to happen and one which will happen soon (Sanjay Kirloskar, Chairman of Kirloskar Brothers).[3]

At the turn of the twenty-first century there were hopes that this millennium was going to belong to the African continent. However, before long focus shifted to the rise of China and India and the pending impact their astonishing growth patterns and increasing presence will have on the geography of the international system and the nature of global politics and diplomatic relations. Nonetheless, as far as Africa is concerned, the debate about whether China and India are engaging in a second scramble has concentrated overwhelmingly upon Beijing's spearheading of the penetration of economies in the developing world. The objective of this chapter is to correct that balance by drawing attention to India as a participant, for good or ill, in the current scramble for African resources and markets.

The new scramble debate is divided between those (Le Pere and Shelton 2007; Naidu and Davies 2006) who perceive China's burgeoning engagement with Africa as benign and constructive for Africa's development agenda; and detractors (Holsag 2006; Lee 2006; Melber 2007) who argue that China's footprint in Africa is exploitative and driven mainly by resource extraction. For them Beijing's behaviour resembles that of a new imperial power with a colonial project that will perpetuate Africa's underdevelopment.

Understanding India's deepening involvement in Africa must start with its government's definition of this relationship and the extent to which it is managed on a mutual basis. Furthermore, India's engagements in Africa must also take into account historical ties. It is only against this background that it is possible to assess how India fits into the new scramble debate.

The answer depends upon the extent to which India's increasing interests in Africa can promote the continent's development. This chapter, therefore, focuses on India's growing relations with Africa by assessing the balance of mutual opportunities and costs. It does this by asking: what are the factors that motivate India's deepening relations with Africa; are these borne out of political expediency or are they based upon economic pragmatism? Where do the lines of complementarity lie and what are the divisions? How much does Africa feature in India's global ambitions? Is there consensus regarding issues of the South and the pursuit of multilateral reform? Or is it a case of differing agendas? First, however, it is necessary to undertake a brief historical overview, followed by analysis of the political and economic dimensions of the relationship.

Historical Relations

Contacts and trade between India and Africa long preceded, yet were deepened by common experiences of British colonialism (Sharma 2007). However, it was during the Cold War that relations moved towards greater political solidarity.

Following independence, India saw its international role as champion of struggles against colonialism and racism. India played a critical role in the Bandung Conference that led to the emergence of the Non-Aligned Movement (NAM) and used the occasion to promote and strengthen Asian-African solidarity. Indeed, Afro-Asian countries became the principal arena for India's policy and diplomacy during the 1950s (Muni 1991: 862). India's friendship treaty with China, based on five principles of peaceful co-existence, was a major reflection of this foreign policy orientation.

Africa was gauged to have a significant role in Prime Minister Jawaharlal Nehru's vision of creating a just international setting. Indeed, he viewed its progress towards independence 'as an important component of the non-aligned force that he was attempting to create in order to minimize the effects of the Cold War' (McKay 1963).

Apart from Nehru's foreign policy principles of 'greater democratization in international relations and free access to available economic and opportunities for the politically weak and economically poor countries of the Third World' (Muni 1991: 862), relations were also founded upon the presence of the large Indian diaspora living in Africa. Settled mainly in eastern and southern Africa as part of the British empire, in many cases having been introduced to the region as imported cheap labour, the hard-working, commercially-astute, diasporic Indian community came to assume an important role as small-scale traders, shop owners and manufacturers. However, although racial tensions were to emerge between Indian communities and indigenous Africans, exacerbated by perceptions of Indian social exclusivity, prosperity and alleged exploitation of African consumers and employees, Nehru's stance was that people of Indian origin should integrate into the fabric of their adopted countries and not seek economic privileges at the expense of local Africans. Furthermore, he urged them to adopt a positive outlook regarding their anti-colonial struggles and political aspirations (Beri 2003). Not surprisingly, Gandhi and Nehru's support for Africa's struggle served as a major inspiration to leaders like Kwame Nkrumah, Kenneth Kaunda and Julius Nyerere.[4]

However, this was generally limited to former British colonies. Thus in West Africa, relations were heavily skewed towards Ghana, while a diplomatic mission was established in Nigeria in 1958, two years before it gained independence (Singh 2007: 3). Nehru followed up by making an historic visit to the country in 1962. Furthermore, 'thousands of students from Ghana and Nigeria attended Indian universities, and a large number of Indian teachers worked in remote towns in both those countries; and official visits by Nigerian and Ghanaian leaders to India had helped to promote such exchanges' (2007: 3). Singh also notes that India offered defence training courses for the Ghanaian military and helped set up the Nigerian Defence Academy (2007: 3). Given the Nehruvian principles and Indian strategic interests in forging ties with Africa, it seemed natural for New Delhi and newly-independent African states to become strategic allies during the Cold War.

India's engagement with Africa was also motivated by its border dispute with China in 1962. Confronted by Africa's mixed reaction to the conflict, New Delhi was forced to realise that it 'did not have the strong ally it had hoped for in Africa and it therefore actively worked towards countering Chinese penetration in Africa' (Serpa 1994: 187). This saw India, first, increasing its 'material support to the liberation struggle in Southern Africa;' and, second, expanding 'economic co-operation with participation of Indian settlers' (Serpa 1994: 187).

It was in partial response to China's burgeoning relations with African states and the difficulties experienced in accessing African markets that led to the launch of the Indian Technical and Economic Co-operation (ITEC). ITEC emerged as a result of a meeting convened by the Indian government of its head of trade missions from Africa and West Asia held in November 1963 to examine ways to improve economic and technical co-operation. ITEC today remains an integral part of Indian development assistance to Africa and elsewhere.

While China suffered in Africa from its Cold War battle with Moscow, India was engaged in its own struggle with China. However, India's profile was undermined by its military humiliation at the hands of China in the border dispute; its 'hesitation in fixing a date for the end of colonialism (on the logic that it was unrealistic) in Africa at the Belgrade NAM Summit in 1961'; its assertion that peaceful means rather than armed resistance should underpin Africa's struggle for liberation; and its vigorous rejoinder to China's growing influence in multilateral forums (Beri 2003: 217–18). All of these factors culminated in African states offering India little diplomatic support.

India's international standing was rendered yet more marginal by the death, in 1964, of Nehru, the chief architect of India's foreign policy of South-South co-operation. As Muni elaborates, this was because the intensifying tensions between the two superpowers shaped the world according to their interests: 'countries like India, which stood for an alternative order responsive to the aspirations of the weak and the underprivileged, were too weak themselves and too disorganized to make their impact felt' (1991: 862). Meanwhile, India also had to grapple with the Cold War on its doorstep as a result of the US-Pakistan military alliance, for this was used to pave the way for rapprochement between Washington and Beijing that blunted New Delhi's initiatives to shape the creation of a new world order. In fact, efforts aimed at containing its effects in its regional neighbourhood preoccupied India for the better part of the Cold War. One consequence was that Africa was rendered increasingly marginal to the major thrusts of India's foreign policy (Beri 2003).

The succession of Indira Gandhi to the premiership following the death of her father in 1964 brought a reassessment of India's Africa policy. This was underlined by her visit to the continent in 1964, which 'was aimed at measuring the depth of African solidarity with India' (Beri 2003: 217). The outcome was that India's engagement moved from treating Africa as a homogeneous bloc to more selective friendship with particular African states. India's treaty with the Soviet Union in 1971, the Green Revolution and the testing of the nuclear bomb in 1974 all aided this change in so far as these factors increased India's confidence and weight internationally. Indeed, India's standing in Africa rose considerably on the back of Delhi's closer ties with Moscow precisely because of the alignment of the continent's major liberation movements with the Soviet Union, a momentum that was maintained by India's increasingly robust support for the anti-apartheid struggles of both the African National Congress of South Africa (ANC) and the South West African People's Organisation (SWAPO) of Namibia in multilateral forums like the United Nations (UN), NAM and the Common-wealth. Furthermore, following the grant of diplomatic status to the ANC as early as 1967,[5] India also provided financial and material assistance to the liberation movements 'through multilateral institutions like the OAU, the UN Fund for Namibia, UN Educational and Training Programme for South Africa and finally through the Action for Resisting Invasion, Colonialism and Apartheid (AFRICA) Fund' (Beri 2003: 218). The AFRICA Fund was established in 1986 by Rajiv Gandhi, who had become India's Prime Minister following his mother's assassination two years previously, under the auspices of the NAM to assist the frontline states in southern Africa to withstand the apartheid regime's strategy of destabilisation.

Nonetheless, although India remained committed to anti-colonialism through the indirect measures it advocated in multilateral institutions, it would appear that the engagement was essentially cursory. This was evident when it came to dealing with the concerns of Indians in Africa. In spite of Gandhi meeting the Indian diaspora[6] during her 1964 visit, India did little to alleviate the fears of that community when Kenya and Uganda adopted their Africanisation policies in the 1970s. Indeed, although the Indian government clearly felt that the support that they were lending to African liberation movements was not being reciprocated, New Delhi remained hesitant to push the issue with its African counterparts, to the immense disappointment of Africa's Indian communities, especially amongst those expelled from Uganda and not welcomed back to their continent of origin.

The socialist system adopted by India had not reaped major dividends for the world's largest democracy, having become associated with relative economic decline and an inward-looking commercial engagement, leading to a 'loss of influence in the years after independence' (Raja 2006: 17). With the international system undergoing an ideological and economic reordering, New Delhi had to assess its response.

In abandoning socialism, New Delhi sought to reconcile its ideological commitments with its emerging strategic economic interests. This became evident in the early 1990s, when annual reports of the Ministry of External Affairs emphasised that 'in the future, new relationships based on concrete economic, technological and educational cooperation [would] assume enhanced significance' (Singh 2007: 10). Underpinning this new trajectory was a strategy of economic liberalisation that facilitated the opening up of the Indian market to inward and outward foreign direct investment and an aggressive commitment to gaining access to overseas markets.

Yet India did not wholly replace its political ideology with geo-economics. Understanding that engagement in the newly multilateralised international system would require a sophisticated blend of geopolitics and geo-economics, New Delhi used its historical platform to consolidate relations with Africa and other regions of the South.

India's orientation towards Africa after the Cold War was about reinventing and rejuvenating the old relationship. In principle, India's relationship with Africa is premised on the moral high ground that it shared Africa's history of subjection to colonisation. According to officialdom, India's contemporary Africa policy is aligned to a confluence of interests around justice in the global order aimed at increasing the leverage of their respective global positions to promote a new international order. To this end, commitment to peace, stability, justice, mutual development and the vision of a fairer multilateral global system became the new genre for India's emerging engagement with Africa.

Nevertheless, India's foreign policy was ultimately guided by its domestic concerns. Thus for all that New Delhi retained its commitment to the principles of non-alignment and South-South struggle against the inequities of the global order, it was also increasingly conscious of its growing need to exploit new export markets and attract foreign capital and technological know-how (Singh 2007:10).

Deepening Economic Engagements
Its deepening engagements in Africa indicate that, alongside other external actors, India 'has discovered that Africa is where the resources and future markets that will fuel its economic growth are'.[7] India's 'quest for resources, business

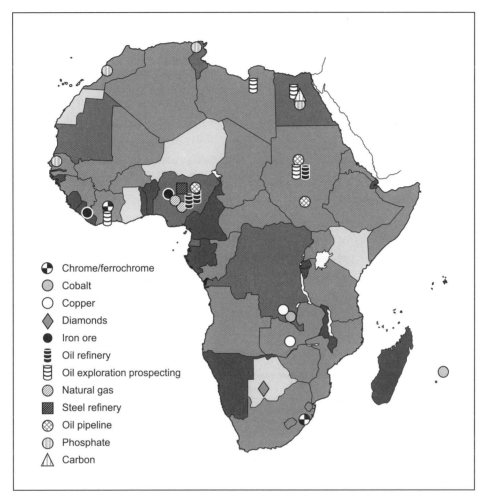

Figure 5.1   Indian energy and mining interests in Africa.

Source: Compiled from various newspapers by the Centre for Chinese Studies, Stellenbosch University

opportunities, diplomatic initiatives and strategic partnerships' (Pham 2007) is seen in the emerging trade, investment and developmental assistance relations that Delhi is crafting with African countries. The map above illustrates this economic footprint, which can be noted in a variety of sectors across the continent, albeit with the extractive industry assuming an increasing dominance.

Since the 1970s, India has made no significant oil discoveries. Consequently, with only 0.4% of the world's proven oil reserves, India's oil needs have to be

financed from elsewhere. Future projections are that by 2030 India is expected
to become the world's third largest consumer of energy, bypassing Japan and
Russia. Furthermore, if forecasts are accurate that India's economy is expected to
expand at an average rate of 5% per annum over the next 25 years, then its
appetite for energy can be expected to grow massively; a situation compounded
by the projection that it will run out of coal, the primary source of its current
energy needs, over the next 40 years. Consequently, the hunt for new and reliable
sources of energy is critical to India's domestic growth trajectories as well as
positioning it as a global economic power. To this end, India's energy footprint
in Africa is becoming increasingly apparent and the continent now supplies 11%
of the country's oil imports, mostly from Nigeria.

The Indian state-owned Oil and Natural Gas Company (ONGC) has in recent
years managed to secure exploration contracts and other related energy projects
in the continent through its international division ONGC Videsh (OVL). Table
5.1 provides an overview.

Table 5.1   Oil and Natural Gas Company investments in Africa.

Country	Indian company	Type of investment	Size of investment
Nigeria	ONGC	Oil pipeline	25% stake in the Greater Nile Petroleum Oil Company (GNPOC) project. Value not available.
Sudan	ONGC	Oil production	24% share in Block 5A & 24% share in Block 5B. Value not available.
Sudan	ONGC	Oil refinery	$1.2 billion
Sudan	ONGC	Multi-product export pipeline	$200 million
Sudan	ONGC	Oil pipeline (part of the Greater Nile Petroleum Operating Company)	$50 million

Source: Newspaper articles

In 2005 OVL entered into a joint venture with LN Mittal Steel (now Arcelor
Mittal), the world's largest steel multinational company, to form ONGC Mittal
Energy Limited (OMEL). OMEL entered into a $6 billion infrastructure deal with
Nigeria in exchange for two offshore acreages. Other OVL activities in Africa
include:

- a 23.5% interest in Ivory Coast's offshore block CI-112;
- a 49% participating interest in two onshore oil exploration blocks in Libya;
- a concession agreement to explore for oil in Egypt's North Ramadan block; and
- identified oil and gas properties in Gabon with potential investments of over $500 million.

In addition, LN Mittal also disclosed its intention in 2007 to acquire a 51% stake in the Port Harcourt refinery in Nigeria that, according to reports, is planned through a separate joint venture with Hindustan Petroleum Corporation Ltd (HPCL) (Shosanya 2007). By pursuing a relationship with HPCL, Mittal is positioning itself and building up a portfolio in the global oil and gas industry. Meanwhile, as table 5.2 demonstrates, other Indian oil companies are also becoming active.

Table 5.2   Other Indian national oil corporations in Africa.

Country	Indian company	Type of investment	Size of investment
Côte d'Ivoire	Unknown (various companies acting as a consortium)	Oil Prospecting	$1bn
Nigeria	National Thermal Power Corporation (NTPC)	Liquefied Natural Gas	$1.7 bn
Nigeria	Indian Oil Corporation (IOC)	Oil refinery	$3.5 bn
Nigeria	Indian Oil Corporation (IOC)	Liquefied Natural Gas (LNG) plant & Oil refinery	$2–4 bn (proposed)
Nigeria	Oil India	25% stake in Sunetra Nigeria OPL 205 Ltd.	
Gabon	Oil India	45% stake (including operatorship) in an onshore block	
Sudan	Videocon Group	Oil Prospecting	$100 m (76% stake)
East and Central Africa	Reliance Industries	Acquired majority stake and management control of Gulf Africa Petroleum Corporation	

Source: Newspaper articles

Apart from energy and gas, Indian companies have also been involved in uranium exploration. In 2007, the government of Niger issued 23 permits to three Canadian firms, three British firms and an Indian company called Taurian Resources to explore for uranium in the southern part of the country. Between them, the firms have invested a total of $55 million in exploration activities over three years.[8] For India, the acquisition of uranium exploration rights is geared to the expansion of its civilian nuclear programme that is officially designed to address energy deficiency and providing clean energy; although, inevitably, critics fear that it is also intended to feed New Delhi's military ambitions.

According to a 2007 survey of the world's 250 best performing energy companies published by Platts, several Indian energy firms featured in the list. ONGC and Reliance Industries were ranked in the top 50, at 23 and 39 respectively, with the former being named the third best performer in Asia. The survey, which rates companies on a combination of assets, revenues, profits and return on invested capital, noted that Indian companies dominated the global leadership position. This signals that Indian oil companies are not just satisfied with being purchasers of oil, but want to be considered global innovators in the industry, especially in terms of upstream and downstream production. To this end, Africa is a strategic priority and Indian companies have become leading exporters of refined petroleum products to the continent. Indeed, Indian firms have also begun to expand their investments to refining projects closer to African oil sources. In 2008 Reliance Industries, one of India's largest private sector companies, announced that it will spend over $11 billion in oil refining, petroleum products and plastics industries in Egypt; while another company, the Essar Group, intends to invest $9 billion in an oil refinery as well as a steel plant in the North African country.

Meanwhile, Indian oil companies are perpetually in the hunt for new energy contracts in Africa. One of the countries being courted is Angola, where Indian companies have found it difficult to penetrate the oil market due to the dominance of Western energy firms and China's relationship with Luanda. Nevertheless, ONGC is seeking to acquire a stake in the Lobito refinery, which produces 200 000 barrels a day (Srivastava 2008).

Even though Indian trade with Africa is still relatively meagre, New Delhi is awakening to the reality that Africa is a priority in its global commercial expansion. India-Africa trade jumped from $967 million in 1991 to over $9.5 billion in 2005 (Sorbara 2007). From 2000 to 2005, Indian exports to the continent increased from $2 billion to over $6 billion. During the same period, Indian imports from Africa increased from $3 billion to over $4 billion. In 2006 exports to Africa amounted to $9.5 billion, while imports from the continent were $12.6 billion (table 5.3 and figure 5.2). Current estimates put India's total trade with the continent for 2007–8 at between $25 and $30 billion.

Table 5.3   India: imports and exports with Africa ($ million).

India	2000	2001	2002	2003	2004	2005
Exports to Africa	2 185.46	2 772.98	2 887.72	3 503.42	4 772.53	6 874.88
Imports from Africa	3 135.41	2 411.63	3 201.41	3 194.76	3 328.86	4 742.67

Source: World Trade Atlas available on Tralac website
          http://www.tralac.org/pdf/20070717_India-Africa_top20s2007.xls

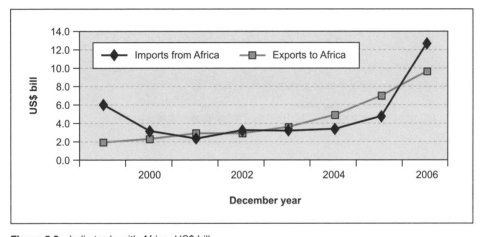

Figure 5.2   India trade with Africa, US$ bill.

Source: World Trade Atlas on Tralac website
         http://www.tralac.org/pdf/20070717_TheAfricanTradingRelationshipwithindia.pdf

India's exports to Africa grew by 120% compared to 76% export growth with the world during the previous five years (Ahmed 2006). Yet in spite of this impressive record, Africa's share of India's global export trade remains negligible despite India's export market shifting southwards. Out of a total of $103 billion for 2006, Africa provided just 7% of New Delhi's export market, whereas Asia and Oceania constituted the lion's share of 47%. Meanwhile, Africa provided only 7.3% of India's imports.

     While Africa's trade with India has improved overall, African exports to India dipped from 12% in 1999 to a low of 3.4% in 2005 and then rose to 7.6% in

2006. This unsteadiness is apparently largely attributable to India's sourcing of oil supplies from other areas (figure 5.3).

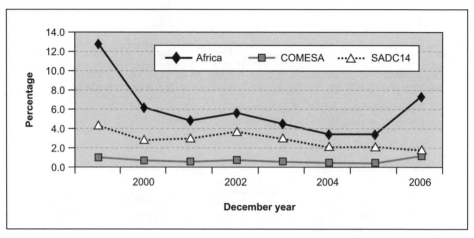

Figure 5.3   Africa's share of India imports.

Source: World Trade Atlas on Tralac website.
         http://www.tralac.org/pdf/20070717_TheAfricanTradingRelationshipwithindia.pdf

By the same token, Indian exports to Africa are less inconsistent and demonstrate a more stable progression (figure 5.4). They consist mainly of manufactured items (49%), chemical products (11%) and machinery and transport equipment (10%) (Ahmed 2006). In terms of the main export partners, South Africa features prominently with exports totalling $2 billion in 2006, followed by Kenya with $1.3 billion, Nigeria at $936 million, Egypt at $739 million and Mauritius with $539 million.

As figure 5.5 shows, Indian imports from Africa are mainly primary goods. Approximately 61% of this constituted oil imports. Gold made up another 13% of the total. From figure 5.5 it is also noticeable that oil from Africa has significantly gained market share, although gold remained the most consistent import during the period under review. The decline in oil imports from Africa between 1999 and 2001 and the sudden increase from 2005 onwards may well explain the uneven trend noted in figure 5.3, reflecting the fact that Nigeria became India's largest African oil import partner in 2006. Imports totalled $5.6 billion from Nigeria followed by Egypt at $1.1 billion, Algeria with $510 million and Angola at $177 million.

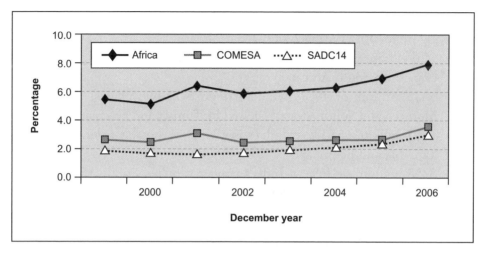

Figure 5.4 Africa's share of India exports.

Source: World Trade Atlas on Tralac website
http://www.tralac.org/pdf/20070717_TheAfricanTradingRelationshipwithindia.pdf

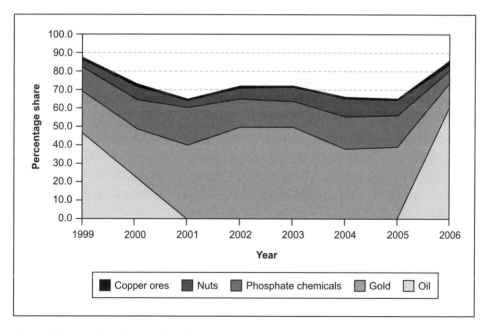

Figure 5.5 India imports from Africa percentage share.

Source: World Trade Atlas on Tralac website
http://www.tralac.org/pdf/20070717_TheAfricanTradingRelationshipwithindia.pdf

Furthermore, table 5.4 and other sources indicate that India imported the following from Africa during 2006:

- $1.6 billion, or 12% of India's total gold imports, of which $1.58 billion came from South Africa;
- $822 million, or 79% of India's imports of phosphates, mainly from Morocco and South Africa, followed by Tunisia and Senegal;
- $363 million, or 91% of India's nut supplies, notably from Ivory Coast, Tanzania and Benin; and
- $258 million, or 16% of India's copper supplies, South Africa, Guinea and Zambia being the major supplying countries.

Table 5.4 India's top five African import partners ($ million).

Country	1999	2000	2001	2002	2003	2004	2005	2006
Nigeria	2 533.96	709.31	73.40	77.12	84.66	52.62	62.46	5 657.89
South Africa	1 776.61	1 255.19	1 396.90	1 931.71	1 933.00	1 766.79	2 651.08	2 477.35
Egypt	235.75	148.63	71.75	195.71	138.43	122.85	219.89	1 407.15
Algeria	17.07	2.62	1.06	1.26	3.29	6.48	13.24	532.13
Morocco	458.59	331.27	252.64	173.85	214.57	247.59	392.97	517.63

Source: World Trade Atlas available on Tralac website
http://www.tralac.org/pdf/20070717_India-Africa_top20s2007.xls

Yet as Jobelius (2007: 6) observes, 'although Indian imports from Sub-Saharan Africa in fact increased by 53% to US$1.73 billion between 2005 and 2006 . . . [it is still] largely restricted to certain countries (South Africa alone accounts for 68% of Sub-Saharan exports to India)'. Nevertheless, India has placed a premium on increasing its trade with Africa through various initiatives so whereas in the 1990s, the government was 'closing down missions in Africa as an economic measure, today it has twenty-five embassies or high commissions on the continent with four others scheduled to open over the next few years' (Pham 2007: 2).

In Ivory Coast, for instance, trade between the two countries reached $500 million over the last two years with investments in mining and oil projects. Currently, the Indian government hopes to see investment of $1 billion over the next five years in mining and hydrocarbons in that country, which it sees as a gateway to West Africa. Meanwhile, there are 262 private Indian firms that have successfully obtained licences to establish industries in Ethiopia and 71 of them are already operational. Other projects under implementation have a total investment of 4.5 billion Ethiopian Birr.

In November 2005 the Export-Import Bank of India (EIBI) and Confederation of Indian Industries (CII) organised a Conclave on India-Africa Partnership entitled 'Expanding Horizons'. This attracted 160 delegates from 32 African countries and over 70 projects valued at more than $5 billion were discussed. This was followed by another meeting in October 2006, attended by 300 African and 375 Indian participants, at which over 300 projects worth $17 billion were featured, with Togo topping the list of investment seekers, requesting $4.6 billion, followed by South Africa ($4 billion), Ghana ($3.7 billion) and Nigeria ($2.6 billion) (Baldauf 2006).

In 2007 the Conclave Partnership Project was extended to three regional meetings that took place between June and July in Ivory Coast, Mozambique and Uganda. These served to strengthen business linkages as well as enable Indian businesses to identify strategic sectors for investment and joint ventures. The targeted sectors looked like a shopping list[9] and included almost all sectors considered catalysts for Africa's development. Twenty Indian companies from the targeted sectors participated in regional conclave meetings, each of them having submitted profiles to the Indian mission so that they could be placed in the sector that dovetailed with their focus and particular region. Meanwhile, regional conclaves also served to augment India's bilateral trade and investment ties with African countries.

From 19 to 21 March 2008, another conclave was hosted in New Delhi and this drew around 500 delegates including government officials from over twenty African countries. The meeting discussed over 130 projects to a value exceeding $10 billion. A number of deals were signed in areas of mutual interest including a memorandum of understanding between the Ethiopian Leather Industries Association (ELISA) and the CII to export high-quality Ethiopian leather to India. The EIBI also extended a $30 million credit line to the African Export-Import Bank (Afreximbank) to finance India's exports to the latter's members. This meeting set the stage for India's first African summit hosted from 8 to 9 April 2008 in the Indian capital.

An unprecedented event in India's African relations, the summit was attended by high-level government officials from fourteen African countries, including heads of state from Ethiopia, Ghana, Kenya, South Africa and Uganda. Outcomes from the summit included India's commitment to the following:

- increasing financial credits from about $2 billion over the previous five years to $5.4 billion over a similar period;

- investing $500 million in development projects across Africa over the next five years;
- establishing an India-Africa peace corps aimed at development, especially in the area of public health;
- allowing duty free imports and preferential market access for primary and finished products, including cotton, cocoa, aluminium ores, copper ores, cashew nuts, cane sugar, clothing, fish fillets and gem diamonds from 34 least developed countries (LDCs) in Africa;
- doubling trade from $25 billion to $50 billion by 2011; and
- increasing the number of scholarships and technical training programmes for African students.

The India-Africa summit marks a watershed: it institutionalises the engagement beyond the historical fluidity of the NAM, setting clear milestones for the fashioning of the relationship in the future.[10]

Focus Africa was launched as part of the EXIM Policy 2002–7 strategy of the EIBI. Through this programme the Indian government provides financial assistance to various trade promotion organisations and export promotion councils in the form of market development assistance. By early 2007, the total operative lines of credit extended to sub-Saharan Africa by the EIBI amounted to over $550 million, targeting regional blocs like the Economic Community of West African States (ECOWAS) and the Common Market for East and Southern Africa (COMESA). Furthermore, in May 2006 EIBI extended a $250 million line of credit (LOC) to the ECOWAS Bank for Investment and Development to finance Indian exports to ECOWAS member states (Sorbara 2007). In terms of the COMESA region, operative lines of credit included $5 million each to the Eastern and Southern African Trade and Development Bank (PTA Bank), the Industrial Development Bank of Kenya and the East African Development Bank (EADB). These LOCs are seen as strengthening and expanding export trade between the respective regions and India through deferred payment terms and should be interpreted as part of the India-Africa Partnership project aligned to the conclave meetings discussed above.

The Indian government has also embarked on a set of initiatives. These include:
- a $200 million LOC to the New Partnership for African Development (NEPAD) under the India-Africa Fund designed to promote African economic integration;

- a $500 million LOC for the Techno-Economic Approach for Africa-India Movement (TEAM-9), an initiative with eight Francophone countries;[11]
- a $1 billion investment in a joint venture with the African Union (AU) to build a pan- African e-network to provide telemedicine and tele-education through integrated satellite, fibre and wireless connectivity; [12]
- letters of intent signed between the state of Andhra Pradesh and Kenya and Uganda to send 500 Indian farmers to cultivate land. [13]

Beyond oil, Indian companies are also beginning to make significant strides across numerous other sectors. India's official investment in Africa in 2008 is around about $2 billion. That of its private sector is estimated to be somewhere in the region of $5 billion, led by the Tata Group, Ranbaxy Laboratories and Kirloskar Brothers. They have mostly focused on markets in South Africa, Nigeria, Egypt and Kenya (Srivastava 2008). In Zambia, Vendanta Resources has a $750 million copper mining investment; while Arcelor Mittal has a $900 million management project for iron ore reserves in Liberia and an investment of $30 million (inclusive of an 80% stake by the Delta Steel Company) in a Nigerian steel refinery.

Overall, the Tata Group has the most extensive presence in the continent. Operating in Ghana, Mozambique, Malawi, Namibia, South Africa, Tanzania and Uganda, Tata claims to employ over 700 people in Africa, with activities ranging from infrastructure development, energy and hospitality services to financial, communication and automotive outputs. Their investments include the following:

- the $800 million renovation of the Taj Pamodji Hotel in Lusaka;
- a $1.2 billion fertiliser plant in Egypt;
- a vehicle assembly plant at Ndola in Zambia;
- construction of a 120 megawatt power plant to supply energy to Zambian mines;
- a $108 million high-carbon ferrochrome plant at Richards Bay in South Africa;
- construction of a $12 million instant coffee processing plant in Uganda;
- provision of 250 buses to the Democratic Republic of Congo (DRC) at a cost of $46 000 per bus; and
- an $18 million export order in 2005 to supply 350 buses to Senegal.

Meanwhile, Indian companies have also begun to invest in Africa's infrastructure as a way of cementing their commercial and commodity presence in the continent.

A leading example is the involvement of Rites Railway and Ircon, two large state-owned infrastructure and engineering companies, in Africa's rail and road development sector through a variety of projects and concessions. Rites has refurbished and leased locomotives in Sudan and Tanzania, whilst supplying technical assistance to rail authorities in Kenya and Mozambique; as well as being involved in design and construction of roads in Uganda and Ethiopia. Meanwhile, Ircon has constructed railways in Algeria and is currently involved in Mozambique; and has also been active in the rail sectors in Sudan, Nigeria and Zambia (Bonnet 2006).

Indian companies are also queuing up to take advantage of Africa's significant investments in power transmission projects. Thus Kalapataru Power Transmission Limited already has a presence in Zambia and is expecting to acquire a major contract worth $35 million from a North African country. According to a company director, 'All these countries are rich in resources such as oil, gas and metals. Therefore when global prices of the resources increase, these countries make more money. Their investment in infrastructure projects has also increased exponentially' (Wadke 2007: 1). Another transmission company, KEC International Limited, has a presence in Algeria, Tunisia, Libya, Kenya, Zambia, Nigeria, Ethiopia and Ghana.

Table 5.5 contextualises the outreach of Indian firms beyond the resource sector at the time of writing in early 2008.
In addition:
- Fouress International Limited has been managing a power plant in Uganda;
- Ranbaxy Laboratories teamed up with Lupin Labs, an Indian pharmaceutical company, to market its tuberculosis drugs in North and West Africa;
- Rites Railway was appointed as consultant for the Adama-Asela road construction project undertaken by a Chinese company in Ethiopia; and
- Kirloskars Brothers have sold $75 million worth of water pumps to various African countries over the last few years with projections that its African business would reach $300 million in 2008.

Between 2002 and 2005, Indian firms topped the list of greenfield foreign direct investment (FDI) projects in Africa at 48 compared to 32 from China (UNCTAD 2007). Underpinned by the increasing global presence of Indian firms,[14] this signals that India is becoming a significant player in the African market. With India one of the 24 non-African members of the African Development Bank,

Table 5.5 Footprint of Indian companies in Africa's non-resource sector.

Company	Country	Investment	Date	Value
Overseas Infrastructure Alliance Pvt. Ltd.	Ethiopia	Supplying Electrical Equipment	2006	$65 million
Mashuli Gashmani Ltd.	Uganda	Commercial Prawn Fishery Plant	2006	$18 million
Ircon International	Ethiopia	Construction of the Dera Mechanra highway	2004	$31.3 million
Ircon International and Rites Railway International Ltd.	Mozambique	Rehabilitation of the Sena Line of the Beira railway system from the port of Beira to Tete	2004	$152 million
KEC International	Ethiopia	Construction of a 132 Kv power transmission project	2005	$40 million
Kamani Engineering Corp.	Zambia	Construction of a transmission line between Zambia and Namibia	2005	$11 million
Rites Railway International Ltd.	Angola	Railway Rehabilitation Project in Huila Province	2004	$40 million credit line from the Indian government
Fouress Engineering	Uganda	Managing a Power Plant		
Bharat Heavy Electricals Ltd. (BHEL)	Sudan	Construction of a 500w thermal power plant	2005	$457 million (US$350 concessional loan from Indian government)
Bharat Heavy Electricals Ltd. (BHEL)	Zambia	Rehabilitation of the Kafue Gorge	2003	$2.57 million
Glenmark Pharmaceuticals	South Africa	Acquisition of Bartlett Bouwer Ltd. from P.D. Pharmaceuticals Ltd.	2005	Undisclosed amount
Alembic Ltd.	Nigeria	Joint venture with US research company, Xechem International Ltd in a pharmaceutical manufacturing plant	2004	$3.6 million
Cadila Pharmaceuticals	Ethiopia	Joint Venture medicine Manufacturing factory with Ethiopian firm, Almeta Impex	2007	$10 million
Mohan Energy (has US$200 million worth of contracts across Africa)	Ghana	Building a rural electrification programme	2004	$25 million
Ranbaxy Pharmaceuticals	South Africa	Acquisition of Be-Tabs	2006	$70 million

Source: Newspaper articles

this footprint is also being propelled by the recent green light given to Indian firms to bid for $4.6 billion set aside by the Bank for infrastructural development projects.

India has also become a significant development partner. Under its ITEC programme, the Indian government has provided more than $1 billion worth of technical assistance and personnel training. Moreover in 2005 India was the first Asian country to become a full member of the African Capacity Building Foundation (ACBF) and pledged $1 million towards the foundation's sustainable development and poverty alleviation capacity building initiative.

In addition, India has contributed to UN peacekeeping operations in Africa. According to the Ministry of External Affairs, India is the largest contributor of peacekeepers to the continent with 3 500 troops in the DRC[15] while the 1 400-strong Indian military contingent constitutes the largest contribution to the UN Mission in Ethiopia and Eritrea. Apart from providing peacekeepers, India has also supplied helicopters and medical and communication equipment.

India has also joined the second phase of the highly indebted poor countries initiative (HIPC II) and to date has written off debts totalling $24 million to Mozambique, Tanzania, Uganda, Ghana and Zambia. Meanwhile, other aspects of India's humanitarian assistance include:

- food donations to Namibia in 2003 and to Chad and Lesotho in 2004;
- the grant of 200 000 mosquito nets to the Republic of Congo; and
- the gift of construction equipment and materials to Seychelles as part of the reconstruction process following the tsunami.

This use of soft power for humanitarian purposes is possibly intended to downplay India's image of scrambling in Africa and instead project New Delhi as a development partner.

Despite their growing involvement, Indian companies appreciate that Africa can be a tough place in which to do business. Recently, ONGC has experienced payment problems with regard to the construction of the petroleum pipeline connecting Khartoum's refinery to Port Sudan. In terms of the agreement, 'Sudan's Ministry of Energy and Mining was to pay back the investment in 18 half-yearly equated instalments of over 14 million dollars each.'[16] But the Sudanese government has delayed payment of the first three instalments. While the agreement makes provision for ONGC to recover its instalments by taking crude oil as a substitute, the Sudanese government has not allowed ONGC to exercise this option.

Meanwhile, the Indian diaspora has often found itself in an invidious position. Their predominantly middleman position in the African market has often led the Indian immigrant community, especially in eastern and southern Africa, into protracted conflicts with indigenous populations. Two decades after the Indian community was expelled by President Idi Amin, Indian businessmen have been encouraged to return to Uganda to exploit booming commercial opportunities. They have not met a unanimous welcome, not least because of the way in which these Indian business elites have conducted their affairs in close collaboration with the political elite. A case in point is the proposed expansion plan by an Indian sugar firm into the protected Mabira rain forest. The fury surrounding the project by the Sugar Corporation of Uganda Limited, part of the Indian-owned Mehta Group, incited mob attacks in Kampala in 2007 against Indian-owned businesses and religious symbols. Two people of Indian descent were killed.

Such tensions suggest that despite the economic prosperity the Indian diaspora may be harnessing, there are still tensions that confront this community. In this regard, it is of note that African markets have become saturated by cheap goods coming from, amongst other regions, the South Asian sub-continent. Over the last few years there has been a mushrooming of petty and informal traders from the sub-continent (including Pakistanis and Bangladeshis) across sub-Saharan Africa. They have sometimes entered the market illegally and are often subject to security checks and raids by local police because of the way they conduct their business and the violation of intellectual property rights associated with the goods that they are retailing, such as DVDs, CDs and electronic products. In short, the burgeoning number of economic immigrants severely complicates the way the Indian diaspora is perceived.

Is India a Scrambler or a Development Partner?

Its proponents argue that India constitutes an increasingly influential development partner in Africa. This is because of its ITEC programme, support for Africa's capacity building and, more significantly, its investment in the rehabilitation of the continent's deficient infrastructure. For these observers, it is not just India's economic and technical largesse that is important, but New Delhi's progressive behaviour within both bilateral and international multilateral institutions. This perspective can be elaborated in several ways.

First, India has taken an aggressive stance regarding the successful resolution of the World Trade Organisation Doha Development Round. Pushing for more equity around trade and market access, notwithstanding some dismantling of agricultural subsidies in the North and the sensitivities of Non-Agricultural Market Access (NAMA) (Srinivasan 2006), shows that India is flexing its muscles on critical issues affecting Africa and the South more generally. The Indian government has also voiced its frustration over the exclusivity of the G8 and is now contemplating initiating a parallel grouping to boost the strength of the South.

Second, India's design of the India-Brazil-South Africa (IBSA) trilateral group demonstrates commitment to promoting a South-South trading market. Not only does IBSA augment the economic strength of its partners, but it also opens a broader market for African producers to penetrate given that the combined IBSA market represents a consumer base of over one billion people. To this end, India's pledge at the 2008 India-Africa summit to enable African products to enter its market duty free provides a platform for expanding the IBSA market. [17]

Third, India has played an important leadership role in promoting South-South cooperation. The recent hosting of the International Conference on India-Africa Co-operation in Industry, Trade and Investment by the UN Industrial Development Organisation in collaboration with the Indian government reflects New Delhi's seriousness in expanding this relationship beyond mercantilism. Indeed, some believe that India's experience in the development of the small and medium enterprise sector as well as promotion of the private sector could offer important lessons to Africa in doing business differently.

Fourth, the affinity of a shared historical experience of colonialism coupled by the fact that India has not deviated significantly from its principles of championing the rights of LDCs in the post-independent period bodes well for consolidation of its reputation as a viable development partner for Africa. Finally, emerging as a rising global power through successful economic pragmatism, it offers hope that Africa could follow a similar path.

On the other hand, critics of the Indian engagement believe that the costs will outweigh the benefits. First, while they recognise that India's strategy is well intentioned, the practical effect of its policies may not be propitious. For instance, although India may be seen as financing Africa's infrastructure rehabilitation generously, this is being done through lines of credit that not only run the risk of adding to the debt burden of African countries, but they also support Indian industries through their procurement criteria. The TEAM-9 initiative is a case in point.

Second, despite fanfare around increasing market access for African goods to the Indian market, much of this is for primary products with low value-added quality. The Indian market still imposes higher tariffs for value-added products.

If a true development partnership is to be garnered, India must reduce its protectionist barriers.

Third, even though India's business acumen can assist Africa with its private sector development and industrialisation programme, the critical issue is how far India is willing to go to advance this trajectory. Indian companies aim to become global innovators and there may be some resistance to competition from Africa's private sector. [18]

Fourth, while India values the support that the African bloc will have in its candidature for a permanent seat in the reformed UN Security Council, there is still uncertainty whether India will speak with the same voice as Africa when it comes to continental concerns or issues of the South. While the rhetoric from both sides suggests a consensus, there are nonetheless indications that India's increasing calibration with the US and China may unsettle this alignment, leaving Africa marginalised. Further, it should not be overlooked that there will be issues where India may react differently to Africa, especially where New Delhi feels its interests are being threatened; for example, the conflict in Darfur.

Finally, critics argue that India's development assistance is primarily aimed at opening more market access for its private sector and warn that Africa will end up merely restructuring the nature of its dependency upon external powers.

Ultimately, it is how African countries themselves define their relationship with India that will determine whether New Delhi is a scrambler or a development partner. At present, India's current political and economic engagement reflects both images. But, if Africa realises that it does not have to allow this relationship to degenerate into one that mirrors the nineteenth century scramble for Africa, then it needs to use current leverage and the nature of the international milieu work to its own benefit. This will require bold leadership and pragmatic decisions.

It means candid and robust discussion on Africa's development needs, how industrial relations should be conducted, vigorous implementation of investment codes of conduct and a regulatory environment, more skills-oriented programmes to improve the technical expertise of the local labour force, more transparency for Africa's public about the deals that are being negotiated and less debt risk. If Africa fails to recognise that the current mantra of the World today is 'the business of business is business,' then it will definitely reinforce the image of a beggar. So whether India is presently scrambling or not in Africa, only time and history will tell. It will depend on how Africa synergises its relationship with India based, as Gandhi wished, on mutual ideas and services and, as Singh contended, on energised initiatives; but, of course, with Africa prioritising its own agenda and interests.

Yet it is hard to conclude that New Delhi's Africa policy does not mask some of the realities that underpin the criticisms levelled against China's presence in Africa. It is from this perspective that this chapter concludes that as India embeds its presence in Africa, it will be difficult to ignore or dissociate India from the new African scramble debate. Even if Western powers are more preoccupied with China, India's growing traction points to the emergence of rivalry that is being set in motion in Africa between China and India with its roots in the regional setting of the Indian Ocean Rim (IOR).

India sees the IOR as a strategic political and economic neighbourhood from which it is able to penetrate African economies through the East Africa region. This region is also significant because of India's 2004 Maritime Doctrine, which enables it to conduct naval and security exercises with its Indian Ocean partners. The IOR is an important shipping lane for Indian exports to and imports from Africa.

Considered as its backyard, New Delhi has become increasingly aware of China's penetration of this region through engagements with Mauritius, where it intends to set up its special economic zone to gain access to COMESA, as well as competing with China in the Seychelles. Thus 'Chinese and Pakistan efforts in the African Indian Ocean Rim are closely monitored by India and concerns about Chinese expansionism have resulted in India looking to deepen its defence and commercial engagement with the Seychelles, Madagascar, Mauritius and Mozambique' (Vines and Ouritmeka 2008: 12).

The second aspect to this emerging rivalry is the hosting of the India-Africa summit, which could be interpreted as a response to China's Forum on China-Africa Cooperation (FOCAC). Whereas Indian government officials have denied this, 'the Minister of State for Commerce Jairam Ramesh was more blunt: "The first principle of India's involvement in Africa [is] unlike that of China. China says go out and exploit the natural resources, our strategy is to go out there and add value"' (Dawes 2008). Advocating that India does business differently is a clear indication that New Delhi wants to entrench its presence in Africa by promoting itself as the better development partner.

Thus, while for the moment India is seen as a junior or negligible player in the new scramble, in the foreseeable future New Delhi's role in the Great Game should not be treated lightly just because of its muted presence, the fact that it shares the same democratic traditions as Western powers and offers better business acumen. Like most emerging Great Powers, India is in the hunt to satisfy resource needs that are vital to its industrialisation and modernisation and where these interests are threatened, as discussed above, it will behave like a scrambler using all kinds of kudos, whether direct or indirect, to exploit Africa's resources for its own narrow economic development. Yet as this chapter has been written the world has entered unchartered waters against the onset of the global financial crisis. Emerging powers like India face daunting challenges in balancing the impact of this manifested crisis on their domestic socio-economic milieu with their global economic ambitions. With questions being fielded around whether the international credit crisis would slow-down China's African engagements, similar considerations should be directed at India, especially in terms of how this global economic crisis may affect India's resurgent behaviour in Africa. Therefore the significant question now in the current eye of the global economic storm is whether it will be business as usual for Indo-African relations.

Notes

1. Cited in Mathews (1997: 1).
2. R. Singh, India, Africa: ready to embrace global destiny. New Delhi: Ministry of External Affairs, 25 Jan. 2006: http://www.meaindia.nic.in/interview/2006/01/25in01.htm.
3. Isaacson (2008).
4. Singh (2007) also notes that in the 1920s the example of the Indian National Congress inspired West African intellectuals to form the National Congress of British West Africa, with Nkrumah paying tribute to Gandhi's efforts at addressing racism in South Africa through the principle of non-violence. Singh argues that the NAM so consolidated Afro-Asian solidarity that by the time the OAU was established, a broad consensus had developed in favour of non-alignment and was enshrined in the organisation's charter.
5. Similar recognition was extended to SWAPO, albeit only in 1985.
6. While there may have been some commercial linkages between the Indian diasporas in East and southern Africa, these were probably confined to social capital networks that were underlined by class, caste and geographical identities. Thus, although the term Indian diaspora is used generically to reflect the presence of the Indian community living in Africa, it is more accurate to state that this is made up of many parts, divided not only by class and caste, but also by distinct and diverse historical experiences of migration to eastern and southern Africa.
7. *The Nation* 9 Feb. 2007.
8. A. Massalatchi, Uranium exploration firms from India, UK make tracks for Niger. Reuters, 2007. http://www.livemint.com/2007/05/14235528/Uranium-exploration-firms-from.html
9. These included: agriculture; agro-processing; construction; minerals; transport infrastructure (roads, railways, waterways, ports and airports); conventional and non-conventional energy; pharmaceuticals; health care; institutional capacity building;

information and communication technology; iron and steel; education and skills development; water and sanitation; housing; oil and gas; turnkey manufacturing projects; tourism; small, medium and micro enterprises; biotechnology; and fast-moving consumer goods.

10. Africa-India Framework for Cooperation, 2008 http://www.meaindia.nic.in/indiaafrica summit/africaframe.php?sec=ia.zl&act=1.

11. The TEAM-9 initiative was launched in Mar. 2004. It is reported that $280 million worth of projects have already been approved against concessional lines of credit. Some of these include: $970 000 for the construction of the national Post Office in Burkina Faso; $30 million for rural electrification in Ghana; $4 million for a bicycle plant in Chad; a $12 million tractor assembly plant in Mali; and $15 million for portable drinking water projects in Equatorial Guinea. Currently, six more countries from the region are interested in joining the initiative.

12. State-owned Telecommunications Consultants India Limited (TCIL) will implement the network, which India will manage for five years before turning it over to the AU.

13. In Kenya the agreement involves 50 000 acres of land while in Uganda there are 20 000 acres. According to the terms of the agreements, Indian farmers will act as entrepreneurs leasing land on a 99-year basis. Land in Uganda will be purchased at $3.75 per acre while the price is still being negotiated with Kenyan authorities.

14. In the first nine months of 2006, investment outflow from India was estimated to be $7.2 billion, up from $4.2 billion in 2005. In the first half of 2007, Indian firms announced 34 foreign takeovers valued at $10.7 billion compared with a total of $23 billion in 2006, which was more than the investments made by foreigners in Indian companies.

15. See http://meaindia.nic.in/interview/2006/01/25in01.htm.

16. 'Sudan delays payment of pipeline instalments to India', *Sudan Tribune* 17 July 2007. http://www.sudantribune.com/spip.php?article22881.

17. Africa-India Framework for Cooperation, 2008 http://www.meaindia.nic.in/indiaafrica summit/africaframe.php?sec=ia.zl&act=1.

18. The immediate impact could be felt by South African corporates. In late 2007 and early 2008 two Indian telecommunication companies, Bharti Cell and Reliance Telecommunications, made separate bids to acquire South African cellular company MTN. Given MTN's expansive presence across the continent, acquiring the company will strengthen the market traction of India's telecommunication giants in Africa. While the Bharti Cell bid failed, Reliance Telecommunication is still negotiating with MTN shareholders around a buy out.

References

Ahmed, S. 2006. 'New opportunities beckon Indian industries'. *Economic Times of India* 1 Nov.

Baldauf, S. 2006. 'India steps up trade ties in Africa'. *Christian Science Monitor* 3 Nov. http://www.csmonitor.com/2006/1103/p04s01-wosc.html.

Beri, R. 2003. 'India's Africa policy in the post-Cold War era: an assessment'. *Strategic Analysis* 27(2): 216–32.

Bonnet, D. 2006. 'India in Africa: an oil partner, a new competitor'. *Traders Journal* 26. http://www.tradersafrica.com/PDF/traders_26_hires.pdf.

Dawes, N. 2008. 'India's African inroads'. *Mail & Guardian*, 10 April. http://www.mg.co.za //articlePage.aspx?articleid=336688&area=/insight/insight__africa/.

Holslag, J. 2006. 'China's new mercantilism in central Africa'. *African and Asian Studies* 5(2): 133–69.

Isaacson, M. 2008. 'An Indian-style pitch for the heart of Africa'. *Sunday Independent* (Johannesburg) 30 March.

Jobelius, M. 2007. 'New powers for global change?: challenges for international development co-operation: the case of India'. In: *Dialogue on Globalization*. Berlin: Friedrich Ebert Stiftung.

Lee, M. 2006. 'The 21st century scramble for Africa'. *Journal of Contemporary African Studies* 24(3): 303–30.

Le Pere, G. and G. Shelton. 2007. *China, Africa and South Africa: South-South Co-operation in a Global Era*. Johannesburg: Institute for Global Dialogue.

Mathews, K. 1997. A multi-faceted relationship: a synoptic view'. *Africa Quarterly* 37(1–2): 1–26.

McKay, V. 1963. *Africa in World Politics*. New York: Harper and Row.

Melber, H. 2007. 'The new African scramble for African resources'. *Pambazuka News* 8 Feb. http://www.pambazuka.org/en/category/comment/39693

Muni, S. 1991. 'India and the post-Cold War world: opportunities and challenges'. *Asian Survey* 31(9): 862–74.

Naidu, S. and M. Davies. 2006. China fuels its future with Africa's riches'. *South African Journal of International Affairs* 13(2): 69–83.

Pham, J. 2007. 'The Indian tiger's African safari'. *Family Security Matters* 19 July. http://www.familysecuritymatters.org/global.php?id=1162076.

Raja, M. 2006. 'India and the balance of power'. *Foreign Affairs* 85(4): 17–32.

Serpa, E. 1994. 'India and Africa'. *Africa Insight* 24(3): 186–93.

Sharma, A. 2007. 'India and Africa: partnership in the 21st century'. *South African Journal of International Affairs* 14(2): 13–20.

Shosanya, M. 2007. 'Indian coy may buy Port Harcourt refinery'. *Daily Trust* 23 Feb. http://allafrica.com/stories/200702230566.html.

Sidhartha, I. 2007. 'Government plans to push trade with Africa'. *Times of India* 11 June. http://www.indiainsouthafrica.com/ShowNews?id=798.

Singh, S. 2007. *India and West Africa: a Burgeoning Relationship*. London: Chatham House.

Sorbara, M. 2007. 'India and Africa: it's old friends, new games and rules'. *The Nation* 8 Feb. http://allafrica.com/stories/200702081111.html.

Srinivasan, G. 2006. 'Çalla to address development challenge of Doha Round'. *Business Line* 29 June. http://www.thehindubuinsnessline.com/2006/06/29/stories/200606 291930800.htm.

Srivastava, S. 2008. 'India loads up presents for African safari'. *Asian Times Online* 12 Apr. http://www.atimes.com/atimes/South_Asia/JD12Df01.html.

UNCTAD. 2007. *Asian Foreign Direct Investment in Africa: Towards a New Era of Cooperation Among Developing Countries*. Geneva: UNCTAD.

Vines, A. and B. Oruitmeka. 2008. *India's Engagement with the African Indian Ocean Rim States*. London: Chatham House.

Wadke, R. 2007. 'Indian power cos flock to Africa, Middle East'. *The Hindu Business Line* 20 Feb. http://www.blonnet.com/2007/02/20/stories/2007022002450300.htm.

CHAPTER SIX

South Africa in Africa

Still a Formidable Player

John Daniel and Nompumelelo Bhengu

Commercial boardings advertising anything from shoe polish to the latest mobile telephones have become a ubiquitous feature of Africa's urban landscapes . . . they signify that the presence of South African companies throughout the continent is here to stay . . . South African business on the continent has, if anything, picked up pace in the past few years and China is not generally seen as a threat to this trend.[1]

We see Africa as a land of unparalleled opportunity . . . Our group [Anglo-American] is actively involved in eight African countries; we are looking at opportunities in five more.[2]

Around the turn of this century, the business media began to take note of a developing new phenomenon in the African political economy – that of a growing South African corporate presence. Shut out by decades of sanctions and general distaste for apartheid, South African capital had been excluded from all but the inner-periphery of southern African states. However, in the early 1990s the iron curtain of exclusion dissolved and South African business, confronted by a saturated domestic market, low or stagnant profit margins, but flush with investible surplus capital (Sanders 2008: 4), moved rapidly to take advantage of new market opportunities in a continent in which most non-African investors seemed, in the wake of the Cold War, to be either uninterested or intent on divesting. A decade later, the *New York Times* woke up and famously observed that the 'South Africans have arrived'.[3]

And indeed they had. Seven years on they are still there and in ever greater numbers. This paper will argue that, other new investors notwithstanding, the South African footprint in the African marketplace today remains considerable and grows each year. A survey of Africa's top 500 companies revealed that nineteen of the top twenty (numbers two to twenty) and 62 of the top 100 were South African. Of the top 500, 53.76 % were South African followed by Algeria at 19.97%.[4]

Another survey of the continent's listed companies found that South African groups constituted seventeen of the top twenty and 55 of the top 100.[5] The top twenty were dominated by South African minerals (mining and metal) groups, little surprise given the boom in commodity prices. Top of the pile was the gold mining operation of Anglo-American (AAC), while its separately-listed platinum holdings group placed fifth. In second, third, fourth and sixth places were SABMiller, Richemont, MTN and Sasol respectively. In seventh place was the first non-South African entity, Egypt's Orascom Telecom.

In 2002, one of the authors of this chapter, along with colleagues at the Human Sciences Research Council (HSRC), began to map South African corporate capital's move into Africa. In subsequent years, four articles on the phenomenon were published in the HSRC's then annual *State of the Nation* series (Daniel, Naidoo and Naidu 2003; Daniel, Lutchman and Naidu 2005; Daniel and Lutchman 2006; Daniel, Lutchman and Comninos 2007). These articles elicited considerable public interest and some critical comment from a cadre of left analysts who concluded that South African capital was intent on a recolonisation of the continent. We challenged that view, arguing that it was mere assertion without convincing supporting evidence, a position defended in the conclusion to this chapter.

In recent times, this voice has fallen silent while public attention has been diverted by the surge of Chinese, Indian and other Asian capital in particular into the African extractive (energy and minerals) and infrastructural sectors. Concomitantly, the activities of South Africa's corporates have slipped from the radar screen while much popular journalism has drawn a picture of something resembling an Asian economic tsunami targeted at Africa. Some have depicted these new investors, and the Chinese in particular, as new imperialists; while others present them as saviours of a failing African political economy.

We do not deny this Asian factor. But we argue in this chapter that its portrayal as rampant to the point of eclipsing all other significant non-Asian players is exaggerated and that South African capital remains a significant player in the African market; perhaps overall for now still the most important. In terms of total volumes of bilateral trade, China has overtaken South Africa. In 2007, China's bilateral trade with Africa (excluding South Africa) amounted to approximately $60 billion while that of South Africa was in the region of only $17 billion. This latter statistic, however, represented an increase of nearly one third over 2006, indicative of a continuing vibrancy to, and growth in, South African-African trade relations. Relevant too, is the fact that the Indo-Chinese penetration of the African economy is niched and confined largely to the sectors mentioned above. The South African move into the continent by contrast impacts on every sector of the African economy from agriculture and mining, banking and financial services to wholesale and retail merchandising, mobile telephony and tourism. This sectoral spread, and its year-on-year growth, gives the South African presence a continuing and particular relevance.

The Economic Salience for South African Capital of the African Market
Investments
The popular media and scholars alike have in recent years obsessively tracked the scramble for Africa's natural resources. The publication of this book, including chapters on China, India and South Africa in Africa, is testimony to that. In much of the popular literature, this development has often been dubbed a new scramble as if nothing much by way of new investment in the continent had happened prior to this decade's awakening to the Chinese and Indian slumbering giants. In fact, as we have tried to show in chapters in *State of the Nation* examining the South Africa in Africa phenomenon, the new giant on the African scene has for more than a decade been South Africa – and, as argued here, it remains a considerable presence.

In the chapter in the 2007 volume (Daniel, Lutchman and Comninos), reference was made to a presentation by then *Business Map* consultant, Reg Rumney[6] (2006), which noted that in 2005 South Africa was the largest source of new foreign direct investment (FDI) into Africa, followed by the United Kingdom, United States, Australia and Canada, the latter two operating almost wholly in the mining sector. China, according to Rumney, ranked ninth but cautioned that this was based on publicly-announced ventures and that if public and non-public ventures were pooled, China would probably move up the table. Since then, China has become much more open about its African ventures and there were many in 2006-7, some spectacularly large and long-term.

Even so, South Africa remained in 2006 the largest single-country investor in the continent. As figure 6.1 indicates, South Africa's total investments in Africa surged in 2006, amounting to R80.02 billion, up by over 117% on the 2005 figure of R36.8 billion. Total investment volumes are calculated by adding direct new cash investments, portfolio acquisitions and a general category. In 2006, direct FDI was up by more than 300% from R19.08 billion to R59.11 billion. This drive was led by the minerals sector with the telecommunications, manufacturing, retail and wholesale, banking and financial services sectors following closely. Virtually across the board, companies reported good returns on their African outlays. Reflective of this, Graham Mackay, CEO of one of the larger South African corporates in Africa, SABMiller, stated that 'if there was any more of Africa, we'd be investing in it'.[7]

Two points, however, are pertinent here, each of which is illustrated by figure 6.2. First, notwithstanding the argument in the paragraph above, South Africa's investment involvement in Africa is comparatively small when put alongside its global performance. At only 6.4% of all outward investment flows in 2006, its African total is dwarfed by 2006 FDI flows into Europe (R82.45 billion) and the Americas (R29.62 billion), in percentage terms, about 66% and 24% respectively. This drive into Europe and the Americas will be discussed in more detail later in the chapter in the section on the internationalisation of South African capital.

The second point is in some ways the opposite of the first and relates to Asia. While in import and export terms, Asian total trade with South Africa has soared in recent times, as a South African investment destination it lags way behind at only 3.2% of the total.

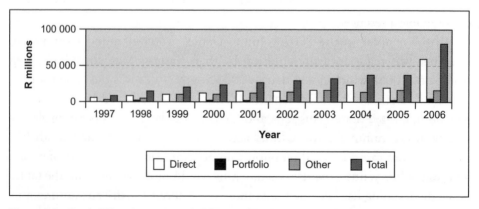

Figure 6.1 South African investments in Africa, 1997–2006.

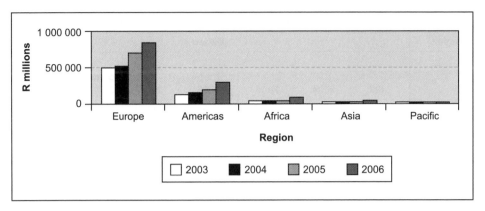

Figure 6.2 South African investments by region, 2003–6.

Exports

From a low base, South African exports into Africa grew rapidly in the 1990s, from 4 to 11%, 1991–2001, reaching 16.7% in 2002. In the process, the African export market overtook the Americas to become South Africa's third largest by region. Since then, the continent's share has declined slightly, even though in Rand value terms it has grown quite significantly. As table 6.1 indicates, the 26% increase in the value of South Africa's exports between 2006 and 2007 was the largest annual percentage increase since 1991. What this reflects is Africa's rising growth rates generated by the price boom in resources.

Even so, in 2007 the Americas regained third place in terms of regional share with a 35% increase in the value of exports. That figure is, however, deceptive: it does not reflect the acquisition of new market outlets, but huge increases in the price of gold, coal and platinum making up the bulk of South Africa's exports into the Americas. Africa, by contrast, purchases far less of these commodities; and a far higher proportion of food consumables and manufactured products where price inflation has been much lower.

What is interesting about these export figures is how little the regional proportions have changed since 2006. The African share has dropped by a statistically insignificant 0.5%. In 2005 the combined Euro-Asian share was 68.3% while in 2007 it was 67.5%, again statistically not significant. What is noteworthy, however, is the shift in the distribution between these two continental regions. While still accounting jointly for just over two thirds of all South African exports, table 6.1 below reveals that Asian exports in 2007 grew by more than twice those

Table 6.1 South African exports by region, 2003–7 (R million).

Region	Exports						
						% change 2006–7	% global exports 2007
	2003	2004	2005	2006	2007		
Africa	39 000	39 037	46 135	53 445	67 477	26.0	15.00
Americas	34 161	36 571	38 345	51 234	69 254	35.0	15.44
Asia	65 176	73 200	86 403	104 975	140 631	34.0	31.35
Europe	92 019	102 969	116 895	139 574	161 299	15.5	36.00
Pacific	6 331	7 921	9 878	9 779	9 901	1.2	2.21
Total	236 687	259 698	297 656	359 007	448 562	24.9	100.00

Source: Department of Trade and Industry (DTI) economic database and the South African Revenue Service (SARS)

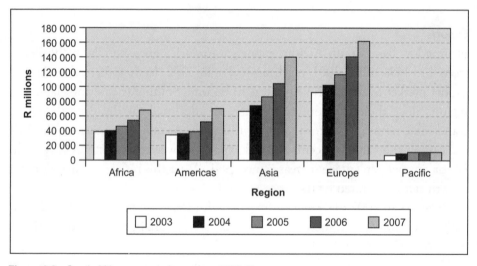

Figure 6.3 South African exports by region, 2003–7.

of Europe and that the gap between the two is narrowing. If this trend holds firm, it is likely that by 2010 Asia will be South Africa's most important export destination.

Imports

Anyone who has walked through a South African market, formal and informal, in recent years will not be surprised to know that the Asian continent is now the largest supplier of goods to the local market. That would also likely be the case now anywhere in Africa, except perhaps in Malawi and Swaziland. Both of them continue to recognise Taiwan and not the mainland. This predominance of Asian imports represents a slight shift over two years. In 2005, Europe and China enjoyed an equal share of the local import market, but since then Europe has slipped behind while the Asian share has held steady. This is likely a product of some of the limited curbs imposed by the Department of Trade and Industry (DTI) on Chinese imports.

As has been the trend now for some years, imports from Africa have since 2005 continued their modest gains, increasing in comparative terms, as table 6.2 suggests, by nearly 3%. It is noteworthy, however, that after fifteen years of unfettered African-South African trade, the continent's most powerful economy generating about 35% of Africa's total gross domestic product sources less than 8% of its imports from its backyard. This speaks volumes to the weakness of the African export sector. Even this modest 3% growth in imports from Africa does not, however, reflect a higher volume of goods sourced from the manufacturing sector; but is almost entirely a result of the fact that South Africa now purchases more of its oil and natural gas requirements from African sources, notably Nigeria and Angola.

In 2005, fuels made up 42.4% of all African imports. By 2007 that figure had risen to around 50%. That Angola had replaced Libya as South Africa's second-largest continental fuel supplier is noteworthy and needs to be seen in the context of the growing trade ties discussed later in this chapter.

Table 6.2 South African imports by region, 2003–7 (R million).

Region	Imports							
	2003	2004	2005	2006	2007	% change 2006–7	% global imports 2005	% global imports 2007
Africa	8 217	13 000	17 250	29 410	42 985	46	4.9	7.7
Americas	36 436	40 158	43 670	58 971	74 599	26	12.6	13.3
Asia	89 131	114 806	139 308	193 627	228 674	18	40.0	40.9
Europe	116 597	129 398	139 564	168 198	200 080	19	40.1	35.8
Pacific	6 765	8 118	8 346	10 824	12 502	16	2.4	2.3
Total	257 146	305 480	348 138	461 030	558 840	21	100.0	100.0

Source: *DTI's economic database and SARS*

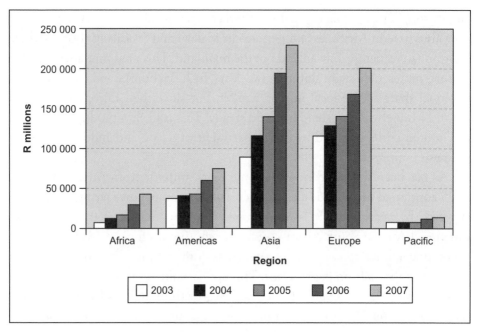

Figure 6.4   South African imports by region, 2003–7.

Trade Balances

Table 6.3 indicates that Africa is the one region with which South Africa has a positive trade balance. In 2005, the ratio stood at 2.67:1, down from 5:1 at the turn of the century. In the last two years that downward trend has continued to dip to 1.8:1 and 1.6:1 respectively. Given increasing oil and gas imports from Africa and their continuing high prices, it is possible that within the next five or so years South Africa's overall balance of trade with Africa will shift from positive to negative. Currently, Nigeria and Angola are the only two African economies with which South Africa has negative trade balances; and for obvious reasons. This scenario is not likely to change in the foreseeable future.

The other point of note from table 6.3 is the widening nature since 2005 of the gaps with Europe and Asia, although in 2007 that with Asia dipped very slightly.

Extraordinarily, perhaps, the identity of South Africa's top ten trading partners in Africa has not changed since the turn of this century. There have, however, been some positional changes in the league table, so to speak. The most notable, but least surprising, has been the toppling of Zimbabwe from top spot. After

Table 6.3 South Africa's trade balances by region (R million).

Region	Trade balance				
	2003	**2004**	**2005**	**2006**	**2007**
Africa	30 783	26 037	28 885	24 035	24 492
Americas	-2 275	-3 587	-5 325	-7 737	-5 345
Asia	-23 955	-41 606	-52 905	-88 652	-88 043
Europe	-24 578	-26 429	-22 669	-28 624	-38 781
Pacific	-434	-197	1 532	-1 045	-2 599
Total	-20 459	-45 782	-50 482	-102 023	-110 276

Source: Data supplied by DTI and SARS.

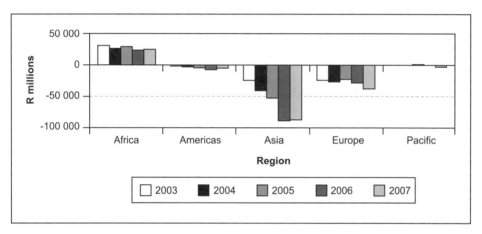

Figure 6.5 South Africa's trade balances by region, 2003–7.

being South Africa's leading trade partner in Africa for more than fifteen years, it slipped to second place in 2006 and down a further place in 2007. There seems little reason why that slide will not continue and accelerate unless political and economic circumstances north of the Limpopo change dramatically in the near future. With the decline of Zimbabwe, Nigeria and Angola have since 2008 been the fastest growing markets for South African investments on the continent.[8]

Nigeria
Unsurprisingly, given its emergence as a major oil supplier to South Africa, Nigeria moved to the top of the table in 2006 and retained that position in 2007. Over two years, the value of Nigeria's oil exports to South Africa increased by 400%,

way in excess of its imports from South Africa. Those increased in the same period by only about 12% and primarily comprised food products, tobacco, sugar and non-alcoholic beverages.

The growing Nigerian-South African trade axis is a natural economic development given that South Africa constitutes the continent's largest economy and Nigeria its largest consumer market. Both parties have for some years recognised the growth potential of their relationship and have spawned promotional institutions in the form of a bi-national commission that meets twice yearly, a joint Chamber of Commerce and a joint Business Investment Forum. A meeting of this forum coincided with a state visit to South Africa in June 2008 by Nigeria's President, Umaru Yar'Adua, who was accompanied by over 300 business people, including a large delegation of representatives of the Nigerian oil, banking, railways and telecommunication sectors.

The business climate in Nigeria is difficult, a product not just of its notoriety for corruption but also of chronic power shortages, a national infrastucture that is overburdened and inadequate, if not archaic, vastly different business cultures and intellectual property issues. Unsurprisingly, therefore, some South African ventures in Nigeria have failed, notably those by Vodacom and South African Airways (Daniel, Lutchman and Naidu 2005: 562). In 2007, the media group Johnnic Communications (Johncom) admitted that its Nigerian operation was under-performing and that it had consequently put a planned Kenyan expansion on hold. In Nigeria, Johncom operates media stores (Exclusive Books) and cinemas (NU-Metro) in Abuja and Lagos as well as CD and DVD manufacturing plants. It also holds part-ownership of the national daily newspaper, *Business Day.*[9] In 2007, the company announced that in 2006 its African operations lost R70 million, up from R48 million a year earlier.

Other South African ventures have, however, done far better in Nigeria, most notably the mobile telephony group, Mobile Telephone Networks (MTN). It is the granddaddy of South African companies in Nigeria, having entered the country in 2001 in defiance of the orthodoxy that foreign entities could not operate profitably there. It has since proved the sceptics spectacularly wrong. As of December 2007, MTN had a subscriber base of 16.5 million, an increase in numbers of 2.5 million and of 3.2 million over one and two years respectively. This represented 43% of the Nigerian mobile telephony market. The 2007 figure for Nigeria also represented 29% of all its African subscribers in sixteen countries, inclusive of South Africa where it had at that time 14.8 million subscribers. Globally in 2007, MTN was operative in 21 African and Middle Eastern states and at the end of that year the Nigerian market represented 26.9% of its global subscription base.[10]

Building on its success in the Nigerian market, MTN has added to its range of operations locally. At the end of 2006 it acquired a 100% shareholding in a cabling and radio telephone service provider (VGC Telecommunications) and followed that up in 2007 with the launch of 3G services and mobile products such as roaming, top-up and Blackberry. It was predicted (Daniel, Lutchman and Comninos 2007: 519–21) that MTN's impressive results could see it become a corporate takeover target. This materialised with confirmation in June 2008 that negotiations were underway with a major Indian operator, Reliance Communications. These ultimately collapsed, but there seems little reason to believe other suitors will not come calling.

MTN's success has encouraged other South African corporates to enter the Nigerian market. In 2003, there were 55 South African companies operating in the country. Some failed and left, but by September 2007 the South African presence had doubled to just over 100 companies. Unsurprisingly, one of these, IT operator Altech Namitech, entered the mobile telephony field, setting up a full subsidiary to supply its pre-paid, top-up vouchers throughout West Africa. Others include a plastics manufacturer (Nampak), fast food dealers (Nandos and Famous Brands), a wholesaler (Game) and a retailer (Shoprite Checkers). The latter opened its first Nigerian outlet in Lagos at the end of 2006 and was profitable within one year. After an absence of several years, the construction giant Group Five re-entered the West African market with contracts to build huge power plants in Ghana and Nigeria. Another group making a big push in Nigeria is Protea Hotels, which operates four hotels with a further eight under construction in mid-2008. A large part of its motivation is to service the growing army of South Africans now working and living there. Once complete, the Protea chain will have 130–40 hotels in Africa, making it by far the largest hotel group on the continent, far bigger than the Sheraton and Hilton groups combined.

A major new entrant into the Nigerian financial sector was Standard Bank of South Africa (Stanbic) with its purchase of a substantial stake, about one third, in the local ITBC Chartered Bank. After a year of operations, its Nigerian affiliate contributed 13% of its Africa-generated revenue, second only to its Namibian operation. Joining Stanbic in the Nigerian financial sector has been the independent retirement fund administrator, Alexander Forbes. In 2008, it acquired a 40% stake in Nigeria's pensions sector. With the Nigerian government announcing that it could no longer afford to meet its pension fund obligations, it outsourced the sector to private operators. With eight million state employees eligible for pensions, Alexander Forbes clearly believes there are huge opportunities for it. At the time of the acquisition, it announced that it intended to acquire a controlling share in the Nigerian group.

Angola

Predictions made in the *State of the Nation* (Daniel, Lutchman and Comninos 2007) suggested that South Africa's ambitions to grow its trade with Angola, to take advantage of that country's return to peace and desperate need for reconstruction, would be difficult to achieve. This was attributed to cultural and linguistic difficulties and the Angolan government's lingering resentment of the apartheid regime's support for the National Union for the Total Independence of Angola (UNITA) rebels. As it turns out, this has been disproved. Though still cautious and far from their potential, trade ties have strengthened since 2005, with Angola willing to sell oil to South Africa. There has been a steady increase in the number of South African companies doing business in Angola and a 500% increase in the level of Angolan imports from South Africa over the last two years.

Amongst the new entrants has been the low-budget, mass-market retailer, Pep Stores, which announced in July 2007 that the first three of a planned 25–30 stores would be opened in southern Angola in 2008. The packaging company, Nampak, announced in October 2007 that it intended to invest over $100 million in a beverage can manufacturing plant near Luanda. It expected by 2009 to produce 700 million cans per year for local and export markets.

This accelerated involvement in the Angolan economy produced a rise of three places up the top ten table from fifth to second. According to an anonymous source in the Department of Foreign Affairs (DFA), this thaw in relations has been the result of a special diplomatic effort launched by the department a few years back as well as to the skilful efforts of the South Africa-Angola Chamber of Commerce headed by Roger Ballard-Tremeer, a former DFA diplomat now resident in Luanda. According to him, there are now several hundred South African exporters supplying goods to the Angolan private and public sectors with between 25 000 and 30 000 visitors entering the country annually.[11]

Democratic Republic of Congo

Also rising three places has been the Democratic Republic of Congo (DRC), despite the fact that it continued to be the worst performer of the big ten in terms of exports into South Africa. In 2006, it sold only R0.32 billion worth of goods to South Africa in contrast with the R4.1 billion worth of goods it purchased. Trade with the DRC was thus a one-way street in favour of South Africa, a telling indicator of the precarious state of the DRC's domestic economy.

It was predicted (Daniel, Lutchman and Comninos 2007) that the DRC would remain a site of considerable South African diplomatic, peacekeeping and economic activity. It was suggested that this would be driven not just by the country's immense mineral potential, but also by South Africa's interest in the Grand Inga hydro-electric project. This massive scheme has been talked about for years as a possible remedy for South Africa's energy deficit. Although there seems to have been little forward movement on Inga despite South Africa's electricity problems, the prediction of intensified economic activity has proved correct.

Unsurprisingly, mining groups are the big South African players in the DRC. These include established majors like AAC, Anglogold Ashanti and Kumba Resources, a zinc and iron ore producer, as well as some relatively new junior mining groups. The busiest of these has been Metorex. Junior miners are often prepared to incur risks avoided by the larger groups and Metorex has dared to venture into the violence-ravaged eastern DRC, while most others have not. It has also opened up across the border in Zambia. In all, Metorex operates copper, cobalt and zinc processing plants and has interests in gold exploration and fluorspar production.

But it is not just mining groups that have opened up in the DRC. Vodacom operates one of its few African mobile telephony operations there while some South African retailers and fast food franchises have also set up in Kinshasa and Lubumbashi. This includes Shoprite Checkers, which in 2007 announced an $80 million investment in the DRC. As of mid-2008 it was operating two stores.

Zimbabwe

As noted earlier, Zimbabwe slipped from first place in 2005 to third in 2007 as a South African trading partner. Given the shambolic state of its economy, it is perhaps surprising that the country features in the top ten table at all, let alone as high as it does. The fact is, however, that in terms of foodstuffs and other consumables South Africa is an essential lifeline and an enormous percentage of the incomes earned by the hundreds of thousands of Zimbabweans working in South Africa is used to purchase commodities for shipment back to Zimbabwe. Then there are sectors of the Zimbabwean domestic economy that are still functional, productive and generating goods for export. In the commercial agricultural sector the sugar giant, Tongaat Huletts, continues to perform well. Huletts operates estates in both the Triangle area and Hippo Valley and in 2007 produced 349 000 tons of sugar, generating a profit of R53 million, down by only R8 million from 2006.

Another corner of Zimbabwe where money is still being made is Victoria Falls. As the rest of the country's economy has crumbled, this old colonial enclave has become a virtually self-governing entity run by its hotel and tour operators, many of them foreign. The South African group Tourvest is one. Its international clientele now fly direct from Johannesburg to Victoria Falls and back; or move onto Zambia and Botswana, not Harare or Bulawayo. All its supplies from food to toiletries are sourced from South Africa and it accepts payments only in US dollars. Were it not for the fact that it employs Zimbabwean workers, there is virtually nothing else about its operation that links it to its host country.

Also profitable is the mining sector, despite production difficulties caused by shortages of parts and uneven supplies of fuel and electricity. South African corporates operate in the gold and platinum sectors and despite their production difficulties have benefited from price booms in these two commodities. For example, Impala Platinum's (Implats) Zimbabwean subsidiary, Zimplats, recorded a gross profit of R854.6 million in 2007, more than doubling its 2006 profits of R317.6 million. In the process. and extraordinarily, its annual production output reached a record high. Likewise, Mzi Khumalo's Metallon Group with its five gold mines has performed well.

Comment was offered (Daniel, Lutchman and Comninos 2007) on the threat of Black Economic Employment (BEE) type legislation pertaining to foreign-owned mining groups. It was suggested that if this legislation were enacted, these companies might put themselves on hold or disinvest altogether. That legislation has now been enacted and foreign-owned groups are required to cede 50% of their holdings to local shareholders without compensation. It has not yet been made operational and rationality suggests that it was no more than an election ploy and will remain in abeyance. This, after all, is a sector that generates sizeable amounts of tax revenue to an essentially bankrupt state.

Elsewhere the 20–30 South African companies – banks, insurance groups and retailers – still operating in Zimbabwe continue to play a waiting game. As the analyst Dianna Games put it, most South African businesses in Zimbabwe 'are ring-fencing operations, keeping financials separate from overall group operations as a way of riding out the storm'.[12] Occasionally they purchase at bargain-basement prices a failing Zimbabwean counterpart and put it on hold, waiting for the day when the tide turns and some form of normal government resumes. This de-Zimbabweanisation of the local economy has now reached the point where domestic ownership of the Zimbabwean economy is at 1960s levels. It is not only the South Africans who have benefited from the steady demise of the local economy. So, too, have Libyans and Chinese who have acquired local companies and farms in what have been essentially barter deals for fuel and weapons.

Mozambique and Tanzania

Even though Mozambique slipped one place in the top ten table, trade between Mozambique and South Africa continues to grow and flourish. In fact, between 2006 and 2007 the total value of trade between the two countries increased by 40%. South Africa remains by far the largest investor in the economy. In fact, between 1992 and 2007 Mozambique attracted 34% of all South African FDI into Africa. A large portion of this went into two mega-projects, the Mozal aluminium smelter and the Temane natural gas pipeline constructed by Sasol. Both are now operational and much of the more recent new FDI has been smaller in size, but pan-sectoral. The net result is that, according to South Africa's DTI, there are now just over 300 South African companies doing business in Mozambique, employing some 50 000 locals.[13]

Two of the larger South African operators in Mozambique are the sugar producers, Illovo and Tongaat-Huletts. Both companies increased their acreage in Mozambique under sugar with the latter spending R1.3 billion in acquiring more land, an additional 2 692 hectares, for cultivation and in expanding their milling capacity. In 2006, the Sugar Associations of South Africa, Swaziland, Zimbabwe and Mozambique each invested $2.5 million in a new sugar silo at the port of Maputo to handle the increasing tonnage of sugar being grown in those four countries and exported to the European Union (EU).[14]

Another important South African investment in Mozambique came in the form of First National Bank's purchase from Portuguese investors of an 80% shareholding in the local Banco Desenvolvimento e Comercio (BDC).

Finally, mention needs to be made of deepening links between South Africa and Mozambique in the field of energy, especially electricity. In a somewhat bizarre arrangement, South Africa currently sells electricity to Mozambique while also purchasing it from the latter's hydro-electric plant at Cahora Bassa. With South Africa experiencing a growing deficit in the supply of electricity, it is now increasing its purchases from Cahora Bassa while continuing to sell power to Mozambique in terms of a contractual arrangement the South African government argues it must honour. Whether it continues to do so or not, the fact is that as demand for power grows in South Africa, the country's dependence over the short-term (6–8 years) on Mozambican supplies is likely to grow sharply.

With all of the top ten countries bar Tanzania total trade volumes increased significantly over the two-year period 2005–7, from R49.4 billion in 2005 to R82 billion in 2007 – about a 15.3% increase. The dip in regard to Tanzania is a result of a fall in the volume of South African exports into that economy. Why that has occurred is not clear. This last fact notwithstanding, the South African expatriate populations in Mozambique and Tanzania constitute the largest of all such communities in Africa.

Table 6.4   South Africa's top ten trading partners (R million).

Country	Exports Nov. 2007	Imports Nov. 2007	Total trade Nov. 2007	Position 2007	Position 2005
Nigeria	4 378 393	12 320 940	16 699 333	1	2
Angola	5 139 445	9 191 483	14 330 928	2	5
Zimbabwe	7 833186	5 407 830	13 241 016	3	1
Zambia	9 225 334	2 369 471	11 594 805	4	3
Mozambique	8 163 657	2 252 974	10 416 631	5	4
Kenya	4 241 416	183 892	4 425 308	6	6
DRC	4 102 651	32 534	4 135 185	7	10
Tanzania	2 561 460	344 909	2 906 369	8	7
Malawi	1 977 917	603 622	2 581 539	9	9
Mauritius	1 751 626	405 708	2 157 334	10	8

Source: Statistics generated by the DTI and SARS

Emerging Trends in the South African-African Relationship

Three trends or factors go beyond the previous analyses.

The Internationalisation of South African Capital

This pertains to the increasingly global, extra-African nature of the operations of a cluster of South African corporates. AAC and De Beers date back to the minerals rush of the late nineteenth century; others like Old Mutual and Standard Bank hark back to the early twentieth century when British capital held sway in the local economy. Still others like the paper and pulp producers Sappi and Mondi, beer producer South African Breweries (SAB), fuel giant SASOL and the media group Naspers grew fat and rich in the apartheid era. A handful, like Sanlam and Rembrandt (now Remgro), were spawned by the apartheid regime's affirmative measures to promote Afrikaner capital. Some like Shoprite Checkers and the Protea Hotels chain saw early opportunities open up in the democratic era and have blossomed into major multinationals; while a few are products of that new era, like Vodacom and MTN.

These companies, along with Dimension Data, the Liberty Group and Bidvest, constitute the first generation of South African multinationals. For some, their international operations are now so much larger than their home-based equivalents that they have moved offshore, listing in places like London and Zurich; and sometimes moving their head offices to these centres of international finance. They include base metal producer Billiton (now part Australian-owned and operating as BHP Billiton), SAB, AAC, Old Mutual and Dimension Data.

Space does not permit a detailed discussion of the international operations of these local multinationals, but the point is that all have African as well as non-African operations. Some like SAB (now SABMiller after its acquisition of the American brewing giant, Miller) moved into Africa and beyond simultaneously, while others have used the success of their African ventures to expand beyond the continent. The two most spectacular, and perhaps most interesting, of these are MTN and the media conglomerate, Naspers.

MTN is a young, post-apartheid creation. A product of the government's BEE initiative, its growth has been rapid. It moved into Nigeria in 2001 and then, only five years later, into what was regarded as an even riskier business environment, the Middle East where it has operations in four states. In a further expansion, the company announced in 2007 that it planned to purchase the entire share capital of the Dubai-based group, Investcom, for $5.5 billion.

The Naspers story is as fascinating, albeit for different reasons. Founded by the National Party and cosseted by it for decades, it grew into a major bastion of Afrikaner capital. With the political change in South Africa, few would have imagined that this ugly duckling of the apartheid era would become a post-apartheid swan, growing and thriving in the new democratic dispensation. But it has and in the process has developed into a major global media player. It blazed a South African path into both China and Russia, has developed extensive holdings in Latin America and Europe, and in 2007 moved into India. While a small part of its empire, Africa has not been neglected. Its M-Net pay television service is Africa's largest, while in 2008 it launched mobile TV services in Namibia, Kenya and Nigeria.

A 2007 survey of the global retail trade listed five South African chains amongst the top 250 general merchandise and fashion retailers in the World. All of them have extensive non-South African operations. They were Pick 'n Pay (ranked 122), Shoprite Checkers (123), Massmart (trading as Makro, 140), Metro Cash and Carry (230) and Edcon (trading as Edgars, 246).

Finally, we need to refer to the growing international role of Sasol. It has been noted (Daniel, Lutchman and Comninos 2007) that the relationship between the company and the South African government was tense with the government threatening to impose a windfall tax on its profits and the company responding by suggesting it might move offshore and seek an overseas listing. Since then, the relationship between the two parties has mellowed considerably. Despite ever-larger profits, the government has shelved its windfall tax proposal while Sasol has dropped its threat and announced plans to deepen its involvement in the local economy. It has also negotiated a much-praised BEE deal and changed the demographics of its management.

In the meantime, its international involvement in the production of synthetic liquid fuels has grown and it operates plants in China, Nigeria, Qatar and the US. It also decided to invest $250 million in expanding its natural gas production project in southern Mozambique, which would double its output production by 2010. With the surge in oil prices in 2008, Sasol was said to be earning tens of millions of dollars per day in profits.

Africa in South Africa

The second point is in some ways the opposite of the first and pertains both to the post-1994 trickle of African companies, as well as to the flood of individual African traders and cross-border shoppers into the South African market.

In 2005, the Nigerian oil company, Oando, set up office in Johannesburg and in November of that year became the first Nigerian company to list on the Johannesburg Stock Exchange (JSE). Two Nigerian banks, including First Bank (Nigeria's largest and Africa's 24th largest company), have set up in South Africa while a newspaper, *The African Standard*, is targeted primarily at the Nigerian émigré community.[15]

Also in 2005, political difficulties at home led the Zimbabwean telecommunications group, Econet Wireless, to move its head office to Johannesburg where it remains. It now regards Johannesburg as a base for its African operations. There is also a Zimbabwean-owned newspaper, *The Zimbabwean*, operating in exile and publishing weekly in both London and Johannesburg.

In April 2008, Nigeria's largest industrial conglomerate, the Dangote Group, purchased at a cost of R3 billion a 45% shareholding in the local African black empowerment group, Sephaka Cement. Dangote plans to build a cement plant geared to producing 2.2 million tons of cement annually by 2010. Cement is in chronically short supply in South Africa and local producers are unable to meet demands generated by the general building boom and the added infrastructural demand generated by the 2010 Football World Cup construction frenzy.

Complementing this small African corporate presence are thousands of African businessmen, refugees and economic migrants, who have set up a range of small businesses – restaurants, spaza shops, fast-food outlets, craft and other market stalls, clothing businesses, hairdressing salons and Internet cafes – that are increasingly giving the downtown areas of major cities a more African feel. A variant on this trade is the extraordinary phenomenon of cross-border retail tourism. This involves not just Zimbabweans crossing the border in search of food supplies, spare parts and the like, but busloads and planeloads (South African Railways no longer operates any cross-border rail lines) of literally tens of thousands of largely southern African traders who descend on Johannesburg in particular and buy up an incredible range of commodities for re-sale in their home markets. Some estimates put the cash injection into the local economy at more than R20 billion. Research by the development group ComMark Trust estimated that in 2005 some 450 000 shoppers travelled by road to Johannesburg, along with about 90 000 air travellers. So huge is this trade that ComMark helped set up a Johannesburg Cross-Border Shopping Association.

While this trade provides a positive financial shot in the arm to small business traders in particular, it has also produced an ugly and lethal streak of xenophobia, especially amongst poorer black South Africans living in informal settlements and the peri-urban areas of the country's larger cities. The upsurge of attacks on African migrants in May-June 2008, in which over 50 African foreigners were killed and tens of thousands displaced, was only an intensification of a trend dating back several years: namely, targeted killings of African immigrant traders operating small businesses in largely black townships. Since 2006, perhaps more than 100 Somali shopkeepers have been killed in attacks on their shops, mostly in townships in and around Cape Town, Port Elizabeth and Durban.

The Awakening of the Financial Services Sector

Finance houses tend to be cautious and conservative; and probably correctly so. They are after all playing with other people's money. Be that as it may, South

Africa's investment brokers have been particularly cautious with regard to the African market. They constitute the one sector that stood aside from the post-1990s drive into Africa. They largely left it to the state-owned Industrial Development Corporation (IDC) to finance the movement of South African corporates into Africa's largely uncharted investment terrain. The IDC has done well with its African ventures and it now seems that South Africa's private venture capitalists have concluded that Africa is a safe bet, a place where they too can do good business. In the last two years, they have embraced this new arena with alacrity, funding not only South African ventures but others where there is no local involvement. Together with a growing South African banking presence on the continent, they make up a spreading network of South African financial institutions active on the continent. They comprise three clusters – banks, venture capitalists, and insurance and retirement brokers.

Daniel, Lutchman and Comninos (2007) noted South Africa's growing footprint in the African banking sector with all four of South Africa's big banks developing services to their growing number of Africa-based clients. These authors commented on the potential offered by the deal between Britain's Barclays Bank and South Africa's largest domestic bank, Absa: Barclays would take over Absa's domestic operations with a 57% acquisition in a first phase; followed by an Absa takeover of all Barclays operations in Africa, bar those in Egypt. It was noted that this would make Absa South Africa's largest bank in Africa. While the first phase of the takeover has been completed, the second has for largely unexplained reasons has been shelved and seems unlikely to materialise.

Consequently, Standard Bank remains South Africa's leading banker in Africa with operations in eighteen countries and market capitalisation of R135 billion. More significantly, in the last two years Standard has deepened its involvement and capacity in the African financial sector with a 60% acquisition of Kenya's CFC Bank, creating Kenya's fourth largest lender, CFC Stanbic Holdings. Likewise in Nigeria in 2007, Standard Bank bought a controlling share in the local IBTC Chartered Bank. Profits from this link up amounted to R1.26 billion in 2007, 13% of Standard's total extra-South African earnings in Africa; making it, along with its banking operation in Zambia, the two most profitable outside South Africa.

Perhaps the deal with the greatest potential was Standard's decision in March 2008 to develop a strategic partnership with the Industrial and Commercial Bank of China (ICBC) that saw the latter take a 20% share of Standard Bank in return for a R36.7 billion cash injection. Standard announced at the time that it intended to use this cash to grow its African business. Standard and the ICBC were working on 80 potential investment and acquisition deals with a particular focus on mining and infrastructure projects in the DRC.[16] Commenting on the deal, Martyn Davies, Director of Stellenbosch University's Centre for Chinese Studies, argued that it 'destroys the stereotype of China Inc being interested in Africa's extractive industries and nothing more'.[17]

The most interesting new development with regard to South Africa's involvement in the African financial sector has been in the area of lending. It is of two types. One is micro-lending, where the market leader is Blue Financial Services. Founded in Durban in 2001, Blue has grown phenomenally both inside and outside South Africa. In May 2008, Blue operated about 200 branches in twelve African countries, including South Africa, and employed over 1 500 workers. In August 2007, its revenue split between South Africa and the rest of Africa was 60:40. It is the biggest firm listed on the JSE's alternative AltX exchange market and is also listed on the Botswana Stock Exchange with applications for listings in Zambia, Kenya and Namibia. In early 2008, Blue linked up with Nigeria's Intercontinental Bank to create Africa's biggest micro-finance bank, while in May 2008 Blue purchased the Zambian mass-market lender, Nedfin, making it the biggest micro-financier in that country.

Blue's activities on the ground in Africa are dwarfed, however, by the actions and intentions of a number of large private equity groups that have suddenly, it seems, discovered Africa. Like MTN, one of these has its origins in the ANC government's BEE initiative in the form of Mvelaphanda Holdings, headed by a senior ANC politician and former premier of Gauteng, Tokyo Sexwale. In January 2008, Mvela linked up with the New York-listed alternative asset manager Och-Ziff Capital Management and a private investment vehicle, Palladino Holdings, to create a multibillion dollar fund called African Global Capital (AGC). With investment teams in London and Johannesburg and fourteen offices on the continent, AGC was looking for investment opportunities primarily in mineral resources, energy, infrastructure and property.[18]

In its operations, AGC will be competing with three other South African groupings. One is the Pamodzi Resources Fund set up by another BEE grouping, Pamodzi Investment Holdings. It has the backing of a US hedge fund, First Reserve. The second is Stanlib Asset Management which in 2007 secured $100 million from the US-based Overseas Private Investment group to establish an Africa Debt Fund. Its third competitor is the Standard Africa Equity Fund which, with a resource base of $1 billion from its Chinese banking partner, intends to target investments in four of Africa's larger economies, Egypt, Morocco, Nigeria and Kenya.

Mention has already been made in the discussion on Nigeria of the entry of Alexander Forbes into the local retirement fund and pension sector. The other interesting development in this area was the decision of South Africa's largest insurer, Old Mutual, to expand its involvement in the African insurance arena by opening operations in the potentially huge but difficult Angolan market, as well as in Swaziland. This development brings to six the number of African markets outside South Africa in which it has operations.

Other South African insurers active in Africa are Sanlam, which operates in nine other African countries, and is looking at the possibility of going into Nigeria; Metropolitan Life, functioning in the Nigerian, Ghanaian and Kenyan markets and in each of the Southern African Customs Union (SACU) states;[19] and the Liberty Group, which operates in the SACU states and Uganda. In late 2007, Liberty, 30% owned by Standard Bank, announced an ambitious expansion programme into the African market. Its CEO stated that it intended to target those countries in which Standard was operating: 'We have a natural strategic competitive advantage in Africa because of our relationship with Standard Bank . . . we would be foolhardy not to exploit that relationship'.[20]

Conclusion

Some contributors to this book have put the issue of the scramble within an ideological framework of imperialism and neo-colonialism. They also suggest that the new scramble is not new at all but a re-run of the nineteenth century rush for Africa's resources. Chameleon-like, the imperial creature has changed its form, colour and modus operandi; but at core it remains exploitative, pillaging the continent's resources in the manner of old. Others offer a more nuanced view, arguing that while there are differences between new and old scrambles, at core the process disadvantages, if not exploits, the continent to the benefit of the current crop of scramblers, old and new.

We have our reservations about these arguments. In our conceptualisation, imperialism is something more than just exploitation, a skewed arrangement or a bad deal between two or more parties. We see it as descriptive of an ongoing power relationship of domination and subordination, which the dominant power seeks to maintain and perpetuate. While we accept that the relationship between Africa and the rest of the world today continues often to be an unequal one, and that there remain some imperialist features in that relationship – such as in the

EU's drive to tie the states of the continent into a series of bilateral Economic Partnership Agreements (EPAs) and George Bush's wish to set up an Africa Command Centre on the continent – we do not believe that it is at core an imperialist one. From the late nineteenth century and for close on 100 years, the Euro-African relationship was an imperialist one, manifesting itself in direct colonial rule. A late twentieth century era of neo-colonialism followed, but to suggest that this imperialist form still expresses the essence of the relationship between Africa and other parts of the world is an argument insufficiently nuanced, if not actually wrong.

It follows that we do not accept, as some suggest, that the new scramble is the same as the old. In our view, it is different in many significant ways and it does not, as some have termed it, take the form of continuing pillage. Pillage is theft, larceny on a grand scale. Pillage is what King Leopold did to the Congo in the late nineteenth century; and theft is what the British did to the Boer Republics in the early twentieth century. Now it is a charge some make with regard to China's exploits in Africa. We may not like or approve of some of the deals negotiated in recent times between China and a range of African governments – like the $2 billion loan to Angola in 2004 that enabled its government to circumvent the International Monetary Fund's good governance strictures – but that hardly constituted robbery: $2 billion is a considerable sum.

Consider also some other recent Sino-African agreements. In 2007, the Chinese agreed to invest $9 billion in infrastructure projects in the DRC in exchange for mineral rights. It will build 3 200 kilometres of railway tracks, 550 kilometres of urban roads, a further 2 700 kilometres of beaten roads, two airports, two electricity distribution networks, and more than 170 hospitals and clinics.[21] Of course, the Chinese will themselves benefit from these inputs, but to dub the arrangement pillage is off the mark. In 2005, the Chinese state oil company, Petrochina, paid its Nigerian counterpart $800 million to purchase 30 000 barrels of oil per day for one year. A year later the Chinese National Offshore Oil Corporation paid $2.27 billion for a 45% share in an offshore oil and gas field. The vastly increased price is an interesting case of an African government flexing its muscles, a symptom of what is often dubbed resource nationalism with the Nigerian government here turning to its advantage factors of supply and demand. Other recent examples of African resource nationalism could be cited from both Algeria and Angola. We do not believe that some contributors to this book have paid sufficient attention to the changing nature of some recent deals negotiated with some of Africa's larger oil and gas producers.

Finally, there is a need to emphasise that these deals so disliked by some are arrangements negotiated between two sovereign entities. They are not cases where outside powers have walked in and helped themselves to Africa's resources, as the notion of pillage would suggest. If they are bad deals, then the local African government is as culpable, if not more so, than its foreign partner. If as a consequence of the deal the locals remain poor and the money finds its way into Swiss bank accounts, is the outside party the one at fault? If the new scramble is a new form of imperialism, then it is imperialism by invitation which is not imperialism at all. What it is, rather, is old-fashioned compradorism.

This leads to a discussion of the nature of South African economic involvement in Africa. As indicated in the introduction to this chapter, some like Bond (2003) have termed it a new form of colonialism. We do not take that view. We do not see it as an imperialist relationship or as some have described it, sub-imperial. What does that term mean anyway: sub-imperial to whom?

In our view, the South African-African economic relationship is primarily a case of market forces at work. It is an evolving situation from the time post-1990 when South African capital found it could venture into a hitherto closed market and do business. With the passage of time, more and more South African corporates have become aware of the potential of this new African market potential and moved into it. Not all have succeeded and some have fallen hard. But for the most part, they have negotiated deals from which, by and large, both parties have benefited. The successes of many South African businesses in Nigeria suggest that the Nigerian consumer wants the quality products Game, Shoprite Checkers, MTN and others offer. The recent xenophobic killings of foreign Africans may have inflamed feelings in Africa, but they have not in retaliation led to the targeting of South African nationals or their businesses.

The point does need to be acknowledged, however, that the growing South African corporate presence in Africa contains within it the seeds for the possible use of state power to its advantage by South Africa or its corporates. Were that to happen, were the South African government to threaten to use economic leverage – to turn off the lights in Zimbabwe, for example – then that would be an imperialist use of power. But it has not happened in the case of Zimbabwe, perhaps to the chagrin of some parties. Nor has there been such a use of economic pressure, or even the threat of it, anywhere else in Africa.

This leads to two conclusions. The first is that what the local corporate sector is doing in Africa is good business. And, second, because that business has, on the whole, been good, the South African corporate footprint on the continent is now considerable and will continue to grow. Local capital will never be able to match the Chinese or Indian investors in the size and value of their contractual arrangements, but the sectoral spread of the South African presence is one which continues, and will continue, to make of it a formidable presence on the continent.

Notes

1. *Africa Report* Apr. 2008: 54.
2. Cynthia Carroll, CEO, Anglo-American Group in *Business Report* 6 Feb. 2008.
3. *New York Times* 2 Feb. 2002.
4. *Africa Report* Apr–May 2008. Largest of the top 500 in the *Africa Report* list was the Algerian state-owned hydrocarbon and energy producer, Sonatrach. The other nine of the top ten were South African corporates Old Mutual (insurance), Bidvest (retail), Sanlam (insurance), Sasol (chemicals and fuel), Imperial Holdings (diverse), Telkom (telecommunications), MTN (telecommunications), De Beers (mining and diamonds) and Barloworld (diverse). The eleventh largest company is Vodacom, South Africa's largest mobile telephony provider.
5. *African Business* Apr. 2008. Common to the two journals' top ten listings were only Sasol and MTN while Old Mutual and Telkom were ranked twelfth and eighteenth of the listed companies.
6. South Africa's FDI flows into Africa: presentation to the National Treasury's Interdepartmental Workshop by R. Rumney, Johannesburg, 15 Feb. 2006.
7. *Business Day* 1 Oct. 2007.
8. *Africa Report* Apr–May 2008: 56.
9. In Oct. 2003 *Business Day* Nigeria launched a daily paper in South Africa entitled *This Day*. Aimed at the upper-end serious newspaper-reading public, it rapidly acquired just over 30 000 daily readers, but it was unable to attract sufficient advertising revenue and develop a reliable national delivery system. It folded after little more than a year. Soon afterwards, Johnnic, publisher of South Africa's *Business Day* newspaper, took a share in the ownership of its Nigerian namesake.
10. Outside Africa, MTN has operations in Iran, Syria, Afghanistan, Yemen and Cyprus. In the latter, it had in December only 113 subscribers and in 2008 it dispensed with its shareholding there.
11. *Business Day* 10 Dec. 2007.
12. *African Business* Aug. 2005: 22.
13. *Business Report* 7 May 2008.
14. While smaller than Tongaat-Hulett in Mozambique, Illovo is the largest South African sugar operator in Africa with estates in Mozambique (4%), Swaziland (9%), Tanzania (9%), Zambia (12%) and Malawi (41%) – the figures in brackets represent percentage contribution to overall profit. In 2007, Illovo announced that it planned to start growing sugar in Mali and would invest R1.4 billion in sugar and ethanol milling plants. It also

planned to double its Zambian sugar production through the acquisition of further land and by expanding its milling capacity. Of the two companies, only Tongaat- Huletts operates estates in Zimbabwe.

15. *African Business* Apr. 2008:18.
16. *Business Report* 6 June 2008.
17. *Business Report* 7 May 2008.
18. *Sunday Times* (Johannesburg), 4 May 2008,
19. The members of SACU are Namibia, Lesotho, Botswana, Swaziland and South Africa.
20. *Business Day* 10 Aug. 2007.
21. *Business Day* 2 June 2008.

References

Bond, P. 2003. *Against Global Apartheid: South Africa Meets the World Bank, International Monetary Fund and International Finance.* Cape Town: University of Cape Town Press.

Daniel, J. and J. Lutchman. 2006. 'South Africa in Africa: scrambling for energy'. In: *The State of the Nation: South Africa 2005–2006*, edited by S. Buhlungu et al. Cape Town: HSRC Press: 484–509.

Daniel, J., J. Lutchman and A. Comninos. 2007. 'South Africa in Africa: trends and forecasts in a changing African political economy'. In: *The State of the Nation: South Africa 2007*, edited by S. Buhlungu et al. Cape Town: HSRC Press: 508–32.

Daniel, J., J. Lutchman and S. Naidu. 2005. 'South Africa and Nigeria: two unequal centres in a periphery'. In: *The State of the Nation: South Africa 2004–2005*, edited by J. Daniel, J. Lutchman and R. Southall. Cape Town: HSRC Press: 544–68.

Daniel, J., V. Naidoo and S. Naidu. 2003. 'The South Africans have arrived'. In: *The State of the Nation: South Africa 2003–2004*, edited by J. Daniel, A. Habib and R. Southall. Cape Town: HSRC Press: 368–90.

Sanders, R. 2008. 'South African investment in Africa: restructuring and resistance'. At *Issue Ezine* 1, May.

CHAPTER SEVEN

The Militarisation of the New Scramble in Africa

Martin Rupiya and Roger Southall

David Harvey (2003) argued that the global hegemony of the US, founded on production, finance and military power in the immediate post-war period, lost its superiority after 1970 and might well now be losing financial dominance as well, leaving it with military might alone. Yet it was hard to imagine that the US would peacefully adjust to the phenomenal growth of China and recognise that the balance was shifting to East Asia as the hegemonic centre of global power. It was in this context that neo-conservative elements within the US political establishment looked to flex military muscle as the only clear absolute power they had, talking more openly of empire as a political option and looking to control oil supplies as a means to counter the power shifts within the global economy. The invasion and occupation of Iraq in 2003 followed. Although this was ideologically justified by the administration of President George W. Bush as a central plank in his war on terror declared following 9/11, Harvey proposes that the primary motivation was to secure control for the US of the global oil spigot in the Middle East and thereby retain effective control over the world economy for the next 50 years. However, for this to happen, the US also needed to extend its potential or actual control over other sources of oil. One strategy was to use Iraq as a base for consolidating its strategic position in Turkey, Uzbekistan and, dangerously, Iran with regard to Caspian basin oil reserves. Meanwhile, another was to secure dominance over Africa's increasingly significant oil reserves, a strategy that had major political and military as well as economic considerations. It is this – along with the response by other key actors – that concerns us in this chapter.

US Strategic Interests and the Scramble in Africa

On 6 February 2007, the Bush administration announced its intention to create a new Unified Combatant Command for Africa (AFRICOM), indicating the continent's increased strategic importance to the US. Carved out of three of the US's five geographic commands,[1] the new command's area of responsibility would include all African countries except Egypt and achieve full operating capability in October 2008. The motivation was officially provided by:

> Africa's role in the Global War on Terror and the potential threats posed by ungoverned spaces; the growing importance of Africa's natural resources, particularly energy sources; and ongoing concern for the continent's many humanitarian crises, armed conflicts, and more general challenges, such as the devastating effect of HIV/AIDS (Ploch 2007: executive summary).[2]

The perceived needs to secure existing investments and to 'fight off the Chinese' (Weinstein 2006) can be added.

The decision to form AFRICOM was the logical conclusion of the gradual build up of a coherent system of US military assistance to Africa from the mid-1990s. This followed a diminution of US interest in the continent after the Cold War, notably following the negotiated settlements that ended the wars in Angola and Namibia in 1988 and 1989 respectively.

In the immediate post-Cold War period, Africa was seen as having limited strategic and economic interest for the US (Alden 2000). Consequently, a commitment to political reform was now allowed to take centre stage with the US joining Britain and France in insisting that future foreign assistance to the continent would be conditional upon democratisation. Declared by Bush to be the onset of a New World Order, this resulted over the next two years in the US cutting off assistance to long-time Cold War allies resisting democratisation (Zaire, Liberia and Sudan) and shifting resources to countries that were now embracing it (South Africa, Ethiopia and Mozambique) (Ploch 2007: appendix 1; Lawson 2007).

The high point of this moment was the decision by the US to authorise the dispatch of military forces to Somalia. Following a resolution on 3 December 1992 by the United Nations (UN) Security Council that the situation in Somalia had become intolerable, the US deployed over 25 000 troops there to secure humanitarian assistance and prevent a total breakdown of law and order. The extent of this involvement by the US was unprecedented, but it did not last long. In October 1993, US Special Operations soldiers engaged Somali militia forces in Mogadishu, an operation that resulted in the deaths of 18 US soldiers and the televised dragging of their bodies behind a militia vehicle through the streets of the capital (Lawson 2007): 'The visceral response of the American public was to demand an immediate withdrawal of US military forces' (Schraeder 2000: A86).

President Bill Clinton subsequently ordered the final withdrawal of US troops from Somalia in March 1994, ironically the same month that 3 600 US soldiers were deployed to Central Africa to assist humanitarian efforts in Rwanda, where violence instigated by the Hutu government against the Tutsi minority was already breaking out. Reeling from the Somalian debacle, the Clinton Administration issued Presidential Decision Directive 25 (PDD25), which sought to limit future UN missions and especially US participation in them. This led to US refusal to heed warnings about the descent of the ongoing conflict in Rwanda into genocide, admission of which would have obliged the US to intervene under the Geneva Conventions. It proved to be a key factor, allowing the genocide to take its course and resulting in the deaths of 800 000 people (Lawson 2007).

Subsequently, the Department of Defense issued a position paper, which asserted that Africa was of 'very little traditional strategic interest' to the US[3], a view that complemented the call of PDD25 for subregional organisations to shoulder the burden of peacekeeping. Consistent with this was US refusal to have any direct involvement in the peacemaking effort by the Economic Community of West African States (ECOWAS) in Liberia, which was being torn apart by a brutal civil war.[4] Indeed, the determination to avoid intervention in African conflicts also dampened US support for democratisation in preference to a strategy of political stabilisation as in Burundi, where the Clinton administration gave its effective backing to the military regime of Pierre Buyoya that seized power in 1996. However, although the US eagerly embraced the politically convenient rhetoric of African solutions for African problems, the lessons of Somalia, Rwanda and Liberia were that the US could not afford complete disengagement. In short, 'it could not do nothing, and could not expect African forces to contain instability on their own' (Lawson 2007).

The initial proposal was for the creation of an African Crisis Response Force (ACRF) of about 5 000 African troops, trained by Western countries, which could be deployed rapidly for peacekeeping operations endorsed by the UN. However, in the face of a cool response from both Britain and France as well as key African countries, notably Nigeria and South Africa, this was reformulated as an African

Crisis Response Initiative (ACRI). It proposed a bilateral training programme, through which the US would assist in the improvement of African military capacity to engage in peacekeeping and humanitarian assistance provision. Some critics pointed out that ACRI's concern with peacekeeping was inadequate in a region where a focus on peacemaking was more appropriate (Omach 2000); while others argued that the real purpose of the initiative 'was . . . to modernize local armed forces and bring them into line with US norms, particularly in response to emerging terrorism in Africa' (Abramovici 2004: 686).[5] Subsequently, between July 1997 and May 2000, ACRI organised training for battalions from Senegal, Uganda, Malawi, Mali, Ghana, Benin and Ivory Coast; provided light equipment, notably for communications; and extended selective military and civilian assistance programmes to individual countries such as Mali and Senegal (Abramovici 2004: 688).

The US perception of the African continent as a potential site of terror was much heightened by the bombing of the US embassies in Kenya and Tanzania in August 1998. The Clinton administration responded with cruise missile attacks on a pharmaceutical factory in Khartoum that it contended was producing precursors for chemical weapons for al-Qaeda, which had been blamed for the bombings (Ploch 2007: appendix 1). Yet it was 9/11 that provided the impetus for a major boost to military investment in Africa, President Bush declaring that terrorists would not be allowed to threaten African peoples, or 'to use Africa as a base to threaten the world' (Abramovici 2004: 688). The outcome was transformation of ACRI into the African Contingency Operations Training and Assistance (ACOTA) programme that, while adding training for peace enforcement to that for peacekeeping, also laid stress on offensive training. This was for regular infantry units and small units modeled on special forces in particular, enhancing their capability to engage in police and counter-insurgency operations. Backed by the provision of standardised attack equipment such as assault rifles, mortars and machine guns, the emphasis had shifted from ACRI's peacekeeping orientation to ACOTA's more offensive concerns. In 2004, ACOTA became a constituent part of the Bush Administration's Global Peace Operations Initiative (GPOI) programme that, with the support of the G8, aims to train 75 000 peacekeepers, mostly in Africa. Indeed, during 2005, the US contribution to GPOI was $96.7 million, two thirds of which went to Africa (Lawson 2007). By 2007, twenty countries had received ACOTA training (Volman 2007; Ploch 2007: 19).[6] It was backed up by related activities such as the International Military Education Program, in which nearly all African countries participate (officers attend military academies in the US for professional training);[7] and the African Coastal and Border Security Program, which provides equipment to African countries to improve their ability to patrol their coastal waters and borders against terrorist operations (Volman 2007).

The more offensive orientation was most visible in the Horn and North Africa. In the former region, US Central Command (CENTCOM) established a joint task force to focus on 'detecting, disrupting and ultimately defeating transnational terrorist groups operating in the region' and provide a forward presence. The resulting Combined Joint Task Force-Horn of Africa (CJTF-HOA), based in Djibouti, is made up of around 1 500 US military (sailors, marines and special forces) and civilian personnel and covers the land and airspace of Kenya, Somalia, Sudan, Seychelles, Ethiopia, Eritrea, Djibouti and Yemen, as well as the coastal waters of the Red Sea, the Gulf of Aden and the Indian Ocean, and works closely with a multinational naval force of ships from France, Germany and other NATO allies (Volman 2007). Emphasis is placed upon the training of the region's security forces in counter-terrorism, intelligence collection and maintenance of critical maritime access, in addition to the provision of advice to peacekeeping operations and support for humanitarian assistance. The last mentioned has included an extensive effort to provide aid such as digging wells and repairing schools and hospitals as part of a strategy of winning hearts and minds and enhancing the long-term stability of the region (Ploch 2007: 17).

However, it is in North Africa where the Islamic composition of the population and culture is deemed to be the most susceptible to the appeal of al-Qaeda. This was underlined by the Department of State's launch of the Pan-Sahel Initiative (PSI) programme to increase the border security and counter-terrorism capacities of Mali, Chad, Niger and Mauritania; and its Mali seminar in September 2003 on combating terrorism in which militaries from Algeria, Chad, Mauritania, Morocco, Niger, Nigeria and Senegal took part. Subsequently, PSI was followed up by the 2005 launch of the Trans-Sahara Counter-Terrorism Initiative (TSCTI) in which US forces work with African counterparts to improve intelligence, command and control, logistics and border control, as well as executing joint operations against terrorist groups (Ploch 2007: 18). Such activities were legitimised by what critics insisted were exaggerated reports by US military intelligence about the alleged al-Qaeda threat to incumbent governments, obscuring the role of US military support in backing dictatorial governments against rebel movements and marginalised minority groups. In a region that is politically complex and fragile, the expanding US military presence was deemed by many to be increasing prospects of instability, negating the possibility of democracy and tightening the bonds of an encircling US imperialism (Keenan 2004a). Meanwhile, in Kenya the Kibaki government, whose displacement of the autocratic regime of Daniel arap Moi had been strongly backed by the US and British, introduced a Suppression of Terrorism Bill in 2003 that, in attempting to roll back freedoms supposedly guaranteed by the constitution, was construed by civil society opponents as having been introduced to follow the wishes of Washington and London (Kamau 2006).[8]

A more constructive outcome of the re-engagement with Africa was the US decision, albeit reluctant, to intervene in the civil war in Liberia in mid-2003 as rebel forces began encircling the capital, Monrovia. With Britain and France, already engaged in UN peacekeeping operations in neighbouring Sierra Leone and Ivory Coast, worrying that the intensifying Liberian conflict would further destabilise their former colonies, Bush agreed to support a Liberian ceasefire, but only if the warlord president, Charles Taylor, resigned and left the country and if ECOWAS provided an initial stabilisation force. With Nigeria's collaboration, and promises of financial and logistical support from the US, these conditions were met; and backed up by the deployment of US warships off the Liberian coast and 5 000 troops, although only 200 of them were to set foot, very briefly, on Liberian soil. The intervention marked a cautious return to direct US military involvement in peacekeeping in Africa and provided the background to the forging of a sustainable ceasefire, internationally-supervised elections in October 2005 and a UN post-conflict reconstruction programme in which the US remains the lead country.

Far more problematic has been the US engagement in Darfur, where Sudanese government-backed 'Arab' Janjaweed militia forces have since 2003 been systematically expelling 'African' farmers from their land and killing, raping and burning villages as they go.[9] Thousands have been killed and millions displaced. It is a conflict many observers regard as driven by the determination of the Sudanese government to protect its control of oil resources in the south of the country in the face of implementation of a constitutional settlement whose goal is to provide for an equitable sharing of power between the Arab north and African South. It is also a conflict that has been depicted as genocide: indeed, in response to popular awareness of the failings of US policy in Rwanda, both Houses of Congress passed a motion in July 2004 stating that genocide was taking place. Subsequently, after visiting Sudan, Secretary of State Colin Powell confirmed to the Senate Foreign Relations Committee that genocide was taking place and stated that as a contracting party to the Geneva Convention, the US would demand that the UN initiate a full investigation. However, rather than place US troops on the ground, diplomatic and financial support has been provided for the African Mission in Sudan of the African Union (AU) and its transformation into a stronger, official UN peacekeeping force. The US has thereby been able to deflect the sort of criticism it received following the genocide in Rwanda, while – significantly – its ability to avoid deeper engagement has been facilitated by the willingness of China and Russia to veto stronger UN action in the Security Council (Lawson 2007).[10]

The establishment of AFRICOM represented the culmination and consolidation of the US post-Cold War strategic approach towards Africa. It followed the report of an advisory panel of Africa experts that identified US interest in the continent over the last decade as shaped by oil, global trade, armed conflicts, terror and HIV/AIDS. The White House followed up with a national security strategy that identified Africa as high priority and declared that the route to US security lay in 'partnering with Africans to strengthen fragile and failing states and bring ungoverned areas under the control of effective democracies' (Ploch 2007: 11). The US interest was subsequently summarised for Congress as follows:

- the need to protect trade between the US and Africa, dominated in particular by the supply of energy resources from the latter, which had tripled between 1990 and 2005;
- with Africa having surpassed the Middle East as the largest supplier of crude to the US, there was a need for security. Nigeria had emerged as Africa's largest supplier of oil, and the fifth largest supplier globally, yet instability in the Delta Region had reduced output periodically by as much as 25%. Given Bush's announcement in the 2006 State of the Nation speech of his intention to replace more than 75% of US imports from the Middle East by 2025, the importance of Nigerian and other African oil supplies was enhanced accordingly;
- given the susceptibility of Africa's coastlines, particularly in the Gulf of Guinea, the Gulf of Aden and Somalia, to illegal fishing, trafficking, smuggling of drugs, people and weapons, piracy and hazardous dumping, the inability of African governments to police their waters had opened maritime commerce and off-shore oil production facilities to security threats. It was therefore in the interest of the US to improve the capability of African navies and for the US navy to increase its operations in the Gulf of Guinea in particular;
- although the number of conflicts in Africa had decreased in recent years, the continent continued to be home to the majority of UN peace operations.

Instability in Africa had therefore demanded substantial humanitarian and
defence resources from the international community and the interest of
the US lay in assisting African forces to enhance their peacekeeping
capabilities;

- Pentagon officials had identified Africa as ripe for acts of terrorism. In
  particular, ungoverned spaces and failed states were identified as potential
  havens for terrorists and as an acute risk to US national security;
- with almost 25 million HIV-positive Africans in 2006 (63% of the total
  worldwide), AIDS was the leading cause of death in Africa and, by
  implication, a threat to security. In particular, concern was expressed at
  the reportedly high rate of infection amongst African armed forces
  personnel, raising concerns about their ability to deploy when needed.
  The Bush administration therefore placed high priority on the combating
  of HIV/AIDS, committing over $15 billion through the President's
  Emergency Plan for Aids Relief (PEPFAR) (Ploch 2007: 13–15).

It was proposed that against the background of existing initiatives in Africa,
described as addressing the root causes of terrorism while providing for military
strikes to destroy terrorist targets:

> AFRICOM would not only allow the US military to better coordinate
> these operations and programs, but would also allow the [Department
> of Defense] to better coordinate with other U.S. agencies, like the
> State Department, the United States Agency for International Devel-
> opment (USAID), Department of Justice, the Central Intelligence
> Agency, the Federal Bureau of Investigations and others, as well as
> with other governments, like those of Britain and France, which are
> also providing training and assistance for African security forces
> (Ploch 2007: 16).

Although it is reported that the US wants two dozen bases in Africa by 2012 to
promote its security interests,[11] for the moment there is no intention that the new
command will have control over large military units on the ground. Rather the
reverse, for the theory is that troops will on the whole be based in the US from
where they can be deployed at short notice to wherever Washington wishes. Indeed,
as indicated by the quote above, the novel structure of the new command reflects
the fact that AFRICOM will be charged with overseeing not merely traditional

military activities, but other programmes funded by the State Department (Volman 2007). US military policy is designed to be as much about winning friends as punishing enemies.

Inevitably, the establishment of AFRICOM, which will assume command of existing programmes such as CJTF-HOA, will require increased financial and human resources. Although it was anticipated that these would be redirected from other commands, the stretching of resources by existing operations in Afghanistan and Iraq might require an overall increase in the military budget. However, according to the official logic, such problems will be eased by the fact that AFRICOM's mandate would be to build the indigenous capacity of African defence forces (Ploch 2007: 21). This found some backing in the fact that the establishment of the AU in 2002 had been accompanied by the creation of a new African security architecture. This included the projected establishment of an African Standby Force, organised around brigades located in the five African regional economic and security communities operating under a continental Peace and Security Council. Subsequently, this had provided for an extension of African peacekeeping operations, notably an important AU presence in the conflicts in Burundi, Liberia, Ivory Coast, Sudan and Somalia. Ironically, however, these have all been crucially dependent upon financial support mainly from the US and European Union (EU). One reason for the timing of AFRICOM's foundation would therefore seem to be the intention of the Bush administration to secure Congressional backing for increased financial resources to be directed to friendly African regimes, especially those with abundant oil and natural gas supplies (Volman 2007).

There is, of course, a sound argument for providing logistical support to regional peacekeeping entities such as ECOWAS and the AU and placing prime responsibility in African operations upon multinational collectivities (Barnes 2005: 243). However, despite numerous official protestations that AFRICOM is neither about US grand strategy, protecting access to African resources, or 'chasing terrorists around Africa,'[12] there is considerable resistance on the continent, even in military circles, to any expansion of the US military role. Although it is fair to say that this view is more pronounced in southern Africa, where South Africa has ruled out the possibility that SADC will host or co-operate with AFRICOM (Swart 2007: 14), there is a wider suspicion of US motives which, for the moment at least, has discouraged the US from the ambition of placing the new command's headquarters physically in Africa.[13] There is a fear that the new body will more systematically militarise US-African relations, as well as those countries in which

a US presence is located as bases will potentially lead to increased support and
sympathy for militants opposed to the US and their deemed collaborators (Swart
2007: 14). Meanwhile, there is a widespread belief in Africa, notably amongst
intellectuals, that Western military initiatives in Africa, and particularly those of
the US, are a cover for neo-colonialism (Njozi 2008).[14] This is a perspective likely
to be reinforced by neo-conservative suggestions such as that which appears to
link prospective recognition of Somaliland to the provision of intelligence to
Washington and willingness to engage in the war against terror (Pham 2008).[15] In
particular, however, the view is that American security policy in Africa is driven
by the need for oil.

Between 15 and 21 February 2008, George W. Bush undertook state visits to
Benin, Ghana, Liberia, Rwanda and Tanzania; a trip that would also have included
Kenya if that country was at the time not undergoing the disputed aftermath of
the 2007 election. Noting the consolidation of US military initiatives into
AFRICOM, Campbell (2008) declared that the motivation behind Bush's trip was
the grand design to 'control the oil resources from Africa' and that US oil
corporations wanted the military to guarantee their dominance.

As particular attention is paid to the US role in the scramble for oil by Obi in
chapter eight of this book, the treatment here is minimal. Suffice it to say that:

- there is a strong case for arguing that the securitisation and expansion of
  access to oil is a central preoccupation of US policy in Africa with key
  military alliances being forged with Nigeria, Algeria, Morocco and Mali
  and being steadily extended to emerging oil exporters such as Angola,
  Gabon, Chad and Sudan (Volman 2003);
- cost and political implications have led to an emphasis upon military
  collaboration with and training of African security forces, but the formation
  of AFRICOM suggests a preparedness to extend a direct physical and
  intelligence presence. Although the unfinished business of the US in Iraq,
  Afghanistan and Israel/Palestine has hitherto discouraged direct American
  military intervention in Africa following the Somalia debacle, the prospects
  of US military force being deployed to ensure the flow of African oil to the
  US are bound to increase (Volman 2003);
- while the war on terror is being used as justification for increased US
  involvement in both North and West Africa, there is considerable evidence
  that much of the evidence to support this contention has been fabricated
  by US intelligence. Collaborative regimes (notably that of Algeria) have
  deliberately manipulated the terrorist threat to increase military support

from the US and to clamp down on their domestic opponents; and the web of US alliances is actually tilling the soil for the growth of anti-Americanism and terrorism and increasing risk and insecurity for all Western interests whether oil and mining companies, commercial concerns or tourists. Indeed, by strengthening the domestic control of Africa's petro-elites, the securitisation of oil is not only promoting the continuation of highly unequal domestic growth patterns, but exacerbating conflicts within oil rich countries and potentially destabilising entire regions (Keenan 2004b; Obi 2005);

- finally, US military initiatives are also motivated by growing alarm at Chinese military backing for its efforts to expand its economic and political influence in Africa (Volman 2007).

Chinese Military Involvement in Africa

During his trip to Ghana in February 2008, George W. Bush sought to calm fears that the US was aiming to make Africa into a base for greater military power or a proxy battleground with China.[16] Yet observers tended to be sceptical, for Bush was speaking as a president who had recently dramatically changed the US approach to Africa, massively upgrading its national security profile with the creation of AFRICOM while simultaneously making the continent the focus of his compassionate conservatism. At the very least, it seemed to many that Bush's altered strategic approach to Africa was driven by a determination to counter China's increasingly formidable presence (LaFranchi 2008). There were, indeed, from Washington's perspective, solid grounds for concern.

The massively increasing Chinese economic presence in Africa is dealt with in chapter three of this book by Henning Melber. Suffice it to say here that, in a thrust which many have suggested is redolent of a new imperialism, China's shift from a Cold War perspective of relative benign neglect of Africa to one of active engagement appears to be based upon a 'classical pursuit of economic self-interest in the form of access to raw materials, markets and spheres of influence through investment, trade and military assistance' (Marks 2006). During the 1980s, Beijing viewed Africa as largely irrelevant to its quest for modernisation and trade relations dropped off dramatically. However, interest in Africa quickened again after the Tiananmen Square incident of June 1989 when, in the wake of intense Western criticism about Chinese offences against human rights, China scrambled to win allies and associates in the Third World. And this was a time when, in a post-Cold War world, the troubled Soviet Union was withdrawing from Africa, there was increased space for friends to be made, and many African countries were beginning to embark upon a period of economic growth. The outcome was dramatic: 'In 1999, the value of China's trade with Africa was $2 billion; by 2004, this had grown to $29.6 billion and in 2005, reached $39.7 billion,' with Chinese officials estimating that trade volumes with Africa would increase to over $100 billion per annum by around 2010 (Taylor 2006a: 3; 2006b). Much of this activity was, and is, driven by China's desire to secure access to Africa's oil and reduce its dependence upon the Middle East as a supplier. Yet China is interested in far more than oil, actively seeking resources of 'every kind: copper, bauxite, uranium, aluminium, manganese, iron ore, etc.' (Taylor 2006a: 3).

By 2005, there were some 674 Chinese companies involved in Africa, investing not only in oil extraction and export, but mines, fishing, precious woods, telecommunications, clothing and textiles, and farming; as well as playing a major role in infrastructure and construction (from hydro-electric plants to hospitals). Africa also constitutes a significant market for cheap Chinese-made goods. Furthermore, while opportunities for African students in Western educational institutions have dried up, for reasons that range from financial stringency to tightening immigration and security policies, this has been matched by concomitant growth of student flows to China. This emerging relationship is warmly embraced by most African leaders – exchange visits between African capitals and Beijing have soared dramatically – notably because it is conducted without strings. But critics see a replay of the relationship between Africa and the West: the trade of unprocessed raw materials in unequal exchange for manufactured goods, capital goods and imported technology (Marks 2007). This massively increased Chinese economic presence has been matched by its growing engagement with African countries as military and strategic partners and as markets for the sale of arms.

During the 1960s and 1970s, China viewed its role as an anti-imperialist counterweight to both the West and the Soviet Union, offering its support to African countries ignored by or overlooked by the two. It took on ambitious projects such as the TanZam railway and concentrated on striking up ideological friendships where possible with non-aligned countries such as Egypt. Yet although China consistently proclaimed its support for the African liberation struggle against imperialism and oppression, and declared the continent as ripe for revolution, Africa's economic backwardness meant that its strategic importance declined markedly during the 1980s at a time when Beijing's socialist modernisation policy was calling for massive foreign investment and technology. 'As a result, non-ideological relations with the United States, Western Europe and Japan, based on expanding trade links and cooperation, took a priority in China's foreign policy formulation' (Taylor 2006a: 2). However, as noted, this was to change following the Tiananmen Square incident and Africa hove into view as a supplier of raw materials and site for profitable investment. This was also a time when China was re-emerging as a Great Power and embarking upon a massive programme of modernisation of its armed forces.

US strategists argue that modernisation of the Chinese People's Liberation Army (PLA) accelerated from the mid-1990s in response to central leadership demands to develop military options for reincorporating what it regarded as the rebel province of Taiwan. Military expansion, from this perspective, was seen as countering third party intervention in cross-Taiwan Strait crises and preventing Taiwan securing sovereign independence or avoiding negotiation of a settlement on Beijing's terms (United States 2005). Today, China's massive military build-up is viewed as having wider regional implications in Asia, and over the longer term, global ambitions. Indeed, between 2001 and 2005 Beijing increased its annual military budget by nearly 126%. It has been building up its nuclear capacity, including developing its own nuclear-powered submarines that can fire nuclear missiles; and it has recently performed a test on an anti-satellite missile that drew massive criticism from the US and the international community. Furthermore, with 2.25 million active-duty members, it has more boots on the ground than any other country. Even so, this represents a reduction in the number of its military by 1.6 million soldiers over the last two decades, reflecting its shift towards more highly-trained, professional soldiery. China's Africa policy has assumed a long-term orientation of striking at the West's underbelly through a pragmatic, and many say unprincipled, mix of soft and hard power.

Central to this thrust, on the one hand, is China's willingness to extend aid and economic co-operation and investment to Africa without strings, apart from an insistence that its African partners downgrade any diplomatic links they may have with Taiwan and recognise Beijing's one China policy. This is in stark contrast to the present Western predilection for linking aid and some investment to good governance, human rights and anti-corruption initiatives. China uses the provision of large-scale infrastructural projects as an accompaniment to its investment strategy, while also extending debt relief, cultural ties and educational assistance to woo African elites to its side (Melber in chapter three of this book). Meanwhile, Beijing combines this with a strategy to extend military co-operation.

Within this context, China's Africa thrust tasks the PLA with 'conducting high-level and technological military cooperation and exchanges, training African military personnel,' supporting military modernisation initiatives and participating in UN peacekeeping operations and 'traditional missions such as combating terrorism, small arms smuggling, drug trafficking and transnational economic crimes' (Puska 2007). Consequently, the PLA now boasts a growing physical presence in Africa, with military to military links in at least 43 countries and between 1 200 and 5 000 troops on the ground. Overall, the relationship is structured as follows:

- in 2007 China maintained bilateral diplomatic military relations with at least 25 countries. These included the posting of military attaches to Algeria, Democratic Republic of Congo (DRC), Egypt, Ethiopia, Liberia, Libya, Morocco, Mozambique, Namibia, Nigeria, Sudan, Tunisia, Zambia and Zimbabwe. In return, eighteen African countries maintain permanent defence attaché offices in Beijing. Seven of these are directly reciprocal. The eleven remaining countries that do not have known Chinese equivalents in Africa are Burundi, Cameroon, Congo, Equatorial Guinea, Guinea-Bissau, Ivory Coast, Kenya, Mali, Niger, South Africa and Tanzania (Puska 2007);
- regular military exchanges: Chinese military leaders visited Africa over 30 times between 2001 and 2006, calling at nearly every country that recognises Beijing. Visits are supplemented by biannual bilateral security consultations (110 between 2001 and 2006) (Puska 2007);
- China is increasingly opening up its military academies, notably its National Defence University (NDU), to African as well as Latin American and Asian militaries. 'While most countries still send their very best, the chief of staff material, to Western academies, many officers reaching less senior positions such as one star and two star generals are increasingly being trained in China . . . All armies in Africa . . . have NDU graduates at the ranking of colonel and brigadier'. Increasingly, the 'dry, ideological' training of the past is being replaced with a modern curriculum backed by impressively modern facilities;[17]
- since 1990, China has increasingly participated in UN peacekeeping operations. Over the years, it has contributed troops to the UN Mission for the Referendum in Western Sahara, established in 1991 and still in existence (13 out of 195 military observers); the UN Mission in Ethiopia and Eritrea, established in 2000 to verify the Organisation of African Unity brokered ceasefire agreement (7 of 202 military observers); the UN Mission in the DRC, established in 1999 to broker the Lusaka Accord, carry out

disarmament, demobilisation, repatriation, reintegration and the facilitation of elections (218 of 16 594 soldiers and 12 of 713 military observers); the UN Mission in Liberia, established in September 2003 to support the Comprehensive Peace Agreement (565 out of 13 841 soldiers and 3 of 214 military observers); the UN Operation in Ivory Coast, established in April 2003 to facilitate the peace agreement of January 2003 (7 out of 200 military observers); and the UN Mission in the Sudan, established in March 2005 to support the implementation of the January 2005 Comprehensive Peace Agreement between the government of Sudan and the Sudan People's Liberation Movement army (446 out of 8 766 soldiers and 14 out of 599 military observers) (Puska 2007).

While the sum total of these activities is relatively modest, anxieties about China's increasing military profile in Africa centre on the overlapping relationship between Chinese military strategy and oil; Beijing's alleged disregard for human rights; and the growth and implications of its increasing arms sales.

China is reported as having sold $142 million worth of military equipment to African countries between 1955 and 1977 (Pan 2007). After a dip in the 1980s, the pace of the sales has picked up significantly with China providing 12.1% of arms sales to Africa during the period 1996–9, 13.31% from 1999 to 2002 and 15.38% during the period 2003–6. Overall from 1996 to 2006 China slipped from second to third largest supplier of arms to Africa, falling first behind Russia and later behind Germany and Russia. Although the recorded value of Chinese arms sales remained around $500 million, the value of arms sales agreements concluded by China with African countries rose from $800 to $900 million during the later periods (Grimmet 2004, tables IC and IE; 2007, tables 1C and 2E). At one level, this increase is an outcome of China's ambition to become one of the World's top arms sellers by 2020. At another, it is a product of the government's conscious use of arms sales as a foreign policy tool.

Beijing claims to be guided by three principles in its international arms sales policy. One is that exports should contribute only to the legitimate self defence needs of any recipient. The second is that sales should not damage regional or international peace and stability. The third is that China should not interfere in the domestic affairs of recipient countries (Taylor 2007b). However, review of the actual practice of Chinese policy suggests that it is in breach of the first two principles, while implementation of the third provides a convenient cover for the pursuit of Chinese state interests.

A major plank of Chinese policy is the use of arms sales to consolidate relationships with oil producing regimes while offsetting the cost of the purchase of Africa's black gold. Key examples of its arms for oil policy are provided by relations with Equatorial Guinea, Angola and Sudan.

Mutual visits between the two armies of China and Equatorial Guinea have taken place since 1970 when the two countries established diplomatic relations.[18] According to Taylor, Beijing has provided military training and dispatched Chinese specialists in heavy military equipment to a regime which has one of the worst human rights records on the continent, yet presides over a country whose oil reserves, in per capita terms, are deemed likely to exceed those of Saudi Arabia (Pan 2007; Taylor 2005).

In Angola, which accounted for half of China's oil imports from Africa in 2005 and currently exports 25% of its oil production to China, 'Beijing has secured a major stake in future oil production with a $2 billion package of lands and aid that that includes funds for Chinese companies to build railroads, schools, roads, hospitals, bridges and offices; lay a fiber-optic network; and train Angolan telecommunications workers' (Pan 2007). Although traditionally purchasing its arms from Russia, Angola ordered eight SU-27 fighter aircraft from China in 2007 and it is thought that further oil for arms deals may result in the importation of Chinese weapons systems and light arms (Chang 2007).

China takes only 1% of its total imports from Nigeria. However, as the largest oil producer in Africa, Nigeria is a target of growing Chinese interest and in 2006 the China National Offshore Oil Corporation invested $2.27 billion to acquire a 45% stake in Nigeria's offshore oilfields. This is reportedly China's largest investment in Africa so far. Meanwhile, Chinese military influence has begun to penetrate and in 2005 Nigeria spent $251 million on the purchase of twelve F-7NI and three FT-7NI fighter aircraft, probably arranged through oil exports (Chang 2007). China has also provided a fleet of patrol boats to protect oil fields in the Niger Delta against attacks by local militants, who have long protested at the rapaciousness of both federal government and oil companies draining their region of its wealth at appalling environmental, economic and social cost (Taylor 2007).

Of far greater political consequence is China's engagement with Sudan. Currently Africa's third largest oil producer, Sudan produced 500 000 barrels of oil per day in 2005 despite internal upheaval and the conflict in Darfur and has proven reserves of some 560 million barrels. Compared with Nigeria, the continent's largest producer (2.5 million barrels a day, with known reserves of between 35 and 40 billion barrels), Sudan's present ranking is modest. However, this is likely to change: the potential for both production and further discovery of oil is inhibited at present as large sections of the potentially oil-rich belt are rendered out of bounds by conflict. Nonetheless, China already absorbs around 65% of Sudan's oil exports and has positioned itself to reap further advantage by the extent of its military engagement with the regime. On the one hand, the China National Petroleum Corporation (CNPC), a state-owned company, owns the largest single share (40%) in Sudan's largest oil venture, which covers 50 000 square miles in the southern non-Muslim region of the country and which, accounting for 40% of the country's known reserves, is expected to produce 15 million tons of crude oil annually. On the other hand, this interest is shored up by major Chinese military sales of tanks, fighter planes, bombers, helicopters, machine guns and other weaponry to the Sudanese regime, whose 'armed forces have the strongest Chinese color in the region' (Chang 2007; Eisenman and Kurlantzick 2006).[19] While other countries decreased their sales in response to a UN embargo, China provided more than $55 million worth of small arms to Sudan during the period 2004–6, or 90% of the total amount imported.[20] According to both Human Rights Watch and Amnesty International, this massive infusion of Chinese weaponry has been used by the Sudanese military and armed militias supplied by the regime to launch attacks on civilians and rebels in both the south of the country and in Darfur. There are also consistent reports of military raids made from CNPC facilities, including bombing raids from CNPC airstrips, and Chinese assistance helping to keep planes and helicopters in the air. It is scarcely surprising that China has been regularly accused of ignoring international law and extending a civil war in Sudan. This has been responsible for over 300 000 deaths in Darfur and has been labelled, by the US administration amongst others, as genocide (Taylor 2005; 2007). For its part, China has responded by consistently buttressing the right of Khartoum to protect its national sovereignty and limit the extent of UN intervention, although in May 2007 it responded to widespread international criticism by agreeing to dispatch a military engineering unit to assist the overtaxed AU peacekeeping force in Darfur.[21]

Other oil-related details include China's provision in 2006 of a $50 million loan and $10 million in aid to Egypt, already a major Chinese arms importer, alongside the signing of a co-operation agreement for oil and natural gas development. Meanwhile, although an international arms embargo on Congo is still in place, its status as China's eighth largest source of oil supplies and a traditional client of Chinese weapons systems suggests that an arms for oil relationship will be in place relatively soon (Chang 2007).

Yet Chinese supply of arms has done more than buttress its access to African oil, for it has also eased the supply of other resources. Chinese weapons were traded in exchange for Liberian timber during that country's civil war and helped shore up the regime of the brutal warlord president, Charles Taylor (Taylor 2007). Chinese arms sales have also proved of major support to the beleaguered government of Robert Mugabe in Zimbabwe. Mugabe's look East policy is a consequence of Zimbabwe's divorce from the West and the regime's increasing reliance upon the military in a country whose economy has been ravaged by government mismanagement, hyper-inflation, systematised official corruption, widespread human rights offences and consistently rigged elections. China can scarcely be unaware of the ultimate fragility of the regime, yet has provided major supplies of arms including $240 million worth of twelve jet fighters and 100 military vehicles in 2004 to replace existing equipment no longer functional as a result of Western sanctions that prevented the import of spares. Meanwhile, China has also provided water cannons and other material to the regime's internal security forces, installed a radar system at Mugabe's mansion in the suburbs of Harare and provided equipment to monitor the Internet and block external broadcasts from independent news sources (Eisenman and Kurlantzick 2006; Pan 2007). Whether or not such assistance works to maintain Mugabe in power much beyond his defeat in the elections of March 2008 and subsequent militarised campaign has yet to be seen. At one level, Chinese strategy is geared to appear as a friend in a time of need. At another it is aimed at the long term, for it is doubtful that Zimbabwe has the hard cash to pay for its arms imports, which are likely to have been financed by the grant of highly favourable concessions to Chinese companies in Zimbabwe's run down mineral sector.

China's arms sales have at other times been indiscriminate, apparently guided by profit rather than strategy. In 1995, a Chinese ship carrying 152 tons of ammunition and light weapons destined for the Burundi army, dominated by the Tutsi minority, was refused permission to unload in Dar es Salaam at a time when former president Julius Nyerere was actively engaged in negotiations to secure a political settlement between the government and Hutu rebel movements and political parties. Other shipments, apparently destined for the war-torn Great Lakes region, were also halted (Taylor 2005). Similarly, despite a UN arms embargo, Chinese corporations sold around $1 billion of weapons to both Eritrea and Ethiopia during the war of 1998–2000, extending their capacity to continue the conflict. Military links with both countries have continued after the war's end, now taking the form of military training, exchange of military technologies and peacekeeping missions.

Chinese arms policy is welcomed by many regimes in Africa because of its lack of conditionality, and for strengthening their hand in relation to the West. Furthermore, while Western sales of small arms are increasingly constrained by UN embargoes and civil society monitoring and protests – and as Western arms sales strategy is increasingly geared to large-scale, integrated, high technology weapons systems – China has emerged as the country of choice for the purchase of light weapons, anti-riot equipment, infantry equipment and items of human restraint such as leg irons, which Western countries no longer produce.[22]

The drivers of Chinese arms sales appear to observers to be contradictory. On the one hand, recent increases in arms sales have been used to provide capital for the expanding defence industry after reforms in 1999 that forced the military to give up its commercial activities. On the other hand, they are used strategically to win friends and secure support for Chinese positions in international forums such as the UN. Neither motivation is doing much for China's reputation internationally as pressure upon Beijing to pay much more attention to human rights and the consequences of its arms sales begins to mount. While Chinese strategy may well win the support of particular governments in Africa and elsewhere, the fact that many of them are kleptocratic and oppressive is likely to increase concerns amongst ordinary people, the victims of the increased capacity of such regimes for oppression, about perceived Chinese imperialism. However, during an era when Chinese arms sales in Africa are guided by Beijing's scramble to extract natural resources, policy fundamentals appear unlikely to change.

The US, China and the Militarisation of Africa

This chapter has pointed to the growing military involvement of both the US and China in Africa as a result of a common aim to increase the supply of scarce and valuable natural resources from Africa at a time of massively heightened demand for oil and minerals. This has been related to the propensity of the US to respond to slippage in its global power by resorting to military action in order to control oil spigots; and to the Chinese military build up and wider challenge to US hegemony, alongside Beijing's determination to stake its claim in Africa.

Direct rivalry between the US and China in Africa has been muted. This is because the strategies and immediate objectives of the two Great Powers are different. Whereas the US has focused upon the construction of a central command, buttressed by collective regional agreements with African states in the war against terror and more local perceived threats to US interests; China has opted for multiple bilateral arrangements with a wider group of African states, backed by its strategy of increasing arms sales in exchange for oil.

A direct clash of interests between the US and China in Africa has been avoided because in the post-Cold War years the continent has constituted something of an ideological and strategic vacuum following the withdrawal of Russia as political player, although not as a supplier of weaponry. Yet an initial decline in military involvement by external powers in Africa is at present in reverse. This is not illustrated by an absolute increase in arms sales, for whereas the total value of arms transfer agreements during the 1996–9 period was $9.5 billion, it actually fell to $4.1 billion in the period 2000–3. However, this decline is principally a reflection of inevitable unevenness in the international arms market involving individual deals worth huge amounts of money. Much of this particular decrease can be ascribed to the fact that South Africa's massive arms procurement order was placed in 1998–9 (Grimmet 2004: 27).

Attention must therefore be paid to qualitative shifts in the military relations of external powers with Africa. One such aspect is current US emphasis on the extension of counter-terrorism measures in Africa. Enthusiastically backed by Britain, this is itself an extension of a growing militarisation of the Western approach to Africa that had already begun under UN and other auspices from the early 1990s. Centred on concerns about internal disorders in fragile states and regional conflicts, this saw an expansion in aid budgets increasingly related to security concerns rather than poverty reduction and development.[23] Another factor was the amorality of the international arms market, within which there continued to be massive competition between the arms companies of leading powers for sales to developing countries, whose orders during the period 1998–2005 constituted 67% of the global total (Grimmet 2007). This was not only associated with extensive corruption involving payment of bribes and commissions to developing country politicians, civil servants and go-betweens,[24] but was also in direct conflict with the spirit of aid policies. Thus while during the period 1999–2004 the Blair government was putting much political capital into attacking the causes of poverty in Africa, British arms sales to Africa almost quadrupled and reached nearly £1 billion, including hidden aspects.[25] These included, for instance, government backing of the sale in 2002 of a £28 million military air traffic control system by British Aerospace to Tanzania that critics insisted was well beyond the country's needs and its means to pay (Porteus 2007: 127).

It is within this wider context that criticisms of China's arms policies in Africa have to be located. It is not only that major Western players such as Britain and France have negated the impact of preaching good governance to African aid recipients by actively blocking or stalling investigations into allegations of corruption around arms deals;[26] but also that Western arms sales have themselves gone to a multiplicity of authoritarian and dubiously democratic regimes. Meanwhile, informed critics also argue that US counter-terrorist policy, notably in North Africa, is doing more to destabilise the countries in which it is implemented than to secure overall – let alone, American – human security (Keenan 2007).

It is argued here that if present trends continue, the continued militarisation of Africa will be the result. It is difficult to imagine that the scramble for oil between the US and other Western powers with China will not intensify. It is equally difficult to imagine, especially in the light of a projected loosening of French ties with Africa under President Nicolas Sarkozy,[27] that the US – whose arms sales to Africa are already beginning to increase off a low base[28] – will not feel disposed to fill the gap. Finally, it is also difficult to imagine that the growing US concern with China's military build up at the global level will not have marked repercussions locally. Within this context, as proposed by Le Pere (2008), it is to be hoped that Chinese willingness to open a dialogue with the US and other Western countries about African development will meet with a positive response and lead to peaceful collaboration and competition for the continent's good. Unfortunately, however, the recent history of Africa suggests that we should not hold our breath.

Notes

1. The European Command (EUCOM), based in Germany, had 42 African countries under its purview; Central Command (CENTCOM), based in Florida, covered eight countries in East Africa (including the Horn); and the Pacific Command (PACOM), based in Hawaii, was responsible for the islands of Comoros, Madagascar and Mauritius (Ploch 2007: 5).
2. Much of what follows is drawn from Ploch's report on the Africa Command, prepared for the US Congress, which provides a comprehensive official overview of US strategic interests and the role of the US military in Africa.
3. Department of Defense, *United States Security Strategy for Sub-Saharan Africa*, Aug. 1995.
4. The US provided a mere $15 million annually between 1991 and 1996 to the Monitoring Group of ECOWAS in Liberia. In contrast, Nigeria shouldered the burden and provided around $1 billion (Lawson 2007).
5. The programme coordinator of ACRI was Colonel Nestor Pino-Marina, a former US officer and Cuban exile who took part in the notorious Bay of Pigs operation in 1961 when the Kennedy administration unsuccessfully tried to overthrow the Castro regime in Cuba. He later served as a special forces officer in Vietnam and Laos and, during the

1990s, took part in clandestine operations against the Sandinistas in Nicaragua (Abramovici 2004: 687).

6. Benin, Botswana, Burkina Faso, Ethiopia, Gabon, Ghana, Ivory Coast, Kenya, Malawi, Mali, Mozambique, Namibia, Niger, Nigeria, Rwanda, Senegal, South Africa, Tanzania, Uganda and Zambia.

7. In 2006, this programme trained 14 732 African military students at a cost of $14.7 million (Volman 2007).

8. Opposition to the bill by civil society was so strident that the government eventually withdrew it. In retrospect, the incident was a first major sign of popular disillusion with the new government that civil society had worked so strongly to bring about, a precursor to the election crisis of 2007 when Kibaki clung to power despite his apparent defeat in the presidential election.

9. The conflict in Darfur is a highly complex one with deep historical roots in land rights and the short-comings of administration. Furthermore, in a region that has suffered drought and famine, it has become a struggle between pastoral and farming groups for diminishing resources. Yet, argues De Waal (2004: 721), it is only over the last two decades that it has begun to make any sense to describe the conflict as one between Arabs and Africans, a consequence in part of the attempt by the Sudanese government to construct a new Arab ideology.

10. In addition, following the resignation of Colin Powell as Secretary of State, the Bush administration was to become more ambiguous about the issue of genocide, acknowledging in 2006 that it had taken place, but reluctant to admit that it was continuing. See, for instance, the *Briefing on US Efforts in Darfur and US Efforts to Lead the UN Security Council and Work with the African Union and Other Nations on a Transition of the African Mission in Sudan to a UN Mission* by Jendayi Frazer, Assistant Secretary of State for African Affairs and Kristen Silverberg, Assistant Secretary of State for International Organisations Affairs, 3 Feb. 2006.

11. C. Moraff, AFRICOM: round one in a new Cold War? 2007. http://www.inthesetimes. com/article/3334/africom_round_one_in_a_new_cold_war.

12. A US official quoted by C. Moraff, AFRICOM: round one in a new Cold War? http://www.inthesetimes.com/article/3334/africom_round_one_in_a_new_cold_war.

13. Consultations with the governments of a number of African countries – including Morocco, Algeria, Libya, Egypt, Djibouti and Kenya – after the announcement of AFRICOM found that none of them was willing to host it. As a result, the Bush administration announced that AFRICOM would be a distributed command operating out of several countries in different regions of the continent (Volman 2007). By mid-2008, AFRICOM had been forced to scale back its plans and announce that it would remain located in Germany indefinitely (*Business Day*, 8 June 2008).

14. Njozi sees George Bush's visit to Tanzania in Feb. 2008 as related to the signing by a US oil company, Helvey International, in collaboration with South Africa's Petronet International, of a $313 million contract for the exploration of oil in Tanzania.

15. J. Peter Pham is an advisor on Africa to US Presidential Republican candidate, Senator John McCain. Noting that the authorities in Somaliland's capital, Hargeisa, had been

approached by the Canadian-owned, but Swedish-based, Lundin Petroleum AB for rights to oil and natural gas exploration, Pham argues that neither Sweden nor Canada would be much of a strategic ally in a dangerous neighbourhood; and that commercial relations with US firms would serve the country's long-term strategic as well as business relations considerably better.

16. 'That's baloney, or as we say in Texas, that's bull'. George W. Bush, cited by Loven (2008).

17. J. Horta, Defense and military education: a dimension of Chinese power, 2006. http://pinr.com/report.php?ac=viewreport&report_id+562&language_id=1.

18. Chinese Foreign Ministry, 'Equatorial Guinea'. *China.org.cn.* 10 Oct. 2006. http://china.org.cn/english/features/focac/183538.htm.

19. The equipment of the Sudanese military is almost completely Chinese, building on a relationship with China that began in 1994. In 2007, Sudan began negotiating the purchase of twelve FC-1 fighters. This followed the purchase of six F-7M fighters from China in 2006. Another two Y-8 transport aircraft are also in service. Other Chinese weapons currently in service include Type 54 122-mm howitzers, Type 59-I 130-mm cannons, Type 81 122-mm rocket guns, Type 59 57-mm air-defence guns, mortars of different calibres, eight J-6 fighters and a number of J-7 fighters (Chang 2007).

20. P. Eckert, 'U.S. report links China arms sales to Darfur carnage'. *Reuters.* 13 Mar. 2008. http;//news.yahoo.com/s/nm/20080314/wl_nm/darfur_china_report_dc.

21. E. Cody, 'Chinese to deploy soldiers to Darfur'. *Washingtonpost.com.* 9 May 2007. http://www.washingtonpost.com/wp-dyn/content/article/2007/05/08/AR20070508006.

22. T. Luard, 'Buyers line up for China's arms'. *BBC News* 16 June 2006. http://news.bbc.co.uk/2/hi/asia-pacific/5086416.stm.

23. Britain's Department for International Development increased its aid budget in Afghanistan from virtually nothing in 2001–2 to around £100 million in 2005–6; in Pakistan from £42 million to £71 million; and in Somalia from £2 million to £19 million over the same period (Porteus 2007: 130).

24. A prime instance was the 1998 arms deal concluded between South Africa and a mix of British, German and French arms companies (Crawford-Browne 2004; Feinstein 2007: 156–236).

25. Share the World's Resources, UK arms sales to Africa reach £1 billion mark [undated]. http://www.stwr.net/content/view/443/36.

26. In 2007 Tony Blair stopped an investigation by the British Serious Fraud Squad into allegations of payments of billions of pounds in bribes and kickbacks in relation to British Aerospace's multi-billion Yamamah contract with Saudi Arabia. The French government has been less than enthusiastic to assist efforts by South African prosecutors to secure evidence linking the French arms firm Thint to payments of bribes to South African politicians to secure its part in the 1998 arms deal.

27. H. Astier, 'Sarkozy's Africa policy shift'. *BBC News*, 26 Sep. 2007. http://news.bbc.co.uk/2/hi/africa/7014776.stm.

28. The value of arms transfer agreements to Africa concluded by the US doubled from $94 million in 1999–2002 to $186 million in 2003–6 (Grimmet 2007: table 1C).

References

Abramovici, P. 2004. 'United States: the new scramble for Africa'. *Review of African Political Economy* 31(102): 685–734.

Alden, C. 2000. 'From neglect to "virtual engagement": the United States and its new paradigm for Africa'. *African Affairs* 99(395): 355–71.

Barnes, S. 2005. 'Global flows: terror, oil and strategic philanthropy'. *Review of African Political Economy* 32(104–5): 235–52.

Campbell, H. 2008. 'George Bush visits Africa to promote the US Africa Command'. *Pambuzuka News*, 14 Feb. http://www.pambazuka.org/en/category/features/46103.

Chang, A. 2007. 'Chinese arms and African oil'. *Space Daily* 5 Nov. http://www.spacedaily.com/reports/Analysis_Chinese_arms_and_African_oil999html.

Crawford-Browne, T. 2004. 'The arms deal scandal'. *Review of African Political Economy* 31(100): 329–42.

De Waal, A. 2004. 'Counter-insurgency on the cheap'. *Review of African Political Economy* 31(102): 716–25.

Eisenman J. and Kurlantzick. 2006. 'China's Africa strategy'. *Current History* May: 219–24.

Feinstein, A. 2007 *After the Party: A Personal and Political Journey inside the ANC*. Johannesburg: Jonathan Ball.

Grimmet, R. 2004. *Conventional Arms Transfers to Developing Nations 1996–2003*. Washington: Congressional Research Service. 26 Aug.

——. 2007. *Conventional Arms Transfers to Developing Nations 1996–2005*. Washington: Congressional Research Service. 23 Oct.

Harvey, D. 2003. *The New Imperialism*. Oxford: Oxford University Press.

Kamau, W. 2006. 'Kenya and the war on terrorism'. *Review of African Political Economy* 33(107): 133–62.

Keenan, J. 2004a. 'Political destabilisation and "blowback" in the Sahel'. *Review of African Political Economy* 31(102): 691–8.

——. 2004b. 'Terror in the Sahara: the implications of US imperialism for North and West Africa'. *Review of African Political Economy* 31(101): 475–96.

——. 2007. 'The banana theory of terrorism: alternative truths and the collapse of the "second" (Saharan) front in the war on terror'. *Journal of Contemporary African Studies* 25(1): 31–58.

LaFranchi, H. 2008. 'Bush trip to a bastion of support – Africa'. *Christian Science Monitor* 15 Feb.

Lawson, L. 2007. 'U.S. Africa policy since the Cold War'. *Strategic Insights* 6(1) ccc.nps. www navy.mil/si/2007/Jan/lawsonJan07.asp.

Le Pere. 2008. 'The geo-strategic dimensions of the Sino-African relationship'. In: *Crouching Tiger, Hidden Dragon? China and Africa*, edited by S. Naidu and K. Ampiah. Pietermaritzburg: University of KwaZulu-Natal Press.

Loven, J. 2008. 'US not seeking military power in Africa'. *Mail@Guardianonline* 21 Feb. www.mg.co.za.

Marks, S. 2006. 'China in Africa – the new imperialism?' *Pambuzuka News* 2 Mar. http://www.pambuzuka.org/en/category/features/32432.

Njozi, H.M. 2008. 'By inviting Bush we are dishonouring ourselves'. *Pambazuka News 345* 14 Feb. http://www.pambazuka.org/.

Obi, C. 2005. 'Oil, US global security and the challenge of development in West Africa'. *CODESRIA Bulletin*, 3 & 4: 38-41.

Omach, P. 2000. 'The African crisis response initiative: domestic politics and convergence of national interests'. *African Affairs* 99(394): 73-95.

Pan. E. 2007. 'China, 2007: Africa and oil'. *Strategic Issues* 26 Jan. www.cfr.org/publication/9557/.

Pham, J. 2008. 'The U.S. and Somaliland: a road map'. *World Defense Review* 28 Feb. http://worlddefensereview.com/pham022808.shtml.

Ploch, L. 2007. *Africa Command: U.S. Strategic Interests and the Role of the US Military in Africa.* Washington: Congressional Research Service, 16 May.

Porteus, D. 2007. *Britain in Africa.* London: Zed Books.

Puska, S. 2007. 'Military backs China's Africa adventure'. *AsiaTimesonline* 8 June.

Schraeder, P. 1992. Continuity and change in US foreign policy towards Africa: comparing the Bush and Clinton administrations'. *Africa Contemporary Record* 24: A80-A97.

Swart, G. 2007. 'The role of AFRICOM: observer, enforcer or facilitator of peace?' *Conflict Trends* 4: 9-15.

Taylor, I. 2005. 'Beijing's arms and oil interests in Africa'. *China Brief* 13 Oct. http://www.jamestown.org/publications_details.php?volume_id=408&issue_id=3491&article_id=2370718.

——. 2006a. 'China's African policy in historical perspective: from neglect to dynamic interaction'. *Inside Asia* 3-4: 2-3.

——. 2006b. *China and Africa: Engagement and Compromise.* London. Routledge.

——. 2007. 'Arms sales to Africa: Beijing's reputation at risk'. *China Brief.* 21 Mar. http://www.jamestown.org/china_brief/article.php?articleid=2373306

United States. 2005. *Annual Report to Congress: The Military Power of the People's Republic of China.* Washington: Office of the Secretary of Defense.

Volman, D. 2003. 'The Bush Administration and African oil: the security implications of US energy policy'. *Review of African Political Economy* 30(98): 573-84.

——. 2007. 'US to create new regional military command for Africa: AFRICOM'. *Review of African Political Economy* 34(114): 737-44.

Weinstein, M. 2006. 'China adjusts its approach in Africa'. *Power Interest and News Research* 3 Nov. www.pinr.com/pop.php? 3 November.

Scrambling for Oil in West Africa?

Cyril I. Obi

This chapter explores the ramifications of the intensified struggle for access to the vital oil and gas resources of West and Central Africa, or the Gulf of Guinea as the area is referred to in global energy strategic terms. Its point of departure is a critical interrogation of the notion of a new scramble or oil rush; particularly in relation to post-Cold war geopolitics, energy security, and the implications of intensified extraction of hydrocarbons for medium- to long-term stability and sustainable development. This involves a discussion of the role of the various actors involved in the struggle for West Africa's oil: multinationals, national and state corporations, independent and indigenous companies, petro-elites and oil producing communities. The impression is often given that the scramble is basically a new competition between an oil import-dependent US, the European Union (EU) and Japan versus energy-hungry emergent Asia, particularly China which has since 2003 become the world's second-largest oil consumer (Alden 2005: 148; Klare and Volman 2006a: 609; Pan 2006; Pham 2006: 251). However, this analysis will demonstrate that the situation is more complex and multi-layered, with far- reaching implications for oil-rich, but poor, African states.

The chapter attempts to capture the nexus between increasing energy dependency in the advanced market economies and emerging industrial powers; a tight global oil market; and the representation of West Africa as an oil gulf, an alternative to the volatile Middle East, critical to global energy security in a post-9/11 world. It is, however, appropriate to note that the scramble for finite hydrocarbon resources is not limited to West Africa. Every drop of oil on land or at the bottom of the ocean everywhere on the planet is being sought to fire the engines of globalised capitalist production, accumulation and power.

The focus on West and Central Africa in this paper is impelled by several considerations. The first has to do with its rising profile in the global energy security calculations of the US (African Oil Policy Initiative Group 2002; Council on Foreign Relations 2006: xii, 8; Foster 2006; Ghazvinian 2007; Klare and Volman 2004: 226-31, 2006a: 609-28, 2006b: 297-309; Obi 2006a: 93-5; United States 2001; Watts 2006). The second relates to the possibility of economic growth and development of oil producing countries. The third relates to the designation of resources for global markets, transnationalisation of elites and the capacity of states to mediate the pressures on them. The last involves the theoretical leverage and agency bestowed upon oil states. Another critical consideration is the need to interrogate the assumptions of the resource curse thesis that the most recent oil boom will inevitably feed into the paradox of plenty: state corruption, violent conflict and poverty.

A logical question that flows from the above is: can 'post-adjustment West and Central African' countries currently poised to enjoy the providential dividends from rising oil prices 'trade their way out of poverty' (Schulze and Edinger 2007: 6-7)? What interests, dynamics and new opportunities are embedded in, or represented by, increased competition for oil in Africa beyond the obvious growth potential of increased oil rents? Does the new scramble offer any prospect of changing the unequal trade patterns between Africa and the world's industrial powers that has resulted in the plunder of the resources of the former over the centuries? What social contradictions are the processes of global extraction and pollution spawning in the region and how can these be resolved? It is these questions and related issues that this chapter addresses.

Framing the New Scramble in Critical Perspective

The notion of the new scramble for Africa has been attributed to an article in *The Economist* in March 2006 on China's business links with Africa (Frynas and Paulo 2007: 230; Mahtani 2008). These are represented as a threat posed to Western and US interests in Africa by growing Chinese penetration and competition for natural resources, oil, markets and strategic influence (Lyman 2005). The notion of the new scramble has also been described by Marks (2007: 4) as 'China's race for Africa,' which is 'certainly due in large part to the same causes as Europe's 19th century scramble - the need for raw materials to fuel industrialisation'.

China's quest for oil in Africa is the logical outcome of its rapid economic expansion in the past decade and its transition from an oil-exporting to an oil-importing nation from 1993. An estimated 30% of its energy demands are met by imports and as a rising global power, China perceives that a critical part of its energy security lies in increasing access to stable oil supplies around the world, including Africa. Part of the concern is to diversify away from dependence on the volatile Middle East and Asia. As the Chinese ambassador to South Africa, Liu Guijin notes: 'China is diversifying to secure its supply, and now imports energy from countries in Africa such as Angola, Nigeria and Sudan'.[1]

Chinese, and other Asian state oil companies, have in the last decade entered the highly competitive African oil sector, long the exclusive preserve of Western oil multinationals, African state corporations and independent companies. Its multi-pronged strategy for winning oil in Africa includes investing in countries in which Western companies have lost ground or have been forced to withdraw as a result of domestic pressure and the policies of their home governments. This was the case in Sudan, where the withdrawal of Chevron in 1992, followed by other Western companies such as Concorp, Arakis, Talisman and Lundin (Patey 2006: 13–32), paved the way for the China National Petroleum Corporation (CNPC) to buy a 40% share of the Greater Nile Petroleum Operating Company (GNPOC), which commenced oil exports in 1999 and is the largest oil company in the country. Sudan, Africa's third largest oil producer, exports between 50 and 60% of its oil to China and accounts for an estimated 7% of the latter's oil imports. It is reported that China 'presently imports 30% of its oil from Africa, compared to 47% from the Middle East' (Chen 2006).

Other strategies include 'financial assistance, prestige construction projects and arms sales' (Alden 2005: 148). Chinese companies have also purchased equity shares in oil fields, invested in energy and infrastructural development and acquired oil concessions across the continent. In 2005, the China National Offshore Oil Corporation (CNOOC) bought a 45% stake in a Nigerian oil-for-gas field for $2.27 billion and also purchased 35% of an oil exploration licence in the Niger Delta for $60 million.[2] The CNOOC acquisition in Nigeria was its largest in the world. This is apart from Nigeria's sale of four oil blocks (two in the Chad basin and two in the Niger Delta) to the CNPC in May 2006 following a visit by the Chinese President Hu Jintao.

China has made inroads into the oil sectors of Nigeria (Africa's largest oil producer) and Angola (its second largest producer), which account for 13% of its crude oil imports. In Angola, the China Petroleum and Chemical Corporation (Sinopec) acquired two oil blocks following a 'soft oil-backed credit facility' of $2 billion to support post-war reconstruction projects (Frynas and Paulo 2007: 239) after the International Monetary Fund (IMF) and Western creditors, citing widespread corruption and the need to keep to the path of macro-economic discipline, had turned down a similar request. Other African countries with

Chinese oil interests include Gabon, Mauritania, Niger, Equatorial Guinea, Algeria and Chad.

China's forays into Africa's oil fields have been viewed with increasing concern by Western strategic thinkers, energy analysts and policy makers. Its bid to secure stable oil supplies has increasingly come up against those of the US and other Western countries in a very tight global market. Of note, is the centrality of West and Central Africa to US national and global energy security interests. Drawing on the Report of the National Energy Policy Development Group (the Cheney report), Klare (2004) notes that 'West Africa is expected to be one of the fastest growing sources of oil and gas for the American market'. The case is underscored by the fact that the region accounts for over 10% of all US oil imports and it is projected that this will increase to 25% by 2020. Leading US policy makers and analysts have emphasised the centrality of oil from West and Central Africa to US efforts to diversify oil supplies from the volatile Middle East, respond to competition arising from a sharply rising demand for oil, and secure stable supplies of oil and gas. The reasons for this lie in the proximity of Africa to US oil markets; and the fact that most of the oil is of the light variety with low sulphur content favoured by US refineries.

In addition, more oil is being discovered and produced in the Gulf of Guinea and US oil companies have vast investments in the region that guarantee stable supplies of oil to the expanding US domestic market, American jobs and profits to shareholders. Thus, the control of West African oil is critical to American energy security and global power (Klare and Volman 2006a, 2006b; Perry 2007 23–5; Turshen 2004). US interests are locked into major oil producers such as Nigeria, Angola, Algeria and Gabon, as well as the new oil boom states Chad, Equatorial Guinea, and São Tomé and Príncipe. Since most of the oil being discovered is offshore, it is viewed in some quarters as having the added advantage of being beyond the reach of protesting oil communities on land: they are capable of disrupting the flow as has been the case in the restive oil-rich Niger Delta since the 1990s (Obi 2006a: 93–4).

Several pressure groups have been pushing the case of Africa's oil as a way of shifting from dependence on the volatile Middle East, seen as a seething hotbed of militant political Islam and anti-Americanism. Thus, the African Oil Policy Initiative Group (AOPIG) report (2002) quotes the US Assistant Secretary of State, Walter Kanstenier: 'African oil is critical to us, and it will increase and become more important as we go forward'. Beyond energy and security considerations, the relationship also provides the US with the leeway to promote neo-liberal values:

free markets, regional economic growth, good governance and democracy that would influence the region in ways that broadly favour US hegemonic interests and security.

In the light of this, US oil corporations have been at the vanguard of the new scramble for West Africa's oil, having been disadvantaged in the first oil rush of the early to mid-twentieth century, recognising the need to compete against European counterparts such as Shell, Total, BP, Statoil and ENI-Agip. The US is also particularly keen on containing the perceived threat posed by Asian national oil companies (ANOCs), particularly the Chinese companies CNPC, CNOOC and Sinopec. They are aggressively making inroads into the region to the consternation of Western strategists worried about the ramifications of the entry of the Chinese dragon into the new scramble (Zweig and Jianhai 2005).

Illustrating the deep involvement of US oil companies in Africa, Gary and Karl (2003: 12) note that 'Chevron Texaco announced in 2002 that it had invested $5 billion in the past five years in African oil and would spend $20 billion more in the next five years' while 'Exxon Mobil signified its intention to spend $15 billion in Angola in the next four years, and $25 billion across Africa in the next decade'. In addition, both companies were investing billions of dollars in Nigeria, the fifth largest exporter of oil to the United States, accounting in 2002 for 600 000 barrels per day of its imports (Valle 2004: 52). Chevron Texaco has also been involved in developing oil and gas fields in Equatorial Guinea, while Exxon Mobil cornered the São Tomé and Principe oil and gas fields (McCullum 2006; Obi 2006a: 94–5). US interest is also represented in the 1 070 kilometre Chad-Cameroon oil pipeline carrying oil from the Doba oilfields in Chad for export through the Cameroon port of Kribi. This is reportedly the 'largest single US private investment in Africa by Exxon Mobil valued at $3.7 billion' (Valle 2004: 53).

Other US oil interests include the West African Gas Pipeline Project (WAGPP) valued at $500 million, designed to transport an estimated 120 million cubic feet per day (Mmcf/d) of gas to Ghana, Benin and Togo from Nigeria's Niger Delta by 2005 over a distance of 1 033 kilometres. The WAGPP is central to plans for power generation and industrialisation along the West African coastal corridor and there are plans to extend it further, possibly as far as Senegal given the right security and economic conditions. Oil companies from the US, other Western countries, China, India, Korea and Brazil are all competing over potential oil interests in Senegal, Ghana, Ivory Coast, Togo and Cameroon.

A core consideration underpinning the US quest for stable oil supplies in West Africa is its concern for the security of US energy interests: uninterrupted supplies, safe international sea lanes for oil tanker movement, protection of oil investments and the protection of American citizens from possible terrorist attack. This brings to the fore the close connection between West African oil and the US-led global war on terror. Evidence to support such concerns has been found in the escalating violence in the Niger Delta region where the abduction of expatriate oil workers and attacks on oil pipelines by militias seeking a greater say over the distribution of oil rents for local development have disrupted the flow of oil and contributed to sharp spikes in global oil prices (Junger 2007; Marquardt 2006; Obi 2005a, 2006c, 2007b; Pearson and Thompson 2007; Ukeje 2001).

Oil is thus writ large in West Africa's place in the post-9/11 global security architecture (Lubeck, Watts and Lipschutz 2007; Obi 2005b, 2007a; Pearson and Thompson 2007). Through a series of strategic partnerships and military assistance programmes, the US has integrated African states into its global counter-terrorist agenda (Obi 2007a: 91). The US President has also inaugurated an American African Command, AFRICOM, expected to become fully operational in 2008. As the US Assistant Secretary of State for African Affairs put it, 'achieving coastal security in the Gulf of Guinea is key to America's trade and investments in Africa, to our energy security and to stem transnational threats like narcotics and arms trafficking, piracy and illegal fishing' (Sieber 2007).

The other, less obvious, dimension of the securitisation of West Africa's oil lies in the hegemonic project of promoting efficient managerial states – under the rubric of democracy and good governance – supportive of US capital and geopolitical interests in the region. This brings out in bold relief the links between the new scramble for oil and capitalist globalisation, represented by the intensified struggles for resources, markets and spheres of influence in Africa in what is gradually becoming a new East-West race.

What this underscores is the fact that China is the catalyst in the new scramble for West Africa's oil, which is clearly dominated by Western oil multinationals. Roughneen (2006) sums up Western anxiety about China's role in Africa: 'Beijing provides an alternative to the supposed consensus built around governance and development policies, giving China an unfair advantage in competing for the continent's resources'. Although some have argued that China is merely following in the footsteps of Western countries that have plundered Africa's resources over the centuries – a new imperialism – others claim that China's policies in Africa provide support – money and arms – for dictatorial and corrupt regimes in complete disregard of the norms of good governance, accountability and respect for human rights. Critics have pointed to China's aid to the Sudanese regime by purchasing its oil and providing it with arms and diplomatic support in violation of United Nations (UN) Security Council sanctions; support for Zimbabwe through investment in the energy and mining sectors and provision of arms; and aid to Angola, accused of a lack of transparency in the management of its oil revenues. This is seen as evidence of an undermining of Western interests and their efforts at development and promotion of democracy in Africa. Lyman (2005) makes the point that 'China challenges areas where US political leverage was once greatest. This is particularly true in the oil and gas sectors'. These are largely concentrated in West and Central Africa.

The challenge arises from the opportunities the new scramble for oil represents for the region. Schulze and Edinger (2007: 8) identify development assistance, trade and investment as various ways in which African states benefit from Chinese engagement. They are also of the view that it 'gives African leaders more leverage to act with increasing confidence towards Western countries due to the Chinese alternative. Second, the state of infrastructure, regarded as one of the major obstacles for business and entrepreneurial opportunities in Africa, will advance as Chinese companies increase investment in extractive and other industries.' Yet, it is clear that even if there are some short-term benefits and costs, the capacity of African states and ruling elites to exploit the opportunities, such as Chinese 'gifts', lies more in internal cohesiveness, socio-political conditions and a strategic pan-African project of socio-economic transformation.

The Scramble for Africa: Bismarck's Ghost?

The notion of the scramble for Africa has several connotations: competition, greed, partition, plunder, imperialism, domination, exoticism and Africa's subordination to an inequitable global division of labour. Its origins lay in nineteenth century European new imperialism (1880–1918) after Otto von Bismarck of Germany convened the Berlin Conference of 1884–5 'to set the broad limits of expansion by the interested powers – Britain, France, Germany, Belgium, Italy, Portugal and Spain, so they would not quarrel in Africa during the race to carve up the continent among themselves' (Davidson 1991: 284).

It represented changes in global merchant capitalism, in which commodities and the search for markets replaced the trade in human cargo from Africa. A logical outcome was the partition of Africa into fiefdoms for each European occupying power. This led to occupation, subordination and rule as Africans resisted the plunder of their resources and labour. The logic that drove the scramble was clearly shaped by global capitalist expansion beyond Europe. As it moved outwards, it shaped the world after its own image and defined Africa within the new global division of labour as a supplier of primary products for manufacturing and a market for finished products. This situation has remained largely unchanged ever since.

This places oil in the context of the scramble for Africa. It assumed increasing significance as a more viable source of energy compared with coal during and after the First World War: colonial attention then focused on the search for oil in Africa. As far back as the second decade of the twentieth century, the search for oil had commenced in Algeria, Egypt and Nigeria. In Nigeria's case, the imperial power, Britain, legislated its exclusive monopoly over oil: as far back as 1889, the colonial administration passed legislation that gave the monopoly over oil concessions to 'British or British-allied capital' (Obi 2006b: 16). Under such legislation, Shell-D'Arcy was granted an oil concession in 1938 covering the entire Nigerian mainland. Shell-BP struck oil in Oloibiri in 1956 and commenced oil exports in 1958.

During the two decades it controlled its huge oil concession, Shell-BP (later Royal Dutch Shell) identified the most promising fields and established a clear start over other Western oil companies such as Mobil, Texaco, Agip (now ENI), Esso (now Exxon) and Safrap (now Total) by the time they were allowed to join the scramble for Nigeria's oil in 1959, when its oil concession was opened up. Shell has managed to retain its position as the largest producer of oil in Nigeria, contributing almost half the country's daily output.

The same pattern replicated itself in other oil-rich colonies, where the imperial power exercised exclusive control of the fields and dominated them after independence. Thus, 'French oil companies dominated the oil industry at independence in Algeria and Gabon' (Frynas and Paulo 2007: 235) as well as the Congo-Brazzaville; while the Italians held sway in Libya before the 1969 revolution. The broad picture across the continent from the 1960s up to the 1990s showed the clear dominance of Western oil companies, often operating in partnership with African state oil corporations after the Organisation of Oil Exporting Countries (OPEC) revolution of the 1970s. Given the opaque nature of such ties, a great deal of competition and corruption was involved as each company, backed by their governments, tried to outsmart others in wringing juicy oil concessions and profits from African petro-states as demand for oil grew rapidly.

This shows that the scramble for oil in Africa was literally embedded in the scramble for Africa. While some commentators interpret the entry of China into the race for raw materials, energy and markets as the sign of a new scramble for Africa, others have asserted that it is 'a very different process' (Frynas and Paulo 2007: 233). Melber (2007: 6) argues that there is nothing new about 'the looting of Africa' (Bond 2006), noting that 'Chinese penetration only presents the ugly face of predatory capitalism. But Frynas and Paulo (2007: 233–5) aptly note that the 'key characteristics of the nineteenth century scramble are missing from the current expansion of interests in Africa. For instance, there are no clear spheres of interest or spheres of control today.' But they concede that a pattern clearly exists in relation to the scramble for Africa's oil, where US oil firms dominate the oil fields of Equatorial Guinea and São Tomé and Príncipe; and French interests dominate Gabon and Congo-Brazzaville. Also, Anglo-Dutch and US oil interests have a formidable presence in Nigeria, while China has established a firm foothold in Sudan. The fundamental issue here is to evaluate the impact of the entry of new actors from China, India, Malaysia, Korea, and Brazil on the nature of the oil trade with Africa and prospects for the continent's development.

One point often omitted from the discourse on the new scramble relates to its connections with the place of Africa in post-Cold War globalisation, particularly the transnationalisation of capital. It implies greater opening up and securing of Africa's oil reserves for transnational exploitation. Yet given the strategic importance of oil to global capitalism and the risk of demand outstripping supply in the near future, African petro-states stand to reap more revenue from the new oil boom and African elites have a greater chance of being integrated into the transnational capitalist elite. Unlike the days of the old scramble, when African states were the exclusive fiefs of foreign powers, they now have considerable leverage and agency to determine who gets their oil, even if they do not directly determine the global price or possess the sophisticated technology for oil production.

The intensified struggle for oil in Africa is not a replay of the partition of the nineteenth century, yet the continent is haunted by a ghost from the past. Its natural resources are being increasingly exploited by competing transnational actors that marginalise and impoverish people in Africa's oil producing countries.

The Resource and Oil Curse

Discourse on the oil-development nexus in Africa is often predicated on the view that oil breeds corruption, poor governance, human rights abuses and violent conflict (Billon 2001: 562; Coalition for International Justice 2006; Gary and Karl 2003; Human Rights Watch 2002; Obi 2007a; Ross 2001). This perception is clearly a spin-off of the Dutch disease and resource curse theses, a mainstream explanation for conflicts and insecurity in Africa. The latter thesis seeks explanations for the causes of violent conflict in huge natural resource endowments. Rather than brighten prospects for development, they paradoxically act as an incentive for armed groups to exploit the opportunity to loot: 'there is a growing body of evidence that resource wealth may harm a country's prospects for development' (Ross 2001: 328). This echoes the views of De Soysa (2001) that seek to draw a relationship or correlation between natural resources, greed and civil war.

The implications of this diagnosis are that even if Africa experiences an increased net inflow of oil revenue from the new boom, the oil curse and the rentier effect will conspire to ensure that it feeds into corruption and violent conflict rather than the development of society. Already the argument is being made that the windfall from oil in countries like Chad, Nigeria, Angola and Sudan has not benefited ordinary people in those countries, but rather the elite and their foreign partners. Also, with the exception of Angola, these countries are embroiled in conflict with insurgent groups. This supports the prognosis that African oil-rich countries appear to be caught in the trap of a paradox of plenty, where more oil wealth will serve to deepen the developmental crisis confronting the continent.

However, in spite of its attractions, the resource curse thesis does not capture the complex dimensions of the politics and international linkages that underpin violent conflict in resource-rich African countries. Neither does it explain why wars break out in resource-poor countries. Instead it exaggerates the role of a single factor as predisposed to violence. Deeper reflection shows that reality is more complex and that the resource curse thesis, even though seductive, could be wrong-headed.

Even when the emphasis is placed on intensified struggles over scarce resources, the fundamental questions about how such scarcities are produced and the distributive inequities that underpin them, are usually glossed over (Obi 2000). A second issue relates to the actors in the conflict. While most of the attention is placed on locals – political elites, militia groups, warlords and weak and inept bureaucracies – very little is paid to the role of external and transnational actors and the lack of transparency that shrouds the extent of their involvement in these conflicts. Such external actors include private security organisations, mercenaries, international traders and companies, arms suppliers and non-African powers pursuing strategic and economic interests.

Resource endowment may be a curse for those who lose their land, homes and oil extraction rights, but it is a blessing for external forces and their local allies that sell the oil on the world market. Oil alone cannot cause conflict. It is transformed through market, social and power relations. By the time it features in conflict, it would have entered other spheres as energy, profit and power. The fundamental questions are: who has the power over these resources and how are the benefits shared? This explains why Norway is not embroiled in resource wars, while Nigeria is confronted by insurgent militia in the Niger Delta.

The issue of whether China's involvement in the African oil rush will increase the earnings of oil-rich states, and worsen poverty, corruption, conflict and impunity, will ultimately depend on local, national and transnational factors, including the role of African states in the development project. The fundamental issue, however, is that the roots of Africa's conflict lie more in historical, social and distributive inequities; and the contradictions spawned by globally-led extraction and accumulation. The impact of China's entry into the race, for better or worse, will ultimately depend on whether African states and their governing elites use the moment for transformatory or non-transformatory ends.

The Emerging Dimensions of the Scramble for Africa's Oil

The new scramble for Africa might more appropriately be identified in new or emerging dimensions to the struggle to exploit Africa's resources and markets. One feature of this scenario is the entry of Asian industrial powers, particularly China and India, into the preserve of Western powers. Clearly linked to the most recent phase of globalisation, this has contributed to the intensification of the exploitation of the continent. But it has also altered the context of exploitation by providing African states with an alternative choice in what had become a unipolar, post-Cold War order. While the West has tried to reinforce its ties with Africa through the G8-New Partnership for African Development (NEPAD) initiative, African Growth and Opportunity Act (AGOA), Global Peace Operations Initiative (GPOI) and Economic Partnership Agreements (EPAs), there has also been a growing closeness in Sino-African relations following the establishment of the Forum on China-Africa Co-operation (FOCAC) in 2000 (He 2006: 39).

The growing profile of China in Africa reached a significant milestone in early November 2006, when 41 African heads of state were hosted by the Chinese leadership to a FOCAC summit in Beijing. According to Naidu and Corkin (2006: 4), the Chinese leadership proposed a robust development assistance package for Africa, based on 'US$3 billion in preferential loans and US$2 billion in preferential buyers credits over the next three years; the doubling of its 2006 aid assistance by 2009; initiating a China-Africa development fund that will reach US5 billion to encourage Chinese companies to invest in Africa'. Other aspects involved agricultural projects, hospitals, training programmes, scholarships and debt forgiveness.

In response to Western charges of support to autocratic regimes through use of investments and development assistance, China has responded that it is guided by its foreign relations principles: mutual respect for sovereignty and territorial integrity, mutual non-aggression, non-interference in internal affairs, equality and mutual benefit and peaceful co-existence (Roughneen 2006). In most of the discussions at FOCAC, China stressed its interest in assisting Africa in its development efforts, while 'African leaders spoke of investment in developing oilfields and copper deposits and building airports and ports. No Chinese speaker mentioned China's appetite for African oil' (Orr 2006: 6). This also makes it clear that China seeks to tap into the goodwill and support of African states as it builds up its influence globally.

An implication of Chinese policy towards Africa is that it undercuts Western policies and domination. For instance, in Sudan the exit of Western oil companies was followed by the entry of the Chinese and Indians. In Angola, the state's rejection of Western aid conditionalities paved the way for the acceptance of Chinese aid and the takeover of an oil block hitherto allocated to Total by a Chinese oil company. In other parts of Africa, Chinese companies are muscling their way into oil-rich countries by undercutting Western competition through attractive gifts of development aid and non-interference. China's entry into the lucrative Nigerian oil sector was attendant on visits by President Olusegun Obasanjo to China and a reciprocal visit by the Chinese premier, following which deals on Chinese investment and development aid in railways, agriculture and oil were sealed. China has also taken advantage of the nationalist instincts of an African elite seeking integration into the global elite on more equitable terms. But this should not subtract from the immense benefits that China is gaining from increased access to Africa's resources. It is also interesting to note that African states have not exchanged Western for Eastern domination. Instead, what we see are examples of more confident African states diversifying their external economic relations as shown by Angola's relations with Western and Chinese oil companies, and the on-going talks about a 'gas mega-deal between Russia's Gazprom and Nigeria' (Mahtani 2008).

Oil Multinationals and Asian National Oil Corporations

Western oil multinationals collectively represent some of the world's most wealthy and powerful transnational companies. According to the Forbes 2000 Global Report,[3] ExxonMobil and Shell, the world's seventh and eighth largest companies, but first and second largest oil multinational companies (OMNCs), recorded profits of $39.50 billion and $25.55 billion respectively. Other OMNCs in the top 20 companies in the world are BP, Chevron and Total. Although most global oil is theoretically controlled by the national corporations of the Middle East, the global reach and might of OMNCs is unmatched. This has been further reinforced by recent mergers that have seen the rise of super OMNCs such as ExxonMobil, Royal Dutch Shell, BP-Amoco-Arco and ChevronTexaco (Davis 2006: 3). The implication of this is that these companies with their immense wealth, global clout and the support of their home governments, have considerable leverage over the petro-states with which they do business, such as Nigeria, Angola, Algeria, Congo-Brazzaville, Equatorial Guinea, São Tomé and Príncipe and Chad. In all these places they operate mostly in partnership with state oil corporations: in Nigeria's case, the Nigerian National Petroleum Corporation (NNPC); in Angola, Sociedad Nacional de Combustveis de Angola; and in Sudan, GNPOC. They also operate in partnership with private indigenous and foreign oil firms. An important consideration is the revolving door relationship between the state and oil sectors. This enables top local OMNC executives to take government positions, or for retired government officials to assume positions on the boards of local subsidiaries of OMNCs. This trend can be illustrated by Shell in Nigeria (Rowell, Marriott and Stockman 2005).

A related point echoed in the literature suggests that the control of oil has shifted in favour of national oil corporations (NOCs). Looking at the size of oil reserves and production controlled by such NOCs as Petroleos de Venezuela, the National Iranian Oil Company, Brazil's Petrobras, Saudi Aramco, the Kuwaiti Petroleum Corporation, Algeria's Sonatrach, the Nigerian National Petroleum Corporation and the Libyan National Oil Corporation, it is possible to argue that NOCs, not OMNCs, control the world's oil.

In the context of the struggle for oil in Africa, two issues are relevant: the security threats posed by the control of oil by so-called kleptocratic petro-states or failed petro-states and their ability to play OMNCs against each other or ANOCs; or even deny access to an oil-addicted world. But ownership of oil reserves and their control by African states are not altogether synonymous. In spite of ownership by African NOCs, a lack of sophisticated technology, limited knowledge about global oil markets and the secrets of oil technology and contracting, coupled with support from the governments of OMNCs all combine to ensure that they control oil production without owning the reserves. What has changed is the increased bargaining power of petro-states to demand more in exchange for access to their oil reserves. Outside the arrangement of global power and accumulation, African petro-states only stand to earn more, which does not amount to real control. It makes the issue of the agency of petro-states a rather complicated subject, varying from one case to another depending on the nature of the state and the policies it pursues, the balance of power between social forces and quality of leadership in the country in question.

Under the regime of economic liberalisation with its emphasis on the withdrawal of state intervention from the economy, many state oil corporations in Africa opened up their oil sectors to more foreign investment and even divested from the downstream sector. This provided opportunities for OMNCs to invest or enter into partnerships with local actors. The overall global picture in the oil sector is that demand is outstripping supply and that in the face of diminishing returns on oil investments, OMNCs have to push into new frontiers and make big new oil discoveries to keep the rate of profit rising. When the factors of a post-9/11 world, increased global production and energy consumption are added, it becomes all too clear why the West will continue to see the control of oil in Africa as a top priority strategic goal for the foreseeable future.

OMNCs clearly dominate the oil sector across Africa. Although this accounts for about only 9% of world's oil reserves, it is nonetheless important given its significance to the energy security of the world's powers and the view that the continent is the least explored and may hold a lot more oil than is presently known. The entry of Chinese and Indian oil companies in the late twentieth century, and their tactics for getting a slice of the African oil pie, has led to the intensification of the African oil rush.

China operates in Africa through three companies: CNPC, CNOOC and Sinopec. According to Fee (2006), Chinese companies are 'most active in Sudan, Angola, Nigeria, Algeria and Gabon, with pre-investment talks ongoing in Chad, Libya and the Central African Republic'. All these companies are state-owned or publicly-listed companies making the transition from national to global conglomerates.

The CNPC operates in Sudan, Angola, Nigeria, Niger and Chad, while the CNOOC, which primarily operates offshore, has interests in Nigeria and Equatorial Guinea. Its attempt in 2005 to acquire Unocal Oil Company in the US as part of its global outreach policy failed as Chevron beat it to the tape. Sinopec was set up in 2000 as a publicly-listed company. According to its website, its turnover makes it the largest listed company in China. It is quoted on the Shanghai, New York and Hong Kong Stock Exchanges and according to Forbes Global 2000, it is listed 41st in the ranking of global companies with a profit of $16.53 billion. Sinopec has invested in Sudan, Angola, Gabon, Algeria, Congo-Brazzaville and Ethiopia.

Another strategic ANOC involved in the scramble for Africa's oil, is India's ONGC Videsh Limited (OVL). Other Indian oil and gas companies involved in Africa are the Indian Oil Corporation (IOC) and GAIL India Limited. According to Ramachandran (2007), 'India imports over 70% of its crude oil needs,' of which the Middle East accounts for about 65%, prompting India's focus on Africa as an alternative source of oil and gas supplies. This is in a bid to diversify its dependence away from the volatile Middle East; and gain access to more oil for trading purposes and the demands of India's rapidly industrialising economy and growing domestic consumer class (Sharma and Mahajan 2007). Quoting M.S. Srinivasan, secretary at India's Ministry of Petroleum and Natural Gas, who claimed that Africa provides 16% of India's oil needs, a figure expected to rise to 20%, Ramachandran, underscores India's keen interest in Africa's oil and gas resources. The article notes that 'India has already tried the aid-for-oil strategy in Africa', achieving success with a $6 billion investment to 'establish a refinery, power plant and railway lines in Nigeria through a joint venture company, ONGC-Mittel Energy Ltd (OMEL)'. Confirming the deal, Alike (2008) noted, 'OMEL had in the May 19, 2006 oil licensing round won Oil Prospecting License (OPL) 279 and 285 after committing to invest $6 billion in 180 000-barrels per day Greenfield refinery, a 2 000 megawatt power plant and an East-West railway line that will run from Lagos to Post Harcourt. OMEL paid a signature bonus of $50 million for OPL 285 and $75-million for OPL 279.'

The same report describes discussions between Mittal and the Nigerian government in January 2008 on a 172 000 barrel per day refinery. Apart from this, Mittel bought into Nigeria's steel mills, while Oil and Natural Gas Company (ONGC) invested $2 billion in Sudan, Nigeria, Libya, Egypt and Gabon. IOC also imports Nigerian crude. The report, however, notes that 'in its competition with China for Africa's oil, India finds itself at a disadvantage. It lacks China's deep pockets, which have proved crucial in swinging deals in Beijing's favour,' suggesting an intra-Asian race for Africa's oil. Another significant Asian player in Africa's oil scene is Japan, which was 'surpassed as the world's largest oil consumer in 2003 by China,' and is currently regarded as 'the world's fourth largest energy consumer' (Mihailescu 2005).

The Other Scramble: Oil Politics in Africa

Oil politics in Africa has several dimensions, but it is often represented as centralised control of oil revenues by a state or dominant elite to the exclusion of other marginalised groups, regions or elite factions. Oil therefore lies at the core of struggles between factions of Africa's political elites for power. This much is clear from the well-known Niger Delta crisis where the struggle by ethnic minorities for autonomy and resource control has assumed insurgent proportions with frequent attacks on oil and government interests by well-armed militias. Apart from the militias, transnational networks trading in stolen crude oil (illegal bunkering) and small arms are also involved. These networks are responsible for the loss of over 20% of Nigeria's oil production annually.

The struggles of the Movement for the Survival of Ogoni People (MOSOP) in the early 1990s have moved to more recent attacks by the Movement for the Emancipation of the Niger Delta (MEND) on Western and Chinese oil interests. A demand for redistribution of federally-controlled oil revenues has been at the heart of the quest by the oil-producing parts of Nigeria to wrest control of oil from a central government believed to be largely dominated by elites from non-oil producing parts of the country (Human Rights Watch 2005; Obi 2001, 2007a: 23–7; Omeje 2006: 141–6; Saro-Wiwa 1995; Timberg 2006; Ukiwo 2007: 590–1).

In Sudan's case, the struggle for oil, located in the central and southern parts of the country lay at the heart of one of Africa's longest civil wars between the central government and southern rebels before the signing of the Comprehensive Peace Agreement (CPA) in January 2005 with the Sudan Peoples Liberation Movement (SPLM) representing southern Sudan. The discovery of oil by Chevron after the grant of an oil concession in 1975 from the central government in Khartoum made it a target of attacks by rebels of the SPLM. A combination of this and pressure from international human rights groups and the US government forced Chevron to withdraw in 1992. Other Western oil companies followed until the Sudanese state formed a joint venture company, the GNPOC, involving the state-owned Sudan National Petroleum Corporation, CNPC, Petronas of Malaysia and ONGC of India.[4] It was the GNPOC that produced oil and commenced exports for the first time in 1999.

Since oil accounts for 70% of Sudan's export revenues, it has influenced the struggles between the Khartoum-based political elites that control the central government and other groups in the country. Although the CPA has provided for equal sharing of oil revenues, its implementation has been delayed and southern Sudan has not been able to obtain its full share.

This underscores the close connection between state and oil power and the nature of factional squabbles over oil revenues that impose a centrist logic on the control and distribution of oil rents. The result of this is both intense horizontal struggles for access to, and control of, a larger share of oil rents; and more fundamentally, vertical struggles between the marginalised and oppressed groups and the ruling oil elite. These struggles underpin the ruling class formation process mostly through strategic positioning in the distributive circuits of the politics of the petro-state often carried out through primitive accumulation activities. The premium on controlling political (and oil) power is very high, leaving virtually no incentive or space for the democratisation. This can be gleaned from politics in Nigeria, Angola, Algeria, Sudan, Chad and Equatorial Guinea (see chapter nine by Massey and May in this book).

Another dimension of the struggle over oil is the relationship between foreign oil companies and national capital in African petro-states. While in the main partnerships with OMNCs and ANOCs operate joint oil ventures and contracts that involve equity participation in national oil companies, there are also competitors and the emergence of a petro-bourgeoisie that seeks incorporation into the transnational capitalist class. This is most visible in Nigeria where the government has since 2000 embarked on liberalisation of the oil industry. Its effort at building an indigenous petro-elite can be gleaned from several policies: the decision of the NNPC to increase local content in the industry to 70% by 2007; divestment of state shares in downstream sector oil companies, sold to indigenous investors (Conoil and Oando); the reservation of a 10% quota for indigenous participation in every oil mining licence (OML) granted to foreign investors; and the more recent attempt by the Nigerian government to get Shell and ExxonMobil to make outstanding payments, valued at over $1 billion, on the production sharing contracts (PSCs) signed with the NNPC for the Bonga and Erha oilfields. There is no doubt that the leverage given to the Nigerian state by the new scramble for its oil has partly fed into a new kind of economic nationalism, driven by the quest for more profit and the political patronage calculations of the national ruling elite.

As well as asserting themselves domestically, Nigerian oil companies are also venturing outside the country. Oando, formed in 1992, acquired National Oil and Chemical Marketing plc, formerly the marketing arm of Shell, and was listed on the Johannesburg Stock Exchange in 2005. Other indigenous oil companies were allocated oil blocks in the joint development zone between Nigeria and São Tomé and Príncipe in 2005. They include Energy and Equity Resources (EER), Water Smith Petroman and South Atlantic Petroleum (later revoked and now the subject of a court case) (Oduniyi 2005). In the same manner, in May 2007, two federal government-owned refineries were sold to a consortium of indigenous companies named Bluestar Oil Services (Dangote 55%, Zenon Oil 25%, Rivers State government 15% and Transcorp 5%). It bought the Kaduna Refinery and Petrochemical Company (KPRC) for $160 million after a bid by CNPC was turned down for being too low, and the Port Harcourt Refinery for $561 million (Badejo 2007). The major equity holder in Bluestar, Dangote, has substantial interests in salt, sugar, cement and oil, particularly in EER, and together with the owner of Zenon Oil are known donors to the ruling People's Democratic Party (PDP). However, Bluestar 'after paying $721 million,' withdrew from the deal and requested a 'refund of the payment' (Ayankola 2007) when it became clear that Nigeria's newly elected president had ordered a review of the sale of the refineries.

What flows from the above is the complex architecture of the scramble for oil and its enmeshment with trans-global processes and actors. Given its place in the class struggles of a rapidly globalising world, oil is destined to be the commodity of choice for power, influence and wealth. Whether the struggle is between OMNCs, or between them and ANOCs, or between both and state and indigenous private oil capital, the contestations are framed within highly inequitable relations of production and distribution that deepen existing social contradictions within Africa and further complicate any prospect of social transformation or the democratisation of state-society relations.

Conclusion

The spirit of the old scramble for Africa continues to haunt the continent as the world's most powerful states, companies and trans-territorial actors continue to seek its resources for power, influence and domination on a global scale. Oil in West and Central Africa is one of the most highly prized strategic interests in the world today. With the collapse of the Soviet Union, US and Western strategists have identified China and, to a lesser extent, India as the next great competitors for resources and influence in Africa. China has refrained from any ideological position in its African diplomacy. Yet, it may well be that China has a long-term strategy behind its engagement, courting African states, tapping resources and markets and building friendship and trust as means of expanding its influence in Africa. Although the road from Beijing is seemingly different, it serves China's national and global interests

The question of a coherent African strategy for taking advantage of the Chinese 'moment' has preoccupied some scholars and policymakers (Naidu and Davies 2006; Taylor 2006a, 2006b). So far, the entry of the Chinese 'dragon' has elicited approval where it has increased national revenues from resource exports; or disapproval and protest where cheap Chinese products have destroyed local industry, or where Chinese investors are accused of indulging in harsh and discriminatory labour practices or policies that destroy the environment or support authoritarian governments.

There is some scepticism that resource-rich African states and their political elites may not have the capacity, or be willing to deploy their agency, to use increased revenues from the oil rush to transform their economies or societies; and are more likely to enrich themselves and their politico-economic networks and seek to entrench themselves in power. The picture that emerges is that while China appears to have its act together, Africa has yet to do so, with the West busy sizing up the Chinese threat and exploring the options for containing and neutralising it. This may be either through amicable agreement over the limits of expansion or spheres of influence in Africa – a Bismarckian ghost – or dialogue directed at making China toe the Western line. An unlikely worst case scenario involves more competition and an East-West clash over competing interests in Africa.

In the final analysis, there can be no easy answers outside a critical reading of the processes of transnational capitalist accumulation, in which oil plays a central role. The prospects for Africa as a result of the struggle for the continent's resources will ultimately depend on the ability of its states to transform themselves through a developmental ethos to act as catalysts both for social transformation and democratisation. More fundamentally there is a need for re-organisation of production in ways that lift Africa out of its marginal position in the globalised division of labour that since the days of the old scramble, has defined it as an object of domination and exploitation by outside forces.

Notes

1. IRIN News, Africa: China's great leap into the continent. 23 Mar. 2006.
2. IRIN News, Africa: China's great leap into the continent. 23 Mar. 2006.
3. Special report: the global 2000. www.forbes.com/lists/2007/18/biz_forbes2000_The-Global-2000_Rank.
4. Pinaud, C. *Oil Fact Sheet on Sudan*, 2006. www.UnderstandingSudan.org; 'ONGC to acquire oil fields in Sudan, Oman'. *Times of India* 21 Mar. 2002. http: timesodindia.india times.com/articleshow/5081744.cms.

References

African Oil Policy Initiative Group. 2002. *African Oil: A Priority for National Security and African Development*. Washington: AOPIG.

Alden, C. 2005. 'China in Africa'. *Survival* 47(3): 147–64.

Alike, E. 2008. 'FG, Mittal discuss 172 000 barrels per day refinery deal'. *Business Day* (Lagos) 5 Jan.

Ayankola, M. 2007. 'The battle for the refineries'. *Nigerian Tribune* 8 Aug.

Badejo, A. 2007. 'Dangote, Otedola buy Port Harcourt refinery for N71.8bn'. *Business Day* (Lagos) 17 May.

Billon, P. 2001. 'The political ecology of war: natural resources and armed conflicts'. *Political Geography* 20: 561–84.

Bond, P. 2006. *Looting Africa: The Economics of Exploitation*. Pietermaritzburg: University of KwaZulu-Natal Press.

Chen, S. 2006. 'China's oil safari'. *Forbes Magazine* 6 Oct.

Coalition for International Justice. 2006. *Soil and Oil: Dirty Business in Sudan*. Washington: CIJ.

Council on Foreign Relations. 2006. *More Than Humanitarianism: A Strategic US Approach Toward Africa*. New York: CFR.

Davidson, B. 1991. *Africa in History*. London: Phoenix.

Davis, J. 2006. ' "And then there were four . . .": a thumbnail history of oil industry restructuring 1971–2005'. In: *The Changing World of Oil: An Analysis of Corporate Change and Adaptation*, edited by J. Davis. Basingstoke: Ashgate.

De Soysa, D. 2001. 'Paradise is a bazaar?: greed, creed, grievance and governance'. *WIDER Discussion Paper* 42.

Fee, F. 2006. 'Asian oils in Africa: a challenge to the international community'. *Alexander's Gas and Oil Connections Company News: Africa*, 11(9).

Foster, J. 2006. 'A warning to Africa: the new US imperial grand strategy'. *Monthly Review* 58(2): 1–12.

Frynas, G. and M. Paulo. 2007. 'A new scramble for African oil?: historical, political and business perspectives'. *African Affairs* 106(423): 229–51.

Gary I. and T. Karl. 2003. *Bottom of the Barrel: Africa's Oil Boom and the Poor*. Maryland: Catholic Relief Services.

Ghazvinian, J. 2007. *Untapped: the Scramble for Africa's Oil*. Orlando: Harcourt.

He, W. 2006. 'China-Africa relations moving into an era of rapid development'. *Inside AISA* 3–4: 3–6.

Human Rights Watch. 2002. *Niger Delta: No Democratic Dividend*. New York: Human Rights Watch.

——. 2005. *Rivers and Blood: Guns, Oil and Power in Nigeria's Rivers State*. New York: Human Rights Watch.

Junger, S. 2007. 'Crude awakening'. *Observer Magazine* 15 Apr.

Klare, M. 2004. 'Bush-Cheney energy strategy: procuring the rest of the World's oil'. *Foreign Policy in Focus: PetroPolitics* Special report, January, http://www.fpif.org/papers/03petro pol/politics.html.

——. 2006a. 'The African "oil rush" and US national security'. *Third World Quarterly* 27(4): 609–28.

——. 2006b. 'America, China and the scramble for Africa's oil'. *Review of African Political Economy* 33(108): 297–309.

Klare, M and D. Volman. 2004. 'Africa's oil and American national security'. *Current History* 103 (673): 226–31.

Lubeck, P., M. Watts and R. Lipschutz. 2007. *Convergent Interests: US Energy Security and the 'Securing' of Nigeria's Democracy*. Washington: Center for International Policy.

Lyman, P. 2005. China's rising role in Africa. New York: Council on Foreign Relations, 21 July. www.cfr.org/publicationj/8436/chinas_rising_role_in_africa.html.

Marks, S. 2007. 'Introduction'. In: *African Perspectives on China in Africa*, edited by F. Manji and S. Marks. Oxford: Fahamu.

Mahtani, D. 2008, 'The new scramble for Africa's resources'. *Financial Times* 28 Jan.

Marquardt, E. 2006. 'The Niger Delta insurgency and its threat to energy security'. *Terrorism Monitor* 4(16) 10 Aug.

McCullum, H. 2006. 'Oil grab in the Gulf of Guinea'. *Africafiles* 3, Jan–May.

Melber, H. 2007. 'The (not so) new kid on the block: China and the scramble for Africa's resources'. In: *China in Africa*, compiled by H. Melber. Uppsala: Nordiska Afrikainstitutet.

Mihailescu, A. 2005. 'China, Japan vie for African oil, space war'. *Spacewar* 17 Nov.

Naidu, S and L. Corkin. 2006. 'Who was the real winner in China?' *China Monitor* (Stellenbosch) 13: 4–5.

Naidu, S and M. Davies. 2006. 'China fuels its future with Africa's riches'. *South African Journal of International Affairs* 13(2): 69–83.

Obi, C. 2000. 'Globalised images of environmental security in Africa'. *Review of African Political Economy* 27(83): 47–62.

——. 2001. 'Global, state and local intersections: power, authority and conflict in the Niger Delta oil communities'. In: *Intervention and Transnationalism in Africa: Global-Local Networks*, edited by T. Callaghy, R. Kassimir and R. Latham. Cambridge: Cambridge University Press: 173–93.

——. 2005a. 'Globalization and local resistance: the case of Shell versus the Ogoni'. In: *The Global Resistance Reader*, edited by L. Amoore. London: Routledge: 318–27.

——. 2005b. 'Oil, US global security and the challenge of development in West Africa'. *CODESRIA Bulletin* 3-4: 38-41.

——. 2006a. 'Terrorism in West Africa: real, emerging and imagined threats?' *African Security Review* 15(3): 87-101.

——. 2006b. *Youth and the Generational Dimensions to Struggles for Resource Control in the Niger Delta*, Dakar: CODESRIA.

——. 2007a. 'Oil and development in Africa: some lessons from the oil factor in Nigeria for the Sudan'. In: *Oil Development in Africa: Lessons for Sudan after the Comprehensive Peace Agreement*, edited by L. Patey. Copenhagen: Danish Institute for International Affairs.

——. 2007b. 'The struggle for resource control in a petro-state: a perspective from Nigeria'. In: *National Perspectives on Globalization*, edited by P. Bowles et al. New York: Palgrave Macmillan: 93-106.

Oduniyi, M. 2005. 'Nigeria is building a new crop of indigenous operators'. *Alexander's Gas and Oil Connections Company News: Africa* 10(14).

Omeje, K. 2006. *High Stakes and Stakeholders: Oil Conflict and Security in Nigeria*. Basingstoke: Ashgate.

Orr, T. 2006. 'Letter from China: FOCAC 2006'. *China Monitor* (Stellenbosch) 13: 5-8.

Pan, E. 2006. China, Africa and Oil. New York: Council on Foreign Relations. www.cfr.org/publication/9557/.

Patey, L. 2006. *A Complex Reality: The Strategic Behaviour of Multinational Oil Corporations and the New Wars in Sudan*. Copenhagen: Danish Institute for International Studies.

Pearson, J. and C. Thompson. 2007. 'Pentagon forming "Africom" amid threats to oil resources'. *Alexander's Gas and Oil Connections Company News: Africa* 13 July.

Perry, A. 2007. 'Africa's oil dreams'. *Time Magazine* 11 June.

Pham, J. 2006. 'China's African strategy and its implications for US interests'. *American Foreign Policy Interests* 28: 239-53.

Ramachandran, S. 2007. 'India turns its energies on Africa'. *Asia Times* 10 Nov.

Ross, M. 2001. 'Does oil hinder democracy?' *World Politics* 53: 325-61.

Roughneen, S. 2006. 'Influence anxiety: China's role in Africa'. *ISN Security Watch* http://www.isn.ethz.ch/news/sw/details_print.cfm?id=15837.

Rowell, A., J. Marriott and L. Stockman. 2005. *The Next Gulf: London, Washington and Oil Conflict in Nigeria*. London: Constable.

Saro-Wiwa, K. 1995. *A Month and a Day: A Detention Diary*. London: Penguin.

Schulze, K. and H. Edinger. 2007. 'China in Africa – can Africa trade its way out of poverty?' *China Monitor* (Stellenbosch) 14: 6-9.

Sharma, D and D. Mahajan. 2007. 'Energising ties: the politics of oil'. *South African Journal of International Affairs* 14(2): 37-52.

Sieber, O. 2007. 'Africa Command: forecast for the future'. *Strategic Insights* 6(1) http://www.ccc.nps.navy.mil/si/2007/Jan/sieberJan07.pdf.

Taylor, I. 2006a. 'China's oil diplomacy in Africa'. *International Affairs* 82(5): 937-59.

——. 2006b. 'China's African policy in historical perspective: from neglect to dynamic interaction'. *Inside Asia* 3-4.

Timberg, C. 2006. 'Militants warn China over oil in Niger Delta'. *Washington Post* 1 May. wwwwashingtonpost.com/wp-dyn/content/article/2006/04/30/AR20060430010.

Turshen, M. 2004. 'The politics of oil in Africa'. *Scholar and Feminist Online* 2.2. www.barnard.edu/sfonline/reverb/.

Ukeje, C. 2001. 'Oil communities and political violence: the case of ethnic Ijaws in Nigeria's Niger Delta'. *Terrorism and Violence* 13(4): 15–36.

Ukiwo, U. 2007. 'From "pirates" to militants: a historical perspective on anti-state and anti-oil company mobilization among the Ijaw of Warri, Western Niger Delta'. *African Affairs* 106(425): 587–610.

United States. 2001. *Report of the National Energy Policy Development Group* [Cheney Report]. Washington: US Government Printing House. http://www.whitehouse.gov/energy/National-Energy-Policy.pdf.

Valle, V. 2004. 'US policy towards the Gulf of Guinea'. In: *Oil Policy in the Gulf of Guinea: Security and Conflict, Economic Growth and Social Development*, edited by R. Traub-Merz and D. Yates. Bonn: Friedrich-Ebert-Stiftung: 51–8.

Watts, M. 2006. 'Empire of oil: capitalist dispossession and the scramble for Africa'. *Monthly Review* 58(4): 1–17.

Wenping, H. 2006. 'China-Africa relations moving into an era of rapid development'. *Inside Asia* 3 and 4: 3–6.

Zweig, D. and B. Jianhai. 2005. 'China's global hunt for energy'. *Foreign Affairs* 84(5): 25–38.

CHAPTER NINE

Oil and War in Chad

Simon Massey and Roy May

In terms of geopolitics and geo-economics, external involvement in Chad is extensive and complex, although the strategies of external actors are increasingly fluid. Perennially insecure, Chad during the early years of the twenty-first century faced a potential descent into civil war exacerbated by violent contagion from the conflict in neighbouring Darfur that has seen the explicit involvement of the Sudanese government and its proxies. Moreover, it is not entirely fanciful to read the dimensions of the conflict as not only dangerous to regional peace and security, but international as well. Arguably, the spillover from the Darfur conflict has laid the foundations for wider conflict setting Western interests, represented by French and American support for Chad's President Idriss Deby Itno against Sudanese and possibly Chinese backing for the Chadian rebels, encompassing such diverse issues as resource conflict and transnational terrorism. Crucially, while security within and beyond its borders was diminishing, Chad became Africa's newest petro-state. The project to extract oil and pipe it to the Atlantic coast for export came onstream in 2003. It is operated by an American-Malaysian consortium with the backing of the World Bank. The conspicuous involvement of non-Chadians in all aspects of this project has been remarkable to the extent that, in the words of Ghazvinian (2007: 251) 'it is hard to think of another moment in history when a sovereign country has allowed foreign players to dictate the management of its internal affairs to such a level of detail during peacetime'.

Currently the target of external powers seeking economic or strategic advantage, the territory that constitutes modern Chad was no glittering prize at the time of the original scramble. This chapter examines how Chad fits into French Africa, the gestation of social and political dysfunction during the period of largely disinterested colonial rule, and the concretisation of racial, religious and factional schisms since independence. It considers the specifics of the current conflict, the formation of the rebel groupings and their intrinsic relationship with the interconnected civil war in Darfur. Ethnic and religious rivalry and resource competition created an environment of conflict that pre-dates colonialism and endures today. However, there is evidence from non-governmental organisations (NGOs) that the onset of revenue flows from the oil project is aggravating violence in the country (Horta, Nguiffo and Djiraibe 2007). The chapter explores the development of Chad's nascent oil industry and its bearing on the various rebellions and deep insecurity in eastern Chad, as well as Deby Itno's strategy to confront the threat to his rule. Finally, the chapter investigates the motivations of the main external actors – the triumvirate of France, the US and the Peoples' Republic of China, as well as the key role played by the World Bank – analysing their links to oil and conflict in Chad.

The French Connection

France's relationship with its former colonies has been of a different quality to that of other European colonial powers in Africa. Criticised by many as archetypal neo-colonialism, successive governments have nurtured political, military, economic, commercial and cultural ties within a framework so familial that it is known ironically as *Françafrique*. Likewise, leaders and elites from francophone Africa have fashioned remarkably close friendships with their French counterparts. The election of Nicolas Sarkozy, whose manifesto promised an end to this cosy relationship, has sharpened the debate over the relationship between the metropole and Africa.

In the economic context, where does France stand in the putative scramble for resources and markets in Africa? Since their independence, France has remained close to its former colonies establishing the Communauté Financière Africaine (CFA) with its currency, the CFA franc, linked to the French franc and since 2002 to the Euro. The French treasury underwrote two central banks for West and Central Africa, the Banque des États de l'Afrique de l'Ouest (BCEAO) and the Banque des États de l'Afrique Centrale (BEAC) and retains influence in the macro-economic affairs of its former colonies. However, two measures taken in the 1990s indicated that this influence was diminishing. In 1994 the French treasury accepted the inevitable and made it clear that it was no longer prepared to prop up the economies of the fourteen members of the West and Central African franc zones and the Comoro Islands, leading to a sharp devaluation of the CFA franc. In 1998, in another significant development, the Ministry for Co-

Operation, the ministry with the strongest links to francophone Africa, was subsumed by the Ministry for Foreign Affairs. Recognising that globalisation had diminished France's influence in francophone Africa, the then Minister for Co-Operation commented that 'it is not really possible to find satisfactory criteria for distinguishing between countries requiring aid for development and countries in which cooperation based on influence should operate'.[1]

France is still an important commercial player in Africa and at least twenty middle- and large-scale enterprises including Bouygues, CFAO (Compagnie Française de l'Afrique Occidentale), Total and Bolloré operate on the continent. However, as France's monopoly of trade in francophone Africa has been challenged by competitors, and as its historical and political connections have become as much a hindrance as an advantage, French capital has become increasingly vulnerable. The long-established French companies that previously controlled more than half of the market in countries such as Gabon, Ivory Coast, Cameroon and Senegal are disinvesting. At present, apart from the oil sector, sub-Saharan Africa accounts for only 5% of France's direct foreign investment. The president of the Council of French Investors in sub-Saharan Africa argues that 'in francophone Africa, our problem is not identifying new private investors, but preventing those that are there from leaving' (Hoh and Vignaux 2006: 12). There is a conspicuous withdrawal of French companies in traditional sectors such as water and forestry in the face of increased investment from Asia. Disinvestment is also heavy in the poorer and more unstable francophone countries. Although the French giant Total remains the largest private oil company on the continent, there is increasing competition from American and Asian companies, whilst Total itself is looking to invest outside the francophone bloc with over half of its daily production coming from Nigeria and Angola. In line with disinvestment, the number of expatriates working in francophone Africa has fallen sharply. For example, the CFAO group that employed over 1 000 expatriates in the 1980s now employs just 200.

In the political and strategic sphere, disengagement has been less distinct. France maintains around 10 000 military personnel on the continent with permanent bases in Senegal, Gabon and Djibouti: 3 000 are attached to a peacekeeping mission in Ivory Coast and over 2 000 in Chad as part of an ongoing operational deployment and most recently as the backbone of a European Union (EU) humanitarian intervention (Hanson 2008). In 1994, France led a controversial mission to Rwanda during which it was accused of colluding with the perpetrators of the genocide. Three years later the Socialist-led government of Lionel Jospin embraced a policy of non-intervention based on the concept of fraternity not paternalism. Yet, Jospin's defeat by Jacques Chirac in the 2002 presidential election and the return to power of a Gaullist government saw a dilution of the non-intervention doctrine. Until his replacement after a year in office, Michel Barnier followed the non-interventionist line, but after this brief hiatus, the tenor of France's Africa policy was set by Chirac and another traditional Gaullist, Dominique de Villepin as Foreign Minister and Prime Minister. Both maintained personal ties with African leaders and opinion formers and advocated a strong unilateralist line in what they perceived as France's sphere of influence. To this end, Paris continued to support a number of Africa's despotic and kleptocratic leaders (Verschave 2003). When Faure Gnassingbé, the son of another long-serving president, Togo's Gnassingbé Eyadéma, rigged his election victory, Chirac was the first to recognise the new government. The French military response to the outbreak of civil war in Ivory Coast was robust. French soldiers from Opération Licorne continue to police a demilitarised zone between the combatants and have shown a willingness to react vigorously if threatened, destroying the Ivorian air force in response to an attack on its positions (Glazer and Smith 2006). And, as will be discussed later in this chapter, French military backing has kept Deby Itno in power in Chad.

France has dominated Chad's history for over 100 years, first as colonial power, then in a neo-colonial role as its external benefactor and protector. For France, the territory that constitutes modern Chad was divided culturally, economically and physically into Christian-animist, fertile *Tchad utile* in the south and Muslim, barren and lawless *Tchad inutile* in the north. French control of southern Chad was loosely consolidated following the defeat of the warlord and slaver Rabih Fadlallah in 1890 and in 1905 Chad was incorporated with Ubangi-Chari, Moyen-Congo and Gabon as French Equatorial Africa, administered from Brazzaville. Paris struggled to exploit or indeed control the periphery restricting itself to growing cotton in the south and using the southern population as a reservoir of unskilled labour for use in more promising African colonies. Even during these early years, France justified its involvement in Chad in strategic terms, as a base for intervention in other French colonies rather than as a self-sustaining commercial enterprise (Nolutshungu 1996: 68).

In variance with its practice in other parts of its African empire, the French administration in Fort Lamy, renamed N'Djaména in 1978, relied on indirect rule in the remote and mountainous Borkou-Ennedi-Tibesti region of the far north and only fitfully sought to exercise law and order over the unruly central areas where slave raids continued until the 1920s. In the south, the French established a system of direct administration and as a result of the cotton industry there was a degree of economic development. Nonetheless, exactions on the local farmers bred an antipathy to French rule that tied hitherto disparate kinship groups into a shared Sara identity. An enduring legacy of France's divisive policies has been a rooted assumption of cultural superiority amongst the Sara and a corresponding perception of discrimination amongst the northern ethnic groups (Bangoura 2005).

The collapse of the country into civil war in 1979 allowed Libya to test French military resolve. Although reluctant to act, President François Mitterrand under American pressure twice ordered French forces to defend the brutal dictator Hissène Habré from Libyan encroachment. In 1986, France established a permanent garrison in Chad as part of Opération Épervier and in 1987 the Chadian army with French support forced the Libyans from Chadian territory. In 1990, uncomfortable with the egregious human rights abuses of the Habré regime, France encouraged a rebellion by the Mouvement Patriotique du Salut (MPS) led by former army commander Deby Itno. The successful assault on N'Djaména, which the French garrison did nothing to prevent, was organised in Darfur and supported by Khartoum. Many of the MPS fighters were Zaghawa from the Sudanese side of the border. With Cold War proxyism in Africa no longer a priority, development assistance was increasingly tied to human rights and political reforms. At the France-Africa Summit in La Baule in 1990, Mitterrand shocked many of the attending heads of state with the forthright message that henceforth France would prioritise countries that show 'the courage to make the step toward democratization;' providing military assistance only to repel external aggression, not to sustain unpopular regimes. Many doubted France's resolution to implement this policy and the undertaking was respected more in the breach than observance both by Mitterrand and Chirac, his successor; and only superficially applied by France's autocratic allies in francophone Africa (Marchesin 1995).

Continuous Conflict

The response in Chad to the La Baule speech was the establishment by the victorious Deby Itno of a democratic transition. Although there was a retreat from the stifling and repressive dictatorship of the Habré years, the pace of change was deadening and fatally hindered by the continued primacy of factions and concomitant reliance on patronage. At independence, Chad's immense ethnic diversity – there are an estimated 127 living languages spoken within its borders

– exacerbated a pre-existing propensity toward factionalism. Furthermore, intra-group relations, especially in the combative north, were highly prone to segmentation. Prior to the coup that brought Deby Itno to power, Charlton and May (1989: 12) noted 'the apparent resilience of the politics of elite factionalism' concentrated on 'regional centres of power based on personalised rule and military force'. Despite the country's tortuous and ultimately truncated democratic transition, the concept of factional allegiance, whether within Deby Itno's Zaghawa/Bideyat governing elite, between the official opposition parties or amongst the armed politico-military factions, remains fluid and personalised.

Deby Itno's core supporters, mostly from the Zaghawa ethnic group that make up just 2% of the population, saw in him the latest in a line of victorious warlords and expected to receive reward and influence. The obligations of faction con-strained his options and prominent Zaghawa soon consolidated an impregnable hold on the majority of senior and middle-ranking positions in the Armée Nationale Tchadienne (ANT) and the governing MPS, now reconstituted as a political party. Within the Zaghawa, Deby Itno increasingly favoured his own Bideyat clan over the Kobe clan attempting to establish a Bideyat *chefferie* that provoked the sensibilities and pride of the wider Zaghawa (Marchal 2006: 476). Disaffection with his handling of the burgeoning oil portfolio and the Darfur conflict, however, eventually led to defections by core Bideyat loyalists.

The registered opposition parties are for the most part highly personalised and divide along ethnic and racial lines. Harassed by the government, they rarely present a common front and are prone to expedient *ralliements* to the regime that prove wholly ineffective. Following a serious assault by armed rebels on N'Djaména in February 2008, discussed later in the chapter, a number of leaders of the constitutional parties were seized by the secret police. Their spokesman, Ibni Oumar Saleh, has since disappeared and is presumed murdered, whilst other senior politicians fled the country on their release (Amnesty International 2008). As a result, the already limited space for constitutional politics has effectively evaporated, leaving opposition to the regime to the armed factions. Although the current threat comes from rebel groups based over the eastern border in Sudan, Deby Itno has during his tenure also faced rebellion from other parts of Chad. He has adopted flexible tactics to confront politico-military factions, alternating rapprochement with repression. Using these methods he has thwarted serious rebellions in the south and north. However, given the high profile of the rebel leaders and the tacit support of external powers including Sudan, and indirectly China, the various rebellions currently based in Darfur constitute the

most serious challenge that Deby Itno has faced. Existing disillusionment with
the president amongst many within the Zaghawa was exacerbated by the handling
of the Chadian dimension to the Darfur conflict and the controversial decision
to engineer an amendment to the 1996 Constitution to remove the two-term
limit, enabling Deby Itno to stand again for the presidency. The move provoked
a predicable outcry from the opposition, but also raised concerns from former
MPS allies and conservative Zaghawa elements in the ruling circle. Willing to
allow him to continue until the end of his original mandate in 2006, key
personalities wanted a change of policy on Darfur and the oil portfolio. They
also had their own political ambitions. Deby Itno's determination to stay in office,
coupled with rumours that he intended to establish a dynasty by ensuring the
succession of his son Brahim (since murdered in Paris as a result of criminal
activities), persuaded a number of key supporters to defect.[2]

Why did a rebellion launched in an isolated and marginalised province of
Sudan against the government in Khartoum have such a decisive effect on armed
opposition to the regime in N'Djaména? There has been rivalry between the
Arab and African populations in Darfur for centuries. Although these identifiers
have no strong ethnographic basis – and relate in essence to the relationship that
individuals and groups have to the land with pastoralists styling themselves Arab
and agrarian farmers identifying themselves as African – the distinction is
fundamental to the conflict. Competition for the best land was intensified by
increased desertification following the drought and famine of the mid-1980s.
The border is porous and African ethnicities, the Fur, Masselit and Zaghawa are
represented on both the Sudanese and Chadian sides. Harbouring a grievance
against the local Arab population favoured by the Khartoum regime, the Sudanese
Zaghawa joined the rebellion against the al-Bashir government that erupted in
June 2002.

The largest rebel group is the Sudanese Liberation Army (SLA) currently
comprising two factions. The majority of its adherents are led by Minni Arkou
Minnawi, a Zaghawa, with the rump of the SLA led by an ethnic Fur, Abdel
Wahid el-Nur. The other rebel group opposing al-Bashir is the Justice and Equality
Movement (JEM) led by Khalil Ibrahim Muhammad. JEM's origins lie in
internecine fighting within the Khartoum government between those loyal to al-
Bashir and supporters of his rival for influence, the charismatic cleric Hassan el-
Turabi. The involvement of ethnic Zaghawa in the fighting in Darfur placed
Deby Itno in an impossible position. Under pressure from many within the almost
exclusively Zaghawa leadership of the MPS and ANT to offer assistance to their

Sudanese kin, he nonetheless understood the potentially calamitous consequences of opposing his powerful neighbour. The al-Bashir government, whilst officially an ally of the N'Djaména regime, had tolerated Chadian rebels on its soil as a political lever against possible Chadian adventurism. With Deby Itno unable to prevent covert Zaghawa assistance in men and materiel across the permeable border, and with anti-Sudanese sentiments emanating from government ranks, al-Bashir concluded that his former ally was no longer dependable and Khartoum's toleration of Chadian rebel groups switched to active logistical support (De Waal 2007: 11).

Chad's propensity to factionalism and expedient alliances makes tracking the armed opposition to the regime in effect conjectural and an assessment of the current standing of the rebellions is at best a snapshot. Individual groups are liable to disband, splinter, change name, ally or indeed rally to the regime overnight. At the time of writing in early 2008, the three main factions operating out of Darfur and posing the greatest threat to Deby Itno are coalitions. At the end of November 2006, the seemingly most competent and successful politico-military faction was the Union des Forces pour la Démocratie et le Développement (UFDD), an alliance of three groups of which the most important is the Union des Forces pour le Progrès et la Démocratie (UFPD) led by Mahamat Nouri, a former pillar of the regime as Minister for Defence and Ambassador to Saudi Arabia. A Toubou like Deby Itno's predecessor, the tyrannical Hissène Habré, Nouri is charismatic, experienced, diplomatically adept and a credible challenger to Deby Itno, although he is widely disliked by much of the populace. In particular Nouri offers key external actors, France and the US a viable alternative if they decide to abandon Deby Itno. His second-in-command is Acheik Ibn Oumar, the leader of the Conseil Démocratique Révolutionnaire (CDR). As last Minister of Foreign Affairs in the Habré government, Deby Itno has used the connection to assert that the UFDD is a Trojan horse for the former dictator.

The second main group is the Rassemblement des Forces pour le Changement (RFC). Zaghawa defectors from the disbanded Republican Guard form the fighting backbone of the RFC. The driving forces behind the coalition are Deby Itno's twin nephews Tom Erdimi, Deby's head of Cabinet and co-ordinator of the Doba oil project, and his brother Timan, a former director of Cotontchad, Chad's cotton parastatal. In March 2006, using intelligence from high-ranking disaffected army officers still in Chad, it plotted to assassinate Deby Itno by shooting down his plane as he returned from a meeting in Equatorial Guinea. The conspiracy was discovered and the French garrison moved to secure the air space.

The other group comprises the remnants of the Front Uni pour la Changement (FUC) formerly led by Mahamat Nour, now regrouped as the Union des Forces pour la Démocratie et le Développement Fondamentale (UFDDF) under the leadership of Abdelwahid Aboud Makkay. The evolution of FUC reflects the extent of external involvement in Chadian politics. Based in Sudan since 1994, Nour was a long-time opponent of Deby Itno and collaborated with the notorious Janjaweed, an Arab militia led by Musa Hilal accused of ethnic cleansing against African groups in Darfur. Hilal considers the Janjaweed a legitimate counter-insurgency force authorised by the Sudanese government. Although there is evidence that the Sudanese armed forces operate in tandem with the Janjaweed, al-Bashir is careful to distance himself from atrocities committed by Hilal's fighters. A member of the small Tama ethnic group, Nour was recruited by Khartoum to enlist fellow kinsmen to fight alongside the Janjaweed. Under Nour the FUC suffered two significant defeats. In December 2005, his fighters were humiliated by the ANT at Adré on the Sudanese border. On 13 April 2006 the FUC launched a more audacious offensive on the capital making a lightning assault across the desert from Darfur and the Central African Republic (CAR) to N'Djaména. On both occasions French military assistance, notably in terms of reconnaissance, permitted the ANT to inflict serious casualties on the FUC, whilst also exposing Nour's military naïveté. The failure of the offensive, coupled with Nour's notoriously authoritarian style of leadership, saw his faction superseded by a more political group led by Makkay. Nour retired to Khartoum, but in mid-December 2006 resurfaced in Tripoli to announce that he was rallying to the regime and that his fighters would be integrated into the ANT. Reaffirming the fluidity and fragility of factional allegiance in Chad, Nour was appointed Minister of Defence, only to be precipitately dismissed in December 2007 as Deby Itno became increasingly concerned at his political ambitions given the presence in the capital of his sizeable Tama bodyguard. Having taken refuge in the Sudanese embassy in N'Djaména, Nour has since escaped and is rumoured to be in contact with his former collaborators in the Sudanese government.

The Oil Boom

Although US giant Conoco signing an agreement to explore for oil throughout the country as early as 1969, the risks involved from persistent conflict dissuaded exploration. It was not until 1988 that generous tax concessions and low royalties persuaded a consortium of international oil companies to accept a convention agreement with the Chadian government that granted exploration rights until early 2004; and a 30-year concession to develop the oilfields around Doba and transport the oil to market (Exxon/Mobil 2004). That the relationship was destined to be intrinsically inequitable was underlined by the original terms of the agreement that greatly benefited the consortium.

The ousting of Habré by Deby Itno resuscitated interest in oil exploration and renewed seismic tests in the Doba area determined the size and extent of the reserves at a workable 900 million barrels. In 1996, Chad and Cameroon agreed to a bilateral treaty that provided for the construction and operation of a pipeline between the Doba fields and the port of Kribi in Cameroon (Massey and May 2005). Overall costs were estimated at $3.7 billion, although the final bill was nearer $4.2 billion. The Chad and Cameroon governments requested financial backing from the World Bank, a request endorsed by the consortium. Although World Bank loans would be a small proportion of the cost, its support was vital to encourage private investment, as well as endorse the ethical validity of the project in the wake of other mismanaged, corrupt and environmentally disastrous oil projects in Africa. During the 30-month consultation process, numerous domestic and international environmental and human rights NGOs evoking the resource curse argued that the project would be disastrous for Chad given its political instability and managerial immaturity. The weight of criticism persuaded the French company Elf and the Anglo-Dutch company Shell to withdraw from the consortium. After five months of uncertainty, Exxon found new partners. The consortium to undertake the project would be Exxon (40%) operating as Esso Chad, the Malaysian company Petronas (35%) and Chevron (25%). In June 2000, the World Bank announced that it would support the project based on a calculation that the benefits in terms of revenue-driven poverty alleviation would outweigh potential social and environmental disadvantages. Its construction and operation would, however, be subject to an unprecedented regulatory arrangement designed to ensure transparency and accountability through sound revenue management and sensitivity to human and environmental concerns.

This framework of revenue management and environmental monitoring was hailed by its architects at the World Bank as a pioneering model for responsible private investment in Africa and the developing world (Ojameruaye undated).[3] A World Bank official stated that 'Chad has got to be different, because we're staking our reputation on it'.[4] It was mandated that the revenues would be lodged in a special oil revenue account at Citibank in London. Withdrawals would be vetted and authorised by an independent oversight committee, the Collège de Contrôle et de Surveillance de Ressources Pétrolières (CCSRP). This body comprises nine members, of which, by law, four are appointed by independent organisations representing civil society and five come from the National Assembly, the executive, the judiciary and the BEAC, thus formalising a pro-government majority. The CCSRP would ensure that 80% of revenue was allocated to key sectors of the country's poverty alleviation strategy, notably health, education, rural development, infrastructure and water management. There was also provision for 10% of the revenue to be placed in a Future Generations Fund and 5% to be spent on regeneration of the Doba region. This left just 5% to flow directly to the treasury, although the agreement did not apply to indirect revenues such as corporate income tax. The project, pipeline construction and extraction were to be subject to an intensive monitoring process following on from the publication of a nineteen-volume environmental management plan. An External Compliance Monitoring Group was commissioned to make four site visits a year to monitor the environmental performance of all involved in the project, while an International Advisory Group of 'persons of eminence' was appointed with a remit to monitor government issues and the management of public finances, as well as social and community aspects of development (Massey and May 2005).

Concern that the project would make Chad vulnerable to the so-called resource curse was voiced from non-governmental, congressional and academic circles as well as, most probably, from the World Bank's Environmental Panel of Experts whose reports to their management remain confidential. Yet, in June 2000, it was concluded that the project was a worthwhile risk and that Chad would comply with the convention agreement. Factors such as political instability, a dismal human rights record and rampant corruption, leading one international official to describe the country as 'pre-developing,' were not considered.[5] World Bank officials continued to maintain that their priority was to consider the economic sustainability of the project and not 'to make a judgment or political analysis'.[6]

It was estimated that the project would generate $2 billion for Chad over a period of 25 years. This, however, was a fraction of the overall estimated profits. Under the terms of an amended convention agreement, described as 'abusive' by the Fédération Internationale des Ligues des Droits de l'Homme (FIDH), the government had agreed that the consortium should keep all the profits from the project with only the 12.5% royalty payment accruing to Chad (Fédération Internationale des Ligues des Droits de l'Homme 2000). The Chadian government would, however, also receive corporate income tax as well as a small amount of pipeline-related income, and income from fees, duties and permits. These indirect revenue flows were not subject to the framework for revenue distribution and transparency agreed with the World Bank. After a debate lasting just three hours the overwhelming MPS majority in parliament passed the Oil Revenues Management Act (*Loi* 001) and the agreement was given legislative status.

The collapse of the Doba model was prefigured before the CCSRP began its work. In January 2001, the government admitted that part of the $25 million signing bonus paid by Chevron and Petronas had been spent on weaponry to counter a rebel offensive in the north. Although outside the agreement brokered by the World Bank, the government had publicly agreed to spend the money in conformity with the revenue plan. The Bank's Director for Chad, Robert Calderisi, announced that he was 'sobered and disappointed' by the affair and stated that it was 'an object lesson on the need for more transparency'.[7] For the first, but not the last, time Deby Itno announced that he was unrepentant: 'I am not going to let our institutions be threatened . . . I need to have peace and stability to make this project a reality'.[8] A government audit has since accepted that the bonus money had been routinely used for off-budget expenditure outside the purview of the revenue management plan.

Institutional immaturity and inefficiency meant that the oversight functions of the CCSRP were slow to be implemented. Following its quarterly visit to Chad between 17 May and 5 June 2004, the International Advisory Group (IAG), the independent body established to monitor the project, reported that 'the mechanism for transferring and mobilizing oil revenues is blocked . . . the revenues have been accumulating in London since November 2003 because the procedures for repatriating them back to Chad have not been finalised'.[9] The first transfer of $35 million eventually reached Chad on 6 July 2004.

By this time serious violent contagion from across the border and the establishment of several rebel camps in Darfur dominated the political agenda and demanded a response. Sudan threatened to topple Deby Itno either directly or by proxy. Slavish adherence to the model would mean that N'Djaména was supposed to be building schools and clinics whilst Khartoum was diverting funds for the overthrow of the government. At this point Sudan was able to outspend Chad militarily by 50 to one (Junger 2007: 76). Necessity provided the pretext for a rewriting of existing arrangements with the World Bank and consortium. In December 2005, Deby Itno unilaterally abrogated *Loi* 001 and scrapped the Future Generations Fund. This decreased the amount to be spent on priority sectors to 70% and increased the amount of revenue going directly to the government to 30%, while including state security and administration as priority poverty reduction sectors and allowing more arms spending. In response, the World

Bank suspended disbursement of $124 million in loans to Chad and froze the country's $125 million assets in the Citibank account. Deby Itno, however, recognised that with the oil flowing and the pipeline constructed, World Bank President Paul Wolfowitz had little or no leverage. When in early April 2006 Chad threatened to stop pumping oil if the World Bank did not release its funds, Wolfowitz was forced to climb down. An interim agreement was reached, franking the government's reworking of the agreement to increase its share of direct revenue and reformulating security as a priority sector. The World Bank reinstated its loans to Chad and released one third of the funds in the frozen account over each of the next three months. These new provisions were endorsed by a memorandum of understanding (MOU) between the government and the World Bank in July 2006. It accepts that as a result of off-budget spending, the figures for revenue expenditure are unreliable. However, figures, revenues and allocations given by the Ministries of Petroleum and Finance, Citibank and Esso Chad indicate a sharp transfer of funds from development to the general budget.[10]

Having ensured much greater access to and control of profits, Deby Itno manoeuvred to maximise the amount of indirect revenue. On 26 August 2006, he ordered Chevron and Petronas to cease operation and leave Chad within 24 hours for alleged non-payment of income taxes. The two firms claimed that the new agreement negotiated when they replaced Elf and Shell authorised them to use a special depreciation schedule allowing greater tax deductions than those afforded Exxon Mobil. However, the government claimed that agreement to be invalid because it was negotiated by officials without proper authority and was not vetted by the National Assembly. At the same time it was announced that a new state-owned company, the Société des Hydrocarbures du Tchad (SHT), would be established to take a majority stake in the current project and any future extraction projects. To date, there has been no negotiation with Esso Chad, the only company actually producing oil in Chad, and it is assumed that the new company was intended to intimidate Petronas and Chevron with the threat that their assets might be seized and transferred to the state or companies from China, with which Chad had recently established diplomatic relations. Deby Itno's strategy was once more successful and the two companies agreed to pay a total of $289 million in back taxes for 2005-6.[11]

Deby Itno is a skilful politician as is evident from his longevity in power. His handling of the oil portfolio has been deft. Even so, that the World Bank was unable to foresee the Chad government reneging on its agreement seems remarkable. Donald Norland, former US Ambassador to Chad and a supporter of the agreement, recognised its extraordinary nature while still commending it: 'The agreement is historic in one major respect. It's an infringement on the sovereignty of a newly independent African country. Can you imagine, yourself, having a major account in the bank but being unable to get at that money? Someone else has to give you permission to get at your own money'.[12]

In the case of Idriss Deby the answer to this rhetorical question was, predictably, no. With the oil flowing, he could negotiate from a position of strength. The issue of sovereignty, downplayed during the original negotiations, was shuffled to the top of the agenda. Following the unilateral rewriting of the agreement, the Minister of State, Adoum Younousmi, admitting that the government was spending a lot on arms, argued that 'like all states [Chad] must buy arms to defend the integrity and sovereignty of its territory'.[13] As the authors have argued elsewhere, a culture of transparency over compliance exists within the World Bank (Massey and May 2005). This has resulted in the most transparent extractive project in the developing world, yet it is correspondingly the least responsive to criticism. Successive reports by the External Compliance Monitoring Group (ECMG) and the IAG have been ignored by the Chad government and the consortium, while the World Bank marginalises or overrules its own reports. In December 2006, the World Bank produced an implementation completion report (ICR) for the Chad-Cameroon project that judged its outcome, the borrower's performance and the bank's performance all as satisfactory, despite rating the project's sustainability as unlikely and its institutional development impact as modest.[14]

As might be expected, the consortium approached the project as a commercial risk. It put in place appropriate machinery to deflect the expected broad criticism of the project that was in line with the climate of disquiet over the record of extractive industries in the developing world. That the World Bank supported the project obviated a proportion of the criticism that the consortium would otherwise have shouldered alone. The level of adverse publicity that surrounded the project during the years of planning apparently convinced Shell and Elf, both of which are or were mired in allegations of corruption and environmental degradation in Africa, to withdraw. At present the debate over the environmental and social validity of the project is in stasis, degenerating into a round of reports and meetings in which the environmental lobby trade allegations and counter-allegations with the consortium's articulate public affairs team. While the specific events that led to the confrontation between Deby Itno and Chevron and Petronas were not predictable, there was clearly potential for such a situation. This is why companies the size of Chevron and Petronas have crisis management teams and contingency funds.

The remnants of the Doba model were dealt a further blow in the wake of the February assault. Under emergency powers, Deby signed decrees nullifying the 2006 MOU and placed the revenues directly under his control, prompting an independent oil analyst to comment that 'the situation is critical . . . the World Bank can do nothing, their role has become almost nil in Chad'.[15] As in 2006, the government was candid that its intention was to divert revenue to buy arms.

Has the onset of oil revenues aggravated violence? Deby Itno needed to act to save his skin. Throughout 2006 the ANT was under increasing pressure, losing control of a number of towns in the east, suffering an attack on the capital and reliant on French military support to resist the rebels. Increased revenue and the freedom to spend it on weaponry reversed that position. Official figures from Esso Chad indicate that to the end of 2006 the project had brought in $1 289 million in income made up of the royalty payments, but also corporate income tax, fees, permits and duties (Esso Chad 2007).[16] According to one unnamed analyst, Deby Itno is now 'swimming in oil money . . . he can basically do what he likes.' New assault helicopters have been purchased, an invaluable resource against an enemy whose sole transport across the desert consists of converted all-terrain vehicles. Oil money has also allowed for an increase in wages for the armed forces, as well as improved living conditions. This has been at the expense of the priority sectors that the revenue was intended to underwrite. Deby Itno has once more proved his reputation for resilience. As one commentator remarked, 'before April [2007] he was Deby couchant; now he has become Deby rampant'.[17]

The World Bank's ICR recognises that 'the tension is likely aggravated by the new petroleum resources, which have raised the stakes associated with power, and by the paucity of tangible results associated with oil revenues to date' (World Bank 2006). The legitimacy of government transfer of oil wealth for weapons procurement aside, it is debatable whether militarisation in the east will prolong and amplify or shorten the conflict. However, the effects of the oil boom on the Doba region itself have attracted little attention. Muslim-on-Muslim antagonism in the east has obscured the religious intolerance still extant in the south. A legacy of the French colonial administration's division of the country into the useful south and useless north is a fundamental distrust between the mostly Christian or animist southerners and the mostly Muslim northerners.

Deby Itno and a majority of ministers and officials are Muslim. Pressure for jobs in the oil sector is forcing the populations together and potentially recreating the climate for a renewal of civil war. On 30 October 2004 serious unrest broke out in the town of Bébedja, the constituency of the southern federalist politician Ngarlejy Yorongar, who has since fled the country, in the heart of the Doba oil fields. A seemingly insignificant quarrel between a northerner and a local trader escalated into a gun and machete fight in which twelve people were killed and sixteen injured. The local community took up arms against the northerners, seen as interlopers. Yorongar put the death toll much higher and claimed that this confrontation was only the latest in the conflict between the two communities, commenting that 'this is what happens because of the difficulty of cohabitation between the indigenous population who are Christian farmers and the Muslim herdsmen'.[18] The extent of ill feeling in the south can gauged by the regular reports of the IAG that address the complaints of the local population, detailing environmental degradation, heavy-handed policing and irresponsive government and consortium officials.

The Scramble for Chad

Although the World Bank and the consortium continue to argue otherwise, the Doba model has unravelled and 'turned into yet another farrago of embarrassing headlines from a dusty corner of Africa where white men had found oil' (Ghazvinian 2007: 272). What does the ease with which the government was allowed to renege on its agreements say about the will and capacity of external actors to demand compliance; and about the overriding lure of oil?

Although oil lies at the heart of external involvement in Chad, France remains a partial exception. As discussed, France's economic self-interest in Chad has declined since independence. That said, the French export credit agency Coface underwrites $200 million of capital investment in the oil project and diverse French companies are still significant investors in cotton, sugar, electricity, water, construction, transportation and other small industries. France is the country's main source of imports; but at 0.4% of total exports, mainly oil, trails a long way behind the US (33.4%), China (10.6%) and even Portugal (2.1%) and South Korea (1.2%) in terms of destination (Economist Intelligence Unit 2006: 5). However, it is for strategic reasons, shared history and prestige as much as economic rationale that France maintains a close relationship with its former colony. Although it is not officially an overseas base, Paris maintains three military garrisons in Chad involving 1 100 troops with airlift capacity, as well as a squadron of Mirage fighters as part of Opération Épervier, deployed since 1986 to contain Libyan expansionism. Chad's location gives France a strategic hub from which to pursue its geo-strategic interests in Central Africa and the ability to use force and patrol the sub-region. However, critics of *Françafrique* are quick to point out the number of times that Paris has come to Deby Itno's aid since France's external intelligence agency helped bring him to power in 1990.

Following the period of strained relations between the two countries during the cohabitation between the French presidency and its socialist government, Chirac unequivocally positioned France's Africa policy in the traditional Gaullist mould of support for the 'big man'. Chirac offered solid support to Deby Itno, underlined when he became the first French president to visit N'Djaména. France has repeatedly claimed that it now adheres to non-intervention in Africa. To explain the relationship between its garrison and the Chadian armed forces, Paris invokes the defence pact between the two countries, suggesting that France offers logistical assistance to Chad, but would not use its offensive capacity to prop up the regime. This is 'diplomatic persiflage' (Massey and May 2006). The French military remains at the heart of Chad's political entanglements and its artillery, armour and air power, in particular, have saved Deby Itno at least three times between 2006 and 2008. A French diplomat with responsibility for Chad describes him as 'a natural ally' and the only guarantee against the Somali-isation of the country and a possible domino effect that would see other French allies, such as François Bozizé in the CAR, forced from power.[19] A former Chadian President, Goukouni Weddeye, is yet more candid, stating that Deby Itno came to power with the support of Paris for economic and geo-strategic reasons and remains, for the same reasons, 'France's man'.[20] Visiting N'Djaména in November 2006, former French Prime Minister Dominique de Villepin acknowledged that France had a 'specific responsibility' to provide 'a framework of dissuasion and support' to defeat the rebels (Louet and Miarom 2006).[21]

During his campaign for the presidency, Nicolas Sarkozy frequently signalled his intention to reorientate France's Africa policy radically. On a visit to Benin in May 2006 he criticised the *Françafrique* policy, denouncing personal ties.

> We have to build a new relationship; cleaner, uncomplicated, balanced, and cleaned of the errors from the past . . . turn the page of complaisance, secrets and ambiguity . . . We have to clean our relationship from networks from another time, from officious emissaries who only have the mandate that they invent. Relationships between modern states should not only depend on the personal links between heads of state.[22]

Does the evidence of his first months in office suggest change or continuity? The two strands of Sarkozy's Africa policy are counterpoised. On one side, and appealing to France's sizeable xenophobic constituency, he has emphasised the immigration dimension, establishing a powerful Ministry of Immigration, Integration, National Identity and Co-Development under the leadership of his close ally Brice Hortefeux with a mandate to stem the flow of illegal and unskilled migration from Africa. On the other side, to offset the perception of chauvinism, he has appointed the founder of Médecins sans Frontières and veteran proponent of the right to intervene, Bernard Kouchner, as Minister of Foreign Affairs. As a priority, Kouchner lobbied Deby Itno to accept an EU humanitarian intervention force with a mandate to secure the east of the country for the delivery of aid, a request to which Deby Itno acceded in July 2007. Highly contentious given the ramifications for the EU's nascent security and defence policy, the deployment of the proposed 3 700 EUFOR troops intended for November 2007 was delayed by problems acquiring soldiers and equipment. Eventually, Ireland offered to supply a battalion and the force commander. Other contingents were drawn from fourteen EU member states notably Poland, Sweden and Austria, although France supplied over half of the force. A shortfall in helicopters, essential given the terrain, was overcome following the offer of eight aircraft and crew by Russia.

The force began deploying in late December 2007. In early February 2008, however, a fresh assault by Chadian rebels based in Darfur put a halt to the operation. Following the FUC's abortive attack on the capital in 2006, and with Nour temporarily rallied to the regime, the other rebel groups reassessed their strategy. In December 2007, the UFDD, the RFC and the UFDDF announced the formation of the *Resistance nationale*, an alliance rather than a merger steered by an executive committee comprising the leaders of the three movements. At the end of January 2008, the new alliance mobilised, advancing on N'Djaména in a column of between 200 and 300 technical vehicles from the east (United Nations Security Council 2008).[23] Avoiding main towns and engagement with the ANT until 50 kilometres from their target, the rebels entered the capital on the night of the 1–2 February and fierce fighting ensued. At one point, the French ambassador reportedly offered to extricate Deby Itno, but the offer was refused. Government forces eventually repulsed the attack on 4 February with the vital support of JEM forces and ANT reinforcements from the Economic and Monetary Community of Central Africa (CEMAC) mission in CAR. French support for Deby Itno seemingly wavered and real-time intelligence of the kind supplied in 2006 was not forthcoming until the rebels were almost in the capital. However,

at some point on 3 February Sarkozy took the decision to intervene to defend the
Chad government. According to Chad, French support was restricted to the
logistical movement of troops and materiel (at the height of the battle French
aircraft flew replacement tank shells into N'Djaména from Libya) and the supply
of intelligence. However, the French garrison also crucially held the airport and,
despite denials from Paris, there were reports in the press of French special forces
intervening directly on the ground.[24] Following the French intervention, *Resistance
nationale* forces withdrew back to Darfur via Mongo and Am Timan and the ANT
consolidated its control of the capital. That the regime anticipates further assaults
is evidenced by the building of a wide ditch around the city and the felling of
N'Djaména's trees behind which rebel troops had taken shelter.

The decision to save Deby Itno lends credence to the doubts expressed by
commentators from Africa and beyond that Sarkozy would bring radical change
to France's policy in Chad and Africa in general. As Touati (2007) points out, 'to
maintain its status as a world power, France cannot accept volatility in its area of
influence, therefore the need to retain stability in some regions has led to a
tolerance, and even support, of dictatorships and their leaders'. A controversial
speech outlining his Africa policy delivered in Dakar, given in the presence of
Gabon's autocratic President Omar Bongo, was met with indignation by many
African intellectuals. Presumably intended to reflect Sarkozy's candour, in some
passages the speech seemingly placed blame for Africa's under-development on
primitivism, alluding to the African peasantry and the 'eternal renewal of time,'
while other passages looked back with nostalgia to the colonial era. Achille
Mbembe (2007) detected in the speech a 'continuity in the running of *Françafrique*'
and predicted satisfaction amongst the numerous authoritarian presidents that
France counts as allies. To this end, Vines (2007) predicts that Sarkozy 'will develop
a policy on Chad that goes beyond supporting President Idriss Deby simply for
being the least bad option'. While France's reaction to the February attack
seemingly corroborates this analysis, a number of factors distinguish the Chadian
case. Sarkozy is well aware of the potential for further violent contagion from the
Darfur conflict and its likely destabilising effect on the wider region. France has
accepted the role of the West's point man to prevent the conflict spreading. In
particular, the amount of diplomatic capital that Sarkozy and Kouchner have
expended on EUFOR provided a powerful incentive to intervene. Yet, at the same
time, France's involvement in pushing back the rebel assault has placed the
European initiative in an invidious position. Despite the EUFOR commander on
the ground, a French general, declaring the force to be wholly neutral, France's

status as a pro-government belligerent in the insurrection fatally undermines the force's supposed neutrality with the rebels threatening to treat EUFOR personnel of whatever nationality as enemy combatants.

American interest in Chad currently rests on three main concerns: oil, terrorism and the conflict in Darfur, all of which have international connotations. The US strategy to source a significant proportion of its oil needs from Africa has been well documented and two of the three members of the consortium operating in Chad are American. Former Assistant Secretary of State Walter Kansteiner believes that 'African oil is of national strategic interest to us, and it will increase and become more important as we go forward' (Institute for Advanced Strategic and Political Studies 2002: 1). The US imported 28.4 million barrels from Chad in 2007. This is small in comparison with the 413 million barrels that the US received from Nigeria and the 561 million barrels from Saudi Arabia.[25]

Currently, sub-Saharan Africa supplies about 15% of North American oil needs. However, the National Intelligence Council projected that Africa will supply 25% of its needs by 2015.[26] Such estimated growth has prompted a reappraisal of US strategic and security policies in Africa. The focus of American-based multinationals and US government diplomatic and military involvement is the Gulf of Guinea. Nonetheless, considerable political capital has been invested in supporting the Doba model. The agreement between the World Bank and the Chadian government was seen as a marriage of entrepreneurialism with development policy, satisfying the commercial needs of the consortium while putting in place an overarching framework to ensure sustainable development. The Bush administration has also been concerned about the negative impact that the project has had on the standing of the World Bank and notably on Paul Wolfowitz, a long time Bush ally. Washington's concern over the collapse of the model led to the dispatch of the Deputy Secretary of State for African Affairs, Donald Yamamoto, to mediate the dispute.

American concern over Deby Itno's assertive oil policy is counter-balanced by Chad's support for the war on terrorism. The US considers Chad a strategically important partner in containing Islamic fundamentalism. The US has been involved in training units of the ANT as part of the Trans-Sahara Counterterrorism Initiative (TSCTI), formerly the Pan-Sahel Initiative. How many of these troops remain loyal is not known, but it is likely that the presence of units with superior skills and training was essential during the February 2008 offensive on N'Djaména. Finally, like France, the US is concerned with the impact on Chad of the conflict in Darfur. The Bush administration has resisted pleas to intervene in Darfur, despite former Secretary of State Colin Powell raising the spectre of ongoing genocide. While the direct involvement of American forces is unlikely given that France and EUFOR are already on the ground, wholesale export of the conflict into Chad would increase pressure on the US to do something at a time when its resources are stretched in Iraq and Afghanistan.

For its part, the Sudanese government continues to play a deft diplomatic game. Adopting the roles of mentor and student, Deby Itno has historically deferred to al-Bashir. For reasons outlined above, the outbreak of the Darfur conflict destroyed that understanding. However, while it is certain that Khartoum has supplied material assistance to some or all of the rebel factions, it has not advertised the policy. Rather Sudan denies charges that it encouraged the Janjaweed to press further into Chad territory and that Sudanese planes have been involved in bombing Chad's border towns. The principal source of Sudanese funding for the rebel groups is its oil wealth and Sudan exports 60% of its oil to China, a percentage that is growing. China would stand to benefit from a government in N'Djaména willing to switch from Western investment in further exploration to Chinese investment and to substitute the Red Sea for the Atlantic as the downstream destination for its oil. There is evidence that China was involved, albeit indirectly, in supporting the anti-Deby Itno rebels. There have been reports that weapons captured during an FUC attack on N'Djaména in April were Chinese and new and that the Toyota vehicles that ferried the FUC to N'Djaména were bought by a Chinese oil company based in Sudan for which Mahamat Nour used to work.[27]

The FUC attack on the capital underlined Chad's military vulnerability to Sudan. Deby Itno acted to bolster his own preparedness by ensuring increased revenue flows and the freedom to spend on defence, while acting to mitigate Sudan's diplomatic advantage. In August 2006, Deby Itno severed diplomatic relations with Taiwan in favour of China. From the perspective of many commentators, including the Taiwanese government, the switch in allegiance was a straightforward attempt to bribe China into easing its support for Sudan (Chang 2006). However, China for some time had been quietly seducing the regime in N'Djaména, looking to achieve a toehold in the country. During the standoff with the World Bank, China intimated that it would be willing to replace Chad's frozen loans with loans of its own, unconstrained by conditions. Beijing's influence also tempered the fraught relationship between Deby Itno and al-Bashir, with the latter making the trip to attend the Chadian president's latest inauguration, although the rapprochement has proved insincere. Where France has the weight of history and its status as a world power as motivations and the

US has the imperatives of the war on terror, China's interests, according to the US Ambassador to Chad, Marc Wall, are 'resources and markets and allies' (Junger 2007: 101). Only 23% of global oil reserves are open for foreign ownership and Beijing is compelled to deal with countries such as Chad in order to meet its growing demand for oil. Beijing has an ambitious African strategy founded on the application of soft power, appealing to African leaders as a fellow colonised nation and offering generous amounts of aid and interest-free loans in exchange for access to strategic resources. In 2006, Sino-African trade reached $40 billion and Chinese aid is expected to reach $10 billion by 2009. China has signed bilateral trade and investment agreements with three quarters of Africa's states and 750 Chinese companies are operating on the continent.

In Chad, although the US-Malaysian consortium currently has a monopoly on production, large swathes of the country remain to be explored. To this end, in January 2007 China National Petroleum Corporation (CNPC) International (Chad) Ltd, a wholly-owned subsidiary of the CNPC, bought exploration rights in an area called Block H from the Canadian firm EnCana for approximately $202 million. Block H is a vast area of territory split between the north and south comprising seven sedimentary basins that have already yielded finds of commercial value. Chinese companies have also been quick to exploit subsidiary industries. Underbidding Western rivals, construction companies pay their workers less and work them harder. The workers, engineers and equipment all come from China as a package (Broadman 2007: 224).

Aside from economic self-interest, if China is to emerge as a bona fide global superpower, it will need diplomatic leverage. In 1971, its replacement of Taiwan as the Chinese representative at the United Nations (UN) and its subsequent acquisition of a permanent seat on the UN Security Council was the result of the votes of newly independent African allies. Beijing, a former client of the North, recognises the importance of Southern solidarity. This is not to say that China still sees diplomacy merely as a numbers game and there are indications it accepts that it is no longer 'in its interests to be the symbolic head of a coalition of despots' (Kleine-Ahlbrandt and Small 2007). China has seemingly encouraged al-Bashir to allow a UN presence in Darfur and with its flag flying in both Khartoum and N'Djaména there is potential for Beijing to mediate the Sudan-Chad confrontation. The reward for China could be increased investment in Chad's oil sector and, possibly, the Holy Grail: the construction of a pipeline between the Chadian oil fields and Sudan, opening up the opportunity to pipe crude for export to the Red Sea coast.

These developments could have far-reaching implications for the US and France. In a very short space of time, Chad has gone from being diplomatically and militarily reliant on France and commercially reliant on the US-led consortium to being part of a three-player game. The speed with which China has inserted itself into Chad's oil sector and become a potential military ally of the Deby Itno regime must alarm American and French policy makers. Will China's assertive policy in Chad lead to an escalation of resource competition in Africa? African oil is now seen as of national strategic interest. In 1980, President Jimmy Carter established as a doctrine the policy decision that the US would use all means necessary to protect its interests in Middle East oil. Could this doctrine be extended to Africa? At the same time, the new government in Paris faces a monumental task in steering EUFOR, an operation that will prove to be militarily and diplomatically intricate.

Conclusion

After independence, Chad attracted interest from external actors greater than might be expected of such a poor, war-torn and largely barren country. An initial draw was its strategic position abutting the Maghreb and east, west and central sub-Saharan Africa. This interest has been compounded by oil. The discovery of workable reserves coincided with increased unease over exploitation, corruption and environmental degradation caused by extractive projects in the developing world. As a result, the Chad government and consortium called on the World Bank to lend its moral authority to the project, subjecting the proposal to an unprecedented consultation exercise and establishing a stringent framework intended to ensure that the profits would be largely given over to priority development sectors. However, as the profits started arriving for disbursement, the government was faced with twin threats – internal unrest resulting from political and economic corruption; and violent contagion from neighbouring Darfur. Deby Itno's response was to rewrite the revenue distribution arrangement unilaterally, ensuring the government much greater freedom over spending and applying pressure on the junior members of the consortium to pay corporation taxes that they had allegedly evaded.

The collapse of the Doba model has seriously undermined the World Bank strategy for the extractive industries in Africa and beyond. French and American involvement in Chad is, to some extent, predicated on countering China's resource-driven expansionism in sub-Saharan Africa. China has significant investments in the Sudanese oil industry and there was circumstantial evidence that Chinese-supplied weapons were being diverted by the Sudanese government to Chadian rebels in Darfur. In these circumstances Deby Itno was well advised to switch his country's diplomatic allegiance from Taipei to Beijing. Chinese companies have bought exploration rights to a large swathe of southern and northern Chad and have discovered commercial reserves. The Chinese way of operating is unlikely to benefit the wider Chadian population any more than the defunct Doba model.

That China should have been able to insert itself into the Chadian economy, not just in the oil industry but in a range of subsidiary ventures, is further testament to the waning influence of France in its former *chasse gardée*. France has a declining commercial interest in Chad and only tangential economic involvement in the oil project. Yet, its continued military presence has proved crucial to Deby Itno's survival. France's military involvement in Chad is as decisive as at any time since independence; although beyond the intangible impulse to maintain global prestige and Kouchner's humanitarian mission, France finds itself in the discomfiting position of providing protection for the interests of other external actors.

Historically a long way down the policy agenda of the US, Africa is now on the radar as a result of oil and terrorism. Deby Itno has proved a useful ally in the war on terror in the past, although the US would not go out on a limb to ensure his survival. While scarcely reliant on Chad's oil, Washington will continue to offer diplomatic support to the American companies in the consortium, keeping a watching brief on China's expansion into Chad's oil sector. For the World Bank, the scramble in Chad has been disastrous. Having staked all on the success of the Doba model, the bank has been forced to audit the project creatively, pronouncing it satisfactory in the ICR. The arrival of the Chinese has further eroded its already precarious leverage in post-pipeline Chad. China's loans and investments on the continent already dwarf those of the World Bank and there is every possibility the Chinese will follow the path they used in Angola and offer Deby Itno an oil-backed loan and preferential rates unencumbered by the sort of restrictions that the bank sought to impose under the Doba model.

The biggest losers in the scramble, however, have been the Chadian people. Since the oil came on stream, and despite the claims of Esso Chad's public affairs team, there is evidence that the environmental and social conditions in the oil-producing region have deteriorated. There is no sign that the revenue is having a significant effect on the wellbeing of the population with Chad still mired at seventh from bottom of the Human Development Index. Oil wealth has seemingly increased tension in the south and has the potential to militarise further the unstable eastern border with Darfur. As Delphine Djiraibe of the *Association Tchadienne pour la Promotion et la Défense des Droits de l'Homme* argues, 'poor people can't wait; they have been waiting for seven years'.[28]

Notes

1. C. Josselin in a speech to the Sixth Conference of Ambassadors, 27 Aug. 1998.
2. 'Show us the money' *Africa Confidential* 45(21) 2004.
3. Ojameruaye, E. Lessons from the Chadian model for distribution of oil wealth in Nigeria's Niger Delta [undated]. www.waado.org/Environment/Remediation/chadian_model_niger_delta>, accessed 28 July 2004.
4. *Economist*, 12 Sep. 2002.
5. *Africa Confidential* 45(21) 2004: 3.
6. Marie-François Marie-Nelly, Senior Programme Manager, Chad-Cameroon Project, World Bank, remarking on 'The Chad-Cameroon pipeline project: a non-completion report', Chatham House, London, 24 July 2007.
7. *Washington Post* 5 Dec. 2000.
8. Public Broadcast Services. *Religion and Ethics Newsweekly.* 30 July 2004.
9. Report of visit to Chad and Cameroon, 17 May to 5 June by the International Advisory Group.
10. World Bank, Chad-Cameroon Pipeline Project: revenue and allocations table, 2007.
11. Energy Information Administration, Country analysis briefs: Chad and Cameroon. www.tonto.eia.doe.gov posted Jan. 2007.
12. Public Broadcast Services. *Religion and Ethics Newsweekly.* 30 July 2004.
13. Public Broadcast Services. *Religion and Ethics Newsweekly.* 30 July 2004.
14. World Bank, Implementation completion report: Chad-Cameroon pipeline, 2006.
15. Reuters report, 28 Feb. 2008: 'Chad decrees avoid World bank controls – analysts'.
16. Esso Chad, Export project update: year end report, 2007.
17. IRIN, Chad: good year for President Deby, bad year for Chad. 28 May 2007.
18. IRIN, Chad: ethnic clash in Chad kills 12, wounds 16. 5 Nov. 2004.
19. *Le Monde* 5 May 2006.
20. *Liberté* (Algiers) 19 Apr. 2006.
21. S. Louet and B. Miarom, Chad accepts UN plan on border force. Associated Press report, 1 Dec. 2006.
22. Ministry of Interior May 2006 at www.interieur.gouv.fr/misill/sections/a_l_interieur/le_ministre/interventions/19-05-2006-deplacement-benin/view.
23. United Nations Security Council, *Report of the Secretary-General on the UN Mission in the Central African Republic and Chad.* 1 Apr. 2008.
24. *La Croix* 8 Feb. 2008.
25. Energy Information Administration, US imports by country of origin. www.tonto.eia.doe.gov accessed Feb. 2008.

26. *Global Trends 2015: A Dialogue About the Future with Nongovernment Experts* published by the National Intelligence Council, 2000.
27. *Journal du Dimanche* (Paris) 23 Apr. 2006.
28. Remark made by Delphine Djiraibe, founder of the *Association Tchadienne pour la Promotion et la Défense des Droits de l'Homme*, at a meeting on 'The Chad Cameroon oil and pipeline project: a non completion report', Chatham House, London, 24 July 2007.

References

Amnesty International. 2008. *Chad: Human Rights Crisis Brewing in Wake of Attack on N'Djaména*. London: AI.

Bangoura, M. T. 2005. *Violence Politique et Conflits en Afrique : Le Cas du Tchad*. Paris : L'Harmattan.

Broadman, H. 2007. *Africa's Silk Road: China and India's New Economic Frontier*. Washington DC: World Bank.

Chang, Y. 2006. 'Ministry regrets diplomatic break'. *Taipei Times* 7 Aug.

Charlton, R. and R. May. 1989. 'Warlords and militarism in Chad'. *Review of African Political Economy* 45-46: 12-25.

De Waal, A. 2007. Sudan: international dimensions to the state and its crisis. Crisis States Research Centre Occasional paper 3: 1-27.

Economist Intelligence Unit. 2006. *Chad: Country Report*. London : EIU.

Fédération Internationales des Ligues de Droits de l'Homme. 2000. 'Tchad-Cameroon: Pour Qui le Pétrole Coulera-t-il?' *Lettre Menuelle de la FIDH* 295: 17-21.

Ghazvinian, J. 2007. *Untapped: The Scramble for Africa's Oil*. Orlando: Harcourt.

Glazer, A. and S. Smith. 2006. *Comment la France a perdu l'Afrique*. Paris: Pluriel.

Hanson, A. 2008. *The French Military in Africa*. New York: Council on Foreign Relations.

Hoh, A-V. and B. Vignaux. 2006. 'L'Afrique n'est plus l'eldorado des enterprises françaises'. *Monde Diplomatique* Feb.

Horta, K., S. Nguiffo and D. Djiraibe. 2007. *The Chad-Cameroon Oil and Pipeline Project: A Project Non-Completion Report*. http://www.forestpeoples.org/documents/africa/ chad_cameroon_proj_report_apr07_eng.pdf.

Institute for Advanced Strategic and Political Studies. 2002. *African Oil: A Priority for US National Security and African Development*. Washington: African Oil Policy Initiative Group, IASPS.

Junger, S. 2007. 'Enter China, the giant'. *Vanity Fair* July.

Kleine-Ahlbrandt, S. and A. Small. 2007. 'Beijing cools on Mugabe'. *International Herald Tribune* 4 May.

Marchal, R. 2000. 'La nouvelle politique africaine de la France'. *Développement et Coopération* 1.

——. 2006. 'Chad/Darfur: how two crises merge'. *Review of African Political Economy* 33(109): 457-82.

Marchesin, P. 1995. 'Mitterrand l'Africain'. *Politique Africaine* 58: 5–25.

Massey, S. and R. May. 2005. 'Dallas to Doba: oil and Chad, external controls and internal politics'. *Journal of Contemporary African Studies* 23(2): 253–76.

——. 2006. 'The crisis in Chad'. *African Affairs* 105(420): 443–9.

Mbembe, A. 2007. 'L'Afrique de Nicolas Sarkozy'. *Le Messager* [Douala] 1 Aug.

Nolutshungu, S. 1996. *Limits of Anarchy: Intervention and State Formation in Chad.* Charlottesville: University Press of Virginia.

Touati, S. 2007. 'French foreign policy in Africa: between pré-carré and unilateralism'. *Africa Programme Briefing Note* (Chatham House, London) Feb.

Verschave, X. 2003. *Françafrique: Le Plus Longue Scandale de la République*. Paris: Stock.

Vines, A. 2007. 'Plus ça change'. *Mail and Guardian* [Johannesburg] 29 May.

CHAPTER TEN

The Mining Boom in Sub-Saharan Africa

Continuity, Change and Policy Implications

Wilson Prichard

The mining sector is of major importance to many countries in sub-Saharan Africa, frequently contributing major shares of both exports and tax revenues. There are sixteen sub-Saharan African countries, excluding South Africa, for which exports of ores and metals either comprise at least 10% of total exports, or are expected to do so in the near future.[1] Sub-Saharan Africa is also believed to be home to roughly 30% of the world's mineral reserves, making it a hugely important, and relatively under-explored, target for mining firms. Consequently, surging mining activity in sub-Saharan Africa since 2002 has attracted significant popular attention and has frequently been seen as part of a new scramble for Africa's primary resources. The new discourse has frequently implied that the recent boom represents a fundamental transformation of sub-Saharan African mining that raises historically unique policy challenges.

It is thus surprising that very little has been written that seeks to address systematically the content, context and potential impact of recent activity. This chapter seeks to do just this by looking at first, the historical evolution of mining on the continent; second, the question of whether the developments of the last five years constitute a historically unique period in mining in sub-Saharan Africa; and third, the main development policy questions raised. An underlying theme is that the recent surge in mining activity has elements of both continuity and disjuncture relative to earlier periods. This demands solutions cognisant of the past, while recognising the uniqueness of the present.[2]

The Historical Trajectory of Mining in Sub-Saharan Africa
Mining during the Colonial Period

Foreign involvement in the exploitation of sub-Saharan African mineral resources is by no means new. Colonial economic policy was built around the desire to open the continental interior to resource extraction and cash crop farming, and minerals figured as the most valuable opportunity for European exploitation. This gave rise to two important economic processes during the early colonial period. The first was the forced introduction of a cash economy, through poll taxes for example, as the need for cash was the most effective way to force local labourers to enter into extractive industries or cash cropping. The second was massive investment in infrastructure, mainly railways, which would open up access to valuable resources in the interior. New railways emerged all over the continent and invariably led directly to major cash cropping regions or valuable mineral deposits: the copper mines of Zambia and the Democratic Republic of the Congo (DRC), the Ghanaian gold fields, tin mines in northern Nigeria and iron ore deposits in Liberia were all prominent examples (Freund 1984).

These processes were successful in so far as European-controlled mines became major global producers and destinations for wage labourers. Yet, mining during this period implied major costs for local communities, while contributing precious little to national development. Costs to local communities included the social dislocation caused by migrant labour and significant environmental destruction. At the same time, the vast majority of benefits flowed abroad to major Northern mining firms. While significant low-wage employment was generated, local sourcing and ownership were non-existent and mining profits consistently flowed back to Europe. Meanwhile, even the major infrastructure construction of the early colonial period was very poorly suited to the needs of the countries in question beyond aiding the export of primary products. Thus, while mining projects prospered they did little to promote sustainable local development (Freund 1984).

Post-colonial Policy and Sovereignty over Mineral Resources

Responding to the fact that the benefits of mining overwhelmingly flowed abroad during the colonial period, post-independence governments adopted an increasingly nationalistic approach to the management of mineral resources. This mirrored changes in economic policy more generally. Thus, the post-independence period saw the formation of state mining firms and the nationalisation of many existing mining operations. The World Bank reports that by 1989, 41.5% of minerals production was under state control, 40.5% was controlled by state-private sector joint ventures operated by private firms, while 18% of activity was under the sole ownership of the private sector. Of these totals, 76.9% of entirely private sector mining activity occurred in Namibia and Zimbabwe, while 86.9% of state-operated production occurred in Zambia and the DRC, primarily in copper (World Bank 1992). Aside from the expansion of state ownership, governments also tended to impose stricter rules relating to local employment, local sourcing of inputs, local beneficiation, taxation, transferability of mineral rights and profit repatriation.

Data compiled by the World Bank indicates that sub-Saharan Africa's share of minerals production across a wide variety of commodities declined markedly during the post-independence period. While the value of minerals production increased during the 1960s, sub-Saharan Africa's share of developing country minerals production fell, based on a sample of ten commodities, from 31.5% in 1970 to 10% in 1987 (Fozzard 1990, Kumar 1990, World Bank 1992).[3] The progressive decline of production during this period was linked to the relative lack of exploration expenditure, which averaged only about 4% of the global total in the 1980s, and a failure to invest sufficiently in existing operations (World Bank 1992).

The World Bank and others attributed this decline to the mismanagement of the mining sector by governments and the existence of major disincentives to private sector involvement. They demonstrated that mines operated by the private sector, including joint ventures with the state in which the latter played a passive role, had expanded production much more dramatically since independence than had state- controlled firms. Private sector firms, they proposed, had adjusted much more effectively to the downturn in global demand in the 1980s. They also tended to focus more effectively on exploration and maintenance, while state firms were often pressured to meet the short-term revenue needs of overstretched governments. Disincentives to private involvement included the prevalence of state mining firms, the lack of stable control of mineral resources and the existence of high rates of taxation and regulation (World Bank 1992).

While the World Bank focused on policy variables, the 1980s were a period of more general decline and crisis on the continent. Factors that likely exacerbated the problems of the mining sector included: severely depressed prices; the onset of a broader fiscal crisis in many African states; and the fact that this period represented a low point in the quality of overall governance and political stability on the continent.

Liberalisation, High Prices and Increased Mining Activities in the 1990s
In the light of the widespread feeling that government intervention had been the central cause of minerals sector decline in the region, the late 1980s and the 1990s saw the majority of sub-Saharan African countries undergo significant liberalisation of their mining sectors. Regulation was made much more amenable to foreign investment, while the direct involvement of states in mineral production was dramatically reduced, either through privatisation of state firms or the selling down of public sector shares in mining operations, a process heavily influenced by the World Bank and International Monetary Fund (IMF). In 1992 the World Bank explained that:

> The recovery of the mining sector in Africa will require a shift in government objectives towards a primary objective of maximizing tax revenues from mining over the long term, rather than pursuing other economic or political objectives such as control of resources or enhancement of employment. This objective will be best achieved by a new policy emphasis whereby governments focus on industry regulation and promotion and private companies take the lead in operating, managing and owning mineral enterprises. That is not to say that only investors should benefit from mining. But in the new policy environment governments should obtain a fair share of the economic rent of the sector through fiscal arrangements that are stable, competitive and fair, rather than through ownership and operation (World Bank 1992: x).

This period of liberalisation coincided with a major recovery in the international price of most mineral commodities, which began in 1988 and continued until 1997. This saw the expansion of private sector activity, along with an increase in investment and exploration in both absolute terms and as a share of global activity. Ghana, Tanzania and Mali were the most prominent success stories, and each of them underwent significant World Bank supported liberalisation.

Despite the growth in mining activity, liberalisation was not without controversy. Many observers argued that it meant a return to the colonial pattern of domination by private firms: a reliance on foreign inputs, extensive exporting of profits abroad and scant concern for environmental damage or for creating local economic opportunities (Campbell 2004). In fact, the World Bank was keenly aware of the potential for the new policy advice to be interpreted as a return to colonial practices and wrote: 'The strategy proposed here should not be interpreted as turning the clock back to the era when host governments were dependent on the patronage of powerful, foreign companies. What is here proposed is an enlightened partnership' (World Bank 1992: 10).

The Late 1990s and the Minerals Boom since 2002

Following the successes of the early 1990s, global prices declined between 1997 and 2002 before registering a much publicised and very rapid rise beginning in late 2002 (figure 10.4). Rising prices have been the result of rapidly expanding demand, particularly due to economic growth in China, which has not been matched by increase in supply, which remains tight after five years of very low investment. The rise in prices has led global investment in minerals exploration to increase dramatically, from a low of $1.9 billion in 2002 to an historic high of $7.5 billion in 2006 (figure 10.1).[4] Yet, while there has certainly been a dramatic increase in exploration recently, the overall level of exploration is probably still less than it was in 1997, as the absolute value of exploration expenditure does not account for inflation nor for higher costs of exploration (Metals Economics Group 2007).

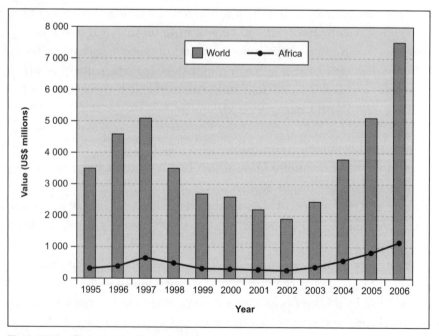

Figure 10.1 Global exploration spending.

Source: Metals Economics Group (2007)

Reflecting increasing integration of the sub-Saharan African mining industry with global markets post-liberalisation, exploration spending in the region has largely followed the global trend. Available data, which includes South Africa in the totals, indicates that the regional share of global expenditure has risen from 12.5% in 2000 to approximately 16% in 2006, but that this level is still slightly less than peaks of 16.45% and 17.46% in 1997 and 1998 (figure 10.2). If we draw on more sporadic country-specific data from the Metals Economics Group and World Bank it appears that the share for sub-Saharan Africa, excluding South Africa, has increased somewhat more steadily: an average of 4% of global exploration spending in the 1980s, 5% in the early 1990s, a peak at about 9–10% during the mid-1990s minerals boom, a decline to about 6% in 2000 and a historic high of 12% in 2006 (Metals Economics Group 2007; World Bank 1992; Onorato, Fox and Strongman 1998).

This pattern is indicative of a steady improvement in minerals sector performance over the past two decades. It is equally indicative of the particularly

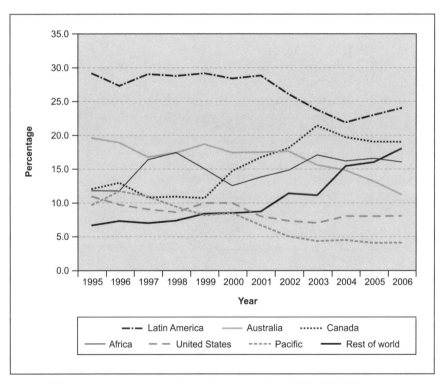

Figure 10.2 Regional shares of global mining expenditure, 1995–2006 (%).
Source: Metals Economics Group (2007)

dramatic cyclical nature of the mining sector in developing regions. Bridge (2004) has argued that during periods of high prices, mining firms tend to expand aggressively into higher-risk mining regions; but that during low periods they tend to dispose of high-risk operations first. The implication is that we should expect the sub-Saharan African share of minerals exploration to be particularly high during boom periods and this is precisely what we observe.

While prices and the level of mining exploration have been up across all commodities, base metals have experienced a particularly dramatic rise, as Chinese demand has been focused on industrial metals (Broadman 2007).

A longer-term trend, dating back to 1997, has been the decline in the share of gold in global exploration, along with a rise in the share of platinum group metals (PGMs). The share of gold in global exploration declined precipitously from 65% in 1997 to 42.5% in 2001. This has been primarily offset by a rise in exploration in the other category, of which over half is PGMs (figure 10.3).

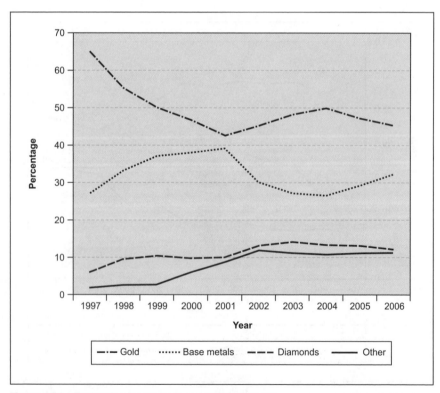

Figure 10.3 Exploration by mineral type, 1997–2006 (%).
Source: Metals Economics Group (2007)

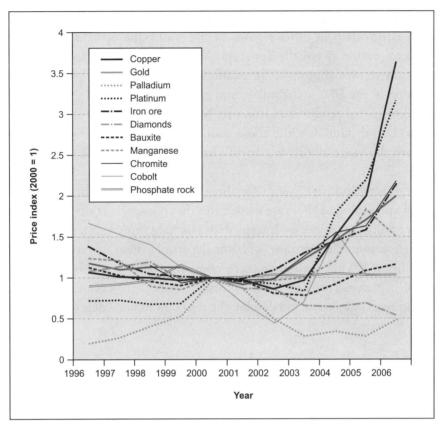

Figure 10.4 Commodity prices, 1996–2006.

Source: Data is derived from annual Mineral Commodity Summaries prepared by the US Geological
Survey (USGS 2007)

The distribution of metals exploration spending across commodities in sub-Saharan Africa differs somewhat from global patterns. In Africa, including South Africa, exploration for gold, diamonds and PGMs has consistently exceeded global shares for these commodities: they represented 86% and 77% of exploration in 2003 and 2004 respectively, as compared to roughly 68% globally in both years. While the production of PGMs is largely concentrated in South Africa, recent surges in gold production in Tanzania, Ghana and Mali, as well as the continued centrality of diamonds in a number of countries, point to the dominance of these commodities on the continent as a whole. This reflects both mineral endowments and the fact that gold and diamond production generally require less developed infrastructure.

Nonetheless, while reliance on base metals has tended to be lower in sub-Saharan Africa than in other regions of the world, the upward trend in base metals exploration is equally apparent. While not yet reflected in aggregate production figures (figure 10.5), examples include rapidly growing copper exploration in the DRC and Zambia, and plans in place to see Liberia re-emerge as a leading global producer of iron ore. Moreover, the potential for expansion seems to be substantial: while these countries are not presently major global producers, they were among the world's leaders as recently as the 1970s (World Bank 1992).

The mining industry comprises three broad types of firm: Majors, intermediates and juniors. Majors are those firms that possess a major presence across a variety of different minerals. Intermediates include firms with a major presence in a single commodity or those with smaller involvement in producing several commodities. Finally, junior resource companies (JRCs) are small firms that specialise in high-risk exploration and prospecting. Both majors and intermediates often conduct exploration and develop the resultant mineral deposits themselves.

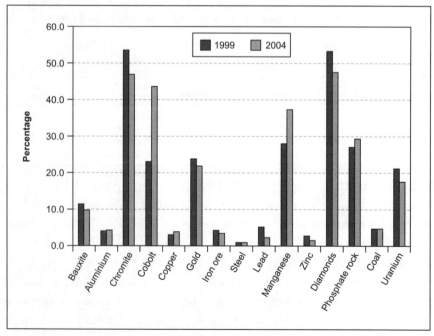

Figure 10.5 African share of global production by commodity (%).
Source: USGS (2007)

By contrast, junior firms seek high-risk venture capital to fund exploration in the hope of eventually selling valuable deposits to larger firms that possess the resources for longer-term mine development. Junior firms will occasionally seek to develop mines themselves, or in partnership with a larger firm, but this is the exception rather than the rule. Because of their smaller size and reliance on venture capital, JRCs play an important role in initiating exploration in lesser-known, and thus higher-risk, areas.

The rapid increase in global mining exploration has seen the share of exploration conducted by JRCs surge from 26.4% in 2001 to 52% in 2006 (figure 10.6). While the magnitude of this expanded role is significant, and appears to be at an historic high, the general pattern is unsurprising: JRCs are expected to

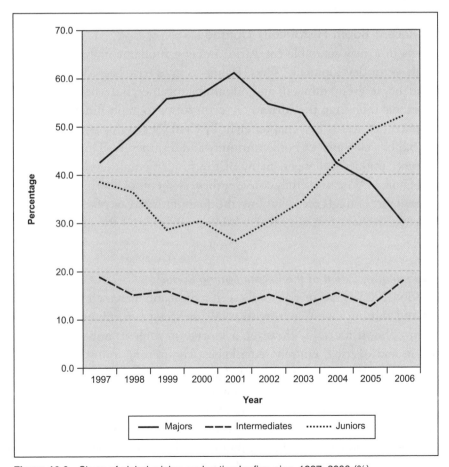

Figure 10.6 Share of global mining exploration by firm size, 1997–2006 (%).
Source: Metals Economics Group (2007)

flourish when prices are high due to the ready availability of venture capital and greater industry interest in the development of higher-risk mines. While conclusive data is not available, both intuition and observations by those in the industry point to the importance of this explosion in JRC activity for mine development in relatively high-risk sub-Saharan African markets.

While the expansion of mining investment globally has involved firms of many nationalities, JRCs have been unique in that they continue to be listed almost exclusively on stock markets in Canada, Britain and Australia. This reflects the fact that JRCs are heavily reliant on their ability to raise capital for high-risk exploration; and that these three countries offer well-developed financial markets with an interest in mining ventures and relatively undemanding accounting and disclosure requirements.

Is the Recent Boom Historically Unique?
Allusions to a new scramble for Africa imply a fundamentally new period of minerals sector development.[5] These claims seem to have been driven in part by the tendency to group minerals and oil mining together, but whereas the sudden international interest in the African oil sector seems to imply fundamentally new development concerns (see chapter eight by Cyril Obi in this book), the mining sector exhibits elements of both continuity and disjuncture. Thus, while it does pose some unique challenges, many of the fundamental development factors remain familiar. We can usefully consider these elements of continuity and change in terms of three broad considerations: the quantitative scope of recent expansion, the particular characteristics of new mining targets, and the characteristics of investors.

The Quantitative Extent of the Recent Mining Boom
The period 2002–6 has undoubtedly seen a dramatic increase in both minerals prices and mining investment, with total investment in minerals exploration increasing almost fourfold. However, a short-term surge in minerals investment is not, in and of itself, entirely remarkable. The mining industry is inherently highly cyclical, driven by the volatility of prices, which in turn reflects uncertain demand and the fact that bringing new mines to production often involves a time lag of five years or more. Recent events are consistent with this view: new Asian demand has exceeded prior expectations, while the supply response has been unusually slow due to the common time lag in bringing new mines into production, the increasing costs of exploration, the effects of very low exploration from 1997 to 2002 and the relative exhaustion of many easy to mine areas.

Because mining is inherently cyclical, the fact that it is currently in the midst of a major upturn does not necessarily imply any fundamental change in the industry. What should interest us are changes in the trend level of mining activity, or in the extremity of boom and bust cycles in the industry. In other words, is this simply a cyclical peak, or are we witnessing a change in the overall trend, with both peaks and valleys expected to be higher than previously? In the first case, the challenges are little different from previous periods: to manage skyrocketing revenues in a manner that promotes long-term growth and poverty reduction and avoids a boom-bust cycle (Labonne 2002). By contrast, if there has been a change in the trend level then we may sensibly discuss the possibility of fundamental changes in the management and impact of mining activity.

The evidence so far is consistent with a particularly dramatic cyclical upturn, rather than fundamental change. As was noted earlier, the level of global mining exploration, while dramatically higher than in 2002, appears to be lower than in 1997, accounting for inflation and higher costs. The sub-Saharan African share of global exploration, using data that includes South Africa, was also slightly less in 2006 than in 1997 and 1998. If South Africa is excluded, the sub-Saharan African share of mining exploration has expanded from roughly 9% in 1997 to 12% in 2006. While significant, this does not represent a fundamental transformation and implies only a modest increase in real exploration relative to 1997 given rising costs. Highlighting the relative modesty of this increase is that fact that the countries grouped by the Metals Economics Group as rest of the world have experienced a much more dramatic transformation, rising from 7% of global exploration expenditure in 1997 to 18% in 2006.[6]

While the data so far is only indicative of a major cyclical upturn, it is possible that the present period could yet emerge as a more fundamental disjuncture in the history of mining if prices, and thus mining activity, remain unusually high over an extended period. Market analysts have produced a large literature debating the future trajectory of global mining activity and minerals prices. Suffice it to echo the most common view, based on historical models of resource use: both demand and prices will remain high, but not at present record levels, for some time, suggesting that the present high levels of mining activity may persist longer than during the boom of the mid-1990s. With that important debate in mind, a reasonable conclusion might be that the scope of the present expansion is distinctive and seems likely to be more persistent than previous expansions; but that the differences are, so far, of degrees rather than of kind and not comparable to the massive changes going on in the oil industry (Broadman 2007; Goode 2006; Naidu and Davies 2006).

The High Risk Character of New Mining Targets

Cross-country data reveals two more specific differences between previous mining booms and the current period: recent years have seen a distinct shift in priority towards base metals; and JRCs playing an unprecedented role. In and of themselves, neither of these observations is terribly significant.

Of greater significance is the combined impact of these two factors on the distribution of mining activity across countries. The increasing importance of JRCs appears to be both a symptom and a cause of a greater willingness to be involved in more isolated and high-risk mining areas, characterised by limited infrastructure, unstable politics and, in many cases, a legacy of conflict. While we have already noted evidence that periods of high prices tend to promote higher-risk exploration, the fact that the level of JRC involvement has hit an historical high is noteworthy (Bridge 2004). Meanwhile, the shift towards base metals has moved the locus of mining activity away from traditional gold mining leaders (Ghana, Mali and Tanzania) and towards major producers of base metals (DRC, Zambia, Liberia, Guinea and Gabon). While this would not seem to have an inherent tendency to increase risk, it so happens that in sub-Saharan Africa these base metals producers are, for the most part, countries that have experienced either very unstable and undemocratic politics or recent conflict.

This tendency of global mining trends to lead exploration towards higher-risk regions of sub-Saharan Africa is being reinforced by patterns of conflict. A significant part of the downturn in sub-Saharan African mining activity from 1997 to 2002 was the result of renewed conflicts, particularly in West Africa and the Great Lakes region, while the return of peace and relatively low levels of instability since 2002 has facilitated renewed activity. Several of these post-conflict regions are also base metals producers (DRC and Liberia, for instance) and are thus experiencing a particularly strong surge in interest.

Despite the cessation of conflict as well as nominal democratisation in many of these countries, these gains have yet to be widely institutionalised and thus risks remain significant. This, though, has not slowed international interest: for example, the DRC, despite ranking near the bottom of virtually every policy and political indicator in the most recent Fraser Institute survey of mining executives, is placed highest among African nations on a composite score of policy and mineral potential (McMahon and Melhem 2006). Furthermore, the state-owned South African Industrial Development Corporation (IDC) is predicting that its next mega-project in the mining sector may centre on the Kolwezi copper and cobalt mine in southern DRC.

Table 10.1 Impact of conflict on minerals output in selected countries.

Country	Duration of conflict	Impact on mining
Burundi	1993–2003	Gold production reached 2 000 kg in 1995, but then collapsed to zero by 2000 before recovering to 2 900 kg in 2004.
DRC	1996–2002	Gold production fell from 9 300 kg in 1990 to 69 kg in 2000, before recovering to 5 400 kg in 2004. Copper production from 509 000 tonnes in 1990, fell to 31 000 tonnes in 2000 and has not yet reached pre-war levels.
Rwanda	1990–4	Gold production was 2 160 kg in 1990 but collapsed to virtually zero by 1995. While gold production has not recovered, overall mining output has risen rapidly since 1995.
Liberia	1989–2003	Liberia was the world's fifth largest producer of iron ore before official production fell to zero by 1995. In 2005 the country signed a $1.2 billion iron ore project with Arcelor Mittal.
Mozambique	1982–92	The value of ore and metals exports increased 500% from the period 1990–5 to the period 1996–2000, while the period 2001–4 saw a 1 500% increase over the previous period due primarily to the Mozal aluminium smelter.
Uganda	1971–85	In the 1960s mining comprised as much as 30% of exports, but the sector collapsed during conflict and is only now hesitantly re-emerging.

Expansion into these high-risk areas is significant for two reasons: the potentially dramatic development implications and the unique challenges presented for mining firms. Positive potential lies in the fact that such areas are likely to have particularly low levels of infrastructure, public services and skills, so mining activity can possibly become a major driver of community development. On the other hand, the quality and accountability of governance in such remote areas is likely to be weak, involving the additional risk that the negative aspects of mining operations will take centre stage: for instance, poor labour practices, environmental damage, corrosive effects on governance and a failure to secure local benefits.

From the perspective of firms, mine development in more remote areas requires unique skills. First, success means developing the ability to manage both political risk and the legacy of conflict. More concretely, it demands an ability to co-ordinate and manage the investments required to develop necessary infrastructure, which may include railways, airstrips, power supply, water supply or port upgrading, among other things. This is no small matter. For example, Randgold encountered serious delays in expanding gold production in Mali when problems emerged with the partner firm responsible for co-ordinating logistics and infrastructure on the project.

New Political Actors and Competition for Access to Resources

The most significant distinguishing feature of the recent mining boom is the emergence of developing country investors. Firms from South Africa and, to a lesser degree, Brazil have become very active investors in the region. Meanwhile Chinese, and to some extent Indian, firms are making increasingly aggressive movements in the region, although this activity has yet to catch widespread popular attention.[7]

The entry of emerging market firms into the sub-Saharan African mining sector has three potentially dramatic implications, the first positive, the other two negative. The potentially positive outcome is that increased competition for access to mineral resources in the region is likely to increase the negotiating power enjoyed by governments seeking to maximise local benefits. There are several recent examples, discussed in greater detail later, in which governments have used this increased leverage to renegotiate existing agreements or impose new requirements. There are, equally, cases in which historically dominant firms have failed to gain access to resources as they have been outbid by developing country firms. In contrast to laments that liberalisation would represent a return to a system in which a small number of major mining firms could dominate poor governments, in reality this increased leverage may be an opportunity to change the terms of engagement.

Against this, the most commonly held concern is that developing country firms will maintain very low standards of corporate social responsibility, as they are free of the new standards and increasing civil society activism that have led to progressive improvements among firms of developed countries. This has two primary dimensions. The first involves upholding labour and environmental standards; the second, the risk of firms becoming involved in mining activities, and the financing of governments, in conflict areas. China has been widely chastised on this account, while there is some evidence to point to similar worries about firms from other countries.

The second concern is that increasing competition for access to mineral rights will result in increasing politicisation of access. It is widely recognised that securing access to mineral resources, and establishing the terms upon which that access occurs, is a political process, while mining legislation in sub-Saharan Africa generally still provides significant latitude to political elites to shape those terms (Etemad and Salmasi 2002; Naito, Remy and Williams 2001). The risk is that increasing competition for access to mineral resources will expand the potential for corruption in the allocation of mining rights and lead to a corresponding decline in local benefits. Whereas the political nature of negotiations over access to oil rights tends to be relatively apparent and observable due to the huge sums of money involved, the particulars of such politicking in the mining sector are much less readily observed. That said, it is widely accepted that politics matters: the Brazilian and Chinese governments have both been increasingly involved in courting political favour in potential mining destinations,[8] while one reason cited by international mining firms for establishing offices in South Africa is the political advantage to be gained by having a regional base.

The following provides a more detailed overview of the involvement of the new emerging market competitors for sub-Saharan Africa's minerals.

China

While China has sought a major ownership interest in the African oil sector, it has so far remained primarily a buyer, rather than a producer, of minerals. While it has expressed a desire to become independent of prices set on the London Metals Exchange, it has so far pursued this goal primarily by entering into long-term purchase contracts.[9] While Chinese firms may eventually play a larger role in minerals production, as they have in the oil sector, ownership ventures have been relatively rare. The acquisition of mining rights, such as those recently acquired to mine iron ore in Gabon, also remains relatively rare but is growing.[10]

Until recently, the one major exception to this trend was Zambia's copper belt. A Chinese firm controls the Chambishi copper mine, while the Chinese government has intensified diplomatic links and pledged to invest an additional $900 million in Zambia from 2007 to 2011.[11] Given that copper has seen the most prolific price increases over the past three years, it is not surprising that it is the mineral in which the Chinese are exhibiting a major interest.

China's experience in Zambia is also indicative of what are perceived to be the benefits and drawbacks of Chinese investment in the resource sector in Africa. The Chinese firm that operates Chambishi was willing to work a mine that most major mining firms considered economically unviable. More negatively, the mine has been controversial locally due to poor safety, including an explosion in 2004 that killed 46 workers, growing labour unrest that culminated in demonstrations during which six people were killed, and the importation of Chinese workers.[12] Planned protests at the Chambishi mine forced visiting Chinese President Hu Jintao to cancel a scheduled visit in February 2007.[13]

More ambiguous is the effect of China's growing political engagement with the Zambian government. China's Prime Minister visited Zambia in February

2007 in order to strengthen diplomatic ties and pledged that China would invest an additional $900 million in the country along with the creation of a special investment zone centred on Chambishi.[14] At the same time, the Chinese also forgave Zambian debts owed up to 2005.[15] The Chinese have trumpeted increased aid and diplomatic ties as positive, but others have raised concerns. Some worry that the reciprocal granting of major investment incentives by the Zambian government will erode the local benefits of any new investment. On the political front, there is concern that the ready availability of major revenues from the Chinese will distort local politics by encouraging compliance with Chinese preferences while reducing incentives for accountability to citizens. It is notable that the visit to Zambia by President Hu Jintao saw opposition political parties centrally involved in protests.[16]

The Chinese have recently made a second, much more dramatic, appearance in Africa, though many of the implications of this deal remain to be seen. First announced in September 2007 and signed in January 2008, this deal will see China invest at least $5 billion in infrastructure projects in the DRC. They will begin in 2008, to be repaid from mining profits generated by Socomin (Société Congolaise Minière), jointly owned by Congolese national mining firm Gecamines (32%) and the China Eximbank (68%), which is providing the loans to the Chinese firms undertaking the construction projects. Initially, 64% of profits are to pay off the infrastructure loans, while the remainder will be split between the shareholders. The mines to be controlled by Socomin are to come primarily from new mineral sites, along with a small portion claimed from Katanga Mining. As with the projects in Zambia the focus is, unsurprisingly, on copper as well as cobalt.

Unlike the Zambian mining venture, which generated relatively little notice from other mining companies, but led to significant criticism from development observers, the venture in the DRC has elicited much more significant concern from mining firms, and initially more positive response from development observers. The concern of international firms stems from the fact that there is fierce competition to secure mining rights in the DRC and the Chinese government can mobilise enormous resources and effective co-ordination across different sectors and political actors, in that effort. The somewhat more favourable reception from development observers derives from the proposed existence of immediate and tangible benefits to the country, as well as provisions for joint ownership, local beneficiation and local employment that seem to address at least some of the concerns often leveled against international mining firms. That said, the actual outcome of these deals will not be clear for many years and the governance implications of China emerging as an enormous source of revenue for DRC government projects remain particularly unclear.[17]

India

Indian activity in sub-Saharan African mining has perhaps been more rumour than substance, with relatively little investment to date. That said, Indian corporations have become involved in some significant ventures on the continent and the pace appears to be increasing. This issue is discussed in more detail by Sanusha Naidu in chapter five of this book and so will not be developed here, save to note the interesting role played by India within the African mining value chain as a competitor for basic beneficiation. India is the world leader in diamond cutting and polishing, but relies heavily on imports from Africa. This would seem to be precisely the type of relatively low-skill, labour-intensive form of beneficiation that African countries should be seeking to engage in (Broadman 2007: 32).

Brazil

The major Brazilian mining firm CVRD has begun to establish an important presence in sub-Saharan Africa with offices in South Africa, Angola, Mozambique and Gabon, and additional activities in Guinea. Its largest project is the $2 billion Moatize coal mine in Mozambique, which will be the largest coal project in the southern hemisphere. In Gabon, CVRD thought that it had secured major iron ore mining rights at Bélinga, only to have those rights subsequently granted to a Chinese firm.[18] Nonetheless, CVRD is leading a major manganese prospecting effort that it hopes to see make Gabon the world's largest exporter of the mineral.[19] Finally, while activity in Guinea is less advanced, there are reports that the firm, with the support of the Brazilian government, has been lobbying aggressively to secure new mining rights. This all comes at a time when a growing number of Brazilian firms in other sectors are beginning to enter the African market, with the government making increasing diplomatic overtures.

While much of its activity in Africa is at a relatively early stage, CVRD argues that it has experience in exploration techniques and processes specifically designed for use in tropical areas. Central to this claim is the ability to manage the infrastructure and political demands of new mining ventures in developing countries. The Moatize coal project required extensive negotiation in order to secure the initial rights, and is poised to involve total investment of $2 billion in order to develop the mine, build a coal processing plant, upgrade the rail link to the coast, rehabilitate a local hydroelectric plant and build new port facilities.[20] The major co-ordination challenges involved in bringing the project into production are indicative of suggestions that developing country firms, with strong links to their governments and a history of managing political risk and new infrastructure, may enjoy important advantages. The Belinga project, in which CVRD narrowly lost out, also involved significant infrastructure construction in a difficult environment, and was, not surprisingly, only contested by developing country firms.

South Africa

South African firms have played a major role on the continent since the end of apartheid, particularly in gold mining. For a variety of reasons conclusive data on the amount of investment is not available (Goldstein and Prichard 2008). That said, the Business Map Foundation, which tracks foreign direct investment (FDI) from South Africa into Africa based on public announcements, reports that from 1994 to 2004 South African corporations and parastatals invested slightly over R13 billion (US$1.814 billion) in the mining sector.[21] Bridge (2004) estimates total mining investment in Africa between 1990 and 2001 at around US$7 billion. While the Business Map estimate amounts to roughly 25% of this total, the likelihood that announced investment overestimates actual investment suggests that South African investment during the period 1994 to 2004 probably amounted to 10–20% of total investment.

The two areas in which recent South African expansion has been particularly dramatic are West and Central Africa. In West Africa, led by Randgold in Mali and the acquisition of Ghanaian firm Ashanti Goldfields by Anglo-American Corporation (AAC), South African firms have become leading players in the mining industry. Observers indicate that they have exploited their experience in African gold mining, as well as relative geographic proximity, to expand their operations rapidly (Goldstein and Prichard 2008). Meanwhile, South African firms have shown a growing interest in expanding in Central Africa, and particularly the DRC, with Metorex the most aggressive to date. This represents new challenges for South African firms unaccustomed to such politically volatile regions. It also poses questions about their commitment to responsible corporate behaviour.

The success of South African firms investing in the region reflects a combination of historical links to countries in southern Africa, technical and managerial expertise suited to the African environment, established local supply networks and valuable formal and informal political support from the South African government (Goldstein and Prichard 2008). There is nothing to suggest that South African firms will not continue to play a major role on the continent (Daniel, Lutchman and Comninos 2007).

On the other hand, the involvement of South African mining firms in sub-Saharan Africa has not been universally successful. The most significant issue is the absence of a significant South African presence among JRCs. Historically, mineral rights in South Africa were considered private, rather than state, property. This allowed the politically influential major mining houses, led by AAC, to maintain control of all of the valuable mining deposits in the country, even when not developing them, thus leaving few opportunities for JRCs. By contrast, Australia and Canada maintained state ownership of mineral resources and introduced use it or lose it provisions that granted access to mineral rights only as long as the mineral deposits were being actively explored and developed. This opened space for smaller firms to step in where larger firms were inactive, thus giving birth to a culture of JRCs. While South Africa has now changed the regulatory context and there is now a junior mining index on the Johannesburg Stock Exchange, the historical legacy means that South African JRCs remain minor players.[22]

Aside from this limitation of South African involvement, AAC, one of the big four global mining companies, has shown a conscious desire to diversify its involvement outside Africa. This includes the recent divestiture of African gold mining assets held under AngloGold Ashanti and the appointment of a non-South African as CEO (Chabane, Goldstein and Roberts 2006). Finally, South African firms have not been without failures on the continent. For example, AAC incurred significant losses from its involvement in the privatisation of Zambian Consolidated Copper Mines (ZCCM), Zambia's national copper mining firm. More recently, Anglo subsidiary Kumba Resources has lost mining rights in Senegal (iron ore) and the DRC (zinc and copper) under controversial circumstances, suggesting the limits of South African political leverage on the continent.[23]

The Mining Value Chain and the Role of South Africa

South Africa acts as a regional platform for mining activity. All of the major mining firms have established offices in Johannesburg, viewing South Africa as a hub from which to conduct business in the rest of Africa. In similar fashion, many large mining services firms have established African offices in South Africa, while South African mining services firms have expanded northward since the end of apartheid.

There are several factors which contribute to this pattern: South Africa has far superior business infrastructure to other sub-Saharan African nations, travel between South Africa and the rest of Africa is easier than from Europe, Australia or North America and there is significant established expertise in South Africa, particularly for working in the African environment. There are equally significant factors which are slightly less obvious: there are likely to be benefits for firms locating together in terms of information sharing, co-ordination and human capital development; foreign firms operating from South Africa may gain political support from the South African government; and the South African IDC can contribute significantly to mining ventures through financing, implicit political risk guarantees and co-ordination (Goldstein and Prichard 2008).

Despite such evidence, some recent private sector research has suggested that South African dominance of regional mining services provision is far from guaranteed. A first, major factor is the tendency of globalised mining firms to enter into global sourcing contracts with individual mining service providers, so that firms with regional expertise may be marginalised. Second, South African mining service providers have struggled to enter into new mining markets at a rate proportionate to the overall growth of mining in these regions.

Finally, there is the question of sub-regional mining hubs as the scope of mining elsewhere on the continent continues to expand. While such operations at present are largely limited to mining equipment importers and fairly straightforward infrastructure firms, emerging mining nations like Ghana are likely to seek a greater upstream role in the sector in the future.

Mining, Development and Emerging Policy Challenges

While the expansion of mining activity in sub-Saharan Africa has been celebrated in many circles as a major contribution to both economic growth and government revenues, other studies have suggested that the long-term impact of mining activities on development may be more modest, or even negative (Labonne 2002). For example, Aykut and Sayek (2007) disaggregate foreign investment by sector and find that primary sector FDI has a neutral, or potentially negative, impact on growth. In similar fashion, economic growth based on minerals sector development has been increasingly criticised on other grounds: the failure to account for major environmental degradation, the enclave nature of benefits, the risk of contributing to civil conflict and a potentially corrosive effect on governance (Campbell 2004; Ross 2004, 2006). In assessing the impact of the recent surge in mining activity in the region it is thus useful to distinguish between the different potential development benefits, as well as between risk factors relating to economic consequences, conflict, environmental impact and governance implications.

The expansion of mining activity in Africa has the potential to produce significant economic benefits, but in practice their extent is case specific (Campbell 2004; Hilson 2004). In what follows, a distinction is made between direct economic benefits, state revenues and infrastructure.

Historically, mining was expected to contribute to local development largely through the generation of employment and the creation of new opportunities for suppliers and downstream beneficiation. Thus, state mining regulations prior to liberalisation emphasised these elements, either provided directly by state firms or as conditions demanded of foreign investors. This could be seen, at least in part, as an attempt to break the colonial pattern in which sourcing and beneficiation occurred largely offshore, to the benefit of colonial firms and governments rather than local populations.

But with the apparent decline of Africa's mining sector in the years that followed, such regulations were identified by the World Bank and others as major constraints to private sector engagement and thus to expanded mining activity. The liberalisation lobby argued that states should no longer focus on deriving direct economic benefits from mining, but should instead focus on maximising tax revenues to the state that could in turn be used to support social programmes and economic development (Onorato, Fox and Strongman 1998; World Bank 1992). While direct benefits were desirable in principle, the policies needed to generate them were felt to impose excessively high costs on firms and be technically demanding for governments to implement. Thus, for example, the level of local beneficiation of minerals production in sub-Saharan Africa has remained extremely low. A telling example of the difficulty of initiating local beneficiation has been Guinea, which is a major producer of bauxite, but was historically unable to persuade international firms to process the mineral into aluminium on Guinean soil (Campbell 1991).

It is now widely accepted that liberalised mining activities in sub-Saharan Africa will create only modest benefits through direct employment and few opportunities for local production of inputs or beneficiation. Benefits are thus expected to be primarily indirect: taxation, new infrastructure and foreign exchange.

With the relationship between mining and economic development increasingly focused on the generation of government revenues, growing attention has been paid to the development of appropriate tax regimes. Two general principles emerge: taxation is preferable to public ownership; and taxes should distort economic incentives as little as possible. But this still leaves the question of how much tax is appropriate and what type of tax is most effective and least distorting.

Despite the general push towards liberalisation over the past twenty years, there are still major variations between countries. They levy very different taxes and do so at different rates, while the most widely praised mining destination in the developing world, Chile, remains home to a major state-owned mining house, Codelco (Daniel, Marr and Payne 1993; Naito, Remy and Williams 2001; Otto et al. 2006). A recent World Bank publication on royalties emphasises the country specific nature of appropriate levels of taxation, due to the role of political risk, mineral endowments and other factors in establishing what constitutes an appropriate tax structure (Otto et al. 2006).

That said, many observers voice concern that despite the avowed focus on generating tax revenues for the state, mining activities have yielded far too little revenue in much of sub-Saharan Africa. To take one example, Ghana has been widely praised for its success in reviving the mining industry and becoming an important global gold producer, with mining contributing 5% of gross domestic product from 2000 to 2005. Yet corporate and individual income taxes collected from mining firms, including all royalties, amounted to an average of only slightly more than 10% of total direct taxes in the country, or only about 3% of total tax revenue.[24] Given that a small number of large taxpayers and their employees pay the overwhelming share of income taxes in the country, it appears very likely that mining firms contribute relatively less to tax revenue than large firms in other sectors. This is attributable to low tax rates, but, more importantly it seems, to extensive exemptions and capital allowances. While the laws on capital allowances in many African states are consistent with those that exist elsewhere, the ability of local tax administrations to monitor the veracity of capital allowance claims is more limited. Thus, for example, many tax administrators point to cases is which firms overvalue their equipment, claim full capital allowances on used equipment that had previously been depreciated in another country and then imported, or claim capital allowances on equipment owned by contract miners that they employ. All of these types of tax fraud reduce income tax liabilities and are reflected in the fact that in Ghana, as in many countries, revenue from mining royalties is offset by exceptionally low corporate tax payments.[25]

On the question of what type of tax is most appropriate, there is a recognised tension between taxes on profits and taxes on revenues: profit taxes are less distorting, but technically demanding and lead to dramatic variations in revenue; while taxes on revenues distort production decisions, but ensure more regular returns. Overall there appears to be a preference for the former in international circles.

The lack of existing infrastructure in many African countries has meant that new mining ventures are often forced to make major investments, while public money may also be invested in improving everything from transportation networks to electricity production. Recent examples in the transport sector include the rehabilitation of railways in Angola and the DRC (Benguela), Zambia (Northwest province), Tanzania and Zambia (Tanzam), Liberia (linking iron ore mines to the coast), Gabon (linking Belinga to the coast) and Mozambique (Moatize to Beira). The development of this new infrastructure could open major new opportunities to local communities, who may, for example, gain vastly improved access to transportation networks. Yet, the historical record from the colonial period invites scepticism about the extent to which mining firms will take an interest in ensuring such access. An early test case on the continent was the construction of the M4 toll road linking South Africa to the Mozambican port of Maputo as part of the project to develop the Mozal aluminium smelter. Significant declarations were made regarding the potential development benefits to communities situated along the new road, but early returns have been mixed at best, with many communities finding the cost of accessing the road prohibitive (Söderbaum 2003).

A major risk presented by mining investments is their potential to fuel regional or civil conflict. Simply put, parties may be encouraged to go to war in order to gain control over mineral resources, while, once at war, the ability to exploit mineral resources, often through illegal exports via neighbouring countries, can be a primary source of revenue to sustain conflict (Ross 2006). The past decade has seen various examples of conflict in Africa in which mineral wealth has helped to fuel the fighting: most notably, diamonds have helped drive civil conflict in Sierra Leone, Liberia and Angola; while competition over a wider variety of minerals has contributed to conflict in the DRC, involving both competing domestic factions and neighbouring countries. While these countries are all presently at peace, that does not eliminate the potential risk. In the DRC, illegal minerals exports continue to fuel conflict in more remote areas, leading the UN to argue that 'until mining [is] brought firmly under state control, it will be impossible to ensure peace and security'.[26] With increased competition for access to those mineral resources the challenge of regulation is likely to become more difficult.

Most indications are that while environmental degradation is a major priority for local communities and for many international bodies, it does not rank highly among the priorities of African governments. Of the 66 jurisdictions considered by the Fraser Institute survey, the ten with the weakest environmental protection include six from Africa, while the two remaining African nations, South Africa and Zambia, rank fifteenth and twentieth. This would seem to reflect not only weak policy frameworks, but also severely limited enforcement capacity and motivation (Campbell 2004).

While the issues discussed above have received the bulk of attention from international bodies, questions of governance play an equally important role in shaping the impact of new mining initiatives. In arguing that the main benefits to developing countries from mining will come in the form of increased tax revenues, proponents of mining liberalisation assume that increased tax dollars will generate improved provision of public goods. While it seems a rather elementary point, the reality remains that the transformation of taxes into development benefits remains tenuous in many countries. It is also clear that because sub-Saharan African states are far more fiscally centralised than in any other region of the world, communities that bear the direct costs of mining activity have few guarantees of reaping a proportionate share of the benefits of increased government revenues, which tend to flow to the central government. For example, local communities are currently expected to reap only 0.4% of tax revenues from the new aluminium smelter to be constructed in Guinea (Labonne 2002).

These problems are compounded by concern that the use of minerals revenues may be particularly unaccountable or may even erode the quality of governance. Moore (1998) has argued that governments are more likely to be accountable to citizens when taxes are relatively more earned, by which he means that their collection involves the development of an effective bureaucracy and the securing of some degree of citizen consent. Similarly, governments that have easy access to revenues that demand neither a reliable bureaucracy nor citizen consent, such as mineral revenues, may feel a diminished responsibility to be accountable. This dynamic is particularly well established in the case of oil revenues (Ross 2006), but there is growing evidence that it may hold more generally.

Policy Options for Increasing Local Benefits

What follows addresses major policy questions at a macro level and divides important policy debates into three broad categories. The first relates to the ongoing debate about the appropriate balance between liberalisation and state intervention and regulation. The second asks whether the recent minerals boom justifies a shift in the balance between liberalisation and government intervention. The third focuses on those aspects of the current boom that are historically unique

– specifically, the implications of movement into higher-risk areas and the entry of developing country firms into the region.

The history of mining in sub-Saharan Africa has seen a series of swings between a laissez-faire and highly interventionist approaches. The colonial period clearly brought too few benefits to local communities in granting total power to international firms, while the post-independence period of intervention resulted in the decline of the sector. The recent phase of liberalisation was a reaction to the failures of the 1960s and 1970s, but has left some observers wondering whether there may be a middle way.

Some critiques of liberalisation are in many ways simple criticism of mining-led development in general, arguing that mining development only benefits an elite at major environmental and political cost (Campbell 2004). This is not without validity, but this approach is not pursued any further here because it would move the analysis in a different direction. Instead, what follows focuses on the more narrow justification for liberalisation in terms of aggregate economic benefits to host countries.

The initial argument in favour of liberalisation rested on evidence that areas of high government intervention in the minerals sector were also the areas of poorest performance. Subsequent evidence of the success of liberalisation lies in the fact that sub-Saharan Africa's share of global minerals exploration spending has steadily increased ever since. The first country to undergo structural adjustment was Ghana and the impact on gold production was dramatic: it rose from 16 800 kg in 1990 to 53 087 kg in 1995 and 72 080 kg in 2000 (Hilson 2004). Countries including Mali and Tanzania liberalised later and experienced corresponding surges in production after 1995 and 2000 respectively (Mitchell 2006), while privatisation in Zambia has coincided with increased activity in copper mining (Craig 2001). While many observers have fixated on the short-term surge in global, and thus also regional, mining activity, many within the industry argue that the more important long-term development has been the increase in the region's share of that activity, which is often attributed to liberalisation. Annual surveys conducted by the Fraser Institute find that mining regulation in sub-Saharan Africa's leading mining destinations now compares reasonably favourably with other developing regions in the eyes of mining executives (McMahon and Melhem 2006). Moreover, given that the region's share of global mining activity still lags far behind its estimated share of global deposits, observers argue that the benefits of increased investment have only begun to be realised.

A plausible counter argument derives from the fact that the evidence presented in favour of liberalisation has been somewhat selective, and has fixated on policy variables to the exclusion of other factors driving activity in the sector. The massive decline in Africa's share of minerals production after 1960, along with the evidence of dramatic underperformance by state mining firms, was overwhelmingly driven by the experience of declining copper production in the DRC (then Zaire) and Zambia (World Bank 1992). Yet, both countries were in the midst of dramatic governance breakdowns at the time, and this should cast some doubt on the extent to which mining sector regulations alone were the source of stagnation. While the underperformance of state operations holds in the remaining cases, it is much less dramatic. Equally significant, the World Bank definition of private firms for the purpose of demonstrating their superior performance includes all privately-operated projects, including those with major government ownership shares. While this does not diminish the finding that these projects were more successful, it does not provide evidence that partial state ownership alone is problematic.

It is also important to note other factors that contributed to the bottoming out of sub-Saharan African minerals investment and production in the 1980s, and to the subsequent recovery. First is the fact that the 1980s were a period of very low minerals prices and such periods are associated with major declines in activity in high-risk areas (Bridge 2004). This tendency can equally be seen in the post-liberalisation period, as Africa's share of global minerals exploration spending fell to between 5 and 7% in the period 1999–2002, after reaching 9–10% at its peak in 1997 and then 10–12% in later years.

Second is the fact that the quality of governance and of economic management reached a historic low in the 1980s, with a wide range of sub-Saharan African countries encountering major debt and more general economic problems. Indeed, it is precisely the depth of the systemic crisis affecting these countries that led to the process of internationally supported liberalisation. While it is certainly true that under conditions of such drastic economic mismanagement reducing public sector involvement would be expected to yield benefits, it is less clear what this implies for countries that are beginning to demonstrate improved governance capacity.

Many of the countries that seem to be benefiting most from the recent boom are those emerging from conflict, most notably the DRC and Liberia (see table 10.1). In fact, the DRC, despite still being ranked very poorly by industry executives on policy issues, has emerged as the most attractive mining destination in the region after attaining a tentative peace. This fact further highlights the extent to which basic political stability is perhaps the single greatest prerequisite for mining investment, but it was increasingly absent in many countries in the 1980s and into the 1990s. Thus we may wonder whether it was liberalisation specifically, or political stabilisation generally, that was most important for increased mining activity.

If one takes the view that it is broader progress in improving political stability and reducing conflict that has been at the root of improved mining performance in the region, then it is equally plausible to conclude that as stability takes root governments can, and should, seek to demand greater benefits from mining ventures. This may take the form of higher taxes, partial ownership or more complex forms of regulation, such as requirements for local employment, sourcing or beneficiation. Looked at another way, political risk is one of the major costs facing mining firms, so as it declines there should be opportunities for increasing other demands. An interesting case in this regard is Indonesia, which initially undertook major liberalising reforms in order to revive a stagnant mining sector, but subsequently gradually increased demands on foreign investors as confidence and existing projects were developed. While observers at the time worried about the consequence of this regulatory tightening for investment levels (World Bank 1992), a recent World Bank study has suggested that the progressive increase in regulation was highly effective (Otto et al. 2006).

Some observers argue that although the general case for liberalisation may be sound, the recent boom in the regional minerals sector implies a fundamentally new regulatory context. The argument is simple: with higher profits being made, host countries should also be demanding more. Consulting firm Country Risk recently reported a growing sentiment of resource nationalism throughout Africa, mirroring the emergence of active manifestations of this sentiment in Latin America, though it argued that major policy changes do not seem likely at present.[27]

Those within the mining industry have consistently argued against countries imposing stricter regulations during mineral booms. They argue that because the mining industry is highly cyclical, investment during low times will only be undertaken if there are assurances that large profits will be allowed during boom periods. This general proposition is undeniably legitimate: the case for reforming mining regulation must rest on evidence of a step change in demand, as opposed to a cyclical boom. If prices, and therefore demand, are witnessing a sustained upward shift then that may present a case for national governments seeking to secure greater benefits. Equally, in so far as a greater number of firms, from a greater number of countries, are now competing for access to sub-Saharan African mineral deposits, regional governments may have greater negotiating leverage than ever before. That said, the evidence for such a fundamental shift remains uncertain, pointing to the need for a gradual approach to regulatory changes until such time as evidence of a sustained upward trajectory becomes more evident.

Particular characteristics of the recent boom seem to raise daunting governance questions. As has already been noted, it has long been recognised that mining firms may have a negative impact on governance in host countries. Competition for mineral resources may lead to conflict, access to large external revenues may erode accountability or firms may bribe government officials, thus leading to mining agreements that generate private, rather than social, benefits. The increasing entry of firms into high-risk and post-conflict regions of sub-Saharan Africa clearly adds to these possibilities.

This is exacerbated by the involvement of firms from a growing array of nations. On the one hand, these new firms may be less concerned with upholding standards of good practice, related to both bribery and to environmental and labour standards, which seem to have seen some improvement, albeit haltingly, among established firms. At least as importantly, greater competition between the expanding number of firms active on the continent means that they may be under more pressure than ever before to engage in unsavoury dealings. All of these issues point to an urgent need for greater attention to the connection between effective political management, through means such as transparency and community participation, and the ability to reap the benefits of expanded mining.

While there has not, as yet, been any wholesale regulatory change in any of the major mining countries in sub-Saharan Africa, there have been several developments of interest to those who advocate more demanding regulation.

One trend is found in countries that have sought to renegotiate mining agreements signed by earlier governments under questionable circumstances. In the DRC, civil society groups demanded a review of all minerals contracts signed during the conflict and the transition to peace. The government announced the creation of a review commission in April 2007, although results remain to be seen.[28] Similarly, on the election of President Ellen Johnson-Sirleaf, the Liberian government renegotiated an iron ore mining agreement signed with Mittal by the previous transitional government, thus significantly increasing benefits to the country.[29] The success of this effort in Liberia would seem to suggest that at least some contracts on the continent could be made significantly more favorable to host countries and that changes in regulatory policy can be successful when they are undertaken prudently.

There have also been intriguing developments in several countries where governments have intervened to insist on the local beneficiation of minerals production. In South Africa, unprocessed chromium was increasingly exported to China before being processed into ferrochrome, thus bypassing South African beneficiation facilities. This practice was encouraged by the Chinese government, which places lower tariffs on unprocessed mineral imports. The South African government responded by banning these unprocessed exports.[30] Soon afterwards, the governor of Katanga province in the DRC declared that unrefined ore, often processed in neighbouring Zambia, would be banned from export while he also announced plans to investigate the export of concentrates. While the outcome in the DRC remains up in the air, it was notable that the measures were celebrated by the leading mining publication in South Africa.[31] Finally, Guinea has recently secured a commitment from Global Alumina to construct an aluminium smelter to beneficiate the country's bauxite. While this did not involve a change in law, it is notable that after decades of seeking local beneficiation it has finally been achieved during the recent boom.[32]

It is worth mentioning far-ranging regulatory changes occurring in South Africa, led by the introduction of black economic empowerment regulations, discussion of royalty taxes and the publication of a Mining Charter. South Africa is actively trying to change the allocation of benefits from mining, while still respecting the needs of the market, which may further the likelihood of other countries considering different forms of intervention. On the whole, these changes have aroused scepticism within the international mining community, but the real test will lie in assessing the long-term impact on South African mining. This remains difficult to judge while the transition is still underway (McMahon and Melhem 2006).

Conclusion

Since 2002 high minerals prices, driven in particular by demand from China, have led to a sharp upturn in mining investment around the world. This process has, not surprisingly, led to some dramatic predictions, both positive and negative, about the likely impact of these events on prospects for economic development in sub-Saharan Africa. Yet, much of this popular attention has been poorly rooted in any systematic analysis of current events or their relation to the history of mining in the region.

This chapter has tried to provide a more balanced view. While the recent surge has been dramatic, the minerals industry is extremely cyclical, and when viewed in historical perspective the rise in investment and prices from 2002 to 2006 is not quantitatively unique. If prices remain high for several more years it might then be possible to claim differently, but even then the challenges facing mining in sub-Saharan Africa would not be unrecognisably different from those that have existed since 1960. The unique characteristic of the recent boom has been the increasing involvement of firms from developing countries, and while this may affect competitive dynamics in the region and raise some challenging governance questions, it does not fundamentally change the regulatory challenge.

What benefit is served by placing the current mining boom in historical perspective? As with so much similar analysis, it allows policy makers to learn from the mistakes of the past. The optimistic days of the 1960s led to dramatic policy reforms that ultimately quashed much of the dynamism of the sector. The low prices and political instability of the 1980s contributed to wholesale liberalisation, leaving host countries with relatively limited benefits from newly expanding mining activity. While recent events have led to some calls for dramatic change, this chapter has suggested that while there is a case for some reform of mining regulation in sub-Saharan Africa, reforms will be best approached gradually, keeping a careful eye on what works, and what does not, elsewhere in the region.

Afterword

This chapter was finalised in early 2008, at the height of the global mining boom. Despite the exceptionally high prices that prevailed at the time, one of the basic arguments of the chapter was that it was important to maintain an understanding of history, and bear in mind the inherent cyclicality of the minerals sector when formulating policy. Recent events have borne out this conclusion as the global economic downturn that began in mid-2008 has led to sharp reductions in many commodity prices, and in corresponding levels of investment. The impact of the downturn has been most acute for diamonds, which are a pure luxury good, and for base metals, precisely the commodities that had benefited most from the mining boom. While it is still too early to fully assess the impact, the African Development Bank has already highlighted the mining downturn as an important contributor to the expected growth slowdown in the region (ADB 2009), while, to take a single example, reports have emerged from the DRC about major job losses as some mining operations have been shut down.[33] The lesson that has been reinforced is that policy frameworks need to be tailored to the cyclicality of the industry, so as to reap large benefits during boom times, while seeking to reduce the volatility that can accompany major price swings. This is not to suggest that African governments could not be reaping greater benefits from their mining sectors, but simply that ad hoc policy making during boom periods is not likely to be an effective solution.

Notes

1. Central African Republic, DRC, Gabon, Guinea, Liberia, Mali, Mauritania, Mozambique, Namibia, Niger, Senegal, Sierra Leone, South Africa, Tanzania, Togo, Zambia and Zimbabwe.

2. Many of the insights provided in this paper, particularly related to the activities and motivations of mining and mining services firms, are drawn from extensive interviews conducted by the author in July 2006, along with intermittent email correspondence since then. These instances are not individually cited in the text in order to avoid pointless repetition and because the interviews were conducted on condition of anonymity.

3. This refers to a sample of ten minerals: aluminium, copper, iron ore, zinc, nickel, lead, tin, bauxite, alumina and gold. Although the data are not available, it is clear that the inclusion of diamonds in these calculations would make the African share significantly larger and would diminish the relative decline. On the other hand, diamond mining poses rather unique challenges and is, perhaps, usefully thought of separately.

4. All exploration data is from the Metals Economics Group (2007). Data on mining investment in aggregated form is both rare and difficult to access and data on exploration activity is most frequently used to gauge levels of mining activity.

5. *Mining Weekly* 13 July 2007.

6. The rest of world group includes Europe, the former Soviet Union, Asia and the Middle East and has been led by activity in Russia, China and Mongolia.

7. Money Web 30 Jan. 2007.

8. *Sunday Telegraph* (London) 5 Feb. 2007.

9. *Purchasing* 14 June 2007.

10. *Business Report* (Johannesburg) 3 June 2006.

11. *Reuters* 23 May 2007.

12. *Sunday Telegraph* 5 Feb. 2007; *Sunday Telegraph* 5 Feb. 2007.

13. *Times Online* 2 Mar. 2007.

14. *Reuters* 23 May 2007.

15. International Monetary Fund, Government of Zambia: Letter of Intent, Memorandum of Economic and Financial Policies, and Technical Memorandum of Understanding, 2007.

16. *Times Online* 2 Mar. 2007.

17. *Mining Weekly* 8 and 10 Feb. 2008; *IPS News* 8 Feb. 2008.

18. *Business Report* 3 June 2007.

19. *Mining Weekly* 6 Aug. 2004; *Business Report* 3 June 2006.

20. *Bloomberg* 17 Aug. 2006.

21. South Africa's FDI Flows into Africa: presentation to the National Treasury Interdepartmental Workshop, Johannesburg, 2006, by R. Rumney.

22. *Creamer's Mining Weekly* 2 Feb. 2006.

23. *Creamer's Mining Weekly* 27 Oct. 2006.

24. International Monetary Fund, Ghana: statistical appendix, 2005.

25. Interviews conducted by the author within the Ghanaian tax administration, Feb.-Mar. 2008.
26. *Reuters* 30 Jan. 2007.
27. *Mining Weekly* 17–23 Nov. 2006.
28. Bretton Woods Project, Congo: mining, conflict and complicity, 2007; Global Witness, Congolese government should ensure transparency and independent oversight in mining contract review, 2007.
29. *Mine Web* 2 May 2007.
30. *Mining Weekly* 9 Mar. 2007.
31. *Mining Weekly* 30 Mar. 2007; *Mine Web* 22 Mar. 2007.
32. *BBC News Online* 1 May 2007.
33. *BBC News Online* 9 December 2008.

References

ADB. 2009. *Impact of the Global Financial and Economic Crisis on Africa*. Tunis: African Development Bank, Office of the Chief Economist.

Aykut, D. and S. Sayek. 2007. 'The role of the sectoral composition of foreign direct investment on growth'. In: *Do Multinationals Feed Local Development and Growth?* edited by L. Piscitello and G. Santangelo. Amsterdam: Elsevier.

Bridge, G. 2004. 'Mapping the bonanza: geographies of mining investment in an era of neoliberal reform'. *Professional Geographer* 56(3): 406–21.

Broadman, H. 2007. *Africa's Silk Road: China and India's New Economic Frontier.* Washington: World Bank.

Campbell, B. 1991. 'Negotiating the bauxite/aluminium sector under narrowing constraints'. *Review of African Political Economy* 18(1): 27–49.

——. 2004. *Regulating Mining in Africa: For Whose Benefit?* Uppsala: Nordiska Afrikainstitutet.

Chabane, N., A. Goldstein and S. Roberts. 2006. 'The changing face and strategies of big business in South Africa: more than a decade of political democracy'. *Industrial and Corporate Change* 15(3): 549–77.

Craig, J. 2001. 'Putting privatization into practice: the case of Zambia Consolidated Copper Mines Limited'. *Journal of Modern African Studies* 39(3): 389–410.

Daniel, J., J. Lutchman and A. Comninos. 2007. 'South African in Africa: trends and forecasts in a changing African political economy'. In: *The State of the Nation: South Africa 2007*, edited by S. Buhlungu et al. Cape Town: HSRC Press.

Daniel, P., A. Marr and P. Payne. 1993. *An International Comparison of Mining Tax Regimes*. Brighton: Institute of Development Studies.

Etemad, H. and K. Salmasi. 2002. *Location-Specific Advantages in Mining Investments in Developing Countries: Empowering and Inhibiting Factors*. Winnipeg: ASEC, University of Winnipeg,.

Fozzard, P. 1990. 'Mining development in sub-Saharan Africa: investment and its relationship to the enabling environment'. *Natural Resources Forum* 14(2): 97–105.

Freund, B. 1984. *The Making of Contemporary Africa*. Basingstoke: Macmillan.

Goldstein, A. and W. Prichard. 2008. 'South African multinationals: South-South cooperation at its best?' In: *Doing Business in Africa*, edited by N. Grobbelaar. Pretoria, South African Institute of International Affairs.

Goode, R. 2006. *Impact of China and India on sub-Saharan African Metals, Ores and Minerals: Issues and Challenges*. Johannesburg, African Economic Research Consortium. http://www.aercafrica.org/documents/asian-drivers-working-papers/GoodeR-MetalsOres Mineral.pdf.

Hilson, G. 2004. 'Structural adjustment in Africa: assessing the impacts of mining-sector reform'. *Africa Today* 51(2): 53–77.

Kumar, R. 1990. 'Policy reform to expand mining investment in sub-Saharan Africa'. *Resources Policy* 16(4): 242–53.

Labonne, B. 2002. 'Harnessing mining for poverty reduction, especially in Africa'. *Natural Resources Forum* 26: 69–73.

McMahon, F. and A. Melhem. 2006. *Fraser Institute Annual Survey of Mining Companies 2005/2006*. Vancouver: Fraser Institute.

Metals Economics Group. 2007. *World Exploration Trends: A Special Report from Metals Economics Group for the PDAC International Convention 2007*. Halifax: Metals Economics Group.

Mitchell, P. 2006. 'Mining and economic growth: the case for Ghana and Tanzania'. *South African Journal of International Affairs* 13(2): 53–67.

Moore, M. 1998. 'Death without taxes: democracy, state capacity and aid dependence in the Fourth World'. In: *The Democratic Developmental State*, edited by M. Robinson and G. White. New York: Oxford University Press.

Naidu, S. and M. Davies. 2006. 'China fuels its future with Africa's riches'. *South African Journal of International Affairs* 13(2): 69–83.

Naito, K., F. Remy and J. Williams. 2001. *Review of Legal and Fiscal Frameworks for Exploration and Mining*. London: Mining Journal Book.

Onorato, W., P. Fox and J. Strongman. 1998. 'World Bank group assistance for minerals sector development and reform in member countries'. *World Bank Technical Paper* 405.

Otto, J. et al. 2006. *Mining Royalties: A Global Study of Their Impact on Investors, Government and Civil Society*. Washington: World Bank.

Ross, M. 2004. 'Does taxation lead to representation'. *British Journal of Political Science* 34: 229–49.

——. 2006. *Mineral Wealth and Equitable Development*. Washington: World Bank.

Söderbaum F. 2003. 'Governance in the Maputo Development Corridor'. In: *Regionalism and Uneven Development in Southern Africa: The Case of the Maputo Development Corridor*, edited by F. Söderbaum and I. Taylor. Aldershot: Ashgate, 57–76.

USGS. 2007. US Geological Survey Minerals Yearbook 2007. Reston, VA: United States Geological Survey.

World Bank. 1992. 'Strategy for African mining'. *World Bank Technical Paper* 181.

CHAPTER ELEVEN

Extractive Orders

Transnational Mining Companies in the Nineteenth and
Twenty-First Centuries in the Central African Copperbelt

Jana Hönke

A boost in global mineral and metal prices has spurred investment in the resource-rich regions of Africa, provoking comparisons with the imperial scramble for Africa at the end of the nineteenth century. Transnational companies played an important role in tapping African raw material resources in the nineteenth and early twentieth centuries as they do today. In the past, companies were not only instrumental in opening up the continent's mineral deposits to supply European industrialisation, but were also significant in the establishment of colonial rule. Imperial and colonial states subcontracted governance functions to concessionary firms who acted as hybrid entities following private, for-profit interests while endowed with state-like powers and functions. Today, large multinational companies, alongside a number of state-owned enterprises, are involved in a new economic scramble for industrial minerals on the continent, driven either by the price boom on the international metal market, or the resource interests of their home states.

History provides appealing analogies to capture contemporary developments: the words new scramble are used in the title of this book and others (Frynas and Paulo 2006). Taking the analogy seriously, this chapter analyses the old and new engagement of international industrial mining companies from a particular angle. Focusing on foreign companies during two periods of an alleged scramble for African resources – the early phase of European colonisation during the nineteenth and twentieth centuries, and the beginning of the twenty-first century – my interest lies in exploring similarities in the role of companies in producing a resource extraction order. Compared to their predecessors mining companies today seem to be much less involved in governing mining regions. However, contemporary companies also operate in contexts of fragmented and weak political order, so similarities can be expected. This chapter analyses how strategies to secure production shape the political, social and spatial order of extraction enclaves and how companies relate to local political authorities.

The analysis draws on the Central African Copperbelt, comprising the Copperbelt province in the north of Zambia and the Katanga province in the south of the Democratic Republic of Congo (DRC), as a case study. Historically, the region was characterised by an economic regime of competitive exploitation (Austen 1987: 155) and it is strongly affected by the booming demand for industrial metals today. The first part of the paper introduces the heuristic perspective from which the nexus of extractive business and political order will be analysed. The second part relates the integration of the region into the global economy to the boom and bust cycles of the international copper and cobalt market, gives an overview of the role of companies in the scramble for Katanga and the Copperbelt in the nineteenth century, and provides background information on the recent investment boom in the region. While acknowledging a number of obvious differences, the third part analyses how companies engage in securing production in the context of weak statehood and carves out similar patterns of ensuring order pertaining to both periods of time.

Changing the Perspective

The modern state is historically and geographically a unique form of ordering that emerged from the particular historical, social, economic and political context of Western Europe, and legitimised a monopoly over the use of force by a single agency (Elias 1997; Tilly 1992; Weber 2006). African states emerged under conditions different from the European context (Clapham 1996). Limited statehood is understood here as referring to a centralised political apparatus that claims to have the monopoly of the means of force in a territory, but does not employ it effectively (Weber 1971: 506).

While contemporary debates about the future of the state suggest that with the demise of the Westphalian system transformation into a multilayered system of global, national and local governance is under way in the West, overlapping spheres of authority were always the norm in Africa (Mbembe 2002). This can be observed in particular in regions, such as the enclaves of resource extraction in the global South, drawn into global economic circuits while part of weak or unstable political orders. Studies on enclaves of mineral extraction such as the oil-producing Angolan region of Cabinda (Soares de Oliveira 2007) and oil platforms in the Niger Delta (Frynas 2001; Zalik 2006) show how particular forms of private order have emerged that seek to protect islands of stability against poor and politically fragile surroundings.

It is surprising, though, that mining regions have rarely been studied from the angle of the maintenance of security. This chapter looks at the role of transnational mining companies in maintaining local order in one of the most important African mining regions. Similarly, across different historical periods, the mining industry has had an important impact on local politics. First, investment in mineral exploitation is capital-intensive, risky and implies long cycles of returns to investment. As a result, the mining industry is oligopolistically structured and vertically highly integrated. Foreign capital plays an important role in any mining operation (Vernon 1971). Second, mining operations rarely have an exit option and are dependent on engaging with local social and political structures. Third, investment in mineral exploitation is often linked to external strategic interests and tends to be intertwined with political interests (UNCTAD 2007: 122). A recent example in this respect is the issue of energy security. Having resurfaced at the top of the international political agenda, companies and states are competing over access to oil. Similarly, recent investment by Chinese companies in industrial mining is backed by active state policy.

Requiring the investment of enormous sums over a long period of time, industrial mineral extraction depends on a minimum of stability and order. The organisation of the means of violence and the regulation of the use of force is a central institutional feature of any political order. Taking the functional claim of the modern state as a starting point, mining companies are analysed in terms of taking up functions usually associated with statehood, such as assuming the 'administrative, policing and military authority within a specific jurisdiction' (Thompson 1994: 150). In the context of the modern state, the police have historically had two functions: first, maintaining an effective monopoly over the use of force internally, and second, the enforcement of regulations and discipline in the interest of public order within a given territory (Schlichte 2005: 81; Zedner 2006). Looking at contexts of plural policing (Jones and Newburn 2006), this chapter describes the role of companies in security governance based on Schlichte's and Zedner's broad understanding of policing, including more indirect patterns of social control and shaping space.

The Scramble for Resources in the Central African Copperbelt

During the late nineteenth and early twentieth centuries, at the height of an economic scramble, the Central African Copperbelt was characterised by the arrival of large foreign companies working in the context of absent or limited statehood (Hopkins 1976b: 274). Today, multinational mining companies are investing in the Zambian Copperbelt and the Katanga province of the DRC in the context of weak state structures. During the nineteenth century, companies proceeded alongside the imperial interests of their respective home countries, building up colonial administrative structures and providing capital for the development of the mineral resources of British Northern Rhodesia and the Belgian King Leopold's Congo Independent State. Today it is the search for industrial minerals by newly-industrialising countries that has spurred foreign direct investment (FDI) in the mineral resources of the region.

Africa's integration into the global economy was based on the extraction of natural resources through a model of predatory production: slavery, ivory, timber and rubber, as well as enclave plantation production and mining (Austen 1987: 97). External demand cycles incorporated African regions into formal and informal global economic circuits.

Following the discovery of gold and diamonds on the South African Rand, mining exploration began in the Central African Copperbelt in the 1890s. The European industrialisation process had increased demand for base metals and subsequently copper mining became a central sector in the African export economy (Austen 1987: 70; Mikesell 1988). While the development of the Katanga mines took off with the arrival of the railway from Kimberley via Bulawayo in 1910, mainly financed by Belgian and British capital, Northern Rhodesia became a strategic sourcing region for copper in the 1920s, attracting large-scale investment from South African, British and American capital. In the Belgian Congo, the Société Général du Belgique acquired a dominant position in the Union Minière du Katanga (Depelchin 1992; Ilunkamba 1984). Copper production in Northern Rhodesia was controlled by the American Roan Selection Trust Group and the South African Anglo- American Group from the late 1920s (Butler 2007: 128). The expansion of large Western mining companies against the background of an evolving colonial order is reflected in the fact that in the early twentieth century, more than 50% of FDI went into extractive industries in developing countries (UNCTAD 2007: 127). Having attained strategic importance in the metropolis, Central African copper production expanded from 1910 and, after the Great Depression in 1929, once again during the Second World War.

After a long-term decline of prices on the international metal markets from the mid-1970s, the demand for industrial minerals such as copper, zinc, bauxite and the platinum group of metals rose enormously after 2004. Considerable price increases also occurred in metals such as aluminium, copper, nickel and zinc due to growing demand in industrialising economies such as China and India (see chapter ten by Wilson Pritchard in this book). As a result, corporate profits soared and international investments rebounded. These investments have gone to politically more risky areas as can be observed from increasing exploration activities in Central Africa, China and Russia. This trend is also driven by restructuring that has taken place within the international mining industry. While until the 1960s Western multinational companies used to dominate the extraction of African minerals, less risk-averse junior companies and corporations from newly-industrialising countries such as India, China and South Africa have increasingly invested on the continent (Tilton 1990; UNCTAD 2007).

In the nineteenth century scramble for Africa, Western firms played an important role both in the years preceding the Berlin Conference of 1884-5, as well as during the period of formal colonial rule afterwards. Until the nineteenth century, European states used private companies to open up new markets for trade and the extraction of resources and to extend their influence and authority outside Europe. Proto-multinational companies (Jones 2005: 17), such as the British and Dutch East India Companies, were officially used to extend the metropolitan sphere of indirect and, later, direct control (McIntyre 1967: 363; Thompson 1994).

These chartered companies received commercial privileges, such as the monopoly over trade with a region or in a particular good. However these companies were created, they were mainly privately financed entities that exercised diplomatic, juridical and military power. To enable them to penetrate new territory, the charter delegated substantial sovereignty to them: they were usually allowed to make treaties, raise arms and make war (Thompson 1994: 10, 35). Commercial privileges were thus associated with governmental purpose (Vernon 1971: 294).[1]

In Central Africa company rule continued 'long after it had become anachronistic elsewhere'. (Martin 1983: 8). European trading companies of the eighteenth and nineteenth centuries extracted slaves, ivory and gold by working with indigenous authorities or strongmen. In the second half of the nineteenth century, trade in rubber and palm oil, which were used in the industrialisation of Europe, transformed Central Africa. The hinterlands of coastal trading posts were increasingly drawn into outward-oriented circuits of production and trade.

The search for potential mineral deposits at the end of the nineteenth century encouraged the exploration of Katanga and the Copperbelt and industrial mining became the major restructuring force for the region's societies (Austen 1987: 68; Martin 1983).

Two types of company rule played an important role in the region, the British model of chartered company, represented here by the case of the British South Africa Company (BSAC) in what later became part of the British colony of Northern Rhodesia; and the Belgian model of concessionary company, exemplified by the Compagnie du Katanga (CdK), jointly run and owned by private capital and the state to open up copper and cobalt reserves of the Congo (Austen 1987: 124).

The British strategy of granting charters to private companies to extend a commercial, indirect empire in the world outside Europe persisted well into the nineteenth century, when interest in the exploration of new markets and precious and industrial mineral deposits increasingly encountered rising competition between European imperial powers over the control of territory. The area north of the Zambezi had remained a backwater of imperial politics for a long time. However, although not showing much interest in the area initially, Great Britain nevertheless granted a charter to Cecil Rhodes' BSAC to explore the area. Rhodes had a substantial stake in the emerging mining economy of South Africa and lobbied for expanding the British empire further north, hoping to find a second Rand comparable to the South African gold fields (Galbraith 1974).

The BSAC operated on the basis of a charter that did not itself grant any mining rights. However, it empowered the company 'to acquire by any concession, agreement, grant or treaty all or any rights, interests, authorities, jurisdictions and powers of any kind or nature whatsoever' (Slinn 1971: 365). Authority and concession rights had to be acquired from local rulers with jurisdiction over the respective territory. In the absence of a state that was recognised by the international system, the company sought operational legitimacy through striking deals with local sovereigns, playing on its hybrid status as a private company working as an agent of its home state (Galbraith 1974: 212; Slade 1962).

Partly as a reaction to public criticism of company governance in Northern Rhodesia, the Copperbelt came under direct British administration in 1924. The BSAC, however, remained the sole owner of mineral rights throughout the region and continued to perform quasi-governmental functions for the mining industry beyond the scarce resources of the newly-established, under-resourced Colonial Office (Slinn 1971: 384). With growing external demand for copper and change in the regulation of mining, this form of joint company-state rule provided the basis to attract large-scale mining investment to the Copperbelt from British, South African and American capital. The discovery of large deposits of copper led to the development of one of Africa's largest industrial complexes during the 1920s and 1930s, controlled by two industrial groups, the South African Anglo-American Group (AAG), in whose Rhodesian operations the BSAC held substantial shares, and the American Roan Selection Trust (RST), a subsidiary of American Metals Climax (Butler 2007; Larmer 2007; Roberts 1976).

To govern the semi-private Congo Independent State, the Belgian King, Leopold II, made extensive use of the second type of company. The Congo having been recognised as his personal fiefdom at the Berlin conference of 1884–5, Leopold developed a privatised regime of indirect management through public-private concessionary companies. Part of the territory was declared an exclusive domain for state enterprises and other parts were given to private concessionary companies in which the state held considerable shares (Jewsiewicki 1983: 97; Stengers 1981).

The CdK received exclusive buying and selling rights as well as unhindered effective control over the south of Katanga. After several expeditions, jointly organised by the CdK and Leopold, the local ruler was overthrown and the region was put under business-state administration from 1900 to 1910. Full administrative authority was accorded to the newly- created Comité Special du Katanga (CSK), in which Leopold and the CdK held shares. After the takeover of the colony by the Belgian state in 1908, Katanga remained under a separate administration. A close relationship developed between the colonial 'état holding' (Vellut 1981) and company interests (Ilunkamba 1984; Stengers and Vansina 1985; Vellut 1983). In 1906 the Union Minière du Haute Katanga (UMHK) was created, jointly owned by the CSK, the Belgian Société Général, the British Tanganyika Concession Limited and other minor shareholders and developed into a 'state within a state' (Depelchin 1992) in the south of Katanga.

Large-scale industrial mining was a driver for the introduction of more direct modes of controlling African territory. Emerging enclaves of mining not only required the mobilisation of international capital to build up industrial infrastructure, but they also needed the administration of the rural hinterland to provide access to labour and cheap food supplies (Jewsiewicki 1983: 98; Vellut 1983: 128). On the Copperbelt this was organised by companies without much state interference, at least until the 1930s (Butler 2007: 24). The mining regions of Katanga remained under the management authority of Belgian private capital (Ilunkamba 1984; Vellut 1983: 129).

The Present Investment Boom in Zambia and the DRC

The recent rise in global demand for African oil and industrial minerals has reminded some observers of the nineteenth century scramble. This interpretation of the mining boom in 2004–8 can only be understood in contrast to previous historical developments: first, the nationalisation of the industry in the DRC and Zambia after independence in the 1960s; and, second, the decline of the industry due to the long-term crisis of global copper prices since the mid-1970s.

In Zambia, the nationalisation of the industry began in 1967 and was completed when the government of Kenneth Kaunda took over management and sales responsibility from private companies in 1974–5. Finally they were merged into the state-owned company Zambian Consolidated Copper Mines (ZCCM) at the beginning of the 1980s (Roberts 1976).[2] Initially earning the bulk of the newly independent state's revenues, Zambia struggled with the long-term decline in global copper demand and its economic dependence on a single commodity. The privatisation process of the ZCCM, pushed through by the World Bank in 2000 in a period of continuously low demand for copper, placed the Zambian government in a poor position to negotiate advantageous contracts with foreign companies (Craig 2001). This was even more so when the major investor in the Copperbelt, the Anglo-American Corporation, pulled out of the country in 2003.

In Katanga, nationalisation of the mining industry under President Mobutu Sese Seko transferred ownership to the state, but changed little else in the new parastatal Gécamines. A study in 1984 concludes that regardless of the nationalisation of the copper and cobalt industry, the colonial model of external control of Katanga's mining industry by the Belgian Société Général, which continued to manage the company on behalf of the state, remained in place (Ilunkamba 1984: 97).[3] The Mobutu regime used Gécamines as major source of revenue nurturing patrimonial networks in the context of declining statehood, without investing in the industry (Braeckman 1992; Young and Turner 1985).

The privatisation of Gécamines started in 1995. After Joseph Kabila had replaced Mobutu in 1996, concessions were given to many small and sometimes doubtful companies belonging to political allies. Due to the general mismanagement of the new government and the outbreak of civil war in 1998, large mining companies abandoned the DRC looking for investment in more stable environments. State structures collapsed with the outbreak of the second civil war, during which the mining sector became part of a regional war economy. After the conclusion of a power-sharing agreement, a transitional government was only established by 2003 and it took until 2006 for a new government to be elected.

There has been a rise in foreign investment in the Zambian and the DRC mining industry since 2004 and 2006 respectively (see figure 11.1 for an illustration of the regional topography of mining). With the resurgence in demand for copper, a number of exploration activities are under way. Initially, medium-sized companies such as the Indian company Vedanta Resources, the Swiss company Glencore, the Canadian company First Quantum Minerals (FQML) and the South African group Metorex invested on the Copperbelt. FQML opened a new mine close to Solwezi, and the Australian exploration and mine development company Equinox Minerals is about to open up the rural North Western province with a greenfield investment in the new Lumwana copper and uranium mine, expected to become the largest open-pit mine in Africa. Zambia has also become a core country in China's search for energy and industrial resources in Africa. The first of five potential special economic zones has already begun to be established around the Chambishi mine, in which the Chinese parastatal Non-Ferrous Metals Industry Corporation (NFC) had already invested.[4]

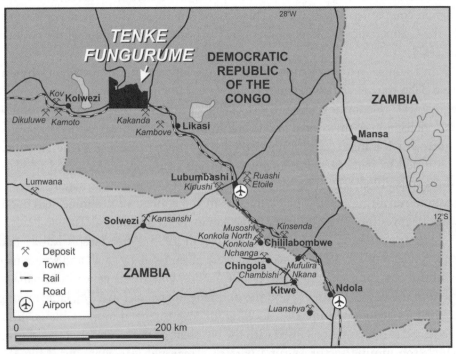

Figure 11.1   Location of major mines and towns in the Copperbelt, Zambia and southern Katanga, DRC.

Source: http://www.tenke.com/s/DRC.asp?ReportID=126093

FDI has been pouring into Katanga's mining industry since 2006. Even though the fighting in the east has not stopped and the DRC has remained volatile, elections gave large multinational mining companies a minimum of legal certainty so that they started re-entering Katanga, joining the scramble for copper, cobalt and uranium resources (UNCTAD 2007). With regard to major global mining companies, the American company Freeport McMoRan has recently acquired the majority share in one of the richest cobalt and copper reserves in Katanga, the Tenke Fungurume Mine close to the mining town of Kolwezi. The world leader in industrial metals mining, BHP Billiton, has started exploration in Katanga and AAG has recently opened regional offices in Lubumbashi and Kinshasa to push exploration for copper, nickel and zinc deposits in the DRC.[5] Junior firms entered the country earlier. Amongst them are Anvil Mining, FQML and Metorex. There are also Congolese companies such as Katanga Mining and Boss Mining, part of the business conglomerate of the former manager of Gécamines, George Forrest. Others are the Central African Mining and Exploration Company (CAMEC), struggling to distance itself from former major shareholder Billy Rautenbach, who has become persona non grata under the new government.[6]

Apart from medium and large industrial mining companies, there are many small cobalt and copper trading companies in the region, many of Chinese origin. A large-scale investment deal with China was concluded in November 2007, comprising enormous investments in the Congolese mining sector and infrastructure.[7]

An economic scramble has recently taken place in Katanga and in the Copperbelt, spurred by the long-term peak of industrial mineral prices and the industrialisation process in countries such as India and China. While economic motivations for the scramble seem to be similar, the nature of the actors involved as well as economic and political structures have changed significantly compared with the nineteenth century. Rather than imperial expansion, African sovereign states are recognised within the international system. Companies are usually less bound to their respective home states and invest in areas of high risk driven by market dynamics and without an explicit legal assignment. Apart from many obvious differences, I argue in the next section, however, that these regions show a particular pattern regarding the order produced through business and state actors. In both periods, a growing external interest in African resources went hand in hand with the operation of large international companies in a context of weak and fragmented statehood. The BSAC and the CdK ventured into areas with fragmented political orders that were destabilised in this process, alongside a colonial administration in the making. Today the DRC is usually referred to as a classical failed state, characterised by conflict, high political volatility and competing elite networks of power (Reyntjens 2007; Young 1998). Zambia exemplifies a typical case of a neo-patrimonial state with a semi-authoritarian regime and selective and weak statehood. There are similar patterns to securing extraction in these different contexts of weak statehood. The profound effects on political, social and spatial structures known from the early colonisation period may teach us about similar patterns today.

Patterns of Extractive Orders

Over time, the private mining industry has depended on alliances with incumbent political elites. This close relationship between mining companies and authorities can be observed at two levels: first, the relation between home state and multinational company; and second, between the company and local chiefs and host governments.

As regards the first, the region's mineral resources were opened up for industrial mining by a close coalition between colonial states and Western capital. Today, such a close relation between companies and state is not as evident. Companies act as private entities and when home countries do get involved, their influence is brought to bear informally. Chinese mining companies, however, are notable for the degree to which their current advancement in the Central African copper and cobalt market is driven by active Chinese foreign policy towards Zambia and the DRC. In both countries, debt relief and large- scale investment packages in infrastructure projects are being combined with special investment and trading conditions for Chinese enterprises (Melber et al. 2007). As the US Economic Co-operation Administration in the 1950s boosted Central African copper production by granting unsecured loans in return for repayment in copper and cobalt, China is linking her loans to future minerals supplies.

On the second level, mining companies need to negotiate with governments and chiefs who are the legal owners of mineral deposits. 'There is no purpose in lamenting about the authorities. You want that copper? Deal with it'. This is how a company security manager perfectly summarised the approach of mining companies towards the local political order.[8] Incited by the prospect of high profit margins, large-scale investments are made in places with high levels of uncertainty and political risk. Obtaining and securing mining concessions is a major concern.

During the 1890s the BSAC and the CdK sent expeditions to the major local rulers to obtain mining rights and recognition of the British or Belgian flag respectively. An historical example of successful collaboration was the BSAC's relationship with the Lozi king, Lewanika. In return for military protection against rival chiefs, the company obtained exclusive mineral rights in his territory in 1891 (Roberts 1976; Slade 1962). In the case of the CdK, relations with Msiri, ruler of the Garenganza kingdom, which controlled the copper trade in Katanga, were more difficult. Refusing to recognise King Leopold's authority over his land and its resources, he was killed by a delegation sent by the company. After a period of political instability, a more effective, joint colonial administration was put in place (Slade 1962: 134).

A two-tier system of indirect rule had developed towards the end of the nineteenth century. Granting companies access to mineral resources and a monopoly on profits in a certain territory, they were charged by their home country to bear the costs of establishing political domination, an administration and basic infrastructure. Confronted with a myriad of sovereignties, the companies sought to draw on existing structures of domination and to collaborate with local authorities. With weak administrative capacities in both concessionary companies and colonial states, such collaboration was imperative (Martin 1983). Therefore the BSAC built its structure on indirect rule (Slinn 1971: 368):

> we must do our best to keep [Lewanika] and his son Yeta on their
> legs. If there should be a reaction against them in a territory as big as
> Germany . . . [it] will be chaos . . . It is our settled policy to administer
> Barotseland through native authorities and not to supplant them . . .
> It would be far more expensive to try and administer so large and
> unhealthy a territory through white officials (Gell to Farnell 26 June
> 1902, cited in Slinn 1971: 269).

Founding the state authority over Katanga on traditional rulers, often appointing ex-soldiers and hand-picked loyalists as chiefs irrespective of existing local tradition, Leopold and the CdK managed to keep control over the copper province (Slade 1962: 172; Stengers and Vansina 1985: 335).

Negotiating mining rights today is a highly politicised issue in Zambia and the DRC. Companies operating in Katanga claim that political and legal insecurity is their major concern. For this reason, good relations with government elites are crucial to secure contracts and investments. In interviews conducted by the non-governmental organisation (NGO), Global Witness, in 2005, companies revealed that it was impossible to operate in Katanga without what is called a political umbrella in Kinshasa (Global Witness 2006: 42). An example of the centrality of such personal ties is the role of Katumba Mwanke, governor of Katanga Province under Laurent-Désiré Kabila from 1998 to 2001 and an important power broker with regard to the allocation of mining concessions in Katanga. He has been instrumental in negotiating the mining contract of the Australian company Anvil Mining, an early investor in the conflict-ridden DRC and was paid in return as a director of the company (Global Witness 2006; International Crisis Group 2006: 10).

The widespread demand for kickbacks and the private interests of a whole network of politicians needing to be involved during negotiations makes the DRC in some investors' point of view one of the 'worst countries to do business in'.[9] 'Elite criminal networks' (United Nations 2002) have a long history, having thrived under Mobutu and then multiplied during the recent civil wars. Similar to other parts of the DRC under the control of foreign rebel groups, state and non-state actors enriched themselves from copper and cobalt production in government-controlled Katanga.[10]

The issue of mining rights is key to company-state relations across time and explains why companies strive for an intimate relationship with incumbent regimes, particularly in a context of weak institutions and personalised rule. During the colonial scramble, companies were complicit either in drawing local sovereigns into the emerging colonial order as collaborators, or overthrowing their rule in the process of establishing a central colonial government based on revenues from mining. Today, taxes and royalties from mining companies are not simply an important contributor to government revenues. Rents in the form of taxes and side payments allow for personal enrichment, support authoritarian regimes and nurture the clientelistic networks of political elites. This has been widely discussed in the resource curse literature (Ross 1999) and theories of the rentier state (Beblawi and Luciani 1987; Moore 2004).

This close interdependence of mining business and political regime has problematic consequences. In Zambia, the importance of high-level political relations became particularly clear with regard to President Levy Mwanawasa's close relationship with China.[11] Government ignored the low level of social and safety standards and this led to protest, particularly around the Chinese-owned Chambishi Mine. First welcomed as new investors preventing the struggling mine from closure, three years later resentment had developed after 51 Zambian workers died in an explosion in 2005. After the incident, government police came to protect the company's property and allegedly shot dead several protestors calling for improved compensation packages. In July 2006, workers destroyed mine property in a violent protest during which mine management opened fire, wounding five workers. Management denies this and no official investigation has been opened so far (Larmer 2007).

In the DRC, NGOs observing malpractices in the mining sector were repeatedly threatened by government officials (Global Witness 2006: 45). In the volatile political context of Katanga, an incident in the town of Kilwa in the north east has received particular international attention as a company was allegedly involved in violence perpetrated by a faction of the army. In October 2004 the company Anvil Mining became complicit in an attack by the Congolese army, the Forces Armées de la Republic Democratic du Congo (FARDC), during which more than 100 civilians died. The company's vehicles and aeroplanes were used to attack an allegedly renegade army officer. Even though the real motives behind the attack have not been fully revealed, a close connection between politicians, commercial interests and the violent attack is manifest (ACIDH 2005; International Crisis Group 2006: 10).

Selective Local Security Governance

Security governance, defined in the sense of policing as enforcement of a political and social order by a variety of actors, forms another important area in which extraction companies engage. They are not only involved in protecting their private property, but also in governing security. Since political authority and economic interests are neatly interwoven, there is conflation of private and state policing in mining regions.

In the nineteenth century, companies built the capacities of an emergent colonial administration and fostered the development of a central police force. As the sovereign body over the territory, the BSAC was responsible for recruiting its own police force. But its approach was minimalist. The small contingent was used to guard government and company property, escort caravans, carry administrative messages to local chiefs and to effect arrests and guard prisons. Later it was instrumental in enforcing the hut tax introduced in 1911 to improve the sparse revenue base on which the BSAC's early administration depended. These examples underline the hybrid character of the company, representing private and state interests at the same time. While full administrative authority lay with the BSAC, the company was placed under the overall authority of the commander of the military in British Central Africa (Wright 2001: 13–21).

Separately managed from the rest of the Belgian Congo, the Committee Special du Katanga had its own police force to exercise authority and its representatives dealt directly with Brussels, often bypassing the colonial administration (Stengers and Vansina 1985: 242).

Companies in the nineteenth century took on state-like functions legally ascribed to them to establish external control and develop new territories for mining. Today international companies do so as a means of private management of security risks. In the context of limited statehood, companies follow a mix of strategies to shape this. They selectively engage with the security agencies of host states and private service providers to manage business security within a web of state and non-state (in)security actors.

To provide for protection of mining sites, companies in Zambia and the DRC draw extensively on the services of private security companies. In most cases, a small contingent of senior in-house security personnel monitors a larger number of private security guards, who carry out the routine tasks such as guarding gates and fences. With the current boom in mining, the private security market has been growing accordingly in the region.

In both countries, however, companies rely on the police for more critical tasks within their private property such as armed patrols and the control of labour protest, as only state police are allowed to carry arms. In Zambia, police are called in on an ad hoc basis; while in the DRC, particular branches of the national police, the Police Minière and officers of the Police de la Justice, have a permanent presence on mining sites (Netherlands Institute for Southern Africa 2006). In Zambia, companies selectively draw on the police to assist them, particularly when combating organised copper theft outside their mining premises. 'Internally, we are quite successful in catching wrongdoers,' but companies complain that they get frustrated with ineffective and unreliable police and the prosecution system. Nostalgically remembering the days of the mine police that exclusively served the needs of the industry, they today resort to private policing and nurture personal relationships with 'reliable police officers' to organise joint patrols and investigations. Local police stations around a company's operations are often supported with fuel, transport or other resources. In this sense, companies engage in selective state building.[12]

The dependence on state security forces binds companies and regime together structurally and is particularly problematic in a context where these forces are known to be corrupt, committing human rights abuses and illegally profiting from mining (Amnesty International 1999; Netherlands Institute for Southern Africa 2006; US Department of State 2006). The risk of such indirect complicity is present in the DRC in particular. State agents are widely involved in making illegal profits from mining. Some engage in the business of protecting mining sites, extracting shares from small-scale miners' earnings. Even though the military is not allowed on mine property, the army is present at many sites. The same is true for the presidential guard, the Guardes Specials de Sécurité Présidentiele (GSSP) (Spittaels and Meynen 2007: 22-25).

How companies deal with security risks depends on the particular issue and context. As a basic principle, however, companies focus on what immediately impacts on them. They turn to private policing or selectively to the public sphere depending on what is perceived as an urgent security problem.

An illustrative example is the control of labour. In the past, recruiting and controlling labour used to be an important area of joint public and private policing. During the nineteenth and early twentieth centuries, the organisation of labour supply as well as the control of a large unskilled industrial labour force was a major security concern for mining companies and linked private strategies with the state. During the early years of the mining industry, forced labour remained common in the Congo. Company agents made arrangements with local chiefs and colonial administrators over weekly or monthly supplies of labour, implying the transfer of people by force (Vellut 1983: 146). With the introduction of a labour tax, the administration later assisted companies in establishing a migrant labour system by pushing people into wage labour (Fetter 1983: 74). Imposing tax burdens on Africans living in Northern Rhodesia, the BSAC made the region an important labour source for the mines in Southern Rhodesia and Katanga, recruiting people and walking them to the mines with the help of the Rhodesian Native Labour Bureau. In the former, the BSAC had direct stakes in the form of shareholdings and revenues from royalties; in the latter through the railway line. Under company rule, a thinly spread administration relying on a few policemen and indirect rule often resorted to extreme violence, such as hut burning, summary flogging and the destruction of food stores to enforce obedience with tax laws and the demand for labour (Butler 2007: 42-4; Roberts 1976: 178).

In Central Africa, mine workers used to live in compounds managed by companies without much state interference (Austen 1987: 167). On the Copperbelt, government stations opened at four mines in 1931, but two of them were withdrawn during economic depression. District officers sent to the Copperbelt had difficulty in playing a strong role in labour affairs. They only supervised Africans living in small settlements outside the mines, but had very little to do with the thousands living in mining compounds on private property under the sole authority of compound managers who ran a hierarchical and authoritarian system (Berger 1974: 26). In Katanga, the UMHK stabilised the labour supply at the end of the 1920s by settling permanent workers close to the mines. In the new mining compounds, two authorities maintained a totalitarian subculture: 'the compound head, responsible for discipline maintenance, and the [catholic] teacher-preacher responsible for morals and learning' (Vellut 1983: 156), supported by the authoritarian colonial state administration (Fetter 1973; Peemans 1997). Compound managers even usurped some of the judicial functions given to government officers under colonial legislation: 'most minor breaches of discipline by Africans on the mines were dealt with summarily in the compound by deduction from efficiency bonuses or, at least on one mine, by corporal punishment' (Berger 1974: 27). Despite formal authority vested in the hands of a British colonial administration since 1924, the lives of African mine workers and their families were mainly governed by a private company regime. The colonial administration only appeared as a tax collector, a punishing agent of last resort who worked closely with the company and the military, which intervened on mine property in the case of labour unrest.

This paternalistic regime of labour discipline and control has profoundly changed since the 1980s (Hönke 2008; Zalik 2006). Yet there are other areas today in which social order is being imposed through joint public-private policing. Building up industrial mining operations often goes along with the displacement of traditional modes of production and small-scale miners. Enforcing concessions acquired by companies against local artisanal miners is a current example of the industrial order of extraction. The situation in Katanga is a case in point. While industrial mining may have potential to improve working conditions and transform mining in Katanga into a more legally regulated business, as hoped by a number of observers, it is currently squeezing out tens of thousands of artisanal miners without offering them any alternative means of making a living (Global Witness 2006: 40). Chasing out small-scale miners from company concessions is a tense issue in Katanga. It is particularly urgent near the new Tenke Fungurume mine and on former Gécamines concessions around Kolwezi. There have been a number of violent confrontations between miners, state security forces and company police in the context of a 'survivalist environment'.[13]

In general, companies become involved in policing in terms of their needs, either engaging with state security forces or keeping their interference at bay as much as possible. In any case, the interdependence of business and state elites produces selective patterns of private and public-private security management. This is highly biased if the provision of security is assumed to be a public good and a benchmark against which legitimate political order is evaluated. Policing in these extraction enclaves takes place within states in which the police and the military have weak capacity to provide security as a public good. They are characterised by bad human rights records and the local population is not only excluded from security provision, but exposed to oppression and insecurity.

Shaping Space

The notion of order does not only comprise activities related to the use of force and the management of physical security. Industrial mining also profoundly shapes the spatial order of a region, entailing the creation of new nodes of power and profit. Industrial mining requires roads, railways and stable energy, water and labour supply to run an operation effectively. Companies engage in infrastructure development where not provided by the state.

Imperialism on the cheap characterised British policy towards Africa in this regard. Authorisation allowing the BSAC to claim the territory that came to be called Northern Rhodesia was a product of government policy that aimed to extend and deepen its influence without being prepared to carry the financial burdens of administration. Direct political control is expensive and was even more so at a time when major infrastructure investments were necessary to explore a potential new mining region and to link it to the global economy. The BSAC was notorious for financial difficulties, mainly due to expenses for administration that were initially not met by commercial returns. Preparing the future extraction of copper and cobalt, the company developed infrastructure such as railways and roads as a priority, while keeping other administrative efforts to a minimum (Galbraith 1974: 310). Relieved of its administrative burden in 1924, but keeping the mineral rights over the copper deposits of the Copperbelt, the BSAC granted exploration rights to large international companies. They, again, engaged in constructing railways, roads and harbours to allow for the transport of raw materials to Europe.

The recent agreement between China and the DRC is an illustration of how an old combined strategy of securing access to resources and developing infrastructure is being adapted to the postcolonial context. Chinese companies will begin this year with infrastructure projects in the DRC costing more than $9 billion. Compared to the DRC's 2007 budget of $1.3 billion this is an enormous amount of money. While the state-owned company Sinohydro was building high-voltage power lines and plants and expanding water supply infrastructure, the China Railway Engineering Company (CREC) was supposed to be renovating the major railway lines between Kinshasa and Lubumbashi up to the border with Zambia and between Kinshasa and the ports in the Gulf of Guinea. According to the agreement, substantial loans will be repaid to China with the copper and cobalt reserves of Katanga. For this purpose, Chinese parastatals and the Congolese state-owned company Gécamines set up a joint venture company, the Société Congolaise Minière (Socomin), which is due to invest another $3 billion in new mining projects. The future profits from these mining operations are supposed to repay both mining and infrastructure investment.[14]

Even though on a smaller scale, private companies behave in a similar way. To transport copper ore for further processing to Zambia, FQML has planned to connect its new tailings dam project in the Congolese city of Kolwezi with its operations near Solwezi on the Zambian side. As in the case of other FQML mines in the border region, extra border posts have been opened and paid for by the company to connect mines and processing facilities in this transnational economic zone.

Such new transport links and production venues imply changes in social structures and patterns of mobility. There are new settlements: urban agglomerations and mining townships in which workers, fortune seekers, petty business people and prostitutes seek to make a living. In the past, a disciplined labour force was maintained by building and controlling parts of these urban structures, including the provision of social services in mining towns. Today, companies refrain from such obligations and, emphasising the purely private, economic purpose of their activity, seek to pull out of any such responsibilities. While they have reduced their involvement in social service delivery, companies continue, at the same time, to invest heavily in transport infrastructure.

Conclusion

This chapter has taken as its starting point increased investment in the exploitation of the vast mineral resources of Central Africa. Even though political and economic structures have changed profoundly, as in the nineteenth century it is the demand for base metals from industrialising countries – today China and India – that has fuelled demand for minerals and spurred investment in the region. In fact, the two periods of high international interest in Africa as a source for minerals show an underlying general pattern of its integration into the world economy as a supplier of raw materials. Since the late nineteenth century industrial metals have become important strategic resources for governments in what are today Zambia and the DRC.

A brief look at the relation between transnational business and political rule at the eve of colonial domination has revealed that, in the absence of an internationally recognised monopoly over the means of force in territories perceived as vacant land, companies and states went into an intimate relationship to open them up and exploit their resources. However, the nature of the companies competing for African resources has changed. Today, they are mostly private multinational companies that no longer have direct relations with their home state. Only Chinese state-owned companies are an exception, sharing remarkable similarities with the mercantile proto-multinationals of earlier times.

However, what is similar is that these companies all take on state-like functions to tackle the problem of security. There are three strategies of producing order in which companies have engaged over time. The first involves nurturing alliances with local rulers. While the early proto-multinationals had to deal with local power holders, modern mining investment requires striking deals with elites of sovereign, but fragile, states. In both cases, incumbent elites who co-operate with foreign investors have been strengthened, usually irrespective of their internal legitimacy. A second pattern is the selective provision of security, as joint policing by company and state focuses on securing extraction by enforcing mining rights, combating product theft and controlling labour. Third, industrial mining profoundly shapes the regional spatial and social order. Creating extraction enclaves with an export-oriented infrastructure, new nodes of power and profit have been established.

The international publicity of cases like the murder of Ken Saro-Wiwa in Nigeria or the financing of warlords fighting in the eastern DRC brought the involvement of extractive companies in human rights abuses onto the global governance agenda. While the adoption of binding human rights norms in the context of the United Nations has failed, voluntary codes of conduct have emerged at the global level that aim to regulate the interaction of companies with local state and non-state security providers in authoritarian and fragile states.[15] Research has began to study large foreign companies as potential agents for improving governance in host states through voluntary company engagement (Wolf, Deitelhoff and Engert 2007).

In contrast to these positive expectations, the analysis presented in this chapter rather points to structural continuities. These suggest how limited such attempts might turn out to be in their impact upon functioning, but dysfunctional states (Soares de Oliveira 2007).[16] Contemporary firms are 'stuck with those who are internationally recognised' where companies in the extractive sector tend to boost the power of the ruling faction (Reno 2004: 614). If the period after the end of the Cold War was interpreted as a chance to overcome the international system of client states (Clapham 1996) and to push for human security and democratisation on a global scale, then the new scramble seems to be another indicator that the window of opportunity might have closed. On the African continent, the new emphasis on stability to combat international terrorism (Duffield 2007; Hönke 2005) and the new strategic importance of the supply of energy and industrial minerals seems to advance client-like relations between external interests and African states, strengthening the position of unaccountable regimes.

Drawing again on an analogy from the early period of European colonisation, the idea of setting up 'liberal protectorates' (Cooper 2004) to tackle the problem of global (dis)order emerged during the war on terror. As opposed to the nineteenth century, however, today the will and the resources to address numerous 'frontier problems' (McIntytre 1967) by imposing direct external domination are limited, whether with regard to supposed safe havens for terrorists or the oil- and mineral-rich regions of Africa. Therefore, indirect modes of global governance may regain importance. Future research should pay attention to the role of private actors in managing areas in the South that are formally independent, but of strategic interest to external actors.

Notes

1. Other early examples are the Russia Company (1554) and the Hudson Bay Company (1670). In the context of the imperialism of the nineteenth century, chartered companies such as the Royal Niger Company (1886), the British South Africa Company (1889) and the British East Africa Company (1888); and concession companies such as the Compagnie Francaise de l'Afrique Occidental (1887), the Companie du Katanga (1891) and the Companhia de Moçambiqe (1888) furthered the influence of European powers across the continent (Hopkins 1976a).
2. Nevertheless, the Anglo-American Group kept 28% of ZCCM shares and enjoyed privileged buying rights in the privatisation process.
3. This is partly due to the fact that Belgian and American forces were central to Mobutu's rise to power in 1965. Both states were eager to safeguard the Congo against influence from Moscow and to secure access to its rich mineral resources (Schatzberg 1991).
4. For an overview see Fraser and Lungu 2007.
5. *Business Day*, 5 June 2007.
6. The joint venture of CAMEC with Prairie International has been interpreted as an attempt to distance the company from its former major shareholder, Zimbabwean

businessman Billy Rautenbach, former manager of Gécamines and beneficiary of the Congolese war economy (*Mining Weekly* 7 Nov. 2007).

7. Vandeale, J., China outdoes Europeans in the Congo. InterPress Service. Johannesburg, 9 Feb. 2008.

8. Interview by the author, Zambia, Oct. 2007.

9. See the Doing Business Classification by the World Bank. Interviews conducted by the Netherlands Institute for Southern Africa (NIZA 2006: 35) with twenty mining experts and company representatives in the DRC.

10. Lutundula Commission Report, 2005, *Rapport des Travaux, 1ière Partie*. Kinshasa: Commission spéciale chargée de l'examen de la validité des coventions à caractère économique et financier conclue pendant les guerres de 1996-97 et de 1998.

11. President Mwanawasa died in August 2008, following a stroke.

12. This information is based on interviews conducted in the region, Oct.– Nov. 2007. They refer to sensitive issues and anonymity was assured to the interviewees.

13. Interview by the author, DRC, Nov. 2007. On the other hand, the recent scramble for copper and cobalt in the DRC has fuelled a flourishing trade in artisan-mined heterogenite. This business is dominated by Chinese, Lebanese and Indian trading houses buying ore from small-scale miners who work under miserable conditions (Global Witness 2004, 2006).

14. *Mail and Guardian*, 5-11 Oct. 2007.

15. See www.voluntaryprinciples.org; Kinley, Nolan and Zerial. 2007 on the UN norms; and Frynas and Pegg 2003 for a critical account of transnational companies and human rights.

16. There are two other lines of criticism this chapter does not address that lie in the nature of the voluntary principles themselves. First, the vague formulation of the norms; and second, the institutional design of the principles as a secretive industry forum that lacks transparency. While raising awareness of risks and human rights abuses entailed in security practices of companies and their relations with host country military and police, it remains unclear what 'implementing the Voluntary principles' actually means (Global Witness 2007: 14-16).

References

ACIDH. 2005. *Rapport Conjoint sur Kilwa: Une Année Après le Massacre d'Octobre 2004*. Lubumbashi: Action Contre l'Impunité pour les Droits Humains.

Amnesty International. 1999. *Zambia: Applying the Law Fairly or Fatally?: Police Violation of Human Rights in Zambia*. London: AI.

Austen, R. 1987. *African Economic History: Internal Development and External Dependency*. London: James Currey.

Beblawi, H. and G. Luciania (eds). 1987. *The Rentier State*. London: Croom Helm.

Berger, E. 1974. *Labour, Race and Colonial Rule: The Copperbelt from 1924 to Independence*. Oxford: Clarendon.

Braeckman, C. 1992. *Le Dinosaure: le Zaire de Mobutu*. Paris: Fayard.

Butler, L. 2007. *Copper Empire: Mining and the Colonial State in Northern Rhodesia, c.1930–64*. Basingstoke: Palgrave Macmillan.

Clapham, C. 1996. *Africa in the International System*. Cambridge: Cambridge University Press.

Cooper, R. 2004. 'The post-modern state'. In: *Re-ordering the World: The Long-Term Implications of 11 September*, edited by M. Leonard. London: Foreign Policy Centre.

Craig, J. 2001. 'Putting privatisation into practice: the case of ZCCM'. *Journal of Modern African Studies* 39(3): 389–410.

Depelchin, J. 1992. *From the Congo Free State to Zaire (1885–1974)*. London: Codesria.

Duffield, M. 2007. *Development, Security and Unending War: Governing the World of People*. Cambridge: Polity.

Elias, N. 1997. *Über den Prozess der Zivilisation, Band II*. Frankfurt am Main: Suhrkamp.

Fetter, B. 1973. *L'Union Minière du Haut-Katanga, 1920–1940: La Naissance d'une Sous-Culture Totalitaire*. Bruxelles: Centre d'Etude et de Documentation Africaines.

——. 1983. 'The Union Minière and its hinterland: a demographic reconstruction'. *African Economic History* 12: 67–81.

Fraser, A. and J. Lungu. 2007. *For Whom the Windfalls?: Winners and Losers in the Privatisation of Zambia's Copper Mines*. Ndola: CCJDP.

Frynas, J. 2001. 'Corporate and state response to anti-oil protests in the Niger Delta'. *African Affairs* 100(398): 27–54.

Frynas, J. and M. Paulo. 2006. 'A new scramble for African oil?: historical, political and business perspectives'. *African Affairs* 106(432): 229–51.

Frynas, J. and S. Pegg (eds). 2003. *Transnational Corporations and Human Rights*. Basingstoke: Palgrave Macmillan.

Galbraith, J. 1974. *Crown and Charter: The Early Years of the British South Africa Company*. Berkeley: University of California Press.

Global Witness. 2004. *Rush and Ruin: The Devastating Mineral Trade in Southern Katanga*. Washington: Global Witness.

——. 2006. *Digging in Corruption: Fraud, Abuse and Exploitation in Katanga's Copper and Cobalt Mines*. Washington: Global Witness.

——. 2007. *The Congolese Mining Sector in the Balance*. London: Global Witness.

Hönke, J. 2005. *Fragile Staatlichkeit und der Wandel der Afrikapolitik nach 1990*. Leipzig: Institute of African Studies, University of Leipzig.

——. 2008. Governing security in enclaves of extraction: private self-help, partnership policing or shadow networks of public-private rule. Paper presented at the American Political Science Association Conference, Boston, 28–31 Aug. 2008.

Hopkins, A. 1976a. 'Imperial business in Africa: part I'. *Journal of African History* 17(1): 29–48.

——. 1976b. 'Imperial business in Africa: part II'. *Journal of African History* 17(2): 267–90.

Ilunkamba, I. 1984. *Proprieté Publique et Coventions de Gestion dans l'Industrie du Cuivre du Zaire*. Brussels: CEDAF.

International Crisis Group. 2006. 'Katanga: the Congo's forgotten crisis'. *Africa Report* 103. Washington: ICG.

Jewsiewicki, B. 1983. 'Rural society and the Belgian colonial economy'. In: *History of Central Africa*, edited by D. Birmingham and P. M. Martin. New York: Longman.

Jones, G. 2005. *Multinationals and Global Capitalism: From the Nineteenth to the Twenty-First Century.* Oxford: Oxford University Press.

Jones, T. and T. Newburn. 2006. *Plural Policing: A Comparative Perspective.* London: Routledge.

Kinley, D., J. Nolan and N. Zerial. 2007. 'The politics of corporate social responsibility: reflections on the UN human rights norms for corporations'. *Company and Securities Law Journal* 25(1): 30–42.

Larmer, M. 2007. *Mineworkers in Zambia: Labour and Political Change in Post-Colonial Africa.* London: Tauris.

Martin, P. 1983. 'The violence of empire'. In: *History of Central Africa*, edited by D. Birmingham and P. Martin. New York: Longman.

Mbembe, A. 2002. 'At the edge of the world: boundaries, territoriality and sovereignty in Africa'. In: *Beyond State Crisis?: Postcolonial Africa and Post-Soviet Eurasia in Comparative Perspective*, edited by R. Beisinger and C. Young. Washington: Woodrow Wilson Center Press.

McIntyre, R. 1967. *The Imperial Frontier in the Tropics, 1865–75.* London: Macmillan.

Melber, H. et al. 2007. *China in Africa.* Uppsala: Nordiska Afrikainstitutet.

Mikesell, R. 1988. *The Global Copper Industry: Problems and Prospects.* London: Croom Helm.

Moore, M. 2004. 'Revenues, state formation and the quality of governance in developing countries'. *International Political Science Review* 25 (3): 297–319.

Netherlands Institiute for Southern Africa. 2006. *The State Versus the People: Governance, Mining and the Transitional Regime in the DRC.* Amsterdam: NIZA.

Peemans, J-P. 1997. *Le Congo-Zaire au Gré du XXième Siecle: État, Économie, Société, 1880–1990.* Paris: L'Harmattan.

Reno, W. 2004. 'Order and commerce in turbulent areas: 19th century lessons, 21st century practice'. *Third World Quarterly* 25(4): 607–25.

Reyntjens, F. 2007. 'Democratic Republic of Congo: political transition and beyond'. *African Affairs* 106 (423): 307–17.

Roberts, A. 1976. *A History of Zambia.* New York: Africana Press.

Robinson, R. and J. Gallagher. 1961. *Africa and the Victorians: The Official Mind of Imperialism.* London: Macmillan.

Ross, M. 1999. 'The political economy of the resource curse'. *World Politics* 51(2): 297–322.

Schatzberg, M. 1991. *Mobutu or Chaos?: The United States and Zaire, 1960–1990.* Lanham: University Press of America.

Schlichte, K. 2005. *Der Staat in der Weltgesellschaft: Politische Herrschaft in Asien, Afrika und Lateinamerika.* Frankfurt am Main: Campus Verlag.

Slade, R. 1962. *King Leopold's Congo.* New York: Oxford University Press.

Slinn, P. 1971. 'Commercial concessions and politics during the colonial period: the role of the British South Africa Company in Northern Rhodesia 1890–1964'. *African Affairs* 70(281): 365–84.

Soares De Oliveira, R. 2007. *Oil and Politics in the Gulf of Guinea.* London: Hurst.

Spittaels, S. and N. Meynen. 2007. *Mapping Interests in Conflict Areas: Katanga.* Amsterdam: Fatal Transaction.

Stengers, J. 1981. 'The Congo Free State and the Belgian Congo'. In: *The History and Politics of Colonialism, 1870–1914,* edited by L. Gann and P. Duignan. Cambridge: Cambridge University Press.

Stengers, J. and J. Vansina. 1985. 'King Leopold's Congo 1886–1908'. In: *The Cambridge History of Africa. Vol.6: From 1870–1905,* edited by R. Oliver and N. Sanderson. Cambridge: Cambridge University Press.

Thompson, J. 1994. *Mercenaries, Pirates and Sovereigns: State-Building and Extraterritorial Violence in Early Modern Europe.* Princeton: Princeton University Press.

Tilly, C. 1992. *Coercion, Capital, and the European States, AD 990–1992.* Cambridge: Blackwell, rev. ed.

Tilton, J. 1990. *World Metal Demand, Trends and Prospects.* Washington: Resources for the Future.

UNCTAD. 2007. *World Investment Report: Transnational Corporations, Extractive Industries and Development.* Geneva: United Nations.

United Nations. 2002. *Report of the UN Panel of Experts on the Illegal Exploitation of Natural Resources and Other Forms of Wealth in the Democratic Republic of Congo.* New York: UN.

US Department of State. 2006. *Zambia: Country Reports on Human Rights Practices 2006.* Washington: Bureau of Democracy, Human Rights and Labor.

Vellut, J-L. 1981. *Les Bassins Minières de l'Ancien Congo Belge (1900–1960).* Brussels: CEDAF.

——. 1983. 'Mining in the Belgian Congo'. In: *History of Central Africa,* edited by D. Birmingham and P. M. Martin. London: Longman.

Vernon, R. 1971. *Sovereignty at Bay: The Multinational Spread of U.S. Enterprises.* New York: Basic Books.

Weber, M. 1971 [1921]. *Gesammelte Politische Schriften.* Tübingen: Mohr.

——. 2006 [1922]. *Wirtschaft und Gesellschaft.* Paderborn: Voltmedia.

Wolf, K., N. Deitelhoff and S. Engert. 2007. 'Corporate security responsibility: towards a conceptional framework for a comparative research. *Cooperation and Conflict* 42(3): 295–321.

Wright, T. 2001. *The History of the Northern Rhodesian Police.* Bristol: BECM Press.

Young, C. 1998. 'Zaire: the anatomy of a failed state'. In: *History of Central Africa: The contemporary years,* edited by D. Birmingham and P. Martin. London: Longman.

Young, C. and T. Turner. 1985. *The Rise and Decline of the Zairian State.* Madison: University of Wisconsin Press.

Zalik, A. 2006. *Subjects of Extraction: Social Regulation, Corporate Aid and Petroleum Security in the Nigerian Delta and the Mexican Gulf.* Ithaca: Cornell University Press.

Zedner, L. 2006. 'Policing before and after the police: the historical antecedents of contemporary crime control'. *British Journal of Criminology* 46(1): 78–96.

CHAPTER TWELVE

The Scramble for Genetic Resources

Carol Thompson

The scramble for Africa did not simply sanction the plundering of the continent's mineral resources, from oil and diamonds to gold and copper, but it also facilitated the removal of its bioresources. Plants and animals comprise the treasures of Africa and they helped to build overseas empires as much as yellow or black gold. Because plants and animals freely reproduce, however, their extraction did not prohibit African breeders from enjoying the fruits of their innovation and labour. What is new in the twenty-first century is not the scramble for genetic resources, but changes in law and science that allow exclusive ownership over nature. Not only are genetic resources removed, but they are privatised so that communities which bred the resources for thousands of years have no rights to access or use. To plant a seed their ancestors developed, they must pay a royalty. To treasure a handful of seeds in storage is illegal. What is new about the twenty-first century scramble is its all-embracing reach.

This chapter begins by explaining the complex legal, political and ecological processes of biopiracy. Biopiracy extends primitive accumulation into microscopic nature through hegemonic interpretations of law and of science that serve the interests of capital. Theories of primitive accumulation, or accumulation by dispossession (Harvey 2003), help to explain the social relations driving these very new expressions of scramble. A few examples of biopiracy from Africa will be analysed to show the diverse means of dispossession. The conclusion reports that communities are not standing by and watching, but continuously resisting. They have rejected the intellectual property rights interpretation of the World Trade Organisation (WTO) and free trade agreements. They are planting their own legal and political seeds to allow their indigenous knowledge to flourish.

Biopiracy

Biopiracy may be a new word, but the act is very old.[1] Understood by us all, piracy is the taking of wealth or looting by force. Swashbuckling and swagger create the anti-hero image of bravado and fearlessness. They loot out in the wilds and often they pillage and burn what they cannot haul away. Biopiracy involves both the taking of plants, seeds and animals for pirate gain as well as pillaging local plant riches by genetic or chemical contamination. Biopiracy is removal of the organism, whether by literally taking the plant, animal, seed or genetic material and claiming ownership, or by destroying it. Piracy refers to refusal to compensate or even acknowledge the original cultivators of the bioresource. Nothing is given in exchange with the excuse, if one is offered, that the plant or animal is wild and free for the taking. Both types of biopiracy, taking and destroying, undervalue the bioresource economically, culturally, nutritionally and spiritually. Such depreciation also degrades communities and their food security, sovereignty and ability to sustain cultures.

At the time of the first scramble for Africa, the field of economic botany flourished, for gardeners and plant breeders worked with governments to develop new strains of plants for industrial use. Every major colonial power – United Kingdom, Belgium, Netherlands, Germany, France – had royal or official gardens as experimental stations for plants brought back from the tropics by explorers, sea captains and navies. Innovative technology allowed glass greenhouses to accommodate palms and bamboos, which could reach a three-storey roof in one growing season. King Leopold of Belgium, for example, entertained in his Winter Garden greenhouse, full of plants taken from the Congo. Climates were controlled in order to work toward improving plant varieties and to develop those adapted to their new temperate ecosystem. This curiosity and experimentation gradually enhanced the diet of Europeans, first for the aristocracy (citrus fruits in the nineteenth century, *l'orangerie*) and gradually for the general population.

The goal was not simply to make exotic foods available during European winters, however. In her seminal work on London's Kew Gardens, Brockway (1979: 6–7) explains as follows:

> Through its research, its dissemination of scientific information, and its practical activities, which included *plant smuggling*, Kew Gardens played a major part in the development of several highly profitable and strategically important *plant-based industries* in the tropical colonies . . . institutions like Kew Gardens were as important

in furthering the national welfare as our modern research laboratories today (emphasis added).

Joseph Banks, the creator of Kew Gardens, promoted the idea that biology could help enhance the growing British Empire (Fara 2003; Hepper 1982). Reigning over the Royal Society for more than 40 years, Banks fostered projects to break China's tea monopoly and to promote the growing of coffee: both tea and coffee became cash crops in British eastern and southern Africa after the first scramble.

Removal of plants is not simply the taking of a seed, for it also usurps indigenous knowledge about plants' characteristics and uses. In transferring the biomaterials for economic gain, the Europeans did sometimes contribute their knowledge in adapting the plants for new climes and new uses. Most often, however, they provided only transport, such as the ships to move rubber trees from Brazil to Malaysia or the cinchona to India, and always under imperial control.[2] The scramble for plants consisted of claiming the wealth of new accessions in the botanical gardens as belonging solely to the new possessors: new strains of bananas or pineapple or rubber became British or Dutch or Flemish, without recognition of previous centuries of breeding. The removal was neither exchange nor free trade, for the Europeans did not compensate rulers, traditional healers or cultivators for their knowledge or plant resource. The taking of plants contributed to the disruption of traditional relations, reducing the economic competitiveness of the communities that had provided the labour, scientific knowledge and raw materials.

Taking control of plants to commercialise them across global markets required land and labour for crop production as well as extensive transport networks. Costs of production were reduced through the use of forced, unpaid labour (for example, King Leopold conscripting labour to collect rubber in the Congo) and through acquiring land and water at no cost after colonial conquest. By the twentieth century, direct colonial rule was deemed too expensive and risky, with unequal exchange under neocolonialism offering a higher rate of profit. The newly independent governments of Africa found their people still grounded in the international division of labour as primary commodity producers shipping unprocessed minerals and crops to Northern markets (Amin 1974). Control over commodity prices was maintained via boards of trade, with the consumers, not the producers most often setting the price: for example, Tanzania and Kenya were beholden to the London tea exchange for the pricing, anywhere in the world, of their high quality tea. Massive consumption of coffee in the US allowed the buyers to manipulate prices for the beans as a monopsony. Even today, Dutch merchants are the most powerful grouping in the negotiation of the prices of cut flowers purchased from African growers, and require the meeting of strict phytosanitary conditions, keeping out all but the most prosperous horticulturalists.

Using market advantage based on unequal exchange to control agricultural trade really only lasted about 35 years, from about 1960 (when most of Africa began to decolonise) to 1995 (establishment of the WTO). From 1980 to 2000, another whole regime was being built, based on the transformation of law and science.

The current approach to intellectual property rights (IPRs) enshrined in the WTO is based on a long, but singular, tradition of Anglo-Saxon thought. Mainly advanced by John Locke, the first argument is that one has entitlement to the fruits of one's labour. A person's labour is inseparable from its product and, therefore, the person owns the product, be it an idea or an object. The second argument refers to just desserts: the labourer deserves to benefit from her or his labour. This argument parallels the utilitarian idea that rewarding the person who is inventive stimulates the progress of science. The innovator is deserving not only of priority use of the product created, but also of a reward (just desserts) if his or her invention has contributed to scientific progress.

In contrast to property, however, knowledge increases if it is shared or consumed. Others can take and use previous information to enhance it. Further, the source of the knowledge is not diminished by someone else using it. Quite the contrary: one could say that knowledge only increases in value if used, for the sharing will most likely engender new knowledge. These characteristics have long been valued by scientists. Jonas Salk, for example, did not expect ownership as part of just desserts from his discovery and development of a vaccine against polio:

> The scientists of previous generations who refused to patent their breakthrough discoveries were neither naïve nor saintly. They were members of a flourishing gift culture, the academy, which presumed . . . that data, research tools, and other scholarly resources should be widely shared and openly scrutinized. There is an expectation that certain standards of rigor, candor and ethics will be met, and that a discipline's work should serve a larger public interest (Bollier 2002: 19).

Debates over the patenting of knowledge (intellectual property) began with the advent of patents in the nineteenth century. Generally, patents were retained for invention of an object. Copyright laws encouraged the sharing of knowledge, for one could take an idea and improve it, just so long as one gave all those involved in the debates full credit. With the introduction of computer software, however, distinguishing knowledge as intangible became more difficult and the term intellectual property rights allowed knowledge – a way of calculating or a discovery – to be patented as private property.

Until recently, patenting living organisms was illegal around the globe because they were considered part of nature, not a human invention. However, in 1980, the US Supreme Court case Diamond v. Chakrabarty decided, by a 5–4 margin, that a strain of bacteria, modified by insertion of new genes, could be patented because the new strain did not occur naturally. Chakrabarty later admitted that he had invented nothing: he had simply shuffled genes. From that date, other patents on life established the legal precedent in the US that new combinations of natural materials could be inventions (Mbeoji 2006).

This new legal interpretation, however, stretches scientific logic to breaking point. Because different components of an organism (for instance, a gene) can be transferred by biogenetic techniques, it is claimed that these components are discrete and thus not dependent on highly interactive processes for life. But living organisms do not have isolated components independent one from another; nor does an organism compute itself from its DNA (Levins and Lewotin 1985: 89). The scientist may be able to extract nucleotides (compounds) or a nucleotide sequence (gene) for observation, but neither can fully function without the dynamic of the living organism, for interaction, exchange and osmosis are vital processes. Yet the notion remains dominant that genes can do everything in and by themselves.

Allowing one gene to redefine a whole organism is not related to the nature of that gene, but to the nature of economic and political power to redefine science. The major reason for the recent assertion of gene discreteness is that such an interpretation takes the first step toward making a living organism patentable: only objects that are distinct can be patented.

With the apparently discrete entity now an invention, two steps were taken toward exclusive ownership of a living organism: organic no longer means holistic and dynamic. However, with seed, the biotechnology industry still had a problem. Seed has inherent qualities that make it even more antithetical to description as property than abstract knowledge. First, seed freely reproduces itself and rarely needs human intervention. Second, it appreciates in value with its disintegration into a plant. Third, it multiplies with use: one seed is able to propagate hundreds, or thousands, of others. The head of one amaranth has about 50 000 seeds.

Some seed varieties, especially hybrids, were of course already commodities, sold under brand names in the market. They propagate for only two or three seasons and must be bought again for planting. However, most seed in the World is not yet commodified and still freely shared among farmers. Over 80% of food crop seed in Africa is still saved seed. The new legal domain certifies the process of inserting a gene or modifying germ plasm as an invention and the new seed as a discrete, unique entity that can be patented. Thus protected, that seed then becomes a commodity that can be used only with the permission of the sole owner. A user must buy the seed in the market from the monopoly seller.

The process is then complete. What was natural has become an invention of one person with rights to sole ownership. What was both a commodity and a representation of traditional knowledge is now just a commodity. What could propagate itself can now only be reproduced by its owner for a profit.

But because a seed may indeed propagate itself, new laws have been devised so that such a seed cannot be saved and planted without paying royalties to the owner of the patent. The corporations helped to write the terms for plant protection under the Union for the Protection of New Varieties of Plants (UPOV)[3] to make them resemble other patent laws. It is thus the protocol of choice by countries of the North for implementing intellectual property rights under the WTO.

If genetic changes are made in only one part of the plant, such as the reproductive propagating part, UPOV allows for full privatisation of the entire plant. Not only that, but it extends private ownership to any other plant or commodity essentially derived from the patented plant. It also extends private ownership over any product resulting from the patented plant, such as flour ground from a strain of wheat or cassava protected by UPOV. Because patent protection is first over a whole plant, not just the part altered, second over any commodity essentially derived from the protected variety, and third over any product produced from the variety, UPOV is the most restrictive law preventing the sharing of new seeds or plants.

Under previous contracts, farmers who originally bought the UPOV plant-breeder seed and therefore paid royalty fees, had the right to save the seed and replant it. They could even exchange the seed informally with neighbours. The major restriction was they could not commercially market the seed without paying royalties. This principle of farmers' rights recognised the importance of farmers in increasing biodiversity through adapting seed to new bioregions and through free exchange. It was also a major marketing tool, for shared seed could create a market for further purchase, increasing demand rather than diminishing it. However, now farmers' rights have been turned into farmers' privilege. Gone is the right to exchange seed informally.

To be eligible for UPOV protection, a plant breeder must give a written description of the new element and submit germ plasm samples, in the form of seeds, dried plant material or live plants, as evidence. This stringent requirement makes sure that plant breeders in laboratories do not cheat each other in claiming new plant parts or a new variety. But such a submission excludes almost all small-scale farmers in Africa from benefiting from UPOV protection. If successfully registered, or privatised, under UPOV, a plant can remain unavailable to anyone for twenty years. Yet if innovation occurs out in the fields and is not registered under UPOV, the new variety is free and available for the taking. The corporations have succeeded in privatising plants in their laboratories, while legally preserving their ability to steal indigenous knowledge and seed from farmers. Because plant breeders must continually go back to parent materials for new breeding, keeping farmers' varieties free and available for the taking by corporations reduces the cost of raw material inputs to zero.

Dispossession, like enclosure of land, requires changes in law; but also, changes in scientific descriptions. Although the exact innovative steps must be disclosed to receive patent rights, no one can accurately describe a new microorganism, for it is a changing, living entity. Therefore, the Budapest Treaty requires instead that an example be put in a depository. The Budapest Treaty, like UPOV, is another instrument used to implement WTO principles, but it also deviates from patent laws as they have been practised for more than a century. Although the WTO and Budapest Treaty allow for microorganisms to be patented, neither international agreement defines them. Further, what is submitted to a depository does not need to be disclosed, for the sample can even be given a symbolic name to keep it secret. The reciprocity of royalty protection in return for full disclosure has been torn asunder. One of the immediate results of no legal definition, along with no enforced disclosure, is that depositories of microorganisms now include human cell lines, embryos, nematodes, DNA and seeds (Rodríguez Cervantes 2008: 34, 37).

Accumulation by Dispossession

Biopiracy refers to one specific act of primitive accumulation: the removal of control from farmers over their seeds. If the farmers can no longer save their seed, or exchange it informally, they must go to the commercial market to purchase it. They not only need cash, a deficit resource across Africa, but also supply of the seed and transport by which to acquire it. Further, the genetic composition of the seed and its attributes are no longer under their careful, scientific selection and adaptation. In the one act of buying a packet of seed, instead of pulling it out of the thatched roof beams or from storage under the kraal, the farmers not only lose control over choices about its desirable traits such as taste, texture, size, colour, soil and water requirements, but also its availability and cost. The loss is biological, ecological, economic and, in very real terms, political. The biological wealth of seeds for a diverse food base must be purchased with capital cash or credit. Even if the cash becomes available, the farmers will still lose genetic biodiversity on their farms and their people will lose diversity in their food. This translates into loss of nutrients, vitamins and minerals. Theories of primitive accumulation, or accumulation by dispossession, explain this process which at first seems like gross exaggeration. How can the simple act of buying seed evoke all these changes?

To summarise briefly what are long debates, the process of primitive accumulation explains, according to Karl Marx, the way in which emerging industrialists first acquired free resources to increase their productive capacity and their rates of profit. The most familiar description, also relevant to the African continent, is the usurpation of land from small-scale farmers. If families can feed themselves, with a bit extra for trade for other goods, then it is not rational for them to work in factories. Therefore, removal of families from the land, or enclosure, is the quintessential example of primitive accumulation. During enclosure in Europe, common land available for livestock was also privatised and hunting was banned (Perelman 2007). In Africa, no game park exists that did not require the removal of indigenous communities, a historical fact that ecotourism tends to hide. Without any means to sustain a family, the small-scale farmers move to the cities to sell their labour. The expropriation of land provided both relatively free input for production for large-scale farming as well as cheap labour for factories.

Marx wrote about this process as an initial stage of capitalist accumulation, as a transition from feudalism to capitalism. Therefore, many theorists argue that primitive accumulation can only occur at the margins of capitalist production, either historically as an initial stage in Europe or geographically, as in Africa, where pre-capitalist relations of production exist next to advanced capitalism. In this interpretation, the act of primitive accumulation is designated as one-time and one- stage: as capitalist relations of production become dominant, it no longer occurs. In fact, accumulation through command over labour power is more efficient. The workers provide continuous surplus value through their unpaid creative production more reliably than the occasional usurpation of land.

Later Marxist theorists, however, emphasise the contradictions of capitalist relations to suggest that primitive accumulation can occur throughout the development of capitalism (Bonefield 2001; Glassman 2006: 21–22; Hart 2006). To sustain an increasing rate of profit, capitalists must exchange products in the market. But if labour is too impoverished to purchase commodities, market demand does not grow sufficiently to increase the rate of profit. Driving down the costs of inputs through innovation, economies of scale, externalising costs or other means can sustain profit, which eventually again increases production, encouraging the cycle to begin again. Robinson (2004: 21) describes the current process as follows:

> Despite the importance of technology and organizational innovation, globalisation is not driven by a technological determinism, as technology is not causal to social change but a dependent variable . . . The dynamic of economic globalisation, including the development of innovative new "globalizing" technologies, has been caused by the drive, built into capitalism itself by competition and class struggle, to maximize profits by reducing labour and other "factor" costs. Competition drives each capitalist enterprise to increase profits by developing new technologies and methods of production that can lower costs

Theorists from Luxemburg (1964), Arendt (1968) and Amin (1974) to Harvey (2003, 2005) therefore see the contradictions of surplus accumulation continuing the process through lowering the cost of inputs even during advanced stages of capitalism. To differentiate this process from a particular stage of capitalism, Harvey has offered the concept 'accumulation by dispossession'. Taking land out of collective or communal production remains central to accumulation through dispossession, but it also refers to the expropriation of many other means of production: 'the conversion of various forms of property rights (common, collective, state etc.) into exclusive private property rights; suppression of alternative (indigenous) forms of production and consumption' (Harvey 2003: 145; see also Sutcliffe 2006).

Legally enshrining private ownership of a living organism allows corporate control over food and medicine, and over the global ecological system. With the total commodification of plants and animals, their exchange value is determined not by tradition, nor the community, nor even by their use value, but by private monopoly control. Privatising seed or animal embryos separates the farmer producer from his or her means of production (Dickens 1996: 115–16; Harvey 2005: 153; Mushita and Thompson 2007). As stated earlier, over 80% of seed used for food (not cash crops) is saved in Africa. With patenting of seed, farmers will have to purchase them every year from the corporate monopolies. If the corporations can control all the farmers' inputs – seed, fertiliser, pesticide and water – then land ownership does not matter, for the farmer is no longer a rural entrepreneur but a rural worker even though on her own land. Enclosure of the twenty-first century will refer more to privatisation of the gene pool than to land.

The most comprehensive enclosure, one that invokes futuristic calamities, is the increasing enclosure of the planet's gene pool, both animal and plant. This enclosure involves privatisation not just of the means of production, but of life itself.

Current Biopiracy

Enclosure of the animal gene pool is only beginning to receive attention, yet the loss of animal biodiversity is occurring more rapidly than that of plants. The Food and Agriculture Organisation (2007 – FAO) recognises about 7 600 breeds, developed over 12 000 years by farmers and pastoralists. But 'twenty percent of classified breeds of cattle, goats, pigs, horses and poultry are now considered to be at risk of extinction, as the world's livestock production has become increasingly based on a limited number of breeds. Since 2001, an average of one breed per month has become extinct' (International Institute for Sustainable Development 2007: 2). Within breeds, the genetic loss may be even more serious. Scientists recommend that 100 unrelated individuals are necessary to avoid inbreeding, but of 3.7 million Holstein milk cows, the US has only 60 individuals for breeding. Other livestock, from beef cattle to ducks, do not fare well.

This dangerous loss of biodiversity, both across and within species, has the same origins as the loss of biodiversity among plants. As the FAO emphasises, 'A number of threats to genetic diversity can be identified. Probably the most significant is the marginalisation of traditional production systems and the associated local breeds, driven mainly by the rapid spread of intensive livestock production, often large-scale and utilising a narrow range of breeds' (Food and Agriculture Organisation 2007: xxxv). As the livestock industry becomes more consolidated, so do the providers of genetic breeding material. Farmers across the globe who market ducks, turkeys, broiler chickens or eggs on a commercial scale acquire genetic material from very few breeders. Breeders of broiler chickens have declined from eleven firms in 1989 to four; and for laying hens, the decline is from ten to two breeders over the same period (Gura 2008: 4).

Searching for a broader genetic base by which to save a livestock industry therefore becomes the impetus for biopiracy. Accessing the gene pool of other animals with favourable characteristics is more crucial than recognising or respecting indigenous knowledge. If the new acquisition succeeds in the market place, the profits are not shared. The following story gives the details of biopiracy affecting one African animal, but it is representative of inequities across breeds and across the world.

Evolving on the African continent along with indigenous wildlife about 7 000–9 000 years ago, the humpless African cattle differ greatly from those brought to the continent from Asia about 3 000 years ago. Descendents of the Kalanga and Nguni dynasties bred the cattle along the Tuli River, which drains southward toward the Limpopo River in Zimbabwe and South Africa. Bred from indigenous strains for more than 1 000 years, the cattle were named tuli, taken from the Ndebele word *utuli*, meaning dust, which depicts the local harsh environmental conditions. Tuli thrive on low-nutrient grasses and minimal water and their lighter colours – golden yellow to pale silver – help them endure intense sunlight and heat (Harvey 1986).

Because ancient peoples were dependent on the meat, milk and blood of their cattle, the cows were bred for docility, designed to facilitate easy milking. As farming of crops began, the cattle were then bred for a larger frame to provide the draft power and endurance needed for ploughing or for transporting goods to local markets. Custodians of the breed, communities developed local knowledge and technologies for improving the cattle within prevailing environmental conditions and for specific social needs. Today's animals represent many generations of selection and crossing for desired improvement.

Commercialisation for the beef industry began in Southern Rhodesia after 1945, but the Tuli Breeding Society was formed only in 1961 to provide higher quality beef for the commercial market of Europe. Tuli characteristics prized for the new cross-breeding programme were many: high fertility; easy calving; early sexual maturity; high growth; resistance to disease, heat and drought; hardiness; adaptability; and above average marblings (Mushita 2003: 8).

In 1987, the Commonwealth Scientific and Industrial Research Organisation (CSIRO), an Australian government agency, and a consortium of Australian cattle producers, collaborated to form the Boran and Tuli Producers Consortium. To initiate a livestock improvement programme in Australia, they approached the Cattle Producers Association of Zimbabwe for embryos of both breeds. In 1988, the government of Zimbabwe approved the export of frozen cattle embryos to Australia and they have been successfully cross-bred for disease resistance. By the 1990s, Canadian Scott McKay traveled to Zimbabwe to choose among genetic strains. The resulting embryos were shipped to Canada and their offspring to Texas. The North American Tuli Association (NATA), formed in 1996, promotes the breed as adaptable to Texas and other places in the western hemisphere. Dr J.W. Holloway, Director of Research at the Texas A&M Research and Experiment Station, signals its high value: 'The Tuli breed can provide the missing link to bridge the gap in cattle genetics, that gap being adaptation to heat and nutritional stress combined with carcass merit.'[4]

This case demonstrates how a government can sign over a bioresource with no reference to the original breeders. Neither the government of Zimbabwe nor the foreign cattle associations consulted the local communities nor recognised their contribution in any way, although Australia, the US and Zimbabwe are all parties to the intergovernmental negotiations designating benefit-sharing for original breeders. Instead, access to the Tuli gene pool was provided by commercial deals among large-scale commercial cattle producers, with no consideration for centuries of selection and breeding by local communities.

This type of access, bioprospecting or biopiracy, is fast becoming a race to acquire the best genes of an animal breed in order to harvest significant profits on the global market. Current competition by industrialised countries to access, research and isolate traits required by the beef industry will soon lead to the patenting of all useful genes of the Tuli cattle without the involvement of the local communities that nurtured the breed for their livelihood. While Tuli traits are hailed as second to none in countries that abrogated international agreements to access the genetic materials, the peoples who developed the breed in the first place are forgotten and left to fight abject poverty alone. Communities in the semi-arid Tuli areas of Zimbabwe live on less than $1 per day, while the cattle they originally bred are contributing immensely to the global beef industry. Those who accessed the genetic materials freely, without regard to international laws, will continue to play a more predominant role in organising, regulating, trading and controlling the political economy of Tuli genes. They continue to disregard any mutually agreed terms for fair and equitable sharing of benefits. While research proves that the Tuli's juicy and tender beef traits are transferable to other breeds, no one is willing to ensure the reverse: juicy and tender benefits going to the custodians and original breeders of Tuli cattle.

The Tuli cattle case raises several contentious, and continuing, issues of biopiracy. First, the impetus for stealing genes comes from industrial breeding that, by focusing on very few desirable traits for the market, quickly narrows the genetic base for commercial breeds of livestock. The very viability of livestock industries requires a wide gene pool, yet desire for quick profit destroys that diversity. This illogical approach has probably survived because new genetic materials have been free for the taking for over a century. The gene pools can be revived through access to lesser- known livestock breeds found outside the commercial markets. Second, the Zimbabwe government and commercial cattle producers both agreed to the export of embryos, with zero regard for the original breeders. The government and commercial sector gave prior informed consent (PIC), but not the breeders. This neglect is why the African Union (AU) model legislation, discussed further below, to protect genetic resources requires dual PIC – from both the central government and the local communities that bred the animals or plants. Neither one can give consent alone. Of course, to the legal regimes of the WTO, World Intellectual Property Organisation (WIPO) or the Budapest Treaty, no biopiracy has occurred, so no benefit-sharing back to the breeders is required. Indeed, quite the contrary, for the third issue is that NATA can patent the new cross-bred strains under American laws, completing the biopiracy circle through legal recognition of new private owners. Accumulation through dispossession is not just a theory: it has become standard business practice.

The removal of marine life abrogates the United Nations Convention on the Law of the Sea (UNCLOS) if it occurs within the 200-mile limit of national jurisdiction. The US has never ratified UNCLOS and was finally removed from the treaty's regulatory bodies. The wide 200-mile band of limited rights, without sovereignty, along coastlines was adopted at the insistence of the US, yet it is often its citizens and corporations who violate that jurisdiction.

Under UNCLOS, removal of marine resources from that band would at least require prior approval from the government whose shoreline has been mined. Most African governments have regulations regarding scientific research, but very few legislate access to marine genetic resources. They do not have adequate coastguards or navies to enforce their jurisdiction. A very preliminary investigation of harvesting activities offers little sign of prior consent or benefit-sharing, even when the material is now patented. Much more work needs to be done in this area: privatisation of marine life has not received much attention compared with land plants and animals. A recent study begins to raise questions and figure 12.1 gives just a sample of marine biopiracy. If permission is not sought to mine these resources, it seems likely that no benefit-sharing will occur when use becomes profitable. The cost of the input or raw material is nothing.

The Scramble for Oil Meets the Scramble for Bioresources

The rain forests of Central Africa remain second only to the Amazon, but for millennia they covered more than three million square kilometres, teeming with life from the largest mammals (elephants and gorillas) to the microbes in the luxurious soil. Scientists do not know how many species thrived in the forests, nor how many are lost forever. The Gamba complex of Gabon, one corner of the remaining forests, extends to about 11 300 square kilometres, along the Atlantic coast and inland for about 100 kilometres. In September 2002, President Omar Bongo established two national parks in the area, but a middle corridor with both forests and oil concessions received much less environmental protection than the parks. The Rabi oil field, for example, lies in the headwaters of the Rabi River, which still yields an inventory of about 69 fish species, but swamps and ditches from oil platform construction and roads have changed the aquatic life network. The Ndogo lagoon complex experiences oil pollution that affects fish and other aquatic life.[5]

With both offshore and onshore oil production in the Gamba complex beginning from 1965, peak production was in 1997 with declining production ever since. Although oil had been pumped for over 30 years, it was 2000 when the Shell Oil Company and the Smithsonian Institution Monitoring and Assessment of Biodiversity (SIMAB) Program started tracing the impact of pumping oil in the middle of tropical rain forests and lagoons. This initiative also pledged to train Gabonese in all aspects of scientific research and biodiversity surveys. According to the Smithsonian, few foreign scientists have worked in the area except for plant collection in the 1990s by a Dutch team from Wageningen University. With Gabon's National Herbarium, they recorded 47 new plants.[6]

Even with this monitoring and relative lack of official collection, in 2003 Aventis, a major biotechonology corporation, patented compounds from a vine

Table 12.1 Marine resources patents with no evidence of benefit-sharing.*

Country	Organism	Owner	Patent numbers	Comment
Cape Verde	Sponge extracts (*Pachastrella sp*)	Harbor Branch Oceanographic Institute, Florida USA	US 6 384 187 (7 May 2002)	From the patent: 'A sample of the sponge [was] collected by dredge at a depth of 1 000 feet off the West Coast of Ilha São Vicente, Cape Verde'.
Mauritius	Sea Hare extracts (*Dolabella Auricularia*)	Arizona State University, USA	US 6 239 104 (29May 2001)	The latest in a long series of patents on dolestatins, a family with anti-cancer potential. The sea hare was collected in 1972; but it and other collections continue to provide patented compounds for Arizona State University.
Mozambique	Bacteria extracts (*Micromonospora sp.*)	PharmaMar S.A., Madrid Spain	US 6 214 793 (10 April 2001); US 5 849 540 (15 Dec. 1997) US 5 681 183 (28 Oct. 1997)	Anti-cancer and antibiotic drugs. From the patents: 'The organism was isolated from an unidentified marine soft coral collected at the Indian Ocean [sic] near the coast of Mozambique'.
South Africa	Tube worm extracts (*Cephalodiscus gilchristi*)	Arizona State University, USA	US 5 583 224 (10 Dec. 1996)	Source of cephalostatins. The patent says: 'In 1972, Cephalodiscus gilchristi was collected in False Bay, Cape Province, Republic of South Africa. All subsequent re-collections were also taken from the same general area'.
South Africa	Sea pen extracts (*Gyrophyllum sibogae*)		None (yet)	PharmaMar (Spain) scientists have recently reported finding anti-tumour compounds in this species.

* A table of known patents would take many pages: these few are representative of the most recent ones.

Source: Partial reproduction of table (McGown 2006: 27–8)

(*Uvaria klaineri*) from this very area of Gabon.[7] The patent application claims that the plant produces chemicals that inhibit cell growth, which may assist in preventing the growth of cancer tumours. Although the patent application designates the plant's origin as Gamba, Gabon, there is no mention how the plant was accessed, nor by whom.[8] Additional Aventis patent applications on Uvaria are pending in Canada, Australia and Europe. WIPO records that Aventis plans to apply for patents in 105 countries, including Gabon (McGown 2003).

Traditional medicines across Africa, from Sierra Leone to Ethiopia to Tanzania, have long used Uvaria to treat jaundice, malaria, stomach aches and bronchitis. The fruit can be important food for travellers. Even though the genus is well known across Africa as both medicine and food, the Aventis specie is not registered in public databases, such as Kew Gardens and the Missouri Botanical Gardens. McGown (2003) suggests, '*Aventis U. klaineri* may be new to Western science or, perhaps, the company has used a novel spelling of the name of another plant, such as *U. klaineana*.'

The extensive patenting of a plant that cannot be found in the public domain raises many questions about the complexity of the current scramble for Africa. Transparency about exploitation of resources is desirable to direct attention and to document the variable impacts. However, biodiversity monitoring can also render whole areas vulnerable to biopiracy. As outsiders learn of the favourable characteristics of a plant, it most often remains free and available for the taking for, as discussed above, current laws favour the biopirate. How did Aventis access the plant? Did indigenous knowledge signal its beneficial attributes? Was PIC given and by whom? What is the effect of the patent on future research with the plant and for availability of medicine to all?

As McGown (2006: iii) concluded in his more recent study: 'It's a free-for-all out there, and until the parties to the Convention on Biological Diversity (CBD) solve the problems of access and benefit sharing, the robbery will continue. They've got to declare a moratorium on access until a just protocol on access and benefit sharing is finished and implemented'.

The removal of a plant or animal from a community without permission and its subsequent patenting is a definitive act, raising questions of PIC and benefit-sharing. The other act of pirates, destruction of the wealth they cannot carry away, is even more contentious. One form of destruction is the loss of biodiversity through narrowly focusing on and nurturing just a few varieties within a few species. This destruction of genetic wealth may not be intentionally malevolent, but it is very predictable. If science and the agricultural industry value only two strains of potatoes – the current commercial production in the US – or a few of wheat, the other varieties may be quickly lost. *Ex situ* gene banks may preserve a few varieties, but for potatoes the Andean peoples have chosen their own *in situ* planting of hundreds of varieties expressly to preserve them. Conservation of food crops is counter to the logic of other forms of savings, from water to cash. To conserve food crops, it is best to use them: then they are valued in both the market and cultures. Industrial agriculture and livestock, however, grow by reducing biodiversity to breed a few varieties of a few species. This dominant mode of food production, used as the example of the only way to provision humans, destroys genetic wealth. Choosing industrial monoculture as the dominant farming system destroys biodiversity just as surely as any pirates burning riches they can't carry away. In Ethiopia, for example, where hundreds of varieties of teff once grew, only a handful now remain.

The other destruction of genetic wealth more closely resembles traditional pirates. Monsanto owns over 90% of the world's patents for genetically modified organisms (GMOs) giving this biopirate a name. Monsanto has taken zero responsibility for the fact that its GM strain genetically pollutes traditional or indigenous varieties of canola, maize or soya. In fact, it does the opposite. If a gene patented by Monsanto is found in a farmer's field and she has not paid royalties, then Monsanto sues the farmer. The genetic pollution of the field could have occurred by wind pollination beyond the control of the farmer. In fact, she should be able to sue Monsanto for contamination of heirloom seed, bred over generations within the family. Instead, the courts in Canada and the US are favouring Monsanto by ruling that the farmer owes royalties and penalties to Monsanto (Mushita and Thompson 2007: 42–3). This pollution is not piracy, for the regimes uphold the destruction as legal. It fits much better into the theory of accumulation by dispossession, which explains how dominant classes seize the means of production from farmers. By depriving the farmer of her prized seed through genetic contamination, Monsanto has destroyed her independent means of production. What is left is seed contaminated by Monsanto's privatising patents.

Virulent GM seed, bred to be open-pollinated, represents biological dominance translated into market power. GM strains cannot sell solely on the basis of their innovative characteristics, but need legal and political power to advance genetic pollution that steals the farmers' original seeds. GM strains that proliferate rapidly as invasive species, with legally-binding royalty payments to honour the conquest, is the innovation, not the plant's short-term resistance to pests or weeds. Conquest no longer takes armies, but simply pollen floating on the wind, backed by courts that recognise the offspring from the cross-pollination as the legal property of the corporation.

Philanthropic Dispossession

In late 2006 the Bill and Melinda Gates Foundation and the Rockefeller Foundation announced an Alliance for a Green Revolution for Africa (AGRA). By mid-2007, Kofi Annan had agreed to be the executive director. The goal of AGRA is to replicate the green revolution of the 1960s in Asia, while avoiding some of the mistakes. The agricultural model of a green revolution focuses on improving seeds for higher yields of very few crops – rice, maize and wheat. In India, yields of wheat increased ten-fold and rice three-fold.[9] India granaries now export food instead of waiting for food aid.

The earlier green revolution did increase yields, but at what cost? The water table in the Punjab has dropped drastically because the new varieties need a great deal of water to yield more than the old ones. The soil and water have been polluted with pesticides and fertilisers and the high yields destroy top soil, requiring more fertiliser. This cycle is highly dependent on fossil fuels, a cost not fully calculated when measuring benefits.

Focus on a few varieties reduced biodiversity, which makes the crops highly vulnerable to disease and pests. New seed needs to be commercially purchased every year. As the breeders need to return to parent genetic materials, loss of biodiversity reduces the gene pool, rendering seed reproduction unsustainable over the long term.

The social lessons are equally sobering. Only large-scale farmers could uphold the industrial production because only they had the cash to provide water, pesticides and fertilisers at exactly the right time. Land ownership was consolidated as the poor sold land to pay for debts incurred from the cost of the inputs. Further, nothing in the revolution could have happened without the extended hand of the state, offering agricultural extension and subsidies.

When championing the increased yields of a green revolution, advocates keep many costs as externalities and do not address whether such production is sustainable over generations. Green revolution high yields

- lower the water table and pollute ground water;
- destroy the organic composition of soil;
- reduce genetic biodiversity essential for seed reproduction;
- render crops more vulnerable to pests and diseases;
- require high inputs of fossil fuels;

- consolidate land ownership;
- commercialise seed sales making monopoly prices possible;
- lower nutrition as commercial food is defined by a few species;
- increase the role of the state in agriculture (infrastructure, subsidies and marketing).

AGRA, the twenty-first century variety of the green revolution designed for Africa, adds the following potential biopiracy:
- the new seed varieties in the 1960s remained in the public sector, but seed can now be patented and fully privatised without recognition paid to the original breeders;
- enclosure of the gene pool as privatised seed means that the germ plasm is not freely available to other breeders;
- many of the new varieties will be genetically modified and their pollen could contaminate indigenous varieties (for example, sorghum and teff) destroying farmers' heirloom seeds.

When questioned about the history of the green revolution and its twenty-first century dangers, the foundations reply that they plan to avoid the mistakes of the past. Yet they have correctly named their initiative, for it is an extension of the model of agricultural production that emphasises high yields of a handful of varieties, at any cost. Projects have already begun to modify seeds genetically and to patent them.

These wealthy and powerful foundations are entering African agriculture after over 25 years during which international agencies removed the state from agriculture. Since the Berg report of the World Bank (1981) receipt of grants, loans or trade from the North has required African governments to privatise agricultural research, extension, land and marketing. As very little cash was forthcoming – one of the few resource deficits on the continent – private foundations will now come to the rescue. Yet these foundations are financing the very type of agricultural system that extends enclosure across geographic territory and across production sectors and enriches the class they represent – whether African, American or European. More ominous for this new century is that scientists now know this production system is ecologically unsustainable. This enclosure to benefit one class not only renders small-scale African farmers an endangered species, but threatens the planet.

The North is gene poor, while Africa is gene rich. The new scramble for Africa is pirating genetic wealth, privatising it and then demanding that African farmers pay to use it or African geneticists pay to explore it. This process is not at all different from the commodity chain for oil: taken from African reserves it ends up as petrol in dilapidated African buses. The commodity chain beginning with columbite-tantalum dug from African soil is processed for laptop computers too expensive for Africans to buy.

Africans Unscrambling

Resistance to enclosure and dispossession does not come from one class in Africa: broader coalitions are emerging and linking easily across old scramble territorial borders. It is in the interest of all but the very elite to have sustainable and sufficient food production, provisioned by regional neighbours, not global markets. Such food reflects cultural heritage, withstands local natural disasters and is sustainable, as it has been for centuries. McDonalds will not disappear, nor will fried caterpillars or termites. Slow food has never disappeared from Africa. Plentiful, localised food production and consumption are quite possible, if the ideology and practice of privatisation meet resistance.

The ideology of patenting life forms is legally enshrined in the WTO, WIPO and Budapest Treaty, as discussed above. Other widely accepted international treaties counter enclosure of the commons and continue to make it difficult if not impossible. The deep seas beyond the 200-mile limit belong to no one, as protected by UNCLOS. It sets a precedent that some aspects of life belong only to the planet or the universe. The CBD gives control over genetic resources to national jurisdictions, with undefined PIC and benefit-sharing as legal principles that need to be moved into legal practice. The newest treaty, the International Treaty for Plant Genetic Resources (Food and Agriculture Organisation 2004), disallows patenting of 64 species. For every legal precept the corporations muster, counter legal regimes can contest their interpretations, a considerable accomplishment given the disparities in wealth and power behind the opposing arguments.

For the African continent, all countries unanimously agreed there should be no patents on life. That message was sent to the Seattle WTO ministerial meeting in 1999. African members of the WTO asked that their unanimous resolution be put on the agenda. The US refused. Yet African members have been among the leaders in disallowing the extension of patents on micro-organisms to all plant and animal life.

The fundamental principle of no patents on life is central to the Model Law on Rights of Local Communities, Farmers, Breeders and Access of the African Union (2000),[10] a working model for all African governments to adapt into national legislation. The AU model legislation uses provisions in the WTO to develop and implement *sui generis* alternatives to protect bioresources. The alternatives will vary across the continent. One common principle, however, is to honour farmers' rights as equal to private property rights. Farmers' rights to exchange, breed, plant and experiment with seed are inviolable, for such innovation sustains and extends biodiversity. African farmers joined Latin American, Asian and other farmers in the South to have that right enshrined in international law. The CBD and the International Treaty for Plant Genetic Resources are incompatible with the WTO and WIPO over patenting and property rights. The AU model law makes it clear where Africa stands on the issue.

Drawing legal lines around genetic resources is no more respected in Africa than the original drawing of lines on a map in Berlin. The geographic demarcations may exist according to the rules of the scramblers, but over 120 years later those borders are daily ignored by millions, as anyone familiar with informal African markets knows well. The geographic boundaries do not contain the languages, the cultures, the people, the commodities, the plants, nor the animals. For this new scramble, Africans are very much at the table, insisting that legal precepts based in their cultures – no private ownership of life and farmers' rights – are equal to any other legal ideas emanating from a different culture.

May (1998: 60, 64) summarises this as follows: 'What intellectual property is, is not fixed but is the function of the need of capitalism to exploit new resources made available by new technologies . . . the tenacity of the argument that "there is one theory of all property" (including intellectual property) is a product of political economic power'.

Scientists do not have one view of nature and many dispute the idea that one gene defines a whole organism. That one perspective is becoming disreputable and endures mainly because distinct genes serve patent lawyers well in their claim for uniqueness. The US National Science Foundation issued a report offering hope – a change in direction – by systems biology, yet also gave a stern warning:

> new systems biology is bringing mathematical and computational methods to bear on genetics, physiology, development and evolution, so as to deal with multiscale complexities without losing sight of them . . . If such a research program is permitted to flourish, in a few years, *the 20ᵗʰ century's gene binge will be just a memory*, and biology will again take its place among the subtle products of the human mind. However, if systems biology spawns a new reductionism of

social integration through molecular manipulation, we may witness another regression into oversimplification . . . that could set back our knowledge of ourselves and the natural world by at least another century. *Another binge on reductionism could be the fatal one, putting not only our science, but our lives and natures, at risk* (emphasis added).[11]

African scientists probably participate across the spectrum of this debate over reductionism, but they have shown considerable unity in following what they know about scientific testing. In many African countries, scientists have protested at the truncated time of laboratory and field tests for genetically engineered crops. In Zimbabwe, they refused to allow Monsanto to bring in its Bt cotton until they had completed the required three-year, confined-field testing. By the end of the period, all the scientific promises of Bt cotton came up short. The quality of the cotton bolls was much less than local strains; and pesticide use was less for a couple of seasons, but then increased as pest resistance to the Bt gene grew. Many other examples across the continent could be cited such as poor performance of GM sweet potatoes. African scientists stand by rigorous testing, not corporate hype, as demonstrated in the acceptance of the Cartagena agreement on biosafety across the continent. Scientists advise their governments that it is best to follow international law that allows protective banning of substances and procedures, even if they cannot yet be proven deleterious. They recognise that when something is released into nature, often it cannot be called back. The biosafety protocol therefore allows the precautionary principle to rule. GMOs can be totally banned, as in Zambia. The country that vociferously denounces this scientific decision to enforce the precautionary principle, the US, has not ratified Cartagena.

Countering legal and scientific definitions and principles, internationally and nationally, is essential, but not effective unless the farmers and their advocates are organised. Those who will stop the new scramble for bioresources and keep their governments and scientists transparent are the communities, farmers and traditional healers who have much to lose. They are the ones organising to demand the PIC of the local community that traditionally bred and protected the bioresource. The AU model law sets up PIC from both community and national government before a bioresource can be used. PIC can be abused either locally or nationally, as a leader sells off community treasures. Consequently, dual consent offers greater insurance.[12]

African communities also work on benefit-sharing, debating what is appropriate. As discussed above, however, little or nothing is returned by the biopirates. The international press heralded recognition and payments to the San people for the global commercialisation of the *hoodia* plant as a success. At least, the traditional knowledge of the San was given credit, as Phytopharm synthesised the plant for general use. However, the payments back to the San have been minuscule.[13]

Legal and scientific resistance is leading the way. What will take longer are steps toward economic equity. No one denies that biotech corporations need to be rewarded for their contributions to human nutrition or health. Resistance is against sole reward or recognition when much of the knowledge and the genetic materials are centuries old. To privatise genes is to enclose the means of production for farmers and for healers. It cuts off sharing of ideas, partial insights, false starts, all necessary to advance knowledge. Most fundamental, privatisation of the gene pools, plant or animal, destroys biodiversity, our collective sustenance.

Notes

1. The term was first popularised by Shiva (1997), but is now used widely among environmental activists across the globe, including the Indigenous People's Council on Biocolonialism. By 2002, at the world summit ten-year assessment of the Convention on Biological Diversity, Biowatch South Africa was hosting alternative sessions on biopiracy ten years post-Rio.
2. Surreptitious removal of plants from indigenous peoples by the British include the famous cinchona plant from the Andes, the source for quinine to cure malaria, so necessary for effective occupation of Africa (Brockway 1979: 53–5, 113–18).
3. UPOV was founded in 1961 by just six European countries in an effort to protect their plant breeders' rights. UPOV 1978 and 1991 brought the agreement to the status of an international treaty because of the increased number of signatories. What is fully in effect now is UPOV 1991, in force only since 24 Apr. 24 1998.
4. Quoted on the homepage of NATA, available at http://www.tuliassociation.com. The website gives the history of Tuli cattle in Africa, but makes no attempt to explain how the breed arrived in North America. Tuli cattle in Texas could also be violating the WTO intellectual property right of geographic indications, which identifies a product as originating in a particular place to which its quality, reputation or other characteristics are essentially attributable. If IPRs were fair, Tuli cattle could no more be bred in Texas than champagne be produced in California.
5. Smithsonian Institution. 2000. *Gabon Biodiversity Program*. http://nationalzoo.si.edu/ConservationAndScience/MAB/conservation/centralafrica/gabon/.
6. Smithsonian Institution. 2000. *Gabon Biodiversity Program*. http://nationalzoo.si.edu/ConservationAndScience/MAB/conservation/centralafrica/gabon/.
7. US patent 6 579 903, 17 June 2003.

8. The full text of the patent can be found on the website of the United States Patent and Trademark Office at http://patft.uspto.gov/netahtml/search-bool.html>. Enter the patent number and view the details.
9. 'A new green revolution for Africa?' *GRAIN Briefings* Dec. 2007.
10. http://www.grain.org/brl/?docid=798&lawid=2132.
11. Converging technologies for improving human performance: report by National Science Foundation and US Department of Commerce, 2003: 12. Available at http://www.wtec.org/ConvergingTechnologies.
12. In Indonesia a prominent biotech firm bribed as many as 144 civil servants in order to have Bt cotton grown commercially (Bassey 2005).
13. Phytopharm agreed to give payments to the South African Council for Scientific and Industrial Research, but arranged to share with the San people only after adverse publicity about biopiracy. The estimated amount for the San is 0.003% of retail sales (McGown 2006: 8).

References

Amin, S. 1974. *Accumulation on a World Scale: A Critique of the Theory of Underdevelopment.* New York: Monthly Review Press.
Arendt, H. 1968. *Imperialism.* New York: Harcourt Brace Janovich.
Bassey, N. 2005. 'Conned with corn'. *This Day* (Lagos) 22 Apr. http://allafrica.com/stories/200504250259.html.
Bollier, D. 2002. 'The enclosure of the academic commons'. *Academe* Sep.-Oct: 18–22.
Bonefield, W. 2001. 'The permanence of primitive accumulation: commodity fetishism and social constitution'. *Commoner* 2.
Brockway, L. 1979. *Science and Colonial Expansion: The Role of the British Royal Botanic Gardens.* New York: Academic Press.
Dickens, P. 1996. *Reconstructing Nature: Alienation, Emancipation and the Division of Labor.* New York: Routledge.
Fara, P. 2003. *Sex, Botany and Empire.* London: Icon.
Food and Agriculture Organisation. 2004. *International Treaty on Plant Genetic Resources for Food and Agriculture.* Rome: FAO.
——. 2007. *The State of the World's Animal Genetic Resources for Food and Agriculture.* Rome: Commission on Genetic Resources for Food and Agriculture, FAO. http://www.fao.org/docrep/010/a1250e/a1250e00.htm.
Glassman, J. 2006. 'Primitive accumulation, accumulation by dispossession, accumulation by "extra-economic" means'. *Progress in Human Geography* 30(5): 608–25.
Gura, S. 2008. 'Livestock breeding in the hands of corporations'. *Seedling* Jan: 2–9.
Hart, G. 2006. 'Denaturalizing dispossession: critical ethnography in the age of resurgent imperialism'. *Antipode* 38(5): 977–1004.
Harvey, D. 2003. *The New Imperialism.* Oxford: Oxford University Press.
——. 2005. *A Brief History of Neoliberalism.* Oxford: Oxford University Press.

Harvey, L. 1986. 'Tuli: Zimbabwe's own breed'. *The Farmer* (Harare): supplement.

Hepper, F.N. 1982. *Royal Botanic Gardens, Kew: Gardens for Science and Pleasure*. London: HMSO.

International Institute for Sustainable Development. 2007. Summary of the First International Technical Conference on Animal Genetic Resources for Food and Agriculture, 3–7 Sep. http://www.iisd.ca/vol09/enb09383e.html.

Levins, R. and R. Lewontin. 1985. *The Dialectical Biologist*. Cambridge: Harvard University Press.

Luxemburg, R. 1964. *Accumulation of Capital*. New York: Monthly Review Press (first published 1913).

May, C. 1998. 'Thinking, buying, selling: intellectual property rights in political economy'. *New Political Economy* 3(1): 59–78.

Mbeoji, I. 2006. *Global Biopiracy: Patents, Plants and Indigenous Knowledge*. Vancouver: University of British Columbia Press.

McGown, J. 2003. *Biodiversity Mystery Theatre*. Washington: Edmonds Institute. http://www.edmonds-institute.org/mystery.html.

——. 2006. *Out of Africa: Mysteries of Access and Benefit-Sharing*. Washington: Edmonds Institute.

Mushita, A. 2003. *Bioprospecting and Commercialising Traits of the Golden Beast of Zimbabwe: The Case of the Tuli Indigenous Cattle*. Harare: Community Technology Development Trust.

Mushita, A. and C. Thompson. 2007. *Biopiracy of Biodiversity: International Exchange as Enclosure*. Trenton: Africa World Press.

Perelman, M. 2007. 'Articulation from feudalism to capitalism'. *Africanus* Nov: 20–35. http://www.nu.ac.za/ccs/files/Africanus%20poli%20econ%20special%20issue.pdf.

Rodríguez Cervantes, S. 2008. 'CAFTA and the Budapest Treaty: the debate in Costa Rica'. *Seedling* Jan: 33–7.

Robinson, W. 2004. *A Theory of Global Capitalism: Production, Class and State in a Transnational World*. Baltimore: Johns Hopkins University Press.

Shiva, V. 1997. *Biopiracy : The Plunder of Nature and Knowledge*. London: South End Press.

Sutcliffe, B. 2006. 'Imperialism old and new: a comment on David Harvey's "The New Imperialism" and Ellen Meiksins Wood's "Empire of Capital"'. *Historical Materialism* 14(4): 59–78.

World Bank. 1981. *Accelerated Development in Sub-Saharan Africa: An Agenda for Action*. [Berg Report]. Washington: World Bank.

CHAPTER THIRTEEN

The European Union and the
International Scramble for African Fish

André Standing

Africa's marine resources are under increasing strain from many directions. Pollution, global warming, offshore coastal mining and rapid real estate developments are all playing a role to varying degrees in most countries. Yet it is undoubtedly expanding and largely unregulated commercial fishing activities that are the primary cause for concern.

African territorial waters are facing massively increased pressure. While historically North America, Europe and Asia have managed to consume a large quantity of fish from their own waters, overfishing and population growth has led, quite rapidly, to a dependence on fish imports from further afield. The European Union (EU), for example, has seen several of its key commercial fish stocks severely depleted by overfishing since the 1970s and now imports over 60% of fish from beyond its borders, primarily from Africa. Yet despite dwindling fish supplies, the industrial fishing fleets of developed nations have failed to shrink accordingly. Indeed, there is now widespread agreement that the international fishing fleet is suffering from chronic over-capacity, with subsidies being blamed for a large part of the problem. Thus, with dwindling fish stocks back home, a bloated fishing industry that supports thousands of jobs, and the growing popularity of fish as a healthy food option, the importation of fish from developing countries has become critical for the global North and Far East.

Important mechanisms that govern foreign fishing in Africa are bilateral trade agreements, of which those entered into between African countries and the EU are the most significant. What makes these so important is not only the scale of fishing opportunities they create, but also their strategic role in the governance of fisheries on the continent. These are popular among African officials and are championed by the EU for their ability to promote sustainable fisheries, good governance and economic development, particularly since they have been reinvented in recent years as partnership agreements.

The aim of this chapter is to review these agreements and consider if they are positive or otherwise for African countries by addressing three interrelated issues: the ecological consequences of EU access agreements; their social and economic impacts; and, finally, political considerations including transparency and democratic governance. First, however, it is necessary to introduce EU access agreements and place them in a wider context.

European Access Agreements in Africa

Bilateral trade agreements emerged as a response to the United Nations Convention on the Laws of the Seas (UNCLOS), signed after several years of negotiations in 1982. Before this landmark agreement, international fishing boats had almost free access to the vast majority of the world's oceans. There was little control over who fished where and for what. However, due to increasingly heated international competition for fish, as well as a realisation that fish were fast disappearing, UNCLOS gave coastal countries and island states ownership of, and responsibility for, the sea stretching in a 200-mile radius from their coasts: the Exclusive Economic Zone (EEZ). The terms of this convention made clear that all countries have an obligation to manage their marine resources in a sustainable way, taking into account the best available scientific data. However, for those countries that are unable to exploit their own fish stocks fully, UNCLOS states that they are obliged to offer access to those who can.

UNCLOS therefore created an environment where foreign fleets and coastal countries had to negotiate access between themselves to parts of the ocean that were previously rent free. The trend since 1982 has been for developed nations to consolidate control of their EEZ. However, due to the skewed nature of global fish consumption and fishing capacity, developing nations have tended to sell fishing rights to developed countries and their fishing fleets. Thus in Africa, European and Asian operators carry out most of the commercial fishing that supplies global fish markets.

Europe's efforts to capture African fish exports have been driven by the need to support its fishing industry, which for a long time has been placed in a precarious position due to the collapse of European fish stocks. Over and above subsidies given to European fishing boats, offering preferential trade tariffs on raw fish exports to developing countries has been one important mechanism to ensure African fish end up being processed, sold and consumed in Europe. However, bilateral access agreements have been the most important means of controlling African fisheries by the EU and these agreements may become more important if both subsidies and preferential trade tariffs are phased out as a result of current World Trade Organisation (WTO) reforms.

The first bilateral fisheries agreement (FA) was signed between the EU and Senegal in 1979, on the eve of UNCLOS. Since then a further seventeen African countries have entered into FAs with the EU. These have been updated many times, although there are certain countries, such as Namibia, Angola and Senegal, that have failed to renew their EU access agreements and there are others that are still being negotiated, by Tanzania and possibly Kenya.

Although the nature of these bilateral trade agreements has changed over time, the basic structure has remained the same for the past 30 years. The EU pays African countries an annual lump sum to guarantee licences for a number of European fishing boats. This sum is calculated as a percentage of the total market value of expected fish landings of these individual European boats, typically 10-12%. Those European fishing boats wishing to exploit this opportunity then buy annual licences to operate in that particular African EEZ. Individual licences cost European fishing boats approximately one third of the value the EU pays to African governments. In effect, the EU pays two thirds of the licence agreement on behalf of the European fishing boats. By far the most numerous European fishing boats that take advantage of these EU access agreements are Spanish, followed by French and Portuguese.

The fixed sum paid to African countries through these agreements is subject to fluctuations in fishing success. For example, the FA being negotiated between the EU and Tanzania is based on an annual payment of €600 000. This fee pays for the annual licensing of 79 EU fishing boats that are expected to catch 8 000 tonnes of tuna. The EU will pay €75 per tonne and individual boat licenses cost €25 per tonne. However, if the 79 fishing boats manage to land more than 8 000 tonnes in a given year, then the EU will increase its payments accordingly and so too will the individual fishing boats – each extra tonne generating a further €75 for the Tanzanian authorities from the EU and a further €25 from the boat owners.[1]

During the 1980s and 1990s, EU agreements represented straightforward cash for access deals. Under the terms of some agreements, a proportion of the money paid to African countries was earmarked for targeted actions, such as support of monitoring and surveillance, scientific studies and the development of artisanal fisheries. Since the early 2000s, FAs have been gradually phased out in favour of Fisheries Partnership Agreements (FPAs). Under these new agreements, the EU distinguishes between funds paid to the government for licences by boat owners and funds transferred by the EU for what it calls sectoral reforms. In essence, FPAs have two distinct components: a transfer of cash between boat owners and host governments to secure fishing rights; and a transfer of cash between the EU and host governments for the development of local fisheries policy and management. Funds for sectoral reforms are managed by joint committees, staffed by European experts and host officials. Other changes between FAs and FPAs include the promotion of joint ventures between European fishing companies and local businesses, as well as a commitment to restrict opportunities for European boats wanting to fish outside these agreements. The European Commission (EC), the ministerial council of the EU, claims FPAs better support the mutual interests of the EU and host countries and promote pro-poor development and good governance.

Despite the decision to move from straightforward, cash for access deals to the more attractively named FPAs, EU-African fisheries contracts remain explicitly commercial. Indeed, since their inception, bilateral agreements have always operated first and foremost as a means for Europe to export overcapacity in its fishing industry to developing countries: the primary aim is protection of jobs and the ongoing flow of raw fish into the EU. This was made clear in 2002 by the EC in an official communication on FPAs, which stated that 'the specific objective of the Common Fisheries policy is to maintain the European presence in distant Fisheries and to protect European fisheries sector interests'.[2]

Access Agreements and Competition for Fish

Access agreements protect European interests due to the loss of fish in European waters. But they are also presented as an important bastion of sustainable fishing in African waters, which is one of the reasons given for moves towards sectoral reforms under FPAs. There are several streams of competition with which the EU is confronted in African waters.

Although European access agreements dominate in Africa and should be considered as the most substantial bilateral trade agreements by far, some African countries also have access agreements with other foreign commercial organisations or governments from outside Europe. The most significant are access agreements signed between various African governments and Asian fishing associations from Japan, Taiwan, South Korea and China. On the surface, these differ from the access agreements with the EU because they are entered into between African governments and private fishing associations – there is no official role played by

Asian governments. Our knowledge of these agreements remains poor, largely because they are closed agreements subject to confidentiality clauses (Mwikya 2006).

For the time being, Asian access agreements do not seem to be as significant as EU FAs. But this may change. For example, China's rapidly enlarging and heavily subsidised fishing fleet will increasingly need new fishing grounds, bearing in mind that its own fish stocks seem to have collapsed, while its population is growing in both size and affluence. As in other primary resource sectors, it seems inevitable that there will be growing competition for the control of African fish between Asian business interests and those of the West. So just as the EU has attached developmental conditionalities to their access agreements, less paternalistic – and possibly even more lucrative – sources of business from the East may be on the horizon.

Most African countries, including those with access agreements, sell private licences to foreign fishing boats. The EU now contains exclusivity clauses in its agreements, meaning in theory no European boats should fish outside access agreements in those countries that have entered into an agreement with the EU. But the same restrictions do not exist for non-European vessels.

Information about many private licences sold by African governments to commercial fishing operators is difficult to obtain and not available publicly in many countries. Furthermore, where government data is available, it may not be reliable. For instance, the fisheries department of one East African nation claims that it had sold approximately 80 licences for tuna fishing, whereas other sources close to the government have privately speculated to the author that the real figure may be closer to 140. Embezzlement of licence fees may be one reason for this disparity in official and actual data. Another problem is that in some African countries semi-autonomous states issue licences independently, and perhaps in competition to, central government authorities. This is of particular concern in Somalia, where authorities in Puntland and Mogadishu are selling licences simultaneously; and in Tanzania, where authorities in Zanzibar and Dar es Salaam sell licences for the same EEZ.[3]

A further way to gain access to African waters involves joint ventures or flag transfers, where foreign companies become locally registered. The transfer of European boats to African flags was encouraged for years by the EU through financial incentives and soft loans, although this policy was phased out between 2002 and 2004. For private companies, transferring to an African flag may be an attractive option due to preferential licensing and less stringent rules on health, safety or environmental standards. Clover describes how Spanish trawlers have cynically latched on to this practice in Senegal:

> In theory, joint ventures between local fishing companies and foreign fishing fleets have to be 51% Senegalese-owned. But no one really complies with this rule. "There are people who one day have problems buying long trousers and the next day are the owners of four trawlers," one Senegalese official marked tartly. All the observers I met had been offered bribes by EU skippers to turn a blind eye to the rules. The EU has said it wants the transfer of EU vessels to foreign flags to stop, but characteristically it has given them a year's grace and, when introduced, the new rules will not be retrospective. Needless to say, joint ventures are proliferating rapidly (Clover 2005: 44–5).

It is possible that such joint ventures are common in other countries: they involve both European and non-European companies and their impact significantly adds pressure to resource competition. Moreover, it is an area, as Clover suggests, where corruption may be problematic. The resulting business ventures may prove stubborn to regulate given inherent conflicts of interest. Somewhat strangely, although the EU phased out subsidies for joint ventures by 2004, the ideal of partnerships between European companies and African businesses has been reinstated through FPAs. How this will be regulated and who will benefit most remains a subject for further research.

Finally, an increasing number of foreign boats simply by-pass regulations altogether and fish in African territorial waters without any licence at all. In Guinea, for example, research claimed that in the first six months of 2005, the authorities arrested eight boats of Asian origin (with some flying under non-Asian flags) for fishing without permission (Environmental Justice Foundation 2005a). In South Africa, unlicensed fishing boats of Spanish origin caught 32 000 tonnes of patagonian toothfish over a two-year period in the late 1990s. This resulted in a collapse of the fisheries, with annual catch limits being reduced to a mere 450 tonnes (Moola 2005).

Although there are now numerous reports on illegal fishing in Africa, almost all are, at best, impressionistic and some are possibly prone to over-exaggeration (Marine Resources Assessment Group 2005). Indeed, because the issuing of licences can be opaque and deliberately obscured, it is extremely difficult for independent researchers to know whether foreign fishing boats are poaching or not.

Nevertheless, it is clear that the EC, along with many international non-governmental organisations (NGOs), considers illegal fishing one of the most severe threats to the sustainability of fisheries in developing countries. Combating illegal fishing is therefore a priority activity for sectoral reforms under FPAs and the EU is also launching a dedicated programme to combat what is now confusingly known as illegal, unregulated and unreported (IUU) fishing.

In sum, whereas EU bilateral access agreements are one of the most important legal mechanisms governing foreign fishing in Africa, they exist alongside non-EU access agreements, private licences, joint ventures, flag transfers and unlicensed fishing. It is clear that this chaotic and competitive environment poses threats to the security of the European fishing industry. The claims that:

> fisheries agreements generate in Europe and the coastal states important, often vital, economic activities . . . The positive impact of the new Partnerships agreements on the Developing Country's local economies should even be more important in the future . . . The situation is amplified by the fact that the LDWF [long distant waters fleet] is evolving in a global context of scarcity and overexploitation of some fish stocks and is becoming less competitive vis-à-vis the fleets of new emerging fishing nations which are operating at lower costs. In the meantime, the generalization of flags of convenience, illegal fishing, lack of transparent rules, effects of direct or indirect public subsidies leads to an increasing distortion of competition and the development of practices that offer fewer guarantees for the maintenance of a sustainable global fishing activity.[4]

The implied message is that the EC is a more responsible partner for African countries and that competitors, such as those from the Far East, are more threatening and less trustworthy. Thus, according to the EC, access agreements are not only vital for Europe, but also imperative for African countries given the scramble for African fish.

The Spirit of Sustainable Fishing

The analysis of threats to sustainable fishing in Africa presented by the EC is convincing. It is certainly the case that the combined impact of illegal fishing, arbitrary granting of licences and the transfer of flags are all contributing to strain on fish stocks. However, despite these various threats to Africa's marine habitat, the EC claims its fishing policy in Africa is sustainable. In 2002, it released an official document providing details of its integrated framework for FPAs with third countries. This stated that the 'Community will, through fisheries partnership agreements, strengthen co-operation to ensure the implementation of a sustainable fisheries policy and a rational and responsible exploitation of the resources in the mutual interest of the parties concerned'.[5] Now all fisheries agreements signed by the EU with African countries contain reference to this ideal of sustainable fishing. For example, in the explanatory memorandum of the proposed EU agreement with Tanzania, the authors claim, 'the spirit of the agreement is in line with the objective of sustainable fisheries'.[6]

For fish to be exploited in a sustainable way, the number of adult fish that are killed must not cause a reduction in the overall biomass of the species, nor must it have an impact on the natural marine ecosystem. Under a constant regime of sustainable fishing, the oceans would be in exactly the same state now that they were hundreds of years ago, taking into consideration natural changes in the environment.

Marine scientists are still refining their understanding of how human activities impact on complex marine ecosystems. Longitudinal models based on single species are considered insufficient because of the intricate dynamics between fish species and their environment. Moreover, developing models of sustainable fishing is made more challenging as data on fisheries has only been accumulated for a few decades and large-scale industrial fishing predates this. Consequently, experts are not sure what pristine marine ecosystems look like.

Despite these problems within the science of sustainable fisheries, there is little doubt that the world's seas have been overfished and are facing an uncertain future. Indeed, a depressing article published in *Nature* in 2002, written by eight leading marine biologists from the University of British Columbia, argued that commercial fishing has never been sustainable (Pauly et al. 2002). Although there may be some recent exceptions, including Iceland, Australia and New Zealand, these authors argue that fishing has been rendered sustainable only by the inability of humans to catch fish, not by deliberate conservation measures. Persistent government subsidies and technological advances in fishing are exacerbating the situation, with the use of digital maps and powerful sonar equipment ensuring that there are no longer areas of the sea hidden from fishing boats.

Statistics describing the world's marine crisis are highly contested. In 2003, a controversial study claimed that the current populations of predatory fish species in the world's oceans had been reduced by 90% since 1950s. The same research showed that it takes approximately fifteen years for industrial fishing to cause reduction in marine community biomass by 80%. Others have disagreed with this data, suggesting that the rate of overfishing is not quite so high, the west Indian Ocean for example (Polacheck 2006), although few credible reports offer a positive prognosis.

Global overfishing seems to have been temporarily masked by the fact that commercial fishing has compensated for dwindling catches by landing higher quantities of smaller fish. There has also been a shift to new species that were previously not in demand. This dynamic is often referred to as fishing down marine food chains and there is now evidence that this has caused irreversible genetic distortions in most oceans (Morato et al. 2006).

Despite displacement effects, since the 1980s global fish landings have decreased at a rate of approximate 0.7 million tonnes a year (Pauly, Watson and Alder 2005). Based on current trends, some have estimated that wild fish catches from the oceans will finally end within 40 years.

Many experts agree that if the oceans are to be saved, a significant reduction in industrial fisheries capacity is needed (Greenpeace 2007) and much larger areas of the ocean need protection from fishing and pollution. Moreover, the management of commercial fisheries will need to be based on very careful scientific modelling, complemented by ongoing monitoring and policing. Stringent limits to what can be taken from the sea are required, combined with measures to reduce or eliminate environmentally destructive fishing practices, including the discarding of by-catch and the destruction of the seabed by bottom trawling. Furthermore, due to the precarious nature of marine science, it is now widely urged that fisheries should operate on a precautionary basis, even if this does not achieve maximum allowable yield.

Concerns in African Waters

The EU's claim to promote sustainable fishing via its access agreements has attracted widespread criticism. There are two broad concerns: the regulation of fishing intensity for targeted species and the approach of the EU to curbing by-catch. In both cases what is of particular alarm is that the EC applies less strict rules for fishing in third countries than it does in its own waters.

Fishing Intensity and Profit Maximisation

Neither the EU nor African coastal states that sign access agreements seem to conduct in-depth scientific audits of the marine ecosystem where European fishing boats operate. Instead, the EU undertakes what it refers to as evaluations to provide indications of how many fishing boats a certain region of the sea may sustain over the duration of the agreement, which typically runs for two to six years. Because evaluations are not published, we can only speculate on the data and methods used. It would seem likely that they are informed by trends in catch data, or they may draw on information about fishing potential passed on by fishing boats.

Evaluations lead to decisions on reference tonnages. This is the amount of fish that the EU will pay for in its advance annual payments to host governments. However, these reference tonnages do not represent what European fishing boats are allowed to catch under the EU access agreements. In the vast majority of access agreements, there are no upper limits at all and boats catch as much as they can.

A superficial understanding of access agreements may mistake limits to the size of the fishing fleet as a conservation measure. However, there is no wording in EU-African access agreements suggesting that the number of licences issued is informed by conservation goals. Indeed, limiting the number of licences as a mechanism to control fishing intensity is widely acknowledged to be a flawed strategy. Information on the capacity of a fishing fleet is insufficient to know what impact it will have on the marine ecosystem. One reason is that boats may transship fish catches several times while at sea. Moreover, whereas the physical size of a fishing fleet may remain constant, the technology influencing its efficiency does not. In the mid 1990s, the efficiency of EU fishing fleets was estimated to have increased by 2–3% per annum since the early 1980s (Johnstone 1996: 18). Likewise, it has been shown (Molina, Areaso and Ariz 2007) that the number of Spanish tuna vessels operating in the Indian Ocean has remained approximately the same since the late 1980s, but total landings by the fleet have more than doubled: in 1990 twenty Spanish purse-seine fishing boats caught 96 666 tonnes of tuna, whereas in 2006, 22 boats caught 200 543 tonnes. This increase in efficiency has been facilitated by EU subsidies that have helped replace older ships with more modern ones. It is also an outcome of dramatic advances in technology, such as digital mapping devices and the use of artificial devices to attract tuna schools.

The outcome of this regulatory approach is that neither the EU nor host governments can be sure in advance what amounts of fish will be caught under access agreements. Both parties proceed in the hope that reference tonnages will be surpassed, otherwise the deals will not be as profitable as they should be. In Tanzania, the EU's current evaluation has set the reference tonnage at 8 000 tonnes of tuna. However, in convincing the EU that the annual fee paid to the Tanzanian government represents a sound investment, the EC state that their 'evaluation suggests that not only will the reference tonnages be reached but it will exceed the reference catch'.[7] In this case, the EC states that it is willing to pay for up to 24 000 tonnes of tuna and other fish per year. If the European fishing fleet manages to catch more than this, then the Tanzanian authorities have to renegotiate the contract to receive extra payment.

The approach to commercial fishing in access agreements contrasts with the situation in Europe and most developed countries, as well as in South Africa and Namibia, where efforts to control fisheries is maintained through total allowable catch (TAC) limits. There is little doubt that a system of TAC is preferable to a system of merely limiting fishing through the number of licences, although due to the combined problems of unreliable scientific data and illegal fishing, TACs have generally not been successful either. Nevertheless, as several commentators have argued, it is inconceivable that the EC would apply the same rules governing fishing intensity in European waters as it does in most African countries (Brown 2005).

The weak regulatory approach to the control of fishing in Africa by the EU makes overfishing of targeted species probable, particularly given the statistics of worldwide collapse in marine ecosystems. It is a system of managing fishing intensity that pays little respect to the precautionary principle that is embedded in responsible fishing. Indeed, nowhere in the proposal between the EU and Tanzania is it considered whether Tanzania's sea can sustain catches of 24 000 tonnes of tuna every year. Nor is the regional impact of this level of fishing considered, given that tuna is a highly migratory species and swims into Kenyan waters, for example.

Data illustrating overfishing by European boats in Africa is in fact hard to come by and reflects the lack of scientific monitoring. However, there are several worrying indicators. For example, an anomaly of FAs is that utilisation rates are increasingly erratic and reference tonnages are not always achieved. Thus in Mauritania, the EU paid for 55 fishing licences in the octopus fisheries, but only 43 boats took up these opportunities. Recent research regarding tuna fisheries (Marine Resources Assessment Group 2007: 89–91) shows that 74% of licences for purse-seine fishing were utilised, 59% of long-line licences and only 26% of pole and line licences. Such low utilisation rates are considered to be indicative of poor management and dwindling fish populations. In this situation predicting potential fishing capacity is extremely difficult.

Meanwhile, the volume of fishing opportunities provided by EU access agreements is shrinking, which again points to decreasing fish populations. For example, in Guinea-Bissau the EU has had a FA since 1980. In the latest agreement, signed in 2007, the number of tuna licences decreased from 70 to 37. In Morocco, the EU decreased its fishing fleet from 500 vessels in the late 1990s, to just 137 vessels in 2007.

Declines in utilisation rates and decreases of reference tonnages are not necessarily reliable indicators of overfishing by EU fleets. This is because such data may be describing the crowding out of EU fishing boats by other participants in the industry, or they may indicate over fishing by non-EU fleets. However, the regulatory system imposed by the EU shows little, if any, commitment to the spirit of sustainable fisheries. The overall impression of access agreements is that fishing intensity is largely controlled by the dictates of the fishing industry itself. It is possible that under a regime of self-regulation participants may have a strong desire for sustainable resource exploitation. However, it is equally possible that a system of governing fisheries defined by short-term profit maximisation, weak scientific data and virtually no limits to catches may foster a competitive mentality that will eventually cause severe ecological degradation.

By-catch and Waste

Almost all industrial fishing activities result in catching non-targeted fish and marine wildlife. This has caused considerable degradation of marine ecosystems and has pushed certain species to the brink of extinction. In 2004 it was estimated that 7.3 million tonnes of so-called by-catch was dumped at sea (Kelleher 2004).

The type of fishing undertaken by the EU in Africa is among the most wasteful in the world. In the tuna fisheries that dominate the majority of European access agreements, licences are available for three forms of fishing: pole and line fishing, long-line fishing and purse-seine fishing. In comparison to the other two methods, pole and line fishing generates very little by-catch. However, it is far less efficient, more labour intensive and therefore less profitable; and thus the other two methods tend to dominate.

Purse-seine fishing, almost exclusively for the canning industry, involves catching schools of fish in an enormous net, up to 1 800 metres in circumference and 240 metres deep. Tuna are found in their highest densities on thermoclines, where cold and warm water collide, and they tend to gather en masse under floating objects at sea, possibly for protection. Whereas in the past boats used to set nets around free swimming schools, increasingly the technique of finding schools of tuna is to set nets around naturally floating objects, which can include whales and whale sharks, or by constructing artificial floating objects, so-called fish aggregation devices (FADs). Attached to these are receivers that send information to ships notifying them of the presence of fish.

The primary target of purse-seine vessels is skip-jack and yellow-fin tuna, both of which are extremely fecund and therefore require heavy fishing to cause a reduction in their populations. Another species is the big-eye tuna, which is much larger and slower to reproduce. The International Union for the Conservation of Nature list big-eye tuna as highly threatened: a dramatic reduction of fishing is needed to avoid extinction.

The technique of purse-seine fishing is extremely efficient, leading to massive landings. Yet it is indiscriminate, as many other species of fish are hauled out of the ocean at the same time, a large proportion of which is discarded overboard. The scale of by-catch generated by purse-seine fishing is poorly documented, as confirmed by recent studies undertaken by the Indian Ocean Tuna Commission (IOTC).[8] Nevertheless, ad hoc reports published by the IOTC indicate that large quantities of marine wildlife are found in the nets of purse seiners, possibly representing 10% of landings.[9] Moreover, the use of FADs seems more destructive than setting on free swimming schools. FADs not only attract a disproportionate number of juvenile tuna, but various non-tuna species as well. Netting hung beneath FADs, designed to increase the number of fish gathering for protection, is also known to drown marine wildlife, including turtles (Fonteneau et al. 2007).

Long-line boats, which tend to supply tuna for the raw fish markets, also generate massive amounts of by-catch. Long-lines, stretching for several miles behind ships and containing thousands of hooks ensnare turtles, birds and other marine wildlife. Indeed, it is thought that worldwide long-line fishing accounts for the deaths of 200 000 loggerhead turtles and 50 000 leatherback turtles, both of which are highly threatened species (Environmental Justice Foundation 2005b: 5). The World Wide Fund for Nature (WWF) reports (2007) that in the Benguela current marine ecosystem alone, stretching from Angola to South Africa, some 40 000 sea turtles are caught on long-lines every year, although presumably this figure will be declining rapidly.

Outside the tuna industry, the EU fishing fleet is also involved in bottom trawling for various species, including shrimps and octopus. Trawling for shrimps, which involves dragging a net across the seabed, can generate up to 90% discards, including turtles, sharks and hundreds of different tropical fish species. It also scars the seabed, destroying critical habitats including coral reefs. Industrial shrimp fishing is regarded as the most destructive in the world, accounting for some 27% of all by-catch (Environmental Justice Foundation 2003).

By-catch and environmental degradation of the marine ecosystem seem to be inevitable outcomes of industrial fishing, but they can be minimised and controlled. In fact, the EU claims to be addressing some of these problems. Thus in the EU-Tanzania agreement it is claimed that there are measures in place for the 'collection of by-catch and that dumping of by-catch is banned'.[10] Yet further reading of the document suggests these objectives will not be achieved. When a fishing boat finds it has landed fish or other marine animals that it does not intend to sell, under the terms of the agreement the boat's captain must notify the Tanzanian authorities. The intention is to supply unwanted fish to the authorities so that it can be used to feed the poor, a donation that may not be welcomed by local fishermen. The Tanzanian authorities then have four hours to dispatch a boat, at their own expense, to collect the by-catch. If the authority's boat does not arrive within four hours, then the EU fishing captain can legitimately dump whatever he wants. However, whether the Tanzanian authorities have the capacity to dispatch such waste disposal boats to reach all EU fishing boats in four hours seems unlikely; and even if they did, that presumes they have the further capacity to keep the fish in a state fit for human consumption.

Indeed, the EU's effort to limit by-catch in Africa has been accused of being one of the worst in the world (Environmental Justice Foundation 2005b). Rules governing access agreements are often less strict than domestic legislation in Africa. In Guinea, EU shrimp trawlers are allowed to catch five times as much by-catch than the local government permits Guinean trawlers (Gorez 2005: 26). Likewise, in Mauritania the government has legislated that total landings of domestic shrimp trawlers can contain only 35% by-catch, yet reports show that European fishing boats in Mauritania produce 85% (CFFA 2006a: 7). Similarly, efforts to stem the rapid decrease in octopus populations have involved limiting fishing to adults that weigh 450 grams or more. However, under the EU access agreement with Mauritania, European boats are allowed to fish octopuses with nets containing a mesh size of 70 millimetres. Scientific studies show that nets of this density capture octopuses much smaller than that. The impact on the ecosystem and on the potential for octopus populations to recover is profound.

The EU's approach to limiting by-catch in Africa contrasts to its attitude to European waters. While European regulations are far from satisfactory, there are numerous laws restricting the type and size of fishing nets to be used in EU waters and several European fisheries are required to use by-catch reduction devices. The Environmental Justice Foundation suggests that the EU should be leading environmentally-friendly fishing techniques globally, and complains that 'there can be little justification for the EU to accept different bycatch standards for fisheries in the North Sea, for example, than for European vessels fishing off Senegal' (Environmental Justice Foundation 2005b: 4).

Fishing beyong their Surplus?

The evolving legal framework governing access agreements is based on a fundamental principle. Coastal states are encouraged to give other countries access to fish stocks that their domestic fishing industries are not catching. In theory, this ensures renewable fish resources are exploited at maximum intensity. By default, in order for coastal states to offer this surplus, they need to understand what the capacity of their national fishing industry is, and to have in-depth accounting of sustainable catch yields. This type of information is absent in most African countries. Furthermore, where there are independent reports showing clear signs of overfishing and over capacity, these are easily ignored. For example, in 2005 the Mauritian Institute of Oceanographic Research and Fisheries published data showing that there was 31% over capacity in the octopus fisheries, yet the EU failed to respond to this warning and merely reduced its own fishing by roughly 6% (CFFA 2006b: 3–5).

Those working on access agreements on behalf of the EU have explicitly claimed only surplus fish are targeted in developing countries. However, in some countries where the EU operates, particularly off West Africa, local fisheries have evolved enough capacity to exploit their marine resources fully, rendering the continued presence of EU fishing fleets untenable. Thus a report by the United Nations Environment Programme (2002b) describes how the first bilateral FA between Senegal and Europe, signed in 1979, coincided with considerable growth in small-scale fishing in that country, largely caused by Senegalese subsidies, including financial assistance for mechanising pirogues, lower fuel costs and export incentives. Due to these policy interventions, the size of small-scale fisheries has increased dramatically; and the growth and power of individual boats increasingly blurs the distinction between small-scale artisan fishing and industrial fishing. Total landings by small-scale fishers in Senegal stood at 130 000 tonnes per annum in the early 1980s, rising to 250 000 tonnes in the early 1990s, and by 2002 it was up to 350 000 tonnes.

Alongside this expansion of the so-called small-scale sector, the Senegalese industrialised fishing fleet has developed more than enough capacity to exploit the vast majority of fish that live further out in the EEZ, beyond the range that is typically targeted by small-scale fishers. This growth seems to have been augmented by joint ventures and flag transfers by European and Asian fishing companies. Thus, there appears to be very little surplus to offer to foreign fishing boats (Brown

2005). Indeed, despite having had access agreements with the EU for over 25 years, Senegalese authorities have recently failed to grant the EU a further agreement due to widespread anger with overfishing and excessive competition.

Industrialised foreign fishing is far from the only threat to coastal communities for whom fishing is culturally and economically important (Wolfgang 2005). Poorly managed small-scale fisheries have also contributed to overfishing. Local fisheries have grown too large in many African countries and become a major threat to the environment in their own right. Furthermore, the fact that African governments allow foreign industrial boats to fish well beyond the surplus may have a profound impact on small-scale fishing. Whereas from the EU's perspective access agreements protect European jobs and livelihoods, the opposite may be true in many African countries. Reports from Senegal, Angola, Mauritania and Madagascar show that local fishermen find it increasingly difficult to land the amount of fish they used to. Moreover, growing competition between small-scale fishermen and industrialised boats has caused an escalation of conflict between them (Bartels et al. 2007: 52; Gorez 2000; Lankester 2002: 8). There are also complaints that industrial trawlers from southern Europe, Russia and the Far East enter closer inshore than they are allowed. Local nets are destroyed in the process and occasionally there are collisions causing loss of life. Such conflict is exacerbated as local fishermen venture further out to sea in order to sustain their traditional catches or compensate for degraded in-shore fishing.

A Cost-Benefit Analysis of European Access Agreements

The EC is obliged to conduct cost-benefit analysis of its access agreements with third countries. The primary reason may be to account for the expenditure of a significant sum of the Commission's funds. However, despite being requested by the European Court of Auditors (ECA) in 1992 to provided detailed public evaluations, to date the EC has only published one external study, conducted by the French consulting firm IFREMER (1997). The ECA undertook an external review in 2001 and although the EC in its response to this review promised to publish an updated and improved cost-benefit analysis by 2005, this has not happened.

Under FPAs, the EC supposedly conducts environmental and social impact evaluations before a new deal is negotiated and after a deal has come to an end. The resulting reports are not made publicly available (Gorez 2005: 24), which is peculiar given the EU's commitment to transparency. Moreover, the organisations used to conduct these evaluations are private European consulting firms and many seem to have close associations with the European fishing industry.

The 1997 IFREMER study is still the most widely cited, although clearly it is dated. Nevertheless, it paints some trends that probably hold true today. The authors acknowledged that a lack of data from both the EC and EU member states severely limited their appraisal. Yet the final report suggested access agreements with Southern countries were profitable from the EU's perspective. European employment generated through Southern agreements was estimated at 13 440 on boats and another 19 400 related jobs, 18% of which were in the canning industry. In total, with an annual value added of €731 million, the study claimed that every euro spent by the EU generated an average turnover of slightly more than €3.

The ECA report published in 2001 dismissed much of this analysis, arguing that weak and inconsistent data made it impossible to be sure about the real value of these deals. Moreover, the share of costs between the EC and member states appeared heavily skewed. According to IFREMER, the EU contributed as much as 87% of the costs for negotiating these deals on behalf of member states, with over 80% of the value added being received by Spain. A recommendation made at the time was for member states to pay far more than they do, although the situation remains largely unchanged. The ECA report also noted that member states increasingly requested fishing opportunities in Southern countries that were not taken up and therefore the EC was paying for fish that only existed on paper. This is clearly beneficial to boat owners who are able to speculate on the best fishing opportunities, knowing that various options are paid for them in advance by the EC.

A further concern raised by both IFREMER and the ECA was the high level of risk to which the EC was exposing itself in the event that access agreements were not renewed or kept at a constant level. IFREMER calculated that if all Southern access agreements were to end suddenly, the EU would have to spend €921 million in compensation and structural adjustment. Indeed, in 2000 the EU's access agreement with Morocco was temporally allowed to expire due to disagreements between the two parties. As a result, the EC paid out €59 million to European boats as compensation for reduced fishing opportunities, with a further €65 million coming from individual governments. The EU's agreement with Morocco in 1999 accounted for 7 000 direct jobs and 470 vessels, most of which were Spanish and Portuguese.

Although the temporary lapse in the agreement with Morocco was thought to have caused a loss in jobs, the same situation may not hold true in other countries. This is because European boats, and perhaps their governing bodies and national governments, have the ability to negotiate private licence agreements themselves. Indeed, there have been a number of access agreements between individual European countries and African states in the past (Mwikya 2006). Thus, if EU access agreements were to be terminated, access to African waters would be negotiated through other means.

IFREMER also argued that during the late 1990s the total cost of not renewing access agreements, presuming this would lead to compensation payments, was of a similar magnitude to the cost of paying for them. In other words, the EC budget used to negotiate access may be sufficient to cover the costs of decommissioning boats and compensating those who lost their jobs. We may therefore assume that the high dependence on access agreements by the EC is caused primarily by political considerations, not purely financial ones.

The benefits of access agreements from the perspective of EU taxpayers are also ambiguous. There is little reason to suspect that without access agreements the flow of raw fish into Europe would decrease or the cost of fish increase. Thus it is those involved directly in the European fishing industry who enjoy the real benefits from these agreements. Access agreements lower the costs of licences and provide security for future fishing rights. Indeed, the EC has effectively provided European fishing boats international access to waters from which they can pick and choose depending on their interests. Nor, as the EC signs these agreements on their behalf, are they troubled by potentially costly and lengthy negotiations in African countries.

The African Experience

To appreciate the benefits of these agreements from the African perspective, we consider first, income from licences and compensation payments; and second, the potential value added to economies through job creation.

Compensation and License Fees

On the surface, a clear benefit of these agreements for African countries lies with annual compensation payments. For some countries, such as Mauritania, Ivory Coast, Seychelles and Senegal, the annual payment made by the EU represents a substantial amount of total government revenue. In Mauritania, funds from EU access agreements have effectively doubled the annual budget of the Fisheries Ministry (Marine Resources Assessment Group 2007: 86). However, in Mozambique, the access agreement with the EU only brings in €900 000 each year, a negligible sum and less than 3% of the annual budget of the Ministry of Fisheries (Marine Resources Assessment Group 2007: 84). As the majority of these funds are targeted at activities within the fisheries sector, little seems to be reinvested in the wider economy and we can presume a significant amount is spent on monitoring and managing foreign fishing boats.

Prices paid by the EU to African governments for fishing licences are actually higher than by other LDWFs on the African continent. According to the official terms of these agreements, the EU pays roughly 10–12% of the value of declared fish catches, whereas other private licences typically account for as little as 3–5% (Marine Resources Assessment Group 2005: 35). However, this does not mean that EU boats fishing under access agreements are paying more to African countries than other LDWFs. In most cases, licences under access agreements are marginally less expensive for boat owners than private licenses. In Mozambique, for instance, private licences for tuna fishing cost €45 per ton, whereas under access agreements they are €35 (Marine Resources Assessment Group 2007: 86).

Despite the fact that access agreements are calculated on the quantity of fish caught, the final sum paid to African governments may not always correspond to actual fishing activities. Utilisation rates can be low, meaning African governments may be paid money for fishing that never takes place. However, it is also thought that there are large amounts of unreported catch. Clover (2005: 48) argued that the declared catch by European trawlers in Senegal was roughly 12 000 tonnes a year, whereas the WWF had estimated that the actual amount was probably nearer to 80–100 000 tonnes. Similarly, a study of European fishing in Guinea-Bissau (Kaczynski and Fluharty 2002) estimated that not only were there high levels of misreporting catches, but substantial amounts of fish and shrimps were caught as by-catch that incurs no fees and is then sold in Europe. The profits made by European boats, and the value added to European countries, may therefore be far in excess of what is often assumed.

This problem of under-reporting catches reflects the inability of most African countries to measure accurately the activities of foreign fishing boats. Often, in contravention of national laws, large quantities of fish will be transshipped at sea or enter and leave African ports with minimal supervision. To a large extent, African governments rely on the goodwill of boat owners to know precisely how many tonnes of fish, and what species, have been caught in their EEZs. Under EU licence agreements both boat owners and the EU have to increase their payments in line with the amount of fish they land, so there is an economic incentive not to be honest. Kaczynski and Fluharty (2002: 87) claim:

> foreign fleet operators do not cooperate with local authorities as prescribed in the Agreement and by the Guinea-Bissau's licence regulations. As a result no statistical data on foreign fleet activity are

supplied and information on catches is routinely denied to the
government. EU fleets do not accept coastal country observers on
board their ships and do not pay agreed fees for tuna harvested in
the country's coastal waters. They also do not visit local ports for
inspections.

There are reasons to suspect that the EC is unaware of this level of fraud. Again
turning to the ECA report, the Commission submitted eight data sheets that
contained information about the activities of member states in third countries.
Four of these sheets had no information at all on catch quantities, and all eight
failed to include data on value (European Court of Auditors 2001: para 18).

There is some cause for optimism: EU access agreements now tend to include
better provision for on-board observers from host countries on European fishing
boats. However, it is unclear whether on-board observers, typically poorly paid
and poorly trained, can ever be effective at policing boats. Observers are isolated
at sea and anecdotes suggest many are easily bribed, intimidated or are conveniently
ushered below deck when irregularities occur. Moreover, observer programmes
enforced under EU agreements are not as strong as they could be. Costs for host
governments can be prohibitive and because they are not mandatory, many
countries, such as Seychelles, choose not to use them.

Undermining increased surveillance and policing by African authorities is
the fact that the governments of European fishing boats appear reluctant to impose
strict sanctions when crimes are committed. In 2006, for example, the
Mauritianian Fisheries Surveillance Unit arrested four Spanish boats for illegal
fishing. Each boat was found to have two different logbooks, one for declared
catches and one for actual catches. In addition, the authorities found large
quantities of juvenile fish that were well below the legal size for landing.
Mauritanian officials wanted to launch an in-depth investigation and
recommended that boat owners found guilty of under-reporting should have their
boats confiscated. It was reported in the media that the Spanish fisheries ministry
opposed these recommendations, describing the infractions as minor, worthy of
a small fine.[11]

High levels of fraud perpetrated by European fishing boats in African waters,
condoned or ignored by European authorities, may be characteristic of the fishing
industry in general. The ECA (2007) recently completed a scathing evaluation of
industrial fishing within European waters, showing large inconsistencies in the
declaration of catches, extremely weak systems of inspection, incoherent data
and very poor levels of sanction and punishment. Indeed, levels of punishment

for infringements by European boats were considered so low that there is 'a risk that the fishing industry may consider penalties imposed for infringements . . . just as an ordinary running cost for the enterprise and see no real incentive to be compliant' (para 94).

Downstream Job Creation

Compensation payments and revenue from private licences represent the most obvious source of income from these agreements. However, the most significant value for African countries comes with potential job creation and the value added to the local economy through fish processing and servicing boats. Here, the experience of African countries differs significantly. In some countries, such as Seychelles, Ivory Coast and Mauritius, a substantial amount of fish taken from their EEZs by European boats is sold back to their governments and processed in local canning factories. The benefits of this transaction may be reduced as allegedly European boats charge a premium on raw fish to African processors in comparison to non-European boats (Ponte, Raakjær and Campling 2007). This is because European boats know it costs African processors less to export European-caught fish to the EU due to lower trade tariffs. Nevertheless, processing fish in African countries generates far more value than the amount received through compensation payments and licence fees, although according to Greenpeace (2007: 19) jobs in canning factories are very badly paid. Over 50% of the workforce in the Seychelles canning industry is supplied by immigrant labour, as locals consider it demeaning employment.

Most countries have very limited potential to process fish and therefore the value added from access agreements is nominal (tables 13.1 and 13.2). A United Nations Environment Programme (UNEP) report claimed that only 12% of the fish caught in Mauritania's waters, by all fishing fleets, is processed within that country (2007: 4). This difficulty in developing local capacity to process fish may simply be a factor of underdevelopment, but an aggravating factor is that despite preferential trade tariffs for African, Caribbean and Pacific (ACP) countries in the EU, many African countries find it difficult to meet strict hygiene and sanitary standards placed on imported processed foods. EU processing factories may have a competitive advantage in this respect due to European subsidies. It may also be that fish imports from non-European sources tend to be subject to far more rigorous inspections than those from Europe (Bartels 2007: 40).

The EU claims it now does more to promote domestic landings in order to stimulate downstream job creation in African countries. Under several agreements

European boats are offered financial incentives, with licence costs reduced by €5 per tonne for catches that are landed locally. Whether such policies are effective or not remains unclear. Unfortunately, evidence points to cynical abuse. In Morocco, the ECA (2001) claimed many Spanish boats benefited from lower licence costs by simply landing their fish at Moroccan ports and then immediately putting the fish back onboard before setting sail for Spain.

A further benefit supposedly accruing to African countries through some access agreements is provision for European boat owners to employ locals on board. Whether the resulting job creation can be considered significant or not is unclear and anyway industrial fishing is not labour intensive. Detailed audits to show that these job offers are actually adhered to have not been undertaken and in some cases, such as Mozambique, the EU has ensured employing locals is optional given complaints by skippers that picking up and dropping off locals is financially burdensome (Marine Resources Assessment Group 2007: 86). Moreover, anecdotal evidence suggests Africans on board foreign fishing vessels are badly treated, paid less than Europeans and are vulnerable to infringements of their labour rights. Deaths and injuries on board are rarely compensated, as documented by the Seafarers Assistance Programme based in Kenya (Mwangura 2005).

The data collated by IFREMER over the period 1993–7 gave an impression of skewed benefits generated by access agreements in Southern countries. Again, it is important to note that the data is not entirely reliable and does not take into account the implications of under-reporting. This may mean the data underestimates the benefits accrued by Europe. Moreover, when comparing jobs, it is possible that the quality of employment between Europe and African countries is quite different. Nevertheless, the disparity between Europe and Southern countries during this period was considerable and there is a remarkable difference in the outcome of agreements, largely reflecting the ability of some states to process fish (tables 13.1 and 13.2).

Reliable data on the value added for either Europe or individual African countries is not available for the years after IFREMER's study. Some changes should be expected. One reason is that the total value of access agreements has diminished, possibly caused by over-fishing. Further, under new FPAs additional funds can be allocated to promote domestic sectoral fishing policy, which may give the appearance of increased value added to host countries. However, there is little reason to suspect the overall economic effect of these agreements has changed markedly over the last decade.

Table 13.1 Annual averages of jobs created in Europe and Southern
countries through access agreements, 1992–7.

	Total jobs for Europeans	Total jobs for host country
Angola	1 129	22
Cape Verde	176	0
Comoros	155	0
Ivory Coast	1 041	2 397
Gambia	68	1
Guinea	387	12
Guinea-Bissau	1 241	53
Equatorial Guinea	283	0
Madagascar	403	1 368
Morocco	18 671	922
Mauritius	91	160
Mauritania	4 448	307
São Tomé	104	0
Senegal	1 484	1 583
Seychelles	3 049	844
Total	**32 370**	**7 669**

Source: IFREMER 1997

Table 13.2 Annual averages for total value added for Europe and Southern
countries through access agreements, 1992–7 (€ million).

	Total value added for Europe	Total value added for host country
Angola	25.86	6.76
Cape Verde	0.72	0.24
Comoros	1.97	0.17
Ivory Coast	7.70	10.34
Gambia	0.08	0.07
Guinea	4.19	0.94
Guinea-Bissau	45.84	4.82
Equatorial Guinea	1.54	0.59
Madagascar	5.11	3.79
Morocco	435.07	36.11
Mauritius	0.39	2.70
Mauritania	132.34	13.80
São Tomé	0.42	0.25
Senegal	29.90	9.13
Seychelles	38.77	8.24
Total	**729.90**	**97.95**

Source: IFREMER 1997

Factoring in the Costs

In relation to the costs of access agreements a lack of data hampers our analysis. However, there are several issues to consider. First, if access agreements reduce fish stocks, this leads to a decrease in long-term potential revenues.[12] For example, the government of Guinea-Bissau entered into a new access agreement with the EU in 2007 that will last for four years and is their ninth fisheries agreement. The EU claimed this agreement confirms its commitment 'to strengthen sustainable fisheries'.[13] Yet in 2007 the number of licences for tuna fishing was reduced from 70 to 37. This has meant that annual payments to Guinea-Bissau from the EU for fishing access have shrunk to less than they were over ten years ago. In fact, compared to the previous agreement that ran from 2001 to 2006, the EU now pays €3 million less to the government of Guinea-Bissau every year. Although difficult to show categorically, it seems possible that the need to reduce the European tuna fishing fleet by almost 50%, and reduce the overall payment to Guinea-Bissau's government accordingly, represents the legacy of overfishing.

Second, the cost of overfishing and degradation of the marine environment may also generate various social and cultural problems. This is an acute problem in those countries, particularly in West Africa, where fish is a local food staple and European fishing boats have, for many years, targeted fish species upon which local markets depend. With dwindling fish catches, African citizens need to replace fish in their diets, which either means turning to other sources of local protein, or relying more on imported food that may be more expensive and subject to volatile price fluctuations. In West Africa, the decline of fisheries has been blamed for a remarkable increase in bush meat trade, leading to the extinction of numerous forest species. It is worth noting that the basic need for access agreements is to compensate for decreased fish stocks in Europe. Yet when fish cease to exist in Africa, African citizens do not have the ability to fish elsewhere.

Dwindling fish stocks and degraded marine environments also threaten local fishing activities, causing strain on coastal communities. This heightens economic insecurity and migration to urban areas. A recent article claimed that overfishing caused by foreign fishing vessels is directly linked to rising illegal migration from West African coastal communities to Europe.[14] Further research is needed to validate such claims, particularly as problems often presented as the outcome of industrial fishing may be aggravated by overfishing by artisans as well (Pauly 2006; Wolfgang 2005).

A further form of cost created by these agreements lies with the potential benefits of different approaches to managing fisheries. In effect, choosing to govern fisheries through access agreements may deny other forms of fishing that could be more beneficial. A mounting literature argues that small-scale fisheries are far preferable to industrial fishing. Pauly (2006) claims that globally small-scale fisheries generate approximately the same annual catch as large-scale industrial fishing – about 30 million tonnes. Yet small-scale fisheries require far less capital investment and are far more labour intensive. Despite landing the same quantity of fish, the large-scale sector employs roughly half a million people, compared to over twelve million engaged in small-scale fisheries. Every single job on board an industrial fishing boat represents a capital cost of up to $300 000 in comparison to a maximum of $3 000 on board a small-scale boat. Similarly, Gorez (2000: 30) reports that in Madagascar industrial fishing generates 42 jobs for every 100 tonnes of shrimp caught, whereas 100 tonnes of shrimp landed by small-scale fisheries generates 230 jobs. Pauly also points out that small-scale fisheries generate very little by-catch, whereas industrial fishing discards up to twenty million tonnes every year. Moreover, industrial fishing consumes far more fuel: 37 million tonnes compared to approximately five million tonnes by the small-scale sector.

It may be argued that it is not feasible for African small-scale fisheries to exploit fish stocks fully in their own EEZ, a job more suited to the powerful modern boats of the EU, particularly in those regions of the seas that are treacherous. With the increased capacity and reach of small-scale fishing, some of its apparent benefits may disappear. However, it is feasible given investment and technical assistance that local, more labour-intensive and environmentally-friendly fishing could successfully replace industrial fishing boats in many areas. This is the view of Greenpeace (2007: 22) who argue that 'providing foreign industrial fleets with access to coastal tuna is the worst possible fisheries develop-ment and conservation option for coastal communities'. Their recommendation is based on a straightforward principle: 'building a domestic fisheries economy is required to maximise the employment benefits of the fishery . . . the best means of doing so for job-starved coastal states is to develop labour-intensive, domestically built and financed, small-scale fishing fleets based exclusively on passive and highly selective fishing gear, preferably hook and line, pots and fish traps'.

In sum, the costs and benefits of access agreements in Africa appear heavily skewed in favour of Europe: the income generated by selling access agreements represents a trivial offset to short-term and costly exploitation.

The Political Economy of Fisheries Agreements

Although bilateral access agreements are business deals designed to protect the interests of European fishing boats, they have long assumed the outward appearance of development projects. For many years a proportion of the money paid to African governments was earmarked for targeted activities that included funds set aside for developing artisan fishing and improving monitoring, surveillance or scientific studies. However, there has been little accountability of the spending of this money and the EU has not appeared interested in conducting audits. Critics have claimed that misuse of funds has been inevitable in many African countries that rank among the most corrupt in the world. Indeed, there is scant evidence to show that a proportion of EU funds allocated to poverty reduction in its agreement with Angola ever reached the poor (Lankester 2002). Similarly, the EU's fishing agreement with Morocco, worth €36 million per annum, allows boats into the waters of the Western Sahara. The EU has defended the deal on the grounds that a proportion of the compensation payments will be used by the Moroccan government to advance the welfare of the occupied Sahrawi people. They have not been consulted about the agreement, nor have they consented to it. Given the stance of the Moroccan government to the people of the Western Sahara, the probability remains high that their welfare will not improve.[15]

Since the early 2000s, targeted payments have been gradually phased out in favour of FPAs. Under these new agreements the EU distinguishes between funds paid to the government for licences by boat owners and funds transferred by the EU for what it calls sectoral reforms that are managed jointly by the EU and the host government. However, evidence suggests that negotiations between the EU and some African governments have been less than cordial. Ndiaga Gueye, the then Senegalese Director of Marine Fisheries, reported that during the negotiation in 2002, 'the EU actively resisted numerous conservation measures and drove a hard bargain on price' (Ilnyckyj 2007: 37). The concept of partnership may be inappropriate.

Detailed plans on sectoral development assistance are not publicly available. We therefore have very little idea as to precisely how FPAs will achieve sustainable fisheries and promote poverty reduction. With the exception of the latest agreement in Mauritania, civil society groups and representatives of artisan fishing communities are not invited to participate, nor are minutes of meetings published. Given that evaluations of the cost and benefits of these agreements are also kept secret, there is doubt about the commitment of the EC or host governments to transparent governance, even if this is repeatedly claimed by the EC and in the FPA contracts themselves.

Such lack of transparency, combined with reports of competitive negotiations, prompts the question whether the EC's interest in assisting African government fisheries policies is benign or is a strategic attempt to protect European industrial fishing interests. For FPAs to be genuinely developmental, funding and assistance should not be tied to granting EU boats access to African territorial waters. However, development assistance provided under FPAs is explicitly conditional on fisheries access and the amount of money supplied is directly related to the value of fishing potential in the host country. Moreover, making industrial fishing a condition of sectoral reform may be counterproductive to sustainable resource exploitation and pro-poor development. Yet it seems highly unlikely that the EU will support sectoral reforms that involve decreasing, or even eliminating, foreign industrial fishing.

Furthermore, FPAs may have created an environment where those representing the EU fishing industry have a strong degree of influence on local policy decisions, scientific studies, inspections and monitoring. In this context, the potential for conflicts of interest could be high, although this has received almost no scrutiny to date. One area that should generate more interest is the EU's role in combating illegal fishing in Africa. This seems a role that may be particularly open to abuse, characterised by less stringent policing for EU boats than others.

The prospect of progressive policy through FPAs becomes even more questionable as dependency on European funding for jobs and departmental budgets may be created. This is also counter-productive for democratic governance: state departments may become less disposed to serving the needs of local stakeholders, who provide far less revenue and therefore have less political influence. In fact, in one report on FPAs (Marine Resources Assessment Group 2007: 48–9) it was argued that countries that have not renewed access agreements have tended to show the most encouraging signs of improvement in fisheries management.

The Threat of Corruption

The assumption that the shift to FPAs may consolidate influence on fisheries management in third countries is contentious. However, this line of thinking is given credibility because of increasing competition for access to fishing in developing countries by non-European boats, mostly originating from the Far East, as well as the chaotic systems of fisheries governance that exist in many African countries. As noted already, competition for the EU takes the form of illegal fishing, flag transfers, private licences and more formalised licence agreements with Asian fishing associations.

The EC has been frank about pursuing sectoral reforms to protect its own interests, although this is presented as a positive policy for both host countries and the EU. Where countries have chosen not to sign access agreements, the EC has shown a remarkable tendency to denounce them publicly, accusing them of being irresponsible. For example, Tanzania's delay in signing a three-year access agreement with the EU prompted the EC to issue a press release that read:

> The failure to adopt the [EU] fisheries agreement is not in the interests of Tanzania nor the region . . . there is little control on fishing as there are no quotas or catch limits and no vessel monitoring. Under the current licensing system, no one knows how much Tuna is being caught in the Tanzanian waters. The EU-Tanzania Fisheries Agreement could have, for the first time, provided the Tanzanian Authorities with important data on Tuna catches . . . used to estimate the value of the fishery and if significant, present an opportunity to extend the controls of the EU-Tanzania Fisheries Agreement to all foreign vessels fishing in Tanzania EEZ . . . Vessels fishing for Tuna stock in Tanzanian waters will continue to be subject to significantly less controls compared to other countries [who have signed EU agreements]. The essence of the Fisheries Agreement is to provide a framework for better governance regimes. Such support is needed to help ensure the introduction of a coherent and integrated long-term policy for resource management and an enhancement of the value of the fishery.[16]

The message repeated by the EC is that it is a more responsible partner for African countries and that its competitors, such as those from the Far East, are more threatening and less responsible. This is an objectionable view given the weak commitment by the EU to sustainable fishing in Africa. Moreover, while the EC shows little commitment to transparency, the costs and benefits of European FAs seem heavily skewed against host countries.

The EU's claims suggest an escalation of competition for control over resources that is likely to increase given the collapse of fish stocks elsewhere. This situation could create an opportunity for African governments to negotiate better deals on behalf of their citizens as they are placed in a strong bargaining position. However, it is equally possible that forms of undue influence may proliferate. Lee Clark puts it simply: 'with resources becoming scarcer and access to them becoming more valuable, incentives for corrupt practices are bound to increase and impatience with the kind of secrecy that attends access agreements also can be expected to rise'. Foreign governments have attempted to win over local officials in Pacific Island states by paying suspiciously well for meetings, entertaining officials on lavish overseas trips and even agreeing to pay for the overseas education of ministers' children. It is possible that similar tactics are used in Africa.[17]

There have also been allegations that the lure of donor funds and trade concessions, or the threat of their removal, has played its role in negotiations for fishing access (Clover 2005: 43–4; Mwikya 2006: 11). Similar concerns have been raised regarding access agreements with Asian companies. Yet whereas the EU is relatively open about its work to protect the European fishing industry, the links between governments and fishing associations from Asia can be less obvious. Several of the fishing associations that have entered into access agreements in Africa are considered private non-state organisations and this ensures that the terms of these agreements are kept confidential. However, as argued by Greenpeace (2007: 12), the relationship between fishing associations, such as the Japan Tuna Fisheries Co-operative Association, and their governments is far closer than some assume, which means the donor activities of their governments in African countries may be intimately connected to the interests of their fishing fleets. Because the public has no access to information, suspicions can run high. As the head of the Artisinal Fisheries Council of Senegal remarked in 2006, 'here and there we see infrastructures being built with the support of China and we say these may be part of the access agreements, but we know nothing about the contents of these agreements . . . a partnership must be based on transparency and participation from the artisinal sector' (Bartels et al. 2007: 81).

Conclusion

Disturbing trends in global fishing strongly suggest the next few decades may be critical for Africa's marine environment. If the pessimists are correct, marine ecosystems will be plundered for short-term profit. The costs of this will spiral in various directions, affecting food security and the economic, social and cultural well-being of millions of people, particularly coastal communities. The disapearence of marine wildlife will also be profound for those who attach a spiritual importance to life at sea.

Industrial fishing promoted by EU access agreements cannot be considered the only cause of concern for this imminent marine crisis. A lack of information, including scientific as well as economic and political data, means the impact of these agreements remains obscure. Yet the claim that they promote sustainable resource use, pro-poor development and good governance seems to contradict the evidence.

Most African governments support these deals as they provide an easy stream of foreign currency, particularly to state departments and ministries involved in managing fisheries. It is also possible that corruption and undue influence play a role. Indeed, any attempt to reform commercial fisheries in Africa has to begin with a careful analysis of the political economy of this sector, a task that remains neglected.

Despite a lack of data and access to information, European access agreements have been denounced for many years by a range of non-governmental organisations, both in Europe and in Africa. These remain unpopular deals and it is remarkable that they have been so enduring. On the surface, improvements seem to have been made under the new FPAs, but further evaluations may show such partnerships to be little different from the deals that preceded them. However, to call for the ending of access agrements between African countries and the EU may not represent the best way forward. If the EU was to turn its back on FAs, private fishing companies from the EU could continue to dominate the commercial fishing sector and a plethora of private licences or bi-lateral trade agreements with single countries might prove more difficult to manage. Without access agreements, commercial fisheries could become even more competitive, prone to corruption and lacking accountability.

The prospect of a domestic, labour intensive and ecologically friendly fishing sector displacing foreign commercial fishing in Africa may seem an alluring policy goal, although this is as likely as artisinal mining replacing foreign mining companies on the continent. Perhaps, therefore, the solution to unsatisfactory EU access agreements lies in improving their terms; putting in place better systems for scientific and economic audits, improving the monitoring and surveillance of ships, introducing stringent regulations for reducing by-catch and minimising the degradation of the marine environment, and so forth. Unfortunately, these reforms may well be slow, challenged by vested interests and undermined by rule breaking. Moreover, it is hard to find evidence of political will in many African countries to make such reforms a reality, even though there is no shortage of support from NGOs and probably the international donor community. Therefore, the best hope for Africa's marine environment is that African governments realise the true value of protecting their oceans before it is too late. Conducting a thorough, independent cost- benefit analysis of bilateral access agreements might be a good place to start.

Notes

1. Proposal for a Council regulation concerning the conclusion of the agreement between the European Community and the United Republic of Tanzania on fishing in Tanzania's fishing zone, European Commission, 2005.
2. Communication . . . on an integrated framework for fisheries partnership agreements with third countries, European Commission, 2002.
3. This situation may be addressed in 2009 with the passing of the Deep Sea Fisheries Act that will result in all off-shore fishing licences being issued from Zanzibar.
4. Communication . . . on an integrated framework for fisheries partnership agreements with third countries, European Commission, 2002: 4.
5. Communication . . . on an integrated framework for fisheries partnership agreements with third countries, European Commission, 2002: 3.
6. Proposal for a Council regulation concerning the conclusion of the agreement between the European Community and the United Republic of Tanzania on fishing in Tanzania's fishing zone, European Commission, 2005: 2.
7. Proposal for a Council regulation concerning the conclusion of the agreement between the European Community and the United Republic of Tanzania on fishing in Tanzania's fishing zone, European Commission, 2005: 29.
8. Report of the third session of the IOTC Working Party on Ecosystems and By-Catch, Seychelles, 2007.
9. Statistics reported by Clover (2005) on the by-catch of purse-seine boats are much higher than statistics presented by the IOTC, with Clover implying as much as 50% of landings is discarded.
10. Proposal for a Council regulation concerning the conclusion of the agreement between the European Community and the United Republic of Tanzania on fishing in Tanzania's fishing zone, European Commission, 2005: 2.
11. Fisheries disagreement between EU and Mauritania about four Spanish boats arrested for illegal fishing. Press statement issued by Nouakchott Info and Voz de Galicia, downloaded from www.illegal-fishing.info.
12. A damning research report on access agreements in Argentina by the United Nations Environment Programme (2002a) illustrated this effect clearly. EU access agreements from the 1990s caused massive overfishing in the hake industry, which had clear negative ramifications for the long-term viability of the hake stock. By calculating the downstream impacts of this overfishing, UNEP argued that EU boats cost the Argentinean economy some $500 million. UNEP also calculated that the potential revenue from well-managed fishing was in the region of $5 billion per annum.
13. European Union concludes fisheries partnership agreement with Guinea Bissau, European Commission press release, 2007 available at: http://ec.europa.eu/fisheries/press_corner/press_releases/archives/com07/com07_39_en.htm.
14. *New York Times* 14 Jan. 2008.
15. Europe looking for fishy partners. See www.illegal-fishing.info.
16. Tanzania failure to adopt EU fisheries deal means loss of sustainable fishing in EEZ. Press release, 9 Jan. 2007 by EC delegation in Tanzania.

17. Addressing corruption in Pacific Island fisheries: report prepared for the IUCN Profish Law Enforcement, Corruption and Fisheries Project by M. Tsamenyi and Q. Hanich, 2008: 10-11 (www.iucn.org).

References

Bartels, L. et al. 2007. *Policy Coherence for Development and the Effects of EU Fisheries Policies on Development in West Africa*. Brussels: European Parliament.

Brown, O. 2005. *Policy Incoherence: EU Fisheries Policy in Senegal*. New York: United Nations Development Programme.

Clover, C. 2005. *The End of the Line: How Overfishing is Changing the World and What We Eat*. London: Ebury.

Coalition for Fair Fisheries Access. 2006a. *Mauritania EU Fisheries Partnership Agreement: What Impacts on Fisheries Sustainable Development in Mauritania?* Brussels: CFFA.

——. 2006b. *Denouncing the EU-Mauritania Fisheries Agreement Protocol: Putting the Fisheries Partnership to the Test*. Brussels: CFFA.

Environmental Justice Foundation. 2003. *Squandering the Seas: How Shrimp Trawling is Threatening Ecological Integrity and Food Security Around the World*. London: EJF.

——. 2005a. *Party to the Plunder: Illegal Fishing in Guinea and its Links to the EU*. London: EJF.

——. 2005b, *What's the Catch?: Reducing Bycatch in EU Distant Water Fisheries*. London: EJF.

European Court of Auditors. 2001. 'Concerning the commission's management of the international fisheries agreements, together with the commission's replies'. *Special Report* 3.

——. 2007. 'On the control, inspection and sanction systems relating to the rules on conservation of community fisheries resources together with the commission's replies'. *Special Report* 7.

Fonteneau, A. et al. 2007. *Species Composition and Free Swimming Schools Fished by Purse Seiners in the Western Indian Ocean During the Period 1990–2006*. Victoria, Seychelles: Indian Ocean Tuna Commission.

Gorez, B. 2000. 'Pink gold, muddy waters'. *Samudra* Apr.

——. 2005 *EU-ACP Fisheries Agreements*, Brussels: Coalition for Fair Fisheries Access.

Greenpeace. 2007. *Taking Tuna Out of the Can: Rescue Plan for the World's Favourite Fish*. Amsterdam: Greenpeace International.

IFREMER. 1997. *Evaluation of the Fisheries Agreements Concluded by the European Community: Summary Report*. Paris: IFREMER.

Ilnyckyj, M. 2007. 'The legality and sustainability of European Union fisheries policy in West Africa'. *MIT International Review* Spring.

Johnstone, N. 1996. *The Economics of Fisheries Access Agreements: Perspectives on the EU-Senegal Case*. London: International Institute for Environment and Development.

Kaczynski, V. and D. Fluharty. 2002. 'European policies in West Africa: who benefits from fisheries agreements?' *Marine Policy* 26: 75.

Kelleher, K. 2004. 'Discards in the world's marine fisheries: an update'. *FAO Fisheries Technical Paper* 470. Rome: FAO.

Lankester, K. 2002. *The EU-Angola Fisheries Agreement and Fisheries in Angola.* Amsterdam: Scomber.

Marine Resources Assessment Group. 2005. *Review of Impacts of Illegal, Unreported and Unregulated Fishing on Developing Countries.* London: MRAG.

——. 2007. *Comparative Study of the Impact of Fisheries Partnership Agreements: Technical Report.* London: MRAG.

Molina, A., J. Areso and J. Ariz. 2007. *Statistics of the Purse Seine Spanish Fleet in the Indian Ocean,* Victoria, Seychelles: Indian Ocean Tuna Commission.

Moola, S. 2005. *IUU Fishing in Africa.* Cape Town: Fiekke.

Morato, T. et al. 2006. 'Fishing down the deep'. *Fish and Fisheries* 7(1): 24–34.

Mwanguru, A. 2005. 'The safety and health of Kenyan fishers on board industrial fishing vessels'. Paper presented at a meeting on safety and health in the fishing industry, University of Nantes, France, 17 March.

Mwikya, M. 2006. *Fisheries Access Agreements: Trade and Development Issues.* Geneva: International Centre for Trade and Sustainable Development.

Pauly, D. 2006. 'Major trends in small-scale marine fisheries, with emphasis on developing countries, and some implications for the social sciences'. *Maritime Studies* 4(2): 7–22.

Pauly, D. et al. 2002. 'Toward sustainability in world fisheries'. *Nature* 418: 689–95.

Pauly, D., R. Watson and J. Alder. 2005. 'Global trends in world fisheries: impacts on marine ecosystems and food security'. *Philosophical Transactions of the Royal Society: Biological Sciences* 360: 5–12.

Polacheck, T. 2006. 'Tuna longline catch rates in the Indian Ocean: did industrial fishing result in a 90% rapid decline in the abundance of large predatory species?' *Marine Policy* 30: 470–82.

Ponte, S., J. Raakjær and L. Campling. 2007. 'Swimming upstream: market access for African fish exports in the context of WTO and EU negotiations and regulation'. *Development Policy Review* 25(1): 113–38.

United Nations Environment Programme. 2002a. *Integrated Assessment of Trade Liberalization and Trade-Related Policies: A Country Study on the Fisheries Sector in Argentina.* Geneva. UNEP.

——. 2002b. *Integrated Assessment of Trade Liberalization and Trade-Related Policies: A Country Study on the Fisheries Sector in Senegal.* Geneva: UNEP.

——. 2007. *Environmental Impact Assessment of Trade Liberalization: A Case Study on the Fisheries Sector of the Islamic Republic of Mauritania: Summary.* Geneva: UNEP.

Wolfgang, S. 2005. 'Are EU access agreements harming Africa's artisanal fisheries?' *Agriculture and Rural Development* 2: 38–40.

World Wide Fund for Nature. 2007. *Marine Turtle Update: Recent News from the WWF Africa and Madagascar Marine Turtle Programme.* Gland: WWF

Zeller, D. and D. Pauly. 2005. 'Good news, bad news: global fisheries discards are declining, but so are total catches'. *Fish and Fisheries* 6: 156–9.

CHAPTER FOURTEEN

The Scramble for Africa and the Marginalisation of African Capitalism

Roger Southall and Alex Comninos

The significant inflow of foreign investment capital into Africa, designed to increase international access to oil, minerals and markets and conceptualised as a scramble, provokes enquiry into the nature of the engagement between external investors and African business. Historically, the relationship between African capitalists and foreign capital has largely been one of dependence and subordination. This poses the questions of whether the latest scramble reinforces this pattern of subordination, or whether in contrast it is laying the foundations for Africa to launch itself upon a self-sustaining path of capitalist development, in which case there is clearly the need for the accompanying development of a class or classes of African capitalists. Hitherto, such classes have been weak and nationally isolated. Yet if the latest scramble posits a new era of economic growth that is to span Africa, then we also need to enquire whether it is matched by the expansion of African capitalist enterprise within and across national borders.

The State and African Capitalism in Historical Perspective

Taking its cue from late-colonial economic practice, Keynesianism and socialism, the development discourse of the early post-colonial period was overwhelmingly statist, and understandably so. First generation regimes regarded the state as the primary vehicle for development, not only because African capitalism had been underdeveloped but because, in addition, African capitalists, such as they were, were generally viewed with suspicion and not a little hostility: as exploiters, unsocialist or as potential rivals for power. Hence, while there was no shortage of African initiative or enterprise on the ground, the emergent post-colonial national bourgeoisies developed largely through public employment and state economic activity via parastatals rather than through economic entrepreneurship within the private sector. The emergent bourgeoisie, managerial rather than capitalist, was therefore from this perspective pursuing rent rather than profit, so the key intercontinental relationships were not just those of aid and trade, but even more between multinational corporations and politicians and bureaucrats.

This perspective was reflected in early discussions about the nature of post-colonial capitalist development. Key to this was the debate initiated by Leys (1975) of neo-colonialism in Kenya. Leys argued that while the nature of the settler economy meant that post-colonial Kenya was somewhat exceptional in the relative dynamism of its capitalist growth, so that an identifiably African capitalist bourgeoisie was developing, this was only under the wing of multinational capital and was subordinate and auxiliary to it, comparable to Latin American compradors. Subsequently, he was to modify his views in response to Swainson (1977, 1980) who insisted that African capitalists were considerably more independent of the multinationals than he had allowed. Their origins lay in successful African commercial enterprise in the native reserves, the subsequent extension of agri-commerce with the Africanisation of settler farms and related African upward penetration of the chain of production. Even though Himbara (1994) was subsequently to argue that it was Indian Kenyans rather Africans who were largely responsible for Kenya's capitalist growth, and that African capitalists remained state dependent, the focus was still overwhelmingly national. This perspective, of African capitalism contained by state borders, was to be replicated by the important comparative literature (Forrest 1996; Kennedy 1988; Leys and Berman 1994) that soon began to take African capitalism more seriously.

Notwithstanding the continuing subordination of local African to multi-national capital, the policy environment of the first two decades after independence reduced the relative strength of foreign companies in many African economies. Parastatals increased in number and scope, invading economic territory previously dominated by colonial companies, and were able to pose a more significant challenge to multinationals than weak national capitalist classes (Tangri 1999). Furthermore, national political control introduced a new element into the equation. Expropriation of the subsidiaries of foreign companies increased from the 1960s through to the mid 1970s, and indigenisation programmes became popular. Whilst politically wary of African capitalist classes, states commonly attempted to create more favourable conditions for local capital by, for instance, barring foreign capital from various (usually low-level enterprise) sectors, maintaining or strengthening certain trade barriers or demanding sale of equity to local investors. Meanwhile, the availability of aid and debt from multinational institutions and Eastern bloc countries strengthened the state. Even so, foreign companies were still welcomed, not just for their investment, but for their employment creation, skills, technology transfer and access to markets. Even public enterprises, many of which were capital intensive, continued to rely substantially on multinational partners to continue operation. For their part, while wanting to retain a presence in African economies, multinational companies tended to view their African operations as marginal to their global strategies (Abdou 2001).

This situation was to be changed considerably by structural adjustment. Following the oil shocks of the early seventies, the level of African indebtedness leapt dramatically (Loxley 1986; Riddell 1992). This enabled global creditor nations and institutions, led by the International Monetary Fund (IMF) and World Bank, to induce far-reaching changes in the trade regimes of African countries, bring about shifts in the structure of investment and production, and demand significant alteration in the mix of state control and market incentives. Key here was the insistence upon deregulation and liberalisation of the economy, privatisation and the shrinkage of the state and increased reliance upon foreign investment. By 1986, adjusting African countries had already privatised around a fifth of their parastatals (Abdou 2001). The outcome was not only a significant diminution of African economic sovereignty, but the adjustment of states to a comprador role on behalf of global capital by providing physical security and access to local resources and markets (Amin 1990). Indeed, in the absence of a dynamic African capitalist class, privatisation meant the transfer of assets to politicians and bureaucrats, who used political connectivity to gain favourable access to capital, or into foreign ownership, reducing further the opportunity for locally-driven development (Tangri 1999).

Although the flow of foreign direct investment (FDI) did increase in absolute terms for sub-Saharan Africa during the period 1980–5, doubling from an average of $1 411 million to $2 879 million through 1992–7, this was substantially less than was the case for all developing countries ($12 634 million through 1980–5, to $100 581 million through 1992–7). In turn, this reflected a marked relative decline in the proportion of such investment going to sub-Saharan Africa compared to all developing countries, decreasing from 11.2% during 1980–5 to as low as 1.9% in 1997 (UNCTAD 1992, 1998).

The failure of structural adjustment to promote sustainable growth, let alone alleviate poverty, is attributable both to global factors, such as the marginalisation of resource- based African countries within the global economy; and internal factors, such as inconsistent implementation of policy, minimal accountability of multinational corporations and donors to host governments, rent seeking and corruption, poor infrastructure, and the continuing lack of a favourable environment for private business (Agboli and Ukaegbu 2006; Pedersen and McCormick 1999). Even so, the constant refrain of the IMF and World Bank remained that, however painful the medicine, structural adjustment was clearing the ground for an increased rate of growth. Not surprisingly they now trumpet the fact that, over the last decade or so, the overall growth rate in Africa, and in many individual countries, has increased substantially. However, the reasons for this appear to lie rather more outside Africa than within.

African Economic Performance and the Current Scramble

Poverty in Africa is chronic and rising. The share of the total population living below the widely-cited threshold of $1 a day is 46%, higher today than in the 1980s and 1990s.[1] While there were some 164 million poor individuals living in sub-Saharan Africa in 1981, this figure increased to 316 million in 2001.[2] African countries remain overwhelmingly dependent upon the sale of primary commodities, yet declining real prices for many, notably agricultural, products have had a negative impact upon indebtedness and investment. Non-oil exporting African countries suffered cumulative terms of trade losses between 1970 and 1997 of almost 120% of Gross Domestic Product (GDP), offsetting increased aid flows after 1973 (World Bank 2000). While trade liberalisation is widely hailed as a panacea, a recent authoritative study suggests gains would probably be quite modest. Full liberalisation of Organisation for Economic Co-operation and Development (OECD) agriculture would add a welcome 0.7% to African annual income, but might force yet further specialisation in agricultural commodities. Unless trade liberalisation is linked to increased investment in industrial and service sectors, short-term gains will prove unsustainable and are unlikely to be shored up by limited-term programmes such as the US African Growth and Opportunity Act of 2000, which has improved access to the American textile market for a number of African countries.[3] Meanwhile, OECD countries regularly make promises of increased aid, but equally regularly fail to live up to them. Official development assistance (ODA) flows (at $19.4 million) were well below their 1990 peak by 2001. Although they have later increased, in 2004 it was estimated that there was an annual shortfall of $20–25 billion of resources needed for African countries to achieve the UN's Millennium Development Goals (MDGs) of halving poverty by 2015.[4] While the Multilateral Debt Relief Initiative (MDRI) announced at the G8 Summit in 2005 promised much needed debt relief for thirteen sub-Saharan countries, it was castigated by the Economic Commission for Africa (ECA) as not enough.[5] The ECA insisted that much more external funding would be needed to help African countries increase growth rates and achieve meaningful reduction in poverty.

Against this bleak background, encouragement has been drawn from an improving economic performance by a significant number of countries. In recent years, African economies have recorded substantially improved growth rates, averaging 4% in 2003, 5.2% in 2004, 5.4% in 2005 and 5.8% in 2006.[6] As many as 25 African countries recorded improvements in growth in 2005, such gains being hailed as a major turnaround from decades of economic decline. Although only ten African countries achieved the 7% growth in 2005 that is needed on a sustained basis to achieve the MDGs, five of them (Burkina Faso, Ethiopia, Liberia, Mozambique and Sierra Leone) were non-oil exporting countries, while four of the worst five performers are either recovering from civil war (Burundi) or remain mired in political crisis (Ivory Coast, Togo and Zimbabwe). Credit for this turnaround is regularly awarded to better macro-economic management, while the long-term impact of liberalisation and deregulation has undoubtedly improved the investment environment for foreign companies. However, the major factors responsible for improved performance appear to be external, political and technological rather internal to African economies. Continentally, four such factors can be emphasised.

First, although the peace dividend of the post-Cold War era failed to materialise (the 1990s was the most conflict-ridden in Africa since independence), there has been a wind-down of wars in Angola and the Democratic Republic of Congo (DRC), two of Africa's largest and most resource-endowed countries, as well as transitions to (relative) peace and stability in Liberia, Sierra Leone and Burundi. Notwithstanding enduring political crisis in Somalia, Ivory Coast, Sudan and Zimbabwe, the reduction in conflict in key countries has significantly improved the continent's prospects of attracting international investment.

Second, the post-Cold war resource boom, occasioned by global shortages heightened by the unleashing of market forces in Russia, eastern Europe, and especially in China and other emerging economies such as India, has sparked fierce competition among multinational companies for important African commodities, notably oil and minerals.

Third, South Africa's transition to democracy has enabled South African capital to reap comparative advantage in terms of resources, experience, local knowledge and proximity to African markets by undertaking a major investment thrust into the wider continent.

Fourth, the recent revolution in information and communications technology (ICT), aided by improving physical communications infrastructure, notably the increasing volume and ease of air travel, has seen (notwithstanding Africa's backwardness globally in this regard) an explosion of investment in areas such as satellite communications and cellular telephony. It is important to ask what impact these developments are having upon African capitalism.

Economic Reform and African Capitalism

Even after three decades of structural adjustment and pro-market economic reform, African capitalism remains exceptionally weak. Despite externally driven programmes of privatisation, 'the state still overshadows the private sector in African economies' (Tangri 1999: 145). Governments remain the largest employers, spenders, borrowers and even investors in most African countries. African politicians have chorused the view propagated by the IMF, World Bank and donor community that privatisation will reduce the scope for political patronage and corruption, a goal also espoused by increased demands from civil society for greater accountability and transparency in government. Nonetheless, for all the shrinkage of the African state, the nature of African politics has remained much as it was before structural adjustment was imposed. In contrast to the successful developmental states of East and South East Asia, African states have been largely anti-developmental.

Although opportunities for entrepreneurs are offered by recent growth, locally owned and controlled private sectors remain limited in size and significance, so African elites continue to give higher priority to control of the state. After independence, politicians used state resources to fuel the patronage and corruption that maintained them in power and state economic decisions were 'driven pre-eminently by political and personal rather than by economic and technical considerations' (Tangri 1999: 139). Hence, while certainly seeking to shift African economies away from statism and socialism towards market-led growth, donor driven programmes of privatisation and good governance were also an attempt to steer towards greater rationality in economic decision-making. However, as long as African political leaders continue to rely on public resources to maintain themselves in power, and public position provides them with the most easily available opportunity to acquire wealth, they will:

only gradually give up some of their control over economic decisions, and only do the minimum to promote accountable and transparent state economic governance. Where they do privatize, they will ensure that ownership of public companies is transferred to loyal elements; and where they do promote "good" governance, they will ensure that designated governance mechanisms are in the hands of loyal supporters and limited in their independence (Tangri 1999: 143).

Despite ritual claims by African governments that structural adjustment programmes have been home grown, the reality is that they have largely been externally imposed. Consequently, there is a lack of sense of ownership of economic strategy, which is compounded by widespread resentment. Something of an exception may be provided by Zimbabwe. Here the Mugabe government has retained heavy state involvement in business, extending to all major areas of economic activity, alongside the movement of cronies with strong connections to the military or the ruling party into the private sector. Heavy demands for the transfer of equity in the name of black empowerment are being made on the private sector.[7] However, whether this will survive political and economic meltdown and the likely future imposition of a structural adjustment programme by a post-Mugabe regime remains to be seen.

The nature of the African state thus remains much the same as it ever was. Nonetheless, the increasing urgency of the crisis that afflicts every single African economy has forced governments into giving much higher priority to modernisation and growth. Thus it is regularly asserted that there is now considerably greater scope for the expansion of African business.

McDade and Spring (2005), in reviewing the literature on African entrepreneurship, confirm that, overwhelmingly, African business inhabits the sphere of petty capital: only 2% of all African businesses have ten or more employees and the majority are small-scale and micro enterprises (SMEs) operating in the informal sector that consist of just one to three employees. Ownership of such SMEs is overwhelmingly black African. However, such small enterprises face numerous obstacles to growth including difficulty in gaining access to capital and markets, lack of productive linkages with other businesses, lack of training and skills, severe competition, and their customers' low income. Consequently, with governments increasingly viewing the informal sector as an engine of growth and employment, they are the targets of considerable amounts of official and non-governmental organisation (NGO) assistance, such as micro-financing, utilities and skills training. In turn, this brings pressure upon them to formalise; yet half of small-scale formal enterprises in Africa with more than ten employees are owned by residents of Asian or Middle Eastern descent.

Notwithstanding the numerical predominance of SMEs, McDade and Spring acknowledge that 'medium to large-scale enterprises owned by Africans are an important part of the entrepreneurial landscape in spite of their small percentage' (2005: 20). They cite one study by Marsden in 1999 that profiled medium-sized concerns. This identified 5 000 formally registered road transport companies in Tanzania and reported that over 2 000 Ghanaian businesses applied for loans from financial institutions where the average investment project funded was $1.5 million. They conclude that perceptions that the middle sector of African economies is missing are overdrawn. Against this, while they suggest that privatisation programmes, which they confirm as having encouraged a category of politically-favoured business bureaucrats, may have facilitated entry into such spheres as beverages, clothing, furniture, rubber, leather products, plastics, soap and toiletries, pharmaceuticals, construction and transport, many large-scale firms in these sectors are owned by non-indigenous minorities such as Asians, Syrians, Lebanese and Europeans. Overall, 'Indigenous Africans own one third or less of large industrial firms,' with the amount varying between countries: 'In Kenya, black Africans own only 3.6% of large firms, whereas in Zimbabwe the percentage is more than 30%' (McDade and Spring 2005: 21).

Although confirming the small size of the African capitalist class in most African countries, McDade and Spring depict a new generation of African entrepreneurs in ten sub-Saharan countries,[8] which they identify as participating in regional business networks from West, East and southern Africa that were initially funded from the early 1990s by various US, OECD and European agencies. Although comprising only a fraction of entrepreneurs in Africa, they claim these business persons (28% of their surveyed network members were women) to be highly influential with regard to commerce, trade and regulatory practices. Their key findings were that most network members were relatively young (20s–40s) black Africans and well educated: half had earned advanced degrees, the majority of them in the US or Europe. They were urban based; were children of parents who were either in business themselves (31%), professionals (17%) or civil servants or politicians; and had earned managerial experience (70%) in other firms (42% in major national firms, 23% in foreign firms). The overwhelming majority (95%) were business owners, the remainder holding high executive positions in large private corporations. Twenty-eight per cent owned one or more companies; and 70% owned firms that operated in the service sector (advertising, computer training, consulting, financial and legal services, ICT, public relations and planning). Only 16% owned manufacturing firms. Inevitably, these operations were medium scale, having between five and 50 employees, and an average annual turnover of $1 million.

This new generation is reportedly highly optimistic about development prospects in Africa, and views the networks as critical to expanding business opportunities across regions and the continent. Intra-African trade may be limited: 'from the 1970s to the late 1990s, intra-African trade was only 4% of African exports and imports, increasing to 7% from 1998 to 2000, and to 10% by 2002' (McDade and Spring 2005: 31). However, while they are interested in developing markets beyond the continent, the main focus of network members is on increasing trade and commerce in Africa. To this end, they view the networks, which they see as based upon shared ethical attitudes, business practices and trust, as vital to expand intra-African trade, improve the business climate, lobby for improved regional integration and create venture capital. A fair number of them trade with, do business in, or own enterprises in countries other than their own.

McDade and Spring conclude (2005: 36) that network members are 'upwardly mobile entrepreneurs who are interested in economic and political reform;' embrace 'profits not profiteering;' and can be distinguished from dominant political, military and trading elites by their ethics and commitment to 'working hard, being self-starters, having business savvy, using network contacts, being transparent, and refusing political patronage'. As such, 'this small but growing segment of the African entrepreneurial landscape may serve as a catalyst to improve economic conditions and stimulate private-sector led development' (McDade and Spring 2005: 38).

Such overviews indicate that the business scene is far from stagnant. Not only does it evince an increasingly transnational African orientation, but this has been facilitated by access to cellphones, emails, faxes, computers, websites and so on. However, while such snapshots imply that African business is, broadly, a beneficiary of recent improvements in the rate of economic growth fueled by the commodity boom, it offers little evidence that it is a direct participant in any new scramble. That is scarcely surprising, for although there are a few exceptions, the capital requirements of this are considerable and the number of African-owned firms that can afford to participate remains extremely small.

African Large-scale Business

Africa's top companies – that is, those that are listed on African stock exchanges, but which are not necessarily African owned – are dominated by South African firms. In 2004, while South Africa had 941 parent corporations, Tunisia had 142, Mauritius sixteen and Swaziland twelve (presumably dating from the relocation of South African firms during the era of sanctions). No other country had more than eight (Page and te Velde 2004: 17).

South African firms were also prominent in lists of developing country multinationals, with one in the top ten and another six in the next 40 (UNCTAD 2004). Furthermore, no other African country is a major investor in South Africa, but South Africa is the third largest foreign investor in Africa following the United Kingdom and US, albeit 90% of this going into southern African countries – that is, members of the Southern African Development Community (SADC) (Page and te Velde 2004: 22). Most South African investment in SADC is in natural resources, followed by basic industries and utilities. In addition, South African companies have in recent years become prominent as investors in the rest of Africa in telecommunications and retail. The United Nations Conference on Trade and Development (UNCTAD) recently listed only six African non-South African companies with subsidiaries in other African countries:[9] Kenyan involvement in traditional sectors such as beverages, plastics, food, banking and finance within East Africa is by far the most prominent (Page and te Velde 2004: 67). Not surprisingly, therefore, South Africa dominates lists of the top African companies. For 2007, a survey lists 38 out of the top 50 African companies (measured by $ market value) as South African; 61 of the top 100; and 101 of the top 200.[10] Meanwhile, according to another ranking of Africa's top 500 companies (measured by turnover, strongly correlated with profit and employment),[11] South African companies were responsible for 60.5% of the turnover of the top 500 for 2006, followed by companies from Algeria (13.8%), Morocco (6.72%), Egypt (5.53%), the Communauté Financière Africaine (CFA) zone (4.82%), Nigeria (2.86%) and Tunisia (1.9%). South Africa also has the continent's five top banks ranked by assets and earnings.[12] Against this, South African companies have been losing places in the top 200 to companies from other countries, most notably to those from North Africa, and in particular in the sphere of telecommunications.[13]

Unsurprisingly, the rankings reflect the commodity boom. In terms of turnover they are headed by Algeria's oil giant Sonatrech, while gas and oil refining companies from Algeria, Morocco and South Africa have all moved into the top 50 company league, which includes a significant presence from sub-Saharan Africa. Thus while Angola's Sonangol was eighteenth in 2006 (but not listed in 2007),[14] Nigeria's private oil company, Oando, powered into the top 100 (at 94) in 2006 and then up to 62 in 2007 after listing on the Johannesburg Stock Exchange and announcing a plan to raise over $3 billion to invest in a Nigerian oil refinery.

Sociétié Ivorienne de Raffinage, an oil refining company, came in at 50 (up seven places from 2006) and Total Gabon moved up eleven places from 2006 to 76 in 2007. In addition, other resource companies are prominent within the corporate vanguard. Although South Africa's De Beers and Anglo-American now have their primary listings in London, their child companies De Beers Consolidated Mines and Anglo American Platinum Corporation (Amplats) were listed at nine and 21 respectively in 2007, with Ashanti Goldfields, a subsidiary of AngloGold Ashanti (Ghanaian and South African) ranked at 29 and Botswana's Debswana at 30. Overall, oil and refining companies account for 17.3% of turnover of the top 500; and mining companies for 7.2%.[15] Distribution, financial services and telecommunications companies account for just over 30% of turnover: 'this is where South Africa's growing dominance of the continent's economy is clearest'.[16] Telecommunications companies alone account for 9.6% of turnover and this figure is seen as likely to rise sharply, with Africa listed by the International Telecommunications Union as the world's fastest growing mobile telephone market.

Identifying firms by membership of national stock exchanges is instructive, yet it is not the same as analysing their ownership. However, four generalisations can be proffered. First, South African firms are largely owned by white capital, mostly in the form of institutional investors. Second, many leading firms throughout the continent are either owned or partially owned by foreign, non-African multinationals or investors. However, third, the principal exception to this is a small number of highly significant companies either fully or majority owned by the state and these include Algeria's oil giant Sonatrach, Angola's Sonangol and the National Petroleum Company as well, of course, as major South African parastatals Transnet (ranked 18), Eskom (12) and South African Airways (24). Meanwhile, fourth, various other companies, especially if they are former parastatals that have been privatised such as Telkom (7) are still subject to official influence as governments retain significant minority ownership. The upshot of this is that indigenous private African ownership of large-scale capital in Africa is minimal. How, then, if at all – apart from being employed as workers – are indigenous Africans in particular participating in any current scramble for Africa?

African Participation in the Scramble

Four principal features define African participation in the current scramble. The first is the continuing centrality of states to economic regulation, with a concomitant need for foreign investors and international institutions to collaborate with government elites. Second, South African capital is by far the most aggressive

African player in the current scramble, with established, white-owned capital working in close harmony with state-owned corporations and increasingly in partnership with up-and-coming, black-owned companies. Third, large-scale African capitalist participation in the scramble is largely limited to the rapidly expanding ICT sector; and fourth, the major opportunity for impoverished Africans to participate in the scramble, except for the relative few who obtain jobs with multinational companies or security operations guarding them, is through illegal or informal mining in conflict-torn, fragile states, an activity that reinforces their subordination to corrupt political elites, warlords or international criminal networks.

State, Capital and International Institutions in the Scramble

Turmoil in the world's oil and gas markets, occasioned by predicted global shortages of fossil fuels, hugely increased demand from China and other major emerging markets such as India and Brazil, as well as the declining predictability of Middle Eastern countries as reliable suppliers of oil to the US and Europe, have seen a frenzied search by the major consuming countries for new and stable sources of supply. Africa, as a treasure trove of unexploited oil and gas resources, is particularly well placed to benefit. Heightened demand for minerals, again driven by the spiralling needs of China and India in particular, is similarly fueling a sustained boom in the mining sector, encouraging significant new investments, especially in the mineral-rich territories of Central Africa – notably the post-war, albeit fragile DRC, Zambia and even conflict-torn Zimbabwe. In turn, exploitation of oil, gas and mineral resources heightens demand for energy, notably electricity, supplies of which are already under pressure from increased demand from industrial and private consumers throughout the continent. This drives the need for massive infrastructural investment, greater access to loan capital and the expansion and rationalisation of the continent's financial sector.

Pressures for economic liberalisation may have increased the attraction of many African economies as sites for foreign investment. Nonetheless, government elites remain central to economic management and act as gatekeepers for access to resources and markets. According to the World Bank, Africa has made considerable recent progress towards deregulation. In a World Bank report (2007) surveying the regulatory hurdles faced by investors across 175 countries, sub-Saharan Africa moved to third place, behind eastern Europe and the OECD countries, but ahead of Latin America, South Asia, East Asia and the Middle East, from last in 2006 in a ranking of regions according to the number of reforms. Forty-five regulatory changes in 30 economies in the region reduced the time, cost and hassle for businesses to comply with legal and administrative requirements. Ghana and Tanzania were ranked the ninth and tenth best performing global reformers respectively in 2007. Conversely, Africa remains by far the most regulated region in the world overall. Only South Africa (29), Mauritius (32), Namibia (42) and Botswana (48) appeared amongst the best 50 performing countries. In contrast, Africa claimed 29 out of the 50 worst performing countries. Significantly, oil and mineral producing countries featured heavily amongst these. Nigeria was ranked 108, but Gabon came in at 132, Equatorial Guinea at 150, Zimbabwe at 153, Sudan at 154, Angola at 156, Sierra Leone at 168, São Tomé at 169 and Chad at 172, while the DRC propped up the entire league table at 175. This means, for instance, that whereas it took only two days to register a business in Australia and three in Canada, the best performing countries on this indicator, it took 35 in South Africa, 124 in Angola, 136 in Equatorial Guinea and as many as 155 in the DRC.[17]

The regulatory maze provides leverage to government elites in their negotiations with potential investors and encourages the latter to maintain access to resources and markets by forging formal business relations with or greasing the palms of politicians and civil servants. It is therefore no surprise that there is a positive correlation between the World Bank report (2007) and Transparency International's (TI) findings. For 2006, out of 163 countries globally, TI rated Botswana (37), South Africa (51) and Namibia (55) as the least corrupt countries in sub-Saharan Africa; whereas Zimbabwe (137), Angola (142), Nigeria (146), Sierra Leone (148), Equatorial Guinea (154), Chad (157), the DRC (157) and Sudan (158) were all firmly clustered towards the bottom.[18]

Notwithstanding their official disapproval, bodies like the World Bank, governments of investor companies and multinational companies prove in practice to be remarkably tolerant of corruption in countries with valuable oil, mineral and energy resources. In country after country, international financial institutions, multinational corporations, governments and politicians form an unholy alliance that, whilst rarely free of tension, enables them to profit from the natural wealth of Africa, often at the expense of impoverished populations.[19]

The South African Role

The expansion of South African capital into continental Africa after 1994 has been elaborated at length (Daniel and Lutchman 2006; Daniel, Lutchman and Comninos 2007; Daniel, Naidoo and Naidu 2004; and by John Daniel and Mpume Bhengu in chapter six of this book). South Africa has become the third highest source of new direct investment in Africa (Page and te Velde 2004) through a range of mergers, acquisitions, joint ventures and greenfield investments; and there has been an across-the-board involvement of every sector (private and parastatal) of capital in African markets, although the large balance of investment takes place in southern Africa. However, the major thrust of outward investment from South Africa has taken place in the spheres of mining (around 22% during 2000–3), oil, gas and petroleum (18%) and infrastructure (27%), the last being a composite of six related but distinct sub-sectors – power, rail, roads, water, sanitation and ports.[20] Furthermore, Daniel, Lutchman and Comninos (2007) predict that South Africa's mining sector will continue to expand into Africa with so-called junior mining companies playing an active role alongside established majors; that the energy sector will intensify its scramble to acquire African oil, gas and hydro-power to overcome South Africa's looming energy deficit; and that despite the DRC's current relatively lowly status as South Africa's tenth largest African trading partner, it will become an increasingly important site of South African activity, much of this driven by the long-term importance to South Africa of the Grand Inga hydro-electric power project.

In the mining sector, South Africa's two largest players are the now global giant AngloGold Ashanti and the medium-sized Randgold and Exploration. Both are involved in gold mining and exploration in Mali, Ghana and Tanzania; while AngloGold also has interests in Guinea, the DRC and Namibia, and Randgold in Ivory Coast, Senegal and Burkina Faso. Meanwhile, the other major South African gold mining group, Gold Fields, has also entered the Malian mining sector by funding the exploration ventures of the Irish group, Glencar Mining, which has three options in Mali. In addition, Anglo-American/De Beers maintain major interests in diamond mining in both Botswana and Namibia.

The expansion of the South African mining sector has been taken by the established majors. However, it is complemented by the entry into the African mining sector of Mvelaphanda Holdings. Founded in 1998 by Tokyo Sexwale, a leading black empowerment magnate, the company today has gross assets exceeding R10 billion and interests across diverse sectors that include banking, financial services, tourism, healthcare, logistics, industrial services and security. Sexwale appears determined to position Mvelaphanda as 'a pan-African minerals and mining company' (Daniel and Lutchman 2006: 491). On the one hand, it has acquired an indirect stake in the mineral sector in Angola, Namibia, Tanzania, Zambia, Burkina Faso, Ghana, Botswana and Zambia through equity holdings in and partnerships with Anglo-American, Anglo Platinum, De Beers, Goldfields and Remgro. On the other, it has built itself into an important player in the mining and energy sector through its various subsidiaries: Mvelaphanda Resources has significant investments in South African assets in the gold, platinum and diamond sectors; and exploration and development joint ventures in other African countries. Meanwhile, Mvelaphanda has recently moved into the African oil and gas sectors through its 50% ownership of Ophir Energy, launching a partnership with the London-listed Fusion Oil and Gas in 2004. Fusion had been instrumental in a series of major discoveries offshore in Mauritania. Today, Ophir has concessions in the Sahrawi Arab Democratic Republic, the Nigeria-São Tomé Joint Development Zone, Equatorial Guinea, Guinea-Bissau, Gabon, Congo-Brazzaville, Senegal, Tanzania and Somaliland as well as South Africa. Sexwale is also involved in major construction projects in Nigeria and Equatorial Guinea.[21]

This activity needs to be put into perspective. First, new exploration activity in Africa is being undertaken by junior companies that reportedly account for over 60% of growth in the mining sector. Most of these are Australian and Canadian companies, with their South African counterparts left far behind. This is even more the case in the oil and gas sectors, where both the capital and technology requirements are far higher. Not surprisingly, therefore, South African, and indeed wider African, participation in oil, gas and the broader energy sector is mainly through state companies, often in partnership with multinationals.

In January 2006 it was said that South Africa was 'losing in the new scramble for Africa' and that the dominance of Australia and Canada in the African mining industry was due to the fact that they had access to cheaper capital.[22] At the end of 2006 the same source noted that the Toronto Stock Exchange, Australian Stock Exchange and London's Alternative Investment market had traditionally been the preferred markets for junior mining companies operating in Africa, 'owing to the historically unfavourable investment ethos towards exploration in South Africa. However, both mining companies' and investors' attitudes towards the South African investment market are beginning to change with the [Johannesburg Stock Exchange] JSE experiencing the most successful run of junior main-board listings in recent years'. Nine mining companies were listed on the JSE in 2006.[23]

South Africa generates two thirds of the continent's supply of electricity, almost all of it by the state-owned utility company Eskom. The latter is Africa's largest energy utility and the fourth largest in the world, producing 90–95% of the electricity generated in South Africa. However, with South Africa facing serious projected power shortages, the Department of Mining and Energy is seeking to ensure future energy security by diversifying its sources from coal to nuclear and hydro-electric power and developing a liquid fuels (processed natural gas) industry (Daniel and Lutchman 2006: 497–505). Thus South Africa is increasing its engagement with neighbouring countries, beyond its established sourcing of power from Mozambique's Cahora Bassa generation scheme on the Zambezi River. Eskom Enterprises, Eskom's international arm, is active in 31 African countries. By far the most significant of these thrusts is the Grand Inga project, the world's largest hydropower scheme that is being implemented in three phases over 20 years. When completed in the 2020s, Grand Inga is expected to generate sufficient power for the entire continent, as well as revenue from the export of electricity to the Middle East and Europe.

State participation is also central to South Africa's engagement in the natural gas and oil sectors. South Africa will soon be purchasing gas from NamPower, the Namibian national power utility, as it has few reserves of natural gas of its own. This may change if there is successful development of new reserves of gas recently discovered offshore in an area that straddles Namibia and South African waters. Known as the Ibhubezi Project, this is 60% owned by two US companies, Forest Oil and Anschutz, and the balance owned by state-owned PetroSA (30%) and Mvelaphanda Resources (10%). Meanwhile, the South African and Mozambican governments are working in partnership with Sasol to construct an 865 kilometre pipeline for the supply of natural gas from the Pande and Temane fields in central Mozambique to Sasol's plant in Secunda, east of Johannesburg. Ultimately, this could lead to 10% of South Africa's energy needs being supplied from natural gas.

South Africa similarly lacks oil reserves and has to import 98% of its requirements. Increasingly, it is attempting to source these from Africa, which presently supplies about a quarter of its needs, mainly from Nigeria, Angola, Cameroon and Gabon. The government is attempting to reduce import dependency by buying into production through a mixture of direct state involvement and state support for South African companies, notably Sasol. State involvement takes place through PetroSA, currently involved in joint venture arrangements in oil production or exploration in Algeria, Angola, Gabon, Nigeria and Sudan. It works with state companies of other countries (Sudapet in Sudan), independent African companies (Moni Pulo in Nigeria) or multinationals (the US company Burlington in Algeria). PetroSA is also negotiating oil rights with the governments of Equatorial Guinea, Central African Republic, Libya and Egypt. Meanwhile, Sasol is engaged in crude oil production in Gabon (a 30% holding in the Etame Marine field offshore) and is negotiating further oil exploration rights. The company has also acquired significant stakes in Equatorial Guinea's state-run energy industry: 10% and 20% stakes in oil and gas fields respectively and a 50% option on two other blocks in the Rio Muni Basin.

South African participation in the energy sector is therefore state driven. First, the South African government recognises the importance of state involve- ment in a sector where profits will be constrained by the need to supply a domestic consumer market including the poor and economically marginalised (Daniel and Lutchman 2006: 56). Second, it is wary of South Africa becoming too dependent upon sourcing supplies in an increasingly energy-starved world from multinational companies. Third, it recognises that the capital requirements in energy are so large that unless black empowerment companies are actively backed by government, they are likely to be squeezed out.

African Capitalist Participation in Telecommunications
The African telecommunications sector is one of few where indigenous capitalist participation has become significant. This has occurred as a result of the confluence of

- the exploitation of market opportunity at the right time by a number of African venture capitalists, albeit backed by a combination of state, private and multinational capital;[24]
- the dismal state of fixed line and telecommunications infrastructure in Africa, largely dominated by state-owned utility companies;
- liberalisation and privatisation of the telephony market, allowing for private sector expansion that bypassed incumbent fixed line operators; and
- the availability of rapidly advancing telecommunications technology.[25]

Furthermore, Africa's ICT revolution was catalysed by the International Telecom- munications Union (ITU), a United Nations agency as well as a lobby group for the telecommunications industry, the Global Systems for Mobile Communication (GSM) Association, the G8's World Summit on the Information Society, the World Bank and various other development agencies. Initial mobile licences in Africa were often funded in part by the International Finance Corporation and similar bodies. The result has been the spectacular expansion of cellular telephony and ICT in Africa since the early 1990s. Indeed, while Africa lags far behind in telecommunications connectivity compared with every other region, it is today the world's fastest growing cellphone market in terms of subscribers.[26] According to the ITU, Africa had an average growth rate of cellphone subscribers of 65% a year between 1998 and 2003, higher than in any other region of the world. Furthermore, by the end of 2003, three quarters of the countries on the continent allowed competition in mobile networks, up from 56% in 2001 and 7% in 1995. In 2001 there were 100 mobile networks in Africa, up from 33 in 1995. As of 2003 there were no countries lacking a cellular network compared with 28 in 1995 (ITU 2001, 2004). According to the ITU (2001: 3):

> it is not State-owned incumbents, multilateral donors and large multinationals that are building Africa's telecommunications networks. Rather, a new breed of pan-African mobile companies is creating the mobile miracle in Africa. These pioneers, such as Mobile Telephone Networks (MTN), Orascom Telecom, and MSI are stringing together regional networks, shattering the conventional wisdom that the problem with Africa is a lack of investment.

In December 2003 the ITU ranked the top six strategic investors on the continent by subscriber numbers as Vodacom, MTN, Orange, Orascom, Celtel and Millicom. Of these, only MTN and Orascom (of Egypt) were fully African-owned, although Vodacom was part-owned by South African interests (Telkom). The African mobile market has grown and changed significantly and MTN, since its acquisition of the Lebanese Investcom group of companies, has become the largest mobile operator in Africa, by subscribers and geographical footprint, with over 48 million subscribers as of 30 June 2007 (now including subscribers in the Middle-East), up from 10.1 million in 2003 (ITU 2004). MTN now claims to be the largest mobile operator in developing markets. However the ITU (2004: 5) noted that:

> The region's strategic investors are unique in that they tend to be focused on Africa. For example MTN and Vodacom have leveraged their South African success and experience to expand into the rest of Africa. Celtel tends to invest in Sub-Saharan Africa whereas Orascom is concentrated on the North African region. Although Millicom is active in other parts of the world, its attention is on developing markets. Econet, which started as the first private mobile operator in Zimbabwe now has investments in Botswana, Lesotho and Nigeria and a recent license award in Kenya. Only Orange has a strategy focused more on developed countries with most of its African investments arising out of former France Telecom holdings in incumbent operators.

Orascom Telecom, Egypt's first multinational, operates mobile networks in the Middle East, South Asia and North Africa, where with major investments in Algeria and Tunisia, it is seeking to dominate the market. Meanwhile, the race for coverage of the sub-Saharan African market has been dominated by MTN and Vodacom, which in 2007 were listed respectively at 16 and 13 in the top African companies by turnover.

The ITU's generalisation that state-owned telecommunications companies are not a major force needs qualification. This is illustrated by Vodacom. The company was launched as a joint venture by Vodafone, the British-based multinational, and South Africa's state utility Telkom in 1994. Today it claims 59% of the share of the South African cellular market, by far the largest on the continent, and has affiliates, partners or subsidiaries in Kenya (where its market share stands at 64%), Tanzania (55%), Egypt (47%), the DRC (38%), Mozambique (33%) and Lesotho (80%). Telkom was partially privatised in 1997, becoming majority owned by the US-based SBC Communications and Telkom Malaysia. However, SBC subsequently sold its interest, which was purchased by the Public Investment Corporation (PIC), a manager of state pension funds. Today, therefore, although operating at a distance from the state, it is effectively majority state-owned, the state's direct 38% shareholding being complemented by the PIC's 13%.

Vodacom has adopted a consistent strategy to seek politicians and their cronies as business partners. In Mozambique, its prominent shareholders include President Armando Guebuza as well as politicians closely associated with his predecessor, Joaquim Chissano. Vodacom Tanzania is chaired by the Speaker of Parliament and its shareholder representative on the board is Rostam Aziz, the ruling party's treasurer and a close associate of President Jakaya Kikwete. In the DRC, Vodacom's 49% partner, Congolese Wireless Network, appears to have won its licence to operate at least in part through the influence of Didier Kazadi Nyembwe, who in 2001–2 headed the national intelligence agency. Apart from having a close relationship with President Laurent Kabila, Nyembwe was fingered in 2001 by the UN appointed panel that examined the illegal exploitation of natural resources and profiteering by the elite from the country's civil war.[27]

Nor was the state absent from the launch of MTN. It was established in South Africa in 1994 after obtaining a licence to operate as a cellular operator and was deliberately established as a black empowerment venture with the original shareholding comprising M-NET (25%); Britain's Cable & Wireless (25%); Corporate Africa, the shareholding company of New African Investments Limited (NAIL) (20%); Transtel, Transnet's communications subsidiary (25%); and

FABCOS, a company associated with the South African Black Taxi Association (5%). MTN was a black empowered company, but was conceived and lead by the Naspers-owned M-NET. By 2004, the bulk of MTN shares (72.5%) were in free float. Held by local and international shareholders, the rest were owned by the National Empowerment Fund (8.89%) and Newshelf 664 (18.7%), the latter being a company formed as the result of a management buyout.

MTN has always enjoyed a high level of political connectivity. Nthatho Motlana, Nelson Mandela's doctor-turned-businessman, was chairman of NAIL (the first ever black group listed on the JSE) at the time of MTN's incorporation. He was instrumental in convincing the government that a second licence was necessary as well as in attracting international investment from the Southwestern Bell Corporation and Cable & Wireless. He served as chairman of MTN 1994–9. Its current CEO, Phuthuma Nhleko, formerly worked for Standard Corporate and Merchant Bank and sits on the boards of Johnnic, Nedbank and Old Mutual; while former African National Congress Secretary-General, Cyril Ramaphosa, its non-executive chairman, was formerly chair of Johnnic and is one of the foremost black magnates in South Africa. Today MTN is one the leading black empowerment companies.

When launched in 1994, MTN did not see itself expanding beyond South Africa. However, the company swiftly turned its attention to Africa, where its strategy was to win a greenfield telecommunications licence and then aggressively boost demand. In 1998, MTN began its expansion into Africa with the acquisition of licences in Rwanda and Uganda. By late 2004, MTN was closing in on Vodacom as the largest cellphone group on the continent as measured by the subscriber numbers, boasting eleven million at the end of September of that year compared with Vodacom's 13.5 million. By this time, its geographical footprint included Rwanda, Uganda, Swaziland, Cameroon and Nigeria and it was well ahead of Vodacom in terms of revenue and profitability, for Vodacom's expansion in southern Africa had yielded nothing like the operational success that had attended MTN's movement into the wider continent. The jewel was Nigeria, where MTN launched operations in 2001 and 4.4 million subscribers had ballooned to 12.2 million in early 2007. In 2005 MTN overtook Vodacom in Africa through acquisitions in Ivory Coast, Zambia, Botswana and Congo-Brazzaville, as well as investing 49% in a second GSM license in Iran (Irancell). In 2006 MTN acquired the Lebanon-based Investcom, giving it operations in Benin, Ghana, Guinea-Bissau, Guinea, Liberia and Sudan as well as in Afghanistan, Syria and Cyprus. MTN now has operations in 21 countries in Africa and the Middle East.

By this time, having also acquired licences to operate in Ivory Coast, Sudan and Zambia, MTN had over 40 million subscribers. With a market value of R70 billion in mid-2005, it was reckoned to be an increasingly juicy target for takeover by one of the major global cellphone operators with ambitions to move into potentially lucrative markets such as Egypt, Angola and Morocco.[28]

MTN's major setback occurred when it was defeated in a bidding war by a Kuwaiti cellular operator, MTC, to take over Celtel, another pan-African cellphone operator that had six million customers in thirteen countries with little overlap with the markets in which MTN was already operating. Celtel itself had an interesting history. It was launched in 1998 by MSI, the consultancy company formed in 1989 by Mo Ibrahim, a Sudanese-born British citizen, after he left British Telecom when, in his view, it was failing to grasp the opportunities by launching vigorously into cellular communications. MSI grew rapidly to a staff of 800 worldwide, creating mobile phone networks for major operators. Its success was such that in 2000 it was sold to Marconi for £570 million, of which Ibrahim himself received £70 million. He proceeded to pour that money into Celtel, whose *raison d'être*, he proclaimed, was to serve the poorest of the poor. Along with its refusal to pay bribes, this may have explained its relatively modest rate of growth. Nonetheless, its wide regional presence was recognised as presenting the opportunity for rapid expansion, so when Ibrahim sold out to MTC, the company went for $3.4 billion.[29]

Disposal of a cellular operator also proved profitable for Rwandan-Congolese businessman, Miko Rwayitare, who sold an 80% interest in Telecel International, then operating in eleven African countries, to Orascom Telecom for $413 million. Rwayitare made history with Telecel by placing the first mobile call on the first African mobile network built in 1986 with a licence granted by his close friend and confidant Mobutu Sese Seko.[30] At the time of his death in September 2007, although partially retired, he was still president of Telecel, then in fourteen African countries and holding around 40% of the sub-Saharan African cellular market outside South Africa; boasted a major interest in the hotel sector in Rwanda; and had a chain of South African investments in hospitality, oil, vineyards and real estate. One of his last acquisitions was a 66% stake in Goal Technology Solutions, which planned to use the South African municipal electricity infrastructure to deliver broadband, TV programming and voice telephony, thereby offering a challenge to Telkom and Multichoice.[31]

The increasing domination of the African cellular market by larger operators means that smaller companies have struggled. One such company is Econet

Wireless. Owned and run by Strive Masiyiwa, a Zimbabwean electronic engineer who after working for the Zimbabwean Post and Telecommunications Corporation (PTC), moved into the private sector. He formed Econet with a view to launching a mobile sector in 1993, initially seeking a partnership with the PTC. However, the latter was reluctant to lose its monopoly and Masiyiwa was destined to become bogged down in a long battle in the courts, claiming that the behaviour of the state operator violated the right to free speech. A Supreme Court judgment eventually went his way, but by this time PTC had developed its own cellular ambitions in partnership with Rwayitare's Telcel and backed by political heavyweights. This defeated Econet in a bid for the grant of the first cellular licence. However, Econet obtained a second licence in 1997 and went on to become the major operator in Zimbabwe. Inevitably, however, political restrictions and economic crisis have had a negative impact upon the company's expansion, which otherwise has major stakes only in the small markets of Lesotho and Burundi. Holding licences and interests in a number of other countries – Nigeria, Burundi, Kenya and even New Zealand – its best prospect may lie in developing its potential in order to be bought by one of the major operators.

Informal African Participation in Mining

African Consolidated Resources (ACR) is a junior mining company, based in Kent in Britain that has in recent years aggressively pursued mineral deposits and exploration opportunities in Zimbabwe. Initially, at least, it was unmoved by the prospects of political meltdown. 'Sovereign risk' was not perceived as high and ultimately 'the world shall embrace the country once again'. Zimbabwe offered a 'world class portfolio of minerals, underexplored by modern techniques,' along with 'an infrastructure and skills base almost unrivalled in Africa'. Furthermore, in order to reduce its political exposure, the company deliberately set out to include 'black indigenous partners' and sought to maintain 'a healthy relationship with Government,' with which it had discussed the design of an acceptable policy of black economic empowerment.[32]

In September 2006, ACR announced the discovery of a rich diamond seam on one of its properties in Marange (Manicaland) it had taken over from De Beers. Within a matter of days, 20 000 people had descended upon the area with picks and shovels. 'They came in droves,' reported ACR's hapless CEO, 'lifting diamonds on a scale never seen. Those stones have found their way into South Africa, the Congo, Sierra Leone, Israel and Lebanon'. A more upbeat picture was offered by one of the illicit miners: 'Our area has been transformed. This is empowerment like you've never seen'. The government was impressed. Within a short space of time, the state-owned Zimbabwe Mining Development, citing pre-existing property rights, seized the site and the government threw up a police cordon around Manicaland, entry to which required permits even from government officials. However, these measures proved manifestly ineffective. Although nearly 30 000 illegal diamond and gold miners were arrested, the informal mining continued virtually unabated and it was reported that the site police themselves were joining in the fun. Then, in early March 2007, the son of the CEO of Zimbabwe Defence Industries, Tshinga Dube, was arrested by police at his Harare home with consignments of diamonds and gold. A partner, a major in the air force, was also arrested and found to be in possession of diamonds worth over $49 million and gold worth $98 million. In addition, William Nhara, a Zanu-PF party spokesman for Harare province, was arrested at the airport for attempting to smuggle 10 773 carats of diamonds out of the country. This latter arrest occurred on the same day that Robert Mugabe announced plans to take control of the entire diamond mining sector, seeking to stem the illegal outflow of precious minerals which, according to the governor of the central bank, was worth as much as $40–50 million a week.[33]

This story is illustrative of a phenomenon which, at one level, is as old as the history of mining under capitalism itself, but which at another has intensified over recent decades in a continent where vicious armed struggle for resources has been the root of devastating wars. The collapse of the capacity of the state to control resource-rich areas can, as the case of the Marange diamond seam illustrates, lead to rich pickings for local people. Yet such gains are usually short term, their extent limited, and the ultimate political and environmental cost can be ruinous to local communities.

Taylor has identified the neo-liberalisation of the global economy and the structural adjustment foisted upon Africa as context for the plunder of natural resources: 'Far from bringing about stability and legitimate growth, impulses generated by globalisation have contributed to the further deepening and development of criminal networks, and decidedly quasi-feudal forms of political economy' (2003: 52). Rulers of weak states who face internal threats and external pressures destroy formal institutions of the state; while outside creditors, foreign firms and even elites from neighbouring states may move in either to support or undermine hard-pressed rulers. In the DRC, for instance, withdrawal of US support for Mobutu following the end of the war saw major US and Belgian multinational mining companies, backed by covert US defence activities, funding the rise to the presidency of Laurent Kabila, who in turn was backed by Rwanda and Uganda. Numerous concessions followed, but it was not long before, having gained power,

Kabila not only frustrated his Western backers by tearing up many contracts he had signed with international businessmen (while forging new deals on an individual basis), but turned on his Rwandan and Ugandan allies who responded with a new invasion of the DRC. This in turn prompted Kabila to construct new alliances with regimes such as Angola and Zimbabwe, whose commitment to driving out Ugandan and Rwandan forces was funded by the award of valuable concessions. Even though their rhetoric was often rabidly anti-Western, they 'had no intention of severing the highly profitable linkages that international capital had constructed in the Congo over many decades, even if it meant that new networks and regional spokes needed to be constructed' (Taylor 2003: 5).

Similarly, today, the illegal mining and export of gold from Zimbabwe – and indeed of other resources from other countries – is dependent upon the existence not only of impoverished local miners who actually dig the resources out of the ground, but networks of participating political elites, smugglers, unscrupulous traders and end-destination purchasers overseas. Inevitably, local miners are at the very bottom of the commodity chain and the benefits of illegal mining flow overwhelmingly to others.

Conclusion

The increased global demand for Africa's resources has seen a surge of foreign investment. At one level, this has been based upon a reinforcement of alliances between international capital and political elites in resource rich territories, entrenching patterns of patronage, corruption and informalised economy sustained by often shady international linkages. At another, it has increased the potential for Africans to participate in the benefits of the resource boom. Ironically, however, although most African governments now mouth the developmental potentialities of market economics, African capitalism is on the whole too weak and undeveloped to move much beyond existing niches in domestically-oriented manufacturing, even if there is some evidence of the growth of a new generation of African entrepreneurs displaying an awareness of pan-African trading and business opportunities. The principal exception is South African private capital, whose outward movement since 1994 has proved an important stimulus to the scramble. South African firms dwarf the private sectors of other African countries, yet even they cannot match the capital requirements of major projects in energy and infrastructure, even if they had the long-term vision to do so. It is only a handful of state-owned or backed companies that have proved able to become significant African players in sectors such as oil and gas, their role now complemented by the increasing reach of major South African parastatals, notably Eskom, across the continent. Even in junior mining, where niche investments provide opportunities for emergent black-controlled mining companies (principally from South Africa but including a politically-backed, African-owned mining sector in countries such as Zimbabwe), the scene is largely dominated by Canadian, Australian and, to a lesser extent, British interests.

The one field in which African capital has proved able to mobilise capital and capacity to become dominant is that of ICT. Yet it has only been able to do so because global telecommunications companies initially perceived Africa as marginal to their expansion and left it as virgin territory for investment by local capital, albeit acting as local stalking horses for, and partners to, the major corporates. However, while the cellphone market was penetrated, or indeed was virtually created by, astute African venture capitalists – all of whom drew upon technical training, experience and financial expertise acquired in the West – it is again South African capital, displaying a significant black empowerment profile, which has become dominant. Even so, as the African market has become increasingly profitable, so the major global players have begun to take it seriously and the prospect is that this sector too will soon fall prey to the financial power of Western capital through takeovers and mergers. Although the profits of such deals would accrue to local owners and shareholders, only experience will indicate whether they will provide a basis for the expansion of African capitalism into other sectors; or, in contrast, be recycled back into the maw of the international financial system.

Notes

1. Economic Commission for Africa, *Economic Report on Africa, 2005: Meeting the Challenges of Unemployment and Poverty in Africa.*
2. *Poverty, Inequality and Labour Markets in Africa: A Descriptive Overview.* Development Policy Research Unit, 2005.
3. Economic Commission for Africa, *Economic Report on Africa 2004: Unlocking Africa's Trade Potential.*
4. Economic Commission for Africa, *Economic Report on Africa, 2005: Meeting the Challenges of Unemployment and Poverty in Africa.*
5. Economic Commission for Africa, *Economic Report on Africa, 2006: Capital Flows and Development Financing in Africa.*
6. Economic Commission for Africa, *Economic Report on Africa, 2006: Capital Flows and Development Financing in Africa*; Economic Commission for Africa, Economic Report on Africa: press release, Addis Ababa, 29 Mar. 2007.

7. E. Bloch, 'Privatization talk without action'. *Zimbabwe Independent* 2 Mar. 2007.
8. Botswana, Ethiopia, Ghana, Kenya, Mali, Senegal, South Africa, Uganda, Zambia and Zimbabwe.
9. The five countries apart from Kenya UNCTAD listed as having subsidiaries in other African countries were Ghana, Nigeria, Djibouti, Tanzania and Zimbabwe, each having one or two operations in the areas of insurance finance and trade.
10. *African Business* Apr. 2007.
11. The rankings are devised by *Jeune Afrique L'Intelligent*, but limited by the failure of some companies (particularly within extractive industries) to report data. For instance, 'Undoubtedly, the giant state-owned Nigerian National Petroleum Corporation would have been among the top ten companies had its audited accounts been submitted on time'. The Egyptian state oil company, another continental giant, also failed to produce data for inclusion in the index. Note also that Zimbabwean companies have been excluded from the ranking. The alarming rate of inflation, which causes such a difference between the official and unofficial exchange rate, means that Zimbabwean companies would occupy positions on the list that bear no relation to actual performance.
12. *The Africa Report* 6, Apr. 2007.
13. South Africa lost seven places in the top 100; kept its balance of 38 companies in the top 50; and lost five in the top 200. Meanwhile, only 163 South African companies made the top 500, down from 188 in 2006 (*The Africa Report* 2, Apr. 2006; *The Africa Report* 6, April 2007).
14. Reason unknown: presumably from failure to submit a company report.
15. *The Africa Report* 6, Apr. 2007.
16. *The Africa Report* 1, Mar. 2006.
17. Even so, the DRC's performance in this regard was considerably better than that of Guinea-Bissau, where it took 233 days. Sources: World Bank, *Economy Rankings*, 2007; World Bank, *Starting a Business*, 2007.
18. Transparency International, *The 2006 Transparency International Corruption Perceptions Index*.
19. See, for instance, the case of Chad, discussed by Simon Massey and Roy May in chapter nine of this book.
20. These proportions are drawn from figure 19.4 of Daniel and Lutchman (2006) that uses data provided by: Whitehouse and Associates in 2004. However, Daniel, Lutchman and Comninos (2007) cite Rumney's 2006 figures, which are somewhat different: telecommunications (24%), mining (19%), electricity (18%), steel and other metals (13%), oil and gas (10%) and other (16%). Note that there is no specific reference to banking and finance, a growing field of activity that is presumably included in other.
21. *Business in Africa* Feb. 2007.
22. *Mining Weekly* 20 Jan. 2006.
23. *Mining Weekly* 15 Dec. 2006.
24. The initial major greenfield involvements and acquisitions by African and Arab companies in this sector happened in the context of developments in Northern cellular and other ICT markets with the burst of the dotcom bubble and the expansion of

Northern operators into costly third generation (high speed data-enabled cellular communications) licences in Britain and Europe. At the time, first tier international cellular operators were pulling back from expansionary activities and even selling off in some instances. This point was drawn to our attention by an interview conducted by Alex Comninos with Alison Gillwald at University of the Witwatersrand, 23 Mar. 2007.

25. The particular technological choice that was important to the spread of global telephony, in particular to Africa, was the use of GSM technology. Africa's late entry into the mobile telephony market meant that it benefited from the adoption of the newest, most efficient and most commonly used standard for cellular communications. According to the ITU, Africa is the world's most GSM-oriented market outside Europe. Africa was one of the last markets in which the technology developed for consumer use. GSM was the first global standard for digital mobile communication (2G or second generation). It was a new technology in the early 1990s, but by the time African mobile operators started spreading on the continent its success was proven and it was the logical choice for new network operators. Technological path dependency meant that in a sense African networks were for a time more advanced than networks elsewhere where pre-GSM technologies prevailed.

26. Although its share of global population was about 13%, at the turn of the century Africa accounted for only 0.22% of the total number of landline telephone connections in the world and only 0.16% of cell phones (Yaú 2004: 14).

27. *Mail & Guardian* 13–19 Apr. 2007.

28. *Financial Mail Corporate Report* 3 Dec. 2004; *Financial Mail* 17 June 2005; *Business Report* 30 Mar. 2007.

29. Of which he poured $100 million into a personal foundation to fund development projects in Africa.

30. Before Telecel, Rwayitare's business history entailed a long-term involvement with Gécamines as well as responsibility for winning the African distribution rights of the Xerox and Hewlett-Packard brands (*Sunday Times* 7 Oct. 2007).

31. *Financial Mail* 13 Oct. 2006; *The New Times* (Rwanda) 19 Sep. 2005.

32. http://www.minesite.com/companies/com_single/company/african-consolidated-reso.

33. *Business Report* 18 Mar. 2007; *Daily News* 9 Mar. 2007; B. Latham, Zimbabwe to nationalize diamond mine after gem rush, 2007 http://www.bloomberg.com/apps/news?pid= 20601087&sid+alUT7x9G53Bw&refer=home.

References

Abdou, A. 2001. *Adjustment and Investment in Africa: A Retreat to Compradorization.* Saskatchewan: Department of Economics, University of Regina.

Agboli, M. and C. Ukaegbu. 2006, 'Business environment and entrepreneurial activity in Nigeria: implications for industrial development'. *Journal of Modern African Studies* 44(1): 1–30.

Amin, S. 1990. *Delinking*. London: Zed Books.

Daniel, J. and J. Lutchman. 2006. 'South Africa in Africa: scrambling for energy'. In: *State of the Nation: South Africa 2005–06*, edited by B. Sakhela et al. Cape Town: HSRC Press: 484–509.

Daniel J., J. Lutchman and A. Comninos. 2007. 'South Africa in Africa: trends and forecasts in a changing African political economy'. *State of the Nation: South Africa 2007*, edited by B. Sakhela et al. Cape Town: HSRC Press. 508–32.

Daniel, J., V. Naidoo and S. Naidu. 2004. 'The South Africans have arrived: post-apartheid corporate expansion into Africa'. In: *State of the Nation: South Africa 2003–04*, edited by J. Daniel, A. Habib and R. Southall. Cape Town. HSRC Press. 368–90.

Forrest, T. 1996. *The Advance of African Capital: The Growth of Nigerian Private Enterprise*. Edinburgh: Edinburgh University Press.

Himbara, D. 1994. *Kenyan Capitalists, the State and Development*. Nairobi: East African Educational Publishers.

International Telecommunications Union (ITU). 2001. ITU Telecommunications Indicators Update, July–August–September–October 2001. www.itu.int/ITU-D/ict/update/pdf/update_3_01pdf.pdf.

ITU. 2004. African Telecommunications Indicators 2004. www.itu.int/wsis/tunis/newsroom/stats/Africa_2004.pdf.

Kennedy, P. 1988. *African Capitalism: The Struggle for Ascendancy*. Cambridge: Cambridge University Press.

Leys, C. 1975. *Underdevelopment in Kenya: The Political Economy of Neo-Colonialism*. London: Heinemann.

Leys, C. and B. Berman (eds). 1994. *African Capitalists in African Development*. Boulder: Lynne Rienner.

Loxley, J. 1986. *Debt and Disorder: External Financing for Development*. Boulder: Westview.

McDade, B.E. and A. Spring. 2005. 'The "new generation of African entrepreneurs": networking to change the climate for business and private sector-led development'. *Entrepreneurship and Regional Development* 17: 17–42.

Page, S. and D.W. te Velde. (2004) Foreign Direct Investment by African Countries, Papers prepared for InWent / UNCTAD meeting on FDI in Africa, 22–24 November 2004, UNECA, Addis Ababa.

Pedersen, P.O. and D. McCormick. 1999. 'African business systems in a globalising world'. *Journal of Modern African Studies* 37(1): 109–36.

Riddell, J. 1992. 'Things fall apart again: structural adjustment programmes in sub-Saharan Africa'. *Journal of Modern African Studies* 30(1): 53–68.

Swainson, N. 1977. 'The rise of a national bourgeoisie in Kenya'. *Review of African Political Economy* 8: 39–55.

Swainson, N. 1980. *The Development of Corporate Capitalism in Kenya 1918–77*. Nairobi: Heinemann.

Tangri, R. 1990. *The Politics of Patronage in Africa: Parastatals, Privatization and Private Enterprise*. Oxford: James Currey.

Taylor, I. 2003. 'Conflict in Central Africa: clandestine networks and regional/global configurations'. *Review of African Political Economy* 95: 45-55.

UNCTAD. 1992. *World Investment Report: Transnational Corporations as Engines of Growth.* New York. United Nations.

——. 1998. *World Investment Report; Transnational Corporations, Market Structure and Competition Policy.* New York. United Nations.

——. 2004. *World Investment Report: Transnational Corporations and the Internationalization of R&D.* New York. United Nations.

World Bank. 2000. *Can Africa Claim the 21ˢᵗ Century?* Washington: World Bank.

——. 2007. *Doing Business Report 2007: How to Reform.* Washington: World Bank.

Yaú, Y.Z. 2004. 'The new imperialism and Africa in the global electronic village'. *Review of African Political Economy* 99: 11-29.

CHAPTER FIFTEEN

International Competition, Public Contracts and Foreign Business Bribery in Africa

The Case of Uganda

Roger Tangri

Apparently reputable companies and multinationals are known to engage in underhand deals with high officials in order to gain advantages against their competitors or to carry out unethical operations (Jerry J. Rawlings, President of Ghana, 2000).[1]

There should be no single sourcing; all contracts must be competed for. Getting bribes from business people is the biggest problem (Yoweri Museveni, President of Uganda, 2006).[2]

International competition for access to Africa's markets and natural resources is an important feature of the contemporary scramble for the continent. Another aspect, less commented on by analysts, is the competition among foreign companies for big, lucrative government contracts in African countries. Western as well as non-Western firms are engaged in at times intense competition in pursuit of government tenders and contracts, principally in the construction, defence and energy sectors. In Uganda, for instance, although competition for its natural resources had been limited until recent growth in the emergent oil sector, nearly every large government contract in the past decade has attracted often fierce struggles among foreign business firms. This chapter focuses on international business competition for Uganda's major public contracts.

The scramble for Africa's natural resources has been seriously tainted by bribery and corruption, especially as foreign firms compete with each other to gain access to mineral and other resources (Commission for Africa 2005: 145–9). Similarly, as suggested by the epigraphs to this chapter, the competition for Africa's large government contracts has involved multinational companies making illegal payments to political leaders and top public officials. It is estimated that of the $4 trillion spent worldwide on government public contracts every year, some $400 billion is lost to bribery (Commission for Africa 2005: 149–51). In this chapter, foreign business bribery of politicians and officials in competition for Uganda's big government contracts is examined. There is also brief comment on international business corruption in the competition for Uganda's oil resources. The role of foreign companies attempting to obtain preferential treatment by bribing Ugandans who control particular government decision-making is highlighted. The motive is to 'turn on its head the perception in first-world countries that consultants are obliged to pay bribes in Africa'. As in the case, for instance, of the construction of the Katse Dam in Lesotho, it was foreign companies 'that offered money' and paid the bribes to obtain lucrative contracts for which they were so ardently competing. In Lesotho, 'it is very important that the briber was convicted,'[3] although this is a rare occurrence among bribe-paying foreign companies operating in Africa.

The impact of foreign business corruption on Uganda and Africa's governance is considered. Through the examples presented, it is argued that corrupt state-business interactions have had deleterious effects on the way the state operates and carries out its decision-making functions. State corruption involves the private sector and state-business transactions should become an area of growing concern for international donors and national anti-corruption efforts.

Foreign Firms and Corruption in Africa

State corruption in African countries is often viewed as a series of illegal actions on the part of public officials and politicians, aimed at acquiring money and other material benefits in return for making favourable government decisions. Thus public officers may solicit bribes from foreign business groups in exchange for favourable treatment in government decision-making. Studies on corruption in Africa show that demands for illegal payoffs have contributed to an uncertain business environment that is detrimental to private sector development. Recent research on Uganda, for instance, has shown that public sector 'corruption has a large adverse effect on firms' as well as having imposed 'a heavy burden' on them by increasing the cost of business through the price of bribes (Svensson 2001: 320). Similarly, demands for illegal payments by African state officials have been considered inimical to foreign private investment. Thus, the chairman of the British-based East Africa Association, Alan Wood, named corruption within the state as an important deterrent to British investment in Uganda (Mugunga 2000).

These studies, however, have missed an important dimension of corruption across the Africa – the role of private firms, especially foreign companies, in public sector corruption. In fact, within Africa there is a view, held strongly by observers, that 'graft in public office is perpetrated by leaders in the corporate world and their agents who canvass for multi-million shilling tenders and government contracts'. As a Kenyan journalist has noted, it is international 'corporate executives who call into public offices with briefcases, sometimes sackfuls of money;' and who are important agents of state corruption in African countries (Munaita 2001).

The empirical evidence for foreign business bribery in African countries is mainly anecdotal and confined to a few journalistic accounts. There are only a few general works on the payment of business bribes by multinational firms to win public tenders and government contracts in developing countries (Moody-Stuart 1997). Yet the importance of foreign business corruption can be seen in the attempts of Western governments and international organisations to criminalise it. For example, there are international conventions and laws that make it possible to prosecute Western private companies for making illegal payments to foreign public officials. Transparency International (TI), the global, non-governmental anti-corruption organisation, has shown in its bribe payers indexes that there are high levels of bribery in developing countries by quite large numbers of multinational firms from Western countries. TI has singled out Chinese, Indian and South African companies as among the worst offenders for their propensity to pay bribes when doing business in developing countries (Transparency International 2006). Moreover, the World Bank claims to have banned over 100 mostly Western companies from participating in its projects in developing countries on account of graft in contracting.

Although clearly not unaware of foreign business bribery, international aid donors have been far more concerned with pressing African governments to combat corruption within their state institutions than addressing the role of international companies as promoters of public sector corruption. Donors have tended to accept the claims of foreign investors that they are obliged to make illegal payments because of the corrupt demands being made on them by grasping state officials. And, partly for this reason, donors have pushed strongly for action to be taken against state personnel demanding illegal payoffs rather than devoting much attention to the role of foreign firms in African state corruption.

A major theme of this chapter is to show through Ugandan case material that foreign business is deeply implicated in state corruption. There is substance to the view of African observers cited above that 'graft in public office is perpetrated by leaders in the corporate world and their agents'. Considered here are a number of cases where international companies competing with each other to obtain large, lucrative contracts have been involved in illicit offers and payments to government officials and politicians to win deals and contracts over competitors. Far from being innocent dupes of public sector corruption, research shows that favour-seeking foreign firms have contributed to, as well as been complicit in, state corruption in Uganda.

This is not to deny that senior Ugandan state personnel have not demanded financial inducements from foreign companies. Although, in the words of a Kenyan journalist, 'it is now widely accepted that the private sector is the supply side of corruption' in African countries (Munene 2002), there is clearly also a desire on the part of some public officials and politicians to benefit from the pressures and imprecations of foreign firms. Not only the supplying side but also the demanding and taking sides are involved intimately in African public sector corruption. What this case study material seeks to show, however, is that at times foreign firms may have initiated the bribe-giving process; while at other times they have shown clear willingness to enter into corrupt relations with public officials and politicians to secure major government contracts. This chapter focuses on collusion between foreign private sector bidders and senior state personnel; and how this contributes to many irregularities in government decision making and has been harmful to the quality of public governance in Uganda.

Foreign Business Corruption in Uganda

A number of cases have been selected to highlight various aspects of the relations between foreign business and Ugandan state personnel that reveal corrupt practices. Three cases are considered in detail and they relate to foreign business bribery in the competition for Uganda's big government contracts in the construction, energy and telecommunications sectors. Further cases consider more briefly foreign business corruption in the competition for Uganda's oil resources. In all these cases, abundant evidence has been collected to illustrate two main arguments. First, there is evidence that foreign firms have offered private benefits to public officials in order to obtain advantages in government decision-making.

This has been particularly the case where international firms have been in competition with each other to win a valuable public contract. Second, collusive interactions have occurred between foreign private interests and state personnel that have been to their mutual advantage, but harmful to the functioning of government ministries and state agencies as well as to Uganda's legislature.

AES Nile Power and the Power Purchase Agreement

Western companies eagerly seek opportunities for new dam construction in developing countries. New dam construction in Western countries has been declining for the past two decades. For example, in Norway there are tight restrictions on the building of new dams. This serves as a major impetus to Western firms to compete with each other for new business in the developing world. Because competition among foreign dam contractors is intense, improper influence of officials in African countries has become common as dam developers lobby for highly profitable contracts.

Large dam construction projects in Africa have been associated with major corruption scandals. The construction of Kenya's $270 million Turkwel Gorge Dam in the late 1980s was alleged to have cost more than twice the original estimates because of large bribes paid by the French contractors to senior government officials (Ozanne 1991). Similarly in Lesotho in the early 1990s major Western companies were accused of paying huge bribes to obtain lucrative contracts in connection with the construction of the multi-billion-dollar Lesotho Highlands Water Project. British, Canadian, German and Italian contractors were found guilty between 2003 and 2006 of bribing public officials in Lesotho to secure these contracts (Darroch 2005, 2006).

In Uganda, as well, allegations of corruption accompanied the award in 1992 of an $84 million contract for the Owen Falls Dam Extension Project. Despite competition from Western firms, the contract was awarded to the Chinese state-owned company SIETCO. Up to 30% of the contract was allegedly paid to bribe officials in the Uganda Electricity Board to give the contract to SIETCO.[4] The Chinese company possessed neither the technical nor the financial capacity to construct the dam and, eventually, the Ugandan government negotiated SIETCO out of the contract, a process that resulted in the bankruptcy of Pan World Insurance Company, the biggest private insurance company in Uganda.

Our specific Ugandan case relates, however, to the Bujagali hydropower project on the River Nile near Jinja, which from the time of its inception in the mid-1990s up to 2004 was shrouded in controversy. In the 1990s, in response to severe power shortages that were constraining economic growth, a number of foreign power companies conveyed their interest in generating and selling power to the government of Uganda. In December 1997 two of them – an American company and a Norwegian consortium – were licensed to invest in the generation of electric power. However, only one of them would be given government backing including the possibility of external funding from the International Finance Corporation. The Bujagali Dam project that was finally approved in 2000 would have been East Africa's largest ever investment, but the process leading to its agreement was one marred by allegations of corruption and improper dealings.

Applied Energy Services (AES) Corporation of the USA is one of the largest hydro-electric producers in the world. It proposed to build a $520–580 million dam at Bujagali Falls that would generate 200–240MW of hydroelectric power. In 1998, its local affiliate, AES Nile Power Limited, entered into negotiations with the Ugandan government that led to the signing of a letter of intent to develop a hydro-electric power production facility on the Nile River. Later, critics of the project would argue that it had not been subjected to a competitive bidding process. The Minister of Energy and Natural Resources, Richard Kaijuka, strongly supported the proposed agreement and in January 1999 took it to Parliament for approval. There the Committee on the National Economy, chaired by Isaac Musumba, examined the agreement. The Committee raised a number of objections to the proposed power deal (Musumba 1999).

One objection was that a Norwegian consortium, NORPAK Power Limited, was offering to construct a hydro-electric dam further down river at Karuma Falls that would generate 200MW of electricity on completion within thirty months of commencement at a cost of $300 million. It was the view of committee members that the AES Nile Power scheme would not only take longer to produce power, but would also do so at much higher expense than the Norwegian one. It was estimated that for the extra 50MW that Bujagali would generate on completion, AES would receive an additional $230 million at least.

Another objection concerned the tariff AES Nile Power wanted to charge, which was considered far too high. The chair of the committee, Isaac Musumba, presented tariff calculations showing that AES Nile Power would earn $96 million per year over a period of 30 years and that this would enable the company to recoup its initial investment in eight years, an especially high rate of profitability.

The parliamentary committee also raised questions about the status of AES Nile Power. Before May 1998, it was known as Nile Independent Power Limited (NIPL). When NIPL was registered in Uganda it had a share capital of one million

Uganda shillings (about $1 000) of which only 20 000 Uganda shillings (about $20) was paid-up capital. Strong concern was expressed that such an insignificant enterprise could be invited to enter into such a major project with the Ugandan government. The committee further reported that in the draft agreement the parent company of AES Nile Power was AES Electric of the United Kingdom, considered by analysts to be financially unsound.

During 1999, the Minister of Energy and Natural Resources, Richard Kaijuka, came three times to Parliament to persuade it to endorse the agreement. But each time legislators rejected the agreement on the grounds that it was seriously flawed. Eventually, a revised Power Purchase Agreement of 8 December 1999 was presented by Kaijuka's successor as Minister of Energy and approved by Parliament on 2 March 2000. The amended version addressed the various objections raised by MPs. These included a reduction of the tariff levels to be charged as well as a guarantee for the project from AES Incorporated of USA and a performance bond of $12 million. However, the allegedly inflated cost of the Bujagali Dam project was not reduced in the agreement. When the confidential agreement was released as a public document a few years later, critics of the project argued that power from the dam would cost $280 million more than necessary because of the unfavourable project contract with AES.[5]

In various parliamentary deliberations in 1999, many MPs considered NORPAK Power's proposal to be more attractive and suitable than that of AES. In terms of costs, financial, social and environmental, the dam proposed for Bujagali was much higher than that at Karuma. In May 1999, NORPAK decided to send six members of the Musumba parliamentary committee to Norway to inspect the funnelling technology it was proposing for its Ugandan project. The parliamentarians were provided with first-class air tickets, shopping money and accommodation at top hotels. Many saw this as an open bribe and the visit affected NORPAK's public standing in Uganda.

The media furore surrounding the visit to Norway diverted attention away from AES Nile Power, which was also avidly soliciting support among parliament-arians for its agreement. During the time he was minister, Richard Kaijuka was regarded as having clear preferences in the competition between AES Nile Power and NORPAK. He was evidently a key supporter of AES Nile Power in the energy ministry and had pressed strongly for Parliament to endorse the agreement. He was also an implacable opponent of NORPAK's proposal and had, allegedly, blocked another US-based company, Enron International, from investing in Uganda's power sector. The Ugandan press alleged that Kaijuka had received a bribe of

$240 000 and that a further $260 000 was promised him on the successful signing of the agreement.[6] Whatever the veracity of these and other allegations – for instance that one of the local representatives of AES Nile Power purchased Kaijuka's loss-making flower farm through a front company at an inflated value – it is evident that thanks to Kaijuka's firm support, AES Nile Power enjoyed favour in Ugandan government circles. Allegations of corruption also dogged relations between AES Nile Power and its contractors and state organisations. It was reported that a British firm, Amis Consultants, acting on behalf of a Scandinavian company that was to become the lead contractor for Bujagali, had given financial inducements to Ugandan MPs to swing their support from the Karuma Falls project to the Bujagali Dam project (Pallister 2003).

In July 2002, AES Incorporated of USA informed the World Bank that it had discovered evidence that its main construction contractor allegedly bribed a Ugandan government official in connection with the Bujagali Dam project (Phillips 2002).[7] In Uganda, some MPs began calling for a probe to find out who could have received the $400 000 said by a former Nile Power Uganda employee to have been set aside as an 'inducement fund' (Kaiza 2002).[8] Subsequently, former energy minister Richard Kaijuka was named in Ugandan newspapers as one of the government officials and parliamentarians who had received bribes.[9] Kaijuka was then an alternate executive director at the World Bank. The Ugandan government recalled him. In addition, the World Bank suspended approval of loans and risk guarantees for the Bujagali Dam until the bribery allegations were fully investigated.

The United States Department of Justice began investigating allegations that people or entities involved with the Bujagali Dam project had made illegal payments in violation of the 1977 Foreign Corrupt Practices Act, which outlaws the bribing of foreign public officials by American companies. In August 2003, AES announced its withdrawal from the Bujagali power project, although denying that its pullout was related to the bribery probes.

Contrary to initial World Bank claims that there was no evidence to substantiate corruption allegations,[10] it would appear that the process whereby AES Nile Power took the deal was marred by impropriety. AES secured the power purchase agreement over its competitors partly because the tendering process was opaque and involved only minimum bidding; and partly because it was more adept than its rivals in reaching and influencing key decision makers. Indeed, there appears to have been collusion between AES Nile Power representatives and individual power-holders that improperly influenced government and parliamentary decision-making as well as compromising the integrity of state institutions. It was only in September 2007, after a seven-year delay, that construction of the Bujagali Dam started under new auspices. The lengthy wait, principally due to international business corruption, plunged Uganda into a deepening energy crisis.

Yet further efforts in 2005 to mitigate Uganda's power crisis by awarding a licence to generate and sell thermal power were also slowed down by nearly two years of protracted court battles between a Norwegian firm, Jacobsen Electro AS, and a rival bidder, Electro-Maxx. Both firms claimed the evaluation and tendering process for the deal worth $300 million was mired in corruption. Once again, foreign companies bent on obtaining a lucrative contract were alleged to have paid bribes to various government officials as well as parliamentarians in an attempt to influence decision-making to their advantage.

Alcon International and Workers' House

First conceived in the early 1970s, the Social Security House project (popularly referred to as the Workers' House project) involved the construction of an 18-floor, twin-tower block in Kampala. The project was abandoned in the mid-1970s but revived by the National Social Security Fund (NSSF) in 1992. Four foreign firms were invited to tender. One pulled out, leaving three – Alcon International, Roko Construction and Concorp International. In their tender evaluation report, the consultants recommended that the contract be awarded to Concorp. However, the Ministry of Labour turned this down, mainly on security grounds as the company was Sudanese-owned. In July 1994 the contract was awarded to Alcon, a company owned by a group of Kenyan Asians. The project was to cost $16 160 000 and be completed within two years. In May 1996 the contract was altered both in duration and cost following a decision by the NSSF to re-design the building. Completion time was extended to March 1998 and the contract sum increased to $25 226 917. Alcon, however, fell behind schedule in its construction work and its contract was terminated in May 1998. By then, Alcon had received payment of at least $28 million from the Ugandan government. The contract was later retendered and won by Roko Construction. Thus, by the time the Workers' House project was completed in 2001, its total cost amounted to over $40 million.

A parliamentary committee inquiring into the affairs of NSSF reported in August 1998 that the project tendering process through which Alcon won the contract had not been open and transparent. The NSSF Board and the Minister of Labour and Social Development, Ateker Ejalu, 'had already settled for Alcon, and the rest of the pre-award activities and processes were make-believe' (Parliament of Uganda 1998: 29). Information provided by NSSF's secretary about Alcon's record in neighbouring Kenya was ignored, as was the fact that Alcon had ceased to exist as a company in Kenya in November 1993 (Parliament of Uganda 1998: 32, 36). Moreover, Alcon, which was incorporated in the United Kingdom, was considered by some financial analysts to be grossly insolvent and highly risky. From the beginning, contended the parliamentary committee, it was obvious that Alcon was a briefcase company.

This was evident as well from the minutes of the NSSF board of directors meeting of 13 June 1994. In spite of serious concern expressed by the board secretary about the suspect corporate and financial status of Alcon, the meeting approved the award of the tender to Alcon. The information presented on the credibility of Alcon was ignored and in the view of board members interviewed this was evidence of improper lobbying carried out by Alcon.

A newspaper editorial stated that the 'NSSF Board then, and people in the ministry had a vested interest in Alcon getting the contract'.[11] In its pursuit of the lucrative construction contract, Alcon was said to have made unofficial payments to a number of NSSF board members and top managers as well as government ministers. Various NSSF personnel and politicians were alleged to have pocketed kickbacks. Alcon officials told a closed session of the parliamentary probe team that they had given $300 000 to a relative of the NSSF managing director in a bid to get the contract (Parliament of Uganda 1998: 47-8).[12] Alcon was also alleged to have bought his land in Entebbe at well above the market price. Public officials and politicians as well as a foreign company had co-operated closely to their mutual advantage, but to the detriment of integrity in state governance.

The National ID Tender

Foreign firms have paid bribes to secure lucrative government contracts to produce national identity cards in African countries. In 2001, for instance, French electronics giant, SAGEM SA, was alleged to have paid bribes to Nigerian cabinet ministers and government officials to win a $214 million identity card contract over its international competitors.[13] In Uganda, as well, foreign business corruption was evident in the national ID tender.

Calls for an expression of interest in the National Population Databank and Identification System project were made in March 2005. Later that year, in November, a South African firm, Face Technologies, emerged as the best evaluated bidder. It beat the Israeli Supercom and the British-based Contec Global for the lucrative $100 million project. But on 19 November, Minister of State for Finance Isaac Musumba wrote to Contec Global, ranked third by the evaluation committee, and invited them 'as a successful bidder to come and negotiate with Government the modalities of execution of the project'.[14] 'Musumba was advised of his irregular action' by senior Treasury officials, whereupon he wrote a similar backdated letter to the other two bidders. A few days later, on 23 December, Musumba accompanied Contec Global officials to meet President Yoweri Museveni. The minister also issued a personal cheque on 6 January 2006 for 28 700 000 Uganda shillings ($15 400) as partial payment for the travel bill for the team that would visit projects of the three companies, although Finance Ministry officials had advised him that site visits were not part of the scoring scheme for the evaluation. In the meantime, the contracts committee held negotiations with Face Technologies and on 10 January reported that negotiations had been completed successfully. The following day, however, Musumba wrote to Treasury officials arguing against awarding the contract to Face Technologies. In a subsequent letter of 27 January, Musumba declared 'The best evaluated bid was of FT who got 81.6% [while Supercom scored 66.7% and Contec Global 65.9%] but the best company evaluated at the post-qualification was Contec Global with 84% score'. After the site visits, Musumba claimed Contec Global should negotiate with government for the contract.

Following complaints of foul play, the Minister of Finance suspended the project, while the Inspector General of Government (IGG), the government's anti-corruption agency, investigated the evaluation and awarding of the contract. In August 2006, the IGG recommended cancellation of the project citing various irregularities in the bidding process. In particular, the IGG accused Musumba of gross interference, manipulation and influence peddling in favour of Contec Global. As a Kampala newspaper had editorialised earlier in the year, 'A minister was reported to have flouted every tendering rule in the book in an apparent attempt to make a company win the multi-billion [shilling] deal to process national identity cards'.[15] The IGG also said that 'multinational companies from the donor countries get involved in influence peddling to get large scale contracts' (Nyanzi 2006). And as a well-informed journalist said to us, 'foreign companies understand well how the system works. They need a political godfather to oil the wheels for the system to turn'.

It was alleged that Musumba was given a kickback of $1.8 million by a foreign company (Kyamutetera 2006). The IGG exonerated Musumba of this particular allegation, but our interviewees insisted that he had received money in cash from Contec Global. Payments to politicians and government officials are impossible to confirm. But several questions can be raised to show Musumba's irregular conduct:

- why and in what capacity did Musumba invite the third-ranked bidder for negotiations?;
- why did he accompany Contec Global to meet the President?; and
- why did he issue a personal cheque for the contract team to carry out a site evaluation?

Answers to such questions provide circumstantial evidence, as confirmed by the IGG's probe report, of Musumba peddling influence and fronting a foreign company.[16]

Some Further Cases

Not only Western companies, but also African firms, are known to make payments to government ministers and bureaucrats to secure contracts. TI has identified South African companies as being particularly prone to payment of bribes when doing business in other African countries, a view endorsed strongly by a seasoned South African business journalist: 'Although many businesspeople claim that bribes are actively solicited in many African countries ... a number of businesspeople from other African countries tell me that foreigners, including South Africans, are quick to offer bribes' (Games 2006). One such firm cited by Ugandan informants was the South African Mobile Telecom Network (MTN). Unlike some other African countries, there was no mobile phone licence auction in Uganda. Instead, MTN was alleged to have secured the licence to operate the mobile phone business in April 1998 largely on account of its connections and corruption. 'Its bribery was so comprehensive,' related a well-placed official describing how MTN's agents paid off government ministers and parliamentarians during the company's intense lobbying to win the contract. According to an impeccable source, President Museveni's brother, Salim Saleh, allegedly received a substantial payment from MTN's agent. MTN obtained a very favourable contract that included an exclusivity clause preventing any other company from entering the lucrative sector for a period of six years.[17]

As implied by the Alcon case study, Kenyan Asian firms also have a reputation for engaging in corrupt practices in African countries. On 4 April 2003, a contract valued at $112 million was signed between the Ugandan government and a Kenyan firm, Bidco Oil Refineries. According to the contract, the government undertook to give Bidco 26 500 hectares of land on a 99-year lease to develop palm oil plantations. Bidco was also given various incentives, including exemption from company tax for 25 years and concessions on water and electricity. The agreement also gave Bidco monopoly status barring any other local or international investment in a similar project. Questions began to be asked as to how Bidco could acquire such highly concessionary terms from government. Well-informed respondents mentioned money being exchanged during private negotiations between government and the beneficiary. Two government ministers were alleged to have come back from Kenya each with around $2 million in cash. Moreover, the report of the parliamentary committee on finance, planning and economic development that investigated the Bidco agreement was not tabled by order of the Speaker. Indeed, the day the report was completed, President Museveni officially launched the project.

Uganda's emergent oil sector is evolving in non-transparent ways, and, with international competition for oil increasing, it is ripe for corruption as has happened elsewhere in Africa.[18] Over a ten-year period, 1997–2007, the Ugandan government signed four production sharing agreements (PSAs) with Western oil companies. PSAs enabled these companies to prospect for oil in western Uganda around Lake Albert. Foreign companies pay signature bonuses on new agreements.[19] In 2004 the signature bonus paid by the Canadian firm, Heritage Oil and Gas for a new PSA was around $6 million. Government officials cite a much lower amount. No public scrutiny of Heritage's agreements on oil exploration has been permitted and the close relations evolving between President Museveni and Tony Buckingham, the CEO of Heritage, whose private security firms in oil- or mineral- rich Angola and Sierra Leone earned him notoriety in the 1990s, raise concern for good governance in Uganda's emergent oil sector.[20]

Moreover, Libyan leader, Muammar al-Qadaffi, has been closely associated with the Toro royal family for several years and many of the prospects for oil are in the territory of the Toro kingdom. The Libyans have acquired rights to build a small refinery in western Uganda and also won a construction deal to extend the Kenya oil pipeline from Eldoret to Kampala. Both contracts were obtained under unclear circumstances. In addition, there have been several other recent Libyan investments in Uganda. These have included Libyan acquisition of 69% of Uganda Telecom, 60% of Tristar (a company set up by Sri Lankans to export garments to the US under the African Growth and Opportunity Act) and 49% of Uganda's largest real estate developer, the National Housing and Construction Company; deals concluded 'under the table, without open bidding'.[21]

Chinese companies have been evident in Uganda in the past two decades, especially in the construction sector. As noted above, SITCO paid bribes to secure a dam construction contract in the early 1990s. Recently, a Chinese company won the lucrative $80 million deal to reconstruct the decaying State House in Entebbe, amid rumours of bribes being paid to government leaders. China is showing interest in the development of Uganda's oil resources, but has yet to commit itself as it has done in neighbouring Sudan.

Conclusion

In this chapter, it has been shown that the existence of potentially lucrative contracts as well as competition among rival foreign firms to win profitable business has generated influence peddling and graft by foreign companies. Foreign firms have offered payments and other material benefits to, as well as colluded with, officials and politicians to gain advantage in government decision-making. As the IGG commented in 2002: 'some multinational companies have been fuelling corruption in the Ugandan public service' and improperly influencing the bidding process for public contracts.[22] Foreign business bribery as well as attendant collusive state-business interactions have had pernicious consequences for state governance in Uganda.

Many foreign business firms evidently do not observe the principles of competitive bidding to attain the contracts they so ardently desire. Instead, international companies may do their utmost to stifle open competition, preferring to influence government decision makers through local intermediaries to gain access to coveted contracts and deals. An early study on Nigeria demonstrated the extent of the use of middlemen by foreign firms concerned with winning government custom (Turner 1976). In Uganda, we have seen how most concerns usually approached government through politically well-connected intermediaries who leveraged the structures of power to acquire desired contracts. Most foreign business concerns used middlemen to make illicit offers and payments on the company's behalf to win major, profitable deals.

Government decision-making has been marred by many irregularities from collusion between state personnel and the representatives of foreign business. Evidence has been provided of foreign companies obtaining preferential treatment from government ministers in order to win contracts and deals over their competitors. Collusion and corrupt transactions can affect the way the state operates and carries out its functions. In particular, connections and bribes have become important in Ugandan government decision-making. Illicit payments, expensive holiday trips or property purchased at above market prices have weakened the building of a reliable, professional public administration. Corrupt and collusive state-business interactions have also undermined the political importance of Parliament in Uganda. Legislators have been bought and their integrity compromised.

A further area in which foreign business payments have had an impact has been as a source of funding for ruling parties in African countries. International companies have quietly contributed to the coffers of the regimes that helped them to profit through corrupt means. They have financed these regimes to maintain them in power. Thus in Uganda, various foreign companies made financial donations to the ruling National Resistance Movement (NRM) candidate in both the 2001 and 2006 presidential elections. Western diplomatic sources claim that the Chinese Communist Party also contributed funds to President Museveni in 2006. Moreover, Uganda's political leaders have used the payments received from foreign firms for other political purposes. In 2004, for instance, they used such money to influence MPs to amend the constitution to enable President Museveni to stand for a third term. In this and other ways, foreign business has helped to keep in power those who have enabled it to win highly profitable contracts and deals.

International aid donors have been conspicuous in their reluctance to confront foreign business bribery in African countries (Hellman, Jones and Kaufman 2000).[23] It is important to distinguish between facilitating payments (payments offered to African officials to expedite routine governmental action) and larger bribes paid to senior state personnel to secure a commercial contract. The former is often initiated by public officials and is usually tolerated by international donors, especially if they are small and the norm. Foreign firms, however, may be more likely to initiate the latter, although public officials and politicians actively seek to benefit from the demands of foreign business. In most Western countries, bribery of foreign public officials is a crime but one for which companies are rarely prosecuted. International donors have tended to view it with remarkable complacency. They have often overlooked it, and, indeed, evinced less than strong interest in addressing the problem of commercial bribery. This donor indifference was evident, for example, when the World Bank disregarded many of the early reports questioning the Bujagali dam's propriety. The result is that private foreign firms run hardly any risks in proffering bribes because they are unlikely to be detected and punished.[24] Another feature is that non-Western firms are emulating this conduct in international business transactions as they make illicit offers and payments to public officials and politicians.

Acknowledgement

I wish to thank Andrew M. Mwenda, managing editor of the Ugandan weekly, *The Independent*, for many stimulating and informative discussions on the topic of this chapter.

Notes

1. J. Rawlings, 'Address to the Special United Nations Millennium Summit'. *West Africa* 10 Oct. 2000.
2. Y.K. Museveni quoted in *East African Business Week* 12 June 2006.
3. These are the words of Guido Penzhorn, an advocate who led the Lesotho government team that secured convictions of several Western firms for paying bribes in the Lesotho Highlands Water Project. The quotations are from *The Economist* 21 Sep. 2002.
4. In a report on Uganda, the World Bank commented, 'The contractor SIETCO, originally awarded the bid for the Owen Falls Hydro-electric Dam Extension Project and subsequently removed for non-compliance, claims that 30 percent of the UShs 84 billion contract price had to be paid in bribes to officials of the Uganda Electricity Board' (Recommendations for strengthening the anti-corruption campaign, Dec. 1998: 40).
5. World Bank dam in Uganda overpriced by $280 million: press release from International Rivers Network, 20 Nov. 2002.
6. *Uganda Confidential* 5 Feb. 1999. The author has seen a letter from three MPs – the chairs of parliamentary committees on works, statutory authorities, and legal affairs – sent to Richard Kaijuka calling for his resignation as he had demanded 'a bribe of $500 000 from Nile Independent officials out of which [he] received $240 000 with the balance to be paid . . . after the signing of the agreement between Uganda Electricity Board and Nile Independent Power'.
7. AES has been tainted with other shady deals in international business. For instance, an investigation carried out by the *Financial Times* showed that in 1988 AES and Enron colluded to rig the auction for the largest electric distribution company in Latin America (Sevastopulo 2003).
8. The accounts manager of AES Nile Power Limited, Harriet Kabayondo, claimed that $400 000 was authorised by the company director to pay bribes to local politicians. The author has seen a letter from seven MPs to the World Bank dated 12 Dec. 2001 alleging corruption in the Bujagali dam project.
9. *New Vision* (Kampala) 8 Sep. 2002.
10. World Bank officials informed the author that corruption allegations linked to the Bujagali project had been fully investigated. The investigations had been unable to find evidence to support the allegations.
11. *The Monitor* 17 Apr. 1998.
12. In its 1998 report, Recommendations for strengthening the anti-corruption campaign, Dec. 1998, the World Bank noted as follows: 'The company constructing a headquarters

building for NSSF alleges that they were required to pay a bribe of US$1 million to obtain the contract. The IGG demands that the company be barred from future government contracts. The NSSF Managing Director is sent on leave but may be reinstated' (40).

13. *Financial Times* (London) 23 Jan. 2006.
14. Unless otherwise stated, this section draws on two leaked letters: one from Isaac Musumba to the Prime Minister, 30 Jan. 2006; and the other from Keith Muhakanizi, Acting Permanent Secretary to the Treasury, to the Prime Minister, 7 Feb. 2006.
15. *Daily Monitor* 24 Jan. 2006.
16. We are unable to consider here allegations of corruption levelled against the South African company, Face Technologies.
17. In 2000-1, MTN was remitting eleven billion Uganda shillings ($6 million a month or around $70 million a year). A number of Ugandan MPs began voicing complaints against the high level of profit repatriation. It is alleged that members of the parliamentary committee on the national economy were bought off to prevent a parliamentary investigation into the matter taking place. More recently, there have been allegations that members of the Communications Commission have been bribed not to enforce regulation of MTN activities. For instance, little has been done to make MTN comply with its obligations to list the company on the local stock exchange. It is also alleged that through spending heavily on advertising in the local media, MTN is able to ensure discreet and selective reporting of its activities in Uganda.
18. For instance, in 2003 executives of France's state-owned company, Elf, were jailed over corrupt practices including illegal payments to African leaders in Gabon to guarantee that French, and not rival Western firms, pumped the oil.
19. In documents made public, it was shown that in 2001 British Petroleum paid the Angolan government a $111 million signature bonus.
20. It is alleged that a partner of Buckingham in the security firm, Executive Outcomes, set up a subsidiary called Saracen in Uganda in co-operation with President Museveni' s brother, Salim Saleh; and that Saracen guarded the gold mining activities of Branch Energy, in which Saleh had a stake.
21. *East African* 17 Mar. 2008.
22. *New Vision* 18 Mar. 2002.
23. The World Bank has, however, occasionally cancelled support for projects where bribery has been involved. For example, in 2000 it cancelled a $100 million loan for a water project in Ghana. It was found that a $5 million bribe had been paid to senior government officials by the US company that had been awarded the contract (*Africa Confidential* 17 Mar. 2000).
24. Testifying before a committee of the US Congress in July 2004, the lead prosecutor in the case in the Lesotho High Court against international firms charged with bribery in the Katse Dam project said that none of the governments whose companies were found guilty of bribery had assisted the prosecution. A Canadian company, Acres International, and a German company, Lahmeyer International, were the only firms placed on the World Bank's list of disbarred firms that violated its fraud and corruption provisions.

References

Commission for Africa. 2005. *Our Common Interest*. London: Commission for Africa.

Darroch, F. 2005. 'Lesotho puts international business in the dock'. In: *Global Corruption Report 2005*, compiled by Transparency International. London: Pluto: 31-6.

——. 2006. 'Lesotho Highlands Water Project: corporate pressure on the prosecution and the judiciary'. In: *Global Corruption Report*, compiled by Transparency International. London: Oxford University Press: 87-92.

Games, D. 2006. 'South Africans among first to grease Africa's palm'. *Business Day* 9 Oct.

Hellman, J., G. Jones and D. Kaufman. 2000. 'Are foreign investors and multinationals engaging in corrupt practices in transition economies?' *Transition* May-July: 4-7.

Kaiza, D. 2002. 'Bujagali dam: fresh claims of bribery could stall project'. *The East African* 8 July.

Kyamutetera, M. 2006. 'ISO asks IGG to probe Musumba'. *Daily Monitor* 24 Jan.

Moody-Stuart, G. 1997. *Grand Corruption: How Business Bribes Damage Developing Countries*. Oxford: World View Publishing.

Mugunga, J. 2000. 'British investors fear Uganda'. *The Monitor* 25 Aug.

Munaita, P. 2001. 'Kaca Bill: govt using wrong tactics'. *Daily Nation* 9 Aug.

Munene, M. 2002. 'Private sector abetting graft'. *Daily Nation* 1 Feb.

Musumba, I. 1999. 'Who is not telling the truth on Bujagali power?' *The Monitor* 25 Feb.

Nyanzi, P. 2006. 'Donors fuelling fraud – IGG'. *Daily Monitor* 15 Sep.

Ozanne, J. 1991. 'Mr. Biwott the businessman: a look at the former Kenyan minister's road to riches'. *Financial Times* (London) 27 Nov.

Pallister, D. 2003. 'Africa dam's passage eased by bribes'. *Guardian* (London) 3 Nov.

Parliament of Uganda, 1998. *Report of the Standing Committee on Commissions, Statutory Authorities and State Enterprises on the National Social Security Fund*. Kampala: Parliament.

Phillips, M. 2002. 'AES uncovers bribery in Bujagali dam project'. *Wall Street Journal* 4 July.

Sevastopulo, D. 2003. 'AES colluded with Enron to rig bid for Latin American energy group'. *Financial Times* 21 May.

Svensson, J. 2001. 'The cost of doing business: firms' experience with corruption'. In: *Uganda's Recovery: The Role of Farms, Firms, and Government*, edited by R. Reinikka and P. Collier. Washington: World Bank.

Transparency International. 2006. 'Bribe payers index'. In: *Global Corruption Report* London: Oxford University Press.

Turner, T. 1976. 'Multinational corporations and the instability of the Nigerian state'. *Review of African Political Economy* 5: 63-79.

CHAPTER SIXTEEN

Conclusion

Towards a Response

Roger Southall and Henning Melber

This collection of essays has presented Africa as the object of a new round of scramble. The major thrust has been one of continued external focus on the extraction of Africa's resources, renewed exploitation, accumulation by dispossession, marginalisation of African economic actors, uneven and niched development, the extension of unfair trade and the corruption of African elites. Yet while this emphasises the cost of the new scramble, there is also a case for saying that it possibly offers opportunity too. Certainly, this is the argument put forward by bodies like the World Bank and African Development Bank, as well as a host of commentators. Their argument is that significantly increased demand for scarce commodities, such as oil, gas, uranium and minerals, activated notably by Chinese, but also Indian and other Southern late industrialisation, provides African countries with unprecedented possibilities of growth, investment and development. Given the more usual focus upon Africa as the backward continent of stagnant economies, poverty, war and declining human development prospects, this shift is clearly to be welcomed – cautiously. Furthermore, it would be naïve to think that ordinary African people do not want more investment, more employment opportunities, improved access to consumer goods and greater involvement in all the benefits the modern world has to offer. So the question is posed: what should the response to the new scramble be?

This new scramble has since the drafting of the contributions to this volume rather turned into a new tumble with the collapse of the global financial markets. The result has since then been a declining demand for some (though not all) of Africa's resources and a corresponding decline of world market prices (such as for copper and diamonds, but also for oil). The global crisis, to which Africa contributed least, has major negative effects for the continent too. Its dependency from asymmetric relations with the outside world and hence vulnerability with regard to external shocks is becoming brutally evident once again. The impressive economic growth rates recorded during the last few years until 2007/8 at least in the resource-rich African economies had to be adjusted in sobering forecasts for the years to come (IMF 2009). This confirms that the short-lived bonanza has failed to trigger more self-reliant socio-economic trends, which would reduce the dependency syndrome. Despite emerging alternatives in a new multi-polar world with new potent global state actors, African countries seem to have not (yet?) reaped any lasting benefits from the temporary boom. This sobering assessment does not, however, render the question irrelevant, of which nature the 'African' interaction with the external counterparts should be.

Imperialism: Pioneer of Progress?

It is appropriate at this point to remind ourselves of the perspective of Warren (1980) whose major text, published posthumously, argued the case that imperialism was the pioneer to capitalism in the countries of Asia, Africa and Latin America. His fundamental lament was that post-Leninist Marxist analyses of imperialism had reversed the views of the founders of Marxism, 'who held that the expansion of capitalism into pre-capitalist areas of the world was desirable and progressive' (1980: 3). Marx and Engels had viewed imperialism as raising the level of productive forces in societies they saw as backward compared with the capitalist West. In contrast, Lenin's theory of imperialism proposed the advent of a new and regressive stage of monopoly capitalism. Critically, this offered not merely a practical, political foundation in the quest of the Bolsheviks for allies against the powerful centres of capitalist state power, but ignored the major analytical achievements of Marxist economics. Whereas the latter acknowledged capitalist penetration of non-capitalist areas, for all its violence, as providing for historical progress; Leninism substituted this insight by a crude theory of under-consumption, that is, the inability of the Western proletariat to provide an adequate market for capital. The outcome was that the projected world revolution against imperialism – 'a fusion of the movement of the working class against its bourgeois rulers in the West and the revolt of the colonial and semi-colonial peoples against the major capitalist powers' – turned out not to be a revolution against capitalism as such, but simply a struggle against particular capitalist countries (Warren 1980: 5).

According to Warren, this misapprehension confused two distinct movements: the socialist working-class movement in the industrialised capitalist countries and the intrinsically bourgeois movement of Third World nationalism; the one striking at the state system in Europe and North America to establish socialism, the other striking at the same target to promote the faster and further growth of industrial capitalism (Warren 1980: 5). One result, ultimately, was the disarming of the working-class movements of Asia, Africa and Latin America in the struggle by bourgeois nationalists for their political and cultural independence. From this perspective, post-war theories of underdevelopment are best regarded as successors to Lenin's *Imperialism*, with the concept of neo-colonialism providing a vehicle for the wholesale transfer of Leninist theory to the post-independence period. Its emphasis on parasitism and pillage of the Third World was perfectly suited to the psychological needs and political requirements of nationalists and, indeed, progressive intellectuals (Warren 1980: 8–9).

After putting forward his empirical case for the historically progressive effects of colonialism – notably advances in health, education and the provision of new consumer goods, all of which are particularly favourable to the expansion of productive forces – Warren tackled what he termed the illusion of under-development by reference to five criteria:

- first, he argued that there has been a substantial, sometimes impressive, rise in the per capita gross national product (GNP) of many Third World countries, compared with both their pre-war record and indeed with many advanced economies;
- second, he suggested that rapid economic progress in the Third World had not been inherently associated with rising inequality as much underdevelopment theorising proposed. While rising inequality had often been associated with the outset of rapid growth, the tendency had been for inequality to decline as growth continued;
- third, contrary to assertions about the increasing marginalisation of Third World populations, estimates of the level of unemployment fairly consistently referred to open unemployment whose calculation downplayed underemployment and work in the informal sector, neither of which could be dismissed as merely parasitic and redistributive because in reality they were often highly productive;
- fourth, far from the rising volume of goods and services available to Third World countries providing luxuries to a few, they increasingly satisfied the

basic needs of the majority. This was indicated by various development indicators based upon reasonably objective factors from life expectancy through to productivity and energy consumption (measures today customarily expressed through the United Nations Development Programme's Human Development Index);

- finally, despite assertions to the contrary, 'the underdeveloped world as a whole has made considerable progress in industrialization', with manufacturing output rising faster in the underdeveloped world than in advanced countries throughout the post-war period (Warren 1980: 241).

Warren's overall conclusion was that 'titanic strides forward' (1980: 252) had been made in the establishment, consolidation and growth of capitalism in the Third World since 1945, with corresponding advances in material welfare and the expansion of productive forces. This did not mean that many of the benefits of development had not been squandered by policy blunders, not least those associated with inappropriate imposition of liberal welfare measures or Soviet-style development prescriptions. Yet the fundamental failure in both much development thinking and in many countries was to recognise that most Third World countries had been developing in a capitalist direction, explicit recognition of which would have allowed for a 'more efficient and humane capitalist development' (Warren 1980: 254). Central to this was the notion that 'as Third World capitalism grows, imperialism (as a system of domination by advanced over less-developed capitalist states) declines' and that 'as Third World capitalism develops, the working class is destined to play its classic revolutionary role' (Sender 1980: xiii).

Looking back from our vantage point of the early twenty-first century, there are solid grounds for arguing that Warren's perspective has, to a considerable extent, been vindicated. After all, development theory today has to account for the remarkable industrial advance of numerous countries especially in East and South East Asia. Furthermore, the new scramble for Africa is heavily constructed around the dramatically rapid late industrialisation of China, India and other emergent markets, as they are so often termed, even if we may take serious issue with his notion of imperialism, as opposed to the notion of the imperialism of particular powers (notably the US) being in decline. However, what is equally remarkable in retrospect, is how little contemporary Africa, and debate about Africa, conforms with Warren's vision.

Responding to Warren

The easy criticism of Warren is that today his eulogy to capitalism in the Third World as progress reads as if it could have been published by the World Bank – rather than by Verso, the publishing house of the *New Left Review*. That may be so,[1] yet we can argue from our present vantage point as follows.

First, as noted, the Third World industrialisation of which Warren writes has largely passed African countries by. There are, of course, a number of countries, such as South Africa, Kenya, Egypt and Algeria that possess significant manufacturing sectors, although in the first of these, at least, manufacturing is today declining. Indeed, the implications of this were the subject of much discussion even as Warren was writing in the late 1970s with, for instance, the important Kenya debate, and that about African capitalism in general, revolving around the characteristics and developmental potential of an emergent African capitalist bourgeoisie. Against this, what strikes the contemporary reader of Warren's text is how little he draws upon African, especially sub-Saharan African, examples to support his generalisations: his Third World is overwhelmingly Asian and Latin American.[2] African countries feature little in his tabulations by country of manufacturing and even per capita income and life expectancy. By contrast, the new scramble perspective, as presented in this book and elsewhere is that:

- Africa's contribution to world manufacturing remains marginal, having been subject to structural adjustment programmes that, whether deliberately or not, have worked to de-industrialise many projects developed under colonialism or during the post-independence phase of import-substitution;
- foreign direct investment (FDI) in Africa largely eschews manufacturing in favour of resource extraction, deliberately cut off as far as it can be from the host society, often physically as well as symbolically by walls, razor wire and the privatisation of security. Otherwise, projects are geared to export platforms (such as the US African Growth and Opportunity Act, AGOA) that have a limited life expectancy and are therefore footloose and highly mobile; use exceptionally low-cost, casual labour; and whose dramatically fluctuating employment levels draw upon a reserve army of labour in the crudest of fashions;
- while the limited amount of FDI going into manufacturing is directed overwhelmingly at industries that are export-oriented (such as textiles), these latter are destined to compete with Asian (notably Chinese) industrial output whose production cost is in the long term likely to be lower;
- the collaborative linkage between international and multinational investors

and African elites is such that more capital flows out of Africa in the form of profits and deliberately obscured expatriation of resources by compradors than enters in the form of investment.

The second major retrospective comment upon Warren is that he was writing before African countries suffered the blitzkrieg of International Monetary Fund (IMF) and World Bank-initiated structural adjustment. The treatment of this in the literature has been vast, balancing the necessity or otherwise of macro-economic reform of African economies during the 1970s and 1980s against the impact: that is, whether or not the medicine was appropriate to the cure (Williams 1994). In chapter two of this book, an important overview of the neo-liberalisation of African political economy has been offered by Vishwas Sitgar. Suffice it to say here that the new scramble perspective has recently been eloquently expressed by Ferguson (2006). He argues that structural adjustment programmes as implemented by the IMF and World Bank were no less ideological, rigid and dogmatic than any application of scientific socialism and for that reason can be usefully depicted as scientific capitalism (Ferguson 1980: 76-9). They were characterised by amorality, economism and pseudo-technicism. However, their initially extremely narrow social and moral frame was later to be filled out by reference to good governance, sustainability, human rights and participation.

The new paradigm was supposed to liberalise structural adjustment away from the rigidity of 1980s-style market discipline and hence to provide it with greater legitimacy. It was based upon the assumption that the blame for economic failure rested upon the corruption and economic mismanagement of African governments. However, the reality was that the failed policies for which African governments were blamed, such as import-substitution industrialisation, had in large measure been pressed upon them by the IMF and World Bank themselves. Furthermore, while African governments were castigated for their lack of popular accountability, the IMF and World Bank complex was itself almost wholly unaccountable to African and Third World borrowers. Consequently, while its notion of good governance was that of a government that was efficient and technically functional, the legitimacy of governments in Africa depended rather upon the notion of ordinary Africans that governments should be morally benevolent and protective of their people. In this sense, governments that had been compelled to reduce their expenditure drastically on such items as health, education and social infrastructure under the rubric of structural adjustment, could scarcely hope to be considered good by the citizens over whom they ruled.

Nor, we may add, could they be said to have carried on the tradition of post-war development, identified by Warren, of developing the productive capacity of their population.

Critically, Africans have become increasingly conscious of the inability of their national governments to control either macro-economic processes or day-to-day living conditions. They are aware of the limitations of African governments to confront, not just market forces, but the strictures of the 'formidable institutions governing Africa from afar: the transnational financial institutions and the associated development agencies as well as non-governmental organizations (many of which are themselves transnational and western-based)' (Ferguson 1980: 87). They are therefore increasingly dissatisfied with the gospel of liberal democracy, recognising that while a change of government can bring important gains – and the importance of the overthrow of dictators should by no means be gainsaid – there is little chance of it increasing the capacity of their governments to make important decisions regarding their economic livelihood.

This leads logically to the third major criticism of Warren's overview, notably its major failure to deal with the nature of the Third World state, a failure particularly relevant to the contemporary condition of Africa. Warren's perspective was that Third World states were vehicles of bourgeois nationalism whose historic role was to sweep away the influences retarding the development of capitalism and to force the path of economic growth. Interestingly, he devotes little attention to the way such states should facilitate development, suggesting that he was little interested in whether a progressively upward path was an outcome of free-market or statist policies. Of course, his analysis pre-dates the growth of literature concerning the developmental state. Yet while a fair number of states in both Asia and Latin America may be said to approximate Warren's vision of historically progressive bourgeois nationalism, no more than a few, if any, African states can be similarly characterised, at least unambiguously so.[3] In contrast, the African state is more usually presented not just as weak or fragile, and hence lacking the capacity to foster development even if it wants to, but largely devoid of internal legitimacy and resting upon a basis of neo-patrimonialism. Rulership rests upon the benefits of patronage dispensed to subordinates, often according to ethnic rather than modern class ties, by Big Men in government, with the president customarily the Biggest Man of all.[4] Furthermore, because of the depiction by underdevelopment theory of African ruling elites as subordinate to the dictates of foreign governments and capital, as well as the availability of ample and solid empirical evidence, African states are typically presented as corrupt.

It is not necessary to dwell upon the fact that definitions of corruption are contested, except to note that there is widespread recognition throughout much of Africa that politicians in power expect to 'eat'. More importantly, in the present context, it is necessary to acknowledge that the predominant view of African states as patrimonial can be said to justify IMF, World Bank and donor calls for good governance. Who, after all, is going to support bad governance? Indeed, it is precisely because the anti-corruption and pro-democracy agendas of the IMF and World Bank chime with the similar ambitions of political progressives and a range of actors on the ground who are missing out and denied the prospect of 'eating', that they enjoy considerable salience.

There is, of course, a good deal of common sense behind the view that a government that adheres to the major tenets of good governance – subjecting itself at regular intervals to re-election and possible defeat; securing the rule of law; and rendering itself accountable – is one likely to appeal to foreign investors. However, it is at this point that the IMF and World Bank argument breaks down, for reality indicates that even if multinational corporations might prefer to work with liberal democratic governments, their investment behaviour is determined by the prospect of profit and the ease of doing business. In other words, while liberal democracy may be desirable, it is also eminently dispensable. Indeed, where it is to their advantage, multinational companies demonstrate no lack of compunction in acting in total opposition to the professed ideological norms of the IMF and World Bank, not least through the systematic payment of commissions and bribes to members of local elites in order to gain or maintain access to resources and opportunity.

It is no coincidence that the highest rates of foreign investment and economic growth are to be found not in countries which score highly on democratic rankings as drawn up by bodies such as Freedom House, but in countries such as oil producers Angola, Equatorial Guinea, Nigeria and Sudan as well as mineral-rich countries like the Democratic Republic of Congo, whose governance credentials are highly dubious but which possess resources that are most in global demand.

Angola enjoyed one of Africa's better rates of economic growth throughout its civil war during the 1980s and has not looked back since. Its oil industry is conducted almost overwhelmingly offshore, very little of its wealth even enters the wider society and despite over a quarter of a century of booming oil production, Angolans rank as some of the poorest people in the world (Ferguson 2006: 198). Equatorial Guinea, a country run by a ruthless government that operates as little more than a trust for the ruling Nguema family, offers a similarly dismal picture and much the same can be said for other resource-rich countries such as Gabon; and even those like Botswana and Namibia praised for at least better, if not good, governance practices.[5] Nor are war and civil disorder a bar to foreign investment where their effects upon production can be contained, as illustrated again by Angola in the 1980s, and Sudan and Chad today. This underlines another, local perspective that due to the material interests involved and the explosive mix of greed and grievances, civil war can by no means always be labeled 'a stupid thing' as Cramer (2006) has provocatively put it, again with prominent empirical reference to Angola. Finally, the neo-liberal discourse of good governance is used to discipline credit-dependent African governments; that is, to proscribe their economic options. In contrast, it is the exception rather than the rule for either resource-rich countries or the multinational corporations collaborating with them to be similarly subject to discipline. The Angolan example can suffice.

In spite of an astonishing revenue stream, the Angolan government is some $11 billion in debt and has such a bad record of repayment that nearly all conventional credit lines have been severed (Global Witness 1999: 6).

> The government has therefore turned (in defiance of the IMF) to commercial banks issuing short-term, oil-banked loans at very high rates . . . This has enabled not just the looting of the revenue from current production, but the mortgaging of future revenues for years into the future. Indeed, oil production is now so fully mortgaged that the government in recent years has had very little net revenue. It can pay for its current operations only by taking new loans (which continue to be offered thanks to the rapid recent increase of new confirmed ultra-deep water oil reserves). The whole system is underwritten by a system of export-credit guarantees (issued by the United States and other rich nations) that provide an effective taxpayer subsidy to investor's risk (Ferguson 2006: 199).

To be sure, Angola has recently sought to reduce its dependence upon the international financial institutions (IFIs) by taking a massive $4 billion oil-backed loan from the China Exim Bank, in exchange for which 70% of public tenders for the construction and civil engineering contracts tabled for national reconstruction will be awarded to Chinese companies approved by Beijing (Corkin 2008). However, critics might argue that while in practice securing the debts owed to Western multinationals, such Chinese assistance seems destined to encourage rather than constrain Angolan government profligacy. It is estimated that around 25% of state revenues disappear annually in Angola, while 'government partners in receipt of aid were not the relevant ministries . . . but the president's office, raising questions as to what proportion of the loan in fact ended in productive investment' (Henderson 2008: 13). Meanwhile, no international banks have yet made a name for themselves by declining to accept the funds systematically siphoned off from the public purse by heinously corrupt ruling elites from Angola or indeed any other resource-rich African country.

This brings us to a final, and perhaps most fundamental, criticism of Warren: the suggestion that as Third World capitalism grows, imperialism declines. Indeed, it is thoroughly remarkable that in a book surveying Third World development written in the late 1970s Warren totally ignores the impact of the Cold War upon the countries of Africa, Asia and Latin America. For instance, the Vietnam War receives not a single mention. Yet there is manifest evidence that the global battle between the US and the Western world against the Soviet Union and China had a profoundly destabilising and devastating effect upon numerous countries in all three continents, while promoting the development of others. This has been so extensively documented that there is no need for any further excursion here, except to illustrate the manner in which the US conspired to oust Patrice Lumumba in the Congo in contrast to the systematic support it offered to white regimes in southern Africa and the massive financial and military aid it provided to countries like South Korea (Harris 1986; Kalb 1982). Indeed, as argued by a multiplicity of Marxist and other writers with whom Warren might have chosen to engage, it was during the first four to five post-war decades that the US established itself as a global imperial power, ultimately confounding the similar but domestically flawed bid by the Soviet Union to do likewise. However, while the collapse of Soviet Communism and its associated empire was hailed by many as providing for a US-dominated, unipolar world and a level of US global hegemony that had no historical precedent, this vision was within a remarkably short space of time to be challenged by enormous changes in the international division of labour and the current rise of China as an industrial power. As argued by Harvey (2003), this transformation was to give rise to the aggressive attempt by the US to use military and political power to shore up the foundations of its economic hegemony that was crumbling under the pressures of rapid Chinese and other Southern industrialisation. It is precisely this context that has laid the basis for the new scramble.

Warren's excessively economistic argument falls short of illustrating that post-war capitalist development has caused imperialism to decline. It was only by effectively excluding politics and the state, whether in the advanced or developing countries, from his analysis that he was able to arrive at such a remarkably myopic conclusion. Yet having said that, it is important not to throw the baby out with the bathwater, for his fundamental argument is that the penetration of capitalism into the Third World is historically progressive. In contemporary African terms, this bald statement needs to be translated as follows:

- first, Africa needs capitalist development to realise its potential, but not the anti-developmental genre of capitalism promoted by the new scramble. This implies an environment favouring development of a progressive African (trans)national capitalist class alongside recognition of the major role that needs to be played by state capital;
- second, African capitalist development requires that African countries maximise opportunities provided by the hugely increased competitive demand for their resources represented by the new scramble. This will entail both confrontations and engagements with imperialisms of whatever hue;
- third, progressive African capitalist development will require appropriate forms of state and governance, and state and business relations, aimed at an investment-driven increase of productivity and value-adding economic activities, instead of mere consumption of profits and revenue income from rent-seeking. None of this is likely to be brought about without an intensification of democratic struggles combined with a certain amount of class-consciousness.

Confronting the Scramble

African development must remain centred on greater industrialisation if the employment and welfare needs of burgeoning African populations are to be met. In an era when the centre of gravity of world manufacturing production is shifting to China and other low-wage countries in the East, this is a bold – even foolhardy – statement to make. Yet we see no other way.

It is hugely unfashionable to call for capitalist development. Traditional left analysis of African development has been hostile to capitalism, equating it with an extension of imperialism. During the 1960s and early 1970s, the outcome was that progressive opinion favoured African or scientific socialist and hence heavily statist modes of development. Subsequently, with the collapse of such models, while the critique of capitalism and imperialism has been maintained, there has been a de-ideologisation of projected African development paths. Aware of the immense intellectual hostility that use of the C word evokes, development strategies and programmes, whether they be national, regional or continental, avoid stating explicitly that they are seeking to promote capitalist development. Indeed, the same goes for official documentation from the IMF and World Bank. Instead, capitalism as a strategy is neutralised by reference to FDI, business and the market. Capitalism is seemingly abolished by a stroke of the pen, or the keyboard, yet ironically all the major actors involved in this charade know precisely what they are about. It is just that it is impolite or incorrect to acknowledge the reality of capitalism. Yet this is simultaneously both dishonest and a block to proper analysis.

There is, of course, a considerable body of scholarly literature dealing with the characteristics of African capitalism. As elaborated by Roger Southall and Alex Comninos in chapter fourteen of this book, the fundamental thrust of analysis has dealt with the historical weakness of African capital and hence its dependence upon metropolitan capital and patronage and opportunity provided by the post-colonial state. In broad terms, it would seem that this situation pertains today, although this requires two important qualifications. The first is that we really don't know. In other words, there is an urgent need for a second round of studies of the condition of African capitalism. The second is that, as Southall and Comninos also suggest, there are some indications of stirrings:

- there is the appearance in recent years of a new generation of African entrepreneurs, businesspersons and capitalists, often with an international education background, who have developed their concerns under market conditions and who are wary of entanglement with the state. Importantly, they have a transnational African perspective, doing business across national borders or owning businesses in African countries other than their own;
- many larger-scale African businesspersons have attained their status as capitalists through favourable political access to capital, denationalised industries and so on. It is very possible, if not probable, that many such enterprises fail once they are deprived of political support. Yet this cannot be assumed. The model of political accumulation may be distasteful, dishonest, immoral, unfair and corrupt, yet there are numerous historical precedents for this route to capitalist development, however crude and indeed brutal it may be, as in Russia today;
- the course of Black Economic Empowerment (BEE) in South Africa has attracted enormous criticism, revolving around its creation of a politically-connected, crony capitalist elite. Much of this criticism is well founded. However, there are nonetheless indications that BEE has some internal momentum and that it is encouraging a genuinely black capitalist class. Significantly, a number of black-owned firms are venturing into other parts of Africa and entering into partnerships with local players.

It is fashionable to suggest that the way forward for African business is into services and, indeed, many of the new generation of entrepreneurs are involved in areas linked to computers and advanced technology. Yet traditionally, African entrepreneurship and capitalism have engaged in enterprise sectors designed to satisfy the consumer needs of the African market, from furniture through foodstuffs to chemicals. There is good reason for this: African businesspersons are far more likely to be aware of local market conditions and demands than external suppliers. Much of such activity will depend upon collaborative market relations, perhaps under franchise, with external capital. The key is whether such relationships are mutually beneficial and provide for profit retention in Africa. Suffice it to say that it is within the manufacturing and some service spheres that there is greatest scope for African capitalist development – because African businesspersons have a comparative advantage (knowledge of market conditions); and these are spheres where multinational companies either do not want to engage directly or to do so through franchises. The promotion of such African capitalist enterprise is progressive, particularly to the extent that industrialisation takes place on the basis of employment conditions that are fair and work that is decent.[6]

However, the new scramble provides two major obstacles to such African capitalist development. First, initiatives such as AGOA and the European Union's Economic Partnership Agreements appear designed to assist penetration of the African market by Western, or other externally-based, capital. Second, Africa is increasingly an outlet for cheaply-produced Chinese goods which, it has to be admitted, are meeting the consumer demands of poorer Africans. Often such goods are sold by locally established networks of Chinese traders who compete highly effectively with players in the African informal market. For instance, a recent overview of the impact of Chinese competition upon prospects for industrialisation in Africa suggests that this is likely to be harmful in both the short- and long-term future. The appropriate response might therefore be for African governments to attempt to insulate their infant industries from global competition, from China and India in particular, perhaps by a retreat to the earlier phase of import-substitution industrialisation, albeit within a regional context. However, it is noted that this may have the cost of reintroducing sub-optimum economies of scale (Kaplinsky 2008: 20). Whether this would be practical, given probable opposition from the IFIs, is another matter.

Whatever the particular response, it would seem to point in favour of: the rationalisation of regional economic arrangements away from the present confusing crosscutting *smörgasbord* (as illustrated by Margaret Lee in chapter four of this book) so as to maximise market opportunities for locally-established entrepreneurs; adoption of appropriate measures of market protection, which may require engagement with the World Trade Organisation; and formation of mutually-beneficial business partnerships with external capital, be that representative of multinational or Chinese companies. In this regard, the state may have an important role to play via the prescription of rules for local empowerment as promoted at the present time in South Africa, as well as the provision of a suitably favourable business environment attractive to FDI so beloved by neo-liberal prescriptions. In this regard, particular attention should be paid to the attraction of foreign African capital. What a weak domestic African capitalist class may not be able to do on its own might well be accomplished by a somewhat stronger transnational African capitalist class.

Worthy of consideration though such prescriptions might be, they do not go to the heart of the matter: that the new African scramble is far more about external scramble for resources than it is to capture limited markets. Here the dilemma is that the extraction of resources such as oil, gas and minerals requires huge amounts of capital and the application of highly advanced technology. In such circumstances, there is no alternative: significant African capitalist participation must be by the state, for it is only the state that is capable of deploying, consolidating and concentrating the levels of capital, expertise and technology needed to forge mutually beneficial partnerships with foreign investment corporations, whatever their origin. This is a fact of life largely ignored by the development literature, dominated as it is by the IMF and World Bank gospel of privatisation and the hollowing out of the state role in the economy. Yet the retention and even expansion of appropriate state companies would seem the major way forward to limit the exportation of surplus (sharing in profit), promoting local beneficiation and acquiring the necessary know-how needed to facilitate further African control over, as well as ownership of, valuable scarce resources. This is not to deny that the running of state companies does not present major problems regarding efficiency and decisional autonomy; but it is to insist that state-owned and aligned companies can and have played a major role in economic development in countries ranging from social democratic Scandinavia and post-war Britain to the developmental states of East and South East Asia.

There is no need for the widespread nationalisation of assets and companies pursued at present by Hugo Chávez in Venezuela. Not only is that likely to cause damaging confrontations with Western powers in which African countries are likely to be the losers, but it does assert the major gains to be made by private-public partnerships.

The African developmental landscape has been transformed by the new scramble, as foreign governments and companies tumble over themselves to secure favourable access to African riches. With global commodity prices for key resources having risen exponentially on the back of Chinese and other Southern late industrialisation, the conventional indicators of economic development in Africa – levels of inflow of capital investment, higher rates of economic growth and so on – have significantly improved. Hence the buoyancy of so much current writing about prospects for economic development in Africa compared with the widespread Afro-pessimism of previous decades.

Yet as analysed here and elsewhere, so much of the activity fostered by the new scramble is blatantly anti-developmental, little more than the looting of African resources by foreign capital in league with state elites without regard to general welfare or the future. Worse, whilst such asset stripping could provide the basis for primitive accumulation by a nascent African capitalist class, the more usual pattern seems to be the wholly unproductive expropriation of economic surplus by local elites and the export of huge commissions and profits to financial havens overseas. Incoming FDI in valuable resources is more than matched by the outflow of African capital to external destinations beyond the reach of local authorities and certainly the empty hands and stomachs of the local people. Thus an econometric analysis by Ndikumana and Boyce indicates that annual capital flight from the 40 sub-Saharan countries over the period 1970–2004 amounted to $420 million (in 2004 dollars), or about $607 billion if imputed interest earnings were to be included. Together, sub-Saharan countries are therefore net creditors to the rest of the world in the sense that:

> their private assets held abroad, as measured by capital flight including interest earnings, exceed their total liabilities as measured by the stock of external debt . . . the region's external assets are 2.9 times the stock of debts owed to the world. For some individual countries, the results are even more dramatic: for Cote d' Ivoire, Zimbabwe, Angola, and Nigeria the external assets are 4.6, 5.1, 5.3 and 6.7 times higher than their debt stocks respectively (Ndikumana and Boyce 2008: 6–7).

Given these dismally skewed proportions, the current increase in economic growth rates for mainly resource-rich economies and the massive investment flows from abroad into extractive industries and related sectors such as infrastructure for transport should not too quickly and uncritically be mistaken as a recipe for overcoming structural deficiencies. According to an IMF outlook for sub-Saharan Africa, private capital flows reached an estimated $50 billion in 2007. Still small compared with global capital flows, private investment for the first time exceeded official aid flows in 2006. But the FDI pattern remains largely unchanged, far from inducing a different way of capital accumulation that could promote a significant diversification of African economies. Even the IMF itself has contributed a note of caution (Deléchat, Kovanen and Wakeman-Linn 2008):

> In Africa, private capital flows occur in the context of large export receipts stemming from higher commodity and oil prices (Cameroon, Ghana, Nigeria, Senegal, and Zambia) and scaled-up official inflows (Uganda and Tanzania), compounding the challenges for policy-makers . . . Private capital flows are poised to replace official aid as the most important source of external finance for sub-Saharan Africa. This is a welcome development, but it puts a premium on sound macroeconomic management, transparent capital account policies, and financial sector reforms to ensure that countries use the inflows productively.

In the light of patterns of capitalist investment and exploitation that have characterised external interest in Africa's resources since the days of the slave trade, this sounds more like wishful thinking than a recipe for overcoming the structural deficiencies that limit the benefits of such development to a local elite.

The issue of asset stripping will be dealt with below. Here it is necessary first to deal with the prior question of how African countries might seek to maximise the opportunities provided by the new scramble. In general, there would seem to be two major routes to take.

The first is that of cartelisation. Massively rising demand for oil, gas, uranium and minerals like platinum and copper in particular provides an unprecedented opportunity for resource-rich African countries to act collectively to negotiate improved terms of business with resource-hungry investing companies and countries. This implies substitution of the short-term perspective that prevails at the moment, whereby African countries compete with each other to attract foreign investors, by a long-term perspective that is prepared to limit access to scarce resources – given the significant degrees of monopoly African countries currently, and for the foreseeable future, enjoy – for steadily upward revision of rewards.

The model of course is provided by the Organisation of Petroleum-Exporting Countries that has provided for surplus oil production to be retained by producing countries.

It may be, too, that such cartelisation would have to proceed upon a much wider South-South programme than any mere inter-African co-operation would allow. Such a course undoubtedly has its dangers, not least the inflationary risks if increased profits are not adequately and productively invested at home; as well as the equally likely hazard that the greed of elites would see burgeoning financial surpluses directed into wholly unproductive expenditure, or simply appropriated and recycled abroad. Indeed, the behaviour of petro-bourgeoisies in African oil-producing countries at present indicates that this latter outcome is almost certainly likely unless their excesses can be contained. However, if these dangers could be overcome, or at least limited, cartelisation offers potentially great advantages, ranging from the capacity for huge internal and regional investment and reduction of net African indebtedness to the restoration of public services butchered by structural adjustment. At the very least, it would provide more than adequate opportunity to ensure that local communities bearing the brunt of the costs of extraction – whether in terms of land loss, destruction of livelihoods or environmental despoliation – receive not just compensation, but proper reward.

The second, related strategy is for African resource-rich countries to singly or collectively play off foreign imperialisms and investors against each other. At one level, this strategy is widely pursued at present anyway as governments seek to sell their wares and investment opportunities to the higher bidder. Yet it is also being conducted at a much higher level in a way that is changing the tilt of the playing field. It is precisely because so much Chinese investment or involvement in resource extraction is devoid of conditionality and accompanied by inducement aid in terms of the provision of infrastructure, scholarships or arms that it is so widely welcomed by African governments. Never before have they been in so good a position to wriggle free of their historic subordination to the West. Yet as is so often pointed out, while the Chinese strategy promises multiple advantages, it nonetheless sometimes comes at a considerable cost to African people, as distinct from the benefits which accrue to their governments, because of Beijing's tendency to disregard human rights concerns and, where it is deemed necessary or convenient to do so, to engage co-operatively with dictators.[7]

Even so, it can be argued that the political and economic costs of this strategy are likely to increase rather than decrease as time moves on. Already, for instance, there is evidence (contrary to the conventional Western media view) that external pressures have propelled China into forcing concessions from the Sudanese government regarding Darfur (Srinivasan 2008), while similarly Beijing is said in some quarters to be increasingly wary of its linkages to rogue regimes like that of Robert Mugabe in Zimbabwe (Sachikonye 2008).[8] Meanwhile, the increasing Chinese presence on the continent forcing other actors to compete may significantly enlarge the space for African manoeuvre. Thus, one seasoned observer of the investment scene in Africa asserts that local businesses, labour, communities and policy makers in FDI-recipient countries are increasingly developing new ways of disciplining incoming capital. In Zambia, for instance, protests by local communities and trade unions against privatisation of state companies that resulted in the shedding of social assets and responsibilities for pension benefits, housing, health care and schools – although sometimes meeting state repression – have led to practical forms of resistance that have resulted in some significant concessions by investors, such as sourcing supplies from the local as opposed to the international market (Saunders 2008).

The counter to this proposition is that imperialisms will compete with each other to carve Africa up into new informal spheres of influence. The dangers of this are already apparent: the US-Soviet Cold War may yet be replaced by US-Chinese tension in which African concerns are trampled underfoot. As elaborated by Martin Rupiya and Roger Southall in chapter seven of this book, the new scramble is already inducing a new round of militarisation and the construction of externally determined military alliances that may yet prove both continentally divisive and, contradictorily, hugely politically destabilising and ultimately a threat to human security. Meanwhile, too, the Chinese preference for dealing bilaterally with African countries suggests that the outcome of Chinese aid might prove extremely haphazard. It is precisely because the potential costs of competing imperialisms or proto-imperialisms are so huge that serious, collective African consideration must be given to negating them.

The strength of IMF, World Bank and Western donor emphasis upon good governance is precisely that so much African governance has been, and is, bad: ineffective, inefficient, misguided, brutal and above all, venal. From this per-spective, the widespread critique concerning the limitations of liberal democracy in African conditions fails to provide alternatives other than that of a deepening of democracy: more popular participation, more accountability, more devolution of power downwards, and so on. To be sure, there are nationalist-cum-Leninist critics of Western imperialism who appear willing to support brutal dictatorships and sacrifice the rule of law in the name of African revolution;[9] yet bluntly put, their intellectual and strategic rationale for doing so is as shallow as their morality.[10] It is also the case that Chinese dismissals of Western-style democracy as unsuitable for Africa imply at best a preference for benign dictatorships in the absence of any seriously socialist oriented governments and at worst a cynical preparedness to shore up despots in exchange for gain. Overall, however, for all its practical shortcomings and for all its ideological linkage to the gospel of free markets, there is every indication that African peoples want more democracy, more entrenchment of liberal rights and more commitment to the rule of law as opposed to the law of individual rulers; and not less.

There is the obvious problem of how to achieve such a desirable end in the face of the steadfast determination of African ruling elites to maintain the style, instruments and fact of their predominance, and ensure that their access to material reward is not undercut or disrupted by a loss of their control over the state. We have no prescriptive answers about how to address this conundrum except to assert the customary package of backing for struggles for democracy and support for social movement struggles, such as those of the Ogoni people, against brutal expropriation of resources by alliances of domestic and foreign elites. In particular, it is clear that a major objective of struggle must be for rents appropriated and expatriated by African political elites to be returned and productively invested, a struggle that has major international implications and will require concerted and highly complicated battles against international banks and the world of global finance. Nor should there be a backing away from philosophical and moral difficulties that such struggles may entail violence, both against corporate property and persons. Moral and philosophical issues are to be wrestled with, rather than to be ignored, for that latter option is to fail to engage with the structural violence to African communities and welfare inherent in so much investment associated with the new scramble.

However, our final assertion ties up with the opening discussion on Warren. This is recognition of the human freedom associated with the existence of the operation of the market. The term free market is to be abjured for every market must be regulated to achieve the legitimate collective aims of society. Note too that the relative freedom of the market must be accompanied by as much commitment to corporate as to democratic governance and that this implies far more application to the tenets of economic democracy and accountability than there has been in Africa hitherto, a struggle unlikely to succeed unless it has a major international component. This would involve greater international commitment to corporate monitoring and necessary linkages between foreign monitors and local activists in trade unions, non-government organisations and social movements. As Birdsall (2006: 35) pointed out, in 'advanced market economies, democratic politics help temper the inevitable tendency for the rich and powerful to set the rules of their own short-term advantage'. But there is no equivalent global polity.[11] Nonetheless, our major emphasis is upon the need for appropriate state and business relations, not only for a genuinely national African capitalism, but for African economies to prosper. We refer in this context to the important recent study by Taylor in which he argues cogently that 'business-state coalitions are essential institutions of late capitalist development' (2007: 3).

Taylor proposes that although structural adjustment programmes implemented by African governments in the 1980s and 1990s indicated that they had embarked 'if haltingly' on a capitalist path, state elites often systematically excluded local business from their plans. 'In short, they consented to reforms but largely eschewed reform coalitions that would enhance the new policies' prospects for success' (2007: 3). To be sure, some businesses did well, especially those owned by politicians, but more commonly states thwarted the capacity of business communities to act collectively. So the question is: why have states acted in such an apparently perverse manner? And what factors contribute to the formation and endurance of reform coalitions?

Taylor argues that while reform coalitions have been abundant in Latin America and Asia, they have been few and far between in Africa. Various reasons are proffered. Ironically, one is that structural adjustment programmes may have themselves undermined the capacity of the state to engage effectively with business. Another is that in many countries, the private sector and its business associations are weak, although there is a dangerous circularity to this line of reasoning, the point being that the official adoption of appropriate policies can provide the opportunity for indigenous business classes to develop. Even so, Taylor stresses that African capital lacks weight and hence retains a deeply ingrained incentive to co-operate with the state, for access is often essential to its prosperity. African states, therefore, ultimately play the decisive role in determining the fate of business-state coalitions. Far too often, state elites have remained hostile to private capital, notwithstanding their implementation of neo-liberal reforms (2007: 10–24).

Upon this basis Taylor advances three arguments. First, the emergence of reform coalitions is most likely when key business actors possess institutional strength and the state perceives that it lacks a power advantage over business. Second, reform coalitions endure provided the relationship continues to have political and economic utility for the state. And third, coalitions collapse when the perception of threat exceeds the political or economic utility of maintaining them (2007: 24).

Taylor's approach builds upon the fashionable idea of the developmental state, and serves as an important counter to the damaging simplicities of crude neo-liberalism and the one-size-fits-all, market-driven policies that have historically been favoured by the IFIs. His fundamental contribution, therefore, is to place an important emphasis upon the political conditions for economic growth. Thereby he provides an important challenge to much conventional Africanist thinking by arguing the potential for African capitalism.

The major criticism of Taylor's work is that he almost wholly writes labour out of the reform coalition, thereby ignoring the major branch of literature which argues convincingly that trade unions have been central to the drive for greater democracy in Africa (Kraus 2007). And political democracy, we are assured by much recent neo-liberal literature, is an important accompaniment of, if not a necessary requirement for, successful economic liberalisation in Africa. Consequently, for reform coalitions to become African developmental states, states capable of both steering and controlling capital and thereby fostering the broad-based economic development that Africa needs, it would appear that somewhat more than just appropriate state and business relations are necessary.

Concluding Note

This conclusion raises more questions than it attempts to answer and is highly schematic. There are no easy answers for a continent that remains in crisis across almost all human development indicators; and where the prospects for economic growth and industrialisation remained severely compromised, not merely by the continuing fact of African political disunity and poverty of governance, but also – as indicated by this book – subject to external impositions by global powers. The challenge posed is: how should the opportunities offered to African people be maximised?[12]

While the responsibility for this lies mainly with the actors inside Africa, we cannot be absolved from our own responsibilities. As Birdsall (2006: 36) concludes:

> We have a potentially powerful instrument to increase wealth and welfare: the global economy. But to complement and support that economy we have an inadequate and fragile global polity. A major challenge of the twenty-first century will be to strengthen and reform

the institutions, rules and customs by which nations and peoples complement the global market with collective management of the problems, including persistent and unjust inequality, which global markets alone will not resolve.

Social forces in any given society will need to be alert and to challenge the global and local structures of exploitation and oppression to obtain a fairer deal for the majority of people everywhere.

Notes

1. Although it must be remembered that Warren died before his manuscript was complete, and that the projected third part of his book was destined to deal with 'The Working Class and Socialist Movements in Third World Capitalism', a topic that would clearly escape the purview of the World Bank.
2. The African countries that appear most prominently are Egypt and Ghana.
3. Perhaps if at all, the singular case of Mauritius, and post-1994 South Africa. Botswana is a further candidate, although its much praised exceptionalism has been cogently questioned by authors such as Good (1994, 2004) and Taylor (2003).
4. We have dealt with aspects of this culture in the political sphere in another volume on African (ex-) presidents (Southall and Melber 2006). For an effort to present the rationale of such neo-patrimonial forms of rule in African states see the widely discussed controversial essay by Chabal and Daloz (1999).
5. This is illustrated by figures and ranks presented in the latest Human Development Report (United Nations Development Programme 2007) for these countries, who are among those with the greatest differences between their rankings according to per capita GDP and the Human Development Index: Botswana (54/124, -70), Equatorial Guinea (73/127, -54), Namibia (78/125, - 47), Gabon (84/119, -35) and Angola (128/162, -34).
6. There is an important debate between those who argue that manufacturing in Africa has no future because of Chinese competition and low-cost labour and those who proclaim the potential for African manufacturing for employment creation via adoption of appropriate industrial policy.
7. For a discussion of potential benefits of the Chinese linkage, see le Pere (2008).
8. The inconsistency of such a tendency is of course illustrated by the infamous ship of shame as discussed in Henning Melber's chapter three of this book.
9. B. Magubane and E. Maloka. 'Zimbabwe – an international pariah!: what are the revolutionary tasks of the South African democratic movement'. Unpublished, reported in *Business Day* 5 May 2008.
10. Pro-Mugabe analysts tend to argue that the limited options available for a post-Mugabe regime would drive the latter into the arms of an IMF and World Bank strategy of

deflation and structural adjustment and should therefore be resisted. However, they thereby ignore the fact that the present level of hyper- inflation, along with the deliberate obstruction by Zanu-PF of the delivery of food aid to government opponents, is a fundamental attack upon the right to life of the majority of the population. Clearly the way forward lies in some serious engagement with the structural adjustment that is both necessary and inevitable in order to ameliorate its impact upon the conditions of living for the poor. This is difficult, but hopefully not impossible.

11. The few and reluctant efforts by United Nations organs to monitor transnational companies and their activities and seek compliance with ethical rules and values are little more than an embarrassment.

12. This concern is well elaborated with regard to a number of case studies in Wohlmuth et al. (2007).

References

Ampiah K. and S. Naidu (eds). 2008. *Crouching Tiger, Hidden Dragon?: Africa and China*. Pietermaritzburg: University of KwaZulu-Natal Press.

Birdsall, N. 2006. *The World is not Flat: Inequality and Injustice in our Global Economy*. Helsinki: UNU-WIDER.

Chabal, P. and J-P. Daloz. 1999. *Africa works: Disorder as a Political Instrument*. Oxford: James Currey.

Corkin, L. 2008. 'All's fair in loans and war: the development of China-Angola relations'. In: *Crouching Tiger, Hidden Dragon?: Africa and China*, edited by K. Ampiah and S. Naidu. Pietermaritzburg: University of KwaZulu-Natal Press.

Cramer, C. 2006. *Civil War is Not a Stupid Thing: Accounting for Violence in Developing Countries*. London: Hurst.

Deléchat, C., A. Kovanen and J. Wakeman-Linn. 2008. 'Sub-Saharan Africa: private capital fueling growth'. *IMF Survey Magazine: Countries and Regions* 22 May. http://www.imf.org/external/pubs/ft/survey/so/2008/car052208b.htm.

Ferguson, J. 2006. *Global Shadows: Africa in the Neoliberal World Order*. Durham: Duke University Press.

Global Witness. 1999. *A Crude Awakening: The Role of Oil and Banking Industries in Angola's Civil War and the Plunder of State Assets*. London. Global Witness.

Good, K. 1994. 'Corruption and mismanagement in Botswana: a best-case example?' *Journal of Modern African Studies* 32(3): 499–521.

——. 2004. 'Resource dependency and its consequences: the costs of Botswana's shining gems'. *Journal of Contemporary African Studies* 23(1): 343–66.

Harris, N. 1986. *The End of the Third World: Newly Industrializing Countries and the Decline of an Ideology*. Harmondsworth: Penguin.

Harvey, D. 2003. *The New Imperialism*. Oxford: Oxford University Press.

Henderson, J. 2008. *China and the Future of the Developing World: The Coming Global-Asian Era and its Consequences*. Helsinki: UNU-WIDER.

International Monetary Fund (IMF), Africa Department. 2009. *Impact of the Global Financial Crisis on Sub-Saharan Africa*. Washington: IMF.

Kalb, M. 1982. *The Congo Cables: The Cold War in Africa from Eisenhower to Kennedy*. New York: Macmillan.

Kaplinksy, R. 2008. 'What does the rise of China do for industrialisation in sub-Saharan Africa?' *Review of African Political Economy* 35(115): 7–22.

Kraus, J. (ed.). 2007. *Trade Unions and the Coming of Democracy in Africa*. New York: Palgrave Macmillan.

Le Pere, G. 2008. 'The geostrategic dimensions of the Sino-African relationship'. In: *Crouching Tiger, Hidden Dragon: Africa and China*, edited by K. Ampiah and S. Naidu. Pietermaritzburg: University of KwaZulu-Natal Press.

Ndikumana, L. and J. Boyce. 2008. *New Estimates of Capital Flight from Sub-Saharan African Countries: Linkages with External Borrowing and Policy Options*. Amherst: Political Economy Research Institute, University of Massachusetts.

Sachikonye, L. 2008. 'Crouching tiger, hidden agenda? Zimbabwe and China relations'. In: *Crouching Tiger, Hidden Dragon?: Africa and China*, edited by K. Ampiah and S. Naidu. Pietermaritzburg: University of KwaZulu-Natal Press.

Saunders, R. 2008. 'South African investment in Africa: restructuring and resistance'. *Atissue Ezine* 8(1) http://www.africafiles.org/atissueezine.asp.

Sender, J. 1980. 'Introduction'. In: *Imperialism: Pioneer of Capitalism*, by B. Warren; edited by J. Sender. London: Verso. xi–xvii.

Southall, R. and H. Melber. (eds). 2006. *Legacies of Power: Leadership Change and Former Presidents in African Politics*. Cape Town: HSRC Press.

Srinivasan, S. 2008. 'A marriage less convenient: China and Sudan, and Darfur'. In: *Crouching Tiger, Hidden Dragon?: Africa and China*, edited by K. Ampiah and S. Naidu. Pietermaritzburg: University of KwaZulu-Natal Press.

Taylor, I. 2003. 'As good as it gets? Botswana's "democratic development"'. *Journal of Contemporary African Studies* 21(2): 215–31.

Taylor, S. 2007. *Business and the State in Southern Africa: The Politics of Economic Reform*. Boulder: Lynne Rienner.

United Nations Development Programme. 2007. *Human Development Report, 2007/2008*. Basingstoke: Palgrave Macmillan.

Warren, B. 1980. *Imperialism: Pioneer of Capitalism*, edited by J. Sender. London: Verso.

Williams, G. 1994. 'Why structural adjustment is necessary and why it doesn't work'. *Review of African Political Economy* 21(60): 214–25.

Wohlmuth, K. et al. (eds). 2007. *Africa: Commodity Dependence, Resource Curse and Export Diversification*. Berlin: LIT.

Contributors

Nompumelelo Bhengu is Assistant Director in the International Trade and Economics division of the Department of Trade and Industry, South Africa (alwandeh@gmail.com).

Alex Comninos is a researcher at the Edge Institute, Johannesburg, South Africa (Alex.comninos@gmail.com).

John Daniel was formerly Professor of Political Science, University of Durban-Westville, South Africa (john.daniel@sit.edu).

Jana Hönke is Research Fellow at the Department of Political Sciences, Freie Universitat, Berlin, Germany (Hoenke@zedat.fu-berlin.de).

Margaret C. Lee is Associate Professor, Department of African and Afro-American Studies, University of North Carolina at Chapel Hill, USA (Mlee400261@aol.com).

Simon Massey is Senior Lecturer, Department of Political and International Studies, University of Coventry, England (Lsx167@coventry.ac.uk).

Roy May is Professor Emeritus, Department of Political and International Studies, University of Coventry, England (R.may@coventry.ac.uk).

Henning Melber is Executive Director, Dag Hammarskjöld Foundation, Uppsala, Sweden (Henning.melber@dhf.uu.se).

Sanusha Naidu is Africa-China Project Co-ordinator, FAHAMU, Cape Town, South Africa (Sanusha@fahamu.org).

Cyril Obi is Research Co-ordinator of the Programme on Post-Conflict Transition, the State and Civil Society in Africa, Nordic Africa Institute, Uppsala, Sweden (Cyril.obi@nai.uu.se).

Wilson Prichard is a doctoral student at the Institute for Development Studies, University of Sussex, England (W.prichard@ids.ac.uk).

Martin Rupiya is Senior Researcher, Institute for Security Studies, Pretoria, South Africa (Mrupiya.cu@defenceacademy.mod.uk).

Vishwas Satgar is Executive Director, Co-operative and Policy Alternative Centre, South Africa (copac@icon.ac.za).

Roger Southall is Professor of Sociology, University of the Witwatersrand, Johannesburg, South Africa (Roger.southall@wits.ac.za).

André Standing is Senior Researcher, Institute of Security Studies, Cape Town, South Africa (astanding@issafrica.org).

Roger Tangri was until recently Associate Professor, Department of Political and Administrative Studies, University of Botswana (rogertangri@googlemail.com).

Carol Thompson is Professor of Political Economy, Northern Arizona University, USA and Policy Analyst for Sustainable Agricultural Biodiversity, Community Technology Development Trust, Zimbabwe (Carol.thompson@nau.edu).

Index